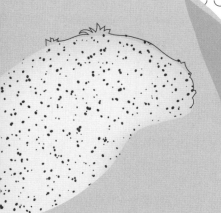
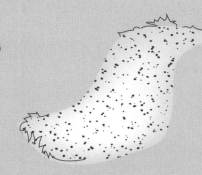

ASSISTANCE

- Maintaining Purpose
- Building Comprehension

REFLECTION

- Evaluation
- Demonstrating Learning
- Extending the Reading Experience
- Retention

PAR Lesson Framework

Graphic developed by Dawn Watson and Walter Richards.

SEVENTH EDITION

Reading to Learn in the Content Areas

JUDY S. RICHARDSON
Virginia Commonwealth University

RAYMOND F. MORGAN
Old Dominion University

CHARLENE E. FLEENER
Old Dominion University

Cengage Learning

WADSWORTH
CENGAGE Learning

Australia • Brazil • Japan • Korea • Mexico • Singapore • Spain • United Kingdom • United States

**Reading to Learn in the Content Areas,
Seventh Edition**
Judy S. Richardson, Raymond F. Morgan,
Charlene E. Fleener

Education Editors: Dan Alpert/Christopher Shortt

Development Editor: Tangelique Williams

Assistant Editor: Stephanie Rue

Editorial Assistant: Caitlin Cox

Technology Project Manager: Julie Aguilar

Marketing Manager: Karin Sandberg

Marketing Assistant: Ting Jian Yap

Marketing Communications Manager:
Shemika Britt

Project Manager, Editorial Production:
Tanya Nigh

Creative Director: Rob Hugel

Art Director: Maria Epes

Print Buyer: Judy Inouye

Permissions Editor: Roberta Broyer

Production Service: Matrix Productions

Copy Editor: Meg McDonald

Cover Designer: Bartay Studio

Cover Image: PhotoLibrary

Compositor: Pre-PressPMG

For product information and technology assistance, contact us at
Cengage Learning Customer & Sales Support, 1-800-354-9706
For permission to use material from this text or product,
submit all requests online at **www.cengage.com/permissions**.
Further permissions questions can be e-mailed to
permissionrequest@cengage.com.

Library of Congress Control Number: 2007936893

ISBN-13: 978-0-495-50606-5

ISBN-10: 0-495-50606-0

Wadsworth Cengage Learning
10 Davis Drive
Belmont, CA 94002-3098
USA

Cengage Learning is a leading provider of customized learning solutions with office locations around the globe, including Singapore, the United Kingdom, Australia, Mexico, Brazil, and Japan. Locate your local office at **international.cengage.com/region**.

Cengage Learning products are represented in Canada by Nelson Education, Ltd.

For your course and learning solutions, visit **academic.cengage.com**.

Purchase any of our products at your local college store or at our preferred online store **www.ichapters.com**.

Printed in the United States of America
1 2 3 4 5 6 7 12 11 10 09 08

To Dan Alpert, our editor for three editions—a wonderful editor and friend.

Judy S. Richardson

To Sue, Jon, and Chris for their steadfast support.

Ray Morgan

To my fellow learners and teachers who bring a sense of special joy and purpose to this work, and to my family and friends for unconditional love, encouragement, and support.

Charlene E. Fleener

Contents

CHAPTER 3

Preparation for Learning   68

CHAPTER 8

Study Skills in the Electronic Age   235

CHAPTER 9

Teaching Vocabulary   287

CHAPTER 10

Writing to Learn in the Content Areas   339

CHAPTER 11

Supporting Diverse Learners in Content Classrooms   389

CHAPTER 12

Teaching in the Affective Domain   435

APPENDIX A

Assessing Attitudes toward Reading   465

APPENDIX B

Readability Information   478

Preface

REFLECTIONS ON THE SEVENTH EDITION

As we reflect on the launching of our seventh edition, we realize how proud we are to have written a text that has weathered six previous editions. We are pleased to have provided what many instructors, teachers, and prospective teachers found useful. Our basic approach to content reading instruction has remained unchanged, but our knowledge of the field grows with each edition. We thank those of you who have weathered these editions with us, and we welcome those of you new to our text. We hope you will find it to be just what you need.

WHO SHOULD READ THIS BOOK?

This textbook is meant for anyone who wants to teach students to learn and think about subject matter. This book is for readers who have never studied reading, as well as for those who have studied how students learn to read, but not how they read to learn and think in subject areas. This book demonstrates how teachers can use reading, discussion, and writing as ways to learn in any discipline.

WHY DID WE WRITE THIS BOOK?

As authors, we enjoy reading about new topics and ideas. Learning is a pleasure for us, and we like to increase our knowledge. But we recognize that many people do not think they enjoy reading and learning. This is often because their instruction in content areas was ineffective and the task of learning created a lasting, negative impression. We don't want learning to be dull or uncomfortable. We want to encourage curiosity, inquiry and investigation, the confidence to read and discover, and ultimately lifelong learning. This is why we have been teachers and college professors for more than 30 years. We believe in what we teach. We realize that all serious learning must be put in perspective. We have ideas about how to share the joys of reading, thinking, and learning with students of all ages. We have ideas to share with you.

Teacher preparation has been criticized. Some say teachers cannot teach their students to think critically or teach students to complete complex tasks required to advance in college or the workplace. Some critics say teachers learn too much content and not enough methodology. Others critics say the opposite. Many critics say teachers have learned to teach content rather than to teach students the content.

This textbook represents an ongoing effort to find positive solutions to such criticisms. We believe that if teachers learn to follow a simple instructional framework and teach strategically by using activities that demonstrate how reading can be a tool for learning, many classroom problems can be alleviated.

SPECIAL FEATURES OF THIS TEXTBOOK

1. Reader involvement is important in this textbook. Each chapter is introduced with a vignette ("Voices from the Classroom") and questions inviting the reader to consider how he or she might respond to challenges and situations related to the chapter's content. These lend relevance, interest, and applications for chapter concepts.

2. We believe that readers need to be prepared to read, need some assistance to understand, and need to be guided to reflect on their reading. So we ask readers to engage in all three stages as they read each chapter of this textbook. We are reader friendly: We introduce new terms first with an activity designed to engage readers, and then within the text in boldface with explanations; we maintain informality to keep our readers comfortable and interested.

3. We take a balanced approach—a realistic and practical treatment of reading and methodology issues, theory, research, and historical perspective. We emphasize the effect of the past on the present.

4. We address teachers of primary through secondary grades. We look at reading in the classroom as a natural tool for learning, no matter what the grade level or content area. We provide examples that show how an activity can work at different levels and in different content areas.

5. We select one instructional framework that reflects current thought but is uniquely ours: PAR (Preparation/Assistance/Reflection). We explain it, compare it, and apply it throughout the book, and it is presented on the front endsheets as well. Readers will appreciate this consistency and our constant reference to the framework.

6. Our organization is considerate of our readers. You can expect to find a graphic organizer at the beginning of each chapter; the "Preparing to Read" section that starts each chapter builds reader background and provides objectives; a one-minute summary (for the streamlined reader) is always provided; and assistance as well as reflection activities provide chapter closure. Throughout each chapter margin notes are interspersed to add emphasis, provoke thought beyond the page, and invite the reader to visit our Web site for additional resources and information.

7. Visual literacy is featured in this textbook. We use many visuals because visual literacy is the first literacy. One important visual is the PAR Cross-Reference

Guide on the endsheets at the back of the book, which identifies specific activities for different content areas and grade levels.

8. Our philosophy is that reading and the other language arts work together. Just as students listen and discuss to learn, so do they read and write to learn. We integrate the communicative arts. When an activity is presented, we explore with the reader how that activity facilitates and encourages discussion, reading, and writing.

9. Ours is also a strategy-based approach. When readers learn about a new activity, they should understand that activity as a strategic means to aid learning. We present the activity as a way to enhance instruction and help teachers see how this activity can be both an instructional strategy and a learner strategy.

10. Ours is a theory-based approach. When readers learn about a new activity, they should understand how and why it reflects sound instruction.

11. This textbook contains several unique chapters. Chapter 2 helps teachers understand assessment and evaluation issues. Chapter 6 has been extensively revised and discusses using resources beyond the textbook, as well as cooperative learning and instruction that goes beyond traditional transmission models. Chapter 7 considers the importance of electronic literacy for learning in today's content classrooms, while Chapter 8 describes ways to approach study skills and tools in the electronic age. Chapter 11 demonstrates how to support diverse learners in the classroom, including at-risk and struggling students and English language learners. Chapter 12 discusses the affective domain of teaching—a topic crucial to learning but so often neglected. All the chapters cover information on the cutting edge of content area instruction.

NEW TO THIS EDITION

This seventh edition reflects the influence of technology on reading to learn and think through the accompanying DVD, which includes many links to Web sites, examples of teachers using technology as they teach their content, suggestions for software, and much more. This edition emphasizes the use of technology throughout the text and specifically in Chapter 7. Both the DVD and the text chapters describe the effective use of the Internet and computer technology in content teaching.

In this edition we have updated and revised all of the chapters from the sixth edition. Chapter 1 presents four examples of the PAR Lesson Framework, from primary through secondary level, showing how technology and literature can be part of good content lessons. Chapter 6 presents the use of multiple resources for teaching that encourage teachers to move beyond standard textbooks. Chapters 9 (vocabulary) and 10 (writing) have been extensively revised. The PAR Framework is presented in Chapters 3, 4, and 5 and demonstrated throughout the rest of the chapters.

Current research and professional resources have been incorporated in our revision. We have endeavored to maintain a theory-to-practice balance. Visuals continue to play an important part in expressing our ideas: Cartoons, diagrams, and examples are provided throughout. All chapters have been revised to include new ideas, activities, and references.

THE ORGANIZATION OF THIS BOOK

The first five chapters are foundational. Chapter 1 discusses research and principles of content area instruction. Here you will discover our philosophy of teaching. It also presents a capsule view of the PAR Framework for instruction and how it works in four different types of classrooms. Chapter 2 considers the role of assessment and evaluation as they influence classroom teachers. Chapters 3, 4, and 5 are PAR Lesson Framework chapters. Chapter 3 demonstrates how to determine reader background and prepare readers to study content material. Chapter 4 is an assistance chapter, demonstrating why and how to provide an appropriate instructional context to develop comprehension. Chapter 5 considers the role of reflection, stressing how to help readers think critically about, extend, and demonstrate their knowledge of their reading.

Chapters 6 through 10 demonstrate how PAR works. We show how multiple resources, cooperative learning, technology, study skills, vocabulary, and writing can be used in all phases of the PAR Framework. Chapter 6 presents the importance of learning with multiple resources and using cooperative learning and transactional methods of instruction within the content classroom. Chapter 7 leads teachers into ways to use technology in their content teaching. Chapter 8 supports and extends the technology chapter by explaining the use of study skills and electronic tools in today's classrooms.

Chapters 9 and 10 describe activities and strategies for effective vocabulary and writing instruction in a variety of content and classroom settings. Chapter 11 explains how to help diverse learners. Chapter 12 discusses the crucial affective domain of teaching.

THE INSTRUCTOR'S MANUAL

The Instructor's Manual summarizes each chapter's main points, theories, and strategies, and also provides test questions. With it, instructors will be able to assign group activities for their classes; assign individual activities to students for homework; guide their students in analyzing content area reading material; select test items for multiple-choice, true/false, and essay tests; and display the authors' graphic organizers and vocabulary inventories for each chapter.

Section I explains the features of the Instructor's Manual. Section II contains recommendations about grouping. Section III contains preparation, assistance, and reflection activities; teaching tips on how to use the activities; and other resources that may be used in class, such as quotes, suggestions for further reading, book lists, graphic organizers, vocabulary inventories for each chapter, and test items. In

Section IV the authors provide possible assignments for the course, such as guides to analyze a chapter in a content area textbook.

DVD

Our seventh edition includes a DVD. We reflect the influence of technology on reading to learn and think through this DVD, which includes many links to sites, examples of teachers using technology as they teach their content, suggestions for software, video that demonstrates content reading in action, and exercises that can be completed using Wadsworth's free subscription (included with the textbook) to InfoTrac.

The entire edition emphasizes the use of technology throughout the text. Both the DVD and the text chapters describe the effective use of the Internet and computer technology in content teaching. At the end of each chapter, and within the Instructor's Manual, suggested electronic literacy activities are provided.

ACKNOWLEDGMENTS

We extend thanks to the colleagues who encouraged us, and aided and abetted us, in this endeavor. We appreciate the comments of our students who used the sixth edition of the textbook and provided handy suggestions.

We acknowledge gratefully the contributions of our reviewers, who gave us such excellent suggestions throughout the writing of this textbook: Jim Johnston, Central Connecticut State University; Marsha Savage, Santa Clara University; Lois Huffman, North Carolina State University; Leonard Johnson, Ferris State University; Kay Dunlap, John Carroll University; Sue Rogers, Averett College; and Adrienne Perry, Stenson University.

Our writing was a more pleasant experience because of the support and kind assistance of our editor, Dan Alpert; assistant editor, Stephanie Rue; and, Caitlin Cox. We also thank Julie Aguilar, technology project manager; our production manager, Tanya Nigh; and our production editor, Merrill Peterson.

If the only tool you have is a hammer, you tend to treat everything as if it were a nail.

MASLOW

Content Teachers and Content Literacy

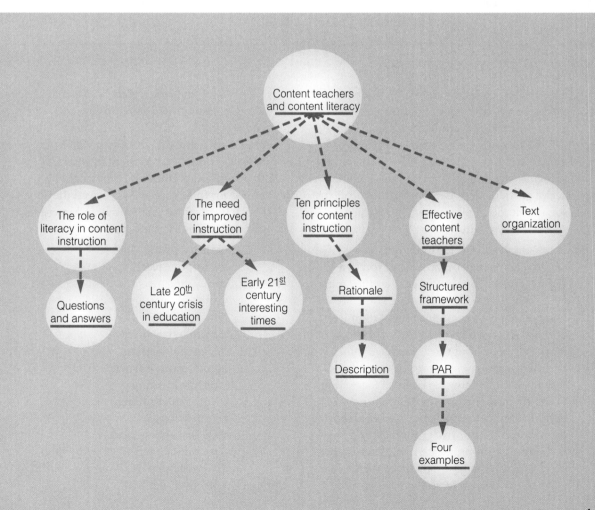

VOICES FROM THE CLASSROOM

It is the first class meeting for a course titled "Reading in the Content Areas." Students gather in the classroom before the instructor has arrived. Some are teachers, having rushed to get to class; they are already tired from a day of instruction, interaction with their own students, driving to get to this class, and finding parking. Others are prospective teachers—either preparing to teach as a first career or entering teaching as a second career.

One turns to another and says, "Well, I'm here; but this course is just another big waste of time." The other responds, "I *have* to take this course to get certified. I can't figure out why." A third chimes in, "But my adviser said this is a really good course and will help me with good classroom ideas." "Well," says a fourth, "we will see about that."

What do you think? Why are you reading this textbook? What do you think this text and the course for which it is assigned reading will be like? Are you feeling resentful or dubious?

PREPARING TO READ

1. How do you currently help your students to discuss, read, and write about the content they study for deep understanding? Make a list of all the ways you guide—or plan to guide when you start teaching—your students. How many of these ways include active participation, demonstration, problem solving, student involvement, assessment of success, and self-initiative?

2. Following is a list of terms used in this chapter. Some may be familiar to you in a general context, but in this chapter they may be used in unfamiliar ways. Rate your knowledge by placing a plus sign (+) in front of those you are certain you know, a check mark (✓) in front of those you have some knowledge about, and a zero (0) in front of those you don't know. Be ready to locate them in the chapter, and pay special attention to their meanings. Decide how you can arrange the terms in four or five groupings, and give each group an appropriate label. There may be several ways to group them, so there is no single right answer. Be ready to explain your

selections. Next, using a piece of paper, make a three-column organizer with the following headings: terms, predicted definitions, chapter definitions. Select 10 terms with which you are least familiar, record them in your organizer, and predict how they might be defined for this chapter. As you read the chapter, verify your predictions and rewrite your definitions as necessary.

_____ NAEP

_____ assumptive teaching

_____ communicative arts (language arts)

_____ visual literacy

_____ new literacies

_____ technological literacy

_____ dependent learners

_____ autonomous learners

_____ strategic learning

_____ incomplete thinking

_____ fix-up strategies

_____ PAR Lesson Framework

_____ preparation step

_____ assistance step

_____ reflection step

OBJECTIVES

As you read this chapter, focus your attention on the following purposes. You will

1. Learn some recent history about research and views of education.

2. Understand why there is a need to improve instruction in schools today.

3. Become acquainted with 10 principles for content reading instruction and understand the importance of each.

4. Understand the use of the PAR Lesson Framework.

5. Learn the characteristics of an effective teacher.

6. Learn why it is important to use a lesson framework when teaching.

7. Become acquainted with the steps in the PAR Lesson Framework.

8. Read examples of the PAR Framework used at the primary, elementary, middle, and high school levels.

9. Learn how this textbook is organized.

© 2007, Brian Basset. Distributed by The Washington Post Writers Group. Reprinted with permission.

WHAT IS THE ROLE OF LITERACY IN CONTENT CLASSROOMS?

 Many teachers wonder why they should complete a course in content reading instruction. After all, when teaching content, they are not teaching reading—or are they? Consider the following questions and answers, and then read more about the role of literacy in content classrooms.

QUESTION: *Why should teachers of subjects such as mathematics, social studies, science, English, foreign language, vocational education, art, music, physical education, and other content areas even think about using reading and writing as a means to learning? Isn't that the job of the language arts or reading teacher?*

RESPONSE:	Reading and writing are the major tools for learning any subject. They help us learn how to learn. So these tools must be used in every classroom, at every grade level, and in every school to provide the application and practice necessary for students to become effective learners.
QUESTION:	*What exactly is reading to learn? Is that like teaching students how to read, with phonics and decoding?*
RESPONSE:	No, we recognize that content teachers teach a subject, not how to read. But within your subject, students will encounter many new words, or words used in new ways, in your subject area. They will have to read with understanding and study effectively to learn your subject. Those skills—vocabulary, comprehension, and study skills—are the ones we introduce in this textbook.
QUESTION:	*Why should content teachers change their instructional practices?*
RESPONSE:	In the past several years, public comment, research, and assessment results have led to concerns and criticism of our educational system. Some criticism states that students are not learning important factual information, are unable to think critically, and cannot apply skills in the real worlds of work and college. This textbook represents an effort to help teachers and administrators find positive, effective solutions to these criticisms.
QUESTION:	*How difficult will it be to implement the content of this textbook into the classroom?*
RESPONSE:	We present a simple instructional framework in this first chapter, and then guide you in applying it as you learn about practical strategies you can use in your classroom almost immediately. Once you have a good grasp of ways to teach strategically, designing activities should flow naturally.

IMPROVED INSTRUCTION—ARE WE THERE YET?

 A major factor in how we measure educational progress is the **NAEP** (National Assessment of Educational Progress), a test authorized by Congress in 1969. The NAEP's mission is to collect, analyze, and present reliable information about student knowledge and practice of that knowledge. The NAEP is administered at grades 4, 8, and 12 to both public and nonpublic students in core subjects. During the last third of the 20th century, many politicians and educators wrote about a crisis in education. They cited evidence that achievement levels were declining in our nation's schools. Test gains on the NAEP had fluctuated only slightly; national results (National Center for Educational Statistics, 2003) for fourth and eighth graders from 1970 to 2003 had shown a decline (although it was slight from 2002 to 2003). Only

Visit the *Reading to Learn in the Content Areas* Web site, Chapter 1, to locate the NAEP site.

31 percent of fourth graders and only 32 percent of eighth graders attained a "proficient" level—a standard that test officials say all students should reach. Thirty-seven percent of fourth graders and 26 percent of eighth graders did not achieve a basic level of reading proficiency as of the NAEP 2003 report. The newest NAEP reports (2007) show that fourth graders scored higher in reading than in any previous year. And eighth graders are also doing better, especially those in the lower- and middle-performing groups. NAEP reports from 2006 showed significant gains in U.S. history and civics, plus math, and science. Also, 12th grade scores in history increased (although 12th grade reading scores declined). Speculation was that test scores were rising because of increased emphasis on intensive teaching of reading as early as kindergarten. Reading scores indicate that many students—even those considered most at risk of failure—have done better in the past few years.

Many educators think that instruction and teaching have improved in recent years. A major finding in recent decades is that the policies states adopt about teacher education, certification, hiring, and professional development matter immensely in how students achieve. Darling-Hammond (2000) found that student achievement, especially in mathematics and reading, is influenced by the qualifications of teachers.

There was a more positive stance about education in the last decade of the 20th century. David Berliner (2001), a prominent psychologist interested in education, maintains that posturing about poor schools and instruction has caused us to waste money, harm already effective school programs, and add to the declining morale among teachers. Berliner challenges many widely held beliefs about schools. He says that schools are not nearly as bad as many reports claim, and he further asserts that schools are doing as good a job of educating our youth as has ever been done in our history. He feels the educational system produces good results in most instances. According to Berliner, problems that exist result from poverty, dysfunctional families, and poor health care. A growing number of researchers (Bracey, 1997; McQuillan, 1998; Whittington, 1991) have agreed with Berliner that children in the United States are reading as well now as they did in past generations, and maybe even better. Godwin and Sheard (2001) provide a history of some policy-making interventions such as vouchers and national testing and speculate about what may come from these initiatives. Glickman (2004) describes several ways we can move forward with best educational practices—such as championing public education; providing policy makers with concrete focus; encouraging and empowering communities and schools; redefining education acts at the federal level; and regaining confidence in pedagogy. Chi (2004), as editor of *Spectrum,* a publication of the Council of State Governments, presents three different perspectives of the recent federal No Child Left Behind Act to encourage ways to move forward with the best suggestions for educational initiatives.

The most recent Phi Delta Kappa/Gallup Poll (Rose & Gallup, 2007)—the 39th annual poll—indicates that the public thinks reforms in education can be accomplished today through the existing system. The public rates schools the highest they have in 39 years. The public thinks that the right amount of emphasis is being placed on science and math but more time is needed for learning about other nations. Much

Visit the *Reading to Learn in the Content Areas* Web site, Chapter 1, for a link to the online version of the Phi Delta Kappa/ Gallup Poll.

of the 39th poll studied the impact of NCLB (No Child Left Behind); more will be considered about this topic in Chapter 2. The 38th Phi Delta Kappa/Gallup Poll (Rose & Gallup, 2006) found that 47 percent of the public said the curriculum needs to be changed—up from 31 percent in 1979. They indicated that the curriculum should not be confined to basics but rather should include a wide variety of courses. However, the public (57 percent) thinks that elementary students do not work hard enough; they also think (73 percent) that high school students need to work harder.

Although NAEP and the Phi Delta Kappa/Gallup Poll indicate steady improvements, debate continues about whether increased scores in some areas really demonstrate the kind of progress educators want to see. A number of past reports and books—still quoted often—have portrayed our nation's schools as being in crisis, questioning the practices and core beliefs of our entire educational system (Bloom, 1987; Hirsch, 1987). Some teachers believe students are experiencing difficulty with higher-level reading and writing skills such as critical thinking, drawing inferences, and applying what is read. This opinion is supported by contemporary research and writing about deep and surface structure comprehension. For instance, Holschuh (2000) found that high performers use more deep-level and specific strategies and seem to know when to use the most appropriate strategies. Learning requires a student-centered approach (Applefield, Huber, & Moallem, 2000). Relying on skills-centered instruction, as a test emphasis tends to do, leaves little time for a student-centered orientation. Simpson and Nist (2000) caution that strategic learning requires mature and complex knowledge, such as task understanding, ability to generalize, and cognitive and metacognitive processing. According to Barnett (2000), the more a person feels in control of his or her comprehension, the more self-regulated about learning he or she will be.

Visit the *Reading to Learn in the Content Areas* Web site for a link to read about the concerns of some teachers.

Gettinger and Seibert (2002) contribute a significant perspective about learning and study by grouping study into four clusters: (1) repetition-based; (2) procedural; (3) cognitive-based; and (4) metacognitive skills. Study skills, according to these authors, contribute to academic competence because they are cognitive skills and processes for effective learning, requiring that we acquire, locate, organize, synthesize, remember, and then use information learned. Study requires specific techniques, intent, and individual decisions, as well as a self-regulatory process. These concerns about deep thinking and self-regulated learning, and their possible clash with an emphasis on testing, are discussed in Chapter 2 and ensuing chapters.

The 21st century has been called the "Information Age" (Frand, 2000). Friedman (2006) explains in his best-selling book that the world is now "flat," having been compressed by the breaking down of physical barriers like the Berlin Wall, as well as the connectivity of the Internet and software that allows interactivity and productivity around the world, new communities without geographic borders, industries that work over physical distance, and information obtained almost instantly. Pedagogy has subsequently undergone radical change in the past several years. We are in an age of technological innovations (Kleiner & Lewis, 2003); accountability (Johnson & Johnson, 2002; Stewart, 2004); high-stakes testing (Afflerbach, 2002; Worthy & Hoffman, 2000); and standards for learning (Valencia & Wixson, 1999). These innovations and issues cross school divisions, states, and nations. Literacy has gained a level of attention far greater than in past generations. It is no longer enough to focus on literacy at only the beginning reader level or in only the elementary school. Educators recognize that literacy permeates learning at all ages and in every classroom.

Questions and concerns remain, though. The adoption of state and national standards may lead to too much emphasis on testing and not enough on learning content (Berube, 2004). Emphasis on the "new" literacy, specifically technology, may alter teacher training for better or worse (Henderson & Scheffler, 2004). As Boyd (2004, p. 105) expresses this new direction, "We are living in what the Chinese call 'interesting times.' Already facing difficult times, public education—and the arts as well—are in real danger of a confluence of forces that could form a 'perfect storm.'"

Teachers need more information and training to instruct in the 21st century.

The result of the many concerns for 21st-century education is that teachers need more information and training to teach higher levels of language and literacy. But often teachers do not have this exposure even though they expect students in their classes to be fluent in processing reading material, making inferences, and reading critically. They assume that students will be able to express their understanding of material orally and on tests. They expect that students will possess a certain amount of knowledge and want to read to learn. This is **assumptive teaching**, described later in this chapter as Principle 7. Such assumptive teaching creates a difficult instructional dilemma.

TEN PRINCIPLES FOR CONTENT READING INSTRUCTION

An obvious first step in new expectations is to encourage teachers to teach language and literacy in content area instruction. To accomplish this, teachers must have principles to follow. In the next section we present 10 guiding principles for facilitating reading to learn. Teachers who can articulate their beliefs about teaching are in a good position to improve their instruction. Like all learners, teachers will alter their approaches if they see a need to do so. We altered our own instruction based on current research. To clarify our own thinking, we encapsulated our approach in 10 principles. By sharing these principles with teachers and demonstrating how they relate to content area teaching, we hope to influence teachers to consider instructional changes in their own classrooms.

These principles are grounded in theory and supported by research. Many teachers think that theory has nothing to do with the classroom—perhaps because theory has been presented to them in isolation from its application. But we think that when teachers ask for "what works," they are also asking why a particular technique works so that they can replicate it in optimal circumstances. Teachers know that imposing an activity on students in the wrong circumstances can produce a teaching disaster. No activity has much merit aside from the construct underlying it (Hayes, Stahl, & Simpson, 1991). Teachers want theory that makes sense because it explains why some activities work well at a particular time during instruction. The 10 principles presented here link the theoretical with good practice in content area instruction.

1. Reading is influenced by the reader's personal store of experience and knowledge. Successful reading depends on numerous factors. The reader's store of knowledge and experience certainly contributes, as well as the reader's attitude toward reading. Even though many people may share the same experience, read the same book, or hear the same lecture, the thinking and learning that occur differ from individual to individual because of what each person brings to the experience. Individuals relate to a common body of knowledge in different ways because of what they already know—or don't know. Thus, for example, converting to the metric system will probably be especially difficult for learners who were taught measurements in inches, feet, and miles. Understanding conflicts in another nation can be difficult when learners do not know the life, climate, geography, and history of that nation. If learners cannot find relevance in a subject, they are likely to ignore it. Thus teachers must become aware of what previous knowledge and experiences their students possess about a particular concept in content subjects.

2. The communicative arts foster thinking and learning in content subjects. The traditional **communicative arts**, or **language arts**, are listening, speaking, reading, and writing. Kellogg (1972) describes the communicative arts as blocks that build on one another. One cannot use one communicative art without also using another. This integration occurs with greater facility as children practice each literacy skill. Yet school environments are often artificial rather than natural in their application of informative communication. Usually teachers talk and students listen so much of the time that little response and interaction can take place. In reviewing the 51 articles about content reading published in *The Reading Teacher* from 1969 to 1991, Armbruster (1992) noted the "emphasis on the importance of integrating writing and reading in content instruction." It is our premise that students can learn better if they spend more time practicing all the language arts in their content subjects. Subject matter and language are inextricably bound.

But the main concern for the subject matter teacher is teaching content. In 1965 Nila Banton Smith reminded readers that the term *primer* did not originally mean "first book to read," as it does today, but referred to the contents of a book as being primary, or foremost. Today the content of a subject is still primary for teachers, as it should be. But using the communicative arts as a major learning tool creates a positive combination for enhancing critical thinking and learning. For example, Richardson (2004) describes several successful content lessons designed by content teachers that incorporate language arts and technology. The communicative arts are essential to teaching content area subjects, and teachers should encourage students' use of all the communicative arts as effective thinking and learning tools. As we present activities in this book, we often identify how they facilitate the use of language to enhance content learning. The role of writing, in particular, is discussed in Chapter 10.

3. Literacy in the 21st century is more than the traditional communicative arts. Although listening, speaking, reading, and writing have been considered the basic communicative arts, sometimes communication occurs most easily through nonverbal, visual literacy. For instance, a picture of a pie divided into pieces may convey the concept of fractions more effectively than a page of explanation. Sinatra (1986) calls

FIGURE 1.1

Stage Three of Literacy Development: Visual Literacy and Its Interactive Relationship with the Oral and Written Languages

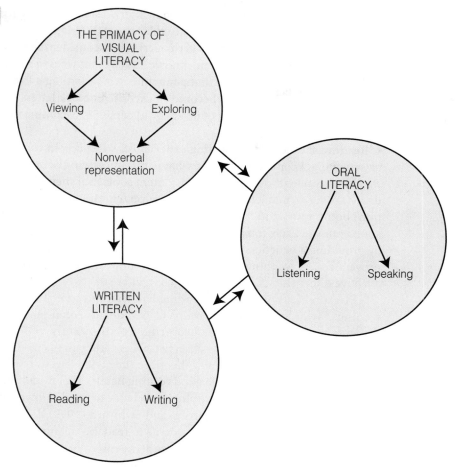

From R. Sinatra, *Visual Literacy Connections to Thinking, Reading, and Writing,* 1986. Courtesy of Charles C. Thomas, Publisher, Springfield, Illinois.

visual literacy the first and most pervasive literacy. Sinatra's model of literacy development suggests the interactive relationship of visual literacy with the oral and written literacies (see Figure 1.1).

Visual literacy conveys emotion through such means as illustration and art. Visual literary precedes listening and helps build experiences necessary to thinking and learning. It is action oriented; the scribbles that young children call writing are a manifestation of visual literacy. Teachers know that when they use visual aids such as graphs, charts, and pictures, they ensure and reinforce learning for many students. An alternative approach is offered for those who excel in visual but not traditional literacy. Because visual literacy has implications for the affective aspects of instruction, it is discussed further in Chapter 12. Many activities presented in this book capitalize on visual literacy.

The term **new literacies** (Luke, 2000) has been used often to describe how the communicative arts are applied in the electronic environment. This term will be dis-

Visit the *Reading to Learn in the Content Areas* Web site, Chapter 1, for a link to the online article "The Handwriting Is on the Wall."

cussed in depth in Chapter 7. While new literacies still employ listening, reading, writing, and speaking, the approach to their use is different due to the electronic environment—so much so that this term alerts us to consider them as almost different experiences. In fact, some lament (Pressler, 2006) that writing has changed so much with the advent of computers that penmanship is becoming a lost art. As keyboards replace pens, manuscript has become an exercise in block letters rather than uppercase and lowercase formation of letters. And cursive is becoming illegible.

4. Reading should be a rewarding experience.   Reading in content subjects should be satisfying. People avoid doing what is not interesting or rewarding in some personal way. Students avoid reading in content subjects if they find it uninteresting and unrewarding. When left to their own devices, children often select content (nonfiction) books to read just as readily as fiction. We have noticed that younger children are even more likely to read for information than are older ones. If teachers can help by providing a beneficial reading environment in content subjects, learning will improve. Because we think this principle is so important, we devote Chapter 12 to the affective dimension of reading in the content areas.

Pleasurable feelings about reading will lead to successful reading and to more reading. Taylor, Frye, and Maruyama (1990) documented that the amount of time students spend reading at school contributes significantly to their level of achievement. The more often students observe teachers and parents reading—and hear parents and teachers read to them—the more they will want to try it. Teachers would like to teach students who have good reading habits. This cannot happen simply because teachers tell, or even implore, students to read. However, it will happen through modeling. Morrison, Jacobs, and Swinyard (1999) documented that teachers who read can better motivate students to read. Modeling takes place when teachers share a newspaper article about a content subject or a book they have read that relates to a topic at hand. Modeling is a form of visual literacy. When teachers model reading visually, they are using one communicative art to promote another. We believe that teachers need to model use of all the strategies we describe in this textbook. Morrison and colleagues (1999) found that teachers who read for personal pleasure report using recommended literacy practices in their classrooms significantly more often than do teachers who report less personal reading.

Good readers read because it gives them pleasure and they do it well; consequently, they get practice in reading and become better at it. In a series of questionnaires we administered over a four-year period to incoming college students, we found a consistent correlation between those who chose not to read and those who perceived that they had poor reading and study habits. This confirms the notion that people tend to avoid reading because it is not easy, pleasurable, or satisfying. There is some evidence that many poor readers get so discouraged that they lose the will or desire to read and thus to succeed. In these cases, teachers need to give more attention to bolstering students' will to learn (Fleener et al., 2000). Improving the will to learn is called *conation* and will be discussed in Chapter 12. It is an important variable in the affective domain of learning, along with attitude, self-concept, and emotions.

5. The practice of critical reading enables better thinking and learning to occur.
Reading is an active, thinking-related process. As soon as readers can pay more attention to the meanings of words than to their recognition, they can begin to think and learn about the material itself rather than about reading it. Yet students often lack critical thinking skills. It is not that students are incapable of critical thinking; they just have not practiced it. In the section about the need for improved instruction, several studies were mentioned that support this principle (Applefield, Huber, & Moallem, 2000; Barnett, 2000; Gettinger & Seibert, 2002; Holschuh, 2000; Simpson & Nist, 2000). By using tools of literacy and being immersed in a thinking climate, students can practice these skills.

Special note: We recognize that literal reading is often a necessary first step toward critical reading. Although we emphasize critical reading, we are not disregarding the importance of factual reading. A reader who understands material at a factual level and can interpret what is read can respond critically with greater success. However, many students who are unable to recall names or dates can predict and infer. It is probably because teachers realize the necessity of literal reading that so much classroom time is spent on literal recall of reading material, to the detriment of higher-level thinking and reading comprehension.

6. Meaningful reading should start early and continue throughout life.   From the first grade on, learning content material is part of most school curricula. Many schools now introduce science, math, and social studies material in kindergarten. The *Weekly Reader,* that ubiquitous early grades newspaper, contains content material. Because most children are still learning to read in the early grades, reading to learn may not be employed as often as visualizing, listening, and speaking to learn. However, both reading and writing to learn are being advocated more frequently for children in the early grades. By the same reasoning, learning about content subjects continues far beyond high school. Content information bombards people daily as they listen to radio and watch television, read the newspaper, and surf the Internet on their computers. The basic difference here is that the learner can structure the environment and choose what to learn and what to avoid. The adults whom teachers meet daily will attest that they continue to enjoy and learn about topics that interested them in school. We develop lifelong learners by introducing them to reading for learning's sake at an early age.

7. Teachers need to refrain from assumptive teaching.   Herber (1978) used the term *assumptive teaching* to describe what teachers do when they unconsciously take for granted that students know how to read and to learn and have the motivation and interest to do so. Teachers may picture all students as having plenty of reading resources and supportive home environments. Unfortunately, these assumptions are not always true.

Some assumptive teaching is necessary. Teachers cannot start all over again every year in a content subject. They may need to assume that a particular skill or concept was covered the year before. Yet if a teacher assumes too much about a student's knowledge or frame of mind, the teacher can act as if what is being taught is already known. Finding the point of familiarity with a concept and guiding students forward is crucial. Content area teachers should be certain about what they are assuming their students already know. By learning to determine and build on students' background, teachers can avoid assumptive teaching.

8. All students, no matter at what level of literacy or learning challenges, deserve instruction in content subjects that enables them to learn.   The "average" student is an elusive creature. Teachers teach students who are gifted, learning disabled, and physically disabled; who speak English as a second language, struggle with reading, and are at risk of failure—to list just a few heterogeneous students. All students in content classrooms deserve instruction that helps them to learn. Chapter 11 describes many diverse students and suggests how to instruct them in meaningful ways within the content classroom. By engaging all learners using research-based strategies, teachers support students as they practice and become strategic and proficient learners.

9. Teachers should use the literacy tools that enable students to learn content material strategically.   Teachers need knowledge and skills—new tools, according to Maslow—that match this time. Yet some teachers have only one tool: the lecture. That is simply not adequate. Teachers must incorporate the full spectrum of the language arts into their instruction: discussion, which combines listening and speaking; reading; and writing. Research in the past two decades shows us that the most effective, and long-lasting, learning occurs when learners of any age are active in the process and think and evaluate their learning. Therefore, teachers need to know how to engage their students in literacy activities that motivate them to learn (Gambrell, 1996; Guthrie, 2000, 2004.) Although many of *us* sat through classes in elementary school, middle school, high school, or college in which the teacher used only the lecture, students today are tuned in to new expectations.

For instance, **technological literacy**—that is, learning to become more proficient in using emerging technology—is one new tool. Ample evidence indicates that technology is changing how people function in society (Friedman, 2006). Emerging and increasingly sophisticated technologies have become so interwoven with every aspect of our daily lives that we do not always comprehend their pervasiveness. Computers are common in the workplace, and their use in homes is certainly growing. A strong argument can be made for increasing the use of computer technology in the schools as a way to ensure that students are adequately prepared for the future (Reinking, 1997). Although computers are definitely one of the greatest technological innovations, fax machines, cellular phones, ATM machines, voice mail, CDs/DVDs, and satellite dishes represent other relatively new tools that we now take for granted. In this text, whenever possible we show technological applications in content area instruction activities. Technological literacy and visual literacy are two important and pervasive forms of literacy that teachers must emphasize to succeed with students. They are discussed further in Chapter 7.

10. Content reading instruction enables students to become autonomous learners. Dependent learners wait for a teacher to tell them what a word is, what the right answer is, and what to do next. Such learners are crippled intellectually. When they need to function independently, they will not know how to do so. Teachers who abandon a textbook because it seems too hard for their students do their students no favor. Teachers who give students all the answers or hand out the notes already organized in the teacher's style bypass opportunities for students to learn how to find answers or take notes. High school can become a place where students avoid responsibility. Schools may perpetuate an environment in which students are excused from learning. The goal of teaching is to move students from being dependent on teachers to being independent in their learning habits—that is, to make them **autonomous learners**. But it is not fair to expect that students can become autonomous in thinking and learning without the benefit of instruction. No matter what the grade level or subject area, teachers can assist students in this transfer of responsibility when they balance the students' level of proficiency and the content to be studied.

To become independent learners, students need to practice a study system to make learning easier. The PAR Lesson Framework, explained in this chapter and used as the basis for this textbook, is a system that can help a teacher show students how to become autonomous learners. The teacher first models PAR and then gradually weans students to independent use of PAR. The four examples presented in this chapter illustrate such independent learning.

As you read this textbook and find activities that you would like to use in your classrooms, use the following checklist to be sure the activity not only works for you in your content teaching, but also is strategic and applies the principles of good teaching:

Activity						
Engages Readers' Prior Knowledge	Uses Communication Skills	Provides Satisfaction in Learning	Enhances Critical Reading and Problem Solving	Enhances Readers' Autonomy and Self-Initiative	Uses Active Involvement and Participation	Provides Feedback

EFFECTIVE CONTENT TEACHERS

Students at all levels need excellent teachers to guide and facilitate their learning. Because the learning process is complex and subtle, students sometimes lack competence and confidence to learn. At such times students need a teacher who can impart both content and the desire and willingness to learn. What constitutes effective teaching? And will principals, supervisors, and especially students value and appreciate the instruction? Good teachers continually explore and learn in an ongoing effort to facilitate student learning. They make their classes relevant by keeping current through their own reading. They provide discussions and activities that link students to the larger outside world. And although they might not be appreciated to the fullest in the short term, they obtain great satisfaction in knowing that their students are challenged to think in an atmosphere conducive to learning.

Effective teachers never rely on simply telling students what they need to know to be successful in a course. Telling is not enough. Effective teachers do not view students as empty vessels to fill with knowledge bit by bit each day. Also, good teachers do not merely assign new chapters or other lengthy reading for homework and expect students to be able to discuss them in class the next day. High-quality teachers use appropriate and effective tools to teach, including strategic instruction, relevant activities, and literacy engagement.

Good teachers often inspire students to think for themselves in deciding how to solve problems, attack reading selections, and evaluate what they are reading. Inspired instruction helps students become autonomous learners—individuals who are independent in their learning habits. Rosemary Altea in *The Eagle and the Rose* (1995) best captured the role of a teacher when she spoke affectionately of her mentor:

> Part of his role as my guide is to teach me to teach myself, so when I ask my question of him, his answer is usually, "What do you think?" He can, and often does, help me to discover answers, like all good teachers; and like all good teachers, he is always there to listen, to encourage, and to steer me gently along my path. (p. 74)

Teachers provide inspired instruction when they guide students by showing them how to learn strategically. **Strategic Learning** uses the methods that are most efficient and effective to suit the learning situation.

Despite the best efforts of teachers, students sometimes misinterpret text in reading. When they do so, they are demonstrating **incomplete thinking**. Students manifest this behavior in a number of ways, such as when they skip important steps in a lesson. A student who has trouble identifying all the steps and who tends to skip steps will have to slow down and rediscover them, or else study will grind to a halt. Such students have no **fix-up strategies** (explained further in Chapter 11)—special intervention strategies good readers have at their disposal to aid in comprehension when they are confused by the reading material.

We appreciate the term *two-finger thinking* used by Edward de Bono (1976) to explain this shortcutting of steps. According to de Bono, two-finger thinking is analogous to two-finger piano playing. A person who plays the piano with only two fingers uses fewer resources than are available. This is fine for playing "Chopsticks" but not suitable for Chopin. In the same way, two-finger thinking uses only part of the brain to perceive and comprehend important reading material. Inadequate use of resources can cause trouble when complex learning skills are required. For instance, two-finger thinking might work on an easy math word problem, but a difficult one will stump a reader used to such shortcuts.

Effective teachers teach students both the content of instruction and, at the same time, all the steps needed for effective thinking and study. Such teachers realize that there is no shortcut to learning and understand the need to provide students reading and writing strategies to help them overcome incomplete thinking. In this text we describe many strategies for training students in reading and thinking. However, the initial step for any teacher is acceptance and use of a framework of instruction as a way to improve learning.

The Importance of Structure through a Lesson Framework

Many mental operations are necessary in reading. For instance, one must sort out relevant from irrelevant information. In addition, readers must be able to summarize information, draw inferences from the text, generate their own questions to be answered in the reading, and monitor their comprehension as they read (Guthrie, 2004). Students who do not think well—that is, who do not adequately perform these mental operations in reading—get great benefit from a well-prepared teacher's structured guidance in learning to better think through a lesson. And students who are poor thinkers cannot afford to be in unstructured classrooms where haphazard teaching is taking place. Poor readers, then, need repetition and structure to learn better habits of thinking and reading. This is what a lesson framework provides.

A framework is the structure around which anything is stretched. It is the systematic arrangement of the basic parts of something. Further, it can represent an organized plan condensed to a series of steps, usually represented by keywords. Such a framework becomes a model for finishing a task. It must be complete and clearly explain all parts of the task.

The framework becomes an aid to learning and a way to activate students to learn. An instructional framework that identifies successful components of a content lesson facilitates the relationships among reading, thinking, and learning. Frameworks for content reading instruction are historically grounded (Herber, 1978; Singer & Donlan, 1985; Vaughan & Estes, 1986) and formulate instruction in a complete and structured way. The most popular content reading frameworks include three basic assumptions:

1. The learner must be ready to learn—thus the teacher must prepare the learner beforehand.

2. The learner must be guided through the learning so that comprehension can be developed during the lesson.

3. The learner should review what has been learned. As part of the third step, the teacher must provide after-reading opportunities to help students retain the learning.

If these basic steps are repeated consistently in the instructional sequence, the learner begins to use them independently of the teacher in a self-instructional manner. It does not matter what keywords are used in a framework as long as they stimulate recall of the steps incorporated in the framework and use words that help teachers adhere to the framework's structure.

PAR: A Lesson Framework for Instruction

PAR stands for "preparation, assistance, and reflection." The **PAR Lesson Framework** is a framework for content reading instruction (see Figure 1.2). PAR is similar to other content instructional frameworks. We coined the acronym *PAR* to develop an

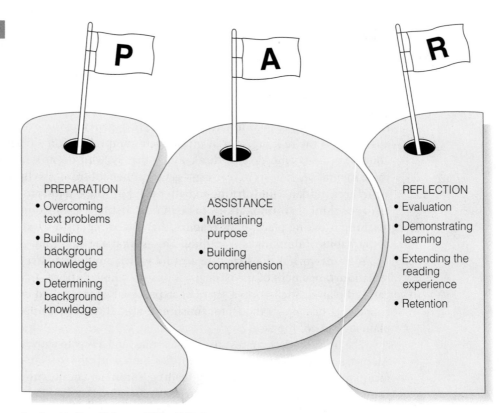

FIGURE 1.2

The PAR
Lesson
Framework

P A R

PREPARATION
• Overcoming
  text problems
• Building
  background
  knowledge
• Determining
  background
  knowledge

ASSISTANCE
• Maintaining
  purpose
• Building
  comprehension

REFLECTION
• Evaluation
• Demonstrating
  learning
• Extending the
  reading
  experience
• Retention

Developed by Dawn Watson and Walter Richards.

association with the golf term *par,* which refers to the completion of a hole or holes by taking only the allotted number of strokes—not exceeding the limit. Golfers usually feel pleased when they achieve par for a course. Likewise, teachers who consistently use PAR to underpin their instruction will be pleased because students will be more meaningfully engaged in their learning. As a by-product, discipline problems that grow from inattention and boredom will be greatly reduced. (Discipline problems represent probably the main cause of teacher burnout.)

In the **preparation step**, as noted in Figure 1.2, teachers need to consider text problems and students' background knowledge. Sometimes students have incorrect or insufficient background knowledge, which makes it difficult for the teacher to have the students begin reading. Instead the teacher needs to choose preparation activities that will build a conceptual base of understanding for students and thereby help them succeed in the reading. The preparation step motivates students to want to read. Put another way, the more preparation a teacher does with students, the more motivated they are going to be to study the topic.

Once motivation is heightened in the preparation step, the teacher moves to the **assistance step**, which provides an instructional context for the lesson. This is a crucial step to help students better comprehend the passage. Teachers many times prepare and motivate students but then tell them to read a passage on their own in class or for homework. Such teachers fail to realize that students who are thinking poorly do not have adequate study skills or do not think critically and need assistance as they read to maintain purpose and build comprehension. Comprehension will improve if strategies are chosen for students to react to as they read. The strategies also help provide a concrete, clear purpose for completing the reading.

In the **reflection step**, teachers use the material that was read to provide extension, enrichment, and critical thinking opportunities. Careful reflection by students is not the same as answering questions either posed by the teacher or listed at the end of the chapter. True reflection occurs when students ask themselves tough questions such as these: "What did I learn from this reading?" "Was it appropriate for me?" "Do I believe what the author said?" "Is this reading material worth retaining?" When students truly reflect on their reading, they retain the material longer and at greater depth.

Using the PAR Lesson Framework improves a teacher's ability to both teach and monitor the reading comprehension of students; however, each phase of PAR is also notable for distinct contributions to the learning environment. As we mentioned earlier, careful preparation for reading enhances students' desire and motivation to learn. In the preparation phase the teacher gets students to *want* to read by awakening natural curiosity. We have seen students in classrooms become very interested in a topic that they cared nothing about before a teacher prepared them with one or more such strategies.

The assistance phase of PAR is the key area for teachers who need to improve students' reading comprehension. When a student is assisted while reading, purpose for the reading is established. Comprehension usually improves when students have a purpose for reading. Finally, using the reflection phase of PAR reinforces students' retention of concepts.

Although we recommend following all the phases of PAR to completion, teachers can emphasize the phase of PAR where their students are having the most difficulty. If students are not motivated, teachers need to do more preparation for the lesson. If students are motivated but not comprehending, teachers need to emphasize the assistance phase. And if students are motivated and seem to comprehend the reading but fail to retain the material, then more emphasis needs to be placed on the reflection phase. Whichever phase is emphasized, the key for the teacher is to consistently model all the PAR steps with the understanding that students will, through such guided practice, significantly improve their reading.

The following sections present four examples of content-specific lessons that illustrate use of the PAR Framework. They provide a sense of how this simple structure can improve any teacher's delivery of content. The PAR Framework can help both the novice teacher and the experienced teacher to become more effective in the classroom.

FOUR LESSONS OF PAR USED IN TEACHING CONTENT

To show that PAR easily accommodates any content area of instruction at any grade level, we chose four lessons—primary, upper elementary, middle, and high school—to illustrate its adaptable nature. All four teachers in these examples use the same framework to lead their learners in a structured and well-paced lesson before, during, and after reading about the assigned subject. These examples provide only an overview; directions for constructing their activities are given in succeeding chapters, where the activities are presented in a larger context. The examples demonstrate how literature, technology, and language arts can be incorporated into content lessons. They help address recent concerns about the reading achievement levels of students at all ages and grade levels.

Example from a Primary Social Studies Lesson

Ms. Alex Seeley, a first grade teacher, incorporated literature into her lesson about school and classroom rules. The lesson would be taught at the beginning of the school year, when first graders are beginning to understand school and classroom expectations, as well as how to be good citizens. She chose the book *David Goes to School* (by David Shannon, Blue Sky Press, New York, 1999). It is about a little boy who is in school but does not seem to understand any of the rules. The book is funny and silly, but at the same time it makes students think about the poor choices David is making and how his choices impact everyone around him, as well as himself. The lesson is intended to coordinate with Virginia Standards of Learning (SOLs) for first grade civics:

The student will apply the traits of a good citizen by

- Focusing on fair play, exhibiting good sportsmanship, helping others, and treating others with respect.
- Recognizing the purpose of rules and practicing self-control; working hard in school.
- Taking responsibility for one's own actions; valuing honesty and truthfulness in oneself and others.

It also coordinates with the Virginia SOLs for first grade English:

- The student will continue to expand and use listening and speaking vocabularies.
- The student will use meaning clues and language structure to expand vocabulary when reading.

To *prepare* her students, she would present this lesson after several days of discussing the rules. To highlight literacy, she would read the title and author of the book and show the children the cover art. By asking students to predict what the book might be about, she would promote discussion and engagement in the reading experience. The children would look at the pictures in the book (picture walk) to make further predictions about David's school experience. During this prereading strategy, the children would be demonstrating their prior knowledge of rules.

To *assist* her students, she would read the story. Next she would construct a cause/effect chart on the board to note what David did and how it affected him and the other children (see Activity 1.1). Then the class would discuss what would happen if David were in their class and how his behaviors would make the children feel. Also, they would comment on how David should be acting.

Next the teacher would write (on a chart, chalkboard, or computer screen) the rule that goes along with what David did wrong. Then she would ask the children to

Cause	Effect	Rule
David did not wait his turn.	Other children had to wait longer.	Everyone gets a turn when we all wait for our turn.
David pushed another child.	Someone got hurt.	No pushing—respect each other.

present other rules that would benefit the class. With each rule they would be asked to explain why it is necessary. The children might even role-play some of these good versus bad behaviors.

To help children *reflect,* the teacher would give each child a piece of drawing paper, folded in half. On one side they would draw a sad face at the top, with a picture below of David breaking a school rule. On the other side of the paper they would draw a happy face and a picture of David following the rule he was breaking. Underneath each picture drawn they would write a sentence about the picture. (If a software program such as *Inspiration* and computers were available, the lesson could incorporate technology as another learning tool.) Afterward they would share their pictures and make a class book to take home and share with their families. The teacher would include a letter inside the front cover of the book to the parents about the making of the book, with the request to read the book carefully with their children to review the rules.

This lesson for young children is about a content subject and uses material that meets state standards for instruction. It also includes several literacy and reading to learn objectives and activities such as predicting, determining cause and effect, and using graphic organizers as it follows the PAR format.

Example from a Fourth Grade Science Class

Ms. Elisabeth Groninger designed a science lesson to help her fourth grade students understand scientific investigations and ecosystems. The class had just finished a unit about botany, so some of the groundwork for the concepts of food chains and food webs had been established. As a result, the students' vocabulary included words to be used within this lesson, such as *producer, photosynthesis, energy, reproduction,* and *ecology.* The lesson would fulfill the following Standards of Learning (SOLs) for Virginia schools:

INVESTIGATING SKILLS

These skills include, but are not limited to, "differentiate among simple observations, conclusions, and predictions, and concretely apply the terminology in oral and written work," "classify into basic categories to organize the data."

This subset also requires that students learn to "create a plausible hypothesis from a set of basic observations, stated in terms of cause and effect that can be tested."

"Illustrate food webs in local area."

"Differentiate between positive and negative influences of human activity on the ecosystem."

"Distinguish between structural and behavioral adaptations."

The lesson would also satisfy language arts objectives for oral presentations, vocabulary and composition, study of nonfiction material, and usage mechanics.

The lesson used two sources of writing. The first selection was "Leopard, Goat, and Yam," an African folktale. This folktale is found in the anthology *Favorite Folktales from Around the World* (Jane Yolen, ed., New York: Pantheon Books, 1986).

The story is a riddle involving a man, two animals, and a vegetable. The riddle and its solution address the question of hierarchy on the food chain. Riddles are fun for all ages; although the answer to the riddle requires some advanced reasoning skills, with collaborative brainstorming and use of drawings on the board to visually depict the possible solutions, the class could attempt the answer. Another appeal of this particular folktale is its African origin, which is a reminder that food chains are found everywhere on Earth, each specific to its ecosystem.

The second selection was the book *Who Eats What? Food Chains and Food Webs* (Patricia Lauber, New York: HarperCollins, 1995). This text is bright, engaging, and to the point. It addresses the concept of food chains and food webs and how animals, plants, and humans are linked ecologically. Although the selection is written more simply than a fourth grade text, Ms. Groninger saw that as an advantage, not a disadvantage. The book supplies basic information while capturing attention. The bright colors, attractive illustrations, and information about different ecosystems accomplish this goal. The text opens with a picture of a caterpillar munching a leaf from an apple tree—a beginning step on the food chain continuum. From there the book continues along the food chain, ending with a boy eating a meal.

For *preparation* the teacher read the folktale "Leopard, Goat, and Yam" aloud. With the teacher's assistance, the class brainstormed about possible answers to this riddle. Because the story describes the possibilities of the farmer's possessions being eaten if not supervised, the class conversation could consider the components of a food chain and, as the second literature selection so succinctly says, "who eats what."

Once the riddle was solved (or the solution given and responses taken), the teacher *assisted* students by reading aloud the second selection, *Who Eats What? Food Chains and Food Webs*. After the selection was read, the teacher put large cards with the words for the unit on the front board. The concepts for these words had been introduced in the read-aloud. The words included *producer, prey, predator, herbivore, carnivore, omnivore, decompose, food chain,* and *food web*. The definitions of these words were discussed, with pictures representing the various terms (such as a picture of a cow for *herbivore*); the students contributed answers based on the information in the read-aloud and the clues from the pictures. The students were then given jot charts to fill out with the terms in the first column, definitions in the second, and examples of each term in the third column (see Activity 1.2). The terms were already listed for the students. The second column was completed by the class. The teacher asked for definitions from

Term	Definition	Example
Habitat	The environment in which a living thing lives	A park, a field, a stream
Herbivore	An animal that eats only plants (producers)	A horse, a cow, a giraffe
Carnivore	An animal that eats only meat	A hawk, a wolf, a crocodile
Omnivore	An animal that eats both plants and meat	A human, a raccoon
Predator	Eats prey	A hawk, a tiger

students as they all filled out the second column, assisting when there were questions or confusion. The students filled out the third column (examples of each term) working in small groups of three or four. Once the charts were completed, the students shared and discussed their ideas for examples of each of the terms; this discussion also reviewed the meanings of the components of the food chain and food web.

The teacher gave each group of four a bag containing small cards with the lesson words on half of the cards and the definitions on the other half. The groups turned the cards face down and collaborated in playing "memory," helping each other to remember which explanations went with each word. This not only provided a fun way to review the words and collaborate about the meanings while playing a game; it also let the teacher evaluate how well the students were grasping the vocabulary.

For *reflection,* a large piece of drawing paper was given to each student. They were asked to choose a favorite meal, showing the parts of that meal across the top of the paper. They then drew and labeled the food chain leading to each final component. The teacher was available for advice and guidance. The students could consult with each other as they thought about their projects. Copies of *Who Eats What?* were also available as reinforcement and for review of examples of pictures of food chains. Again, the teacher could evaluate how well the students understood the concepts in the lesson and could plan additional teaching and review if necessary. The students then shared their drawings and conclusions for the food chains that comprised their meals. The papers were displayed around the room.

For additional reflection, the students were given papers with the following questions to answer in writing for homework:

1. List some animals and plants that live in your neighborhood. Are the animals herbivores, carnivores, or omnivores?

2. What would happen if the sun were taken out of the food chain?

3. What would happen if the food chain lost a part (for instance, if all the plants died)?

4. What is the role of a producer in the food chain? Name one.

5. Why are carnivores important in the food chain?

6. Why are herbivores important in the food chain?

7. A hawk is bigger than a robin. Which do you think needs more energy to live?

8. Make a list of everything you eat in one day. What other animals might eat each of these foods if they had a chance?

Ms. Groninger also supplied some interactive Web sites for the students to visit, just for fun.

Example from a Middle School Mathematics Lesson

Mr. Michael Tewksbury, a middle school mathematics teacher, designed a lesson to teach the difference between ratios and fractions. In his experience, he had found that many students cannot differentiate between what they learn about fractions and ratios. However, from a practical and conceptual standpoint the two are quite different. In short, all ratios are fractions, but not all fractions are ratios. A ratio is a comparison between two quantities. A key developmental milestone is the ability of a student to begin to think of a ratio as a distinct entity, different from the two measures that make it up. Recalling a book he had read to his own 5-year-old son, he selected it as the basis for this lesson (*If You Hopped Like a Frog* by David M. Schwartz, Scholastic Press, New York, 1999). This picture book highlights the amazing abilities of animals by showing what children could accomplish if they were capable of taking on the speed, strength, and size of certain animals. Following the story, the book provides a detailed section that delivers proof of the outlandish claims found in the first 24 pages. These two aspects of the book make it an attractive preliminary instructional activity on ratios. For instance, "If you hopped like a frog…you could jump from home plate to first base in one mighty leap!"

Mr. Tewksbury *prepared* his students with a brief overview about ratios and the course of study for the unit, using a What-I-Know Activity (WIKA) about ratios. Students were asked to list what they already knew about ratios and what they needed to know. The list could be short, but it could be reviewed later for follow-up and additions at the end of the lesson. The teacher also used this preparation activity to assess and build background knowledge. As the ratio lessons continued, the WIKA could be reviewed and updated.

After the WIKA activity, Mr. Tewksbury read *If You Hopped Like a Frog*. As mentioned, the first 24 pages were read by the teacher, but with student interaction as the story progressed. This helped introduce important mathematical concepts, consistent with the following Virginia Standards of Learning (SOLs):

The student will identify representations of a given percent and describe orally and in writing the equivalence relationships among fractions, decimals, and percents.

The student will describe and compare two sets of data, using ratios, and will use appropriate notations, such as *a/b, a to b,* and *a:b.*

The student will compare and order whole numbers, fractions, and decimals, using concrete materials, drawings or pictures, and mathematical symbols.

Visit the *Reading to Learn in the Content Areas* Web site for the link.	Fabulous site with a plethora of information specific to this lesson and other math activities.
Visit the *Reading to Learn in the Content Areas* Web site for the link.	Interesting and fun facts about 20 animals.
Visit the *Reading to Learn in the Content Areas* Web site for the link.	This is a great source of information for this study of ratios and proportions.

For *assistance,* students selected one of the comparisons made in the book and brainstormed a number of ideas about how this comparison could be visually represented (numerically, graphically, or any way they chose). After the discussion, the teacher shared all 12 sets of actual ratio information detailed at the end of the book. Students incorporated this information into their jot charts. Next students were assigned to work in groups of three to find and develop an original animal/personal comparison. To determine specific examples, students needed to research statistics and facts from one of several Internet sites (see Activity 1.3).

After their comparison and facts were identified, students designed visuals to represent their ratios and wrote explanations describing what their representations meant and why they selected particular representation methods. When students had completed the written portion of this task, each group was asked to share their findings, explanations, and justifications as part of a class discussion. The teacher's primary objectives during this *assistance* activity were to assess student understanding, clarify misunderstandings, maintain a focus of relevant discussion, and build comprehension of the concepts of relationships and ratios. The process of focusing discussion and building comprehension was accomplished largely by providing divergent questions aimed at helping students develop a conceptual understanding of ratios.

For *reflection,* students returned to the What-I-Know Activity. This served as a review and preparation for the next lesson about ratios. The specific items reviewed included what they knew now, what they still wanted to know, and interesting and important concepts. This lesson was meant to help students independently formulate their own working conceptual framework and connections for ratios. The hope was that much of this would occur as a direct result of opportunities created for listening, reading, writing, and speaking.

Example from a High School Health/ Physical Education Class

A ninth grade health and physical education class co-taught by James J. DiNardo III and Yogi Hightower Boothe began with students taking their seats near other students with whom they were grouped. The teachers frequently regrouped the students heterogeneously based on their reading ability. (The students had been told only that the grouping was randomly assigned, and they had no reason to question this because they could see no pattern to the groups.)

The *preparation* phase began immediately as the students entered the room. Students began the class even before the teachers told them to by copying into two-column notes the three objectives for the day, written on the chalkboard. They were accustomed to starting each class this way, and no communication was necessary from the teachers. Once this was done, the students were instructed to take a few moments to preview the passage they would be reading that day. Each student then perused the reading, noting features such as title, subtitles, boldface and italicized words, pictures and captions, review questions at the end of the reading, and any other clues that might help them make sense of the text when they later read it.

The teachers then asked the students to close their books. They handed out, one to each student, single sheets of paper, which they called an anticipation guide (see Activity 1.4). Mr. DiNardo explained to the students,

> What good readers do when they read a text such as this is that they make predictions about what the text will say. They make such predictions based on prior knowledge. Then when they go into the text, it really does not matter whether they find out that their predictions are true. Having made the predictions helps them stay engaged in the text. Today we are helping you in this process because we have made some predictions for you in this anticipation guide. All you need to do is, before you read, place a check mark next to the ones you think might be true. Don't worry at this time about whether you are correct. Remember that you are just practicing the habit of predicting before reading. In fact, some of these statements you will later find to be correct; some will be incorrect, and some will be arguable. That is, some of you may interpret them to be true and have evidence to prove them so, while others in the room will have evidence that disproves them. We will have to resolve those issues at that time.

The students were then given a few minutes to check the statements in the anticipation guide. However, the students were told not to open their textbooks; instead, they worked in groups to discuss what they had checked and to try to come to consensus on their understanding of the statements in the guide. In fact, when Boothe and DiNardo worked with the school's communication skills teacher to construct this anticipation guide, they kept in mind four characteristics that make anticipation guides work well to help students interpret difficult text material:

- Rephrase important concepts in the language of students.
- Include a few statements that are intuitively appealing to students but will prove to be inaccurate during a reading of the text.
- Write in such a way as to force students to interpret large segments of text, such as a paragraph or two. This prevents the reading experience from turning into a simple decoding exercise, which is what many textbook worksheets are.
- Word the guide in such a way as to provoke critical thinking about the key concepts. Make statements somewhat vague or subject to interpretation, rather than just true/false statements. Based on their prior knowledge or on the material

NAME _____ DATE _____

ANTICIPATION GUIDE: THE DIGESTIVE SYSTEM

Instructions: Before reading pages 172 through 176 in your textbook, place a check mark (✔) in the space to the left of each of the statements with which you agree. Then, during or after the reading, cross through statements you wish to change, and check any new ones you find to be true. *Be sure you are able to refer back to the text to provide evidence for or against each statement.*

_____ 1. Saliva is important to digestion.

_____ 2. If you ate standing on your head, it would be more difficult for you to swallow and for the digestive system to function properly.

_____ 3. You digest food in your mouth.

_____ 4. Your digestive system could still function properly if the middle 10 feet of your small intestine were removed.

_____ 5. A combination of hydrochloric acid, enzymes, and mucus turns food in your stomach into a thick gooey mush called *chyme*.

_____ 6. If you are preparing to participate in an aerobic sport such as distance running or biking, you should eat a big meal (such as a hamburger, fries, and shake) at least one hour before you do it.

_____ 7. Both the pancreas and the liver produce digestive juices that are stored in the gallbladder.

_____ 8. Capillaries and villi play a major role in the digestive process.

_____ 9. All remaining undigested food passes through the large intestine, which separates fecal waste from water and prepares it for elimination through the rectum.

_____ 10. Diarrhea and constipation are problems of the large intestine.

_____ 11. You could die from diarrhea.

_____ 12. Ulcers, ulcerative colitis, and heartburn are all caused by the same things.

By Mark A. Forget, Yolanda Hightower Boothe, and James J. DiNardo III.

being presented, students might disagree and provide valid evidence for either side of arguments, both before and after the reading. (Anticipation guides are further discussed in Chapter 3.)

Next the *assistance* phase began. The teachers reminded the students to begin silent reading without distracting either themselves or others while reading the chapter about nutrition. The students were reminded to note the pages, columns, and paragraphs that they were using to interpret whether a statement was provable.

The room became quiet as the students read to find out whether their predictions were correct. Boothe and DiNardo either read at the same time or quietly moved around the room to monitor student work with the anticipation guides. One or the other occasionally stopped to whisper encouragement to a student, but they were cautious to avoid any distractions during the reading time.

After about 20 minutes, many of the students were stirring, anticipating the next step: meeting in their groups to attempt to come to a consensus. The teachers instructed them to do just that, reminding the students that coming to consensus differs from attempting to find a majority. They said this to be sure that all voices would be heard and that all students would participate. Once again the teachers moved around the room to monitor and assist. In addition, they reminded students that they must act like "attorneys presenting evidence to support their claims."

This was the *reflection* phase of the lesson. The room was loud as students argued vociferously over statements such as "You digest food in your mouth." Although few checked that statement before or during the reading, some students found evidence that because saliva is important to digestion, the mastication process is also important to digestion, and the digestive process at least starts in the mouth. Many such arguments occurred in the small groups.

The teachers identified the first group to achieve consensus, and they noted the statements that group members believed should be checked now that they had read and discussed them. The teachers placed check marks next to those statements on the transparency of the anticipation guide they had on the overhead projector.

The final phase of the discussion occurred when the teachers turned on the overhead projector and asked for the attention of all the students in order to attempt to come to a classroom consensus. Now the students who had practiced in small group discussions sorted out their differences over the few statements about which all the class had not yet achieved consensus. This process took a few more minutes, and the students obviously relished their abilities to present their interpretations of the evidence they had found in their textbooks. The discussion was orderly and mature, and all students seemed interested in the outcome.

After achieving consensus, the teachers asked the students to report by a show of hands how many felt that using the anticipation guide to make predictions about the reading beforehand had made the passage interesting and desirable to read. All the students raised their hands. In this way the teachers reminded the students of the skills they used to engage themselves in the reading.

The class was nearly over. The teachers reminded the students that they must go back through the reading as a homework assignment to complete their notes based on the objectives that were on the chalkboard at the start of the class, which each student had copied into his or her notebook.

Students usually like the health and physical education classes of Boothe and DiNardo. They say, "We always get to *think* in their class. It's more interesting." These teachers are used to letting the students learn through techniques that encourage them to set their own purposes for reading and then pursue knowledge from the text and reflect on it through discussion or writing. They can see the students develop their own understandings of the text. At the same time they know that active pursuit of these understandings will help the students retain the information and apply it in their own lives. They also know that their students have practiced a learning skill that they will be able to use in any class. Boothe and DiNardo are happy to be reading-to-learn teachers.

The Organization of This Text

The 10 principles presented earlier are an integral part of the discussion in every chapter of this book. The first six chapters are foundation chapters; they present the basic theory and rationale for the approach used in this text. Chapter 2 presents information about the trend for accountability and evaluation for students in content classrooms through standardized testing. Chapters 3, 4, and 5 focus on preparing students to learn, assistance, and reflection. Applications for teachers are provided, as well as examples from several content areas and grade levels. Chapter 6 presents ways to teach with multiple resources beyond the traditional textbook, including cooperative learning. Chapter 7 introduces technological literacy and how to use it in content classrooms. Chapters 8, 9, and 10 discuss how PAR works with study skills, vocabulary, and writing. Chapter 11 describes the many different types of learners in content classrooms and ways to help them. Specific strategies and activities are provided. Chapter 12 describes how to create an affective learning climate.

In each chapter we employ the PAR steps by asking readers to prepare themselves to read, assist themselves in their reading, and reflect on their comprehension. We recommend that you, the reader, now select a subject topic to aid you in creating practice activities. The topic should be one that you are currently teaching or may use in the future as you teach. The books you select will be resources for completing some of the assignments given at the end of each chapter. On completion of this textbook, you should be able to analyze any resource or textbook for its suitability for learners; its effective qualities; and whether it is amenable to the PAR Lesson Framework, its study skills and vocabulary aids, and its attention to different learners. In addition, you should be able to construct activities that help you teach content through a reading-to-learn approach.

When teachers use the PAR Lesson Framework, they facilitate improvement in students' thinking ability. This type of teacher intervention and guidance is a necessary step in improving cognitive ability. In 1983 Pearson and Tierney assessed the instructional paradigm most used by teachers. They found that the key elements of instruction featured the use of many practice materials, little explanation of cognitive tasks, little interaction with students about the nature of specific tasks, and strong emphasis on one correct answer, with teachers supplying answers when confusion remained. Not surprisingly, Pearson and Tierney concluded that such a paradigm was ineffective. We have had much experience since that time observing the type of teaching occurring in schools. We find the same practices prevalent today that they observed. Applying the PAR Lesson Framework to teach specific strategies and skills will help improve how teachers teach. Use of this framework will make teachers more effective in content area classrooms.

ONE-MINUTE SUMMARY

This chapter has provided a short historical overview of the status of education and reading in the late 20th and early 21st centuries. Ways that teachers can be effective in teaching reading, writing, and thinking in their content area classrooms were introduced briefly to launch the book focus. Next the chapter summarized the authors' beliefs about reading to learn and provided the foundation for this textbook by describing 10 core principles for content reading instruction. The goal of good content reading instruction is to aid students in becoming autonomous learners in the classroom. Well-planned reading instruction can help alleviate incomplete thinking on the part of students, when, out of frustration, they sometimes skip important parts of a lesson. The PAR Lesson Framework provides a way to overcome incomplete thinking and poor student learning by offering a structured plan for teachers to deliver content in an effective and organized manner. This chapter provided four examples of the use of the PAR Lesson Framework and documented the need for improved reading instruction as evidenced by failures in reading achievement at all levels of education from kindergarten through adulthood. It also cited studies of researchers who have documented the many achievements of our educational system. Finally, a plan for how we apply these 10 principles and the PAR Lesson Framework throughout this textbook was provided.

PAR ONLINE

For further information about—and activities dealing with—Chapter 1, go to the *Reading to Learn in the Content Areas* Web site and select the Chapter 1 resources: http://academic.cengage.com/education/richardson.

Visit *Reading Online* and read Guthrie's article about engagement and motivation in reading. (The URL is located in the references for this book.)

While at *Reading Online,* read the article by Richardson (the URL is located in the references for this book), from which the PAR examples in this chapter are drawn.

Go to the National Center for Educational Statistics Web site and read some of the statistics about literacy in the United States. (The URL is located in the references for this book.)

END-OF-CHAPTER ACTIVITIES

Assisting Comprehension

1. Look at the list you made at the beginning of this chapter of all the ways you guide—or plan to guide when you start teaching—your students. Add to this list and respond again to this question: How many of these ways include active participation, demonstration, problem solving, student involvement, assessment of success, and self-initiative?

2. Is the PAR Lesson Framework similar to, or different from, any way of teaching that you have used in the past? What associations with other frameworks or other forms of teaching can you make? How do you think you will be able to apply this framework to your teaching?

Reflecting on Your Reading

1. The International Reading Association (2003) has developed a set of standards that identify the performance criteria relevant to classroom teachers. Standard 1 delineates four elements of foundational knowledge that a classroom teacher should possess. Three of these were addressed in this chapter. Teachers should

   • Know foundational theories related to practices and materials they use in the classroom.

   • Recognize historical antecedents to contemporary reading methods and materials.

   • Articulate how their teaching practices relate to reading research.

   How were these elements addressed in this chapter? How does being informed about these elements aid in content instruction?

CHAPTER 2

Often teachers are required to operate under government mandates without government support. It is the "impossible" that leads to resourcefulness. You do not teach for your government; you teach for your students... and for yourself.

MEDITATIONS FOR TEACHERS BY GREG HENRY QUINN, APRIL 15 ENTRY

Assessment and Evaluation Issues

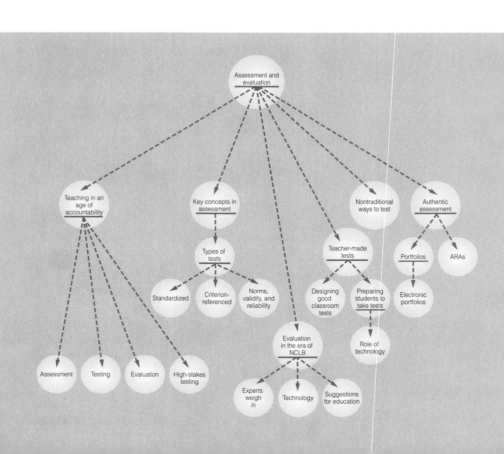

VOICES FROM THE CLASSROOM

It is near the end of the school year. An entire week is being devoted to testing, and everyone is nervous. The students worry that their scores will be low and they won't pass; the teachers worry that low scores will reflect on their performance ratings; the administrators worry that their schools and districts and states will receive failing or borderline results. And teachers are resigned to the fact that after this week, not much real instruction will occur—"everyone knows" the year is over after tests are taken to "prove" that students learned enough, so what's the point of more instruction now?

"Everything" has already been done: Theories and workshop advice have driven instruction; children have been encouraged to get a good night's sleep and eat healthful foods...the students are arriving for the testing. As they walk into the classrooms, they receive peppermints!

The "peppermint theory" (Warm, Dember, & Parasuraman, 1991; Dember, Warm, & Parasuraman, 1996) indicates that focus is improved and affect is engaged when one sniffs peppermint. It's worth a try!

What is familiar to you about this scenario? What issues might trouble you about the week for testing, the anxieties created, and the stakes being wagered on the testing results? What is unfamiliar to you about the solutions to apply?

PREPARING TO READ

1. Before reading this chapter, read the International Reading Association Standard 3, along with the four elements that the IRA expects classroom teachers to be able to perform. How do you rate your knowledge at this point? Could you do these tasks? Standard 3 is presented in the end-of-chapter activities.

2. Following is a list of terms used in this chapter. Some may be familiar to you in a general context, but in this chapter they may be used in unfamiliar ways. Rate your knowledge by placing a plus sign (+) in front of those you are certain you know, a check mark (✓) in front of those you have some knowledge about, and a zero (0) in front of those you don't know. Be ready to locate them in the chapter, and pay special attention to their meanings. Select three terms for which you wrote 0 and create a possible

sentence—a sentence using the term that seems to make sense (that is, it's possible) but may not reflect the meaning of the term.

_____ assessment
_____ testing
_____ evaluation
_____ high-stakes testing
_____ informal assessment
_____ standardized test
_____ norm-referenced test
_____ validity
_____ reliability
_____ criterion-referenced test
_____ NCLB
_____ AYP
_____ highly qualified
_____ value-added assessment
_____ nontraditional test
_____ SCORER

_____ test-wise   _____ portfolio
_____ authentic assessment   _____ ARA

OBJECTIVES

As you read this chapter, focus your attention on the following purposes. You will

1. Define the term *high-stakes testing* and describe its influence on assessment.

2. Understand why the content teacher must take a large role in assessment, testing, and evaluation in today's classroom.

3. Describe traditional tests, including standardized, criterion-referenced, and teacher-made tests.

4. Understand the problems of traditional tests and learn some suggestions for improving them.

5. Understand how to design a test whereby students complete a self-rating of their performance.

6. Understand the importance of nontraditional testing.

7. Understand how being test-wise affects student performance on tests.

8. Learn about practical forms of authentic assessment for the content classroom.

9. Learn about the value of portfolios and how to use them for effective assessment.

10. Consider the role that technology can play in testing, test preparation and/or review, and portfolios.

Reprinted by permission of H. L. Schwadron

Teaching in an Age of Accountability

We are living in an age of accountability (Johnson & Johnson, 2002; Stewart, 2004); high-stakes testing (Afflerbach, 2002; Worthy & Hoffman, 2000); and standards for learning (Valencia & Wixson, 1999). These expectations for accountability, testing, and standards cut across school divisions, states, and nations. It is no longer enough to focus on one's own content in one's own classroom. Educators recognize that all teachers must be accountable to a set of standards that permeate every classroom. For instance, the International Reading Association has prepared a set of standards for assessment, diagnosis, and evaluation specifically targeted at classroom teachers. (In Preparing to Read Activity 1, you were asked to review this standard and its elements before reading this chapter.) Knowing more about accountability issues is clearly becoming part of every content teacher's responsibility. Such knowledge helps teachers discuss standards for learning, evaluation, assessment, and high-stakes testing in a manner that helps all learners to receive the best education and all educators to provide it. In this chapter we present information about assessment, testing, and evaluation as it pertains to the content teacher. Both formal and informal means of assessment are discussed, and suggestions are provided.

"**Assessment** is the gathering of information about students from multiple measures or sources at multiple points in time" (Gottlieb, 2003, p. 2). The purpose of assessment is to make educational decisions by collecting data (Salvia & Ysseldyke, 1998). Assessment is an ongoing process; it can include such data as formal test scores, but often it does not. Each time a teacher begins a new unit of instruction, assessment should occur. We call this process "determining background," which we describe in Chapter 3, along with several assessment procedures. **Testing** is a part of assessment; it is one event, or data source, from one instrument given at one point in time. Tests are a "proxy for accomplishment" (Afflerbach, p. 9) because they provide a sketch—not an entire profile—of how a general population is doing on the factors being tested. Theodore Sizer has commented, "Tests tend to test how one individual performs on that kind of test. It's like taking a temperature in a hospital. It's one important index, but it's only one. We're judging kids on the basis of their temperatures" (Oppenheimer, 2003, p. 282). Tests are useful in providing a point of comparison and one measure of evaluation. **Evaluation** is a term usually reserved for making judgments about educational performance based on collected assessment data. A test is one piece of data for an evaluation. When teachers give tests in their content areas, they use the results to evaluate student knowledge. However, teachers often use many more sources of data in evaluating student learning. When *one* instrument is used to make an educational decision, that process is labeled **high-stakes testing**. According to the International Reading Association, "*high-stakes testing* means that one test is used to make important decisions about students, teachers, and schools" (1999, p. 1). That single test is given specifically to determine how well students know content information.

Teachers are constantly assessing learners because they collect information about their students' performance regularly. In the past, such **informal assessment** has been used to evaluate students and assign grades that should reflect student learning

Visit the *Reading to Learn in the Content Areas* Web site for a link to the article "The Power of Peppermint Is Getting Put to the Test."

and success. However, today such informal assessment is not considered adequate to demonstrate student progress. Uniform assessment procedures at the state level are now required to provide evaluation of educational progress. A formal measure, usually a designated test, is selected as the way to determine whether students have learned what they "should know." Because of this trend toward consistent, uniform testing with one test as the only measure of success, all teachers must be aware of information provided in this chapter; being informed is the first step toward appropriate assessment. Teachers must understand how to balance informal and formal means of assessment.

KEY CONCEPTS IN ASSESSMENT AND EVALUATION

Testing involves quantitative assessment; that is, its purpose is to quantify or ascribe numerical results to performance. Several types of tests are available to assess students. Aptitude tests predict potential for learning. Diagnostic tests designate areas of strength and needs. Suppose a student was not achieving and the teacher suspected that the student could do much better. An aptitude test might verify this observation and lead to an effective educational plan for that student, such as a program that challenges gifted students. Suppose a student was below grade level in reading performance but specific ways to help were not apparent. Then a diagnostic test could help pinpoint the areas of need. In these examples, the tests assess and the findings help activate an instructional plan. Usually guidance personnel or specialists administer such forms of assessment, which can be informal or formal measures. The initial observations of the teacher, often including informal assessment of student class performance, start the testing process.

What are the three types of tests discussed here?

Achievement tests are intended to show what students have achieved or learned about a specific area. Teachers give informal achievement tests all the time. Most schools have participated in annual evaluations of student achievement for decades. Such evaluations have focused on creating a picture that informs us about student progress, especially in math and reading skills. One national example, cited throughout this textbook, is the National Assessment of Educational Progress (NAEP), which publishes results of nationwide testing. School systems have systematically administered tests to determine how their schools are doing, but the tests they have used—and thus the information they have gathered—have differed from state to state and even from district to district. Decisions about individual students' progress, or a school's standing, have seldom been made from the results of such tests. Teachers of content subjects may have helped administer such tests in their classrooms, but in the past they were not held accountable for the test results. In today's content classrooms, however, teachers are being held accountable for test results.

Standardized, Norm-Referenced Tests

Tests can be standardized and norm-referenced, or criterion-based and/or norm-referenced. A **standardized test** measures ability or achievement against an expectation (a norm or standard). The major purpose of standardized, norm-referenced tests is to evaluate the amount of information that students know about a subject. Examples you may know are *The Scholastic Aptitude Test* (SAT) and the *Graduate Record Examination* (GRE), developed and published by Educational Testing Service (ETS); or *The Stanford Ten* (the 10th edition of the *Stanford Achievement Test*). Such tests usually consist of multiple-choice or closure questions, which are readily and quickly scored by scan sheets or sometimes by hand. One correct answer is expected per item. Many classroom teachers follow the formats used on standardized tests as they construct classroom tests. Standardized tests are used to compare the performance of groups, such as the results from one school compared to those of a school system, or a system to the state, or the state to the nation. The tests are designed with care by a group of experts and are pilot-tested on a representative sample of students. The results are studied, the test is modified, and a set of norms is developed. The norms become the basis for comparing results; hence the term **norm-referenced test** is often used to describe standardized tests. Scores on a standardized test are given in percentiles, stanines, standard score equivalents, grade equivalents, or normal curve equivalents.

Not all standardized tests are equally satisfactory to all users. Perhaps the norming groups are not representative of the particular population to be tested. Perhaps the items on the test do not reflect the content taught to the students tested. Perhaps the test purports to test content that it in fact does not really test. Standardized tests, however, are subject to a system of checks that helps users make appropriate selections. These measurement concepts include validity and reliability. **Validity** is the "truthfulness" of the test—a check of whether the standardized test actually measures what it claims to measure. **Reliability** is the "consistency" of the test—whether it will produce roughly the same results if administered more than once to the same group in the same period. Reliability checks how dependable the test is. Both validity and reliability contribute to confidence in a quantitative measure. The higher the validity and reliability, the better a test is reported to be.

A school system should select the standardized test best suited to its system by asking these questions:

1. Does this test measure what has been taught?
2. Can we depend on it to give about the same results if we administer it today and tomorrow?
3. Is the norming group similar to our group of students?

Unfortunately, as information presented in this chapter demonstrates, the decision to use a standardized test usually does not reside at the school level at all; it is the choice of a state or national mandate.

Criterion-Referenced Tests

Criterion-referenced tests are less formal than standardized tests, although their format is much like that of standardized tests—usually multiple-choice or closure questions. Criterion-referenced tests can be standardized, but their major purpose is not comparison, so they often are not normed. Because they are less formal, short-answer, true/false, and other objective items might be included. The purpose of criterion-referenced tests is to measure whether a student can perform a specific task or knows a specific body of knowledge. Thus their purpose resembles that of classroom tests.

The criterion is the level of performance necessary to indicate that a student knows the task. The clients decide this criterion. Thus two schools could use the same test but set different criteria. One school might set 85 percent as a passing score, and the other might set 90 percent as passing. The level of performance on the task is the score: A score of 85 percent means that the student responded correctly to 85 percent of the items. No grade-equivalent scores, stanines, or other scores are provided.

Because criterion-referenced tests indicate mastery of a task, they should be based on specific objectives. For example, the objective might be stated as follows: "The student will demonstrate mastery by correctly identifying 48 of 50 states and their capitals." A student who has been taught 50 states and capitals and can identify 48 on the test has demonstrated mastery of the criterion. A school system that elects to use a criterion-referenced test developed by an outside source can select an appropriate test by asking these questions:

1. Do the objectives and criteria match our objectives in this content?
2. Are enough items included to indicate whether our students have met the criteria?
3. Do the test items reflect the way in which we taught the information?

Criterion-referenced tests are not new, but their evolution into more uniform, formalized tests is. In fact, the concept of criterion mastery is what individual teachers rely on as they design classroom tests that are criterion-referenced but are for individual classroom use. Unfortunately even criterion-referenced tests in today's world of testing are not selected at the school level; this choice is made by a state or national mandate.

EVALUATION IN THE ERA OF NO CHILD LEFT BEHIND

For many years, a perception has existed that public education in the United States is not adequate. Information cited in Chapter 1 demonstrates why this perception has formed. During the last third of the 20th century, national results (National Center for Educational Statistics, 2003) for fourth and eighth graders showed a decline: Only 31 percent of fourth graders and only 32 percent of eighth graders attained a "proficient" level—a standard that test officials say all students should reach. Thirty-seven percent of fourth graders and 26 percent of eighth graders did not achieve a basic level of reading proficiency according to the NAEP 2003 report. Many experts wrote that our schools were in crisis and standards had to be established as a benchmark for all students. Such authors as Bloom (1987) and Hirsch (1987) led this charge several years ago; today politicians are taking the lead. Legislation at the federal and state government levels has raised awareness of assessment and evaluation in schools

Visit the *Reading to Learn in the Content Areas* Web site, Chapter 2, for a link to the NAEP.

today. Godwin and Sheard (2001) have noted some of these policy-making interventions, such as vouchers and national testing. While many experts contest the perception that public education is failing (Berliner, 2001; Bracey, 1997; McQuillan, 1998; Whittington, 1991), the voices of concern have led to new federal interventions such as the No Child Left Behind Act (**NCLB**) of 2001. As President George W. Bush stated when signing this act,

> Our schools will have higher expectations—we believe every child can learn. From this day forward, all students will have a better chance to learn, to excel, and to live out their dreams. (Committee on Education and the Workforce, 2002)

NCLB was incorporated into the reauthorization for the Elementary and Secondary Education Act (ESEA), which indicates in part that stronger accountability is expected, as well as use of "teaching methods that have been proven to work" (www.ed.gov/programs/readingfirst/legislation.html).

NCLB has required a significant amount of testing in schools, beyond the requirement to administer the National Assessment of Educational Progress in grades 4 and 8 in every state.

With this legislation, huge amounts of federal funds have been provided to states to ensure strong education for all students—and for teachers as well. A major goal of this act is to ensure a strong emphasis on reading instruction, especially for children in the first few grades. Some professionals argue that this emphasis takes away support needed for older students who need reading instruction, and also for those who have special needs, as described in Chapter 11 (Paul, 2004; Conley & Hinchman, 2004). This funding has come with a condition: Schools must demonstrate that the education resulting from funding has been effective. The way this demonstration takes place is through the results of mandated testing in grades 3 through 8. NCLB states that schools must show **adequate yearly progress** (**AYP**). AYP requires schools to demonstrate at least minimal progress for every student in every school; if AYP is not being met after two years, parents may move their children to other schools, and federal dollars may be taken away from low-performing schools. Adequate yearly progress must be based on scientific and research-based instruction and evaluation. Also, teachers must be **highly qualified**—that is, specifically endorsed to teach the subjects they are hired to teach.

Did you realize that the NCLB act repeats the words *scientific* or *scientifically* 115 times and the word *research* 245 times? (See pages 240 and 436 of Oppenheimer's *The Flickering Mind*.)

How has NCLB effected evaluation procedures?

What makes one test so important?

Many states have decided, in the wake of NCLB, that they should require all schools to use a designated test that will better determine mastery of content deemed important in their states. They have created—or commissioned creation of—criterion-referenced tests that match their state standards for education; or they have chosen a nationally recognized standardized test they believe will demonstrate such competence. This has created a situation new to many content teachers, in which high-stakes tests are now a greater part of their instructional considerations.

In the past few years, national test scores have gone up, especially in reading (NAEP, 2007), as noted in Chapter 1. Some people believe that this rise in scores is the direct result of NCLB; certainly the Phi Delta Kappa/Gallup Poll (Rose & Gallup, 2007) indicates that some—31 percent—have a favorable impression of NCLB. Others believe it is the result of increased attention to student performance and effective teaching.

Experts Weigh In

Does your professional organization have a position statement about high-stakes tests?

Standardized and criterion-referenced tests have an important place in the evaluation process. They also create some concerns. Many experts in education are quite concerned about the emphasis NCLB seems to place on the use of high-stakes tests, as this article title reflects: "The train has left: the No Child Left Behind Act leaves black and Latino literacy learners waiting at the station" (Paul, 2004). Houston (2005) questions whether different learning styles can be accommodated with an emphasis on standardized tests, and whether the joy of learning might be impeded. Calkins, Montgomery, and Santman (1998) explain that tests are not necessarily the "enemy"; but they warn that teachers must learn how to understand what they can and cannot reveal about individual performance. Now that NCLB has been in place for several years, analyses of its effectiveness are indicating that its success is, at best, uneven (Liston, Whitcomb, & Borko, 2007; Rose & Gallup, 2007). Critics wonder whether conceptual understanding can truly be assessed on tests selected to meet the goals of NCLB (Liston, Whitcomb, & Borko, 2007). Some professional organizations have developed position statements that raise cautions about high-stakes testing (American Psychological Association, 2001; International Reading Association, 1999; National Council of Teachers of Mathematics, 2000). Director Bushaw and International President Fujloka of Phi Delta Kappa have published a statement titled "Rethinking assessment and reforming NCLB" (Bushaw & Fujloka, 2006). They point out that while most Americans agree with the underlying purpose of NCLB, they want schools to focus on yearly student improvement rather than on a school's scores.

A paper about NCLB, written by Seenu Samala, is posted at the *Reading to Learn in the Content Areas* Web site, Chapter 2.

One important group of experts has voiced opinions in the Phi Delta Kappa/Gallup poll (Rose & Gallup, 2006, 2007). As noted previously, some think that NCLB has helped, but there seems to be a caveat: In 2007 40 percent had an unfavorable impression, and in 2006 39 percent (up 9 percent from the 2005 poll) indicated that there was too much emphasis on testing. In 2007 Rose and Gallup noted that "what the data say to us is that the public, despite its desire for high standards and accountability, does not approve the strategies used in NCLB" (p. 36). The polls from 2006 and 2007 also show that participants place great confidence in teachers. Another group of experts, Parent Teacher Associations (PTAs), has shown that one in three PTA members believes that NCLB has been effective for his or her children, but also that too much pressure is being placed on schools and teachers (Robelen, 2005).

Uzzell (2005) is an expert from the legislative side of the picture; he is a former member of the U.S. Department of Education and of the U.S. House and Senate Committees on Education. He points out that there is a danger schools are reporting inaccurate and imprecise data in order to meet the provisions of NCLB—and perhaps concealing accurate results of standardized tests.

One concern about any standardized testing is the *washback* effect of tests (Bardovi-Harlig & Dornyei, 1998). Because of constant exposure, students and teachers become very familiar with the language of tests; this familiarity itself can influence test results. The adoption of state and national standards may lead to too much emphasis on testing and not enough on learning content (Berube, 2004), so students may end up learning more about how to take tests than what they should be learning. A major concern is that one size truly does not fit all. Often questions about what test to choose (such as those we have suggested be asked) do not yield satisfactory answers for a school system; nevertheless school systems use the tests as a measure of performance. They do so because comparisons can be made across schools, divisions, states, and nations. They also do so because demand for national testing, using the same test throughout every state, is increasing. This concern leads to the *high-stakes issue*: More educators and politicians are questioning why students should achieve a passing grade in a content class when they perform poorly on a designated test. They want the test to be the common denominator and the grade to be consistent with the test score.

A Web site posted by Susan O'Hanian and devoted to NCLB—a critical perspective—is posted at the *Reading to Learn in the Content Areas* Web site, Chapter 2.

But are high-stakes tests appropriate measures of academic success? They seem today to be "major influences on curriculum and instruction, on teachers and their professional development, on community–school relationships, and on levels of school funding" (Afflerbach, 2002, p. 1). Gross (2003) points out that sometimes panic sets in when a statistic seems troubling—such as a ranking that places the United States lower in education than in other countries—and the wrong choices are made, causing "American education flu." Should one test be used to make decisions about performance when other indicators, or a combination of other indicators, might better reflect progress? Will test results be used to take money from students such as those discussed in Chapter 11? Can a test really capture the learning that "involves complex, recursive processes of interpretation and meaning construction" (Afflerbach, 2002, p. 12)? Can tests really replicate the daily tasks that students will be expected to perform after having graduated from high schools? Thornburg (2001) encourages educators to "put the pencils down" because standardized test items "decontextualize" learning. He notes that test items focus on isolated facts that are often not at all applicable in real-world knowledge.

On the positive side, NCLB has brought to the surface an increasing need for more standardized means of determining at least some measure of success and needed areas of improvement in instruction. NCLB has improved awareness that many diverse students need more instructional attention. This can mean that subgroups such as English language learners (ELLs) and learning-disabled, at-risk, and poverty-stricken children (see Chapter 11) will receive much more attention and that teachers instructing them will be better qualified to do so. Another benefit is that uniform testing will be provided so that learners and groups of learners can be consistently compared on the same measure. Because so many people have voiced concerns about NCLB, including teachers, parents, superintendents, and politicians, the way the law is interpreted is changing. The recent Commission on No Child Left Behind (2007) has recommended significant levels of support for teachers and principals, as well as accurate and fair accountability and quality student options for demonstrating competence. For content teachers, the emphasis on demonstrating adequate yearly progress through standardized testing means that *all* teachers must become involved!

How Are High-Stakes Tests Constructed and Used?

In the state of Virginia, these are called Standards of Learning (see Chapter 1 for some examples of these standards within the PAR examples). A link to California's Standards for Reading Assessment is posted at the *Reading to Learn in the Content Areas* Web site, Chapter 2.

The essential learning of content information that students "should know" is determined by a group of experts. This group of experts may include content teachers, administrators, state education department personnel, and citizens. The "essential content knowledge" is usually written in the form of standards and competencies that all students are expected to meet.

Once such standards are developed and accepted by a state, they are used to formulate a test that students must take to demonstrate mastery of content. To meet the requirements of NCLB, such tests would be given in grades 3 through 8; but many states also test mastery at the end of content courses to make sure students know specific content before graduating from high school.

If students do not demonstrate mastery of the test material, they and their teachers are held accountable. The consequences of poor scores on this one test are often disturbing. Funding for a school may be withheld by the district, state, or nation; students may not be able to pass a grade or graduate until they pass the test, even if their grades in the content courses are passing; teachers may be asked to explain why their students have "gained so little" in their classrooms. Students who do not pass a mandated test are usually required to repeat the test until they do pass it. Schools—and teachers—whose students consistently do not pass the test are being asked to explain why not and to provide remediation for their students. Many schools have come under fire for low test scores. Because it appears that only one measure of knowledge, the designated test, is being used to judge student, school, district, or state performance, the stakes are indeed high.

What Role Can Technology Play in Assessment, Testing, and Evaluation?

Oppenheimer provides an example of one comprehensive computerized assessment program, *STAR,* in his book *The Flickering Mind.* See page 284 of his book.

Technology programs have been created to perform assessment, testing, and evaluation tasks. Such software programs often compound the problems we have discussed. Russell (1999) examined the effect of taking a test on computer or on paper. His results show that the mode of administration influences student performance. To make sure that the test items are the important factor, not the mode of administration, electronic aids for assessment, testing, and evaluation must be selected using the same criteria as for any other testing method presented in this chapter. Elaborate software that includes assessment procedures, placement into computer learning environments, and evaluation after learner interaction within the program is certainly available; but few of these computer programs are adequate right now. This is probably because such programs must rely on mostly quantitative means of assessment and evaluation and are subject to the same pitfalls as use of isolated tests rather than several sources of assessment data. An appealing quality of computer-based assessment is that after the software or online registration is purchased, individual learners can participate and their results can be computed, saved, and reported quickly without much time invested by the teacher or school. One drawback is the great cost of the more sophisticated programs. Another is that results are subject to the same issues of norming, validity, and reliability as any paper testing.

WHAT EDUCATORS CAN DO IN THE AGE OF ACCOUNTABILITY

 Formal testing provides valuable information; it is a part of good assessment and evaluation of instructional success. What can content teachers do in this age of accountability? Professional organizations provide sound advice for teachers within their position statements (American Psychological Association, 2001; International Reading Association, 1999; National Council of Teachers of Mathematics, 2000):

- Teachers should explain the appropriate use of tests whenever they can. Teachers can point out the importance of using multiple measures. One recommendation (of the IRA position statement) is that teachers "construct rigorous classroom assessments to help outside observers gain confidence in teacher techniques" (p. 1). Such action might demonstrate to outsiders that because instructional quality is high, extreme measures of accountability (that do not really account for progress) are not necessary. Teachers need to explain to parents and policy makers that classroom assessment is important and reflects students' achievement. Teachers need to teach students about tests, but not teach to a test. Informal and authentic assessment should be incorporated into instruction, as will be described in the following sections of this chapter. One school recently took a stand that it will not teach to any test (Fisher, 2004). The principal explained that teachers had been spending too much time preparing students to take the test rather than on deepening student learning and integrating art and music into the classroom. The diversity of the students in this school (77 percent English language learners) meant that more creativity rather than less was necessary. The school expects to do well on the high-stakes test, but it will no longer gear all of its instruction toward this one measure. Richardson (2002) found that high school students who had experienced a humanities curriculum (focusing on the impact of history on literature, philosophy, and art) with little emphasis on a high-stakes test did as well as or better than students who had experienced concentrated test preparation.

- Teachers should understand the purpose of a test—or any other means of evaluation—well enough to describe it to parents, students, and other stakeholders. If an "assessment team" (Murray, 2002) consists of students, parents, teachers, and administrators, everyone can share this job, and all can be ready to help describe the how and why.

- Teachers need to practice accountability by choosing formats for assessment and evaluation that match the content being learned and making sure that the formats are as authentic and representative as possible. This includes technological formats.

- Informed teachers might argue that some of the conflicts raised by high-stakes tests result from trying to equate different sources of data meant to demonstrate different aspects of education. By consistently raising questions and balancing test results with other measures, teachers can keep the role of standardized tests in perspective for themselves—and, we hope, for administrators and the community.

- The most effective solution should be excellent instruction and multiple means of assessment that lead to solid evaluation.
- As Bushaw and Fujloka (2006) suggest, the emphasis should be on **value-added assessment** that looks at a student's growth and achievement over time. The emphasis would no longer be on comparing students to each other, but on comparing a student's past achievements to newer marks of achievement.

How do teachers today cope with high-stakes testing in their classrooms? Hughes (2007) writes about how teachers at his school persisted through many principals and mandates for testing—some effective and some not so effective. They trudged on, building relationships with students, parents, and community. Their school has remained instructionally sound through it all. For some teacher voices, refer to Activity 2.1.

When Teachers Make Tests

Teacher-made tests are one way of increasing accountability. Teachers should test to determine what their students have learned and still need to learn. Their tests should reflect high academic standards but be based on what was taught. Tests are the culmination of periods of study about a content topic. Tests come in many forms—from

---

ACTIVITY *2.1* COPING WITH HIGH-STAKES TESTING IN CONTENT CLASSROOMS

"NCLB is an ironic term because so many children are left behind because their needs are not considered when it comes to testing. How is it that a child who is not on grade level for reading has to take the grade level test anyway? Yes, there is a student who reads at a first grade level in my daughter's class, and by law he must take the fourth grade test for reading. We know this student will not pass. Why put him through the frustration? *Why can't a student take the test that is appropriate for him regardless of his grade level? There still would be a statistical means of showing adequate progress.*" Lori Levy

"As a kindergarten teacher (and former fifth grade teacher), I felt like I was going to explode when I gave the students their first social studies assessment with no pictures and way too many words. It was from the same computerized test generator used for my fifth grade class—some of the questions were even the same! *Thankfully, we've had many conversations with the head of social studies and each year the tests have become more appropriate.*" Ginger Banta

"It was decided the teachers would make chapter tests for every book read for every level reading group, based on the questions used in the reading passages of the test. This was a lot of work; we did not use any materials provided through the school system. Far more detrimental than the teachers' workload was being a part of sucking the joy out of reading for these students. Reading was not for pleasure and stories were not to enjoy; they were to dissect and beat until the pulp was taken out. *We hoped for the 'washback' effect; we wanted students to be familiar with terminology of the tests and use it to influence their answering.*" Ginger Banta

informal observations of student learning to formal final examinations. Students' ages and the topics covered influence the type of evaluation. Teachers do need to test in some way; that is part of their instruction.

Tests should match the learning, not vice versa. Beyer noted in 1984, "Much so-called teaching of thinking skills consists largely of giving students practice in answering old test questions, a procedure that probably focuses students' attention more on question-answering techniques than on the specific cognitive skills that are the intended outcomes of such activities" (p. 486). Unfortunately the situation may not have changed much in recent decades. For instance, Walton and Taylor (1996) created workshops to help teachers at the elementary level produce more relevant tests for the test takers that stretch their minds. Kahn (2000) found that high school English teachers tended to teach students to think critically and analyze literature, but then gave tests of factual knowledge. Such inconsistencies confuse students about what to learn, how to take tests, and why tests matter. Rather than giving practice with stale questions, teachers should seek ways to improve their tests, thereby eliciting the cognitive skills that are the ultimate goal of instruction. A teacher's main purpose in giving a test is to evaluate whether students have learned. Traditionally teachers ask questions about what they have taught, and students answer them. Teachers then evaluate the answers as a gauge of how well students have learned the material. A secondary purpose is to provide test grades as one sign of progress in a report to students, parents, and administrators.

In addition, students' performance on a test should tell teachers how well they have presented content material. Overlooked in the past, this testing purpose has the greatest potential for creating an optimal classroom learning environment. If students can produce fine responses to questions, teachers may conclude not only that students are confident with the topic but also that they as teachers are presenting the content in ways that assist comprehension effectively. If students cannot produce satisfactory answers, the material may need to be retaught with different instructional strategies. Teachers who consider tests as a way to evaluate their own instruction, as well as to evaluate students' knowledge and to assign grades, often alter their instruction and revise their tests. The result is that both teachers and students improve at their respective jobs. But changing the evaluation to match instructional practice is difficult. Teachers need support and time, as well as good reasons, to do so (Liston, Whitcomb, & Borko, 2007). The next sections of this chapter suggest several new ways of thinking about assessment and evaluation.

The Role of Pop Quizzes

Pop quizzes have often been popular with teachers. Teachers may think that pop quizzes provide a means of control over "making" students learn. They may think that such quizzes demonstrate their instructional rigor. The usual scenario for pop quizzes is to find out whether students have read an assignment. But what if students tried to read the assignment and experienced difficulty? A pop quiz may penalize students for not understanding rather than for not reading the material. Students may require assistance before they will be able to demonstrate learning.

Nessel (1987, p. 443) comments that question-and-answer sessions that do not develop understanding "amount to a thinly disguised test, not a true exchange of ideas." Developing a conceptual understanding of a topic is difficult to do with just one homework assignment completed; discussion and thought are required. The question "How did you know the answer was boxcar?" (Walton and Taylor, 1996) may convey the complexity that good questions and discussions require before any measure of knowledge can be made fairly. Most pop quizzes leave no room for such development. When question-and-answer sessions become drills, teachers cannot determine whether a question has been misunderstood or poorly phrased or whether the student has difficulty constructing a response. Unless teachers use pop quizzes for instruction rather than for grading, they will defeat their own purposes and send an incorrect message to students: It's not important to understand the material, just to recount it!

Instead pop quizzes should be used to evaluate what teachers can be reasonably sure has been achieved. For instance, rather than "popping" questions for a grade, a teacher could check to see whether students followed instructions for reading an assignment. A teacher could also use a writing activity (such as the activities described in Chapter 10) to make certain that homework was attempted. If understanding the homework was the problem, the students' written comments will show the teacher that the attempt was made. If students do this, they demonstrate that they tried to read for the assigned purpose. This demonstration will accomplish the same purpose as a pop quiz.

One middle school mathematics teacher, Mary Broussard, allows students to accumulate points toward their final grade by doing homework. The students are also tested, and the homework points do not outweigh the test grade. This teacher encourages students to try, knowing that they can get some credit for doing so, and she uses the class review to clear up confusion. Activity 2.2 shows a homework comprehension sheet designed by a middle school social studies teacher to indicate whether students attempted their homework and also to help the teacher focus the

---

ACTIVITY *2.2* HOMEWORK COMPREHENSION SHEET

On this paper (front and back) I want you to answer the following questions as completely as you can.

1. How did you study pages 192–194 in Social Studies?
2. What did you learn from these pages?
3. Do you see any similarities between your life and the life of the people mentioned?
4. Were there any passages, terms, or concepts you found difficult to understand?
5. What part of this reading did you find most interesting?
6. How do you feel you answered these questions?
7. Why do you feel the way you do?

Developed by Charles Carroll.

lesson. Before assigning the reading as homework, the teacher asks the students to survey the reading and write three questions that they expect to answer from it. When they arrive in class the next day, the teacher distributes this exercise. The teacher can rapidly review the responses to the homework comprehension sheet to find out who completed the assignment. Areas of student confusion as well as student interests can be ascertained. This activity serves as a check of homework and also as a way to determine student background for the rest of the lesson.

A high school foreign language teacher uses "proverbia" to encourage students to keep up in classwork. She thus accomplishes what many teachers think pop quizzes should do while showing her students that practice for their quizzes is important, interesting, and challenging. Activity 2.3 provides an example.

We encourage teachers to think carefully about why they plan to administer a pop quiz, then design the quiz to achieve their objectives. If the objective is to promote student independence and responsibility, then the social studies teacher's solution works well. If it is to "catch" students, we ask teachers to think again about assisting versus evaluating comprehension.

TRADITIONAL TEACHER EVALUATION

Traditional test items include objective questions, essay questions, or a combination of these. Objective tests include multiple-choice, true/false, matching, and completion questions. Teachers find such items easy to grade but difficult to phrase. Students sometimes label objective items as tricky, confusing, or even too easy. Essay tests require students to write about a given topic. Students sometimes call essay questions confusing, too hard, or unfair. Essay formats are also labeled as subjective because teachers must spend time considering responses carefully when grading. However, essay questions are not subjective or difficult to grade when questions are written clearly and carefully. Furthermore, essay questions offer a viable way to evaluate critical thinking and the applied level of comprehension.

ACTIVITY 2.3 PROVERBIA FOR HIGH SCHOOL LATIN STUDENTS

Proverbium #1: Members of an avian species of identical plumage congregate.

Answer: Birds of a feather flock together.

Note: I encourage students to share the proverbia with their parents. Parents may give suggestions to their children regarding problem-solving strategies but must not give the answer.

Correct answers count + 1 toward the quiz!

Note: Proverbs use English words, which are derived from Latin words. They serve as vocabulary builders and critical thinking exercises while also taking the place of pop quizzes.

Developed by Amy Nowlin.

Creating Effective Teacher-Made Tests

The single greatest problem with traditional tests is that the grades students receive often disappoint teachers. We think that the single best solution to this problem is for teachers to stop giving tests before students experience the preparation and assistance phases of the PAR Lesson Framework. Yet even allowing for this solution, many other problems with traditional tests have been identified.

A few decades ago, *Captrends* ("Window on the Classroom," 1984) reported a study of 342 teacher-made tests in a Cleveland school district. Administrators, supervisors, and teachers representing all subject areas reviewed tests from all grade levels. The format that these reviewers found throughout the tests was similar to the format that we described: objective, short-answer questions. Only 2 percent of all items in the 342 tests were of the essay type. The researchers found many problems with the presentation of the test items. Directions were often unclear and sometimes nonexistent. Poor legibility, incorrect grammar, and weak writing made some items difficult to read. Point values for test items and sections were noticeably absent. Ambiguity in questions led to the possibility of more than one correct response or student confusion about choices to make in responding to items. In addition, the types of questions asked were predominantly literal. Almost 80 percent of the items concentrated on knowledge of facts, terms, and rules. The middle school tests used literal questions even more than did the elementary or high school tests. Questions at the application level of comprehension accounted for only 3 percent of the questions asked. The situation has not changed much since then (Ayers, 2001; Kahn, 2000; Walton & Taylor, 1996).

One eighth grade English teacher took a hard look at her own test and found the following:

> The primary comprehension focus was a mixture of all three levels, but more literal and inferential than application. . . . "Comprehension was dependent on recall more than real learning. . . . The test was too long and looked hard. . . . I neglected to give point values or the weight of the test in the final grade." (Baxter, 1985)

This teacher revised her test and summarized her satisfaction with the new version:

> All in all, I feel that the best feature of my redesigned test is that it captures many concepts and is a more appealing form. In relation to the original test, I feel this test allows the student to demonstrate more of his/her knowledge of the material covered in the unit by giving specific responses, especially in the discussion section. I feel this test will net better student response because it appears shorter, looks more appealing, and is different from usual tests I would have given in similar teaching situations before. (Baxter, 1985)

We see five problems as characteristic of teacher-designed classroom tests:

1. Textbooks tend to bombard learners with an abundance of facts without incorporating enough in-depth explanation.

2. Teachers seem to rely on the objective format, and factual questions dominate their tests. We infer that teachers find such items relatively easy to construct.

Perhaps they think knowledge of facts is especially important to test. Students won't learn how to think critically if they are not required to demonstrate such thinking on tests. Note how Activity 2.4 provides a check of whether students understand a third grade mathematics lesson by asking students to demonstrate learning through interpretation and application.

3. Teachers seem to have difficulty expressing themselves clearly when they write questions and construct tests. Perhaps teachers need practice in constructing good questions.

4. Students may not be ready for a test because they have not developed enough understanding of a topic. This problem might occur because teachers need to provide more assistance or because students have not assumed enough responsibility for their own learning.

5. Students must be responsible for demonstrating their learning. They need to take an active role in designing assessments that help them demonstrate what they know in relation to real-life situations. If teachers are always the ones designing tests, students have a limited role: regurgitating information for the teacher. This is why so many students tend to quit rather than study; they don't see any point to a test that doesn't seem real to them.

ACTIVITY 2.4 DEMONSTRATING LEARNING THROUGH INTERPRETATION AND APPLICATION, THIRD-GRADE MATH

SUMMING UP YOUR MEASUREMENTS

These activities are designed to determine how well you have understood the chapter on measurements. You will demonstrate your knowledge and understanding by performing the following activities.

The first activity will be done with your assigned group. The next three will be performed on your own. Be careful and have fun!

1. Read the recipe first. Make the individual assignments. With your group, make a vanilla pudding.
   - Who will read the recipe?
   - Who will assemble the cooking utensils and cups?
   - Who will mix the ingredients?

   - Who will pour the hot mixture into the cups? (Use pot holders!)
   - Who will place the cups in the pan and take them to the refrigerator?

2. Read the outdoor thermometer at three different periods of the day (morning, midday, afternoon). Record the temperature at each period.

3. Use the scales to weigh your empty lunch box, your mathematics book, and your wallet/purse. Record each weight.

4. Measure the perimeter of your desktop, your closet cubbyholes, and any other item on the classroom floor. Record each.

Developed by Bessie Haskins.

How to Improve the Design of Tests

Many teachers like to use traditional tests. There is great value in what is known and experienced. By reviewing the flaws discovered in many tests, teachers can improve traditional tests immensely. Coombe & Hubly (2004) offer several suggestions for constructing classroom tests. Among them are that teachers need to test to course outcomes—to how and what has been taught; to prepare unambiguous items, write clear directions, and take the tests themselves! The following general guidelines will help; they are a compilation of our experience, and that of other professionals such as Ayers (2001):

1. The content to be evaluated should be carefully selected to match not only the teachers' content goals but also those of any standards (such as of a professional organization or a state-mandated criterion-referenced test) to be met.

2. Questions on a test should reflect a balance among the three basic comprehension levels. The difficulty of questions should be related to the task required. Recall is harder than recognition; production is harder than recall. Questions with several parts are more difficult than questions with one part. Selecting is easier than generating. Teachers should try to vary their use of difficult and easy questions within a test.

3. Sometimes the answer that a student gives is unanticipated but better than the expected response. Teachers should write questions carefully to avoid ambiguity but still encourage spontaneous critical thinking.

4. The best-worded test items do not provide secondary clues to the correct answer. Teachers often give inadvertent clues to students, who are very facile at discerning such giveaways. For instance, students may learn that correct answers on a multiple-choice test are often keyed to choice *c* and that the longest choice is most likely to be the correct answer. Also, the stem often signals an obvious match among the multiple choices. Students realize that for both multiple-choice and true/false items, positive statements are more likely than negative statements to be correct choices. Teachers sometimes give answers away with grammatical clues. Teachers should express themselves carefully.

5. When wording test items, teachers need to consider their students' language proficiency. A well-worded test that does not match the students' knowledge of language will result in poor comprehension even though the students' learning may be excellent. Make sure instructions and items are clearly written. Also, balance gender and ethnicity in creating scenarios; don't stereotype.

6. Include distractors if they will test careful reading, content understanding, and critical thinking; do *not* include them if your intention is merely to trick students.

7. Once the test is constructed, create a table that helps you see if you accomplished your objectives:

Question	Does content tested match a standard?	Comprehension level?	Ambiguity?	Secondary clues?	Language match?	Distractors?

8. Ayers (2001) recommends that at this point of test development, the teacher should ask a colleague to review the test and provide comments. She notes that creating a good multiple-choice test takes a lot of time; but a good test can be used to generate new tests, so it ultimately saves time for the teacher—not to mention giving students a fair opportunity to demonstrate their own success.

Preparing and Assisting Students to Take Tests

Chapter 7 describes uses for technology as a learning tool, such as creating an online or disk database that students can access on their own. The use of study questions can be facilitated by such an electronic database.

By using the PAR Lesson Framework, teachers can fulfill much of their instructional role in readying students to take tests. We find that some other techniques also prepare and assist students in test performance.

USING STUDY QUESTIONS

Teachers who encourage students to use study questions find this technique helpful. Study questions can be used in a variety of ways. The teacher can prepare a list of questions to be included on the test and distribute the list at the beginning of a unit so students can refer to it throughout the unit. Or the teacher can suggest possible test questions as instruction proceeds and then review all of the questions after completing the unit. This list can become the pool for essay test items. The teacher might tell students that the test will include only questions from this list. Such a technique has merit for two reasons: A test bank is acquired as the unit progresses, thus eliminating last-minute test construction; and students have a study guide that is familiar, thorough, and not intimidating. If the teacher creates questions that follow the question construction guidelines and cover representative content, the technique works well.

Some teachers tell students before testing what the specific test questions will be. This technique works better with essay questions than with objective questions. Although many teachers hesitate to provide questions in advance, fearing that students will not study everything, this can be a wise way to prepare and assist students. In fact students cannot study everything, and they certainly cannot remember everything for a long time. If the essential information is covered in the proposed questions, then a question list can be effective. A pool of essay questions from which the specific question for a particular test is drawn can also be provided in an electronic environment.

Having students themselves create the questions for a test is sometimes a good technique. This option requires that students understand the content thoroughly and also understand how to write good questions. An alternative for younger students and those not proficient at question construction is to have students use brainstorming to predict possible test topics and then informally generate questions. A first grader could speculate, "I think you might ask me to explain how fish breathe." Students can construct possible items for an objective test as well as an essay test, or they can review items from sample tests that the teacher provides. Teachers who encourage students to create possible test questions should be sure to include some version of the students' questions on the actual test.

Any variation on student construction of the test questions will let students practice questioning and answering, provoke critical thinking, and promote the students' responsibility for their own learning. Another bonus is that students who are familiar with the teacher's way of designing a test will be less anxious about being tested. Test anxiety accounts for much poor test response.

> A threaded discussion at a teacher's Web site can allow students to share their possible test questions with one another. Other students can respond, and the teacher can interject as well.

USING OPEN BOOKS OR NOTES

Teachers find that allowing students to use open books or open notes—or both—lets students concentrate on producing the best response on a test and assists them in the actual test-taking process. This technique encourages good note-taking strategies and clear organization of information by promoting recognition and production rather than recall.

> If students take their tests in an electronic environment and they cannot use notes, be sure that the computer is clean of any aids and that the medium for saving the test (keydrive, disk, or the like) is also clean.

Teachers can employ technology to demonstrate the types of questions students will encounter on a test. Electronic quizzes for practice, such as those on the Web site accompanying this textbook, are a means for independent practice in test-wiseness. A classroom response system (CRS) that uses an electronic device often called a "clicker" promotes engagement and class participation, and it has potential for enhancing learning and test readiness. Clickers use infrared or radio frequency technology that transmits and records what the students click into their remote devices. Teachers receive the responses at a portable station and can immediately produce a bar graph that summarizes responses from an entire class. According to EDU-CAUSEConnect (2005),

> Interaction and engagement are often limited by class size and human dynamics (a few students may dominate the conversation while most avoid interaction). Interaction and engagement, both important learning principles, can be facilitated with clickers. Clickers can also facilitate discipline-specific discussions, small work group cooperation, and student–student interactions. Clickers—plus well-designed questions—provide an easy-to-implement mechanism for enhancing interaction. Clicker technology enables more effective, more efficient, and more engaging education. (Abstract)

For instance, multiple-choice or true/false problems that require careful thinking and application of knowledge can be presented to students, who respond by clicking answers on personal response devices. The class answers are compiled electronically into graphs that the teacher can then present to the class. This procedure lets the teacher understand how the students are reasoning and whether more instruction is necessary. It also allows the students to become familiar with how to think about test items with greater clarity and less nervousness. Activity 2.5 contains two such questions (and a diagram to accompany one question) that pose problems crucial to understanding introductory physics and dental hygiene. Using clicker technology makes learning the concepts enjoyable while teaching test skills.

ACTIVITY 2.5 QUESTIONS FOR A CRS/CLICKER ACTIVITY

Two identical beakers are filled to the same level with water. One of the two glasses has ice cubes floating in it. When the ice cubes melt, in which glass is the level of the water higher?

A. The glass with the ice cubes.

B. The glass without the ice cubes.

C. It is the same in both.

The frequency of brushing your teeth is the most important factor in the prevention of tooth decay.

A. True   B. False

Developed by Jeff Nugent, Center for Teaching Excellence, Virginia Commonwealth University.

NONTRADITIONAL WAYS TO ASSESS

 Everyone appreciates variety. Teachers may be pleasantly surprised to find that students increase productivity when an evaluation device looks more like the strategies that have been used to instruct than the same old test format (refer back to the guidelines for designing tests). We encourage teachers to use new strategies for assessment, testing, and evaluation; even when poorly made objective tests are redesigned, they do not correlate with the type of achievement required in a world where concepts are more important than facts. We must alter our testing procedures if we want to produce critical, thoughtful readers. Creative thinkers often perform much better on tests that are nontraditional and reflect nontraditional instructional activities.

By employing some of the strategies that we present in this book, teachers can construct tests that contain few traditional items. The most **nontraditional test** would eliminate questioning altogether and rely on student application of knowledge. Although teachers may not wish to design an entire test with no questions, some nontraditional items might spark interest. Primary teachers are often especially attracted by nontraditional tests, and intermediate and secondary teachers may prefer adding some nontraditional items to a more traditional test. The possibilities are as numerous as the types of activities presented in this text.

The following activities can be used as nontraditional test items. Teachers who have designed tests using such items report that they elicit more critical thinking from their students. We are sure teachers will see the possibilities for designing many activities as nontraditional test items.

Graphic Organizers

Graphic organizers are used to begin each chapter of this textbook. Their construction is explained in Chapter 3.

Student- or teacher-produced visual representations of learned concepts and relationships are called *graphic organizers*. Research (Katayama & Robinson, 2000; Robinson & Schraw, 1994) has shown that notes and partial notes recorded as graphic organizers help students comprehend better than fully formed outlines. We feel so strongly about the worth of graphic organizers that we begin the chapters in this book with them. At the end of some lessons, the organizers can be repeated, but with gaps; the reader should identify what is missing and recall where it should be placed within each organizer. This activity encourages readers to remember what they have read. Similarly, a teacher can instruct by using a graphic organizer, map, structured overview, jot chart, or any such visual aid and then present the organizer with blanks on a test, where it becomes a nontraditional test item for eliciting responses that demonstrate knowledge of facts. Such is the case with the example in Activity 2.6, designed by an 11th grade teacher. If the teacher provides a list of terms that could complete the organizer, then recognition of facts is tested. Such is the case in the example in Activity 2.7, designed for an elementary social studies class.

If the teacher asks students to explain why they positioned words at certain points on the organizer, the interpretive level of comprehension is being tested. If the teacher asks students to create an organizer using terms they learned during the lesson, the applied level of comprehension is demonstrated. No traditional questions are asked, yet comprehension can be evaluated and graded. The test item might read as follows:

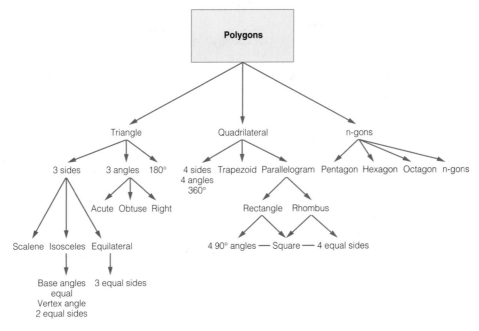

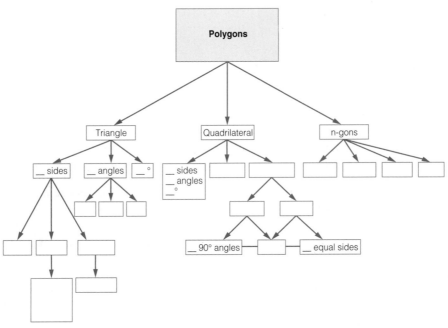

Developed by Fraces Reid.

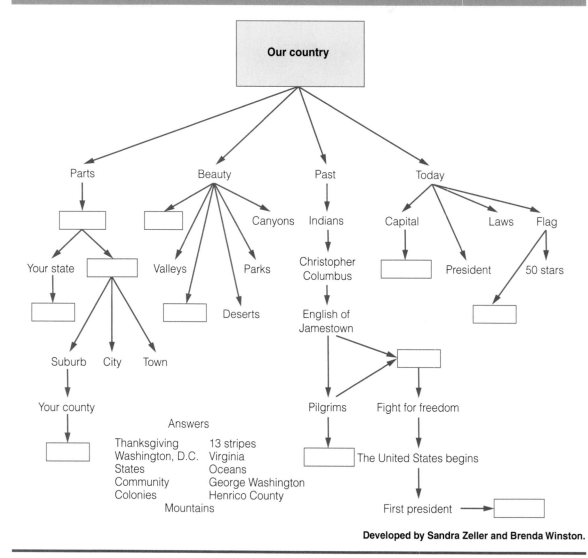

Developed by Sandra Zeller and Brenda Winston.

Study the organizer I have drawn for you. It is like the one we studied in class, but in this one there are several blank spaces. Using the list of terms attached, fill in the term that fits best in each space (1 point each). Then write one sentence beside each term listed; this sentence should explain why you think the term belongs where you put it in the organizer (2 points each). Next, write an essay that includes the information in this organizer. Your first paragraph should provide four (4) details. Your last paragraph should summarize by telling what new information you have learned by reading this chapter (25 points).

Note that the directions are specific and that point values are given for each procedure. Factual knowledge is tested, but some interpretation and application are also required.

Writing an essay is also part of this question. Because the components of the essay are defined, grading it should be simple. It is also possible to prepare a rubric for this essay:

> An A essay will contain three or four paragraphs that fully explain all the information on the organizer. Students not only will demonstrate factual knowledge but also will show inferences and applications. The entire list of terms will be appropriately placed and thoroughly defined. The essay will have a clear beginning and end.

> A B essay will contain two or three paragraphs that explain the information on the organizer. Students will demonstrate factual and interpretive knowledge. The entire list of terms will be appropriately placed and adequately explained. The essay will have a clear beginning and end.

Factstorming

Factstorming is explained in Chapter 3 as a good preparation activity because students identify familiar terms about a topic before they study further. Students can add to the list produced by factstorming after their studying is completed; the additions become an evaluation of new learning. If students are asked to explain each addition, they are demonstrating interpretation of information. If students categorize the already known and new information and then write an essay about this categorization, application is demonstrated. The use of factstorming as a test item is similar to the last step in a What-I-Know Activity (WIKA), but it is graded (see the example in Chapter 1; WIKA will be further explained in Chapter 4).

Other strategies discussed in this text can be used as tests. A number of strategies for writing that are explained in Chapter 10 can be used as effective tests. Some of these are cubing, quick-writes and free-writes, and student-generated questions (also discussed in Chapter 5).

Designing a Test with a Self-Rating

Teachers can design tests that include self-ratings. This technique originated years ago, when Hoffman (1983) suggested this rating technique for journal entries, and Richardson (1992b) created a version for tests. The first questions on a test might resemble these: How did you study for this test? How much did you study? How well do you think you will do? The answers show how the students prepared. Before the test is returned, a second set of questions should be asked: Now that you have taken the test, was this test what you expected and prepared for? What grade do you think you will receive? These questions can help the student take responsibility for studying and producing a good test response. The third set of questions promotes reflection. It is answered after the teacher returns and reviews the test with the students: Now that you have gone over your test, would you say that you studied adequately? Was your grade representative of your learning? Why or why not? What have you learned about taking tests?

Such a three-step process built into the testing procedure sends the message that the student is ultimately responsible for demonstrating learning. If teachers use the procedure often on tests, students should begin to take a more active role. Teachers will also be enlightened by students' views of studying and taking tests and can apply this information in their instruction and when constructing tests.

One requirement for designing good tests is to use previous tests as the basis for constructing new ones. Students learn how to take an individual teacher's tests by learning that teacher's style. Teachers should learn how to design tests based on students' styles of learning as well. Did students need clearer directions? Did they use appropriate study procedures? Do they need reminders about certain test procedures?

HELPING STUDENTS BECOME TEST-WISE

The tried-and-true acronym **SCORER** (Carmen & Adams, 1972; Lee & Allen, 1981) refers to a test-taking strategy. High SCORERs **s**chedule their time; identify **c**lue words to help answer the questions (the directions should contain them); **o**mit the hardest items, at least at first; **r**ead carefully to be sure they understand and fully answer the questions; **e**stimate what to include in their responses, perhaps by jotting down some notes or an outline; and **r**eview their responses before turning in tests. Teachers might teach SCORER to students and then insert the acronym into test directions or include it as a reminder on tests. Students could even be asked to account for how they used SCORER while completing a test. This strategy places responsibility on students to take a test wisely, in an organized and comprehensive manner. SCORER can be used as part of any test design.

There are other ways to teach students to become **test-wise**—that is, able to use a plan of attack regardless of specific test content. Students become used to taking tests. They become confident because they understand how tests are designed and can capitalize on that knowledge to demonstrate their learning. Being test-wise means knowing the system. When students know how to take a test, they can concentrate on answering the items. Being test-wise helps alleviate test anxiety. Panic—the blank mind syndrome—can be avoided. The older mammalian brain can send encouraging messages to the newer mammalian brain, and the student can then apply thinking skills to show knowledge.

Carter's (1986) study indicated that students discern the inadvertent clues teachers give in test items; this is a test-wise ability. Many teachers provide a bit of information in one question that can help students answer another question. Students who watch for these clues are SCORERs. Studies (Ritter & Idol-Mastas, 1986; Scruggs, White, & Bennion, 1986) indicate that instruction in test-wise skills can help students perform better on tests. An instructional session that reviews a list of test-taking tips is helpful, particularly with older students, in improving results on standardized tests. When a teacher wants students to improve performance on classroom tests, such test-wise instruction is best done in the content teacher's classroom with application to a particular test. The following list of test-taking tips indicates the kinds of suggestions that teachers can give to help students become proficient test takers:

1. Be calm.
2. Read through the entire test before answering any items. Look for questions that might provide clues to other answers.

Take a minute to consider when and how you became test-wise.

3. Plan your time. If one question is worth several points and others are worth much less, spend most of your time on the question or questions where the greatest number of points can be made.

4. Answer first the questions for which you are most confident about your answers.

5. On objective tests, remember to be logical and reasonable. Consider your possible answers carefully. Look for "giveaway" words that indicate extremes: *all, none, never, always.* They probably should be avoided when you select the correct answer. On multiple-choice items, think what the answer should be; then look at the choices. Also, eliminate implausible responses by thinking carefully about each choice.

6. For essays, jot down an outline of what you intend to write before you start writing. Be sure you understand the teacher's terms: *List* means to state a series, but *describe* means to explain the items. *Compare* means to show similarities; *contrast* means to show differences. Make sure you answer all the parts of a question.

A CHECKLIST FOR DESIGNING A TEST

The following questions constitute a checklist for test construction. The checklist is useful for teachers who want to review previously designed tests that have produced unsatisfactory results.

1. How did you prepare the class to study for this test? If you suggested certain study strategies, are you asking questions that will capitalize on these strategies? For instance, if you suggested that students study causes and effects by using a pattern guide, are you designing test items that will call for a demonstration of causes and effects?

2. Are you including SCORER, a self-evaluation of test preparedness, or some other way of reminding students about their responsibilities as test takers?

3. Do the items on your test reflect your goals and objectives in teaching the content? Test items should test what was taught. If a major objective is that students be able to name states and their capitals, how can this test measure that objective?

4. What is your main comprehension focus? Why? If you think factual knowledge is more important on this test than interpretation or application, can you justify this emphasis? Remember that many tests rely too much on factual questions at the expense of other levels of comprehension. Be sure whether the factual level is the most important for this test.

5. Do you require comprehension at each of the three levels? What proportion of your questions addresses each level? What is your reasoning for this division? Remember that tests imply the kind of thinking that teachers expect of their students. Have you asked your students to think broadly and deeply?

6. What types of responses are you asking of students? Will they need to recognize, recall, or produce information? A good balance of responses is usually preferable to only recognition, recall, or production. More thinking is required of students when production is requested.

7. Did you phrase your test items so that comprehension depends on the learned material rather than on experience or verbatim recall? Remember that although the preparation stage often calls for students to identify what they already know before a topic is taught, your test should find out what they have learned since then.

8. Is the weight of the test in the final grade clear to students? Is the weight of each item on the test clear? Is the weight of parts of an item clear within the item?

9. Did you consider alternatives to traditional test items, such as statements (instead of questions) or graphic organizers? Is writing an important part of your test? Why or why not?

10. For objective tests, what format have you selected (multiple-choice, true/false, incomplete sentences, short answers) and why? How many of each type did you include? Why?

11. For essay tests, have you carefully asked for all the aspects of the answer that you are looking for? Are descriptive words (such as *describe* or *compare*) clear?

12. Is the wording on this test clear? Is the test uncluttered, with items well spaced? Does the test look appealing?

13. Have you been considerate of the needs of mainstreamed students in your test design?

Authentic Assessment

Links to the NBPTS and VGLA are posted at the *Reading to Learn in the Content Areas* Web site, Chapter 2.

Many authorities (Herman, Aschbacher, & Winters, 1992; Wiggins, 1989) in education have pointed to "alternative assessment" as the solution to the dilemma of traditional testing. The advice to move to such forms of assessment waned with the push for high-stakes tests in the 2000s with the era of NCLB. But with reconsideration of how to regulate NCLB, alternative assessments are also being reconsidered. For instance, the National Board for Professional Teaching Standards (NBPTS, 2007) encourages such alternatives to standardized tests. An example of such an alternative assessment is the VGLA (Virginia Grade Level Alternative, 2006), which allows students to demonstrate their knowledge in another form than a standardized test—usually via a portfolio. The alternative assessment movement is motivated by the feeling that alternative assessment methods facilitate good teaching, enhance learning, and result in higher student achievement (Linn, Baker, & Dunbar, 1991). Wood (1996) has noted that traditional multiple-choice tests may not suffice in today's educational climate of learning outcomes, higher-order thinking skills, and integrated learning. We prefer the term **authentic assessment** to *alternative assessment*. Authentic assessment offers a viable solution. This term often refers to assessment that takes place in naturalistic situations that resemble the settings in which a skill or knowledge is actually used or applied. Teachers take an active role in observing learner activities that demonstrate what the learners can do. While the term *assessment* implies finding out what students already know, authentic assessment is broader in application, including informal evaluation procedures as well as determination of prior knowledge. In this section we describe ways to use authentic assessment as a means of evaluating what students have learned.

When teachers employ some nontraditional test items, they are moving toward authentic assessment, which is alternative, performance based, and process oriented. Traditional tests are specific measures given at specified times. Authentic assessment measures or samples student performance over time to see how student learning develops, matures, and ultimately reflects knowledge of the concepts learned in a real context. Brady (1993) suggests that authentic assessment builds relationships among the physical environment, the people who live in that environment, the reasons for beliefs about completing activities in that environment, and the manifestations of these beliefs in human behavior. In short, authentic assessment is a means of showing students why they are learning, as well as a means of showing educators what students have learned.

Authentic assessment emphasizes realistic and challenging material used over time (Biggs, 1992) as evaluation and can link previously taught material and current instruction. As Hager and Gable (1993) indicate, the increased use of observational and performance-based measures and process instruments, as well as content- or course-specific instruction, is essential to authentic assessment. Students can help decide what should be assessed, thus gaining an important role in demonstrating their own learning. Students enjoy creating authentic projects. In 1995 a group of middle school students wrote a script for and produced a video about the hazards of drugs. As they graduated from high school in 1999, these students were still talking about the fun they had making the video. It is doubtful that they would have remembered the information learned about drug hazards so well if a test or paper assignment had been the measure of evaluation.

The context for authentic assessment might include observing a performance or simulation or completing a task in a real-world situation. Students will want to do well because the real-world consequences are clear. For instance, actually driving a car yields a more authentic assessment than taking a paper-and-pencil test in a driver education course. Encouraging a student to show what steps were followed to complete a math problem is a way of demonstrating the logical processing of information. The process of completing the task reveals as much (or more) about the student's learning as the product recorded as a test grade.

Lund (1997) has written about the importance of using authentic assessment in every classroom. She gives the following as characteristics of authentic assessment:

1. Worthwhile tasks have meaning for the student and are designed to broadly represent a field of study.

2. The emphasis is on higher-level thinking and more complex types of learning.

3. Criteria are always given in advance so students know how they will be graded.

4. Assessments are deeply embedded in the everyday workings of the curriculum so that it is hard to distinguish between assessment and instruction.

5. The role of the teacher changes from dispenser of knowledge (or even antagonist) to facilitator, modeler, and ally in learning.

6. Students know that there will be a public presentation of the work that has been accomplished.

7. Students know that there will be an examination both of the processes they used in learning and of the products that resulted from the learning.

Developing Authentic Assessments

Tierney (1998) has written about the reform in assessment practices. He points out that developing better evaluation means more than just creating new tests. He argues that if the point of literacy is to become immersed in text rather than to "be subjugated by it" (p. 375), we must be thoughtful about how we incorporate authentic assessment into our evaluation procedures. Because learning is a complicated process, evaluation must consider many complex ways to represent itself. Should observation be an assessment component? How? For how long? Under what conditions? Should learners select for themselves what will illustrate their learning? Worthen (1993) suggests that activities based on learning logs (explained in Chapter 10), and observation notes can reveal much about student performance over time. We know teachers who keep gummed labels on a clipboard; as they walk around the classroom, they make notes on these labels, which they later stick into students' folders. These notes often reveal important learning patterns. Such notes can be kept in any content classroom; they could be particularly useful during science labs, reading or writing workshops, cooperative group work, or library work. Performance measures might include oral debates, post-graphic organizers, or even presentations developed using the *PowerPoint* (see Chapter 7).

Rhodes and Shanklin (1991) suggest three ways to increase the authenticity of assessment in the classroom from the very start:

1. Let students use language in natural social contexts.

2. Give students choices in materials and activities to ensure they will discover genuine purposes for reading and writing.

3. Follow students' natural leads to focus on communication through interaction with others.

Portfolios as a Means of Authentic Assessment

Even though educators have for years realized the value of portfolios—Green and Smyser (1996) found that portfolios help students take a much more active role in their own learning—portfolios were all but abandoned in the last decade. A recent edition of the *Journal of Adolescent and Adult Literacy* (Goodson, 2007) reintroduces

For Web links about portfolios, visit the *Reading To Learn in the Content Areas* Web site, Chapter 2.

the place of portfolios in authentic assessment, especially in electronic form. A **portfolio** is a representative sampling of artifacts that demonstrates a feature or specialty about a person. It is not simply a collection but a showcase. A student might collect many samples of work, but only one artifact might be selected for inclusion in the portfolio because it demonstrates best what the student is showing about herself or himself. Unlike traditional tests, many portfolios demonstrate growth over time.

Portfolios can be used at any grade level. Wagner, Brock, and Agnew (1994) advocate the use of portfolios in teacher education courses to help students develop a greater understanding of themselves as readers and language users. Young and associates (1997) explain how portfolios can engage secondary students more effectively in their academic work.

Portfolios work well with both elementary and secondary students (Abruscato, 1993; Cleland, 1999). Activity 2.8 is an artifact selected by a third grader to show the many facts he learned over 12 weeks while he studied animals. Activity 2.9 is a list of history books that a fourth grader included in his portfolio to show how much he had read in four weeks.

ACTIVITY *2.8*

My
Fantastic
Animals

Did you know that snakes eat bats?

Did you know that the Indian Python is one of the largest snakes in the world?

The smallest snakes can fit in your hand.

Hummingbirds can fly backward and hover motionless.

This is my mini-page about animals. I wanted to include this page in my portfolio to show what I learned about animals.

This page was created with *The Writing Center*, from The Learning Company, 6943 Kaiser Drive, Fremont , CA 94555.

Books I read in History:

Meet Martin Luther King, Jr.

Meet Maya Angelou

The Story of Harriet Tubman, Conductor of the Underground Railroad

The Story of George Washington Carver

If You Traveled on the Underground Railroad

I chose this list of books I read to put in my portfolio because I never liked to read before. I did not know very much about history, but now I have practiced reading and learned a lot too! I like to read about real people and find out about real things.

When students are involved in an authentic assessment plan from the start of the grading period, they become more active participants in the learning process. Wilcox (1997) notes that an active portfolio, in which the student, teacher, and even possibly the parents are actively engaged in the selection and presentation process, is a "working portfolio that changes and grows with new input as it creates and generates new input" (p. 96). Students should be encouraged to develop goals for their progress during the period and indicate possible ways in which they can demonstrate their growth at the end of the period. Teachers, in consultation with their students, can guide students toward realistic and reasonable goals. Students then collect their own evidence of their learning from the beginning of a grading period.

If portfolios are created as paper-based products, teachers should supply each student with a folder; then teacher and students can decide together what types of work will be kept in it. At the end of a specified period, students designate which pieces of work in the folder show progress or demonstrate a particular accomplishment. It is a good idea to keep the portfolio folders in the classroom in a storage file at all times. This ensures that papers will not be lost and provides easy access for students wishing to peruse or upgrade their portfolios. Products they select may reflect their learning much more fully over a long time than a traditional test—which captures only one moment in time—could do.

If portfolios are created as electronic products, there are many possibilities for presentation. When portfolios are to be freely shared and open to the public, blogs (explained in Chapter 7) might work best (Fahey, Lawrence, & Paratore, 2007). But if an element of privacy is desired, portfolio spaces can be created within course authoring tools such as BlackBoard. Activity 2.10 is a screen capture of a portfolio window created in BlackBoard.

What types of samples should be collected during each week? What types of samples should be collected to demonstrate the achievement of course goals? Some measures of prior knowledge of topics, such as recognition pretests or anticipation guides, would provide baseline measures (see Chapters 3 and 4). For instance, pre- and post-unit attitude surveys might be the first and last pieces collected. Work samples—such as jot charts (explained in Chapter 4), two-column notes (explained

in Chapter 8), and graphic organizers—might be included. Quizzes, tests, and corrections could be saved. At grading time, the most representative piece and a best piece could be selected. Both process activities and products can be collected. If a student is demonstrating that a standard has been met, the activity that demonstrates this would be included in the portfolio. For instance, John may be unable to compute a problem about fractions on the mandated test because of his learning disability, but he can tell in his own words how he would solve it and draw a picture.

Portfolios should include evidence of problem-solving and communication skills. Samples for a portfolio that demonstrates writing ability could be a table of contents, a best piece, a letter, some creative writing, a personal response, a prose piece from a content area, and an on-the-spot writing sample. Samples for a portfolio that demonstrates math ability could be several best pieces, such as puzzles, a letter to the evaluator, and a collection of math work.

Here are some general guidelines for assembling a portfolio:

1. Organize with a table of contents and section divisions. Select categories to best represent progress, such as "favorite activities," "activities I did not like," and "what I am most proud of."

2. Include representative samples of work over time. Be sure to date the samples and make clear why they are included.

3. Annotate each sample to explain why it is included. The focus here is on individual samples, not the total progression.

4. Conclude with a reflective but brief summary that explains progress in relation to the portfolio contents: What were the goals? What was learned? How, overall, do these artifacts demonstrate this?

5. Make sure that the number of samples is reasonable and representative of the depth and breadth of learning (at least one sample per week during a 10- or 12-week grading period).

This portfolio will count as 25 percent of your grade. Include pieces that YOU think best represent your learning about Early American History and Literature.

You should have at least eight pieces, one per week. Each should be annotated to explain why it represents your learning for this marking period. You may include more than one piece of the same type (two–three maps), but there should be some variety also.

You should write a summary of no more than two pages that explains how you met the objectives for this unit.

Suggestions for Selections:

Completed jot chart of Early American authors: their work, language style, and representative vocabulary

Quizzes taken

Essays written—this can include any drafts that you think show your progress in writing and thinking about the topic

Three-level guides completed and annotated

Notes from any day's discussions

Postgraphic organizer of *The Crucible*

Favorite quotes from *The Crucible*

Maps of *The Crucible*: acts, characters

Teachers need to establish what they expect their students to demonstrate in their portfolios. Will specific knowledge be expected? Will some example of weekly progress be necessary? How will the portfolios be graded, if at all? Will they constitute the total grade or a portion of the grade? Who will read the portfolios—just the teacher and student, the parent, the principal, other students? After making the expectations clear to students, teachers need to encourage students to take ownership and make their own choices within the established parameters. It is a good idea to hold at least a mid-point conference so that students can practice articulating their choices and the teacher can guide the process. Activity 2.11 is an example of a portfolio guideline for high school English students.

Getting Started with Authentic Assessment

Managing and analyzing authentic assessment results are facilitated by use of an electronic database and templates so each student record can be quickly updated.

In the classroom, content area teachers can begin focusing on authentic assessment by keeping a checklist of essential developments that they want students to demonstrate. The checklist presented in Activity 2.12 can be modified as new criteria are added and then removed as students' developmental needs are met. Such a checklist can help teachers keep an ongoing record of subtle developments in the students' reading, writing, and thinking abilities.

A small start such as using a checklist is the easiest way to begin authentic assessment. At this level the students' development—trial and error, dialogue, self-criticism—can be assessed most readily. Samples can be taken over time, and students can be involved in designing the assessment and collecting the samples. Also, the teacher can make certain that both process and product are measured and that audiences—such as

ACTIVITY	*2.12*	CHECKLIST FOR ASSESSMENT OBSERVED OVER THE MONTH OF _____

★ Excellent √ Good × Average ♦ Lacking—needs to improve

Name	Student Self-Evaluation	Decision Making	Questioning	Problem Solving	Attitude and Motivation	Inferential Thinking	Clarity of Writing
Bobby	√	★	★	√	★	√	×
Felicia	×	√	×	♦	√	×	×
Beverly	★	√	★	★	√	√	★
Joan	♦	♦	×	♦	√	√	×
Juan	×	√	×	×	√	√	♦

the students, their parents, and administrators—will be able to understand the samples and how they demonstrate progress in learning. Authentic assessment is the ultimate nontraditional evaluation. It is a challenge that can bring new enthusiasm to learning in every content area.

Once a teacher tries a few of these ideas for nontraditional testing and authentic assessment, the next step might be combining the data collected with the test data required by NCLB or state evaluations. Boyd-Batstone (2004) suggests that teachers can fill in gaps left by questions about what a test score means for instruction, and also attend to immediate classroom needs, by collecting informal observations and data and matching these collections to state and national standards (as might be on state and national test assessments). This might be described as standards-based teaching in which the standard, the test of the standard, and the classroom performance can be integrated. He calls his method **ARA** (anecdotal records assessment). Teachers can organize this electronically by creating templates with a standard listed and several notes collected over time for each student that describe how the student is meeting the standard. In this way, what the learner knows and can do is featured; but the learning is also matched to the standard and should substantiate any testing. As Boyd-Batstone writes, "A quality assessment is like a well-woven fabric" (p. 236).

ONE-MINUTE SUMMARY

Assessment and evaluation are crucial components of ensuring good instruction. In the age of accountability in the United States, content teachers must play a larger role in assessment than ever before. Federal legislation and state standards have become a prominent influence on classroom instruction. In this chapter we presented key concepts about testing. We discussed the design of successful tests and the role of tests in the larger picture of assessment and evaluation. We presented viewpoints from several experts about the impact of NCLB on assessment in this era. These viewpoints, and the expression of them in professional journals and to legislators, have influenced the implementation of the NCLB legislation. Educators have begun to view assessment and evaluation more broadly and to select assessment methods suited to different purposes. We described teacher-made tests and authentic assessment as ways to measure whether desired learning outcomes are taking place. We explained ways to evaluate both traditionally and in a more authentic manner, especially by introducing portfolios—both paper-based and electronic—into classroom instruction, and incorporating anecdotal records with standards-based instruction.

PAR ONLINE

For further information about—and activities dealing with—Chapter 2, go to the *Reading to Learn in the Content Areas* Web site and select the Chapter 2 resources: www.cengage.com/education/richardson.

Look at a Web site that provides information about some aspect of assessment that attracted you. Describe to others in your class how this Web site can be useful in your content instruction.

Post a threaded discussion to share your ideas about high-stakes testing and the role of authentic assessment.

END-OF-CHAPTER ACTIVITIES

Assisting Comprehension

1. Select one way to introduce authentic assessment into your content classroom. Relate this assessment to a standard about which you need to instruct. How can using and recording student performance on this authentic assessment technique demonstrate student progress in achieving the standard?

Reflecting on Your Reading

1. The International Reading Association (2003) has developed a set of standards that identify the performance criteria relevant to classroom teachers. Standard 3 delineates four elements of assessment, diagnosis, and evaluation that a classroom teacher should possess. The teacher should

2. Read about the following:

   • NCLB (link at the *Reading to Learn in the Content Areas* Web site, Chapter 2 resources).

   • Your professional organization's standards for teaching important content ("Google it" by typing in the name of your organization).

   • A history of testing starting with Binet (p. 276 of Oppenheimer's *The Flickering Mind*).

   3.1 Select and administer appropriate formal and informal assessments, including technology-based assessments. They understand the requirements for technical accuracy of assessments and can select technically adequate assessment tools. They can interpret the results of these tests and assessments.

3.2 Compare, contrast, and analyze information and assessment results to place students along a developmental continuum. They recognize the variability in reading levels across different subject areas. They can identify students' proficiencies and difficulties. They recognize the need to make referrals for appropriate services.

3.3 Analyze, compare, contrast, and use assessment results to plan, evaluate, and revise effective instruction for all students within an assessment/evaluation instruction cycle.

3.4 Interpret a student's reading profile from assessments and communicate the results to the students, parents, caregivers, colleagues, and administration.

How were these four elements addressed in this chapter? How does being informed about these elements aid in content instruction?

3

The only way to learn how to read is by reading, and the only way to get students to read is by making reading easy.

FRANK SMITH

Preparation for Learning

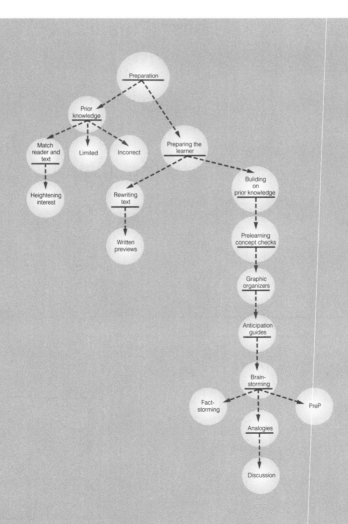

VOICES FROM THE CLASSROOM: A MIDDLE SCHOOL CLASS WITH A PROBLEM

A well-behaved class of all minority seventh grade students from an inner-city middle school sat attentively and waited for the teacher to tell them how to proceed in reading from the textbook. The teacher sat at his desk with pencil and grade book and called on each student in the class to orally read a paragraph of the passage. He put a grade in his book each time a student read. When the first student finished reading his paragraph, he put his head down and went to sleep—he knew his time to perform in the class had come and gone. The next few students were counting the paragraphs to see which was theirs; when they found their paragraphs, they began to whisper audibly as they practiced reading their own paragraphs. The teacher went around the room in this manner and called on students to read; but he skipped over some students. They were the ones that everyone knew couldn't read.

The topic in social studies for this inner-city class of seventh graders was hubris, Greek pride, and the Delphi oracle. Pardon the bad pun, but this was totally Greek to these students. They had no understanding of what was happening in the class. They had no prior knowledge about the topic, and orally decoding the print wasn't helping them much that day. In addition, there was no discussion of the topic, and students didn't seem to be really listening to other students as they read.

Have you ever seen a class like this? More of these classes exist than you might believe. What could the teacher have done to improve the situation?

PREPARING TO READ

1. a. What is the importance of prior knowledge in reading comprehension?
    b. How does a teacher determine students' prior knowledge?
    c. How can teachers overcome misconceptions students may have about a topic?
    d. Are there strategies a teacher can use to prepare students to read?

Think about how you would answer these four questions. This chapter will help you answer these key questions about learning.

2. Predict which of the following three meanings is most similar to the term being given:

    perceptual field
    a. The organization of one's thoughts.
    b. The validity of perceptions.
    c. A grass field where games are played.

    schema
    a. A devious person.
    b. Thinking done after reading.
    c. One's mental blueprint for constructing reality.

    cognitive dissonance
    a. Inconsistency of one's thoughts.
    b. Display of feelings and emotions.
    c. Being mad at someone else.

    graphic organizers
    a. Written outlines of a chapter.
    b. Realistic depictions in paragraph form.
    c. Visual representations that show relationships between concepts.

    anticipation guide
    a. A prereading study guide that teaches literacy.

b. A teacher who guides students orally through a lesson.

c. A written guide used after reading to improve comprehension.

analogies

a. Pointing out differences between concepts.

b. Comparisons between familiar and less familiar concepts.

c. Analog timepieces.

OBJECTIVES

As you read this chapter, focus your attention on the following purposes. You will

1. Understand the importance of building on students' prior knowledge.

2. Learn why it is sometimes difficult to build on students' prior knowledge.

3. Identify pertinent research that supports the concepts of schema theory and prior knowledge.

4. Learn how to adapt texts for the needs of your students.

5. Become acquainted with several activities that help build the match between readers and the material being read.

6. Understand the decisions that teachers must make in building on prior knowledge while using text materials to guide readers appropriately.

Few would deny the importance of literacy in today's fast-paced world. But beyond teaching basic literacy in the early elementary school years, most schools do not place a high priority on developing literacy skills for future success in the academic and business worlds. National standardized tests (National Center for Educational Statistics, 2003) provide evidence that over 60 percent of students in schools today are reading below a basic minimum level. The authors of this book maintain that students are having difficulty in reading because they are not receiving the right reading experiences in school. Most of the time students are asked to answer end-of-chapter comprehension questions or fill in endless worksheet spaces. In addition, most reading that is done in class is oral reading with one student reading the text aloud and all other students listening, as in this chapter's opening scenario. With such boring exercises passing for reading, it is no wonder research shows that students do not like to read textbooks and try to avoid such reading at all costs (Maria & Junge, 1993; McKeown, Bede, & Worthy, 1992; Purcell-Gates, Degener, Jacobson, & Soler, 2002).

We are in this unenviable state because students are simply not motivated to read. In addition, they don't read to learn; rather, they read to please a teacher, get a grade (as the students were doing in the scenario), or find answers to questions that they find inherently uninteresting. Motivation doesn't happen for students as they are reading or doing dull exercises. The student has to be motivated prior to reading. Students have to be taught to think about a topic in various ways before they start to read. Teachers need to both determine students' prior knowledge before reading and build on that knowledge to frame a lesson in a proper learning context. What students learn is greatly determined by the knowledge they bring to the lesson (Byrnes, 1995; McDonald & Stevenson, 1998).

An analogy will shed light on preparation and learning. The preparation phase of learning is much like practicing for a basketball game. Playing the game actually takes up the smallest amount of time; the greatest amount of time is spent in workouts, strategy sessions, viewing game films, and concentrated practice—all intended to ensure success in the game itself. After the game, more time is spent analyzing what occurred on the court, and then preparation for the next game begins. Questions are asked: "Why did we do well in this game?" or "Why didn't we do well?" So it is with reading. A proficient reader spends time getting ready to read by determining and building background. Instead of plunging into the reading, the reader must prepare. Good comprehension is a natural result, just as playing a game successfully is the natural result of hard work in practice. Teachers who are aware of this phenomenon and help students in the preparation stage of reading are like good coaches. The coach is there at every step to assist and encourage students as they take responsibility and work through lessons. Students who realize that preparation for reading is like basketball practice will reap benefits in higher achievement and better grades.

In this chapter we discuss the importance of determining prior knowledge in preparing learners to read. In addition, we explain how teachers can build on limited stores of student knowledge to allow students to learn and better retain information while reading.

THE IMPORTANCE OF DETERMINING PRIOR KNOWLEDGE

Many studies have shown the importance of prior knowledge in reading (Alexander & Murphy, 1998; Hmelo, Nagarajan, & Day, 2000; Muller-Kalthoff & Moller, 2003; Verkoeijen, Rikers, & Schmidt, 2005). Within this context, researchers (Reynolds, Sinatra, & Jetton, 1996) have placed a strong emphasis on the social construction of knowledge and the idea that students have to pull from shared knowledge to complete a task. In problem solving, it has been found that students with considerable prior knowledge of a subject can use strategies more effectively than those with little prior knowledge (Alexander & Judy, 1998). More specifically, learners with rich prior knowledge can focus on what is important in a learning task, whereas those with inadequate prior knowledge often search in a frantic mode because they cannot distinguish relevant and irrelevant material. Research (Last, O'Donnell, & Kelly, 2001; McDonald & Stevenson, 1998; Muller-Kalthoff & Moller, 2003) has indicated that prior knowledge plays an important role in how well students find and understand material on computers and perform computer research. Hogan, Natasi, and Pressley (2000) studied the processes involved with eighth grade students in the construction of shared understanding. They determined the prior knowledge of groups of students about a science topic and then examined which groups improved significantly in knowledge and why. Prior knowledge was found to be very important in how well a group finally understood the topic; further, the most successful groups agreed with, confirmed, and accepted others' ideas.

Researchers also have found that students with little prior knowledge of a topic are unable to formulate learning goals adequately (Last, O'Donnell, & Kelly, 2001) and often have trouble asking questions concerning the material (Miyake & Norman, 1979). For all these reasons, teachers must be able to determine the prior knowledge of their students about any relevant topic to be studied. To accomplish this, teachers must be adept at seeing instruction through the eyes of their students. As Ball and Cohen (1999, p. 8) have noted, teachers need to see students as being "more capable of thinking and reasoning, and less as blank slates who lack knowledge." Borko and Putnam (1996) have said that acquainting teachers with the content area thinking of children should become an important component of teacher preparation programs.

The Problem of Matching Reader with Text

Good readers feel comfortable with how they read. Good readers usually browse before they start to read because they want to see how familiar they will be with the material. They take note of how much they already know about the topic, how interested they are in the topic, and what strategies they might employ to read the material. They size up the material by asking, Is it easy to follow? Is the content clear? Do I have a purpose in mind for reading this? Good readers also assess the relative difficulty of the text. They ask questions such as these: Is it easy to read, like a story (narrative style)? Is it somewhat more difficult, like a newspaper article (journalistic style)? Or is it challenging to read, like many textbooks (expository style with many new facts and concepts)? After determining the difficulty and amount of challenge, they next ask, at what speed should I read this text? Should I take notes as I read? A reader who knows what lies ahead and can chart a course feels more confident than a reader who opens a book and plunges into the text.

Think about your teaching. Are you matching students with texts?

Mature, proficient readers may make such assessments almost automatically and unconsciously. Poor readers are not proficient readers, and they do few or no self-assessments like those just mentioned. Studies (Mesmer, 2005) show that many students are not well matched to texts, often having the dual problems of not being able to recognize words efficiently and not being able to comprehend material. Achieving a good match between readers and texts makes sense. Present studies are seeking a better way to match students to appropriate texts through use of quantitative measures of readability (Walpole, Hayes, & Robnolt, 2006). But until matching procedures are perfected, teachers are still on their own in dealing with the great deal of variability between ability levels of students in content area classrooms.

The most important way a teacher can succeed in a classroom with a wide variation in reading ability is to plan each lesson to include adequate preparation time to introduce the lesson and determine and build on prior knowledge. Teachers need to carefully prepare readers beforehand through discussion of the text and through use of strategies such as those we explain in this chapter. Teachers and readers who ignore this step neglect a crucial part of the overall process of reading.

SCHEMA THEORY AND PRIOR KNOWLEDGE

Often students' prior knowledge is not adequate in and of itself to make necessary connections in learning content material. A number of researchers (Nuthall, 1999) believe that some students learn more than others because they can create mental representations or images of the new learning that are linked to knowledge structures already in their memories. Psychologists stress that learning new information depends on relating the new to something already known. That is, learning is better organized for good learners in a meaningful pattern of the mind. This meaningful pattern is called the **perceptual field**: a fluid organization of meanings existing for an individual at any instant. It is the basis for a person's reactions to any new event. To make sense of the world, the learner attempts to relate new information to already known information by drawing a **schema** (plural *schemata*), or mental blueprint, of the way in which reality is constructed. One's schemata can be thought of as the sum of the personal knowledge and information one has accumulated, and the information a learner acquires about a topic that is organized cognitively into the framework.

This framework grows to include other topics, thus creating larger and larger schemata, arranged in a hierarchy. Learners retrieve information by understanding how newly encountered material links to what they already have organized cognitively. Interrelationships among schemata aid understanding. Rumelhart (1980) stresses that schemata, which may be likened to diagrams or drawings stored in the brain, are fundamental to all information processing. Often our diagrams are incomplete, but we create fuller pictures as more information is found to complete them.

Learning occurs in a process of planning and building information in the brain. Frank Smith (1994) explains the process this way: Just seeing words (page to eye) or even saying words (page to eye to mouth) is fairly superficial. Connecting the intent of the words to what is already stored in one's schemata (eye to brain) is real reading. Thus what learners already know helps them read more effectively. Smith concludes that the eye-to-brain connection is far more complex than the mere intake of information.

Gestalt psychologists probably introduced the term *schema* in the 1930s (Anderson & Pearson, 1984). Bartlett (1932) used the term to explain how information that has been learned is stored in the brain and, with repeated use, becomes part of a system of integrated knowledge. Bartlett contended that learners chunk knowledge in an organized fashion by connecting a new segment to what they already know. Only by so doing can a learner move the new chunk of information from short-term memory to long-term memory. Bartlett felt that the process of memory retrieval involved reconstruction, which is brought about by the frameworks that people already have in their heads. Thus memory is both selective and interpretive, involving both construction and reconstruction, and therefore sometimes can be inexact (Butler & McManus, 1998, p. 35).

There are excellent sections about how the brain chunks information in Chapter 8 on memory training and in Chapter 12 on the affective domain of learning.

Schema theory is mostly accepted today as a bona fide theory of how children learn, even though it has been criticized for its vagueness and lack of a clear definition (Sadoski, Paivio, & Goetz, 1991) and its lack of clear empirical verifiability (Beers, 1987). Despite such criticism, schema theory can help teachers understand how children think as they prepare students to read an assignment. Sousa (2005) describes three ways schema theory can be useful to teachers as they structure their lessons. Sousa maintains that students might need to have a teacher help them add new information to their already existing and fairly stable schema. Sometimes, however, teachers might have to help students alter their existing schema to come into line with new learning in a reading assignment. Finally, Sousa posits that sometimes teachers must help students completely restructure or replace their prior knowledge with new schema.

As an example of the second Sousa directive, one middle school mathematics teacher created a discovery activity designed to build her students' background by helping them see relationships between what they already knew and what they were about to learn. She was preparing them for a unit about the properties of quadrilaterals, showing them how to use what they already knew about parallel lines, perpendicular lines, and angles. This activity (see Activity 3.1) exemplifies the concept of building prior knowledge by connecting the known to the new while making the content interesting.

The Role Prior Knowledge Plays in Heightening Interest

We are reminded of an old story, told by one of our reading professors, about a little girl who goes to the library and asks for a book about penguins. Excited that this

---

ACTIVITY 3.1 ACTIVITY TO DISCOVER PRIOR KNOWLEDGE

WHAT'S IN A SHAPE? THE PROPERTIES OF QUADRILATERALS

The procedures were as follows:

1. Introduce students to a new chapter by having them read only one page of that chapter.

2. Ask students to point out examples of the different types of quadrilaterals using pictures on pages in the chapter—squares, rectangles, parallelograms, trapezoids, rhombuses.

3. Have students put their desks together with a partner; then give each pair a compass, protractor, ruler, and worksheet.

4. Read the worksheet directions aloud: "Find as many true properties about quadrilaterals as possible. Draw lines, measure with a ruler and a protractor, and use a compass to assist in making conjectures. List at least four conjectures for each type of quadrilateral."

5. After group work, discuss the conjectures. Create a master list and have the class agree or disagree with each conjecture.

6. State that conjectures will be verified by information in the chapter.

Developed by Jeannette Rosenberg.

B.C. Reprinted with permission of Johnny Hart and Creators Syndicate, Inc.

See Chapter 12's discussion about the affective domain of learning, where we offer suggestions for determining interests and attitudes, as well as activities to stimulate positive feelings.

small child is requesting information, the librarian selects a large volume about penguins and offers it to her. The child takes the book, almost staggering under its weight, and trudges home. The next day she returns it. "How did you like that book about penguins?" the librarian eagerly asks. "To tell you the truth," the girl replies, "this book tells more about penguins than I want to know." A similar situation occurs when teachers misinterpret a little interest as a lot and thus do not match a reader with a suitable text.

Our lack of schema can also cause a lessening of interest. Notice the protagonist in the comic reproduced on this page. She reads the first step for making an angel food cake. She expects the verb *separate* to mean "set or keep apart." In her schema, the verb *separate* does not include a picture for "detach," so she puts each egg in a different location rather than detaching the egg whites from the yolks. If she were in a home economics class, the teacher would need to help her build a more sophisticated schema.

Drum (1985) found that fourth grade science and social studies texts that were equal in vocabulary frequency, syntactic complexity, and overall structure were not equally easy for the study's fourth graders to read. Prior knowledge seemed to play a significant part in making the social studies texts easy for these students. In other words, no matter how well written material is, if readers do not possess background knowledge or interest in reading material, they will find it hard to read.

If learners cannot find relevance in a selection, they are likely to ignore it. Thus teachers must become aware of their students' knowledge about and experiences with a particular topic and build on that knowledge. Discovering whether students have developed any schemata can help a teacher generate content reading lessons that are directed, meaningful, and highly personal. For example, going from an easy text to a more difficult one can build and strengthen schemata. Gallagher (1995) had much success pairing adolescent literature with adult literature by "bridging" (Brown & Stephens, 1995). Studying the theme of the power of love in Harper Lee's novel *To Kill a Mockingbird* made it easier for students to grasp that same theme in Nathaniel Hawthorne's *The House of the Seven Gables*.

Remember that the reader has a primary problem when there are deficiencies in prior knowledge and a lack of interest in reading. The author does not cause the problem, just as one cannot fault the author of the angel food cake recipe because the protagonist in the comic does not know the meaning of the verb *separate*. The responsibility belongs to both the reader and the teacher to overcome any problems with prior knowledge and lack of interest.

Even the most proficient reader can experience difficulty in understanding and thinking about a subject when there is lack of interest in the topic. Studies indicate that interest in a topic plays a very important role in students' comprehension (Lin, Zabrucky, & Moore, 1997; Schumm, Mangrum, Gordon, & Doucette, 1992; Wade & Adams, 1990). When asked to address textbook issues, 41 percent of teenage respondents commented that they would "include topics in their textbooks that would interest them" (Lester & Cheek, 1998).

If teachers recognize that their students bring little interest or negative attitudes to content material, they can use many activities to stimulate interest and appreciation for the subject. A teacher who simply assumes that students are interested in a subject is likely to be disappointed in students' reactions to it. For example, students often experience psychological tension when new information clashes with their previously acquired knowledge. This situation can be seen as a form of **cognitive dissonance**, defined in *A Dictionary of Reading* (Harris & Hodges, 1995, p. 34) as "a motivational state of tension resulting from an inconsistency in one's attitudes, beliefs, perceived behaviors, etc." Because students may feel conflict due to cognitive dissonance, they may lose interest and assume a negative attitude. Sternberg (1997) calls for teachers to make material presented in class relevant and practical for students. Teachers need to show students that their knowledge does apply to the real world. Sternberg says that when this is done students will become more interested in topics and will have better learning experiences. In the next two sections we discuss the two problems students can have with prior knowledge: They often bring to the learning environment limited or incorrect prior knowledge. Both situations offer great challenges for the content area teacher.

Put another way, cognitive dissonance brings about unclear and disorganized thinking on the part of students.

Think about how teaching background knowledge can be a positive experience for you as well as students.

Limited Prior Knowledge

Students usually have some prior knowledge about almost every topic.

Readers usually have some experience related to or information about any topic they are to study. The students in the scenario at the beginning of the chapter probably had some ideas about the ancient Greeks and their customs. Even if readers know little about specific content, they may understand a related concept. For instance, fifth graders may not know much about the Pilgrims, but some of them may know what it's like to be uprooted and have to relocate to a strange place. Such students would have some background that the teacher could use in introducing the reading.

The following dialogue about golf illustrates how difficult it is to understand material when one has limited background in a subject:

"Do I deserve a mulligan?" asked Bob.

"No, but don't take a drop," said Al. "Use a hand-mashie, then fly the bogey high to the carpet and maybe you'll get a gimme within the leather."

"You're right," said Bob. "I'll cover the flag for a birdie and at least get a ginsberg if I'm not stymied."

(Morgan, Meeks, Schollaert, & Paul, 1986, pp. 2–3)

Unless you are a golfer, reading this dialogue might be more an exercise in pronouncing the words than in understanding the text. Try to answer the following questions about the passage:

1. Does Bob deserve a mulligan?
   a. Yes.
   b. No.
   c. Maybe.

2. What does Al think Bob should do?
   a. Catch a gimme.
   b. Take a drop.
   c. Use a hand-mashie.
   d. Fly a kite.

3. What does Bob decide to do?
   a. Cover the flag.
   b. Take a drop.
   c. Birdie-up.

4. How can Bob get a birdie?
   a. By getting stymied.
   b. By getting a ginsberg.
   c. By covering the flag.

5. If Bob is not stymied, what will he get?
   a. A hickie.
   b. A birdie.
   c. A mulligan.
   d. A ginsberg.

The answers are *b, c, a, c,* and *d.* The test was factual in nature. You probably scored 100 percent because you were able to look back at the passage and find the facts. But you were simply decoding the sounds and using the syntax or structure of the passage. Many researchers maintain that is what students often do when they read unfamiliar material (Opitz & Rasinski, 1998; Worthy & Broaddus, 2002).

Even though you may have decoded the passage and scored well, do you really know what this passage is about? To comprehend it fully, you need broad prior knowledge about golf. For instance, what is a mulligan? What is a birdie? Readers who don't know golf may try to create meaning for these words by calling on their store of information. Likewise, many students can answer rote questions after a reading without really understanding the passage. The following translation shows how paraphrasing by using more familiar language—more likely to be present in one's background—makes the passage meaningful:

1. "Do I deserve a mulligan?" asked Bob. Bob was asking if he deserved a second shot without a penalty.

2. "No, but don't take a drop," said Al. "Use a hand-mashie, then fly the bogey high to the carpet and maybe you'll get a gimme within the leather." Al said no but

warned Bob not to take the option of moving his ball from a difficult location and dropping it at a better spot, which could cost him a penalty stroke. Another (but illegal) move is to kick the ball out of trouble with his foot (a "foot-mashie" or "hand-mashie"). He then might be able to hit the ball with a high trajectory to the green, or "carpet" (where the hole is). If Bob were to get the ball within 18 inches of the hole, or cup ("leather"), he would be able to pick up his ball and give himself one stroke (a "gimme") rather than having to actually putt the ball.

Can you think of some other topic that someone has discussed or you have read about where you had limited knowledge, as might have occurred in the golf passage here?

3. "You're right," said Bob. "I'll cover the flag for a birdie and at least get a ginsberg if I'm not stymied." Bob was saying that he would try to hit the ball close to the hole for a chance at a "birdie" (one stroke under par). If he reached the green, he could lay up his putt to the hole ("get a ginsberg"). In earlier days, golfers did not mark their balls, so they could get stymied by another ball—that is, have to shoot around the ball of another player. Bob was being facetious here. In modern golf a player cannot get stymied by another player's ball on the green.

Incorrect Prior Knowledge

Sometimes readers have incorrect knowledge about material to be studied. Grace Hamlin, a teacher, wrote this "telegram" to illustrate how incorrect knowledge can influence one's reading:

won trip for two st. matthew's island pack small bag meet at airport 9 am tomorrow.

Readers who "know" that islands are tropical, have a warm climate, and are surrounded by beaches for swimming and sunbathing will pack a suitcase with sunglasses, shorts, bathing suits, and suntan lotion. St. Matthew's Island, however, is off the coast of Alaska, where the average temperature is 37 degrees. Incorrect knowledge in this case will impede comprehension. Similarly, readers who "know" that the dinosaurs were destroyed by other animals will have difficulty reading and understanding a theory proposing that dinosaurs were destroyed by the consequences of a giant meteor.

Maria and MacGinitie (1987) discuss the difference between having correct, though insufficient, prior knowledge and having incorrect prior knowledge. They conclude that students are less likely to overcome a problem of incorrect knowledge because the new information conflicts with their supposed knowledge, bringing about cognitive dissonance. In this situation, building students' knowledge is essential because material will be most unreadable to the students who try to refute the material as they read.

PREPARING THE LEARNER THROUGH BUILDING ON PRIOR KNOWLEDGE

 Preparation is the major factor in building on prior knowledge of students and in improving the quality of interaction with a text. Many activities can help teachers and students prepare for texts. In the rest of this chapter we describe a number of activities that prepare readers by building on prior knowledge. The activities represent possibilities but are not an exhaustive list. All of these activities should help students with limited or faulty prior knowledge.

Prelearning Concept Checks

One way to give students a sense of responsibility and a feel for the reading to come is through the use of prelearning concept checks. These are simple and easy to construct, exposing students to key vocabulary in the reading and allowing the teacher to find out how much students know about the topic. Prelearning concept checks are simple lists of terms important to a reading. Students can be asked to rate what they know about the topic, from "know a lot about the concept" to "know very little about the concept." Students can also come back to the list after the reading, or the next day, to recheck their knowledge of the words. Besides their simplicity and ease of construction, the advantage of using these checklists is that they give students with limited prior knowledge a chance to consider what they know about key vocabulary in the new learning and talk about the terms in groups or as a whole class. Notice that we use prelearning concept checks to begin chapters of this textbook to clarify thinking about vocabulary terms in the chapters and to help you prepare for the chapters. Activity 3.2 is a prelearning concept check for words to be learned in an elementary civics class on taking part in a court hearing. This activity is similar to the word inventories found throughout this book.

Rewriting Text

When students have a difficult time comprehending text, teachers can try the strategy of rewriting text in an easier form. Research has shown that text structure and

---

ACTIVITY 3.2 PRELEARNING CONCEPT CHECK

TAKING PART IN A COURT HEARING

Following is a list of terms used in this chapter. Some may be familiar to you in a general context, but in this chapter they may be used in unfamiliar ways. Rate your knowledge by placing a plus sign (+) in front of those you are sure you know, a check mark (✓) in front of those you have some knowledge about, and a zero (0) in front of those you don't know. Be ready to locate them in the chapter, and pay special attention to their meanings.

_____ defendant	_____ witnesses
_____ plaintiff	_____ opening statement
_____ jury	_____ direct examination
_____ judge	_____ cross-examination
_____ attorneys	_____ closing statement

organization, word familiarity, cohesion, and sentence length can influence reading comprehension (Meyer, 2003). Rewriting can address some or all of these problems and can help prepare students before introducing them to the original material. By using rewritten material to introduce text, teachers can simplify writing styles and clarify concepts that students may have difficulty understanding. However, in returning to the original text, teachers will still be using required materials, and students will receive the message that the text material is important.

Siedow and Hasselbring (1984) found that when eighth grade social studies material was rewritten to a lower readability level, the comprehension of poor readers improved. Currie (1990) rewrote text by shortening sentences, replacing unfamiliar words, changing metaphors to more literal phrases, and clarifying. Teachers using these materials reported that students, whether high or low achievers, significantly improved their grades. Beck and associates (1991) revised a fifth grade social studies text to create a more casual and explanatory style, then compared students who read the original version with those who read the revised version. Students who read the revised version recalled and explained the events better and answered more questions correctly.

The assignment to revise Virginia Woolf's essay "Professions for Women" (1966) illustrates rewriting (see Activity 3.3). Rewriting this essay was a desperate move. The teacher had assigned the essay to stimulate the writing of a freshman college English class. The students interpreted Woolf's metaphoric angel literally and thought that Woolf had a ghost looking over her shoulder. They also could not understand why Woolf mentioned buying an expensive cat. Woolf's writing was not at fault; the readers did not possess the appropriate background for the essay. Their backgrounds apparently did not include the metaphors or experiences that Woolf had selected, and they did not know how to relate to the allusions in her essay. Rewriting was chosen because the essay was required reading for the course.

Students read the rewrite first as an introduction; then they read the original essay and compared the two versions. The results were satisfactory. Students understood clearly the concepts Woolf was conveying; and as an unexpected bonus, they realized how much better written Woolf's essay was than the rewrite. As a preparation strategy, rewriting in this case proved successful.

Rewriting can bring down readability levels, sometimes to a significant degree. In the case of Woolf's essay, the original was found to be at ninth grade level and the rewrite at seventh grade level (according to the Fry graph). Sometimes a revision does not lower the readability level but does clarify difficult material. The goal should be to present necessary material in an understandable form as a prelude to reading the original, not to show a change in a readability formula (see Chapter 6 for more about readability formulas).

Like so many other activities, rewriting can be used at every step of the PAR Lesson Framework. If a rewrite is used in place of original material, then it is no longer being used to prepare the reader; in this case rewriting assists comprehension. One teacher rewrote portions of the Georgia Juvenile Court Code because the code was too hard for 10th graders to understand in its legal form (measured at the 14th grade level). The rewrite (to the seventh grade level) enabled students to read with

I was asked to speak to you about women as professionals and tell you about what has happened to me. This is difficult because my experiences in my job as a writer may not be that outstanding. There have been many famous women writers before me who have learned and shown me the best way to succeed at writing. Because of their reputations, families today accept women who become writers. They know that they won't have to pay a lot of money for writing equipment or courses!

My story is this. I wrote regularly every day, then submitted an article to a newspaper. The article was accepted, I got paid; I became a journalist. However, I did not act like a struggling writer who spends her hard-earned money on household needs; I bought a Persian cat.

My article was a book review. I had trouble writing it and other reviews because something nagged at me. I felt that because I am a woman, I should be "feminine": have sympathy, be charming, unselfish, keep the family peaceful, sacrifice, and be very pure. When I began to write, this is what women were supposed to be like, and every family taught its girls to be this way. So when I started to write criticisms of a famous man's novel, all of the things I had learned about being a woman got in the way of my writing critically instead of writing just nice things. This problem was like a ghost whispering in my ear. I called this problem ghost "The Angel in the House" because it was always there, in my "house," telling me to be nice rather than truthful.

I got rid of this problem. I realized that being nice is not always the most important thing. Also, I had inherited some money, so I felt I didn't have to do what others expected of me in order to earn a living! I had to get rid of this obsession with being feminine rather than being truthful in order to write clearly. I killed my problem ghost before it could kill my true thoughts and reactions. This is really hard to do because "feminine" ideas creep up on you before you realize that what you're writing is not a true criticism but something you were raised to believe. It took a long time to realize what was my idea and what was society's idea about what I should write.

Readability as measured by the Fry formula:
Original passage = 9th grade
Rewritten passage = 7th grade

---

attention to the main points. Rewriting can also be used as a reflective reading technique. A teacher might ask students to think about the material and try to rewrite it for younger students. In this way, students gain writing practice and demonstrate their learning, and an integration of the communicative arts takes place. Rewriting can also be a useful tool for the at-risk reader who needs to learn the same content as classmates but has difficulty reading at their level.

The biggest drawback to rewriting is the time it takes. For one rewrite of a 15-page social studies selection, one teacher spent four hours. The Woolf rewrite consumed two hours. Because a teacher's time is precious, teachers will want to weigh their options carefully in attempting to overcome text-based problems. If rewriting is the best choice, we suggest these steps:

1. Read and restate the ideas in your own words.

2. Identify the concepts that are especially important for students to know.

3. Keep rewrites short and to the point.

4. Explain difficult concepts in the rewrite. Reformulate particularly difficult words into words that you think students already know.

5. Make sentences short, and use the active voice whenever possible.

6. Underline specialized vocabulary to make it easier to note difficult words.

Written Previews

Graves, Prenn, and Cooke (1985) suggest that teachers write brief previews of material to be read by students. These previews—especially valuable for difficult material—provide a reference point and offer students a way to organize new information. A written preview should be fairly short and usually is read aloud to the class before silent reading of the original material. Teachers can use information gained from their own previewing of material to write a preview. In writing previews, a teacher can follow these steps:

1. Select a situation familiar to the students and relevant to the topic. Describe the situation and pose questions that will enhance interest in the topic.

2. If the material demands background knowledge that students do not have, include a brief section providing the necessary information.

3. Provide a synopsis of the material.

4. Provide directions for reading the material to facilitate comprehension.

Activity 3.4 is a written preview constructed by a high school government teacher about a section of the chapter called "Why Is Government Necessary?" Notice the

---

ACTIVITY 3.4 WRITTEN PREVIEW FOR "WHY IS GOVERNMENT NECESSARY?"

HIGH SCHOOL GOVERNMENT CLASS

Have you ever been involved in a situation where an authority figure forced you to participate in an action that you would not have been involved in otherwise? How about an organized team or an academic club? For example, I recall a situation in my life when I was named captain of the football team and then told by the coach that my first task as captain was to do all within my power to force one particular young man to quit the team. Even though the player was a great running back, the coach did not like him. He was using his governing authority to get someone to do what he couldn't bring himself to do. I refused to help the coach, and he came down very hard on me. We had heated discussions about it, and when I would not compromise, the player stayed with the team. To this day, I feel that the extra work I had to do to overcome this problem contributed to my getting a football scholarship and gaining my undergraduate degree.

How do you handle conflicts that arise over leadership, loyalty, and duty? How do you respond when you do not agree with those in authority (those who are governing you)? How comfortable are you in a situation where you feel your voice and opinion have no value, and you are at the mercy of the "authorities"? How do you resolve personal conflicts and disagreements with authority figures?

Developed by Travis Sturgill.

---

questions at the end of preview provided by the teacher to heighten interest in the reading.

Written previews are less time-consuming than rewrites, and they accomplish similar purposes. They build on readers' prior knowledge and help them organize forthcoming text material. If a teacher writes previews carefully, the structure of a text will be more apparent to its readers.

Written previews take time to prepare. However, they are worth the effort in heightening student achievement and interest.

Look for different forms of graphic organizers presented throughout this textbook.

Clarifying Thinking with Graphic Organizers

Many students have difficulty with the challenge of reading and interpreting expository text (Bryant et al., 2000). Researchers (Bos & Vaughn, 2002) have recommended the use of graphic representations, especially for students with learning disabilities. **Graphic organizers** visually represent relationships among concepts, thoughts, and ideas. They are also called concept maps, story maps, advance organizers, story webs, or semantic maps (Callison, 2003). Graphic organizers are presented in a number of places in this text. Like written previews, graphic organizers help the reader prepare for reading by presenting a pictorial road map of the text. Promoting *visual literacy*— the ability to interpret visual and hierarchical information—a graphic organizer is effective because readers are asked to interpret a concise, comprehensive, and compact visual aid. A study by DiCecco and Gleason (2002) found that graphic organizers, along with intensive instruction and summary writing, benefited students with learning disabilities. Forget (2004, p. 212) notes that by helping students "to see that written text by others can be deconstructed into a visual graphic that not only shows complex interrelationships from the text, but also is easy to study, teachers are helping to make difficult reading easier for students to handle." At the beginning of each chapter in this book we present a graphic organizer to help readers see the relationships among the concepts and the key terms in the chapter through a visual representation of its content.

One type of graphic organizer that is normally used in the preparation phase before reading is constructed in the form of a hierarchical diagram of words, sometimes described as a *tree diagram*. Such graphic organizers are constructed by teachers to be displayed for students before the reading, whereas other types of graphic organizers may be constructed by students (or by teachers and students together) in the assistance and reflection phases of the lesson. Activity 3.5 shows a graphic organizer in the form of a tree diagram of cloud formations for an elementary science class.

Activity 3.5 was created with *Inspiration*.

A number of studies (Lambiotte & Dansereau, 1992; Rakes, Rakes, & Smith, 1995) support the use of graphic organizers and displays to aid in organizing students' thoughts. Shapiro (1999) found that such overviews also help learning during hypermedia lessons. When readers understand the relationships among concepts in a selection, they can begin to connect the new relationships to their previous knowledge. Robinson's (1998) review of 16 studies on graphic organizers indicates that they facilitate memory for text. This outcome is most likely because they connect schemata and help students see connections between the new and the known.

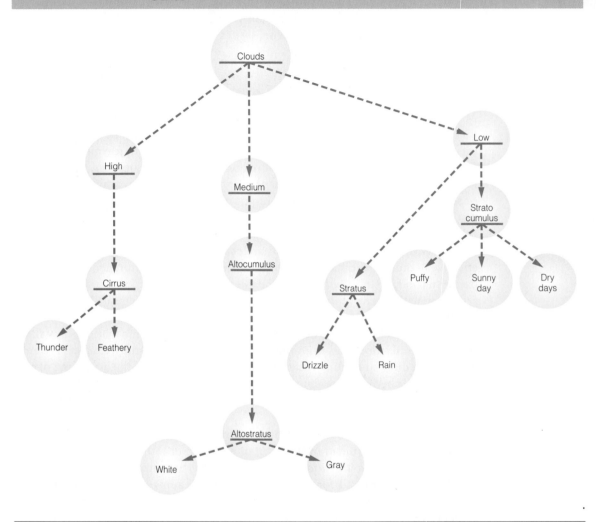

Teachers usually find graphic organizers challenging to prepare but very much worth the effort. To construct one, follow these steps:

1. Identify the superordinate, or major, concept; then identify all supporting concepts in the material.
2. List all key terms from the material that reflect the identified concepts.
3. Connect the terms to show the relationships among concepts.
4. To show relationships between new concepts and already learned ones, add any terms from previous lessons or that you feel are part of students' prior knowledge.

5. Construct a diagram based on these connections, and use it to introduce the reading material.

When developing a graphic organizer, you do not have to include every word that might be new to readers. Some new words may not contribute to the diagram. Including words already known to the students is useful when these words represent key concepts—familiarity will aid understanding. Teachers should explain to students why they prepared the graphic organizer as they did, noting the relationships. This presentation should include a discussion to which students can contribute what they know about the terms as well as what they predict they will be learning, based on the chart. Students should keep the organizer available for reference while they are reading, so they can occasionally check back to see the relationships as they encounter the terms.

After reading, students can use the graphic organizer as an aid for refocusing and reflecting on their learning. It can even be used as a check of comprehension. Thus the graphic organizer can be useful at each of the PAR steps and promote integration of the communicative arts. Activity 3.6 is an example of a graphic organizer for elementary social studies.

Anticipation Guides

An **anticipation guide**, sometimes called a reaction guide or prediction guide, is a prereading strategy that teaches both content and literacy, along with reading skills appropriate for all learners (Kozen, Murray, & Windell, 2006). Students react to a series of statements prepared by the teacher. In reacting to these statements, students anticipate, or predict, what the content will be. Once students have committed to the statements, a purpose for reading has been created. Students' curiosity about their predictions can help maintain their purpose for thoughtful reading. In this way the guide assists learners while they read. In the reflection phase of the lesson, student group and teacher-led discussions attempt to come to final consensus on the answers to the guide. Conner (2003) notes that while some statements should be true/false ones, some should be vague enough to provoke disagreement and "challenge students' beliefs about the topic" (p. 1). Remember that if some statements are intentionally vague to arouse curiosity and discussion, consensus might not be reached in all cases. Here are some reasons why anticipation guides are valuable:

1. Students need to both connect what they already know with new information and realize that they may already know concepts that will help them comprehend.

2. Students exposed to anticipation guides tend to become interested and participate in lively discussion, which motivates reading.

3. Reading and writing instruction are easily integrated when anticipation guides are used.

4. Many students enjoy argument, and a well-structured anticipation guide leaves enough room for doubt about topics to generate healthy debate.

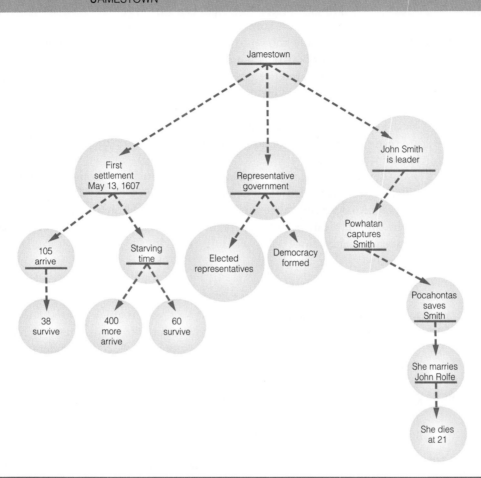

5. Students need to learn to predict outcomes of their reading, and this strategy is an excellent one for teaching this important skill.

Suppose a high school vocational education teacher has introduced the term *high amperages* to an unenthusiastic class in automobile mechanics. In fact, no one is sure what the term means. In discussing the larger concept of automobile batteries it becomes apparent that students think they know about batteries; but they don't have a schema for important terms like *amperage, conductance, plates,* and *voltage regulation*, among others. To overcome misconceptions about how a battery operates, the teacher prepares an anticipation guide (Activity 3.7). As groups of students discuss the guide, they talk about their prior knowledge and begin to formulate more precise knowledge concerning the topic.

NAME _____ DATE _____

Before reading the pages in the text: In the space to the left of each statement, place a check mark (✓) if you agree or think the statement is true.

During or after reading: Add new check marks or cross through those about which you have changed your mind. Keep in mind that this is not like a traditional worksheet. You may have to put on your "thinking caps" and read between the lines. Use the space under each statement to note the page(s), column(s), and paragraph(s) where you find information to support your thinking.

_____ 1. An automobile battery is, in many ways, like a long flashlight with several D-cell batteries inside.

_____ 2. The amount of current and voltage a battery can produce is probably related to the actual size of the battery.

_____ 3. The chemical liquid in a battery is a conductor that allows electrons to leave one type of plate in the battery and move toward another type of plate.

_____ 4. The plates inside a battery are soft and squishy and must be separated by a nonconductive material.

_____ 5. When you are driving down the road, you are actually charging your battery by increasing the number of electrons in the liquid inside the battery.

_____ 6. When buying a battery, it is better to spend a few extra dollars; you should keep in mind the saying that "you get what you pay for."

_____ 7. A battery that has both high amperages and a long reserve capacity probably has more plates inside it than a battery of lesser capacity.

_____ 8. The liquid inside a battery can disappear.

Developed by Mark Forget. Used with permission.

Creating templates in a word processing program for anticipation guides can save teachers' time.

Anticipation guides involve students in discussion and reading and also can ask students to respond in writing to the statements. Many teachers have students refer to the guide as they read, which enhances comprehension. If students return to the guide after reading, to clarify or rethink previous positions, every phase of PAR is applied throughout administration of the guide. Anticipation guides are excellent for developing critical thinking and cultural understanding, and they are well received by both teachers and students.

Making an anticipation guide takes some thought but becomes easier with practice. Here are the basic steps for constructing an anticipation guide:

1. Read the content passage, and identify the major concepts to be learned in the lesson.

2. Decide which concepts are most important to stimulate student background and beliefs.

3. Write three to six statements about these concepts. The statements should reflect the students' background and be thought-provoking. Choose statements

that might make students disagree with one another and provide valid evidence for a side of an argument. General statements, rather than statements that are too specific, work best. Well-known quotations and idioms are successful.

4. Use some statements that are intuitively appealing to students but that will prove incorrect on reading the text. Keep the exercise from turning into rote decoding by writing statements that require students to interpret large segments of text.

5. Make your statements read more easily than the text.

6. Display the guide on the chalkboard, with an overhead projector, or on worksheets. Give clear directions. (These will vary depending on the age group and variations in the guide.) Leave space for original student responses.

7. Conduct class discussion based on your concept statements. Students must support their responses—yes and no are not acceptable answers. Tell students to argue based on their experiences and always explain any decisions they make. Students should be asked to "think like lawyers" to argue their points.

8. After reading with the assistance of the guide, students should form small groups and attempt to come to consensus on the answers to the guide. The teacher brings the class back as a whole to discuss group answers. Here the teacher attempts to bring closure to the lesson. Students discuss what they have learned, and the teacher clarifies any concepts that are still unclear.

9. The teacher may take the opportunity to review and reinforce the use of the skill of predicting. Here the teacher may point out to students that they can use this skill while reading in any subject area to engage themselves and to make the reading more interesting by setting a purpose for reading.

Activities 3.8, 3.9, and 3.10 are anticipation guides constructed by teachers of primary science, geometry, and elementary English classes, respectively. There is no right way to create a guide. Anticipation guides that reflect sound instructional principles and research are developed every day by enterprising teachers.

Factstorming

Factstorming is an excellent activity to determine prior knowledge of students and to build background. The whole class can participate at once as the activity proceeds from a single generative question. Factstorming is similar to brainstorming but focuses on facts and associations pertinent to the topic, whereas brainstorming focuses on problem solving. The teacher asks students to say anything they can think of about the topic to be read—for instance, "Tell anything you know about the country of Egypt and the region known as North Africa." Responses are written on the chalkboard or on a transparency and are discussed as they are entered.

PreP STRATEGY

A sophisticated version of factstorming is PreP, a prereading plan (Langer, 1981). PreP has three phases:

Directions: Read these statements to yourself as I read them aloud. If you agree with a statement, be ready to explain why. We will check all statements we agree with in the prereading column. Then we will read to see if we should change our minds.

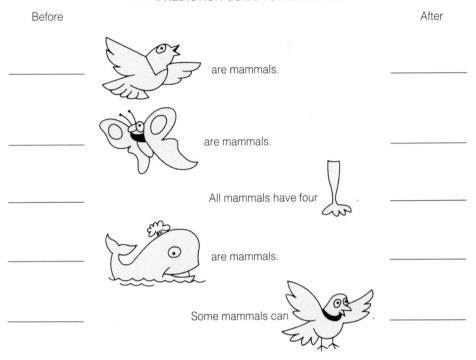

1. Initial associations with the concept, as in factstorming.
2. Reflections on the initial concept, when students are asked to explain why they thought of a particular response, thus building awareness of their prior knowledge and associations.
3. Reformulation of knowledge, when new ideas learned during the first two phases are articulated.

PreP helps ascertain prior knowledge and also builds background. Its steps encourage the reader to use whatever prior knowledge is available by listening carefully to the opinions of others. Misperceptions can be corrected in a nonthreatening way, with whole-group discussion as a supportive environment for expression. Listening, speaking, and reading all take place in a PreP activity. In Activity 3.11 students generate words from the main topic *wounds* in a health education class. They categorize the words they have generated during the PreP into three general categories: health facilities, types, and reasons it happened. Students then use the categories to guide their reading.

NAME _____ DATE _____

PREDICTION GUIDE: PROVING THEOREMS ABOUT ANGLES

Before reading, place a check mark (✓) next to the statements you think will be verifiable in the reading on pages 2–35 to 2–39. Then, during or after the reading, change any that you wish by crossing through checked ones you think not to be true, and by checking any new ones you now agree with. Be prepared to defend your interpretation by specific reference to the text. Use the space under each statement to note pages and paragraphs or diagrams you are referring to in order to prove your interpretation.

_____ 1. Congruent angles have the same number of degrees in them.

_____ 2. The ways that runways point at airports differ from one airport to another.

_____ 3. Two supplementary angles always add up to the same number of degrees.

_____ 4. Proving theorems about angles is easy—it just requires using common sense.

_____ 5. Any two-column proof can also be written in paragraph form.

_____ 6. The term *complementary angle* is like the term *supplementary angle*.

_____ 7. If Jennifer had three pieces of pizza, and Shenika had four pieces, then Jennifer consumed fewer calories than Shenika did.

Developed by Mark Forget. Used with permission.

Modified Cloze Procedure

In Chapter 6 we will introduce *cloze* as a means of determining reading comprehension and as an assessment tool. Cloze passages can also be constructed to help teachers determine students' prior knowledge. Teachers here actually make up the passage themselves and leave blanks wherever key concepts are needed. Instead of deleting words at predetermined intervals, as when measuring readability and checking students' reading ability, teachers construct a passage that closely mirrors the text reading. In this technique teachers are creating their own cloze passages of 50–100 words to assess students' knowledge of vocabulary and concepts for a certain topic. Activity 3.12 presents a passage of approximately 70 words constructed to assess students' knowledge of crocodiles in Africa. Students can fill in the blanks individually, then discuss their answers in small groups. The best, or most unusual, answers can eventually be shared with the entire class.

Analogies

Comparisons can be made between familiar and less familiar concepts by the use of **analogies**. These are like previews in that both begin with a connection point to the

NAME _____ DATE _____

ANTICIPATION GUIDE: STRATEGIES FOR READING POETRY

Before reading: In the space to the left of each statement, place a check mark (✔) if you agree or think the statement is true.

During or after reading: Add new check marks or cross through those about which you have changed your mind. Keep in mind that this is not like a traditional worksheet. You may have to put on your "thinking caps" and read between the lines. Use the space under each statement to note the page(s) and paragraph(s) where you find information to support your thinking.

_____ 1. In poems, the words at the ends of the lines usually rhyme with each other.

_____ 2. Poems actually say more than the words they are made of; they can cause the reader to experience emotions.

_____ 3. Only someone who is an expert in poetry can enjoy reading poems.

_____ 4. Poets paint pictures with words.

_____ 5. You sometimes can tell when a poem was written just by reading it, but this is not always true.

_____ 6. When two people read the same poem, they will usually understand it in the same way if it was well written.

_____ 7. Hearing a poem read aloud can cause you to interpret it differently than if you read it silently.

Developed by Mark Forget. Used with permission.

reader's background. However, analogies carry out a comparison, whereas previews focus more directly on the material to be read.

Analogies are excellent tools for content reading teachers because they are simple to create and highly relevant for students. Researchers (Glynn, 1997; Yanowitz, 2001) have found that analogies are a successful strategy for content area teachers, especially in science classes. They can be presented in oral or written form as an informal introduction to content material. They also promote listening and speaking; and if students are encouraged to write their own analogies after reading certain material, then analogies become useful reflection and writing activities as well. The example in Activity 3.13 was developed by a third grade teacher.

Analogies are powerful tools to use in reading. When a high school junior resisted reading a history chapter that explained the circumstances leading to the American revolution, his parent tried this analogy:

"Suppose," the parent suggested, "that your parents decided to go to Europe for six months, leaving you on your own at home. You would have the car and access to money;

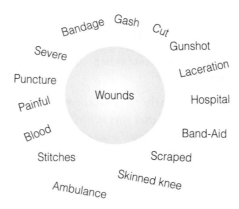

Categories:

Health facilities   Types of wounds   Reasons wounds happened

ACTIVITY **3.12** CROCODILES: MODIFIED CLOZE PROCEDURE

This article is about crocodiles, which live mainly in _____.

Crocodiles eat _____ and are ferocious, sometimes reaching a length of over _____ feet and a weight of _____ pounds. A full-grown crocodile can _____ a man while the poor fellow _____. There are

probably about _____ crocodiles alive today. They believe in _____ their young and often have fun _____ with other crocodiles. Crocodiles are known for their _____ and _____.

you would be able to make all your own decisions. What would your reaction be?" As you might imagine, the high school junior thought this would be an excellent arrangement. "However," the parent continued, "we would arrive home again and take charge once more. We would want our car back, and you would have to ask for permission to do the things you'd been doing freely. Now how would you feel?" The junior did not like this turn of events. "Would you still love us?" the parent inquired, assuming, of course, that teenagers do love their parents even though they have funny ways of showing it.

"Well, yes," the junior reluctantly agreed. "But I'd be insulted, and family life wouldn't be the same."

"Exactly," agreed the parent. "That's the way it was with the British and their American colonies. The British had to attend to problems in Europe and in their own

Goal: To enable students to connect new knowledge with existing knowledge.

Directions: Read the following paragraphs as a primer for small-group discussion comparing cars with bodies.

Materials: Paper
Pencils

"Your body is very similar to a car in the way that it acts. You may have been told to 'rev up your engine' one time. When a car revs up, it begins to go.

"A car needs many different substances to keep it running well. It might need oil for the parts and air for the filters, as you would need oil for your joints or air for your lungs.

"Actually, there are many other things that a car and your body have in common. A car needs gasoline to make it go. What do you need?" (food)

Now divide the students into small groups and let them list on paper the ways that cars and bodies are similar. Some suggestions that you will be looking for are:

Fats/oil
Protein/gasoline
Carbohydrates/spark plugs
Vitamins/fuel additives, super grade gasoline
Minerals/paint, rustproofers
Air/air conditioning
Muscles/wheels
Heart/engine

Return to the class in 15 or 20 minutes and share the group information. Write the analogies on the board. Ask for comments or changes.

Developed by Kathy Feltus.

---

government. They let the American colonists have free rein for a while. Then they turned their attention back to the Americans. But the Americans didn't appreciate the intervention after this period of time. Many of them still 'loved' the British, but they deeply resented the renewed control. While you're reading this chapter, you might want to keep in mind your own reactions to this hypothetical situation and compare those feelings to the reactions of the colonists." Much later in the month, this junior grudgingly reported to his parent that the chapter had turned out to be "pretty easy to read" because he understood the circumstances better than for most of the other chapters in the book.

This on-the-spot analogy was simple enough to construct. The teacher/parent understood several characteristics of 16-year-olds and applied them to building an analogy that would hook the reader to the content material. The informal analogy was a simple preparation strategy. It worked because the reading took on new meaning for the student. His comprehension was enhanced—enough so that he admitted it to a parent!

Changing Student Misconceptions through Discussion

Researchers have for some time examined the use of reading discussion groups and have chronicled numerous successful approaches to such groups, such as literature response groups, book clubs, and literature circles, to name a few (Cantrell, 2002;

Daniels, 1994; Speigel, 1998). Students in these groups interpret text based on their own life experiences. Participation in such groups may offer the best solution to overcoming prior knowledge misconceptions on the part of students. Maria and MacGinitie (1987) conducted a study in which they asked students in the fifth and sixth grades to read two types of materials. The first made specific reference to the misconceptions that the researchers had identified during a pretest and contrasted those misconceptions with correct information. The second was written with the correct information but no direct refutation of predetermined misconceptions. The researchers found that student recall was significantly better for the text that confronted the misconceptions.

Guzzetti, Snyder, and Glass (1992) conducted a meta-analysis of studies about children's misconceptions. They found that some type of intervention was enough to establish for students a degree of discomfort with their prior beliefs (p. 648). Three strategies were found to be effective means of intervention:

1. Using refutational text—providing a passage directly refuting the misconception.

2. Using augmented activation activities to stimulate discussion and then to supplement the material generated with the correct information—similar to what might occur with brainstorming and PreP or anticipation guides.

3. Constructing a web (graphic organizer) whereby students must articulate and defend their positions by referring to the text and discussing results of the visual representation with peers.

Regardless of which specific activity is used, dissatisfaction with incorrect prior knowledge must be created before misconceptions will be altered.

As a final point, the authors would like to remind our readers that preparing students to read through determining and building on prior knowledge is always a worthy goal but is not always easy to do. This is true precisely because students are so special and unique, enigmatic, and often refreshingly unscripted in their thoughts and habits. One of the authors was visiting a first grade class in which the teacher was getting students to ask questions about the lesson. The author posed a question to the class: Who made the first American flag? None of the 14 students seemed to know, and no student ventured a guess. Fully 10 minutes after the question was asked and seemingly forgotten by all, the visiting author told the class goodbye and started to leave. While the visitor smiled, waved, and walked toward the door, a small, red-faced, smiling boy, seated in the front, ran up and tugged on the pants of the visitor and whispered in an almost inaudible voice, "Betsy Ross."

ONE-MINUTE SUMMARY

This chapter has noted the importance of students' prior knowledge in reading and the necessity of building on prior knowledge throughout reading lessons. Careful preparation by teachers may help to overcome both students' limited or incorrect prior knowledge about a topic and their lack of interest in the topic. We described the problem of mismatches between readers and texts and how teachers must overcome such mismatches through strategies that better prepare students for reading.

We discussed many activities—some developed by classroom teachers—for building on students' prior knowledge in reading. Although textbook material sometimes needs adaptation, it should not be eliminated from the curriculum. Preparation activities can promote reading, writing, speaking, and listening. We emphasized that how a teacher uses an activity is more important than rigorous adherence to prescribed steps, and we included variations of activities that demonstrated the creativity of the teachers who constructed them. In this chapter we described strategies to prepare the learner such as prelearning concept checks, rewriting, written previews, graphic organizers, anticipation guides, modified cloze procedure, factstorming, PreP, and analogies. We also described the importance of teacher discussion and reading discussion groups for learning.

PAR ONLINE

Visit the *Reading to Learn in the Content Areas* Web site at http://academic.cengage.com/education/richardson for links to the Web sites mentioned in this chapter, tutorial quizzing, and other resources.

Go to *Reading Online* and locate the article by Thomas Bean about social constructivism. Read it and share your comments with classmates.

Create a template for one of the activities presented in this chapter, such as the anticipation guide or the structured overview.

Visit one of the Web sites where teachers post their activities (provided on the Web links option of the Chapter 3 resources on the book companion Web site). Select what you think is a good preparation activity and be able to explain why you like it.

END-OF-CHAPTER ACTIVITIES

Assisting Comprehension

1. Look over these four questions we asked at the beginning of the chapter:

   a. What is the importance of prior knowledge in reading comprehension?

   b. How does a teacher determine students' prior knowledge?

   c. How can teachers overcome students' misconceptions about a topic?

   d. Are there strategies a teacher can use to prepare students to read? Are you better able to answer these questions now, after having read the chapter? Formulate answers to all four questions to help you remember this chapter.

2. Select a chapter from a content area textbook. Using the following questions as a guide, reflect on what your text offers to help you as a teacher build on your students' prior knowledge for reading the text:

   a. What aids are provided in the text chapter to help you build on students' prior knowledge?

b. Is there a chapter preview or summary that could be used to build on it?

c. Are there any statements, such as those identifying objectives, that could be used in an anticipation guide?

d. Is there a graphic organizer?

e. Are these aids suitable for your students?

f. Are these aids sufficient for your students?

g. As a teacher, should you construct some aids to help yourself build on students' prior knowledge? If so, what will you construct?

Reflecting on Your Reading

1. To help you remember the main content of this chapter, write a 30-word summary of the chapter. Check it against the graphic organizer at the beginning of the chapter to see how many of the main concepts of the chapter you were able to remember.

2. The International Reading Association Standard 1.4 asks classroom teachers to recognize the major components of reading.

One important element they list in this standard is building the prior knowledge of students. They maintain that the classroom teacher should know and be able to articulate the research that supports the importance of background knowledge and prior knowledge in reading. To help you in your deliberations on this, think about the research we cited on all of these topics:

a. Matching reader to text.

b. Schema theory in reading.

c. Limited background knowledge.

d. Incorrect background knowledge.

e. Heightening interest in reading.

f. Cognitive dissonance.

From the study of these topics, try to formulate a coherent vision and purpose statement about why building on prior knowledge is the most important aspect of preparing learners. This vision and purpose statement should be goals you can articulate to others in the teaching profession.

I hear and I forget. I see and I remember. I do and I understand.

CONFUCIUS

Assistance in Learning

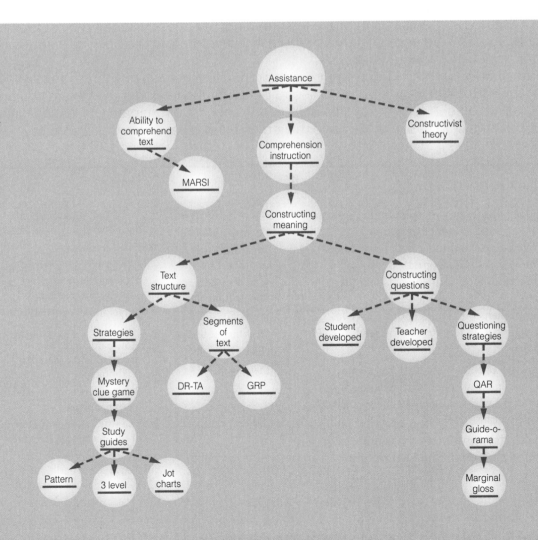

VOICES FROM THE CLASSROOM

The class is a well-behaved group of children who listen to their teacher and always follow her instructions without complaining. Ms. Cramwell as a teacher is fairly stern, always presenting an austere yet professional demeanor. Her English class is studying the novel *Great Expectations* and is currently on Chapter 52 of 59 chapters of the classic Dickens novel. The routine is always the same. She assigns one chapter for homework and for the next day prepares questions about the chapter on a handout to be answered individually by the students at the beginning of class. After this opening assignment, the next chapter is studied each day in class. She calls on "star" readers (her term) to read orally as a way to cover a chapter during class. There are no discipline problems in this class because the students seem "beyond the discipline thing." Most are barely attentive in class while listening to the chapter being read aloud, and many seem to drift off into a daydream state. Some of the students are never called on to read. The teacher discusses what to read but never how to read or how the students can improve their reading. The class is labeled by students as boring and, by the end of the novel, there is little interest in the book or in reading another book by Charles Dickens.

Can students improve their reading comprehension in a class such as this? Why isn't there instruction in how to comprehend better for those students who are having reading problems in this class? Have you ever seen or participated in a class like this? Could the students who are never called on to read have reading problems?

PREPARING TO READ

1. Did anyone assist you in reading when you were a young student by teaching you strategies for learning? Did anyone teach you how to ask appropriate questions while reading? Did anyone tell you that there are at least three levels of comprehension? Think about your own background in learning as you read this chapter.

2. Can you predict what this chapter on "assisting comprehension" will be about? How and why would we help a student to comprehend?

3. Match the words in the left column with their definitions in the right column:

1. Adjunct strategies
2. Constructivism
3. Superordinate information
4. Subordinate information
5. Segments of text
6. Structure of text
7. Discourse analysis
8. Metacognition

a. The act of thinking about one's own thought patterns.
b. Small sections of subcategories of texts.
c. Strategies used to assist someone in reading.
d. Large overall concepts of a chapter of text.
e. How paragraphs are arranged and ordered in a textbook.
f. Smaller concepts, specific to a given content.
g. The study and identification of organizational structure in written material.
h. Active construction of meaning by the learner.

OBJECTIVES

As you read this chapter, focus your attention on the following purposes. You will

1. Be able to define *reading comprehension,* using a historical perspective when forming your definition.

2. Understand constructivism, constructivist learning, and the theory underlying the construct.

3. Be able to help students construct meaning while reading.

4. Learn strategies for teaching short segments of text.

5. Learn the importance of teaching the structure of text.

6. Learn a number of activities that assist and guide students to better understand text.

7. Be able to use questioning strategies to teach comprehension.

Shoe. Reprinted with permission of Tribune Media Services.

ASSISTING COMPREHENSION: THE CONSTRUCTION OF MEANING

Edmund Burke Huey was a pioneer in the field of psychology and reading, and his writings still seem fresh today.

An important step in the PAR Lesson Framework is the assistance phase, in which students develop and deepen their understanding of any learning activity. Consider your response to this chapter's opening scenario: Didn't you think the teacher needed to help students *as they read in class* to better understand the material they were reading? If teachers are to provide assistance to students in this important phase, they must first understand what it means to comprehend in reading.

Although historically the study of reading comprehension has reflected different schools of thought at different times, the changes in definition over time exhibit more continuity than contrast. Huey (1908/1968) and then Thorndike (1917/1932) defined *reading* as a thinking process, implying that comprehension is not only recognizing letters and words but also thinking about what those symbols mean. Sixty years later, Hillerich (1979) drew the same conclusion when he identified reading comprehension as "nothing more than thinking as applied to reading" (p. 3). A little earlier, Frank

Reading is more than simply a basic skill. It involves complex thinking in the learning process.

Smith (1971), drawing from his study of communication systems, argued for a definition of *comprehension* as "the reduction of uncertainty" (p. 17). Smith explained that as readers gain information by reading, they rely on what they know to "reduce the number of alternative possibilities" (p. 17). Pearson and Johnson (1978) pictured reading comprehension as the building of bridges between the new and the known. The continuity among these definitions, which span 70 years, is apparent.

Teachers need to know that reading is more than simply a basic skill. Mature readers take part in a complex process that is analytic, interactive, constructive, and strategic (Guthrie, Schafer, Von Secker, & Alban, 2000; Lederer, 2000). Fluent readers are independent readers who sample text, predict, confirm hypotheses, and self-correct quickly (Schoenbach, Greenleaf, Cziko, & Hurwitz, 1999). In addition, apprehension and reflection are requisites of comprehension. A reader must apprehend and ponder the significance of the content. This analysis must be active, generating strategies that aid the reader now and in future reading. Mature readers must also set their own purposes for reading, maintain meaning over time, cope with the complexities of text, draw inferences, and respond critically to an author's meaning (Whitehead, 1994). To demonstrate how complex the reading act can be, in Activity 4.1 we present one high school government teacher's answers when questioned by one of the authors about how he reads and studies when starting to read a challenging text. Notice carefully all the ways he prepares himself to read.

ACTIVITY 4.1 COMMENTS OF A TEACHER ON READING DIFFICULT TEXT

Think about the last time you read a challenging text. What strategies did you use to understand it?

When reading a challenging text, I implement a number of reading strategies. First, I examine the passage, looking at all the subheadings, textbook margins notes, illustrations, and highlighted material. I do this in order to gain an informative overview of that which I am about to read. By doing this, I access my prior knowledge schema on the subject matter. Secondly, I identify and note the main idea presented by the passage so my reading is focused on development of the principal idea being elaborated. Thirdly, I organize all the sections of a passage by reading the summary or conclusions provided in the text, and thoroughly examine the objectives given by the author in order to prepare myself to think critically and analytically about what is going to be read. Fourth, I quickly read the passage, taking notes around the centralized idea(s) that I have previously identified in my notes, and write my own questions that I desire to have answered through reading. Fifth, I reread the text, more slowly and methodically in order to focus attention specifically on the concepts presented in the reading objectives. Next, I connect all my notes, coupled with illustrations, text margin notes, and highlighted material so that all of my data flow nicely and make sense to me as a reader. Finally, I answer the end-of-chapter questions. If I am satisfied with my answers and such answers were easily recalled and developed, I move on to the next section of the reading. If I am not satisfied with my answers to the questions, I read the passage again until I am satisfied with my understanding of the text, and successfully accomplish the objectives.

Did You Organize the Information?

Yes, I always organize the information, particularly when reading a text that I find difficult. I do this by reviewing the title, subheadings, pictures, charts, maps, graphs, and other visual illustrations given in the text, and make note of each of these items. Next, I review the objectives, summary, and conclusions given by the author and organize my notes so they revolve around the central premise of the information presented. Finally, I complete the end-of-chapter questions to ensure that my organization of the information was accurately accomplished. That is, I ask myself whether I accomplished the objectives that were established.

Did You Ask Yourself Questions?

When reading, I often ask myself questions, and write those questions in my notes. I ask myself such questions as "What do I already know about this topic?" and "How will my previous knowledge of the subject help in my reading, and how will my knowledge be further developed?" I also ask myself, "What is the author trying to communicate to me in this passage?" and "How well do the notes I have taken support the objectives given?" Further, I convert each subheading within the text reading into a question that I want to see answered, thereby focusing my reading on the conceptual notion given by the content subheadings.

Developed by Travis Sturgill, high school government teacher.

Other important factors determine how much a student comprehends. Both novice and expert readers use existing knowledge to construct meaning from text. That is, a reader's world knowledge and specific knowledge of a topic play a crucial role in the comprehension process (Alexander & Jetton, 2000). In addition, not all readers will interpret the same reading material in the same way. Differences in background knowledge and experiences can cause different interpretations and even lead to invalid interpretations of text (Pressley, 2002). Also, we are just beginning to understand the importance of motivation as it applies to reading comprehension, in the manifestation of reading habits. Motivation and emotions seem to play a pivotal role in the achievement of students with reading comprehension difficulties (Sideridis, Mouzaki, Simos, & Protopapas, 2006). Hall (2007) explains that motivation plays a significant role in struggling readers' ability to comprehend text. In one study, this researcher found that poorly performing students refused to take part in certain classroom reading activities when such activities compromised an image of success that they were trying to project to peers.

It should be noted that a mature reader's ability to use strategies in a coordinated fashion does not necessarily develop simply by providing students with opportunities to read, such as oral classroom reading. Students benefit most from being taught comprehension strategies that are based on sound research (Neufeld, 2005). Teaching such strategies and reinforcing them over time helps students learn in a self-regulated fashion.

COMPREHENSION STRATEGY INSTRUCTION

There is strong evidence that students can be taught comprehension strategies and that such instruction is an excellent way to improve their understanding of authentic texts they read (Duke & Pearson, 2002; Kropiewnicki, 2006; Pressley, 2000). Unfortunately, much research evidence also shows that comprehension instruction is not occurring in many content area classrooms across the country (Neufeld, 2005; Pressley, 2002a; Pressley, Wharton-McDonald, Hampson, & Echevarria, 1998). Pressley (2002b) and his colleagues found that students were given opportunities to practice comprehension strategies but were not taught the strategies or why it was important to use them. We feel it is the instructor's role to teach students about comprehension and provide comprehension instruction as well as text information (Fielding & Pearson, 1994). One way to accomplish this is to first test for the behaviors a mature reader should exhibit. One such test, the *Metacognitive Awareness of Reading Strategies Inventory (MARSI)* by Mokhtari and Reichard (2002), is designed to help content teachers know what reading strategies their students use. The MARSI uses a self-report instrument that relies on students' awareness of reading and perceived use of reading strategies for learning. Activity 4.2 shows the test questions along with the Lickert Scale used.

After giving the MARSI, teachers can pick strategies for instruction that coincide with problem areas students have noted on the test. For instance, if students say they do not summarize, take notes, scan tables and figures, or even have a clear purpose for reading, the teacher can design instruction that will concentrate on these problem areas. Or if students say they do not use context clues to learn new words (item 19 on MARSI), the teacher can teach the important skill of context clue discovery (see Chapter 9 about vocabulary).

ACTIVITY *4.2* METACOGNITIVE AWARENESS OF READING STRATEGIES INVENTORY

All items graded on a 1 to 5 Lickert Scale:

1. I never or almost never do this.
2. I do this only occasionally.
3. I sometimes do this (about 50 percent of the time).
4. I usually do this.
5. I always or almost always do this.

_____ 1. I have a purpose in mind when I read.

_____ 2. I take notes while reading to help me understand what I read.

_____ 3. I think about what I know to help me understand what I read.

_____ 4. I preview the text to see what it is about before I read it.

_____ 5. When text becomes difficult, I read aloud to help me understand what I read.

_____ 6. I summarize what I read to help me reflect on important information in text.

_____ 7. I think about whether the content of the text fits my reading purpose.

_____ 8. I read slowly but carefully to make sure I understand what I am reading.

_____ 9. I discuss what I read with others to check my understanding.

_____ 10. I skim the text first by noting characteristics like length and organization.

_____ 11. I try to get back on track when I lose concentration.

_____ 12. I underline or circle information in the text to help me remember it.

_____ 13. I adjust my reading speed according to what I am reading.

_____ 14. I decide what to read closely and what to ignore.

_____ 15. I use reference materials such as dictionaries to help me understand what I read.

_____ 16. When text becomes difficult, I pay closer attention to what I am reading.

_____ 17. I use tables, figures, and pictures in text to increase my understanding.

_____ 18. I stop from time to time and think about what I am reading.

_____ 19. I use context clues to help me better understand what I am reading.

_____ 20. I paraphrase (restate ideas in my own words) to better understand what I read.

_____ 21. I try to picture or visualize information to help remember what I read.

_____ 22. I use typographical aids like boldface and italics to identify new information.

_____ 23. I critically analyze and evaluate the information presented in the text.

_____ 24. I go back and forth in the text to find relationships among ideas in it.

_____ 25. I check my understanding when I come across conflicting information.

_____ 26. I try to guess what material is about when I read.

_____ 27. When text becomes difficult, I reread to increase my understanding.

_____ 28. I ask myself questions I like to have answered in the text.

_____ 29. I check to see if my guesses about the text are right or wrong.

_____ 30. I try to guess the meaning of unknown words or phrases.

From Mokhtari, Kouider, & Reichard, Carla A. (2002). Assessing students' metacognitive awareness of reading strategies. *Journal of Educational Psychology, 94*(2), pp. 249–259. Used with permission.

Look for ways to teach comprehension as you continue to read this chapter.

A number of the strategies we cover in this chapter, such as directed reading instruction and questioning strategies, are important for covering many of the potential problem areas in comprehension noted on the MARSI. The MARSI will help teachers design reading comprehension instruction that meets the needs of students who are having comprehension difficulties due to their lack of sophistication with using authentic textbook material.

Teachers need to reinforce learning during reading (the assistance phase) in addition to doing so before or after reading is completed. Teachers use **adjunct strategies** (strategies during reading) more often than pre- or postreading strategies (Rakes & Chance, 1990). Of the students polled by Rakes and Chance, 78 percent (of 182) at the secondary level and 59 percent (of 156) in the elementary grades said that teachers had taught them strategies to use as they read. How the teacher presents the content material makes a difference in how well students learn the material. In the remainder of this chapter we focus on ways to help students comprehend as they read content material.

CONSTRUCTIVISM AND LEARNING

When students can make sense of their learning by developing a knowledge base or constructing their own purposes for reading a selection and developing tasks on their own that demonstrate their learning, they are constructing meaning. That is, knowledge is not passively received but is actively constructed by the learners on the basis of prior knowledge, attitudes, and values (Betts, 1991). This is called **constructivism** or the constructivist theory of learning. This theory emphasizes the important role of the learner in literacy tasks, allowing readers to feel comfortable with learning because they are so fully integrated in putting it all together. In constructivist theory, students are asked through active consideration and assimilation to internalize material and reshape or transform information into thought that makes sense in their world (Brooks & Brooks, 1993). Constructivism emphasizes a student's ability to solve practical, real-life problems. The teacher's role in this theory is to assemble required resources and act as a guide for students to formulate their own goals and learn themselves (Roblyer, Edwards, & Havriluk, 1997). Concerning this theory, Sparks (1995) has said,

In a constructivist classroom, higher-order thinking skills are emphasized.

> Constructivists believe that learners build knowledge structures rather than merely receive them from teachers. In this view, knowledge is not simply transmitted from teacher to student, but is instead constructed in the mind of the learner. From a constructivist perspective, it is critical that teachers model appropriate behavior, guide student activities, and provide various forms of examples rather than use common instructional practices that emphasize telling and directing. (p. 5)

In a constructivist environment, students must be encouraged to use higher-order thinking skills to find meaning in classroom experiences. Teachers do not stress the "one correct answer" to every question, with that answer being the one supplied by the teacher. Student questioning must be encouraged, and a variety of possible interpretations will have to be accepted by the teacher in certain situations. Teachers who stress constructivism cannot simply rely on factual recall to questions and factual recall–type tests as the central proof that learning has taken place in their classrooms. Betts (1991) has called for teachers in constructivist classrooms to reduce the amount of time spent in drill and practice exercises, increase open-ended questioning and discussions, and increase heuristic, trial-and-error type learning whereby teachers focus discussion on the reasoning that supports a variety of student-generated interpretations.

Liaw (2004) has noted how Web-based learning, with such popular strategies as distance learning, interactive multimedia, graphic displays, and WebQuests, can be used innovatively to teach constructivist learning. Web-based learning environments can provide an excellent opportunity for the teacher to act as a facilitator to help students discover from their own background knowledge any new learning that must take place.

Constructivist learning can take place at any level of education. An example occurred when three professors separated geographically were implementing online instruction and shared insights over a threaded discussion (Richardson, Fleener, & Thistlethwaite, 2004). By talking with each other online, each built new understandings and applications of what a threaded discussion could add to their courses. Chapters 7 and 8 provide more information about Web-based learning.

In a construc-
tivist class-
room the stu-
dent makes
meaning and
the teacher
acts as a
facilitator or
helper.

Ideally, in a constructivist classroom, students are educated to demonstrate their knowledge not through rote memorization and regurgitation of information but by performance-based learning (Dunlap & Grabinger, 1996). Through sharing and reflecting on learning, the emphasis moves from recalling information to a shared production of knowledge through class participation, contribution to group tasks, research, and shared team roles and responsibilities.

Honebein (1996) gives seven pedagogical goals needed for classroom teachers to implement constructivism:

1. Give students knowledge of the learning process.
2. Provide students with experience in appreciation of multiple perspectives.
3. Make learning realistic and relevant.
4. Encourage ownership and voice in the learning process.
5. Provide a social context for learning.
6. Encourage use of multiple modes of representation.
7. Encourage self-awareness on the part of learners.

Dalgarno (2001) has noted that constructivism is emerging as a significant learning theory that emphasizes a student-centered approach to learning. In a constructivist model, teachers are not transmitting knowledge to passive learners; instead learners are building information from the assistance that teachers provide (Weaver, 1994). The reader must actively construct meaning by relating new material to the known, using reasoning and developing concepts. The process is not only individual but also social because "by articulating ideas and experience through writing, speaking, and/or visually representing, students deepen their thinking and construct and organize their understanding of new material" (Gill & Dupre, 1998, p. 95). In addition, some recent research suggests that constructivist learning is useful for improving interactivity in online learning (Rudestam & Schoenholtz-Read, 2002). By discovering what readers do as they read and how they constantly strive to construct meaning while reading, we can design strategies for assistance that enhance their learning. This can be illustrated by an encounter one of the authors had in helping an elementary school youngster read a passage about log cabins. The boy could not say the two words *oil lamp* as he read the passage orally. Throughout the reading he was not given the pronunciation of these two words. After the reading the boy was asked several questions to help him recall the story, including one concerning what kind of lighting was used in the log cabin. The child quickly answered, "Oh, they had an oil lamp." This child was thinking as he read, trying to piece together the clues. He was processing what he knew were unknown data. When he reached the stage of retelling the story, he realized that he did know; he had successfully put the clues together. If the teacher had interpreted as a final product his failure to pronounce the words while he was reading, he would have thought the boy did not know the words. In fact, all along the boy was constructing meaning. Ultimately his processing led to a correct understanding. As this experience illustrates, we must give our students every chance to process information, thus discovering meaning as they read, before we measure their understanding.

There are some cautions for teachers who are contemplating using a constructivist approach.

In being fair and looking at every aspect of this theory, we need to relay a cautionary note about constructivism. Researchers (Green & Gredler, 2002; Vermette et al., 2001) have noted that while constructivist theory is worthy of serious consideration and perhaps implementation, there is still no strong research base concerning the theory to prove its efficacy in the content classroom. It is still just a theory based on the work of John Dewey, Piaget, and Vygotsky. Proponents of constructivism do not even agree on what makes for good constructivist teaching (Ali, 2004). Radical constructivists hold the view that learners should work almost entirely on their own with little aid from the teacher, whereas more moderate proponents recognize that all learning has to take place in a formal and structured environment (Dalgarno, 2001). Vermette and colleagues (2001) note that despite this caution and the multiple interpretations of the theory, constructivism has swept the country. They note that there were over 200 articles written about this topic in the past few years, and constructivism was the cover story of the November 1999 issue of *Educational Leadership,* arguably the leading education journal. This topic is discussed greatly and is generally accepted as being important and worth the necessary time involvement. However, teachers should incorporate only those parts of the theory with which they feel comfortable.

CONSTRUCTING MEANING

Comprehension is influenced by how much teachers help students to understand the way texts are organized and presented. Students need to first understand that a text is organized through the presentation of **superordinate information**, which is information spread over whole chapters and sections of chapters. Put another way, superordinate concepts are the overall concepts the author wishes to impart to readers. **Subordinate information** consists of smaller ideas that are specific to the major concepts.

Readers need to keep in mind the major thrust of the material to understand the relationships among superordinate ideas and subordinate information. For instance, in this textbook, the major (superordinate) theme is the PAR Lesson Framework. Each chapter explains aspects of the framework—subordinate information.

Mapping is one adjunct strategy whose use has been effective in organizing information into major and subordinate ideas (Ruiz-Primo & Shavelson, 1996; Zeilik, Schau, Mattern, Hall, Teague, & Bisard, 1997). This activity, sometimes called *concept mapping,* provides a way for both the teacher and student to remember and organize key elements of knowledge (Romance & Vitale, 1997). Furthermore, mapping can assist readers in understanding concept relationships and thereby avoid fragmented or simple rote learning outcomes (Romance & Vitale, 1999). Mapping has in fact become a very popular activity for helping readers develop comprehension. Just as travelers use a map to find their way, readers can use a diagram that shows the route to understanding a passage, and they themselves can make maps to show their understanding.

Look at the templates and examples in *Inspiration* to see many ways that mapping can be useful.

The primary purpose of mapping is to visually portray the relationships of major and supporting ideas. Because maps encourage students to refer to the reading material and engage in interactive learning, reading educators recognize their value in assisting comprehension. Mapping can be used to teach vocabulary and to introduce

outlining and note taking, as well as being a study aid (see our vocabulary and study skills chapters). Mapping can also introduce a topic before any reading takes place. In such a case, the teacher probably has already made the map or is relying on students' prior knowledge to construct the map; thus the strategy is to use prior knowledge to prepare the readers. Mapping also can aid reading reflection because after the map is made it becomes a study aid. The following are suggestions for developing a map:

1. Identify the main idea of the passage. (Sometimes just the topic or a question may stimulate map generation.) Write the main idea anywhere on the page, leaving room for other information to be written around it.
2. Circle the main idea.
3. Identify subordinate categories, which may be chapter subheadings.
4. Connect the subordinate categories to the main idea.
5. Show supporting details.
6. Connect supporting details to the idea or category they support.
7. Connect all notes to other notes in a way that makes sense.

Although mapping a whole chapter may be time-consuming, we recommend it for portions of a chapter that a teacher identifies as important to help readers understand the superordinate/subordinate relationship.

Maps engage readers as they read, reread, and study; and they demonstrate the hierarchical nature of exposition. Once teachers have mapped several times with students, they will become proficient at making their own maps. Because a map is a diagram of information, it is a visual learning aid. Often, especially for younger readers, drawings added to the map will stimulate learning. Such visual reinforcement capitalizes on visual literacy and right brain functions. Activity 4.3 shows a map about "black holes" for use in a middle school science class.

Integration of all the communicative arts occurs when mapping is used. Class discussion must take place for the map to be developed. This requires students to listen to one another and speak about the topic. Reading is the source of the information mapped, and writing can be incorporated if the teacher asks students to use the map as a frame of reference for writing about the reading topic. For instance, students could be assigned to write a six-paragraph essay about the parts of a computer, as generated from a map. A science teacher who wants students to write a report could have them use a map like the one in Activity 4.3. Students could refer to both primary and secondary sources to find out more about each portion of the map.

COMPREHENSION INSTRUCTION USING SEGMENTS OF TEXT

Authors usually organize text by dividing it into meaningful sections or segments. These are usually signified by subheadings. Readers must pay attention to these **segments of text** to gain information and focus on important information. Teachers can use strategies that provide directed readings over small segments of text. Two important strategies for doing this are explained next: the directed reading–thinking activity and the guided reading procedure.

ACTIVITY **4.3** MAPPING ACTIVITY FOR A MIDDLE SCHOOL SCIENCE CLASS

TOPIC: BLACK HOLES

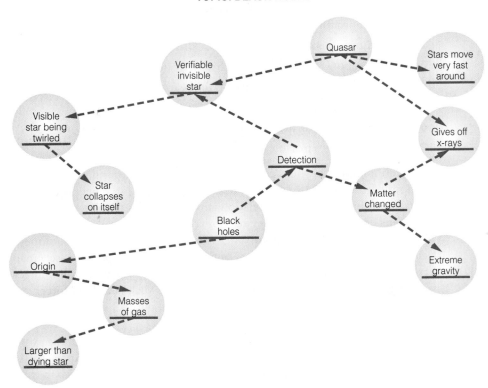

Directed Reading–Thinking Activity

The Directed Reading–Thinking Activity (DR–TA) is an activity that helps students understand that each segment of text can help them figure out the next segment. Because the text is divided into smaller portions, students can focus on the process of responding to higher-order questions (Fisher & Frey, 2008). As advocated by Stauffer (1969a), the DR–TA has three basic steps: predicting, reading, and proving. Predicting involves asking readers to use not only what they already know but also whatever they can learn from a quick preview of the material to predict what the material is going to be about. Predicting prepares the reader for comprehension. It is a very important DR–TA step, but it cannot stand alone. Because students can be encouraged to predict aloud and to justify their predictions, the DR–TA offers a lively listening and speaking opportunity within a social context. Although an overall prediction may be made,

The DR–TA is important because it teaches the correct reading process: predicting, reading, and proving that the reading has occurred. Also, the DR–TA uses all three phases of the PAR Lesson Framework.

teachers encourage readers to make predictions about specific portions of text and then to read the appropriate portions to confirm or alter the predictions. Students reflect aloud on those predictions before going on to read another segment. If teachers are worried that students will be reticent to make predictions, they can use a simple prediction guide, shown as Activity 4.4. Students predict in the left column and write what actually happened in the right column. This also can show the teacher whether the student is actively predicting and taking part in the process. The teacher guides the DR–TA process, making sure that each student is actively involved in understanding each segment before continuing to the next.

Figures 4.1 and 4.2 outline the DR–TA steps to apply to fiction and nonfiction material, respectively. Note that Step 2 in the fiction DR–TA requests that readers read to find out whether the predictions they made were accurate. Step 4 in the nonfiction DR–TA requests that readers read to find the answers to questions they have generated, and Step 5 calls on students to think critically by defending responses. These steps focus on purposeful reading; they are the foundation for a successful DR–TA. A teacher must decide in advance how to segment the material for a DR–TA. The organization of the material is the key factor affecting this segmentation.

The prediction step of the DR–TA builds purpose for reading. When readers are asked what they think might happen next and then read to verify their prediction, they are being encouraged to read purposefully. Readers become very excited about

ACTIVITY **4.4** DR–TA PREDICTION GUIDE

My Prediction	What Really Happened

FIGURE 4.1

DR–TA for
Fiction

1. Previewing
   Preread: Title
   Pictures
   Subtitles
   Introduction (if story is long enough)
   Close book and make hypotheses: What do you think will happen?
   Why do you think that? (What gives you the clue?)

2. Verifying
   Read: To find whether predictions were right

3. Reflecting on reading
   Developing comprehension by
   Checking on individual and group hypotheses
   Staying with or redefining hypotheses

FIGURE 4.2

DR–TA for
Nonfiction

1. Previewing
   Study: Title
   Introduction
   Subtitles
   Pictures
   Charts
   Maps
   Graphs
   Summary or conclusion
   End-of-chapter questions

2. Decision making
   What is known after previewing?
   What do we need to learn?

3. Writing
   Writing specific questions students need to learn

4. Reading
   Finding the answers to students' written questions

5. Reflecting on the reading by
   Determining answers to students' questions
   Having students defend their inferences by referring to text
   Finding out what we still need to know

this predictive involvement in their own reading. Often they share their predictions orally before the individual reading occurs. This activity incorporates listening and speaking. If students are asked to write on the prediction guide what they predict during various portions of the reading and then review those written predictions at the end of the DR–TA, writing is used as a way to determine purpose within the DR–TA.

Our experience with the DR–TA shows that students are quite imaginative when formulating predictions about fiction but can be dreadfully boring when trying to do the same for nonfiction. The reason for this difference may lie in the fact that they are not predicting the nonfiction outcome in the same way they do for fiction. The procedure for nonfiction DR–TAs is to survey, question, and then read for answers. The result, without proper preparation, can be similar to just "doing the questions at the end of the chapter." This defeats the purpose of the DR–TA, which is to allow students to create their own purpose in reading. One way we have found to help students write higher-level questions is through use of the "higher-level questioning bookmark," adapted from one developed by the Maryland State Department of Education and shown as Activity 4.5. Students are given this bookmark to keep and use with each nonfiction reading and use it to think of more creative and interesting prediction questions for the reading. Roughly analogous to Bloom's (1956) taxonomy of cognitive objectives—knowledge, comprehension, application, analysis, synthesis, and evaluation—the bookmark can teach students to see the importance of asking probing questions that tap higher levels of thought.

ACTIVITY 4.5 HIGHER-LEVEL QUESTIONING BOOKMARK

QUESTION MARK: QUESTIONING FOR QUALITY THINKING

Knowledge: Identification and recall of information
Who, what, when, where, how _____?
Describe _____.

Comprehension: Organization and selection of facts and ideas
Retell _____ in your own words. What is the main idea of _____?

Application: Use of facts, rules, principles
How is _____ an example of _____?
How is _____ related to _____?
Why is _____ significant?

Analysis: Separation of a whole into component parts
What are the parts or features of _____?
Classify _____ according to _____.
Outline/diagram/web _____.
How does _____ compare/contrast with _____?

What evidence can you list for _____?

Synthesis: Combination of ideas to form a new whole
What would you predict/infer from _____?
What ideas can you add to _____?
How would you create/design a new _____?
What might happen if you combined _____ with _____?
What solutions would you suggest for _____?

Evaluation: Development of opinions, judgments, or decisions
Do you agree _____?
What do you think about _____?
What is the most important _____?
Prioritize _____.
How would you decide about _____?
What criteria would you use to assess _____?

Maryland State Department of Education; adapted by Mark Forget.

It is important for teachers to know how to teach both fiction and nonfiction DR–TAs. We have included examples of both in this chapter. We present a dialogue in Activity 4.6 that gives teacher and student responses in a fiction DR–TA for the story "The Wildest Ride in the World" by Paul Gallico. Also, in Activity 4.7 we present the DR–TA steps in an elementary lesson through the use of a What-I-Know Activity (WIKA). In this particular reading activity students are given a five-column sheet and

---

ACTIVITY 4.6 DR–TA TRANSCRIPT: STORY OF "WILDEST RIDE IN THE WORLD"

Teacher: What would you guess the "wildest ride" in the world is?

Students: A roller coaster ride.

A bucking bronco.

I think it is a roller coaster too.

An Indy 500 type race at 200 miles an hour.

I think it is being in a little boat in the middle of the ocean in a hurricane.

Teacher: OK, let's read the first page to see if anyone is correct in their prediction. Don't read past the first page, now. Close your books when you get to that point. . . . Was anyone right in their prediction?

Students: No.

Teacher: Then read the part that shows what the wildest ride really is. (One student reads out loud about what the Cresta Run is and that a 59-year-old is going to try to race a steel skeleton down the run.) What is unusual about the man?

Student: He is old!

Teacher: Yes, 59, which may be old to you but is not extremely old. Anyway, what do you think might happen to him in this race?

Student: He is going to win.

Teacher: Why do you think that?

Student: Because it says he is "qualified." He just didn't decide to do it at the last minute. He has had practice.

Teacher: Good thinking! Now what else could happen to him?

Student: I think he will make it down and be proud because he is writing about it and wants to brag a little.

Student: I think he will win also.

Teacher: Why do you think that?

Student: Because I just think so. I don't have a reason.

Student: I think he will have an accident.

Teacher: Why do you think that?

Student: Because he is too old to do this.

Student: I think that is true and I think he will have a minor accident too. Maybe just some bumps and bruises.

Teacher: Good predictions! Now let's read to see if anyone is correct in their prediction. Read the next two pages of the story down to the word "saying" on page 134.

Note: After reading, the teacher asks if anyone is correct, and the students who said that he was going to "just make it down" say they are correct. The teacher asks them to read orally the part that shows they are correct. After this they predict a third, and last time, about the author's second run down Cresta. The author does have an accident, and several students predicted the accident. These students seem to take delight in orally reading to the group the part that describes the accident. They are happy that they made the correct prediction.

Next the teacher asks the students whether they liked the story. All said they did like it. The teacher asks each student to read a part of the story either where the main character did something they particularly liked or where there was a good descriptive paragraph or paragraphs that they liked.

are asked to fill it in as they go through the reading. In the first two columns students, before reading, discuss what they already know about the topic after completing the preview and formulate questions to be answered in the reading. A third column can be added to the WIKA four-column design to ask students to jot down interesting concepts they learned in the reading. In the fourth column they use the time during and directly after the reading to answer the questions they generated. The questions that cannot be answered are placed in the fifth column called "what I still would like to know." The traditional four-column What-I-Know Activity will be discussed in Chapter 6.

ACTIVITY 4.7 DR–TA RESPONSES

WEATHER AND WEATHER-RELATED ACTIVITIES: ELEMENTARY SCIENCE

Before Reading	Before Reading	During Reading	After Reading	After Reading
What I Know after Previewing	What I Would Like to Know	Interesting or Important Concepts from My Reading	What I Know after the Reading	What I Still Would Like to Know
Air pressure is air that is pushing down on the earth.	Where does air come from? Is air pressure the same as gravity?	Tornadoes are fast-moving windstorms.	Air pressure is connected to gravity.	Is air pressure the same as gravity?
Wind is air that is something that blows when it is cold.	Is wind fast-moving air? What causes air pressure?	Hurricanes and tornadoes both have fast and strong winds.	Wind can blow during summer and winter.	What causes air pressure?
Temperature can be measured.	What causes temperature changes? Why are there four seasons?	The earth rotating on its axis can cause temperature changes.	Seasons of the year can cause temperature changes.	Why are there four seasons?
Sometimes it rains and sometimes it snows.	Why does it sometimes rain and sometimes snow? Will there ever be more than four seasons?	Precipitation forms depend on outside air temperature.	Temperature affects whether it rains or snows. Temperature can be measured with a thermometer.	Will there ever be more than four seasons?

Developed by Lori Lambert.

When you teach the DR–TA and ask students to predict, you are teaching higher-level thinking—specifically convergent inference. When you ask them to tell you why they liked or disliked a story, or ask them do some creative follow-up activity, you are teaching divergent inference.

One point to note when adhering to the DR–TA process in fiction is that the predictions themselves show whether the students are adequately comprehending the story. The postreading reflection phase enables the teacher to have students do higher-level thinking in evaluating whether they liked the story. Such evaluation and concomitant critical thinking are needed for students to truly understand and appreciate a story. Of course, in nonfiction reading, the students answer their questions in the "what I know after the reading" column, and this tells the teacher how well they comprehended.

DR–TA lessons help teachers model the reading process at its best. This method is also compatible with the constructivist theory discussed earlier in this chapter. What good readers do as they read is predict and speculate; read to confirm; and stop reading and carry on a mental discussion of what they understand. Students are very active during reading. Through using the prediction process, the material is divided into manageable units. DR–TAs provide a vehicle for figuring out content as the reading occurs; they emphasize reading as a constructive process rather than a measurement of comprehension. DR–TAs also build readers' self-concepts. When readers understand that predictions help them understand better and that everyone's speculations are important whether or not they are proven to be what the author concluded, they feel more confident about their reading. At the elementary level, teachers can encourage readers to become "reading detectives." Playing a game of detection motivates students to read and to take charge of their own reading. We cannot stress enough the pervasive benefits of using DR–TAs in teaching both fiction and nonfiction.

One final note is that the DR–TA uses all the phases of the PAR Lesson Framework. The teacher does not have to worry about whether she is preparing and assisting students because this is an integral part of the strategy. Also, there are plenty of opportunities to reflect about the reading and learning in the DR–TA.

Guided Reading Procedure

The guided reading procedure (GRP) (Manzo, 1975) offers an excellent way to teach students to gather and organize information around main ideas. GRP uses brainstorming to collect information as accurately as possible and then rereading to correct misinformation and fill in conceptual gaps. The second reading is important because it heightens motivation—students read to prove that their statements are correct or disprove fellow students' statements. In conducting the GRP, we have noted students' intensity of purpose and focus during this second reading segment. According to researchers Colwell and associates (1986), GRP is a very effective teacher-directed technique. It can be used to help students become more independent in their thinking and studying. Following are the steps teachers use to apply the guided reading procedure:

1. Prepare the students for the lesson by clarifying key concepts about the reading; assess students' background knowledge. The teacher may ask students to explain vocabulary terms or make predictions concerning concepts inherent to the reading.

2. Assign a selection of appropriate length, and ask students to remember all they can about the reading. Manzo (1975) gives these general guidelines for passage length: primary students—90 words, 3 minutes; elementary students—500 words, 5 minutes; junior high school students—900 words, 7 minutes; high school students—2,000 words, 10 minutes.

3. After the students have completed the reading assignment, have them close the book and relate everything they know about the material they just read. Then list statements on the board without editing, whenever possible assigning two students to act as class recorders. Using student recorders makes it easier for the teacher to monitor and guide the class discussion. Of course, for early elementary classes the teacher will have to do this recording.

4. Direct students to look for inconsistencies and misinformation, first through discussion and then through reading the material.

5. Add new information. If reading a narrative, help students organize and categorize concepts into a loose outline. For nonfiction, students can put information into two, three, or four categories and title each category.

6. Have students reread the selection to determine whether the information they listed is accurate.

7. To strengthen short-term recall, test students on the reading.

Activity 4.8 lists students' facts and concepts while taking part in a guided reading procedure in an elementary science class on the topic of tornadoes. Part I of Activity 4.8 lists the statements that students made in the first phase of a GRP. Listed in Part II of the activity are the categories in which students chose to group the facts they listed. Students placed the facts in Part I under one of the three categories listed. In this manner students created their own categories of learning as an aid to comprehension.

ASSISTING STUDENTS IN LEARNING TEXT STRUCTURE

Steven King (2002), in his book *On Writing*, says that the basic unit of writing is the paragraph. It is certainly true that once children learn the basics of reading, most print language they encounter will be in paragraph form. There is research evidence that the **structure of text**—how paragraphs are arranged and ordered—can affect the reading comprehension of students (Goldman & Rakestraw, 2000). There is also evidence that students who are taught text structure will use this knowledge to improve their writing and reading comprehension (Goldman & Rakestraw, 2000). Informational texts are written in a variety of text structures. We now know more about the ways in which these types of expository textbooks are organized. Following are the five most prevalent organizational formations of text, with examples of a paragraph written in the structure.

SEQUENTIAL OR CHRONOLOGICAL ORDER

In sequential or chronological order, a logical order of presentation is important. Henk and Helfeldt (1987) explain that even capable readers need assistance in applying the

ELEMENTARY SCIENCE

Part I

These are the statements taken from students in science after reading a passage about tornadoes.

1. Thunderstorms develop in advance of cold fronts.
2. Tornadoes can latch onto tropical storms.
3. Waterspouts are tornadoes that form over water.
4. Tornadoes can take different shapes and sizes.
5. Tornadoes can have winds of over 200 miles an hour.
6. Most tornadoes don't last very long.
8. Tornadoes happen most in this country in the Midwest and the states that border the Gulf of Mexico.

9. Most tornadoes happen in spring and early summer.
10. Tornadoes form when warm air rises rapidly ahead of a storm line and then the warm air begins to rotate.
11. In the United States tornadoes whirl in a counterclockwise motion.
12. Tornadoes are often transparent until dust and debris are picked up.
13. Two or more tornadoes can happen at the same time.
14. No place is safe from tornadoes.

Part II: Categories

Causes of tornadoes

Features of tornadoes

Where tornadoes occur

---

sequence structure used in directions. Some words that signal this structure are *first, second, next, before, during, then,* and *finally.*

> **Example:** "Gray's may be the simplest and friendliest of the taxonomies. Gray said that one must first read the lines and then read between the lines; then one can read beyond the lines."

ANALYSIS

Analysis takes an important idea (superordinate information) and investigates the relationships of the parts of that idea (subordinate information) to the whole. Some words and phrases that signal this structure are *consider, analyze, investigate, the first part suggests,* and *this element means.*

> **Example:** "Consider how the child concluded that the word he had been unable to pronounce was *oxygen.* The first portion of his behavior, when he skipped the word, indicated that he did not know the word at all. Yet he was able to recognize it when he

had a context for it during the recall stage. This means that he was processing information all along."

CAUSE AND EFFECT

In cause and effect, there is an event or effect (the superordinate information), and certain theories are presented as causes (subordinate information) of that event. The effect is thus shown to be a result of causes. Some words and phrases that signal this structure are *because, hence, therefore, as a result,* and *this led to.*

> **Example:** "When teachers prepare students to read content material, they help students understand better. As a result of such preparation, teachers will see that students are more interested, pay more attention, and comprehend better."

COMPARISON AND CONTRAST

Sometimes a writer seeks to highlight similarities and differences between facts, events, or authors. The basic comparison or contrast is the superordinate information, and the specific similarities and differences are the subordinate information. Some words and phrases that signal this structure are *in contrast, in the same way, on the one hand, on the other hand, either . . . or,* and *similarly.*

> **Example:** "On the one hand, a checklist offers less mathematical precision; on the other hand, it provides more qualitative information."

ANALOGY/EXAMPLE

Sometimes a writer uses an example—a specific instance or a similar situation (subordinate information)—to explain a topic or concept (superordinate information). Analogies are a type of example. Some words and phrases that signal this structure are *for example, for instance, likened to, analogous to,* and *is like.*

> **Example:** "Reading is like a game of basketball. To play one's best game, lots of preparation and practice are necessary. In reading, this is analogous to preparing by determining and building background for the material to be read."

One way to help students see a structure is to ask them to underline or highlight the signal words. If the text material can be posted electronically, students can use the highlighting feature of a word processing program to experiment with locating signal words.

Often more than one structure is apparent in a single section of text. A writer may analyze by means of a comparison and contrast. A writer may show cause and effect accompanied by example. Some structures appear frequently in particular content subjects. Table 4.1 suggests text structures of some content area subjects, but it is only

TABLE 4.1	Some Organizational Structures Used Frequently in Content Area Textbooks			
Science	**Math**	**Social Studies**	**English**	**Health**
Sequence	Sequence	Cause/effect	Cause/effect	Comparison/contrast
Cause/effect	Analysis	Example	Comparison/contrast	Cause/effect
Comparison/ contrast	Example	Analysis	Example Sequence/chronological	

a guide. Also, teachers need to consider the grade levels they teach and the specific materials they use because different structures may dominate at different grade levels and in different subjects.

The study and identification of organizational structure in written material, as well as student and teacher verbal interaction and reaction to text structure, are called **discourse analysis**. Gee (1996) has noted that students use discourses such as networking, talking, and interacting to learn about the world. Chinn (Chinn, Anderson, & Waggoner, 2001) includes in discourse analysis such behaviors as teacher and student turn taking in discussions, teacher questions, taking authority in decision making, and control of the topic of discussion. Chinn recommends the use of a technique called *collaborative reasoning* (Waggoner, Chinn, Yi, & Anderson, 1995), which was found to be better than recitations in improving student engagement and in teaching higher-level thinking. Collaborative reasoning is an approach to literature discussion intended to stimulate critical thinking. After reading a selection, the teacher poses a central question that is worded in such a way as to force students to take a position for or against the question. Students discuss the question and must in the end defend the position they take concerning the question. In this manner, students collaboratively construct arguments through a complex network of reasoning and through shared evidence (Chinn & Anderson, 1998). After getting the discussion going with the central question, the teacher acts only as a moderator and mostly stays out of the discussion. Students are encouraged to weigh evidence offered and decide whether to maintain or change their original positions. As stated earlier, this strategy has been found to be effective in teaching critical reading and thinking.

> Collaborative reasoning was first used in literature classes to stimulate discussion in higher-level thinking.

Strategic instruction shows readers how to identify text structure (Garner & Gillingham, 1987). Overall comprehension of the text is enhanced for the readers. One simple activity to raise awareness of organization is to have students peruse the table of contents of a textbook and ask, "How did the author organize this writing? What overall structure of organization do you see in the table of contents?" Also, a teacher may simply ask students to identify the text structure used in a chapter, a section, or even a paragraph. Teachers can devise activities to assist readers in identifying structures, as we explain in the next section. When readers learn to recognize text structure and the relationships between superordinate ideas and subordinate information, they take a major step toward independence in reading.

Activities for Teaching an Understanding of Text Structure

When the teacher uses activities to boost understanding of text structure, reading to learn is much easier. Activities help students and create an interesting learning environment. Here we present some of our favorites.

MYSTERY CLUE GAME

The group mystery clue game is designed to help readers understand sequence. It works well when it is important for students to understand a sequence of events. The idea for this activity comes from *Turn-ons* (Smuin, 1978); we have adapted it to fit content materials:

1. To construct a mystery clue game, the teacher first studies the sequence of events in the material and writes clear, specific clue cards for each event. More than one card may be made for each clue.

2. The teacher divides the class into small groups and gives each group member at least one clue card. Each group can have one complete set of cards, but each group member is responsible for his or her own cards within that set.

3. No student may show a card to another in the group, but cards can be read aloud or paraphrased so that all group members know what is on each card. In this way, students who are poor readers will still be encouraged to try to read and to participate.

4. Each group of students must use the clues the teacher gives them to solve the mystery. For example, they must find the murderer, the weapon, the time and place of the murder, the motive, and the victim. Or they must find the equation that will solve a problem, or the formula that will make a chemical.

5. A time limit is usually given.

6. A group scribe reports the group's solution to the whole class.

7. Students are instructed to read the material to find out which group came closest to solving the mystery.

Visit the *Reading to Learn in the Content Areas* Web site for a link to the Great Cities Universities video of Kenya Brown teaching a mystery clue game: Select "Secondary Modules"; select Module Four and then Video.

This cooperative activity promotes oral language as well as reading, and it works well in most content areas. For instance, science teachers can write clues to performing an experiment, mathematics teachers can write clues to deriving a formula, and social studies teachers can write clues to sequencing historical events. The goal of the activity is for students to approximate the sequence of events before reading and then read with the purpose of checking their predictions. It is not necessary for students to memorize specific details. As they read, they will think back to their clues and construct meaning.

Activity 4.9 is a mystery clue game for a French lesson to help students master the Paris Metro. Students in small groups have to read (translate) the 10 clue cards (without referring to their textbooks) and put the cards in the correct chronological order. In doing so, students learn the logical steps in taking the Paris Metro and grasp the relationships among the Metro, the grammar, and the vocabulary presented in the French textbook.

Teaching Text Structure through Comprehension Guides

PATTERN GUIDES

Pattern guides (Herber, 1978) are most useful in helping students recognize a predominant structure such as cause and effect or comparison and contrast. To construct them, the teacher locates the pattern, chooses the major ideas to be stressed, and designs the pattern-oriented guide.

Pattern guides can help students see causal relationships. Students need to learn to distinguish cause and effect when reading text materials—especially in social studies, science, and vocational education. Simply asking students to search for causes is often unsuccessful; students tend to neglect—or worse, misunderstand and misuse—

Luc et Jérome veulent aller au Louvre pour apprendre quelque chose pour leur classe d'art.

A la bouche du métro ils regardent le plan et ils comprennent qu'il faut prendre une correspondance.

Ils prennent la direction Porte de Clignancourt et ils prennent une autre correspondance aux Halles.

Bon! Ils sont là!

Après le musée, ils font des achats.

Ils n'ont pas de voiture. C'est trop loin—ils ne peuvent pas aller à pied ou prendre leurs vélos. Le taxi est trop cher, ainsi ils veulent prendre le métro.

Ils vont au métro—c'est la station Maubert-Mutalité. Ils achètent deux billets de seconde.

D'abord, ils prennent la direction Boulogne–Point de St Cloud, et ils changent à Odéon.

Ils prennent la direction Pont de Neuilly. Ils descendent à Louvre.

Ils entrent dans le Louvre où ils voient la Joconde (Mona Lisa) et la Vénus de Milo.

ENGLISH TRANSLATION IN CHRONOLOGICAL ORDER

1. Luke and Jeremy want to go to the Louvre in order to learn something for their art class.
2. They don't have a car. It is too far—they can't walk or take their bikes. A taxi costs too much, so they want to take the Metro.
3. At the Metro entrance, they look at the map and they understand that they will have to transfer to another line on the Metro.
4. They go into the Metro station "Maubert-Mutalité." They buy two second-class tickets.
5. First, they take the "Boulogne–Point de Saint Cloud" direction, and they change at "Odéon."
6. They take the "Porte de Clignancourt" direction, and they make another change at "Les Halles."
7. They take the "Pont de Neuilly" direction. They get off at "Louvre."
8. Good! They are there.
9. They enter the Louvre, where they see the *Mona Lisa* and the *Venus de Milo*.
10. After the museum, they run errands.

Developed by Laura Clevinger.

this pattern without the teacher's intervention, support, and patience. Moreover, finding causal relationships is difficult because the cause of an event or situation may not be known or may be not traceable. Even so, students should endeavor to distinguish cause and effect for practice in the thinking it affords. Activity 4.10 provides an example of a cause-and-effect guide to conserving resources in high school level history. Teachers can also encourage students to make comparison–contrast maps such as the one shown as Activity 4.11. These graphic organizers or concept maps stress similarities and differences, here comparing brown recluse spiders with black widow spiders. Teachers may help children by constructing some of the map to get them started. Or teachers can talk students through the map and in this way build the map with the students. Such maps provide excellent ways to teach patterns of organization inherent in print material.

3 + LEVEL STUDY GUIDES

An excellent tool to teach comprehension is the three-level study guide developed by Harold Herber (1978). The guide is an effort to connect and integrate three distinct levels of comprehension through the use of a series of statements designed for student reaction. The guide aids students in discerning the interconnectedness of literal, inferential, and applied learning.

Here are the steps in making the guide:

1. Begin with making Level 2 of the guide (interpretive level). Five or six statements are ideal. At this level the teacher asks, "What are the main ideas and concepts I want to teach?" List them in statements that will be certain to elicit the interest of the students. Teachers can put "The author means…" in front of each statement to ensure that the statements truly belong in the interpretive level.

ACTIVITY 4.10 CAUSE AND EFFECT STUDY GUIDE

CONSERVING RESOURCES

Effects	Causes
_____ 1. President Theodore Roosevelt called a national conference on conservation in 1908.	**a.** Franklin Roosevelt realized the need for conservation.
_____ 2. We live in a technological age.	**b.** Cattle raisers and farmers led the western movement.
_____ 3. Crops were abundant in the new land.	**c.** In the early 20th century concern began to grow about the preservation of our natural resources.
_____ 4. Early settlers pushed to slaughter the Great Plains buffalo.	**d.** Early settlers felt America's natural resources were limitless.
_____ 5. After 1901 the United States began to build up its force of forest rangers.	**e.** Leaders began to realize that an ever-expanding economy had drained America's natural resources.
_____ 6. Recent presidents have been more aware of our conservation problems.	**f.** Most of the U.S. climate is temperate, with enough water and good soil.
_____ 7. The Tennessee Valley Authority was begun in the 1930s.	**g.** People felt more force was needed by government to ensure the regulation and preservation of timber.
_____ 8. The Civilian Conservation Corps was created in the 1930s.	**h.** People needed to be put to work during and after the Great Depression.

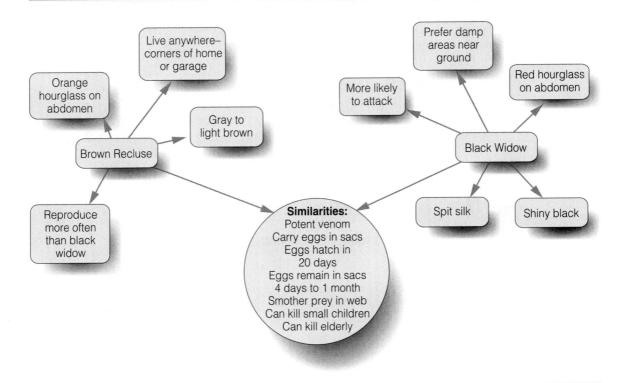

2. Go back and pick up the facts that support the interpretations you wrote in Step 1. Teachers can put "The author says…" in front of each statement to ensure that the statements truly belong in the factual level. Then add "distracters"—statements that are untrue at this level. When finished, you should have five or six statements at this level.

3. As a final step, the teacher can ask, "What universal truths are depicted in this reading?" General statements of application are listed in the third level, the applied level of the guide. Teachers can put "We can use…" in front of each statement to ensure that the statements truly belong in the application level.

4. Finally, add student directions to the guide.

We believe that a fourth level can be added to the guide to teach original Internet research on the topic (hence the designation 3+ level study guide). When students read a passage and react to the three-level guide, we feel they will really become interested in the topic. We have seen this happen in many classrooms where these guides are used. With this heightened interest, it is a natural progression for them to go to the

Web and conduct research on the topic. An example of a 3+ level guide is given in Activity 4.12 for a high school English class on the poem "The Road Not Taken" by Robert Frost.

Jot charts can be filled in by students working in pairs or small groups.

ORGANIZATIONAL (JOT) CHARTS

Jot charts organize text information by showing comparisons and contrasts. Students complete a matrix as a way to see how ideas are alike and different. Jot charts are relatively simple to construct and can be used at any grade level and in any content area.

ACTIVITY 4.12 HIGH SCHOOL ENGLISH 3+ LEVEL STUDY GUIDE

ON "THE ROAD NOT TAKEN" BY ROBERT FROST

Instructions: After reading the poem, check those statements with which you agree. Be prepared to discuss why you chose the statements you did, and be prepared to refer to the poem to defend your answers.

I. Check the statements of fact in the poem.
   _____ **1.** The narrator had come to a fork in the road.
   _____ **2.** Only one of the roads was well used when the narrator arrived at the fork.
   _____ **3.** The horse did not understand why they were stopping.
   _____ **4.** Both roads had the same amount of use by others in the past.
   _____ **5.** The poem took place in summer.

II. Check the statements that are possible interpretations of the poem.
   _____ **1.** One can always go back and start over in life.
   _____ **2.** A person may always wonder whether choices made were the best choices.
   _____ **3.** The narrator is pleased by the choices he has made in life.
   _____ **4.** What appears simple is often complex.
   _____ **5.** Knowing oneself is a lifetime endeavor.

III. Check statements that show how this poem has application to our own lives.
   _____ **1.** Life is a journey with no clear destination.
   _____ **2.** Hindsight is always 20/20.
   _____ **3.** Like a poem, life should begin in delight and end in wisdom.
   _____ **4.** Following the crowd may be easy in the short term, but in the long run this may prove foolhardy.

III.+ Go to this source on the Internet (see our *Reading to Learn in the Content Areas* companion Web site, Chapter 4, for a link) and check which of the following statements are true:
   _____ **1.** Frost graduated from Harvard University.
   _____ **2.** Frost taught at the high school level for six years.
   _____ **3.** Frost was an English professor at Dartmouth College for 22 years.
   Short answer: Frost went to England early in his life. Why was this trip so important in his development as a writer and poet?
   Was Frost ever accorded any accolades or awards in his lifetime?

INVERTEBRATES: ANIMALS WITH NO BACKBONE

Type of Invertebrate	Describe It	How It Eats and Uses Food	How It Moves	Escape or Defense	Other Information
Sponges					
Stinging cell animals					
Flatworms					
Roundworms					
Segmented worms					
Animals with spiny skins					
Arthropods					

The teacher usually sets up the matrix and encourages students to fill it in as they read. In this way, students understand the relationships and build meaning as they read. When completed, jot charts become a good study aid. If they are filled in by groups of students, the social aspects of learning are also included in the activity.

We present two examples of jot charts to demonstrate their diversity in activating comprehension. The chart in Activity 4.13 was developed for an elementary science class. Activity 4.14 depicts a chart of mathematical formulas.

IMPROVING COMPREHENSION THROUGH QUESTIONS AND QUESTIONING

Many researchers feel that dialogue between teachers and students should be the most important medium for teaching and learning (Hillocks, 2002; Langer, 2001). The best dialogue may come in the form of teacher–student questions. Classroom questioning strategies and questioning instruction can help with memory for what was read, can improve information-finding abilities of students, and can lead to more in-depth processing of text (McKeown & Beck, 2003). When questioning works, it works well. Studies show that the most effective teachers encourage higher-level thinking through questioning techniques (Taylor, Pressley, & Pearson, 2002). Questions can help teachers know whether students understand text and can guide readers to consider many aspects of material. Question-generated discussions help create meaning for readers (Alvermann, O'Brien, & Dillon, 1990; Barton, 1995). Questions are excellent probes.

Shape	Picture	Perimeter/Surface area	Area/Volume

2-dimensional

Shape	Picture	Perimeter/Surface area	Area/Volume
Circle		$2\pi r$	πr^2
Triangle		$a + b + c$	$\frac{1}{2} bh$
Square		$4x$	x^2
Rectangle		$2l + 2w$	lw

3-dimensional

Shape	Picture	Surface area	Volume
Cone		$\pi rh + \pi r^2$	$\frac{1}{3}\pi r^2 h$
Rectangular box		$2(lw) + 2(lh) + 2(hw) =$ surface area	lwh

Developed by Serena Marshall.

Robert Sternberg (1994) argues that the ability to ask good questions and to know how to answer them is the most essential part of intelligence. Well-considered questions are essential to guide students' thinking and reasoning abilities (Marashio, 1995). Often, however, questioning does not work well because teachers fall into the common trap of writing questions that focus on literal comprehension. Gusak (1967) reported that 78 percent of the questions asked in second grade were literal, 65 percent in fourth grade were literal, and 58 percent in sixth grade were literal. Observing at the upper elementary level, Durkin (1979) found that teachers asked mostly literal questions, expecting specific responses. Durkin (1981) then studied teachers' manuals for basal reading instruction and discovered that low-level literal questions with one correct response were the major instructional strategy provided for teachers. Newer research shows that this emphasis hasn't changed. Armbruster and colleagues (1991) studied science and social studies lessons for fourth graders and found that 90 percent of the questions were teacher-generated and explicit. In a study of two American history classes, Sturtevant (1992) found that teachers stressed textbook reading and factual information. Reutzel and Daines (1987) reached the same conclusion after a study of seven major basal readers. When Young and Daines (1992) looked at the types of questions that students and their teachers asked, they found that students were more likely to ask interpretive questions, whereas teachers asked literal questions about the same material.

Getting little practice in answering higher-level questions, students are ill equipped to think critically. Elementary students are trapped into expecting only literal questions; secondary students remain in this trap because literal questions have been their previous experience. Research shows, however, that when instructional strategies are altered so that the focus is on inferences, critical thinking, and main ideas, students respond with improved recall and greater understanding (Hansen, 1981; Hansen & Pearson, 1983; Raphael, 1984). Cooter, Joseph, and Flynt (1986) were able to show that third and fourth graders who were asked no literal questions in a five-month period performed significantly better than a control group on inferential comprehension and just as well on literal comprehension. Menke and Pressley (1994) encourage teachers and their students to use *why* questions because their use greatly increases factual memory.

Another trap that teachers sometimes fall into is misjudging the difficulty of the questions they are asking or failing to match questions to students' abilities. Generally, questions are simplest when students must recognize and locate answers in a text rather than close their books and try to recall the same information. Easy questions also include those asked during or shortly after reading, questions that have only one or two parts, oral questions rather than written ones, and those that allow students to choose an answer from among several alternatives. We are not suggesting that all questions should be asked in the simplest manner; we are cautioning that many times teachers do not consider the difficulty of their questions and their students' abilities to answer them.

A final trap that often snares teachers is focusing more on the questions asked and the responses expected than on the students' actual responses. Recall that Durkin's research cited earlier in this discussion found that teachers too often expect

Studies often show that teachers, when asking questions of students, give higher achievers longer than lower-achieving students to think of an answer.

one response and do not consider an alternative. As Dillon (1983) remarks, we should "stress the nature of questions rather than their frequency and pace, and the type of student response rather than the type of teacher question" (p. 8). Students' answers can tell a lot about their understanding of the topic. We need to listen for answers that let us know how well we are assisting the development of comprehension.

Don't fall into the trap of listening for an expected response and ignoring the real responses of students.

Student-Developed Questions

When students are encouraged to develop their own questions, they develop higher-level understanding. Van Blerkom and colleagues (2006) found that students who read and generated questions comprehended authentic text better than those who read and took notes or read and highlighted. Ciardello (1998) argues that the process of asking questions helps students to focus on and learn content, as well as develop cognitive strategies that will help them understand new and challenging material. Ciardello describes a technique called TeachQuest, in which the teacher guides students through a series of steps to identify and classify divergent-thinking questions. The goal is for students to generate their own divergent-thinking questions. Crapse (1995) reports that "through the experience of honest questioning, I have observed students celebrating their own insights and solutions to problems posed" (p. 390). Remember that students can also develop their own questions using the "higher-level questioning bookmark" discussed earlier in this chapter and shown in Activity 4.5.

Constructing Good Questions

We have learned much about how to question from extensive studies of reading comprehension conducted over the past few decades. Although much of this research has been conducted with elementary students, the implications are relevant for secondary instruction as well. Students who have not received a firm foundation in reading comprehension in elementary school will not be well equipped in secondary school. To help teachers construct good questions, we summarize here what we consider the most important research considerations:

Study carefully these ways to construct good questions.

1. Simplify your questions! Although teachers want to challenge their students, they should challenge within a range that allows students to succeed. Consider using these guidelines:
   a. Identify the purpose of each question. (Will it measure fact, implication, or applied levels of comprehension? Is there a particular organizational pattern? Is there a superordinate or subordinate idea?) Is this purpose justified? Does it contribute to a balance of comprehension levels within the lesson?
   b. Identify the type of response demanded by the question (recognition, recall, production, or generation of a new idea from the information). Is this expectation justified, given the ages and abilities of the group? Have you provided an example of what you want? If you wish students to produce a modern dialogue for a character in *Hamlet,* can you give them an example first?

c. Might the question elicit more than one reasonable response? If this is a possibility, will you be able to accept different responses and use them to assist instruction?

d. Does this question contain several parts? Will these parts be clear to the students, and can they remember all of the parts as they respond?

e. Write the question clearly and concisely. Then decide whether to pose it orally or in writing.

2. Share with students the reasons for your questions. Let them know the process you use to develop questions and the process you would use to answer them. This knowledge helps them see what types of questions are important to you. It also helps them understand how they should be thinking when they respond and what you are thinking when you question. This process—thinking about thinking—is called **metacognition** (Babbs & Moe, 1983). It uses two important operations in the learning process: self-appraisal and self-management (Jacobs & Paris, 1987). Research points to the value of teaching students metacognitive behaviors during and after reading (Mevarech, 1999). Helping students think about both their own reasoning and their reading processes should produce large rewards in learning. This sharing is a form of think-aloud (Davey, 1983) and think-along (Ehlinger & Pritchard, 1994). These two metacognitive activities are useful for students. Think-alouds will be discussed in Chapter 5.

3. Encourage students to ask questions about your questions and to ask their own questions. Students will thrive when they can participate in classroom questioning more directly than they do in the typical classroom. Remember that teacher-dominated questioning inhibits student independence and limits thinking.

In Chapter 11 of this textbook we discuss the ReQuest strategy. Look for this strategy, which is an excellent way for students to practice questioning techniques.

4. Provide plenty of practice in answering questions at different levels of comprehension. Check yourself occasionally to make sure you are not leaning on the literal level too heavily. Training and practice result in student learning and in a greater sophistication of understanding. Students' depth and breadth of understanding improve when they are asked challenging questions. Also, students who learn to take another's perspective may become better readers as a result. But students must have opportunities for practice to master this ability.

5. Allow discussions, which give students practice in asking and answering questions (Alvermann et al., 1996). Chapter 5 contains many suggestions for generating student discussions to facilitate critical thinking.

6. Ask students the types of questions you know they can answer. Try not to expect too much too soon, but do expect as much as students can do. For example, research indicates that students can identify main idea statements earlier than they can make such statements (Afflerbach, 1987). If students seem consistently unable to answer a certain type of comprehension question even after you have followed these suggestions, we suggest that you review the most recent research findings for clues.

Questioning Strategies

THE QUESTION–ANSWER RELATIONSHIP

Raphael (1984, 1986) has studied and applied a questioning technique called *question–answer relationship (QAR)*. This has been found to be a practical way to teach students how to formulate questions at different levels of cognition (Mesmer & Hutchins, 2002; Raphael & Au, 2005). QAR is a four-level taxonomy: (1) right there, (2) think and search, (3) the author and you, and (4) on your own. The best way to introduce QAR is with a visual aid showing the QAR relationship. Figure 4.3 shows one teacher's illustrated introduction to QAR. After introducing QAR, the teacher uses a short passage to demonstrate how QAR is applied. To model the use of QAR, the teacher provides, labels, and answers at least one question at each QAR level. The teacher then moves gradually to having students answer questions and identifying the QAR for themselves. At various times throughout the school year, the teacher should refer to QAR. Activity 4.15 lists QAR questions and answers for a poem intended for high school English.

Because QAR is a straightforward procedure that is easily implemented, quickly beneficial to students, and useful at any grade and in any content area, we encourage content teachers to use it in their instruction. QAR has been proven to increase students' comprehension more than several other questioning strategies (Jenkins & Lawler, 1990). QAR fosters listening, speaking, and reading; and if students write their own questions, it also offers opportunities for writing. Raphael and Au (2005) recommend QAR as being especially helpful in schools with diverse populations. They maintain that it helps students with poor reading skills while at the same time teaching higher-level thinking skills. Also, they see the technique as a way for teachers to organize reading instruction on comprehension and comprehension strategy learning.

GUIDE-O-RAMAS AND MARGINAL GLOSSES

We hope you notice that we are using such glosses (notes to the reader) throughout our textbook!

A guide-o-rama (Cunningham & Shablak, 1975) alerts the reader to notice certain information in a reading passage. The teacher creates directions for these passages and encourages students to use the directions as they read. For instance, if the teacher sees that the word *perverse* is used in an unusual way, he might write this: "On page 13, second paragraph, third line, the word *perverse* is used a little differently from what you'd expect. Pay attention to the meaning." When a teacher prepares several directions such as this and gives them to readers to refer to while reading, readers have a panoramic view of the reading—hence the name *guide-o-rama*.

Marginal glosses (Singer & Donlan, 1985) are often found in content textbooks. Glosses are comments that authors make to their readers as asides, sometimes in the margin of the page. Because the comments are intended to help readers understand the passage, they assist readers in developing comprehension. Teachers can write their own marginal glosses if texts do not include them or if additional ones are needed. Also, a guide-o-rama can be designed as a gloss.

FIGURE 4.3

Introduction to
QAR

Q A R

I. Where is the answer?

Right there!
_____

Words are right there
in the text.

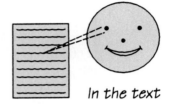

In the text

II. Where is the answer?

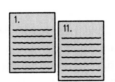

Think and search!
_____

Words are in the text but not
spelled out for you. Think about
what the author is saying.

*Hmm! Gotta
think about this.*

III. Where is the answer?

What I know

You and the author!
_____

Think about what you have learned
and what is in the text.

*What the
author says*

IV. Where is the answer?

On your own!
_____

Answer is in your head!

FOR POEM "ONCE UPON A TIME"

BY GABRIEL OKARA

Question 1: Right there!
To whom is the father speaking in the poem?

Answer
His son.

Question 2: Think and search!
What does the speaker seem to regret most?

Answer
Changing from an innocent young man to a hardened man of the world.

Question 3: You and the author!
In this life should we consider mainly ourselves or the good of the community?

Answer
Readers have to decide that themselves, but it appears the speaker longs for the "good old days" of strong community ties.

Question 4: On Your Own!
Is it too much to think that people can maintain a childlike innocence all through adult life?

Answer
It can be done, but there is a fine line between innocent sincerity and hypocrisy.

Here are some suggestions for making marginal glosses:

1. Fold a sheet of paper next to the margin of a text.
2. Identify the book page at the top of the master copy, and line up numbers beside the teacher remarks and notes.
3. Write the marginal notes on the sheet of paper.
4. Duplicate and give students copies of these notes to match to text pages for use as students read.

Marginal glosses and guide-o-ramas are like having the teacher go home with the students and look over their shoulders as they read, guiding their reading attention. These strategies can help students use features of texts as well as help teachers facilitate comprehension by questioning. We suggest that the teacher select either very difficult portions of text to gloss or beginning portions, when the reading may be tougher. Making guide-o-ramas or glosses for use throughout a text would be time-consuming. However, to provide assistance in developing comprehension of challenging reading, they are worth the time. Activity 4.16 is one for high school earth science.

How can I use this information?

1. Vocabulary word _____
   Definition in your own words:
   (Use the picture for help, if needed.)

2. What do you think *mass* is?

3. Why do you think ice floats in water?

4. Why do you think the average Earth
   density is greater than the average
   density of the Earth's crust?

5. Given a rock with a mass of 550g
   and a density of 2.75 g/cm³, calculate
   the volume of the rock.

6. BRING A ROCK TO CLASS
   TOMORROW—no larger than an egg!

7. What brand-name product
   has used density of the
   product in its advertising?

Place on top edge at p. ____ in binding.

Complete this side first.

Part I: What do I know?

Topic heading:

Vocabulary word:

Using words, give the
density formula:

Recall: Volume = length × width × height

Average Earth density (include units):

Average density of Earth's crust (include units):

Recall from Chapter 1 two (2)
materials found in the Earth's
core:

1.

2.

Developed by Nancy S. Smith.

ONE-MINUTE SUMMARY

This chapter has described activities to be used in the assistance phase of the PAR Lesson Framework. All the strategies in this chapter help greatly in the teaching of reading comprehension. To understand text, students must construct meaning by using their prior knowledge when encountering new information. To facilitate comprehension, students need to be taught to be active seekers of knowledge, use constructivist principles of learning, understand how to study segments of text, and know how to use text structure to their advantage. In addition, students need to learn questioning strategies to enhance comprehension. Teachers, in turn, need to use good questioning strategies to involve students more in the learning process. We introduced several strategies, such as the QAR, to show how text features and questioning strategies can lead students to the effective apprehension of deep meaning.

In this chapter we described the directed reading–thinking activity and the guided reading procedure. Both are excellent for teaching short segments of text. We also explained and gave examples of study guides, such as pattern guides, which are excellent in assisting students to comprehend difficult reading material. Finally we described strategies such as guide-o-ramas and marginal glosses, which can help students to better understand reading materials.

PAR ONLINE

Visit the *Reading to Learn in the Content Areas* Web site at http://academic.cengage .com/ education/richardson for links to the Web sites mentioned in this chapter, tutorial quizzing, and other resources.

END-OF-CHAPTER ACTIVITIES

Assisting Comprehension

1. See how many of the five types of text structures for paragraphs described in this chapter you can locate in a content area textbook. Are they easy or hard to find?

2. Having read this chapter, can you discuss some good ideas for activities to teach comprehension to your students?

3. Can you give some ways you can use questioning strategies better now after having read this chapter?

Reflecting on Your Reading

Standard 1.4 of the International Reading Association Standards for Teachers and Reading Professionals (2003) states that teachers need to demonstrate knowledge of teaching comprehension, a major component of reading. Take some time to reflect on how this chapter has better prepared you to assist students in better learning the comprehension process.

CHAPTER 5

There is one art of which man should be master—the art of reflection.
COLERIDGE

Learning through Reflection

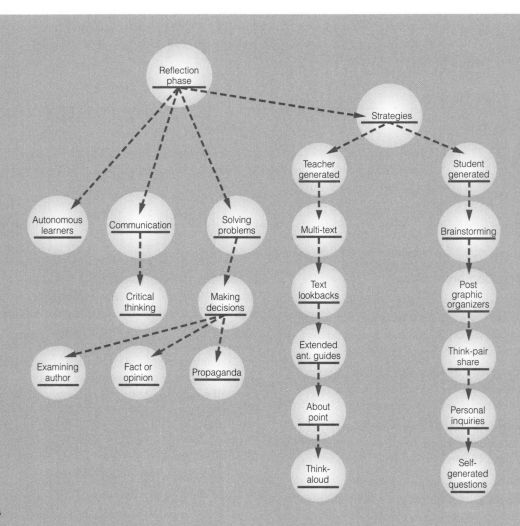

VOICES FROM THE CLASSROOM: THE OVERPROTECTIVE PARENT

The parents of one of your students make an appointment with you about their son. The mother says, "My son says you are always teaching them that they must think reflectively during and after their reading. But to do that students are always asked to talk things over. I don't know about this reflective thinking thing. I don't want him thinking about things he can't do anything about. I want him to pass the state standardized test at the end of this year." Both parents are adamant that their son is wasting his time in school and taking part in too many discussions with peers and with the teacher.

How would you refute their claim? How would you assure them that what you are doing in the class is purposeful and helpful for their son? Read this chapter, which might give you some excellent ideas on how you could answer.

PREPARING TO READ

1. Why is it important to reflect about learning after we finish reading?

2. Why do you think solving problems and making decisions would be two concepts talked about in a chapter about reflection in reading? Use your predictions to motivate you to read this chapter.

3. Following is a list of terms used in this chapter. Some may be familiar to you in a general context, but in this chapter they may be used in unfamiliar ways. Rate your knowledge by placing a plus sign (+) in front of those you are sure that you know, a check mark (✓) in front of those you have some knowledge about, and a zero (0) in front of those you don't know. Be ready to locate them in the chapter, and pay special attention to their meanings.

_____ reflective thinking
_____ autonomous learners
_____ comprehension monitoring
_____ free rides
_____ group-and-label
_____ propaganda
_____ brainstorming
_____ multitexts
_____ post-graphic organizers
_____ text lookbacks
_____ extended anticipation guides
_____ student-generated questions
_____ think-alouds

OBJECTIVES

As you read this chapter, focus your attention on the following purposes. You will

1. Be able to help students construct meaning while reading.

2. Understand why it is important to help students become autonomous learners.

3. Learn why decision making and problem solving are important skills to teach students.

4. Understand the importance of the reflection phase in reading and learning.

5. Learn specific thinking skills that are important in reflection.

6. Understand a number of strategies that help foster reflective thinking.

THE REFLECTION PHASE OF LEARNING

A reporter once asked Coach John McKay, "What do you think about the execution of your team?" After little reflection, the coach replied, "I'm all for it." We are not certain that Coach McKay reflected sufficiently before answering, but we know that reflective thinking is important in life. Purmensky (2006) has stated that true reflection turns experience into learning. The third step in the PAR Lesson Framework is reflection, which takes place after reading has been completed. Many agree that postreading reflective strategies are crucial for extending comprehension beyond the literal level (Marzano, 2003; Massey & Heafner, 2004). But reflective thinking, for most students, does not develop naturally without teacher intervention to actively promote this skill in students.

Whereas the preparation phase of lessons helps motivate students and the assistance phase helps build comprehension, the reflection phase helps clarify thinking and focus understanding. In this phase, students learn better how to retain information. Full understanding cannot be achieved until students reflect in a meaningful way about their reading. Although teachers may guide students by providing instructional support, the students' role is crucial at this stage.

This third phase also has several important by-products. First, it helps students think critically about what they have learned and have yet to learn about the lesson. Much has been written about the necessity of critical thinking in the reading process. John Dewey is considered to be the first educator who introduced the term *reflective thought* into the literature (Shermis, 1999). He considered **reflective thinking** to be careful thought persisting toward a goal of coming closer to the truth (Dewey, 1933). Recent research has shown the importance of critical thinking in changing students' misconceptions in a learning environment (Kowalski & Taylor, 2004). Educators have emphasized, however, that such critical thinking takes time and a sustained mental effort—a fact that is sometimes lost on teachers in our rushed, test-driven classroom environments (Jaimes, 2005). Teachers need to take the time to allow students to think critically because this will lead to the connection of prior knowledge with new ideas to bring learning into sharper focus for students.

A second by-product of reflective thinking is that it helps students retain material they have read. The more we reflect on reading material or on the lesson at hand, the longer we will remember it, and the more likely we will be to use the knowledge we retain. In this manner knowledge is related in a meaningful way to what is already known so that it will be retained and become the basis for further learning. A third by-product is that reflection provides a demonstration of one's learning through some system of evaluation. In this chapter we discuss all these aspects of reflection.

Reflection Helps Create Autonomous Learners

Reflective thinking is important for all students—not just for the gifted, talented, or high-achieving ones. Teachers can help all students in this endeavor by modeling reflective thinking in their own teaching. This will aid students in taking charge of their own learning. Hawkes and Schell (1987) caution that teacher-set reasons to read may encourage dependence and a passive approach to reading. If students determine their own reasons for reading, they are more likely to read actively and ultimately independently. Students need to practice reading behaviors that take the form of discussion, debate, lab application, writing, reorganizing, rehearsal, and other similar activities that let students process ideas and contemplate complex interactions concerning schemata and knowledge (Forget, 2004). It is important for students, after reading, to confront new information, process ideas, and make sense of what they have read. This continual practice in reflection helps students become **autonomous learners:** students who are self-regulated learners. Such students are not restricted in their learning because they know how to read for meaning, study, take appropriate notes, and organize information. Often teachers do not teach with a goal of making all students autonomous learners, even though they should.

An example of the importance of autonomous learning can be found in Robert O'Brien's *Mrs. Frisby and the Rats of NIMH* (1971). "By teaching us how to read, they had taught us how to get away," observe the rats in this children's novel. In this story scientists conduct experiments to teach rats to read. Because the rats are fed a drug to make them smart, the scientists anticipate that the rats will learn some letter–sound and word–picture relationships. They do not expect that the rats will actually understand and apply what they read. They underestimate what reading is about. These rats want to escape from the lab, and their goal is vital: They are willing to work at reading so they can use this new skill to escape. The rats use all their communication skills. They study pictures presented to them; they listen to clues to the meanings of the pictures; and they consult with one another about what they are learning—the connections between letters, sounds, pictures, and words. And then they read! Later, in their new home, they even begin to keep a written record of their progress.

This story demonstrates how cooperative study and the communicative arts can produce reflective readers who think critically, enrich their environment, and use reading as a lifelong process. The key to the rats' success was that they became autonomous learners, and no test of their success could demonstrate their learning better than the self-supporting community they built. The rats had a great desire to escape NIMH and plenty of opportunities for practice as well as plenty of clues in their environment. The natural result was both comprehension and escape. The scientists, to their misfortune, did not realize the important role of the learner in the success of their experiment.

Principle 10 in Chapter 1 states, "Content reading instruction enables students to become autonomous learners." As we wrote earlier, teachers can help students achieve this independence by allowing students, as soon as possible, to take active, responsible roles. However, students may be left stranded unless teachers guide them toward independence by showing them how to use their own communication skills.

Remember that we said in Chapter 1 that a major goal of education is to create autonomous learners.

In this chapter we teach important ways to help students become autonomous learners.

Kletzein (1991) investigated adolescents' use of strategies for reading. She found that students used many strategies when they were reading independently, but students with poor comprehension were less flexible. Good readers can pause and demonstrate their comprehension by retelling and analyzing what they have read and by using certain strategies consistently. In this way they are practicing **comprehension monitoring:** keeping mental track of their own learning. In contrast, poor readers seem to lose track of their reading and to have no particular strategies for comprehending. Research by McInnes and colleagues (2003) found children 9 to 12 years of age with attention deficit hyperactivity disorder (ADHD) were poorer at comprehending inferences and at comprehension monitoring of instructions than were children without ADHD. Research (Winne & Perry, 2000; Zimmerman & Schunk, 2001) has reiterated the critical importance of comprehension monitoring to effective study, and recent researchers (Wiley, Griffin, & Thiede, 2005) suggest that the kinds of expository texts used may be a critical factor in comprehension monitoring.

Because poor readers often do not function independently, we recommend that students be given more control over their strategies so they can gain independence. Bohan and Bass (1991) helped students in a fourth grade math class become independent by taking **free rides** in solving problems about fractions. "After the teacher covered multiplication of two fractions, the class was told the next type of problem, multiplying mixed numbers, was a free ride—a situation in which they were solving a seemingly new type of problem, but one that was not really new because they had previously acquired the knowledge needed to find the product" (p. 4). The next day, a student volunteered another case in which free rides could apply. This situation exemplifies the elements of reflection: The teacher provides a context and encourages students to manage their own learning at the application level. In this way students become self-managed and acquire skills to enhance their own attending, learning, and thinking. In the next section we examine some important skills necessary for reflective thinking on the part of students.

IMPORTANT SKILLS FOR REFLECTION

Communication Skills

The National Council of Teachers of English (1996) has called for the creation of classrooms in which all children seek to become strategic, critical, independent, and lifelong readers and writers. Researchers (Duffy & Hoffman, 1999; Villaune, 2000) have asserted that the key to successful teaching of communicative arts is the training of independent and spirited teachers who understand that their job is to use methods and materials in ways that accommodate student needs. Such teachers realize that just as students read to learn, they listen, speak, and write to learn—and that students use all the communicative arts to make sense of the world.

Oppenheimer (2003) illustrates the importance of learning as communication by describing a team of American researchers who journeyed to Japan in the late 1990s to investigate why Japanese children rank near the top of all countries in standardized achievement tests. What they found surprised them. Instead of classes steeped in memorization and rote learning, the researchers found classes where students were engaged in "active exploration, argument, analysis, and reflection" (p. 360). Further, they found that Japanese students didn't rush from topic to topic (as in the United States) but worked in depth on discrete problems, examining some questions for weeks at a time. Oppenheimer notes how much the classroom environment in Japan is at odds with America's notions of what happens in Japanese schools. And it appears that Japanese schools, with the highest-achieving students in the world, are conducting classes that are compatible with the guidelines called for by the NCTE.

More than at any other stage, reflective learning depends on informative communication. A 15-year-old high school student recently said, "We need more class discussion. You can read stuff out of the book and answer questions, but you never really learn it unless you talk about it. We need more time to ask questions." Teachers have to let go, learn not to talk, and encourage students to ask their own questions and cooperate with one another in their learning. For a student, listening and speaking reflectively about reading reinforce learning in a social context (Summers, 2006). By listening to and considering the viewpoints of other participants, students may gain different and deeper insights about a topic. Other examples surface and new connections are made. Most important, students gain control of their own learning. Richardson (1999b) reports that students prefer discussion to lecture as a means of deep learning, although many students she interviewed reported that few discussions occurred in their classes. Students are aware of how discussions help them understand what they read. In a recent Australian study, Gillies and Boyle (2006) found that teachers need training to use communication skills in promoting student thinking and to scaffold student learning. They trained teachers specifically to challenge student perspectives, ask more cognitive and metacognitive questions of students, and provide scaffolds for student learning. They found that students modeled many types of discourse used by the teachers in the study, and the group communication skills that were used contributed to the students' sense of security in learning.

> The lecture method of instructing is not as popular with students as one might think. Students like discussion and questioning better.

Teachers must realize that the key element of the reflection phase of the PAR Lesson Framework is the type of communication just described. All of the communicative arts are present in some form in good communication. Next we will describe what we feel are the most important skills students need to practice in the reflection phase of learning.

Critical Thinking

Critical thinking as an important dimension of learning is emphasized in textbooks, in the research literature, and in published programs. Unks (1985) said that the ability to think critically is one of the most agreed-on educational objectives. But even though almost everyone agrees that some elements of critical thinking need to be taught across the curriculum, the concept itself remains so vague that educators are not certain about its meaning, about the best ways for classroom teachers to teach it, or even about whether it can be taught. After examining a textbook that contained practice examples in teaching critical thinking, a reviewer once remarked, "It was a good book but it really didn't contain much critical thinking." This comment underscores the subjective nature of the concept.

> Two views of critical thinking are prevalent in the reading literature.

The literature, in fact, supports two interpretations of critical thinking. One is a narrow definition of critical thinking as the mastery and use of certain skills necessary for the assessment of statements. These skills take the same form as logic or deduction and may include judging the acceptability of authority statements, judging contradictory statements, and judging whether a conclusion follows necessarily from its premises (Beyer, 1983). A more encompassing definition includes these skills as well as inductive types of skills, such as hypothesis testing, proposition generation, and creative argument (Facione, 1984; Sternberg & Baron, 1985). Clark (1999) offers a definition that is more in line with this latter view of the construct. Clark says that such reflective and critical thinking "is thinking for an extended period by linking recent experiences to earlier ones in order to promote a more complex and interrelated mental schema" (p.1). We agree with this latter, more inclusive definition and emphasize critical thinking in this broader sense throughout this text.

As we have said, everyone agrees that one of the most important ways to emphasize reflection in reading is to ask students to think critically about what they read. Yet Parker (1991), in a literature review of the pervasiveness of teaching critical thinking in social studies, found that the goal of teaching students critical thinking strategies was largely unrealized. Parker's findings mirror recent studies and national reports showing that critical thinking remains a neglected part of instruction (Jaimes, 2005). Sternberg (1994) laments the lack of correspondence between what is required for critical thinking in adulthood and what is being taught in schools today. Hynd (1999) encourages teachers to expose middle and high school students to historical documents and multiple texts.

Critical thinking is a buzzword in education today. Everyone seems to be talking about how to teach critical thinking. Some popular terms are spurious, but critical thinking is a real construct. Many of our students don't think critically as they read.

This is now a much easier undertaking because many primary source documents are available on the Internet. In this way, students can read different or even opposing views and begin to think like historians. As students experience the process that historians use in researching and writing about history, they may be able to apply this thinking process to other subjects as well. Students have to consider the sources of information and when it was published to determine how to use it as a resource. Thinking like a researcher enables students to think critically. By reinforcing the reading experience through critical thinking, teachers can challenge students to think about content material in new ways.

Too often, however, classroom teachers, especially at the elementary level, shy away from teaching critical thinking. One reason for this is that there is no clear definition of the construct. Another reason is that teachers mistakenly believe that *critical* means to find fault and emphasize the negative. Also, critical thinking is a difficult construct to measure through teacher-made tests, and critical thinking skills are not mandated for minimum competence in many subjects. Gronlund (1993) has found that teachers are not well trained in the skill of test construction in general, much less in testing for critical thinking. In addition, some teachers have the notion that at-risk learners are not capable of critical thinking. Finally, teachers often say that they do not have adequate time to plan instruction in critical thinking and lack appropriate materials and books to teach it properly. Despite these perceived obstacles, teaching critical thinking should not be neglected at any grade level. This important ability leads to greater success in academic subjects and will be useful to students after graduation. In short, critical thinking is a skill that will aid students in all facets of life.

We can clarify our view of critical thinking by studying what happens when this skill is put to use. Duke and Pearson (2002) list the attributes of good readers, and almost all of them involve the types of critical thinking that we describe. These researchers say that good readers

- Are active readers.
- Have clear established goals in mind.
- Constantly evaluate whether the reading is meeting their goals.
- Look over the text to determine text structure.
- Frequently make predictions.
- Read selectively, making decisions about what to read carefully, what to read quickly, what not to read, what to reread, and so on.
- Construct meaning as they read.
- Revise and question meanings while reading.
- Determine meanings of unfamiliar words and concepts as they read.
- Draw from and use prior knowledge before and during reading.
- Monitor their understanding of the text.
- React emotionally and intellectually to text by evaluating the value and quality of the reading.
- Read disparate texts differently.
- Understand settings and characters in a narrative.
- Summarize what they have read in expository text.
- Process text even after they complete a reading.
- See reading as a consuming, continuous, and complex activity.
- Get satisfaction from reading and view it as productive.

Remember that educators have been talking about critical thinking for decades.

All of these reading behaviors include critical thinking in its broader sense. Remember that students think critically when they monitor comprehension, determine text structure, read selectively, revise and construct the meanings of words and concepts, use prior knowledge to evaluate and analyze text, concern themselves with the value of what is being read, summarize text, and in general regard reading as a satisfying and complex activity.

In our complex and rapidly changing society, the abilities to think critically and to be skeptical when weighing evidence before making decisions is of great importance. More than 70 years ago John Dewey (1933) spoke this way about the importance of reflective thinking:

> When a situation arises containing a difficulty or perplexity, the person who finds himself in it may take one of a number of courses. He may dodge it, dropping the activity that brought it about, turning to something else. He may indulge in a flight of fancy, imagining himself powerful or wealthy, or in some other way in possession of the

means that would enable him to deal with the difficulty. Or, finally, he may face the situation. In this case, he begins to reflect. (p. 102)

Students in kindergarten through 12th grade are seldom taught to reflect, to solve problems by "facing the situation," except in published programs on thinking or in "critical thinking" sections of basal reading materials. But Reyes (1986), in a review of a social studies series, found that publishers did not deliver material that developed strong critical thinking, even though they promised it. In another study, researchers (Woodward, Elliott, & Nagel, 1986) found that the critical thinking skills emphasized in elementary basal materials were those that could be most readily tested, such as map and globe skills.

Evidence (McPeck, 1981) indicates that teachers do not need published "thinking" programs and that they cannot depend on basal reading materials to teach critical thinking skills. However, they must integrate their own critical thinking lessons with those of the textbooks they are using. For example, to teach critical thinking, teachers might present study guides that emphasize critical thinking and then have small groups of students practice a problem-solving exercise. In this manner, students can be taught critical thinking in a concrete context of carefully guided thinking. Studies indicate that, especially in early adolescence, formal reasoning and thinking can best be taught through the teacher's use of guided prompts such as graphic overviews and study guides, which help students structure their thinking (Arlin, 1984; Strahan, 1983). More recent studies (Dixon, Cassady, Cross, & Williams, 2005) show that the use of computers can improve critical thinking, especially for boys. Through guided prompts and use of computers (See Chapter 7), teachers are scheduling time to model intelligent and thoughtful behavior in the classroom by emphasizing critical thinking during class sessions.

Critical Literacy

How can newspapers, magazines, advertisements, and the Internet be used to teach critical literacy?

Another aspect of readability and the provision of multiple texts and resources is critical literacy. Critical literacy is about analytical reading and reading between and beyond the lines. The number of resources and writings now available at "the touch of a finger" stirs a sense of urgency to encourage students to become active readers rather than passive recipients of randomly discovered text (Devoogd, 2006; Knickerbocker & Rycik, 2006; Molden, 2007). Considering and questioning authors' purposes and stances for writing add dimensions to reading and understanding (McLaughlin & Devoogd, 2004). The idea is not to encourage skepticism but to give students tools for investigating and becoming informed, rather than gullible, readers. Molden explains that by critically examining a text, readers think about the author's motivation for writing it; consider how the reader is being persuaded to understand ideas through emphasis, de-emphasis, facts, and opinions; and recognize that the author's perspective is merely one. McLaughlin and Devoogd offer several strategies for making connections and detecting bias. *Juxtapositioning* is one such strategy, in which learners compare and contrast two texts having opposing perspectives. In so doing, viewpoints can be clarified, thus helping the reader come to a deeper and greater understanding for forming his or her own perspective.

Solving Problems and Making Decisions

Research (Montague & Applegate, 2000) attests to the importance of problem-solving skills in content area subjects. Critical thinking leads to problem solving, which in turn leads to effective decision making. Students who use critical thinking are more effective thinkers; both their creative and contemplative abilities improve. We offer the following steps in problem solving:

1. *Gather ideas and information:* Students brainstorm to generate enough information to begin defining the problem. They can play a "reading detective" game or do research to gather information from all possible sources.

2. *Define the problem:* Students recognize the need to resolve a situation that has no apparent solution. They should be asked to clarify the nature of the task and completely describe the situation in writing.

3. *Form tentative conclusions:* This is a creative phase in which students suggest possible solutions from available data.

4. *Test conclusions:* Students discuss in groups which conclusions work best as solutions to the problem. Poor choices are eliminated until workable solutions remain. Students may also establish criteria for evaluating outcomes.

5. *Make a decision:* Students select one of the remaining solutions and give reasons for their choice.

Study guides, such as the one in Activity 5.1, can be constructed by teachers to provide cognitive activities to assist students in using these problem-solving steps. It is especially important to start these types of activities in early elementary classrooms

---

ACTIVITY 5.1 CRITICAL THINKING GUIDE: PROBLEM SOLVING

- Problem arises.
- Why do we need to solve problem?

Ways to Solve Problem	Reasons for Choosing Method
Method 1	Positive outcomes Negative outcomes
Method 2	Positive outcomes Negative outcomes
Method 3	Positive outcomes Negative outcomes
Best way to solve problem	Reasons for choosing to solve problem in this manner

Adapted from a decision-making model by J. McTighe and F. T. Ryman, Jr. (1988), Cueing Thinking in the Classroom: The Promise of Theory-Embedded Tools, *Educational Leadership* 45(7), 18–24.

because unsophisticated learners seldom let their minds journey across stories to think about possible similarities.

Group decision making can also be taught through the use of a **group-and-label** technique. The teacher begins by writing the topic on the board and telling students that they will be reviewing important terminology. Then students volunteer any terms they can think of that fall under the topic heading. The teacher may ask leading questions or even eliminate this step by preparing a list in advance on the board or on a worksheet. Students reorganize the list into smaller lists of items that have something in common. Each of these sublists is then given a label. Students may work individually or in small groups to reorganize and label the words. Activity 5.2 shows how grouping and labeling might work for a first grade social studies unit on communities.

ACTIVITY *5.2* GROUP-AND-LABEL TECHNIQUE: FIRST GRADE SOCIAL STUDIES

From a jumbled list of words, the students will be asked to divide the words into four groups, according to their similarities. The teacher will write these four groups of words on the chalkboard. The students will label these groups. These labels will be written by the teacher on the board as titles for the groups of words.

Getting to School

school bus   "The bus driver brings me to school."

walking   "I walk to school with my sister."

Mom's station wagon   "My mom drives me to school in her station wagon."

Daddy's pickup truck   "My daddy drives me to school in his pickup truck."

Bicycle   "I ride my bicycle to school."

Things Used at School

ruler

books   "I learn to read in first grade."

writing tablet   "I write in my tablet."

pencils   "My teacher sharpens my pencil every day."

crayons   "I like to color pictures with my crayons."

glue

scissors   "I cut the paper with my scissors."

Rooms at School

office   "I'm scared to go to the principal's office."

classroom

library   "I like to check out books at the library."

cafeteria   "We eat in the cafeteria."

nurse's clinic

auditorium

gymnasium   "I play in the gym."

People at School

teacher   "My teacher helps me to read."

coach   "The coach is my friend."

librarian   "The librarian always reads us a story."

principal

secretary

nurse   "The nurse is nice."

bus driver

cafeteria workers

janitors and cleaning workers

guidance counselor

Developed by Gail Perrer.

Examining the Author

Rarely are students asked to examine an author's background to determine whether the author is noted for a particular bias. However, as students evaluate content information, they should note the source of that information. Most important, they should ask who the writer is and what his or her qualifications are. This analysis is especially important for information obtained from the World Wide Web. Anyone can post a Web site, but discriminating readers must decide whether the author is qualified to do so. The following questions can be given to students to learn more about the author of a reading:

1. Is the author of this book living? Is he or she currently writing?
2. What are the author's qualifications to write this book or article?
3. What is the reputation of the publisher? Is this a recognized publishing company?
4. Does the author use mainly facts or her or his own or others' opinions?
5. Does the author use propaganda techniques?
6. Does the author show bias in any of this writing?
7. Is the author trying to persuade you to take a stand in a certain direction?
8. Use a search engine to find the author on the World Wide Web. Can you find out any more about him or her there?

Students can think about and discuss these questions in groups after they read a narrative or an expository selection. Also, students can be supplied with multiple-choice items, such as those in Activity 5.3, to help them learn to ascertain an author's qualifications for writing accurate and unbiased statements on a subject. Such an activity can be used to begin class discussion of a reading or to initiate debate after reading.

Determining Fact and Opinion

Determining fact and opinion is another higher-level thinking skill that can be taught to students starting in the early elementary years. Young learners may have difficulty with this because they feel that if they believe something to be true, then it is a fact, not an opinion. For example, a few years ago one of the authors of this book put several statements on the board for her fourth graders to identify as fact or opinion. One student raised his hand and with confidence declared that the statement "Saturday is the best day of the week" was definitely a fact. To teach this skill, teachers must help students to see relationships between and among facts to grasp subtle implications, and to interpret the deeper meanings an author has in mind. Often readers must bring to bear past experiences and background to derive accurate interpretations. With frequent practice, students can become adept at interpreting an author's point of view and detecting biases. Activity 5.4 presents a study guide for fact and opinion—to help students distinguish one from the other and to give students practice working in this important area.

Supply students with multiple-choice items like the following. The student checks the source that is the most reliable of the three suggested.

1. Japan has the highest per capita income of any country in the world.
   _____ **a.** Joan Armentrag, salesperson at Bloomingdale's
   _____ **b.** Bob Hoskins, star golfer
   _____ **c.** Dr. Alice MacKenzie, economic analyst, the Ford Foundation

2. Mathematics is of no use to anyone.
   _____ **a.** Bob Brotig, high school dropout
   _____ **b.** Bill Johnson, editor, *The Mathematics Teacher*
   _____ **c.** Susan Winnifred, personnel, the Rand Corporation

3. We have proved that honeybees communicate with each other.
   _____ **a.** John Bowyer, salesman, Sue Ann Honey Co.

   _____ **b.** Jane Maupin, high school biology teacher
   _____ **c.** Martha Daughtry, bank teller

4. Forty-six percent of all married women with children now work outside the home.
   _____ **a.** Sue Ann Begley, electrician
   _____ **b.** Carol Radziwell, professional pollster
   _____ **c.** Joe Blotnik, marriage counselor

5. We must stop polluting our bays and oceans.
   _____ **a.** Clinton Weststock, president, Save the Bay Foundation
   _____ **b.** Marjorie Seldon, engineer, Olin Oil Refinery, Gulfport, MI
   _____ **c.** Carl Kanipe, freelance writer of human interest stories

Detecting Propaganda

Skilled readers know how to absorb important information and throw away what is of no use. They are especially adept at recognizing **propaganda**—persuasive, one-sided statements designed to change beliefs or sway opinion. Propaganda can be glaring or subtle; students need to be made aware, even in their elementary years, of the effects propaganda can have, particularly in the marketplace. The following are the most common forms of propaganda:

1. *Appeal to the bandwagon:* Aimed at the "masses"—to join a large group that is satisfied with an idea or product. Readers of this kind of propaganda are made to feel left out if they don't go along with the crowd.

2. *Emotional language:* This plays on the subtle connotations of words carefully chosen to evoke strong feelings.

3. *Appeal to prestige:* Associating a person, product, or concept with something deemed important or prestigious by the reader or viewer.

DISTINGUISHING FACT FROM OPINION: THE RENAISSANCE

Directions: Place an F by the statements of fact and an O by the statements of opinion.

_____ 1. Music, architecture, essays, and philosophy are all manifestations of culture.

_____ 2. Wealthy Renaissance women were well educated.

_____ 3. Before the 15th century, the only books were handwritten manuscripts in Latin.

_____ 4. Rich people in 14th-century Italy imitated the cultures of people who had lived more than 2,000 years before.

_____ 5. One of the first books read widely was about how narrow-minded many educated people were in the early 15th century.

_____ 6. There was a strong desire for power on the part of political leaders during the Renaissance.

_____ 7. As books became inexpensive and easier to get, the average person's awareness of the world expanded enormously.

_____ 8. All Renaissance men were smart, athletic, witty, and generally interesting.

_____ 9. The height of the Renaissance occurred during the late 1400s and early 1500s.

_____ 10. Even at the height of the Renaissance, all the new ideas of the era were accepted by relatively few people.

4. _Plain-folks appeal:_ The use in an advertisement of people who seem typical, average, or ordinary (sometimes even dull). The idea is to build trust by depicting people as "regular" folks.

5. _Testimonial:_ The use of a famous person to give heightened credibility to a concept, idea, or product.

Propaganda is rampant on the World Wide Web. Locate a Web site about a topic in your content area and determine if it meets any of the tests listed here.

Teachers at all grade levels need to prepare students to recognize propaganda techniques. After the basic techniques have been explained, students can be asked to bring in examples of advertisements from newspapers and magazines. In literature classes, students can be asked to discover examples in plays, short stories, and novels. _A Tale of Two Cities,_ for example, contains examples of each of these propaganda techniques. Master storytellers like Charles Dickens know how to use such techniques deftly to develop complicated plots.

When discussing environmental issues in a science class, would proponents of industry be likely to take a different position than Greenpeace? How might this difference be manifested in propaganda techniques? Activity 5.5 provides a sample activity for teaching students to recognize propaganda. Students are asked to match statements to the propaganda technique they employ.

Match each statement with the propaganda technique used.

    a. Appeal to bandwagon
    b. Emotional language
    c. Appeal to prestige
    d. Plain-folks appeal
    e. Testimonial

_____ **1.** Come on down to Charlie Winkler's Auto before every one of these beauties is sold.

_____ **2.** Michael Jordan, former star basketball player, thinks Nike shoes are the best.

_____ **3.** You'll be glowing all over in your new Evening Time gown.

_____ **4.** Why, people in every walk of life buy our product.

_____ **5.** Join the American Dining Club today, a way of life for those who enjoy the good life.

_____ **6.** Already, over 85 percent of our workers have given to this worthy cause.

_____ **7.** I'll stack our doughnut makers up against any others as the best in the business!

_____ **8.** Even butcher Fred Jones likes our new frozen yogurt coolers.

_____ **9.** One must drink our wine to appreciate the truly fine things in life.

_____ **10.** Lift the weights that Arnold Schwarzenegger lifts—a sure way to a better body.

STRATEGIES THAT PROMOTE REFLECTION

Brainstorming

Note these "group-worthy" performance tasks.

Group interaction and discussion offers important ways for students to use reflective thinking in the content classroom. But such discussion has to take place with what Lotan (2003) calls "group-worthy" tasks for students to perform. Lotan says such tasks should

- Be open-ended and require complex problem solving.
- Provide students with multiple entry points to the task.
- Provide students with multiple opportunities to show intellectual competence.
- Deal with intellectually important content.
- Require positive interdependence.
- Include clear criteria for the evaluation of the group's product.

We feel that Lotan's criteria for discussion are sound and should be adhered to by teachers when students are allow to take part in **brainstorming**—whole-class or group discussion of a topic in order to reach consensus or solve a problem. Brainstorming sessions can last from 10 minutes to an hour and can be designed to teach any of the skills discussed in this chapter. An especially productive brainstorming session is one in which small groups of students list as many possible alternative solutions to a problem as they can. Group captains are chosen to report findings to the entire class. The teacher lists on the chalkboard alternatives that the students deem worthy. Discussion then centers on how to narrow the choices to one or two and why the final choices are the best ones. An important consideration is the size of the brainstorming group. Five-person groups seem to work best (Gillies & Boyle, 2006); however, three- and four-person groups are also suitable. The most vocal students tend to dominate groups of six students or more.

The "ready reading reference bookmark" (see Figure 5.1) developed by Kapinus (1986) can be used to get students ready to brainstorm after reading a passage. In the section "after you read," students can use brainstorming to perform the five thinking operations called for: retelling, summarizing, asking, picturing, and deciding. Students also can brainstorm the "while you read" and "if you don't understand" operations at other points in the lesson—before reading, for example, or after reading specific sections.

FIGURE 5.1

Ready Reading
Reference
Bookmark

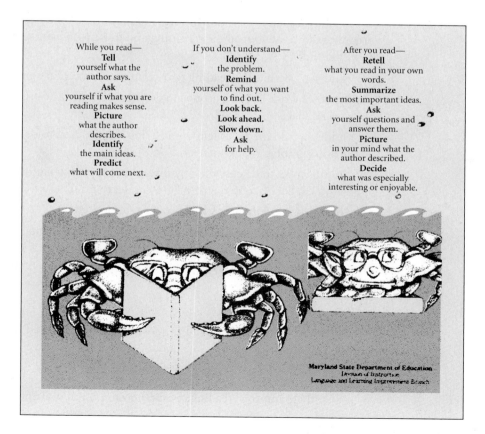

While you read—
Tell
yourself what the author says.
Ask
yourself if what you are reading makes sense.
Picture
what the author describes.
Identify
the main ideas.
Predict
what will come next.

If you don't understand—
Identify
the problem.
Remind
yourself of what you want to find out.
Look back.
Look ahead.
Slow down.
Ask
for help.

After you read—
Retell
what you read in your own words.
Summarize
the most important ideas.
Ask
yourself questions and answer them.
Picture
in your mind what the author described.
Decide
what was especially interesting or enjoyable.

Maryland State Department of Education
Division of Instruction
Language and Learning Improvement Branch

Multitext Activities

Teachers can use **multitexts**—multiple textbooks at more than one level of difficulty—as an important tool to motivate students. Many teachers' manuals suggest multitext activities as a way to encourage reflective thinking. Often teachers feel too rushed to cover curriculum and skip this enriching resource, although research supports the use of many reading materials to solidify learning about a topic. A multitext approach also helps readers reflect by extending their knowledge of a topic after study. We discuss multitexts in greater depth in Chapter 6 (on exploring nontraditional resources) and Chapter 11 (on working with diverse learners).

Post-Graphic Organizers

Students benefit from working cooperatively to construct their own graphic displays to summarize meaning retained from a text reading. These visual images are an easier way for students to show relationships that are often too difficult to visualize mentally. A graphic representation can present a holistic picture of the text reading, creating concrete images of complex ideas and concepts. When students make graphic representations after the reading, these are called **post-graphic organizers**. Designing post-graphic organizers represents another reflection activity that students of all ages enjoy.

We recommend the following steps to help students produce their own graphic organizers to create purpose for reading and to help one another construct meaning from the text:

1. Students preview the reading to determine the structure and main ideas.
2. Students work in small groups to decide what form the graphic organizer should take.
3. Students read the text silently, gathering information to be included in the group's graphic representation.
4. Groups meet to discuss the organization of the information each member has gathered. Each group makes a large model to present to the class.
5. Groups present their finished products to the class.

Activity 5.6 is a graphic organizer called "Maps and Continents" for a first grade class. Activity 5.7 is a post-graphic organizer completed by a group of several college students after completing a reading about how best to construct graphic representations.

Text Lookbacks

Recent research on repeated readings—students in pairs reading and rereading text orally—has shown that such oral reading activities improve oral reading, fluency, and comprehension (Devault & Joseph, 2004; Yurick, Robinson, Cartledge, Lo, & Evans, 2006). We feel that it is just as important for students to repeat reading passages silently to improve reading comprehension. Both oral and silent repeated read-

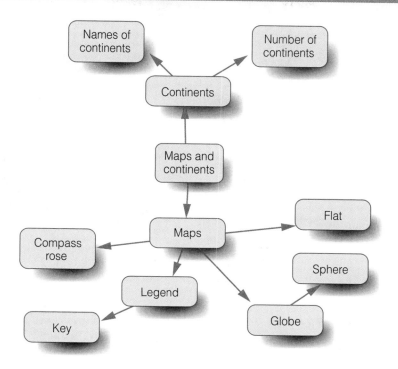

Many students feel it is wrong to reread a passage they have read one time. Try to get students out of this mind-set.

ings get students to look back over text to gain comprehension—a practice we feel strongly will improve comprehension. Some years ago Garner and colleagues (1985) discussed the importance of reexamining text—backtracking, or **text lookbacks**—in overcoming memory difficulties. There is evidence that both children and adults fail to use this strategy (Garner, Macready, & Wagoner, 1985), even though research (Amlund, Kardash, & Kulhavy, 1986) shows that reinspection of text makes a significant difference in recall.

Ruth Strang, the great reading educator, once remarked that she was disappointed when she entered a school library and found students reading for long periods without looking up to reflect on what they were reading and not glancing back over material during their study. We recommend that teachers ask students to use the lookback strategy after a reading by working in groups to clarify confusing points. For instance, students in a social studies class can reinspect a chapter about Athens as a democracy to find out why, in the supposedly strong democracy of Athens, there were so many slaves and so few citizens. Students can then be asked to write a group summary of what the text says about the positive and negative aspects of Athenian democracy.

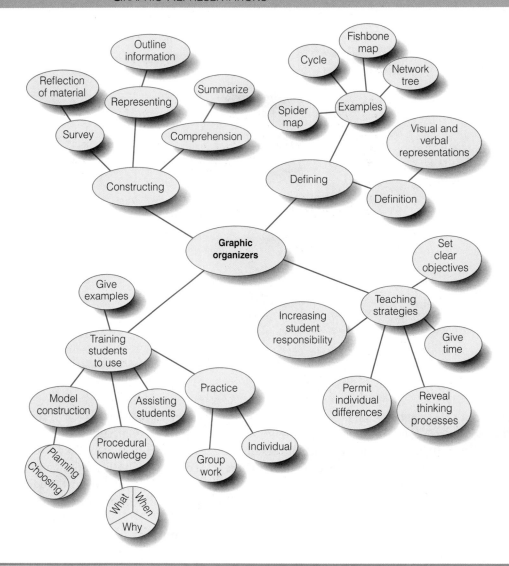

For both summaries and text lookbacks, Garner and colleagues (1985) stress the
following:

1. Some ideas are more important than others.

2. Some ideas can be ignored.

3. Students need to be taught how to use titles and topic sentences.

4. Students need to learn that ideas cross boundaries of sentences.

5. Piecemeal reading that focuses on comprehending one sentence at a time is not conducive to gleaning a wealth of ideas from text.

6. Rules of summarization need to be learned and practiced.

7. Students must be taught how and when to apply both summarization and lookback strategies.

8. These strategies cannot be adequately accomplished in a hurried classroom atmosphere or environment.

9. Students need to practice these strategies in a number of content areas to effect transfer.

Garner and associates (Garner, Hare, Alexander, Haynes, & Winograd, 1984) also maintain that readers should be taught the following: why to use lookbacks (because readers can't remember everything); when to use them (when a question calls for information from the text); and where to use them (where skimming or scanning will help one to find the portion of the text that should be read carefully). Next, readers should practice rereading for answers to questions asked after the reading is completed. Lookbacks are necessary when readers realize that they didn't understand all of what they read. Good readers evaluate their reading and decide whether to look back. But poor readers rarely have this skill, so deliberate text lookbacks will give them greatly needed practice in this aspect of critical thinking.

Group Summarizations

A number of researchers address the importance of summarization for the study and retention of reading material (Garner, Macready, & Wagoner, 1985; Scardamalia & Bereiter, 1984). Garner notes that summarization involves judging ideas deemed important, applying rules for condensing text, and producing a shortened text in oral or written form. A study by Friend (2001) found that student summaries were improved when students looked for ideas in the text that were repeated a number of times and tried to write summaries by generalizing—that is, keeping the gist of the passage uppermost in their minds. Studies consistently show that skilled readers know how to summarize, whereas unskilled readers almost always lack this ability (Brown & Smiley, 1977; Garner, Macready, & Wagoner, 1985; Scardamalia & Bereiter, 1984). To learn to write effective summaries, students can be asked to work in groups and use the following six rules, suggested by Brown and Day (1983):

1. Delete all unnecessary material.

2. Delete redundancies.

3. Substitute a superordinate term for a list of items.

4. Use a superordinate term for a list of actions.

5. Select topic sentences from ones provided in the text.

6. Construct topic sentences when they are not provided explicitly in the text.

One way to have students summarize in groups is for group members to develop a concept map based on the ideas they believe to be important in a chapter or a portion

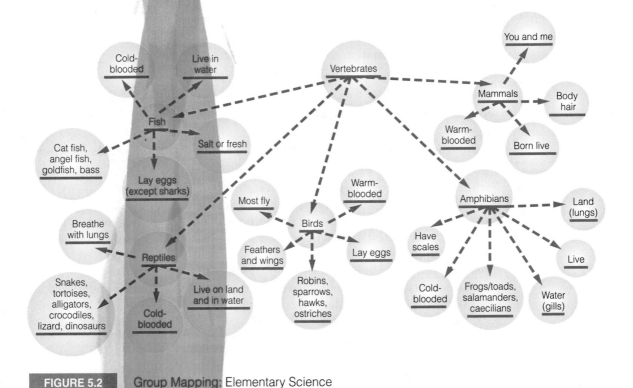

FIGURE 5.2 Group Mapping: Elementary Science

of a chapter. Groups can share their mapping exercises on the board, and discussion can center on why groups chose different concepts to map. An example of an elementary student group's science concept is shown in Figure 5.2. Mapping can be an excellent, cooperatively generated activity for small-group interaction. Davidson (1982) suggests that such concept maps are "low-risk" activities for even the most limited students and can be an unobtrusive way for students to summarize what they learned in a reading. Finally, group summarizing can be accomplished through the use of the GIST (Cunningham, 1982) procedure described in Chapter 10 on writing. Students can work in small groups to make group GISTs and can share these with the entire class. The GIST procedure provides an excellent way to teach needed summarization skills.

Think–Pair–Share

Think–pair–share (McTighe & Lyman, 1988) is a reading activity that stresses reflective thinking and cooperative learning. The activity starts with a prompt given by the teacher to probe student thoughts about reading material. In mathematics, it might be a question such as "How do you find the absolute value of a number?" In science, it might be "How can we tell if an oxidation number of an atom is positive?" Students are asked to take some time to think about the question and then to write down an answer. Next students form pairs and discuss their answers. During this phase, students help each other to improve their own answers and work to formulate joint answers to these questions. Finally, in the sharing phase, the teacher brings the students together to obtain input from the entire class in discussing the topic. Then all students read to see if the text is helpful in answering the question.

Irvin and colleagues (Irvin, Buehl, & Klemp, 2007) cite this strategy as being particularly good for teaching reflective thinking, saying that it allows "time for thought and reaction as well as providing for a fuller, richer, and more thoughtful discussion" (p. 51). This strategy is effective because it can be modified to teach other skills like prediction, summarization, visualization, and elaboration. The key to think–pair–share's effectiveness is that students have peers help them decipher tough questions about text. Also, by transcribing learning into their own words, students use comprehension monitoring in their reflection about the text.

Personal Inquiries

A personal inquiry is a strategy whereby students conduct original research from questions they ask as a result of exposure to a topic. It is similar to the old-fashioned term paper traditionally required at the high school level, when students may be given a choice of topics to research. But with personal inquiry the students select their own topics and are encouraged to develop their own questions. Whereas most lessons are teacher-generated, personal inquiries are student-generated.

Emphasis on inquiry learning has increased over the last two decades (Rasinski & Padak, 1993; Todd, 1995; Zimmerman & Schunk, 2001). Examples have been available for many years, especially in literature. Omri, in *The Indian in the Cupboard* (Banks, 1990), finds himself so immersed in reading books about the Iroquois Indian who appears in his cupboard that he doesn't hear the school bell ring. Usually Omri expresses great dislike for both school and reading. In *Canyons* by Gary Paulsen (1990), Mr. Homesley convinces Brennan to start collecting bugs; they learn about each one together. As a result, Brennan goes to Mr. Homesley when he needs help to find out about the skull he found in the canyon. When materials arrive from Mr. Homesley's friend, Brennan stays up all night reading to unravel his mystery.

Personal inquiry approximates how adults learn. We have a question, and we search for an answer. Our answers are often the result of using literature to learn; most likely we use the World Wide Web or reference books, not textbooks, as our source material. Content teachers who approximate this lifelong learning technique may hook their students on learning just as both Omri and Brennan were hooked. Perhaps the best way to begin supplementing content instruction with personal inquiry is to collect questions that students ask, encourage them to find answers, and promote sharing what is learned with all the students. Teachers who use authentic assessment in the form of portfolios can ask students to demonstrate within a portfolio the results of such inquiry.

To fully understand the value of personal inquiries, conduct some of your own. Questions can run the gamut. A teacher of drama and literature asked, "Can I make puppets that can be used effectively for telling stories, expressing different personalities in a variety of plots?" A geometry teacher asked, "What geometric properties are exhibited in soap bubbles?" A physics teacher asked, "What are the areas related to the topic of sound?" Davis (1998) tells how a beehive in a classroom generated questions that students set out to answer: Which one is the queen bee? Where is the queen? What does she look like? How is she different from other bees?

Extended Anticipation Guides

Another technique that can foster reflective thinking is the **extended anticipation guide** (Duffelmeyer & Baum, 1992). As noted in Chapter 3, anticipation guides can help students predict outcomes. The extended guides can spark discussion and reinforce or verify information that students have learned and can enable them to modify predictions to take into account new insights and information. Activity 5.8 includes both an anticipation guide for high school students to complete individually before reading Upton Sinclair's muckraking novel *The Jungle* and an extended guide to be completed by students working in groups after reading *The Jungle.*

ABOUT/POINT

Teachers are always looking for a simple yet effective way to teach students how to get the main idea of a paragraph and how to recognize subordinate detail. The ABOUT/POINT strategy represents an easy way that students can learn to think reflectively about relationships in a paragraph. In this activity, the student concentrates on "what the passage is about" and what "main points" are covered in the reading. Simple study guides can be given to students to help them categorize the passage in this manner. In kindergarten and first grade, teachers can use this technique as a listening and speaking aid after reading a story aloud to students. An example of its use in first grade (in the form of a study guide) is shown as Activity 5.9. The student is identifying the sun as the source of light and heat. In upper elementary and middle school grades, students can work in groups to recall information from more than one paragraph of content material. To use the ABOUT/POINT strategy in this larger context, teachers ask students to reread a passage and then to decide in groups what the passage is "about" and what "points" (details) support their response. A good example of an upper elementary school study sheet is provided as Activity 5.10 on health education.

Self-Generated Questions

Students seem to improve their understanding of texts when they generate their own questions either before or after reading. This strategy, called **student-generated questions**, succeeds because it provides a monitoring strategy for students. A recent study (Van Blerkom, Van Blerkom, & Bertsch, 2006) asked 100 college students to participate in an experiment in which students were randomly assigned to one of four groups: reading and copying, reading and highlighting, reading and taking notes, and reading and generating questions. Students who generated questions achieved better than two of the other three groups on a 20-item multiple-choice test about the reading material. In a much earlier study MacDonald (1986) found that groups instructed in methods for asking questions had comprehension scores higher

PART I: ANTICIPATION GUIDE

Instructions: Before you begin reading *The Jungle,* read the statements below. If you agree with a statement, check the Agree column. If you disagree with the statement, check the Disagree column. Be ready to explain or defend your choices in class discussion.

Agree	Disagree	Statement
		1. Anyone who works hard can get ahead.
		2. An employer has a responsibility for employees' safety and welfare.
		3. Companies that process packaged food should be responsible for policing themselves for health violations.
		4. Immigrants were readily accepted into the American system at the beginning of the twentieth century.
		5. Unions can remedy all labor grievances.

PART II: EXTENDED ANTICIPATION GUIDE

Instructions: Now that you have read *The Jungle* and information related to the statements in Part I, get into groups to complete this section. If you feel that what you read supports your choices in Part I, check the Support column below. If the information read does *not* support your choice in Part I, check the No Support column and write a reason why the statement cannot be supported in the third column. Keep your reasons brief and in your own words.

Support	No Support	Reason for No Support (in your own words)
1.		
2.		
3.		
4.		
5.		

than the scores of groups without this training. Activity 5.11 presents questions generated by students in an elementary science class studying mammoths.

Think-Alouds

Educators have recently been asking for more information about having students and teachers perform **think-alouds,** in which a reader orally "thinks through" a reading by verbalizing his or her thought processes about the passage at any given time.

NAME ___Porche v.___

Directions: Read the paragraph. Then ask yourself, "What was this selection about and the main idea?"

> The sun is a very big star. It heats the earth and moon. The sun lights the earth and moon, too. We play in the sunlight.

This paragraph is ABOUT ___Sun___
and the main idea is ___Sun heats___
___and lights the earth.___ .

Developed by Dana S. Jubilee.

ACTIVITY **5.10** ABOUT/POINT STRATEGY STUDY SHEET

THE CARE AND MAINTENANCE OF YOUR TEETH

This reading is ABOUT:
How to care for and maintain good hygiene for your teeth.
And the POINTS are:
You can get holes in your teeth by not brushing.
Plaque and tartar can do great harm to your teeth.
Plaque combines with a common food substance to form acid that can eat away at the enamel of your teeth.
Fluoride applied to your teeth can reduce your chances of having cavities.

ACTIVITY **5.11** STUDENT-GENERATED QUESTIONS: THE PREHISTORIC MAMMOTH

Was a mammoth an elephant?
How big was the mammoth?
When did they live on the earth? How long ago?
Did the mammoth have tusks?
The caption under the picture calls them "woolly" mammoths.
Why are they called "woolly" mammoths?
How many mammoth fossils have been found?
Where did the mammoth live? Which continents?
Why did they die out?

In a think-aloud a reader may stop and reflect on the thinking he or she is doing to understand the text. Readers talk about visualizations they are making and how prior knowledge is affecting their reading. This brings thought processes into the discussion so that positive learning processes can be replicated in the future (Oster, 2001). First developed by Davey (1983), this procedure represents a modeling technique to help students improve their comprehension. Research on the benefits of think-alouds has shown that they are particularly effective as a diagnostic tool to assess students' ability to use inferences as they read (Laing & Kamhi, 2002). Another study by Baumann, Seifert-Kessell, and Jones (1992) found that think-alouds were as effective as directed reading–thinking activities in teaching the skill of comprehension monitoring. In addition, students who performed the think-aloud strategy demonstrated deeper comprehension-monitoring abilities. Finally, a study by Anderson and Roit (1993) found that students who verbalize their thoughts while reading score significantly higher on comprehension tests. All of this research suggests that think-alouds are an important reflective learning strategy for teaching reading.

At first teachers need to show students how think-alouds work. To carry out a think-aloud, teachers verbalize their thoughts as they read aloud—modeling the kinds of strategies a skilled reader uses during reading and pointing out specifically how they are coping with a particular comprehension problem. The teacher models these reading comprehension techniques, although not necessarily at one session:

1. Forming hypotheses about a text's meaning before beginning to read.
2. Producing mental images (spontaneously organizing information).
3. Linking prior knowledge with a new topic.
4. Drawing inferences from the reading.
5. Reading ahead, rereading, restating, and summarizing paragraphs.
6. Using context clues to decipher meanings of words and phrases.
7. Using strategies to monitor comprehension.
8. Identifying active ways to "fix" comprehension problems.

In think-alouds the teacher talks through a lesson to verbally share the thought process in reading with students.

Using a difficult text, the teacher "talks" it through out loud while students follow the text silently. This training helps struggling students realize that text should make sense and that readers use both information from the text and prior knowledge to construct meaning. Teachers can make predictions and show how to develop a hypothesis; describe the visual images that come to mind; share analogies and otherwise link new knowledge to prior knowledge; discuss confusing points or problems; and demonstrate fix-up strategies such as rereading, reading ahead to clarify a confusing point, and figuring out word meanings from context. Activity 5.12 is an example of a teacher's think-aloud in a high school history class. The teacher is thinking aloud about a letter sent from James Madison in 1781 in reply to an evangelist's request to speak at an Anglican church.

After the teacher models think-aloud a few times, students can work with partners to practice the strategy, taking turns in reading orally and sharing thoughts.

EXCERPT OF A LETTER FROM JAMES MADISON, 1781

(The actual letter is printed with the thinking of the teacher in italics. Parentheses show the thought processes.)

Letter of James Madison 1781

For want of opportunity and leisure, I have delayed till now answering your letter relative to your preaching in the Pine Stake Church. When the Vestry met, I forgot to mention your request to them, as I promised you, till it broke up. Then I informed the members present what you required of them; Who, as the case was new and unprecedented, thought it had better remain as it then stood less the members of the Church should be alarmed that their rights and privileges were in danger of being unjustifiably disposed of.

(There is another paragraph to the letter that is not reproduced here)

I am, Sir, your humble Servant
James Madison
August 23, 1781

I am predicting that this is a letter from one of the colonial Founding Fathers, James Madison, to an evangelist preacher's request to speak at Madison's Anglican church (prediction). *But as I start to read it I remembered that Madison lived well into the 19th century* (prior knowledge) *and would probably have been too young to be an elder of a church at the time of this letter. I am guessing the author is one of Madison's older kin. Maybe it was his father or an uncle* (prediction).

When the Vestry met, I forgot to mention your request to them

What is a Vestry? I picture (imaging) *a group of very old men who run the church. From the context, I would guess Vestry means the leaders of the church* (context clues). *Why would Madison forget to mention this man's request until the very end of the meeting? Could it have been on purpose?* (inference) *Perhaps evangelical preachers would not be welcomed in the staid, old Anglican Church, I am guessing* (prediction). *So maybe he conveniently forgot?* (inference)

The Vestry . . . thought it had better remain as it then stood less the parishioners of the church should be alarmed that their rights and privileges were in danger . . .

Why would the members of the church feel in danger of losing their rights and privileges? Could it be they would fear any influence coming from outside the Anglican Church? (inference)
I think overall (monitoring comprehension) *this letter is a not-so-subtle rebuke of evangelicals of the time and is an attempt to keep the "status quo"—keeping things as they are—on the part of the leaders of one Anglican Church in colonial times. I do know that evangelical preachers at that time were making big inroads in the colonies and were drawing crowds wherever they went* (prior knowledge). *Maybe the Anglican Church feared this* (inference).

HOW AM I DOING ON MY THINK-ALOUDS?

Think-Aloud Strategy	Not Often	Sometimes	Often	Always
Made predictions				
Formed mind pictures				
Used comparisons				
Used prior knowledge				
Drew inferences from the reading				
Read ahead, or reread				
Monitored comprehension				
Used fix-up strategies				
Summarized the paragraph or passage				

Using think-alouds is an excellent way to teach the thinking process to students.

Block and Israel (2004) explain an excellent activity that pairs students for practice in think-alouds, which they call the Peer Think-Aloud Game. The teacher writes think-aloud strategies on flash cards (the researchers have a list of their own, but the think-aloud strategies we just listed could be used), and the students place the flash cards face up so both students can see the strategies. Then one student begins to read orally from the text. The student will stop reading and perform one of the think-aloud strategies when he or she gets to a point at which this is possible. After completing the think-aloud, the student holds up the flash card naming the strategy just completed. If the listening partner agrees that the think-aloud has been completed, the first student gets a point. Then the students switch roles, and the game continues in rotation. Block and Israel recommend practicing only certain designated think-aloud strategies in a session. Students can let the teacher know which strategies they need more practice with and which need to be retaught.

The think-aloud strategy can become an excellent reflective study technique. To extend the Peer Think-Aloud Game, teachers can give the paired students a checklist to self-evaluate their progress, as shown in Activity 5.13.

ONE-MINUTE SUMMARY

This chapter has described activities to be used in the reflection phase of the PAR Lesson Framework for improving comprehension and retaining learning. Whereas the preparation phase of the lesson helps motivate students, and the assistance phase helps build comprehension, the reflection phase helps clarify thinking and focus understanding. In this phase students learn better how to retain information. Full understanding cannot be achieved until students reflect in meaningful ways about their reading. Although a teacher may guide students by providing instructional support, the student's role is crucial at this stage.

In this chapter we discussed the importance of decision making in reading. We explained how all phases of PAR, but especially the reflection phase, help create autonomous learners. We also discussed how communication is a key element of the reflection phase of learning, along with a student's ability to think critically through the learning process. In addition, the key reflection skills of problem solving and analyzing authors' writing techniques were explained. Finally, strategies to teach reflection were described, such as brainstorming, self-generated questions, postgraphic organizers, think-alouds, and text lookbacks.

PAR ONLINE

Visit the *Reading to Learn in the Content Areas* Web site at http://academic.cengage .com/education/richardson for links to the Web sites mentioned in this chapter, tutorial quizzing, and other resources.

END-OF-CHAPTER ACTIVITIES

Assisting Comprehension

1. After reading this chapter, do you have a better idea of why problem solving and decision making are important for teaching reflective thinking? Have you learned how to teach these important skills?

2. Having read this chapter, what ideas for appropriate activities have you learned to help you to reflect on reading with your students?

3. Why is it important to get students to reflect on their reading?

Reflecting on Your Reading

Standard 1.4 of the International Reading Association Standards for Teachers and Reading Professionals states that teachers need to demonstrate knowledge of teaching comprehension, a major component of reading. Take some time to reflect on how this chapter has helped you to teach reflective and critical thinking in reading.

CHAPTER 6

*Through literature I become
a thousand people and yet
remain myself.*

C. S. LEWIS

*We are each of us angels with
only one wing, and we can
only fly by embracing
one another.*

LUCIANO DE CRESCENZO

Moving beyond the Traditional Textbook and Transmission Methods

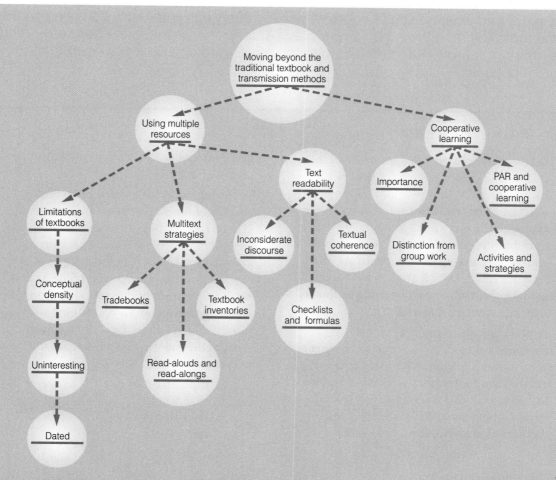

VOICES FROM THE CLASSROOM

Ms. Carson is an energetic and innovative fourth grade teacher in her second year at Urban Elementary. She is about to plan and prepare a science unit about hurricanes and tornadoes. She wants her students to understand the differences between the two storm types, the principles behind their formation, and safety tips and information for dealing with each. She also thought she might find some way to use the same topic to develop math, social studies, and reading lessons.

Her class of 25 includes three students reading well below grade level and four reading well above grade level. Three of her students, Jorge, Maria, and Juan, are English language learners. Although Ms. Carson's school is located on the Atlantic coastline, many of her students have never experienced a hurricane. Only four pages in her science textbook are devoted to the topic, and the copyright date of the text is 1998. She wants to locate some resources that may help, and she wants to try using some peer grouping strategies during instruction.

Where might she find appropriate resources, and what special considerations must she make to provide for the needs of all her students? How might she use grouping, and what must she consider when creating groups? How can she use the same topic to teach the other disciplines? Answer these questions before reading this chapter; then revisit them following the reading to decide if you need to modify your responses.

PREPARING TO READ

1. Do the textbooks provided for use with the courses and classes you teach work for all your students? Why or why not? How do you select materials and resources that will appropriately prepare, encourage, and enrich learning while contributing a sense of inquiry and wonder among your students? As you read this chapter, think about how you can use its information when selecting textbooks and other content material.

2. How do you go beyond traditional transmission models of instruction to engage your students in interactive social and cultural learning experiences? While reading this chapter, look for ways to assist students in developing habits of cooperation and collaboration as they learn how to make decisions and accept responsibility for their own learning.

3. Following is a list of terms used in this chapter. Some may be familiar to you in a general context, but in this chapter they may be used in unfamiliar ways. Rate your knowledge by placing a plus sign (+) in front of those you are sure that you know, a check mark (✔) in front of those you have some knowledge about, and a zero (0) in front of those you don't know. Be ready to locate them in the chapter, and pay special attention to their meanings.

_____ multitext
_____ read-alongs
_____ read-alouds
_____ trade books

_____ readability
_____ inconsiderate discourse
_____ textual coherence
_____ dumbed-down text
_____ rule of thumb
_____ readability formulas
_____ independent-level reading
_____ refutational texts

_____ cloze
_____ maze
_____ positive interdependence
_____ individual accountability
_____ equal participation
_____ simultaneous interaction
_____ jigsaw
_____ interactive guide

OBJECTIVES

As you read this chapter, focus your attention on the following purposes. You will

1. Learn why a textbook cannot stand alone as the only classroom text for reading.

2. Understand the importance of using multiple resources in classrooms.

3. Understand how to determine the match between readers and material to be read.

4. Be able to make appropriate use of readability scores and book leveling.

5. Learn the benefits and techniques of read-alouds for adolescents as well as young children.

6. Improve your own ability to select textbooks and other resource materials.

7. Know the factors that distinguish cooperative learning from working in groups.

8. Learn about the research and practices related to effective cooperative learning.

9. Be able to select and use some cooperative learning techniques to teach reading in the content areas.

Shoe. Reprinted with permission of Tribune Media Services.

Reading in today's content classrooms cannot be limited to course textbooks. Literacy is being redefined to take into consideration the growing number of texts such as CD-ROM encyclopedias, interactive videos, and Web sites (Leu, 2000; Richardson, 2004), as will be discussed in greater detail in Chapter 7. Preparing students to be educated citizens in the 21st century must of necessity include the understanding and ability to negotiate the meaning of text in numerous forms and mediums. Leu and colleagues (2004) recommend combining children's literature activities with the Internet to expand the response to reading in new and more powerful ways. Coiro (2003) maintains that such a combination prepares students for the new literacies that will increasingly define their future. Because understanding these new text formats requires cognitive processing that is similar to reading traditional texts, researchers (Tyner, 1998) are postulating that it is more important than ever to learn how meaning is created in both traditional textbooks and the new technologies. To this end, Thoman (1999) identifies a number of critical thinking questions teachers need to consider when dealing with alternative texts:

1. Who created the message?
2. Why did they create it?
3. What points of view are represented?
4. What techniques are used to attract attention of the reader?
5. How might the message be interpreted differently by different readers?
6. What is missing from the message?

These questions are equally relevant for alternative and more traditional texts.

Textbooks are still the most frequently used teaching resources along with handouts, manipulatives (such as those used in mathematics), and workbooks (National Education Association, 2002). However, many teachers are diverting from the old norm and choosing books and text readings apart from, or in addition to, the designated or assigned textbooks. They are doing this because research (Guthrie, 2004) is demonstrating that students are more motivated when texts and readings are interesting. This chapter has several purposes: to validate the use of books and texts apart from the traditional textbook, to explain ways to determine how readable any chosen text is, to suggest ideas for raising awareness of the need for helping students select and read materials critically, and to provide reasons and strategies for cooperative learning that goes beyond traditional transmission models of instruction. Much of this chapter's content represents the teacher's first step in PAR: preparing learners. Without planning for appropriate resources to teach content, teachers and students will not be prepared to use the vast information resources now available for supporting rich learning experiences. Although we are not advocating abandonment of traditional textbooks, certainly teachers need to explore other book and nonbook options for reading. Dove (1998) suggests that "it is no longer unrealistic to consider the textbook as only one of several resources that teachers can use to plan instruction. . . . Given the diversity of students in today's schools, the one-textbook approach is no longer viable" (p. 29).

Why Textbooks Cannot Stand Alone

The Limitations of the Traditional Textbook

Learning today is often "disjointed and piecemeal" (Jetton & Alexander, 2000). Total reliance on textbooks as the single resource for learners contributes to this disjointed, abbreviated, piecemeal approach. The strength of a textbook is that it can provide within one source a breadth of information, or overview, covering a range of grade- or course-specific topics. But inherent within that strength is a problem: the inability (because of space issues) to provide depth and interest that pique student curiosity and make concepts and content memorable. Textbooks present condensed information about topics and thus are somewhat like encyclopedias. They offer an overview of a topic; they do not offer in-depth reporting. They are often secondary sources that are necessarily brief and condensed. In secondary reports much of the story behind a topic is omitted, and the flavor of any original authors' enthusiasm and style is necessarily lost.

Generally, when teachers assign homework to guide students to find out more about a topic, they want students to research multiple resources. However, teachers are often frustrated when students submit reports for which the obvious only source was an encyclopedia. They would prefer that students read widely about a topic and read primary sources (those written by the authors who originally considered or researched the topic) rather than secondary sources (material written as brief summaries). But by using textbooks as the single classroom resource, teachers model a single-resource approach, and learners tend to imitate this.

Using a solitary Web site for information is much like using only the dictionary.

Because textbooks condense information, their treatment of subject matter can be dry and boring. Hiebert (1999) makes the analogy between a variety of reading resources and a balanced diet. Someone using only one type of reading material may not receive all the nutrients needed to nourish the reading experience—or, we add, balanced knowledge about a content area. Guillaume (1998) proposes complementing textbooks with a multiplicity of resources, including trade books, fiction with content information, magazines, newspapers, and computer software.

Textbooks have also been criticized for their conceptual density (Hurd, 1970) and for their doggedly factual presentation of material (Calfee, 1987). They have been characterized as difficult for students to read and comprehend because the presentation lacks coherence (Armbruster & Anderson, 1984). Too many textbooks are bland collections of facts with not enough emphasis on showing students the relationships among facts or concepts. Textbook writing is often uneven, resulting in some sections that are much harder to read than others. Furthermore, the expository writing found in textbooks is often more difficult for readers than a narrative or journalistic style. The textbook provided for use in any given class may not be the one the teacher wants or needs for that particular class; rather, it may have been chosen by a textbook adoption committee or by the teacher who formerly taught the class.

At times teachers use textbooks that are old and outdated and contain numerous errors in light of factual and conceptual changes within a field of study. NEA (2002) found that one-third of teachers reported using some textbooks 10 or more years old. While teaching in the 1980s, the fourth grade science text a teacher was issued predicted, "Someday we may put a man on the moon," well after our first historic steps there. Living in times when televisions were rolled into classrooms to watch space launches, these students got quite a chuckle at a text that was clearly out of date. This type of problem lends to disinterest, devaluing text, and exposure to incorrect information (Hunter, 2006; Villano, 2005).

The traditional notion of using one textbook for all classroom assignments limits student success. Villano (2005) recommends that textbooks be used as a *guide* for curriculum rather than being allowed to *become* the curriculum. Some teachers have found that because of curriculum changes and prescribed standards and objectives for grade levels, textbooks are not purchased frequently enough to match the changes. Thus outside resources have to be located to assist with the teaching of objectives not addressed within the textbooks students are issued. To add to the problem, NEA (2002) found that one out of every six teachers reported they do not have enough textbooks to issue one to each student. The problem is even more pronounced among urban schools and schools with high populations of students from low-socioeconomic homes, creating what appears to be an economic divide. For various reasons students from urban and low-socioeconomic environments frequently struggle with reading and along with English language learner (ELL) students often need resources beyond the textbook to add interest and facilitate understanding through the power of stories, visuals, and alternative perspectives (see Chapter 11).

Don't forget about electronic resources!

The Strength of Using Multiple Resources

See Chapter 11 for more discussion about diverse learners.

The American student population is growing ever more diverse. It is not unusual for a classroom to include a half dozen nationalities and cultures or for students to speak several languages. There is growing concern that teachers in all content subjects must be adept at offering reading choices that reflect students' interests, cultures, and customs (see Chapter 11). A **multitext** approach is necessary.

USING MULTIPLE RESOURCES IN ADDITION TO TEXTBOOK INSTRUCTION

 How can the resources we have discussed be used to support, augment, and move beyond textbooks? Excerpts of literature, such as read-alouds and read-alongs, are good ways to start. All of these can capitalize on literature and technology.

Read-Alongs and Read-Alouds

Literature and technology can be easily incorporated into existing instruction with no major restructuring of lessons. The teacher can collect and use excerpts of literature as adjuncts to the content being taught. Two plans of action are read-alongs and read-alouds. Using **read-alongs**, the teacher shares an excerpt with students, who

Look for annual book lists posted on the Web sites of several professional associations like the National Council for the Social Studies, the International Reading Association, the National Science Teachers Association, and the National Council of Teachers of Mathematics.

read the piece individually, in small groups, or with the teacher. Using **read-alouds**, the teacher generally reads the excerpt, story, or article to the entire class.

Teachers need to be on the lookout for passages of literature that illustrate concepts in their fields of study. Over time, teachers can compile a collection of examples. Several professional organizations publish annual lists of literature selections appropriate for supplementing or enriching studies and concept development among students. These are often available on organization Web sites. The National Council for the Social Studies, the National Science Teachers Association, and the International Reading Association offer recommended book lists through publications and Web sites. The National Council of Teachers of Mathematics Web site provides lesson plans and information about selected books. Many book lists are annotated and organized by topic and grade. Content teachers might start their personal database of literature selections to augment a content topic. As they come across an appropriate excerpt, they can enter it into the database along with suggestions for its use.

Read-alouds sometimes work more effectively than read-alongs, at least initially, because the teacher can stimulate interest and observe how much attention is given to the excerpt. Read-alouds have been shown to be effective in engaging students in learning (Erickson, 1996; Richardson, 1995a, 2000a; Villano, 2005; Palmer & Stewart, 2005; Ariail & Albright, 2006). Besides promoting a love of reading and modeling fluent reading, teachers cite several reasons for reading aloud. Enhancing understanding, developing interest, demystifying text structures, and reinforcing concepts and content have all been listed as important reasons (Ariail & Albright, 2006). Reading aloud carefully selected passages and stories can build needed background and schemata for greater concept development, thus letting students learn content before having to negotiate texts for themselves (Villano, 2005). While teaching a high school reading improvement class some years ago, one student in particular, Malique (pseudonym), was adamant that the teacher read aloud a portion of the day's reading for the students before they began reading for themselves. When asked why this was so important to him, he responded, "When you read to us, then I know how it is supposed to sound in my head when I read so that I can understand it." Known to be a motivating factor, reading aloud can encourage those who can read but choose not to read (aliterate individuals) to gain new or renewed interest in reading (Lesesne, 2001). However, teachers seem to abandon this practice by the time students start middle school, even though students of all ages enjoy and learn from it (Fisher, Flood, Lapp, & Frey, 2004; Richardson, 1994).

A social studies teacher tried read-alouds to help her students understand myths, legends, and fairy tales of different cultures. After listening to read-alouds, students were expected to read stories from Eastern and Western cultures and then write their own myths. These students were ninth grade honors level, resistant to "baby" activities. Every day during the first unit on India, and every other day during the second and third units on China and Japan, the teacher read a myth, a legend, or a fairy tale during the last 5–10 minutes of class. The class then discussed the characteristics of these stories, as well as their historical merit. Next came the study of ancient Greece, after which students wrote their own myths, legends, or fairy tales based on one of the civilizations studied.

Students were given two weeks to complete their writing assignments, which were worth a test grade; students also could present their stories orally for a quiz grade. The products generated were of high quality. Although good work is expected from honors students, the enthusiasm with which these students participated was greater than usual for this unit. They began to remind the teacher when to start the daily read-aloud time. When the teacher asked her students to evaluate the read-alouds, 63 percent responded that they would like them to continue for other units, and this percentage probably understated their enthusiasm. The teacher recalled, "I really believe more students enjoyed this than even said they did, because they kept looking at each other's papers. I had several students talk with me about the survey after we completed it. The comments orally were much more positive."

Visit the *Reading to Learn in the Content Areas* Web site, Chapter 6, to locate links that support these examples.

In science, one teacher found an Internet site that described the very expensive error in calculations made when the Mars *Climate Orbiter* was sent into space. It never reached its target because one set of scientists calculated using kilometers while the other group used miles. This site provided the perfect read-along "hook" to entice the students into real-world reasons to study metric measurement systems. Another science excerpt can be drawn from Robert C. O'Brien's novel *Mrs. Frisby and the Rats of NIMH* (1971), in which a science experiment works better than expected. Here the scientists divide rats and mice into three groups—control, experimental A, and experimental B—and then inject serums and conduct experiments. The serum works so well for group A that those rats and mice escape and set up their own society. Because this excerpt is several pages long—a whole chapter—it might best be shared through students reading silently and then discussing what constitutes experimental design.

Teachers can find several literature excerpts and many instructional uses for read-alouds in the column "Read It Aloud," which appeared in the *Journal of Adolescent and Adult Literacy* four times a year (Richardson, 1994–1997), or in the monograph *Read It Aloud! Using Literature in the Secondary Content Classroom* (Richardson, 2000a).

ISSUES RELATED TO USING MULTIPLE RESOURCES IN THE CLASSROOM

The classroom physical environment can facilitate the use of literature and technology to support the textbook because the way a classroom is arranged affects the climate for learning and teaching (Kowalski, 1995). According to Gambrell (1995), the availability of books, opportunities not only to read but also to choose what to read, and curiosity appear to motivate both good and poor readers. A classroom arranged to entice readers meets these criteria. When teachers provide bookshelves with literature, folders with newspaper clippings, magazines on racks, and baskets of books about topics being studied, students will be as enticed as any learners who browse in bookstores or libraries and feel the itch to pick up a book. A designated quiet reading spot is a friendly, encouraging touch. If possible, at least five or six computers should be available in the classroom so students have easy access when they need to practice, write, enter data, send or receive mail, or find information on the Internet.

Locating and obtaining these resources may be less difficult than it might seem. In this textbook we mention several resources located by other teachers. Many parent organizations raise money for purchases. Libraries—either public or school—often lend books for extended classroom use. Families may donate books. Sometimes teachers receive bonus books with book club orders. If a school cannot afford several computers for each classroom, perhaps it can establish a mobile or stationary computer lab.

As teachers integrate more literature into their content teaching, they should include multicultural literature. Bieger (1995) describes a four-level hierarchical framework for teaching multicultural literature: (1) looking at the contributions of people from other cultures; (2) adding information about other cultures to the curriculum; (3) changing the curriculum to help students see different cultures from new perspectives; and (4) identifying as well as proposing solutions to social problems that occur in multicultural environments.

Supporting textbooks with literature and technology enhances teachers' abilities to distinguish between the relevant information that textbooks offer and any incorrect, outdated, or abbreviated information that they may present. Exemplary programs do this all the time. For instance, Lafayette Township School in New Jersey was granted the International Reading Association Exemplary Reading Program award (Mahler, 1995). The school integrated instruction in numerous ways—for example, by organizing a Renaissance fair where middle school students read about the Renaissance era, wrote stories, built inventions inspired by Leonardo da Vinci, staged a play, and coordinated activities for students in the lower grades to learn more about the Middle Ages. Mahler points out that this school developed a literature-based program for grades 2 through 8. Alvarez and Rodriguez (1995) describe how high school students in a project called "Explorers of the Universe" learned not only subject matter but also how to think and ask questions as a result of searching in teams for information beyond the classroom textbooks. One group of students began to correspond with two astronomers via telecommunications.

Visit the *Reading to Learn in the Content Areas* Web site, Chapter 6, for a link to this site.

Teachers need to know ways to encourage students to respond to supplemental literature through writing, discussions in response groups, and even art and drama renderings. Later in this chapter we describe drama and cooperative learning response groups; in Chapter 10 we discuss writing activities and learning logs; and post-graphic organizers and other visuals are addressed in Chapters 5, 8 and 10, along with ways to guide students to respond through directed readings.

USING LITERATURE IN THE CONTENT CLASSROOM

Over the past several years, the use of trade books has increased dramatically, especially in elementary and middle schools. **Trade books** are books that are considered to be in general use, such as books borrowed from a library or bought at the local bookstore, rather than textbooks bought and studied as a major course resource. Most trade books are written in either a journalistic or a narrative style; they are interesting resources but are not specifically intended as instructional tools. Trade books are often literature but can also be informational books. Sloan (1984) sums up the importance of the literature component of a classroom:

> The literate person . . . is not one who knows how to read, but one who reads: fluently, responsively, critically, and because he wants to. . . . Children will become readers only if their emotions have been engaged, their imaginations stirred and stretched by what they find on printed pages. One way—a sure way—to make this happen is through literature.

Certainly the familiar story structure found in fiction or historical fiction adds interest and aids comprehension when connections are made to concepts being studied. Students are often drawn to nonfiction as well because of their curiosity about nature and the ways things work (Palmer & Stewart, 2003, 2005; Pappas, 1991). Though narrative has long been the primary genre in use for primary aged students, Pappas's (1993) classic study questioned that practice and introduced the value of including expository text in the early grades. Duke's (2000, 2003) seminal research with first grade students has shown that young learners can effectively process and appreciate informational texts. As more quality books and materials have become available for young students, even emergent readers can find choices that appeal to their interests. Texts written at a variety of levels make it easier for teachers to find supplemental materials to support and enhance the curriculum.

Calfee (1987) notes that trade books offer causal relationships between concepts and provide a better framework in which students can answer their own questions about the reading. Although trade books may have uneven readability, they possess several advantages over textbooks. Guzzetti, Kowalinski, and McGowan (1992) confirm that using trade books improves the affective domain of learning for students; the researchers were impressed "with students' enthusiasm for self-selection of 'real books'" (p. 115).

Haussamen (1995) stresses the value of reading literature for pleasure and interest versus reading to extract information. Because textbooks lend themselves to extraction-type reading, the aesthetic is often lost, and thus any act of reading is devalued. Allowing personal responses to literature can lead students to value reading (Villaune & Hopkins, 1995). "When students are captivated by a particular text, in a specific situation, with a host of environmental supports, they are enjoying a moment of situational interest" (Guthrie, Hoa, Wigfield, Tonks, & Perencevich, 2006, p. 2). Guthrie and his colleagues (2004, 2006) find evidence that situational interest, though not sufficient alone, can work together with other practices to increase long-term motivation for engaging with text. Textbooks can be supplemented by fiction—novels and short stories—and nonfiction trade books in psychology, philosophy, religion, technology, history, biography, and autobiography. Also useful in a broad-based literature approach are reference books, magazines, and teacher-created materials from outside sources such as newspapers. Richardson (2000a) shows teachers how to present lessons that integrate literature with content topics. When teachers bring complementary reading selections to their students, they can help revitalize instruction by opening new avenues for students and teacher alike.

ASSESSING THE READABILITY OF TEXTBOOKS AND RESOURCES

This chapter so far has stressed the importance of using multiple resources instead of relying entirely on a textbook to convey content information. Unfortunately, some studies indicate that as much as 95 percent of classroom instruction and 90 percent of homework assignments for elementary students are based on textbook materials (Sosniak & Perlman, 1990). From our personal experience the situation seems to be similar at the secondary level. Too often teachers organize their instruction around the textbook rather than around the topic. Apple (1988, p. 85) writes, "Whether we like it or not, the curriculum in most American schools is not defined by courses of study or suggested programs, but by one particular artifact, the grade-level-specific text." It makes sense that any textbook or resource material being considered by a teacher needs to undergo thorough examination. Wilson (2004) has called for classroom assessment to be the cornerstone of accountability for teachers. We feel that an important aspect of classroom assessment that often goes lacking is assessment of the textbook and ancillary resource materials. Teachers need to determine what the textbook (or other supplementary content material) has to offer—but also assess possible barriers that may interfere with comprehension and learning. One common barrier is the reading level of the text. Readability considerations when selecting texts and materials can be one useful measure for determining the appropriate match of materials to students within a classroom. If the match is not a good one, the teacher must consider finding materials that better match the readers' background and expertise. Doing otherwise handicaps the readers.

What is this notion of readability, and how does a teacher determine a readability match? Simply stated, **readability** is the match between reader and text. Readability suggests that content is clear, well expressed, and suited to the reader.

Readability is not a formula. It is an exploration of what characteristics within the reader and within the text will create a successful marriage. By examining readability, teachers can appropriately prepare readers to learn. Professional judgment is essential in determining readability; no score or formula can do more than help teachers understand the problems that may arise with reading material. Too many factors are involved for teachers to settle for simple solutions. For instance, careful thought about grammar and its complexity is necessary when considering why students find written material more difficult than oral discussion of a topic. Unsworth (1999) discusses how English writing "packs" many content words into expository text—many more than in the spoken form. One can determine the lexical or grammatical density of a piece of writing by using Halladay's (1994) formula, which divides the number of lexical items by the number of clauses. Unsworth notes that this technique requires a functional grammatical perspective on English.

> Readability is a great deal more than a formula.

Another practice that has gained acceptance and popularity within elementary schools is that of using leveled texts. Various guidelines and leveling systems are used to organize and package sets of books targeting readers at specific levels. Other factors like text formatting, content, predictability, and literary features that go beyond

How does determining readability differ from book leveling?

those generally included in readability formulas are criteria often used in determining these levels. This can be a useful tool for classroom teachers but when used to excess can be a concern (Dzaldov & Peterson, 2005). Dzaldov and Peterson found that "teachers' familiarity with their students' backgrounds, interests, and sociocultural identities is at least as important in identifying appropriate books for students as are lists based on book, print, language, and literary uniformity" (p. 228).

Inconsiderate Discourse

"Your ring adjusters will shape to fit you right by following these simple steps." Wait a minute! Are the "ring adjusters" going to follow some simple steps? As this is written, the subjects, *ring adjusters,* are going to follow simple steps. Doesn't the author mean the reader is supposed to follow simple steps? And will the ring adjusters change shape to fit the reader, or fit the ring, or help the ring fit the reader? The author has written a clumsy sentence in which the relationships between subject, verb, and direct object are confused.

Readers need to work extra hard to understand the meaning of text passages such as these. When confronted with such careless text, the reader must make a decision. Too often students decide that the text is simply not worth the energy. How many readers abandon or postpone mastery of a new software program because its documentation is poorly written or presented? How many parents become exasperated with poorly written instructions for assembling toys? Similarly, some content material, particularly that found in textbooks, may be poorly written and therefore place unnecessary stress on a reader. If this is the case, teachers must identify the difficulties in the material to help readers expend the least energy for the greatest gain.

Poorly written material is recognizable because of its loose organization, its lack of a discernible style, its incorrect syntax, and its incoherent passages. Armbruster and Anderson (1984) call such material **inconsiderate discourse.** When Olson and Gee (1991) surveyed 47 primary grade classroom teachers about their impressions of expository text for their students, 23 percent of them identified text characteristics such as "sentence length, page format, inadequate arrangement and unfamiliar presentation of topics, and lack of aids on how to read expository text" as the greatest problems, whereas another 69 percent cited unfamiliar words. College students indicated in a survey (Smith, 1992) that textbooks are generally boring because passages are too long, the writing style is hard to follow, graphics don't seem to relate to text, and information is either too detailed or repetitive. High school students who were asked to rate their textbooks and indicate how often they read and studied them said that they used mathematics texts most often, followed by social studies, science, and English texts. However, they reported the text they liked *least* was the mathematics text because it was "hard to understand, boring, not specific enough, and poorly arranged" (Lester & Cheek, 1998).

Fortunately, textbooks are changing for the better. Walpole (1999) found that newer science texts are more enticing to readers. She compared science textbooks for third graders written in 1992 and 1995 and found significant improvements in format, organization, text coherence, and illustrations. These factors all enter the mix that makes texts considerate or inconsiderate, coherent or incoherent.

Textual Coherence

For a text to be readable, it must exhibit **textual coherence** (Beck & McKeown, 1988). Textual coherence—the clear presentation of material to facilitate comprehension—can be divided into two categories: global coherence and local coherence.

Global coherence refers to the big picture. Major ideas should span the entire text so that readers are made aware of the global nature of the material and can follow the ideas without becoming confused. The way a text is structured can ensure global coherence. For example, the organization of ideas according to logical patterns, such as clear sequences of cause and effect, aids global comprehension. The style of text is also significant. A narrative style is usually easiest for readers, followed by a more journalistic style. Hardest to read is exposition. It is confusing when a writer mixes exposition and narrative style but doesn't cue the reader. "This is a story about" or "The following description explains" provides clear cues to the style of text to follow. The frequent use of one style also helps the reader recognize and understand the structure of a text. Of course, the content of the material and how well the author matches it to its structure are also important for global coherence.

Local coherence involves the many kinds of aids that connect ideas at the more immediate, or local, level. These aids include cues within sentences—phrases or clauses, for example—between sentences or within paragraphs. When an author clearly identifies the subject and then uses a pronoun to refer to that subject, coherence is much greater than when the pronoun referent is vague and the reader is forced to guess to whom or what the author may be referring. Consider these passages, which Lederer (1987, p. 156) quotes as an example of text ambiguity:

> Guilt, vengeance, and bitterness can be emotionally destructive to you and your children. You must get rid of them.

> After Governor Baldwin watched the lion perform, he was taken to Main Street and fed 25 pounds of raw meat in front of the Cross Keys Theater.

Another type of poorly written text is that in which the author oversimplifies the context. Former Secretary of Education Terrell Bell (Toch, 1984) expressed concern over such textbooks, calling them "dumbed down." In **dumbed-down text**, global coherence may be so simplified that the author can't do justice to the content, and local coherence may be absent because there isn't enough complexity to the text. When important points and intricacies are missing, the reader loses both content and cues. To determine whether textual coherence is a problem, students are often the best resource.

What is the difference between global and local coherence?

HOW TO DETERMINE READABILITY OF TEXTBOOKS AND RESOURCES

Checklists

One way to determine the readability of text material is to use a checklist in judging its overall strengths and weaknesses. Creating an evaluative checklist, which the teacher can use as a guide, ensures both "readability and relevance" (Danielson, 1987, p. 185). One fairly extensive checklist to help teachers consider readability carefully and efficiently is Bader's (1987) textbook analysis chart (see Figure 6.1), which identifies several areas of concern and lists specific items for teacher evaluation. The user is encouraged to summarize the textbook's strengths and weaknesses after completing the checklist and then to decide the implications of the summary for teaching the material evaluated.

The Bader analysis encourages teachers to consider several factors that contribute to readability. The category "linguistic factors," for example, describes word difficulty in six ways, whereas a readability formula considers only the length of a word. The "writing style" category considers four measures of style, whereas a readability formula considers only sentence length. The four other categories are not considered at all in a formula. "Conceptual factors" and "organizational factors" include criteria that many authors identify as having a crucial effect on text difficulty. In addition, the teacher is asked to think about "learning aids" because such aids can make otherwise difficult material easier for students to handle. This category also gives teachers direction in how to guide the reading of otherwise difficult material. For instance, visual aids often make difficult material readable. Because features such as typography, format, illustrations, and book appearance can enhance meaning in a text, Bader includes these items in her last category.

We must issue several cautions when promoting the use of checklists. First, no single checklist can cover all teaching factors. In addition, checklists must be general and rarely cover instructional content. But armed with tools such as those presented in this chapter, and with some knowledge of why determining the difficulty of reading material is important, we believe that teachers can proceed wisely.

The Rule of Thumb

A quick, reader-centered way to determine readability is to teach students to use the **rule of thumb** (Veatch, 1968). Younger students are told to select a book they want to read and to open to a middle page. If they spot an unknown word while reading that page, they press a thumb on the table. For each hard word, they press down another finger. If they press down five or more fingers by the time they finish the page, the book may be too hard. Three or fewer fingers indicate a more reasonable challenge. No fingers means the book might be very easy. Older students can determine readability by using two hands and closing their fingers into fists. One closed fist indicates that the book is just right; two closed fists may indicate difficulty; and only one or two closed fingers may indicate easy material.

Of course students should read the chosen book even if it appears to be too easy or too hard, if that is their wish. The rule of thumb is not scientific and is intended only to help readers make decisions. It is not intended to discourage a reader from trying any book. Its value is that it encourages the reader to be responsible for determining difficulty. This involvement of the reader promotes independence.

FIGURE 6.1 Bader's Textbook Analysis Chart

+	✓	−
Excellent/	Average/	Poor/
Evident	Somewhat	Not
Throughout	Evident	Evident

Book Title _____

Publisher _____

Grade Level _____

Content Area _____

Linguistic Factors

Comments

_____ _____ _____ This book is generally appropriate
to intended grade level(s)
according to _____ formula. _____

_____ _____ _____ Linguistic patterns are suitable to most
populations and fit intended level(s). _____

_____ _____ _____ Vocabulary choice and control are suitable. _____

_____ _____ _____ New vocabulary is highlighted, italicized,
in boldface type, or underlined. _____

_____ _____ _____ New vocabulary is defined in context. _____

_____ _____ _____ New vocabulary is defined in margin
guides, glossary, or beginning or end
of chapter. _____

Conceptual Factors

_____ _____ _____ The conceptual level is generally
appropriate to intended grade level(s). _____

_____ _____ _____ Concepts are presented deductively. _____

_____ _____ _____ Concepts are presented inductively. _____

_____ _____ _____ Major ideas are highlighted, italicized,
in boldface type, or underlined. _____

_____ _____ _____ Appropriate assumptions are made
regarding prior level of concepts. _____

_____ _____ _____ New concepts are sufficiently developed
through examples, illustrations, or
redundancy. _____

_____ _____ _____ Sexual, racial, economic, cultural, and
political bias are absent. _____

Organizational Factors

_____ _____ _____ Units, chapters, table of contents, and
index present clear, logical
development of subject. _____

_____ _____ _____ Chapters of instructional segments
contain headings and subheadings
that aid comprehension of subject. _____

_____ _____ _____ Introductory, definitional, illustrative,
and summary paragraphs/sections
are used as necessary. _____

_____ _____ _____ Topic sentences of paragraphs are clearly
identifiable or easily inferred. _____

_____ _____ _____ Each chapter/section/unit contains a
well-written summary or overview. _____

(continued) ➤

FIGURE 6.1 *(Continued)*

+ Excellent/ Evident Throughout	✓ Average/ Somewhat Evident	− Poor/ Not Evident		Comments

Writing Style

+	✓	−		Comments
____	____	____	Ideas are expressed clearly and directly.	____
____	____	____	Word choice is appropriate.	____
____	____	____	Tone and manner of expression are appealing to intended readers.	____
____	____	____	Mechanics are correct.	____

Learning Aids

+	✓	−		Comments
____	____	____	Questions/tasks are appropriate to conceptual development of intended age/grade level(s).	____
____	____	____	Questions/tasks span levels of reasoning: literal, interpretive, critical, values clarification, and problem-solving.	____
____	____	____	Questions/tasks can be used as reading guides.	____
____	____	____	Suitable supplementary readings are suggested.	____
____	____	____	The book is clear and convenient to use.	____
____	____	____	Helpful ideas are presented for conceptual development.	____
____	____	____	Alternative instructional suggestions are given for poor readers, slow-learning students, and advanced students.	____
____	____	____	The book contains objectives, management plans, evaluation guidelines, and tests of satisfactory quality.	____
____	____	____	Supplementary aids are available.	____

Binding / Printing / Format / Illustrations

+	✓	−		Comments
____	____	____	Book size is appropriate.	____
____	____	____	Cover, binding, and paper are appropriate.	____
____	____	____	Typeface is appropriate.	____
____	____	____	Format is appropriate.	____
____	____	____	Pictures, charts, and graphs are appealing.	____
____	____	____	Illustrations aid comprehension of text.	____
____	____	____	Illustrations are free of sexual, social, or cultural bias.	____

Summary

+	✓	−		Comments
____	____	____	Totals	____

The strengths are:

The weaknesses are:

As a teacher, I will need to:

Original text analysis chart by Dr. Lois Bader, Michigan State University. Used with permission of Lois Bader.

Readability
formulas are
a narrow
measure of
readability.

Readability Formulas

Readability formulas are frequently used for determining the difficulty of material. Fry, a noted expert on readability formulas, quotes Farr as estimating that "over 40 percent of the state and local school districts in the United States use readability formulas as one criterion in textbook selection" (Fry, 1987, p. 339). Readability formulas are fairly reliable starting measures for making instructional decisions about texts.

A quick first look at material to spot potential problems with difficulty can be accomplished by using a readability formula. Because formulas identify a certain grade level of difficulty, they are used most often to report information about textbook difficulty in terms of reading-level scores. A formula can be helpful when a prediction of difficulty is necessary, such as when a textbook adoption committee considers several texts but cannot try out the book with real students. Similarly, a formula may be useful and efficient when a teacher wants to assess the difficulty of several materials that students are to read on their own in the library. A readability formula offers a fairly quick measure and can be used independently of student interaction. However, teachers must not rely on the grade level obtained as an exact measure; it is only a predictor.

HOW READABILITY FORMULAS WORK

Over the years, reading researchers have developed and statistically validated many readability formulas. Some are cumbersome in that they necessitate checking long lists of words. Both the Dale and Chall (1948) and the Spache (1953) measure "word familiarity"—that is, whether students should be expected to know a word within a given passage—by relying on lengthy word lists. The Lexile Framework developed in the mid-1980s is based on the words found in textbooks. Mosenthal and Kirsch (1998) developed a comprehensive measure that focuses on the structure and density that create complexity. Their measure demonstrates that difficulty in reading a document may be due more to the document's complexity than to the reader's abilities.

Essentially, two measurements are used for almost all of these formulas: sentence difficulty and word difficulty. The underlying assumption is that longer sentences and words create harder material. Usually this assumption holds true; sometimes, however, it is questionable. For instance, in William Faulkner's novel *The Sound and the Fury,* several sentences are as much as one and a half pages long, and most readers would agree that the length of Faulkner's sentences makes challenging reading. But could one say that because Ernest Hemingway's sentences are shorter, his material is easier to read? In these cases, one reads to understand style and theme, and sentence length is of little importance. These two sentences better illustrate the point:

> The children played on the playground with the elephant.
>
> We reneged on all prior briefs.

A readability formula would score the first sentence as more difficult, but would it be more difficult for children to comprehend?

The syntactical structure of sentences probably deserves more attention than it receives in readability formulas. For example, sentences in the active voice may be easier to understand than those in the passive voice. Readability formulas do not measure with such sensitivity. Also, word length may be a fairly accurate indicator of difficulty. Just as short sentences seem easier to read, short words generally also seem easier on a reader. First graders recognize a lot of one-syllable words. But *elephant* might be an easier word for young readers than *the*. *Elephant* may be longer, but it's a lot easier to picture an *elephant* than to picture *the!* Because mentally seeing words facilitates comprehension, the longer word is easier in this case. Few readers wish to encounter a lot of long words all at once, but they will be bored by too many short ones. Given these qualifiers, the way most readability formulas measure reading material is common, if not common sense. A few formulas remain popular because they are easy to apply and seem reliable. We describe the Fry readability formula here and the SMOG formula in Appendix B.

THE FRY READABILITY GRAPH

The Fry readability graph (see Figure 6.2) was developed by Edward Fry in the 1960s for African teachers who taught English as a second language. In 1977 Fry revised the graph to include explanations, directions, and an extension to the 17th grade level. The Fry graph offers a quantifiable, efficient way to measure text difficulty.

To use this graph, teachers select at least three 100-word passages from different parts of the material (see direction 1 in the list that follows). For each 100-word passage, two counts are made: the number of syllables and the number of sentences (directions 2 and 3). The three counts of syllables are added, then averaged; the three counts of sentences are added, then averaged (direction 4). The teacher next locates the average for the number of syllables across the top of the graph and the average for the number of sentences along the side of the graph. The point at which these two averages intersect is the readability score. The point will fall within a fanlike, numbered segment on the graph; this number corresponds to the grade-level score. Fry says to count all words, including proper nouns, initials, and numerals (direction 1), and he defines *word* as well as *syllable* (directions 6 and 7). If a point falls in a gray area, the score is unreliable and should be recalculated by using additional 100-word passages.

EXPANDED DIRECTIONS FOR WORKING THE FRY READABILITY GRAPH

1. Randomly select three (3) sample passages and count out exactly 100 words each, beginning with the beginning of a sentence. Count proper nouns, initializations, and numerals.

2. Count the number of sentences in the 100 words, estimating the length of the fraction of the last sentence to the nearest tenth.

3. Count the total number of syllables in the 100-word passage. If you don't have a hand counter available, an easy way is to simply put a mark above every syllable over one in each word; then when you get to the end of the passage, count the number of marks and add 100. Small calculators can also be used as counters by pushing the numeral 1 and then pushing the + sign for each word or syllable when counting.

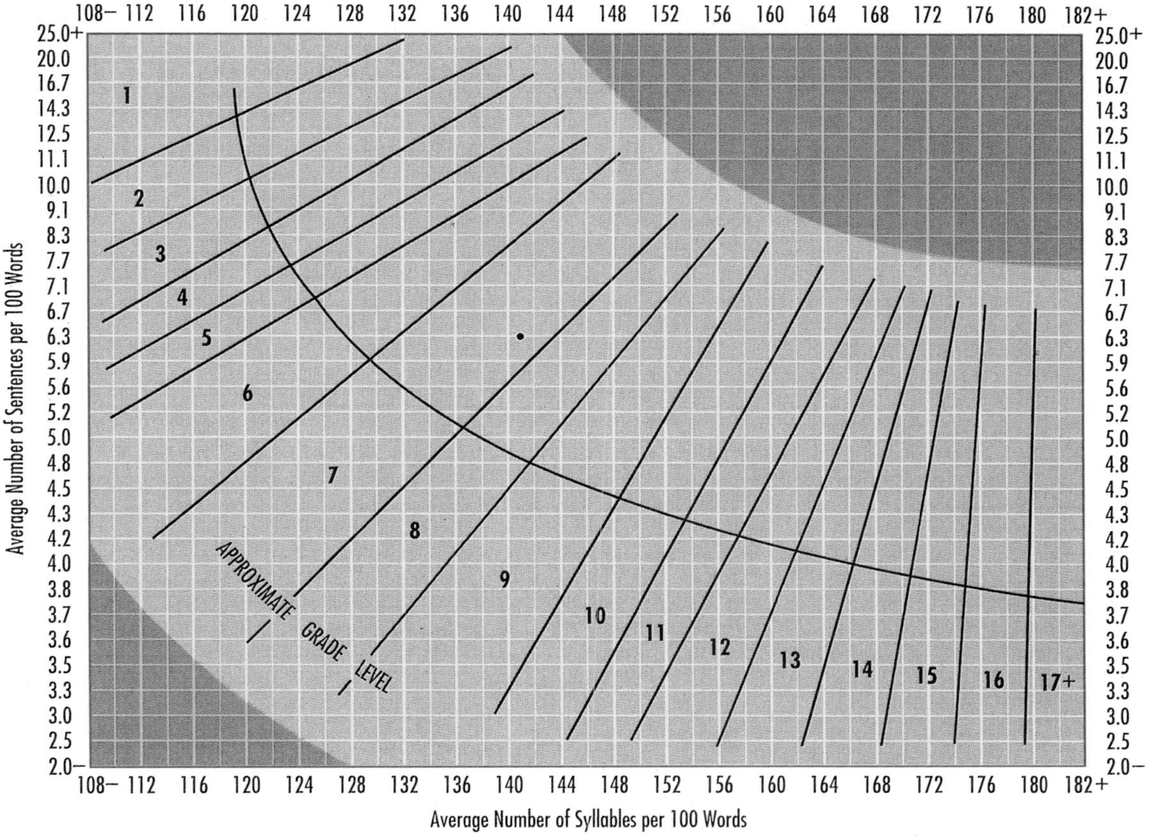
108– 112 116 120 124 128 132 136 140 144 148 152 156 160 164 168 172 176 180 182+
25.0+ 20.0 16.7 14.3 12.5 11.1 10.0 9.1 8.3 7.7 7.1 6.7 6.3 5.9 5.6 5.2 5.0 4.8 4.5 4.3 4.2 4.0 3.8 3.7 3.6 3.5 3.3 3.0 2.5 2.0–
Average Number of Sentences per 100 Words
Average Number of Syllables per 100 Words
APPROXIMATE GRADE LEVEL
1 2 3 4 5 6 7 8 9 10 11 12 13 14 15 16 17+

FIGURE 6.2 The Fry Readability Graph. From *Journal of Reading, 21*, 242–52.

4. Enter the graph with the *average* sentence length and the *average* number of syllables; plot the dot where the two lines intersect. The area where the dot is plotted will give you the approximate grade level.
5. If a great deal of variability is found in syllable count or sentence count, putting more samples into the average is desirable.
6. A *word* is defined as a group of symbols with a space on either side; thus *Joe, IRA, 1945,* and *&* are each one word.
7. A *syllable* is defined as a phonetic syllable. Generally there are as many syllables as vowel sounds. For example, *stopped* is one syllable and *wanted* is two syllables. When counting syllables for numerals and initializations, count one syllable for each symbol. For example, *1945* is four syllables, *IRA* is three syllables, and *&* is one syllable.

The Fry formula is more usable for upper elementary and higher-level material than for lower-level material because at least 100 words are needed for computation. Forgan and Mangrum (1985) developed a way to adapt the Fry formula for shorter materials, and their procedure is described and illustrated in Appendix B.

What is the
difference
between the
Fry and the
SMOG?

For **independent-level reading**—material that students will read on their own with 90 percent or more comprehension—the SMOG formula of McLaughlin (1969) may be used. Directions for using it are presented in Appendix B. In choosing between Fry and SMOG, remember that these two formulas are used for different purposes and that the readability scores they yield are interpreted differently. The Fry formula measures the readability of material used in an instructional setting. Because the teacher explains difficult words and sentences, the Fry score is based on students' understanding 65 to 75 percent of the material at a given grade level. The SMOG formula is intended to measure the readability of material that a teacher will *not* be teaching, such as material that the teacher has suggested a student use independently. Because the teacher will *not* be explaining difficult words and sentences, the SMOG score is based on students' understanding 90 to 100 percent of the material. If a Fry and a SMOG were calculated on the same material, the Fry score probably would be lower.

READABILITY STATISTICS FROM YOUR WORD PROCESSOR

Word processing programs such as WordPerfect and Microsoft Word provide readability statistics for any document being processed. In WordPerfect they can be found under "Grammatik" on the toolbar. In Microsoft Word they can be found by clicking on "Tools" and then clicking on "Options," "Spelling and Grammar," and "Show readability statistics."

Both provide the Flesch–Kincaid grade level, which measures readability based on the average number of syllables per word and the average number of words per sentence. The score is reported as a grade level similar to the Fry grade-level score. Some programs provide various measures with which to compare the Flesch–Kincaid grade-level scores. By typing a few passages into a computer and using these readability measures, you can get a feel for the readability of text without counting words and syllables.

CAUTIONS ABOUT READABILITY FORMULAS

In recent literature, professionals warn teachers to be aware of the limitations of readability formulas. They are not precise determiners of the difficulty of material; they merely predict how difficult material might be for readers.

1. A readability formula gives a grade-level score, which is not a very specific measure of difficulty because grade level can be so ambiguous. Cadenhead (1987) describes this ambiguity as the "metaphor of reading level" and claims that it is a major problem of readability formulas. What does *17th grade level* mean when applied to a topic such as "electrical attraction of dielectric insulation" without consideration of the reader's interests, background, and knowledge? A grade-level readability score gives teachers a start in their considerations of text difficulty—not a complete picture.

2. The lengths of sentences and words are convenient and credible indicators of readability and fit neatly into a formula but are not comprehensive measures. The various factors that make a text coherent are difficult to quantify. Remember that readability formulas cannot get at the depth of the ideas inherent in a text. One cannot compute such factors in a simple mathematical formula.

3. Measures of word and sentence length are sometimes not the most accurate indicators of difficulty. We refer readers to noted author E. B. White's (1951) essay "Calculating Machine," which recounts White's reaction when he received a "reading-ease calculator" developed by General Motors and based on the Flesch Reading Ease Formula. "Communication by the written word," writes White, "is a subtler (and more beautiful) thing than Dr. Flesch and General Motors imagine" (p. 166). His point is well taken: It is dangerous to reduce language to such simplistic evaluation. (For further information about the Flesch formula, refer to the references.) Additionally, background of experience and cultural differences can assist or hinder when reading new material. Reading a text describing space travel and research may prove less challenging for students living in a community of people employed primarily by the National Aeronautics and Space Administration. Reading difficulty may be increased as students who are English language learners struggle with the added challenges presented by figurative language and language structures unlike those of their native languages.

4. The fewer the sections of material measured, the less consistent and reliable the resulting score is likely to be. Even three sections may be too few. If three or fewer sections are measured, a teacher should be cautious about accepting the results. We include the Fry Short Formula in Appendix B but ask the reader to realize that it is already a shortcut. The Fry Short Formula should be used only when material contains fewer than 100 words, such as in books for young readers. However, almost always in such a case, the teacher can assess readability efficiently by relying on checklists and professional judgment.

There is more to readability than readability formulas. Much research has been conducted about texts and text-related matters since readability formulas were developed in the 1920s (Davison, 1984). We know enough to move beyond rigid adherence to mathematical formulas. Although formulas can tell us some things—they yield levels based on the percentage of readers who have performed well at those levels—they tell us a lot less than we want to know. Fry (1989) argues that some reading professionals may not like formulas because they are "so objective." When others argue that readability formulas are not comprehensive enough, his response is, "Readability formulas do not deny all this; they simply state that in general, on the average, the two inputs of sentence length and word difficulty accurately predict how easily a given passage will be understood by the average reader" (p. 295).

A report by Guzzetti and colleagues (1995) recommends that students themselves give considerable input about the readability of texts. The researchers found that a broad sample of students in science classes prefer **refutational texts**, in which both sides of an argument are presented and debated. Also, they found that students prefer expository texts over narrative ones. The students gave researchers specific ideas about how the sample text material they were reading could be improved. The researchers recommend that teachers send students' critiques and suggestions to publishers to make textbooks more interesting and comprehensible.

The concept of readability and the efficacy of readability formulas stir much controversy. We maintain that formulas provide only one measure and should be used with checklists and commonsense criteria to judge the readability of a text for a group of students.

ASSESSING STUDENTS' ABILITY TO USE BOOKS

 Several activities can help teachers assess students' comprehension of text and general background knowledge. The cloze procedure, the maze, pretests, and self-inventories are usually constructed by the teacher. As students understand their own role in the process, they will discover that they can play an important part in their own learning by using THIEVES and completing WIKA sheets (both described later in this chapter).

The Cloze Procedure

The cloze procedure offers an interactive way to assess the match between readers and texts. The term **cloze**, first used by Wilson Taylor in 1953, reflects the gestalt principle of closure, or "the tendency to perceive things as wholes, even if parts are missing" (Harris & Hodges, 1995, p. 33). In the cloze procedure, a passage is cut up so that students can fill it in. The premise is that readers rely on prior knowledge and use of context as they close, or complete, the cut-up passage. Ebbinghaus (1908), in the late 1800s, used a modified form of closure when he conducted his verbal learning and retention studies (described in Chapter 8).

Cloze is from the German word meaning "to cut up."

When Taylor designed the cloze procedure, as we now use it, his purpose was to determine the readability of material for different readers. In the strict format that Taylor designed, a passage of 250 or more words is chosen and words are deleted at regular intervals—every 5th, 10th, or *n*th (any predetermined number) word. The beginning and ending sentences remain intact. Blanks replace the deleted words, and no clues other than the context of the material are provided to the reader, who must fill in those blanks. The cloze procedure can be useful at any grade level if the pattern of deletions is sensitive to the students' familiarity with language. We generally recommend that every 10th word be deleted for primary students because young students need more clues than older, more proficient readers with greater reading experience. Every fifth word should be deleted for older students (fourth grade and above) because they have had more experience with reading and using context.

USING CLOZE TO DETERMINE BACKGROUND KNOWLEDGE

By using a cloze test, a teacher can find out whether students have prior knowledge about upcoming material and are able to adapt to the author's style. The readers demonstrate their prior knowledge because they have to apply it when choosing the best words to insert in a cut-up passage. Their background knowledge helps them fill in gaps; their prior knowledge of language also helps them make good choices. If students complete the cloze with ease, they achieve an *independent-level score,* indicating that they can read the material on their own. If they can adapt when the teacher provides instruction about the material, they achieve an *instructional-level score.* A *frustration-level score* indicates that the material is difficult for readers to understand even with instruction.

Because the purpose of the cloze procedure is to help a teacher quickly see whether students have adequate background knowledge and understand the language clues used in the material in question, scoring should be rapid and efficient. When cloze is used to determine prior knowledge, students are not expected to see the cloze exercise again, and the teacher should not use it as a teaching tool. When cloze is used in this way, exact word replacement is the most efficient scoring procedure. In Taylor's presentation of cloze, only the exact word that was deleted is counted as a correct answer, and research (Bormouth, 1969) indicates that the exact word score is the most valid. When synonyms are accepted, the scoring criteria must be raised and the cloze must be modified. Although scoring seems stringent, the criteria for achieving an instructional level of readability are quite relaxed to compensate for inadequate prior knowledge and the synonym factor. A score of 40 to 60 percent correct is acceptable.

Here are directions for constructing a cloze test to ascertain readers' comprehension in kindergarten through third grade:

1. Select a passage of about 125 words.
2. Leave the first sentence intact.
3. Consistently delete every 10th word thereafter until a total of 10 deletions occurs. Make all blanks uniform in length.
4. Leave the last sentence intact, or include the remainder of the paragraph to give the passage continuity.
5. Make a key of the exact words that have been deleted.
6. Write directions for your students that stress the purpose of the activity—to determine prior knowledge, not to test them. Explain that they are to fill each blank with the word they think the author might have used. Make certain you familiarize your students with the topic by brainstorming about the topic to be covered in the cloze. Remember that it is your job to get real scores from the students, not inflated or deflated ones. Therefore it is important to "warm them" to the task to get the most accurate picture you can of their reading abilities.
7. For each student, count the number of correct responses and multiply by 10 (if 10 blanks were used) to express a percentage.
8. Use these scores to determine whether students will (a) be independent in reading the passage, (b) simply be able to understand the passage, or (c) be frustrated in their reading. A score of 60 percent or higher indicates the independent level; a score between 40 and 60 percent indicates the instructional level. The material is suitable for teaching students with those scores. A score of less than 40 percent indicates the frustration level; the material may be too hard for students achieving

The *use* of the cloze activity determines the scoring procedure.

such a low score. It may be helpful to list your students under each of these three levels, as follows:

Independent	Instructional	Frustration
(scores above 60%)	(scores 40% to 60%)	(scores below 40%)
Material is easy	Material is suitable	Material is too difficult
(list students)	(list students)	(list students)

Here are directions for constructing a cloze test for use with students in the 4th through 12th grades:

1. Select a passage of 250 to 300 words.
2. Leave the first sentence intact.
3. Consistently delete every fifth word thereafter until a total of 50 deletions occurs. Make all blanks uniform in length.
4. Leave the last sentence intact, or include the remainder of the paragraph to give the passage continuity.
5. Make a key of the exact words that have been deleted.
6. Write directions for your students. Go over the directions and discuss the topic with your students before they perform the cloze.
7. For each student, count the number of correct responses and multiply by 2 (if 50 blanks were used) to express a percentage.
8. Use these scores to determine whether students will (a) be independent in reading the passage, (b) simply be able to understand the passage, or (c) be frustrated in their reading. A score of 60 percent or higher indicates the independent level; a score between 40 and 60 percent indicates the instructional level. The material is suitable for teaching students with those scores. A score of less than 40 percent indicates the frustration level; the material may be too hard for students achieving such a low score. It may be helpful to list your students under each of these three levels, as follows:

Independent	Instructional	Frustration
(scores above 60%)	(scores 40% to 60%)	(scores below 40%)
Material is easy	Material is suitable	Material is too difficult
(list students)	(list students)	(list students)

EXAMPLES OF CLOZE TO DETERMINE BACKGROUND KNOWLEDGE

An English teacher facing a new textbook and 11th graders in a school new to her wondered how the students might perform with the textbook and what accommodations she might need to make. These students had been labeled "high ability," but she knew that labels often do not indicate true performance. So she developed a cloze on a 300-word passage from the introduction to the textbook. The passage compared the origins of early American literature to people landing on the moon: Both were adventures and initial explorations of a new era. Would her students have sufficient background to understand this analogy? Would they have enough language skill to read this and ensuing passages with facility?

She administered the cloze during the first week of school, before issuing textbooks, so that she could anticipate difficulties before starting the year. Students were instructed to do their best to fill in the words they thought would fit as a way to help the teacher get to know them better; the teacher assured them that they would not be graded. She never returned the cloze to the students; the exercise was for diagnosis, not instruction. She scored it using the exact-word criterion. In this way she was able to develop a quick profile for 55 students in two sections. One student scored at the independent level; two scored at the frustration level. She decided that with proper guidance the majority of students would bring adequate knowledge to the textbook. She made a note to watch the two students who scored poorly, as well as the high scorer.

As the first weeks passed, she learned that one of the low-scoring students came from an abusive home and could not concentrate on academics even though he was capable. The other low scorer was unhappy to have been placed in a high-ability class because all she wanted to do was play in the band and coast through school. The teacher was able to find appropriate help for each of them. The high scorer continued to perform almost flawlessly on the assignments during the beginning weeks of school. The teacher discovered that this student was new to the school but had been in advanced classes in her previous school. Within the first three weeks, the teacher was able to recommend that the student be placed in an advanced class; the cloze results provided supporting documentation.

The teacher might have missed an opportunity to help these three students had she not administered the cloze. Helpful diagnostic information was learned from an activity that took little time: It was administered to 55 students in 15 minutes.

Activity 6.1 is a cloze for an elementary level social studies chapter about St. Petersburg, Russia. Activity 6.2 is an example of a cloze for high school reading from a technology textbook on the construction of small gasoline engines.

Caution: A cloze procedure can reveal what students already know about a subject and can indicate whether the material is appropriate. The better students do, the more they probably know about the topic. If most students fall in the frustration level, the material is inappropriate because they may not bring enough background to it. Ashby-Davis (1985) warns, however, that a cloze procedure is not like the usual reading that students do. Reading speed, eye movements, and use of context are likely to be different when reading a cloze. Therefore, although a cloze may be a helpful indicator of a student's background in a particular topic, it should not be relied on to tell a teacher about a student's specific reading skills.

USING CLOZE TO BUILD ON BACKGROUND KNOWLEDGE

When a cloze is used for instructional purposes instead of for assessment, the range of possible cloze constructions increases. Instead of exact replacement of vocabulary, synonyms can be considered. In constructing an instructional cloze, the teacher

A VISIT TO ST. PETERSBURG, RUSSIA

St. Petersburg was first called Lovingood. It is on the delta of the Neva River. __1__ is at the eastern end of the Gulf of __2__. The city is built on both bodies of the __3__ and on islands in the river. It is the __4__ largest city in Russia. The city is a major __5__. St. Petersburg is famous for its elaborate palaces and __6__. One of the city's most visited attractions is the __7__ Palace. It was the winter home of the Czars __8__ the 1917 Russian Revolution. The Hermitage is a museum. __9__ has a great art collection. Visitors to St. Petersburg __10__ its beauty and history. It is a majestic city.

ANSWER KEY:

1. It
2. Finland
3. Neva
4. second
5. seaport
6. churches
7. Winter
8. before
9. It
10. love

---

leaves beginning and ending sentences intact, but the deletions can serve different instructional purposes. For example, the teacher may delete all the verbs and then ask students to predict what part of speech the words to replace deleted words must be. Such a cloze activity builds awareness of verbs and helps students become proficient readers of their grammar books. An instructional cloze can also include clues. For example, in Activity 6.3 the teacher deleted important terms about the making of the cell and provided a diagram of an animal cell. Clues from the reading help give a student the answers. At the same time the student gets visual clues in the drawing to help in decision making.

Whatever the design, an instructional cloze can help teachers learn what their students already know and, along with discussion of the choices made, build their knowledge of the material. Discussion also should whet readers' appetites for the reading material that follows, thus giving students a purpose for reading and assisting their comprehension of the material. Because discussing the students' choices is an obvious part of the activity when it is used for instruction, cloze also fosters listening and speaking opportunities. Although word choices are limited to single-word entries, some writing occurs as well. Some teachers find cloze useful as a technique for reflection. Such an interactive cloze procedure is explained in Chapter 9's discussion of vocabulary.

The Maze

A strategy similar to cloze but easier for students to respond to is a **maze** (Guthrie, Burnam, Caplan, & Seifert, 1974), which is especially useful for ascertaining students'

Student Directions: Below is a passage taken from your technology textbook. Some of the words the author wrote have been deleted. Your job is to write in the blank the word that you *think* the author might have used in the same space. Your choices will help me get to know you as readers of this textbook. Good luck and do your best!

CONSTRUCTION OF THE SMALL GASOLINE ENGINE

The internal combustion engine is classified as a *heat* engine; its power is produced by burning a fuel. The energy stored in __1__ fuel is released when __2__ is burned. *Internal combustion* __3__ that the fuel is __4__ inside the engine itself. __5__ most common fuel is __6__. If gasoline is to __7__ inside the engine, there __8__ be oxygen present to __9__ the combustion. Therefore, the __10__ needs to be a __11__ of gasoline and air. __12__ ignited, a fuel mixture __13__ gasoline and air burns __14__; it almost explodes. The __15__ is designed to harness __16__ energy.

The engine contains __17__ cylindrical area commonly called __18__ *cylinder* that is open __19__ both ends. The top __20__ the cylinder is covered __21__ a tightly bolted-down plate __22__ the *cylinder head*. The __23__ contains a *piston*, which __24__ a cylindrical part that __25__ the cylinder with little __26__. The piston is free __27__ slide up and down __28__ the cylinder. The air/fuel __29__ is brought into the __30__, then the piston moves __31__ and compresses it into __32__ small space called the __33__ chamber. The *combustion chamber* is __34__ area where the fuel __35__ burned; it usually consists __36__ a cavity in the __37__ head and perhaps the __38__ part of the cylinder. __39__ the fuel is ignited __40__ burns, tremendous pressure builds __41__. This pressure forces the __42__ back down the cylinder; __43__ the untamed energy of __44__ is harnessed to become __45__ mechanical energy. The basic __46__ within the engine is __47__ of the piston sliding __48__ and down the cylinder, __49__ *reciprocating* motion.

There are __50__ many problems, however. How can the up-and-down motion of the piston be converted into useful rotary motion? How can exhaust gases be removed? How can new fuel mixture be brought into the combustion chamber? Studying the engine's basic parts can help answer these questions.

Answers:

1. the	10. fuel	19. at	27. to	35. is	43. thus
2. it	11. mixture	20. of	28. within	36. of	44. combustion
3. means	12. When	21. with	29. mixture	37. cylinder	45. useful
4. burned	13. of	22. called	30. cylinder	38. uppermost	46. motion
5. The	14. rapidly	23. cylinder	31. up	39. When	47. that
6. gasoline	15. engine	24. is	32. a	40. and	48. up
7. burn	16. this	25. fits	33. combustion	41. up	49. a
8. must	17. a	26. clearance	34. the	42. piston	50. still
9. support	18. the				

From George E. Stephenson (1996). *Power Technology* (4th ed.). Albany, NY: Delmar Publishers, Inc. Reprinted with permission of Thomson Learning.

CLOZE ACTIVITY ON CELLS

Cells are made of smaller parts that do certain jobs. Look at the animal cell on the next page. It is about 1,600 times larger than the actual size of the cell. Notice the cell has a large (1) _____ floating in cytoplasm.

The cell has an outer covering called the (2) _____ _____. The cell membrane lets nutrients, water, and other materials in and out of the cell. The inside of the cell is filled with cytoplasm—a clear, jellylike material. Cytoplasm is mostly water, but it also contains dissolved nutrients and cell parts called (3) _____.

The organelles in the cytoplasm have different jobs. Some organelles help make proteins in the cell. Others release energy from nutrients.

The saclike organelles in the picture—called (4) _____ —store nutrients, water, and wastes.

Find the nucleus in the cell. The nucleus is a large organelle. It has a membrane that surrounds a mesh of structures called chromosomes. The chromosomes are made of (5) _____ —deoxyribonucleic acid. The chromosomes contain instructions that control all the cell's activities. For example, chromosomes control how fast the cell grows and when the cell reproduces.

Different kinds of organisms have different numbers of chromosomes in their cells. Most of your cells have 46 chromosomes. A crayfish has 200 chromosomes in most of its cells, while a sunflower has 17 chromosomes in most of its cells.

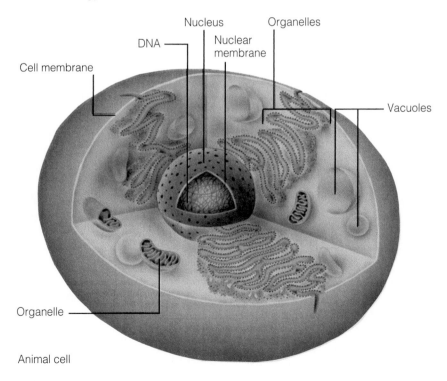

Animal cell

From *Scott Foresman Discover Science, Grade 6,* by Michael R. Cohen et al. Copyright © 1989 Scott Foresman and Company. Reprinted by permission of Pearson Education, Inc.

prior knowledge and understanding of a subject. The teacher selects a passage of 100 to 120 words from a representative part of the textbook and deletes every 5th or 10th word. The students are then given three choices: (1) the correct word, (2) a grammatically similar but incorrect word, and (3) a distracter, which is a grammatically different and incorrect word. Because a maze is easier for students to complete than a cloze, the scoring criteria are more stringent. A maze is a bit harder to construct than a cloze because the teacher must provide three choices for each deleted word; nevertheless many teachers prefer it. Activity 6.4 shows a maze for primary science material.

What are the differences between a cloze and a maze?

Like cloze, a maze builds background as it reveals it. Because choices are given, students who lack prior knowledge have some material to react to. This interaction

---

ACTIVITY 6.4 A MAZE FOR PRIMARY SCIENCE STUDENTS

WHAT CAN MAKE THINGS MOVE?

Air can make things move. It can make a toy frog jump. Squeezing pushes {art / are / air} through a tube.

Air fills the legs under the {frog. / fig. / from.} The legs push the frog to make it jump. {And / Air / At} can make a horn blow.

Squeezing pushes air through {the / them horn. / tug} Then the horn makes a sound.

Moving air {also / as / ago} makes this party blower work. Moving air is a {poor. / push. / pin.}

Wind is moving air. Wind can fill the sails {of / on / or} a boat and push it across the water.

Wind {cane / coat / can} push a pinwheel and turn a windmill. Water can {made / make / mask} things move, too.

Water can make a water wheel {turn. / torn. / told.} It can also push people and things.

Developed by Marvette Darby.

promotes the use of partial associations. Many teachers prefer a maze to a cloze for building background because it is less threatening to students and better promotes discussion. From the maze, students can move right into reading the whole material, practicing the use of context clues.

Pretests of Knowledge

Pretests of knowledge are quick, sensible ways to discover students' background knowledge. Students' self-perceptions on such tests are important factors in how likely students are to achieve. Teachers construct the tests for students to take before they begin reading. The tests are not graded; the teacher and students use them to see what students already know and what they should learn. Pretests can be developed in various ways.

RECOGNITION PRETESTS

Recognition pretests provide a good way to find out what students know about content to be taught. Holmes and Roser (1987) recommend the recognition technique as an informal pretest. Teachers can use the subheadings in a chapter as stems for a multiple-choice format; alternatives are derived from chapter content. Sometimes a teacher designs a pretest from the important points to be learned in a text. One high school drama teacher wrote questions about 10 major ideas in a chapter about the origins of the theater (see Activity 6.5). Student answers helped him see what points needed the most emphasis in the lesson.

KWL ACTIVITY

Another activity designed to find out what students already know about content to be studied is KWL (Carr & Ogle, 1987; Heller, 1986; Ogle, 1986). The *K* stands for what students know, or *think* they know, before they begin to read. The teacher asks students to state facts they know in the first of three columns. The *W* stands for what students want to know. When students tell the teacher this information, the teacher can determine what they think is important about the material. These responses are recorded in the middle column. The *L* stands for what was learned. After reading, the students correct misunderstandings and add new information learned to the third column; they compare and match what they knew in advance with what they wanted to learn and with what they did learn. This activity not only helps the teacher and students determine prior knowledge; it also models an appropriate reflection strategy after reading has occurred.

The What-I-Know Activity is a variation on KWL.

WHAT-I-KNOW ACTIVITY

An alternative to KWL is the What-I-Know Activity (WIKA). Here the steps that students employ better reflect the terminology and steps of the PAR Lesson Framework. To use this activity (see Activity 6.6), students, before reading, discuss what they already know about a topic in the first column. In the second column they formulate questions about what they would like to learn from a reading. During and after the reading they record, in the third column, the answers to their questions. If they can't

WHAT I KNOW ABOUT THE ORIGINS OF THEATRE; OR IT'S ALL GREEK TO ME!

Directions: Circle the answers you think are correct.

1. The Great Dionysia was
   a. a famous Las Vegas magician.
   b. Celine Dion's first stage name.
   c. a Greek celebration with play competitions.

2. "Komos" is
   a. Kramer's last name on *Seinfeld*.
   b. a Japanese robe.
   c. the root of the word *comedy*.

3. The "skene" was used for
   a. making skinny Greek actors look good on stage.
   b. Greek acne medication.
   c. scene building.

4. Thespis was
   a. the first Greek scholar to write a thesis.
   b. Memphis's original name before Elvis.
   c. the first actor.

5. The "chorus" was
   a. that awful group of singers before the Show Choir.
   b. a virus during Greek times.
   c. an important element in Aeschylus's plays.

6. The "deus ex machina" was used to lift a
   a. rude and self-centered actor off the stage.
   b. rude and self-centered director off the stage.
   c. "god" from backstage and plop him in the middle of the action.

7. Greek audiences loved to
   a. pay attention and absorb the whole theatrical experience.
   b. go to Augustus Starbucks after the play.
   c. applaud, hiss, cheer, and even get into fights over the action on stage

8. True or false?

   Women sat alone and in the back of Greek audiences.

9. True or false?

   The altar was always in the center of the stage.

10. Euripides' play *Medea* was
    a. about the media.
    b. about medical miracles of the time.
    c. the Greek equivalent of *The Young and the Restless*.

Developed by Stephen D. Rudlin.

find an answer to a question, it gets shifted to the fourth column, "what I'd still like to know."

When students fill in the column labeled "what I already know," they give the teacher information about their prior knowledge. If students are encouraged to add to their own list after listening to and learning from class discussion, they build background by using other students' knowledge. This information can be placed in the "what I'd like to know" column. Another way to complete this column is to make questions of the subheadings in the material. "What I know now" is the column in which students record information learned from the text. Completing the "what I'd still like to know" column encourages development of comprehension and reflective thinking. The class discussion and recording of associations integrate the communicative arts.

Activity 6.6 represents the results of a What-I-Know Activity produced by a reader of a chapter about the basic telephone system. The reader already knows some information, and she uses her knowledge to create questions based on the

Before Reading		During Reading	After Reading	
What I Already Know	**What I'd Like to Know**	**Interesting or Important Concepts from My Reading**	**What I Know Now**	**What I'd Still Like to Know**
The telephone works by electricity.	How does electricity make the phone work?	Electrical circuits.	A circuit is completed.	I need a simpler book about this topic!
You shouldn't use the phone in a lightning storm.	Why shouldn't you use the phone in a storm?	Electricity travels and current jumps.	The current might jump—electricity might be conducted beyond the normal current by lightning.	A clearer explanation about telephones and lightning.
I can hear another voice and speak in return.	What is the role of vibration in carrying sound from one place to another?	There is a diaphragm in my telephone!	Sound vibrates and causes changes in air pressure. When air pressure hits the diaphragm, it vibrates again, reconstructing the original sound.	I need to be able to explain about the diaphragm.

subheadings in order to complete the second column. In the third column, she answers the questions posed in column two. In the fourth column, she indicates the gaps in her knowledge.

Textbook Inventories

At the beginning of a school year, content teachers might use a textbook inventory as a class activity to help them learn about their students' proficiency in using textbooks. This activity assesses students' knowledge of the parts of a book and can be effective at any grade level—K through 12. Activity 6.7 is based on the "Textbook Treasure Hunt" (Bryant, 1984) and could be used with this very textbook. THIEVES (Manz, 2002) (see Activity 6.8) is a text previewing strategy that uses a memorable acronym. It can be used for most textbooks to encourage students from grade 5 through college level to sneak in ". . .to take as much as they can" (p. 434). Manz suggests questions for use with each component to help students make connections and predictions based on prior knowledge and clues found within the text. Watch for Activity 8.5 in Chapter 8, which illustrates an example of a parts-of-the-book search developed to help students in a computer class become familiar with a word processing manual.

TEXTBOOK TREASURE HUNT

There are many hidden treasures in your textbook. After you have completed the path below, you will have discovered some interesting facts! Write your answers and the page number(s) on which you found the information on a clean sheet of notebook paper.

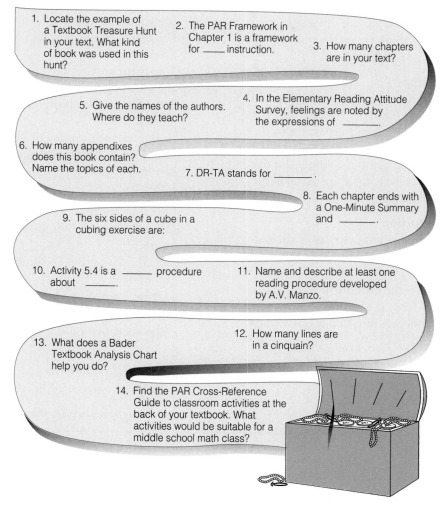

1. Locate the example of a Textbook Treasure Hunt in your text. What kind of book was used in this hunt?

2. The PAR Framework in Chapter 1 is a framework for ___ instruction.

3. How many chapters are in your text?

4. In the Elementary Reading Attitude Survey, feelings are noted by the expressions of _____.

5. Give the names of the authors. Where do they teach?

6. How many appendixes does this book contain? Name the topics of each.

7. DR-TA stands for _____ .

8. Each chapter ends with a One-Minute Summary and _____.

9. The six sides of a cube in a cubing exercise are:

10. Activity 5.4 is a _____ procedure about _____.

11. Name and describe at least one reading procedure developed by A.V. Manzo.

12. How many lines are in a cinquain?

13. What does a Bader Textbook Analysis Chart help you do?

14. Find the PAR Cross-Reference Guide to classroom activities at the back of your textbook. What activities would be suitable for a middle school math class?

Wray (1994) describes the roles of text author, student, and teacher as interactive. He encourages students to consider the author's role in clarifying meaning through text. This can be done only when teachers support students in becoming critics rather than remaining passive recipients. As students thoughtfully examine texts while making decisions and taking action, knowledge and its application goes

T—Title
- What is the title?
- What do I already know about this topic?
- What does it have to do with the preceding chapter?
- Does it express a point of view?
- What do I think we will be reading about?

H—Headings
- What does this heading let me know I will be reading about?
- What is the topic of the paragraph beneath it?
- How can I turn this heading into a question that is likely to be answered in the actual content?

I—Introduction
- Is there an opening, perhaps italicized?
- Does the first paragraph introduce the chapter?
- What does the introduction let me know I will be reading about?
- Do I know anything about this already?

E—Every first sentence in a paragraph
- What do I think this chapter is going to be about based on the first sentence in each paragraph?

V—Visuals and vocabulary
- Are there photographs, drawings, maps, charts, graphs?
- What can I learn from them?
- How do the captions help me better understand the meaning?
- Is there a list of key vocabulary terms and definitions?
- Are there important words in boldface type throughout the chapter?
- Do I know what the boldfaced words mean?
- Can I tell the meaning of the boldfaced words from the sentences in which they are embedded?

E—End-of-chapter questions
- What do the questions ask?
- What information do they mark as important?
- What information do I learn from the questions?
- Let me keep in mind the end-of-chapter questions so that I may annotate my text where pertinent information is located.

S—Summary
- What do I understand and recall about the topics covered in the summary?

Adapted from Manz, 2002, pp. 434–435.

beyond the classroom walls. Lent (2006) reminds us that often when students reach high school they become disengaged from learning and may look upon it as something they are *made* to do rather than as something beneficial and enjoyable:

> For students to become engaged in a subject, they must be both immersed in it and intrigued by it—and they must believe that their new learning has relevance to their lives. Consider why adults think critically: to solve a problem, satisfy curiosity, or increase knowledge. Rarely do we dig into learning just for the purpose of passing a test. (p. 69)

One way of enlisting students to become active learners is to plan and involve them in collaborative and cooperative learning endeavors.

THE IMPORTANCE OF COOPERATIVE LEARNING

Cooperative learning has been found to be both an effective instructional method (Slavin, 1996; Johnson, Johnson, & Stanne, 2000; Roser & Keehn, 2002; Rohrbeck, Ginsburg-Block, Fantuzzo, & Miller, 2003; Madrid, Canas, & Ortega-Medina, 2007) and a successful way to enhance social and academic development among children (Slavin, 2000; Deen, Bailey, & Parker, 2001; Johnson & Johnson, 2003; Boaler, 2006). The end product of cooperative learning is collaboration and joint ownership. Studies show that cooperative learning benefits students by getting them more actively involved (Slavin, 1995). Also, researchers have found that students not only feel more engaged but also perceive that their learning task is more important when working in a small group rather than during large-group instruction (Peterson & Miller, 2004).

Slavin (1991) reviewed 60 studies that contrasted the achievement outcomes of cooperative learning and traditional methods in elementary and secondary schools. His conclusions were as follows:

1. Cooperative learning improves student achievement. The groups must have two important features: group goals and individual accountability.

2. When students of different racial or ethnic backgrounds work together toward a common goal, they gain liking and respect for one another. Cooperative learning improves social acceptance of mainstreamed students by their classmates and increases friendships among students in general.

3. Other outcomes include gains in self-esteem, time on task, attendance, and ability to work effectively with others.

In contrast, some studies show that collaboration doesn't always happen in cooperative groups (Blumenfeld, Marx, Soloway, & Krajcik, 1997). Success of the groups depends, in large measure, on the cohesiveness of students in the group, individual students' willingness to complete the task, and whether the task is considered worthwhile (Leonard & McElroy, 2000). Students with special needs may not benefit if certain aspects important to their participation are not monitored (McMaster & Fuchs, 2002, 2005). If well-meaning or impatient group members complete tasks for their less able peers, they remove the opportunity for those children to make a contribution. Care must be taken to assign tasks with appropriate levels of difficulty so all learners can provide input important to meeting group goals. Each student must be held accountable for participating and learning. Mastropieri and her colleagues (1998) studied the effects of cooperative learning during a seven-week science unit among three classes of fourth graders. Cooperative learning was used in one of the classes, and within that class there were five learners with special needs. These learners were placed in groups with classmates known to work well with peers having special needs. Students in the cooperative learning class outperformed those in the two comparison classes on posttests, and those with disabilities scored near the average score in their own class and above the average score of the comparison classes.

The value of cooperative learning for gifted students has been questioned because of research that suggests these students benefit both cognitively and affectively from working in homogeneous groups (Feldhusen, 1989; Kulik & Kulik, 1990; Fiedler, Lange, & Winebrenner, 2002). Because cooperative groups are typically heterogeneous, the value of their use with gifted students has been under scrutiny. Some are concerned that it is unfair to expect these students to always be the tutors taking on the role of teacher (Robinson, 2003). Boaler (2006) found that although higher-ability students initially complained about having to spend too much time explaining things to peers, they thought about it differently over time. Students felt their own understanding deepening through the explanations and examples they devised to help peers. They also gained new respect for their peers as previously unrecognized strengths and talents surfaced as they worked on a variety of projects. Huss (2006) points out that the purpose or objectives of the tasks assigned can make a difference. Many of Slavin's (1990) and Johnson and Johnson's (1974) structures are designed to work with a transmission model of instruction, letting students practice and master skills and information. Other structures are open-ended and lend themselves to a transformation model, letting students solve problems and create products and ideas. Huss contends that when working with gifted students, "heterogeneous groups should be reserved for challenging, creative, open-ended, and higher-order thinking tasks" (p. 20). Basic information can be gathered and used to make decisions and design solutions that provide a challenge for all the learners. "Collaborative formats that emphasize the development of higher levels of understanding and that require students to explain and justify their ideas can promote the learning of both gifted and nongifted students as they interact together" (Patrick, Bangel, Jeon, & Townsend, 2005, p. 103). Cooperative groups can also allow students to develop leadership skills. Time can be allotted for homogeneous groupings for specific topics and purposes. Hancock (2004) found that students who work together appear to have a higher regard for school and for the subjects they are studying and are more confident and self-assured. As a result, both motivation and achievement improve.

Distinguishing Cooperative Learning from Group Work

Cooperative learning is more than grouping students together to work. It is predicated on the ideas that small groups of students work together to accomplish shared goals and that each group member accepts responsibility for helping fellow group members learn. Teams are formed and ground rules established so that students understand the basic principles:

1. **Positive interdependence:** Group success is positively correlated with the success of individuals within the group. Members of the group must understand that they are in the project together—and that by taking responsibility for their parts and helping each other, they all gain.

2. **Individual accountability:** Each group member is responsible for his or her role or task and will ultimately have to demonstrate his or her understanding and learning. So while students can work as a team to learn the skills, concepts, or information, the teacher may choose to formally grade only individual assignments.

3. **Equal participation:** Turn allocation or division of labor can be used to structure group tasks so that each contributes and no one receives a "free ride."

4. **Simultaneous interaction:** Tasks are structured so that everyone is working at the same time. This is quite unlike most classroom structures, in which one student at a time may be called on to perform while all the others sit and listen (Kagan, 1994).

Another feature that distinguishes cooperative learning from group work is the development and use of interpersonal and social skills that contribute to positive interaction among students. Students learn the skill of working together as they discuss what and how material can best be learned. However, it cannot be assumed that students have the social skills to work productively as a group. These have to be taught. Helping students realize and understand appropriate comments, questions, tones, and behaviors that contribute to rather than interfere with learning is important to the success of cooperative learning. Taking time to explicitly teach and scaffold these skills is well worth the effort. For younger students this may involve demonstrations and role-playing. Having older students decide the ground rules as a class (usually no more than five) and posting them as reminders works well.

Upon completion of a task or project, students can use checklists or criteria for analyzing and evaluating how well they functioned as a group. After debriefing, new team goals can be set for future cooperative work. McKeachie (2002) makes these four points concerning ways to improve what he calls "peer learning":

1. Have students discuss what makes a group effective and why it is valuable to work together as a team.

2. Make sure students know exactly what the task is. To check on this, have students report on the nature of the task and what all the parameters are.

3. Move around the room a great deal to monitor the groups and make certain students are on the right course.

4. Help students develop the skills necessary for effectively working together.

Why Cooperative Learning Is Effective

Weinstein (1987) suggests that cooperative learning strategies are successful in aiding comprehension and retention because they fall into one or more of what she calls "categories of learning strategies"—processes and methods useful in acquiring and retrieving information. Weinstein proposes five categories of learning strategies:

1. *Rehearsal strategies:* Techniques discussed in this chapter include cooperative reading activity and think–pair–share.

2. *Elaboration strategies:* Techniques discussed in this chapter include jigsaw, paired reading, and three-step interview.

3. *Organizational strategies:* Techniques discussed in this chapter include cooperative graphing and cooperative webbing.

4. *Comprehension-monitoring strategies:* Techniques discussed in this chapter include rallytable and numbered heads together.

5. *Affective strategies:* Techniques discussed in this chapter include paired reading and the positive rewards of learning in groups.

In underscoring the importance of cooperative learning, we wish to reemphasize a point made frequently throughout this book: Learning is difficult in a hurried, pressured classroom environment. A first grader recently complained, "The teacher never lets me finish. I never have enough time to finish." This is a lament that holds true in all too many classrooms. Jeremy Rifkin, in his book *Time Wars* (1987), argues that we appear to be trapped in our own technology. Rifkin maintains that the constant pressure to become more efficient causes Americans to feel that they do not have enough time to get things done. This pressure, which permeates classrooms, is detrimental because all types of classroom effort succeed best in a calm, unhurried atmosphere in which students are free to explore ideas, develop creativity, solve problems, and be thoughtful and reflective.

PAR and Cooperative Learning

With cooperative group structures, we recommend a stylized three-step process analogous to the steps in the PAR Lesson Framework described in Chapter 1. In the preparation phase, individual students should commit to something, usually written, to be shared later with the group. In this individual phase of the lesson, the teacher attempts to get a *commitment* from the student. This can be difficult because students today often do not wish to commit to anything; they sometimes prefer not to get involved in classroom activities. However, a sense of involvement is crucial to successful group interaction. Lack of commitment is the reason so much group work degenerates, with students getting away from the subject to be discussed or the problem to be solved. Rarely will commitment be generated by teacher assignment and threat or reward of a grade. Students need to be invested in their learning, and a commitment accomplishes that (Leki, 2001).

The second phase involves the actual work to be done in groups. The key word here is *consensus.* In the group phase the students should share what they have done individually and arrive at a consensus, whenever possible, on the best possible answer. The teacher provides much assistance in this phase by moving from group to group to help students with areas of difficulty and to make sure groups stay on topic.

In the third phase, involving reflection, the teacher may lead a discussion with the groups—an exercise in *arbitration.* The teacher acts as a judge or a mediator to resolve difficult points of the lesson on which students could not come to consensus. Also, in this phase groups may give reports to the whole class on their findings.

To recap, here are the three phases of good group process:

Phase I: Individual phase; key concept—commitment.

Phase II: Group work; key concept—consensus.

Phase III: Teacher-led discussion; key concept—arbitration/mediation.

Teachers often express frustration with the results of group work. One solution is to have students role-play different scenarios in which certain members of a group

Try to practice the three steps for better grouping in your own classes in the near future.

might sabotage the group effort. When students consider for themselves possible obstacles to the success of their group work and possible solutions, they become more productive in groups. Swafford (1995) describes a technique she uses with college students. Groups are given one of three scenarios in which one person in a group is not participating at all, underparticipating, or overparticipating. By discussing these problems and acting out solutions for the rest of the class, everyone experiences the process of commitment, consensus, and arbitration in a friendly atmosphere.

Learning is enhanced when cooperative learning teams are emphasized in content teaching (Abrami, Chambers, d'Apollonia, Farrell, & DeSimone, 1992; Johnson & Johnson, 1987; Meloth & Deering, 1992; Vermette, Harper, & DiMillo, 2004). Australian researchers Gillies and Ashman (1998) trained first and third grade students in formal and informal collaboration techniques during the teaching of 10 social studies units. These students learned more content while in cooperative teams and thereby improved decision making. The study points to the benefit of teaching young children to learn cooperatively and use decision-making techniques. Roser and Keehn (2002), in a study of student collaboration and inquiry during a social studies unit on the Texas revolution, found that student knowledge increased significantly. Misconceptions decreased, and a positive motivation effect was found as well.

Activities for Promoting Cooperative Learning

In the remainder of this chapter we explain reading, writing, and listening activities that involve sharing, collaboration, and cooperative learning. They all work best in a relaxed classroom atmosphere where teachers can guide students in their efforts to work cooperatively. Some of the more basic strategies like rallytable, numbered heads together, and paired reading can easily be adapted to various content areas and can be used at any stage of PAR.

RALLYTABLE

For rallytable (Kagan, 1994), just as for jigsaw, an open-ended question or problem is posed. Within teams of four, students are paired. Each pair passes one piece of paper back and forth. Each time the paper is received, the student writes an answer until time is called. Pairs then share and compare answers. Teams can categorize and illustrate their responses using a graphic organizer.

NUMBERED HEADS TOGETHER

This strategy (Kagan, 1994) is most often used for prior knowledge assessment or review before an exam. Students in teams of four count off so that each has a different number. The teacher gives a question or problem and a time limit for reaching a solution. All four students work together to determine an answer and make sure that everyone on their team knows the answer or a series of answers if the question has several parts. The teacher then randomly calls a number from 1 to 4. All students with that number raise their hands, and the teacher calls on one of them. Two variations on this strategy can increase participation. First, allowing think time before working together gives struggling students a better chance to arrive at an answer. Another variation is to provide white boards or slates for teams to record answers that can be held up simultaneously by the team members from each team when their numbers are called.

PAIRED READING

A strategy that works well with middle school and secondary students is paired reading, developed by Larson and Dansereau (1986). Students begin by reading a short assignment and then divide into pairs. One partner is designated a "recaller" and the other a "listener." The recaller retells the passage from memory; the listener interrupts only to ask for clarification. Then the listener corrects ideas summarized incorrectly and adds important ideas from the text material that the recaller did not mention. During the time the listener is clarifying, the recaller also can add clarification. In this manner, the two students work together to reconstruct as much as possible of what they read. The pair can use drawings, pictures, and diagrams to facilitate understanding of the material. Students alternate the roles of recaller and listener after each reading segment, which may number four or five during one class period. Wood (1987) notes that paired reading succeeds because it is "based on recent research in metacognition, which suggests that without sufficient reinforcement and practice, some students have difficulty monitoring their own comprehension" (p. 13). Paired reading is also based on elaboration strategy, which, according to Weinstein (1987), helps students learn new concepts by drawing on their prior experiences.

THREE-STEP INTERVIEW

Another multipurpose strategy designed for groups of four but adaptable for other group sizes is the three-step interview (Kagan, 1994). A question or topic is proposed for interviews. In groups of four, members partner for the first step. Partner one interviews partner two. For the second step, partner two interviews partner one. Finally, each of the four team members shares with his or her group what was learned. This strategy is useful for exploring prior knowledge, making predictions, or sharing personal connections related to a topic in the preparation phase of a lesson. It may also follow a lesson or unit in the reflection phase to examine knowledge gained, lesson applications, or remaining questions. Affective as well as cognitive aspects of the objectives being taught can be explored. This strategy provides a structure for role-playing when students consider how a character in a story might respond or how positions or viewpoints of historical figures might shape their answers. Or they might consider how different people from various professions can use a particular mathematical formula, procedure, or operation.

JIGSAW

Aronson (1978) describes a cooperative learning strategy called **jigsaw**, named for its resemblance to a jigsaw puzzle. In this strategy, each student in a five- or six-member group is given unique information about a topic that the group is studying. After reading their material, the students meet in "expert groups" with their counterparts from other groups to discuss and master the information. In a variation called jigsaw II (Slavin, 1980), all students are first given common information. Then student "experts" teach more specific topics to the group. Students take tests individually, and team scores are publicized in a class newsletter.

Jigsaw uses two distinct grouping patterns: heterogeneous study groups and homogeneous discussion groups. Study groups are arranged heterogeneously by ability or age level to learn about subtopics. The purpose of the study groups is to allow each member to become expert in a particular topic in common with other group members. Discussion groups are arranged homogeneously by ability or age level to discuss the different subtopics that members studied in their study groups. The purpose of the discussion groups is to allow each member to share his or her expertise with others who share a common perspective.

The number of members in each discussion group must equal or exceed the number of study groups. This is to ensure that at least one discussion group member is in each study group. For example, a class of 22 students might be divided into three groups by reading ability—say, one group of seven grade-level readers, a group of six low-level readers, and a group of nine average-ability readers. These could be the homogeneous discussion groups of jigsaw. Discussion groups would then count off by fours to establish the heterogeneous study groups, thus ensuring equal representation of the reading groups in each study group.

Suppose the topic under discussion is "the life of the Native American," and the subtopics are "traditional myths and legends," "occupations and products," "lifestyles," and "origin and history." Each study group is assigned one of the subtopics to research, dividing the available materials and informational resources among its members. After each member completes his or her assignment, the study group meets for a sharing session. Each member teaches the other members what he or she learned about the subtopic, so that all members become experts on the assigned subtopic. They bring the results of their study back to the discussion group for sharing with students who have become experts on other subtopics. In this way, all students have the opportunities to do a small amount of research, to present their findings, and to listen to and learn from other students.

Another technique similar to jigsaw is called *group investigation,* developed as a small-group activity for critical thinking (Sharan & Sharan, 1976). In this strategy, students work in small groups, but each group takes on a different task. Within groups, students decide what information to gather, how to organize it, and how to present what they have learned as a group project to classmates. In evaluation, higher-level thinking is emphasized.

COOPERATIVE READING ACTIVITY

Opitz (1992) describes a strategy for emphasizing cooperative study called *cooperative reading activity (CRA),* which he offers as an alternative to ability grouping. It entails locating a reading selection and breaking it into sections, having students individually read and identify important points of particular sections, and forming groups in which students who have read the same section come to an agreement on essential points. Each group, in turn, is expected to share its findings with the rest of the class. Opitz suggests the following steps for constructing a CRA:

1. Choose selections that are already divided by headings into sections roughly equal in length. A selection with an interesting introduction is helpful.

2. Count the sections of the selection and determine the number of students in each group. Generally groups of four are ideal.

3. Prepare copies of the text you will use for the CRA. Prepare enough copies so that each group member will have a cut-and-paste version of the proper section and a card with the section heading, which will be used to assign students to groups.

4. Design a form that readers can use to record important information learned from the reading (see Activity 6.9 for an example from elementary science).

To carry out a CRA, research suggests that students first read their sections and record important concepts. When students finish reading and completing their record sheets, they get into groups and each person reads the important points out loud from his or her record sheet. After everyone has a turn, each group lists important details, using a marker on a piece of chart paper. If details are similar, students still write them on the group list. Then other details that students feel are important are added. Students must come to an agreement before a detail goes on the list.

When the work is completed, each group in turn reads its list to the class. Students are held accountable for all the information presented. Lists are then posted for all to see. In this manner, the groups construct cooperatively the essential meanings of the text.

COOPERATIVE INTEGRATED READING AND COMPOSITION (CIRC)

Slavin (2001) describes a way of teaching reading and writing in upper elementary grades through stressing cooperative groups. In *cooperative integrated reading and composition (CIRC),* teachers use basic reading texts and traditional reading groups

---

ACTIVITY 6.9 INDIVIDUAL RECORD SHEET FOR A COOPERATIVE READING ACTIVITY IN ELEMENTARY SCIENCE

NAME *Samika*   SECTION *Three Types of Rocks*

FOUR IMPORTANT FACTS OR DETAILS:

_____ 1. Igneous, sedimentary, and metamorphic rocks are the three main types.

_____ 2. Igneous rocks form from molten rock that can cool slowly if it is below the surface of the earth, or quickly if it is near the surface.

_____ 3. Sedimentary rocks form in layers that are made when pressure is put on sediments.

_____ 4. Metamorphic rocks are formed when lots of pressure is put on old rocks way below the surface of the earth.

---

but assign pairs of students from different reading groups to meet and work on specialized tasks. For instance, students in the pairs might read to each other, make predictions about the reading, summarize stories, write responses to stories, work together on getting the main ideas of stories, and work on vocabulary skills. Writing is especially stressed in the groups—with the stated goal being to publish student writing. The teams have regular quizzes on their work, but one unique feature of this approach is that students do not take the quiz until teammates say they are ready. Slavin says research shows CIRC to be highly effective in teaching reading and writing to elementary children.

INTERACTIVE GUIDE

Wood (Wood, 1992; Wood, Lapp, & Flood, 1992) offers the **interactive guide** as an effective solution for teachers who find that groups of students within a class need additional help with a difficult reading passage. The interactive reading guide allows a combination of individual, paired, and small-group activity throughout a learning task. According to Wood, such a guide is based on two assumptions: (1) Students need differing amounts of time to complete a task; and (2) sometimes the best way for students to learn a subject is through interacting with other students.

After teachers explain the use of the guide, students are given group assignments and are asked to work portions of the guide individually, in pairs, in small groups, and with the class as a whole. The teacher may use the guide with the whole class or with a portion of the class that needs a slower pace on a particular phase of the lesson. Activity 6.10 provides an example of an interactive reading guide used in mathematics.

COOPERATIVE GRAPHING

Another excellent activity for teaching cooperative study can be termed *cooperative graphing*. Students work in groups to rate the importance of concepts in a chapter; the ratings appear in the form of a graph. In the second part of the lesson, students work cooperatively to justify their ratings.

Teachers can construct study guides for a cooperative graphing exercise such as the one shown in Activity 6.11. The activity can be modified for English classes or whenever story structure is being studied by changing the "most important–least important" continuum of the graph to "most liked–least liked" to let students rate how they empathized with characters in the story. This is an excellent activity for teaching both cooperative study and graphing.

COOPERATIVE WEBBING

This structure provides a vehicle for discussing and clarifying understanding before or after reading a text or passage. The group should first discuss and draft a list of ideas before making a larger poster-sized web. The discussion helps clarify understanding and eliminate duplication. The draft encourages consensus on the shape and structure the web will take to demonstrate relationships among the elements.

Each student in a group should use a different marker color to record his or her ideas on the common web. A legend can identify color designations for the students.

△ Work individually   ⊠ Work in groups

△△ Work in pairs   ☐ Work as a whole class

Factoring

☐   1. Discuss instructions for each set of problems pp. 179–180.

☐   2. Review important vocabulary; check for inclusion in notes.

△   3. Work problems 9 & 10, p. 179.

△   4. Work problems 21 & 22, p. 180.

⊠   5. Complete problems 1–4. Discuss which factor is needed.

△△   6. Complete problems 5–8. Compare with group and discuss results.

△△/⊠   7. Continue working problems 11–20. Check with other group members for accuracy.

⊠   8. Work even problems 22–42. If disagreement occurs, first check g.c.f., then verify by distribution.

☐   9. Question-and-answer time for general concerns. Time for extension problems.

Developed by Cheryl Keeton; adapted from Wood (1992).

GAMES INVOLVING COOPERATION IN LEARNING

The activity TRIP (think/reflect in pairs) is a way to help students think reflectively and review before a test. Activity 6.12 shows TRIP cards developed for the study of Shakespeare's *Othello;* students must work cooperatively in pairs to think reflectively, work together, practice writing, and hear each other's views about the play.

In Chapter 8 we describe note-taking procedures. Cooperative group work is very helpful for teaching two-column note taking. After students record and reduce their notes, the teacher has students form pairs or small groups to compare their

COST FACTORS THAT INFLUENCE DECISIONS

Part I. Make a graph of how important the following concepts are, from most important to least important. An example is done for you.

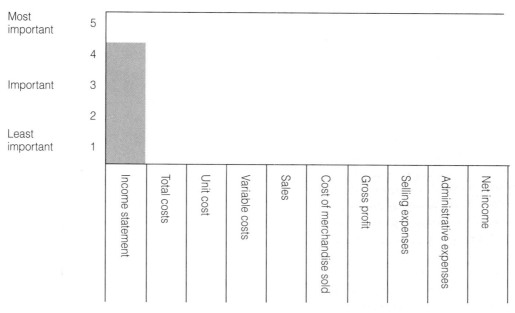

Part II. Work in small groups to justify your answers.

I gave _____ an importance of 5 (most important) because
_____
_____ .

I gave _____ an importance of _____ because
_____
_____ .

I gave _____ an importance of _____ because
_____
_____ .

I gave _____ an importance of _____ because
_____
_____ .

I gave _____ an importance of _____ because
_____
_____ .

I gave _____ an importance of _____ because
_____
_____ .

(*continued*) ➤

Activity 6.11 *(continued)*

I gave _____ an importance of _____ because
_____
_____ .

I gave _____ an importance of _____ because
_____
_____ .

I gave _____ an importance of _____ because
_____
_____ .

I gave _____ an importance of _____ because
_____
_____ .

ACTIVITY **6.12**   TRIP CARDS FOR OTHELLO

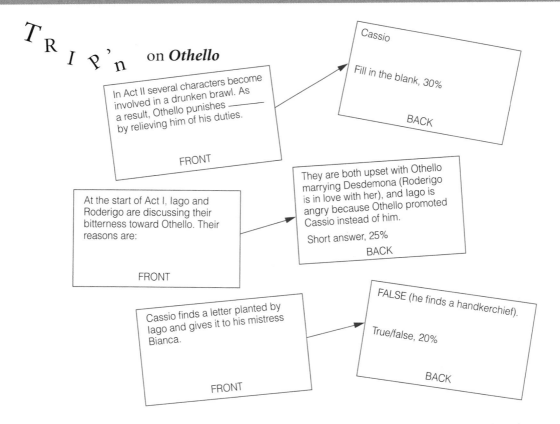

T R I P'n   on *Othello*

In Act II several characters become involved in a drunken brawl. As a result, Othello punishes ———— by relieving him of his duties.

FRONT

Cassio

Fill in the blank, 30%

BACK

At the start of Act I, Iago and Roderigo are discussing their bitterness toward Othello. Their reasons are:

FRONT

They are both upset with Othello marrying Desdemona (Roderigo is in love with her), and Iago is angry because Othello promoted Cassio instead of him.

Short answer, 25%

BACK

Cassio finds a letter planted by Iago and gives it to his mistress Bianca.

FRONT

FALSE (he finds a handkerchief).

True/false, 20%

BACK

Developed by Shawn Nunnally.

reductions. By discussing cooperatively what reduction terms each person in a group decided on, all group members learn from each other not only about the process of reducing notes but also about the material in the notes.

A physics teacher who wished to engage his students in discovery through group work devised an activity he calls "The Shover and the Shovee" (see Activity 6.13). The activity begins with students organizing themselves into groups of three; two people are "shovers" and one is the "shovee." One of the shovers gently pushes the shovee

ACTIVITY **6.13** DISCOVERY THROUGH GROUP WORK IN PHYSICS

THE SHOVER AND THE SHOVEE

[Step 1] Shover #1

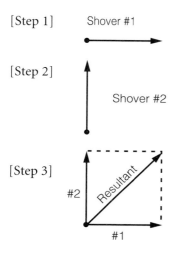

[Step 2]

Shover #2

[Step 3]

[Step 4] Various combinations

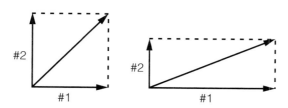

[Step 5] For constant #2, time to wall doesn't change, regardless of the magnitude of #1

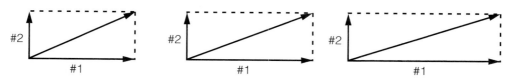

Developed by Jim McLeskey, Jr.

toward a wall. The students are then asked which way the shovee went, which is toward the wall. The vector (arrow) represents this motion as drawn on the chalkboard. The second shover now pushes the shovee toward a different wall. Again direction is established and the vector drawn. Now both shovers gently push the shovee toward their respective walls, and this additional information is added to the chalkboard drawing. Next students are asked what the effect of the shovers pushing with different relative velocities would be. Various combinations are illustrated. Finally, shovers experiment with the time it takes to go from a particular point to one wall while gently shoving the shovee at different speeds toward the second wall. They can see by doing so that the time to go from the starting point to the wall will be the same in each case, thus illustrating the independence of perpendicular vectors. Activity 6.13 shows what would be drawn on the chalkboard.

ONE-MINUTE SUMMARY

This chapter has addressed the importance of going beyond the traditional textbook and traditional instruction models in the content classroom. Textbooks can no longer stand alone; multiple resources are necessary to aid learning. There are numerous ways to supplement traditional textbooks; this chapter suggested multiple resources and solutions for issues that may arise.

Several factors must be considered when selecting textbooks, trade books, and resources to ensure an appropriate match for students. Cooperative learning offers powerful tools and strategies for teaching content, social skills, and critical thinking. Cooperative learning and working in groups are not the same, and their differences were clarified. Retention of content is enhanced when cooperative strategies are used and opportunities are provided for students to practice, under a teacher's guidance, five important categories of learning: rehearsal, elaboration, organizational thinking, comprehension monitoring, and affective thinking. Cooperative learning requires an atmosphere of serious purpose, confidence, assistance, and above all, commitment to disciplined inquiry and study. In this chapter we presented a stylized three-step procedure for group process to help cooperative groups function better. Finally, many actual reading and writing strategies that stress cooperative learning were described.

PAR ONLINE

Visit the *Reading to Learn in the Content Areas* Web site at http://academic .cengage.com/education/richardson for links to the Web sites mentioned in this chapter, tutorial quizzing, and other resources.

Many Web sites provide high-quality resources for planning and developing lessons and activities for enhancing instruction. Visit our companion Web site, Chapter 6, for direct links and information.

Try a threaded discussion on cooperative learning with fellow teachers. Listen to what other teachers say about what grouping schemes and processes they use.

END-OF-CHAPTER ACTIVITIES

Assisting Comprehension

1. Think about why it is important to use both a Fry readability formula and a cloze procedure with your students to get an accurate measure of how readable any text is for your students. Why do the two go together? Which do you feel better about—readability formulas or cloze? Why?

2. Think about and list ways in which you might change the daily operations of your class to incorporate some or all of the techniques described in this chapter.

3. Try specific cooperative learning activities in your classes, and evaluate how well students receive them.

Reflecting on Your Reading

1. Standard 2.3 of the International Reading Association for reading specialists and classroom teachers states that teachers should plan for the use of a wide range of curriculum materials in the classroom. Furthermore, according to the IRA guidelines, the curriculum materials should be chosen to accommodate the developmental, cultural, and linguistic differences of students.

   Consider this chapter, and reflect on how it has helped you think about using multiple resources to aid in curriculum development. Ask yourself two central questions: In what ways did this chapter help you plan to use a range of curriculum materials? Also, in what ways will this chapter help you select resources that accommodate the developmental, cultural, and linguistic differences in your students?

2. Standard 2.1 of the International Reading Association Standards for Reading Professionals and Teachers states that teachers should use appropriate grouping options, such as individual, small-group, whole-class, and computer-based grouping plans. Classroom teachers are asked to model and use scaffolding procedures so that students learn to work effectively in groups. Strategies we described in this chapter were mainly targeted at small-group instruction. Several strategies were described in the chapter that can be used in cooperative learning classrooms. Which strategies do you feel will be most useful for individual learning activities or for whole-class learning activities? Explain your response. Also, do you think any of the strategies can be used for computer-based instruction? Why or why not?

CHAPTER 7

It don't muss things or scatter ink blots around.

MARK TWAIN, 1865

Technology in Today's Content Classrooms

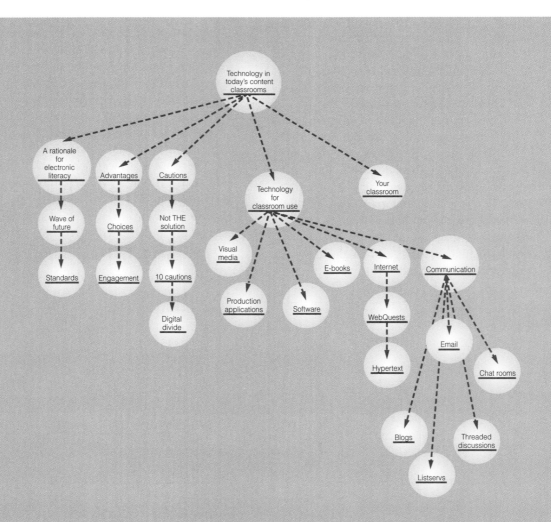

VOICES FROM THE CLASSROOM

The Voice of America (VOA—the official news service of the U.S. government that has broadcast around the world since 1942) has shut down and limited its services to many countries worldwide. VOA is now shifting its focus to newer technologies than high-frequency radio broadcasts, as well as aiming at audiences in the Middle East and North Africa. Satellite TV, FM radio, and the Internet are used so much more frequently than shortwave radio that VOA can no longer afford to serve audiences through that medium.

What do you think this shift in technology and audience indicates about technology and reading to learn? What are some advantages and disadvantages of this new policy?

PREPARING TO READ

Following is a list of terms used in this chapter. Some may be familiar to you in a general context, but in this chapter they may be used in unfamiliar ways. Decide how you could group the terms in four or five groupings, and give each group an appropriate label. There may be several ways to group them, so there is no single right answer. Be ready to explain your selections. Next, using a piece of paper, make a three-column organizer with the following headings: *terms, predicted definitions,* and *chapter definitions.* Select 10 terms with which you are least familiar, record them in your organizer, and predict how they might be defined for this chapter. As you read the chapter, verify your predictions and rewrite your definitions as necessary.

Look for the Web link to a similar story (found in *The Washington Post* on 2/23/07) at the Web links option of the Chapter 7 resources on this book's companion Web site.

_____ technological literacy
_____ electronic literacy
_____ information literate
_____ Net savvy
_____ electronic text
_____ socnet
_____ database
_____ podcast
_____ VoIP
_____ electronic book, e-book
_____ e-classroom
_____ WebQuest
_____ hypertext
_____ synchronous
_____ electronic mail, e-mail
_____ instant messages
_____ chat rooms
_____ discussion group
_____ threaded discussion
_____ asynchronous
_____ blog
_____ listserv
_____ digital divide
_____ distance learning

OBJECTIVES

As you read this chapter, focus your attention on the following purposes. You will

1. Understand the need for complementing content area instruction with technology.

2. View some activities that can apply and adapt electronic literacy in K–12 classrooms.

3. Learn about several technology resources used in classrooms.

4. Appreciate the value of electronic communication for students.

PRICKLY CITY by Scott Stantis © 2005 Dist. by Universal Press Syndicate. Reprinted with permission. All rights reserved.

It's a Flat World

 The quote we used to start this chapter is from Twain's first fictional piece, "The Celebrated Jumping Frog of Calaveras County," which appeared in the last issue of the *Saturday Press.* Twain was the first author to type a manuscript and also to double-space it for his editor's convenience. The quote refers to Twain's admiration for his Remington typewriter! Even though Twain wrote before the world of electronic literacy began, he used the newest forms of technology at the time and was quite pleased with the results. In the same way, teachers and students today have new technologies and need to learn how to embrace these tools.

As Linda Gambrel notes, "The times, they are a'changin" (2005, p. 588). Perhaps no one has shown us how much the times are changing better than Thomas Friedman, whose book *The World Is Flat* (2005) remained on the bestseller list for at least two years. Although the book is a fine introduction to the technological changes taking place, the book had to be updated in 2006—one year after its initial publication—in an attempt to match the pace of technological innovations. And by the time this textbook is published, newer technologies will be available than are presented within this chapter. The printed page has many advantages over the electronic page, but delivery speed is not one of them! The authors will endeavor to update this book's Web site with recent Web sites and commentary so as to retain the best of both paper and electronic text. The aim of this chapter, then, is to introduce some possibilities and help you find ways to engage readers in learning as they use the new technologies of the 21st century.

The word *technology* is derived from the Greek word *techne,* which refers to the "clever manipulation of natural artifacts to reach a desired goal" (Dwight, 2001, p. 22). **Technological literacy** is "the ability to use computers and other technology to improve learning, productivity and performance" (U.S. Department of Education, 1997). Oppenheimer (2003) notes that Arthur Luehrmann coined the term *computer literacy* in 1971.

To indicate how pervasive technology has become in our culture, consider a study in which Yahoo! (a search engine) participated. Researchers wanted to find out how people would respond to having no Internet access for two weeks. The researchers, recounts Barnako (2004), had a tough time finding people who would agree to participate—almost no one was willing to give up Internet access! Of those who did participate, across all age, income, and ethnic groups, the participants recounted feelings of withdrawal, loss, frustration, and discontent. We have indeed become dependent on this global technology (Bean & Readance, 2002; Schaeffer, 2003). Friedman (2006) calls this globalization a "flattening process" in which creativity, connectivity, communication, work, and play can be instantaneous.

Education today must respond to a widely networked society (Davis, 2000). Cornu (2001) notes that society, schools, and students are changing; we must change as well. There is a great need for practical information about integrating technology in K–12 instruction (Gambrell, 2005). In this chapter we discuss **electronic literacy**, which refers specifically to a means of reading in a technologically literate environment. Although we cannot provide a deep study of instructional technology here, we give a brief history of technology and address some of its advantages and disadvantages, forms of technology that contribute to electronic literacy skills, and applications for the content classroom.

A BRIEF RATIONALE FOR ELECTRONIC LITERACY

Two great waves of change influenced human history up to the 20th century, according to Nettle and Romaine (2000): the development of agriculture and the industrial revolution. A third wave, which Rifkin (2002) calls the "hydrogen economy"—to account for a new source of fuel that will change the way we live—is that of the 21st century. Each wave of change has influenced cultures and literacy, changing how we view the importance of literacy and how we use it. Expectations for readers now include being **information literate** (Henderson & Scheffler 2004)—that is, able to find and use information in any paper or electronic form. Lorenzo and Dziuban (2006) use the terms "**Net savvy**" and "Net generation" to describe the current generation of students, who have never known life without the Internet. Although teachers may have had different experiences as they grew up—with perhaps no or limited Internet access—they cannot afford to maintain an "industrial age mindset" (Frand, 2000) today. To avoid a clash of cultures and miscommunication that can arise between teachers with an industrial age mindset and students with an information age mindset, teachers must use and implement technology in their instruction. Paper text is not enough; **electronic text** is also needed now.

The challenge is to discover how seamlessly technology can be used, along with literacy, to create academically engaging content lessons. Most teachers realize that they need to become electronically literate, and they recognize how difficult this can be. In one study (Watts-Taffe, Gwinn, Johnson, & Horn, 2003), three beginning teachers were followed for a year as they strove to incorporate technology in their classrooms. They found themselves using technology for multiple purposes, such as software to create graphic organizers and encyclopedias on CDs to gather information. They found that they could integrate technology more easily as they practiced and gained confidence with it themselves. Their students became more motivated and engaged in learning as they incorporated technology. By the end of their first year, these teachers had lots of ideas for what to do with technology in their next year of teaching.

Visit the Reading to Learn in the Content Areas Web site, Chapter 7, to view the NETS.

Standards

Standards for instructional technology have become a national reality. The National Educational Technology Standards (NETS), developed by the International Society for Technology in Education (ISTE), outline core technological competencies that teachers, as well as students and administrators, should meet. In fact, 90 percent of the United States has now adopted, or relies on, the NETS in developing state technology plans (Loshert, 2003).

Visit the Reading to Learn in the Content Areas Web site, Chapter 7, to view the NCES data.

The use of technology in schools has increased exponentially, as a visit to the Web site of the National Center of Educational Statistics shows; the percentage of schools with Internet access increased from 35 percent in 1994 to 99 percent in 2001 and to nearly 100 percent in 2005.

The International Reading Association and National Council of Teachers of English have set the following standard for students, thus assuming that teachers can instruct accordingly: "Students use a variety of technological and information resources (e.g., libraries, databases, computer networks, video) to gather and synthesize information and to create and communicate knowledge." Technology is here to stay, and we must use it effectively in content classrooms.

ADVANTAGES OF ELECTRONIC LITERACY

No teacher can compete with the pace and lure of new technologies; all we can do is keep in mind that new technologies can be the medium for engaging students in the real work and joy of learning. Technology presents choices in instruction that educators have not had in the past.

At socnet sites, there may be pop-up ads and questionable language (especially for younger children). However, the Net savvy generation seems to take this in stride.

Locate the URL for the YouTube video (visit the *Reading to Learn in the Content Areas* Web site) and view the video "Web 2.0...The Machine Is Using Us!"

1. Technology is a viable means to learning—one that fascinates the Net generation. Electronic literacy seems to promote literacy in ways that paper cannot.

2. The social aspect of electronic literacy engages students. By using **socnets** (networks for social communication such as Facebook, YouTube, and MySpace), students have learned to talk to almost anyone in a variety of electronic media. This social and cultural dynamic (Luke, 2000) has the potential to shift instruction into the emotional zone, where cognition and affect can be used to full advantage in capitalizing on students' interests, along with familiarity with their own medium, in creating learning activities within this social space. (See Activity 7.1.) Children today have a "lifeworld" (Gee, 2000) orientation where discourse is done in social language. Teachers can take advantage of this discourse for instruction. By so doing, they invite students to use a popular way of communicating to bridge into more academic communication.

YouTube is "cool" according to Trier (2007), who uses McLuhan's term "cool" (McLuhan, 1995) to mean a medium that is highly participative. At YouTube one can view and post videos. Trier suggests several activities that help teachers use YouTube in academic settings, such as showing videos from this site to introduce a new topic and provide it with relevance for today's Net savvy generation; assigning students to hunt for videos that illustrate a topic; or having students post their own videos after studying a topic. (See Activity 7.2.)

3. Teachers and students can communicate from great physical distances with a rapidity not dreamed of in earlier times. Learners can locate information without traveling to a physical library; instead they can visit virtual libraries by accessing

---

ACTIVITY 7.1 CULTURE AND GEOGRAPHY ON A SOCNET

Select a socnet, such as Facebook for teenagers or Club Penguin for young children, that you belong to or would like to join.

Once you are logged on, chat with someone by asking, Tell me about where you live; explain one holiday you like the best and why. Try something like this:

4:22 p.m.
Nadifa,

I'm learning how to use Facebook. I want you to tell me something special about Somalia—what is a custom or tradition that you have in Somalia that is different from in the United States?

9:10 p.m.
Judy,

Sorry it took me a while to answer this. A custom or tradition that I have in Somalia but different from there? Well, we obviously don't have the same holidays or traditions. We have different foods, beliefs, and religion. Does that answer your question?

8:11 a.m.
Nadifa,

Could you select ONE holiday that is different and tell me about it or select ONE food that is different and tell me about it? Thanks

What did your online friend tell you? Now look for information in another resource, such as a Web site that presents Somalia and tells about its customs and traditions.

First think of questions you have about the Internet and what Web 2.0 is. Next watch the video "The Machine Is Using Us!" See how many of your questions are answered during this viewing. Then write notes about what you learned and your impressions of the video. Note any questions you still have. Now watch the video again to find more answers to your questions.

What else do you want to know? Select two other places (books, video, Web sites) that can help you find the answers.

Visit the *Reading to Learn in the Content Areas* Web site, Chapter 7 to find Standard 8, and to view the technology standards for instructional personnel in Virginia.

Visit the *Reading to Learn in the Content Areas* Web site, Chapter 7, to read Ruddell's online article about project-based learning in an electronic environment.

the Internet and searching for information by typing in a query on a search engine. People can hold conversations in real or virtual time over distances. Voluminous records can be kept within a tiny memory drive and transported on a key chain. Learners can "be there" without leaving their homes.

4. Technology "shifts power into the hearts of children" (Maurer and Davidson, 1999, p. 460). Maurer and Davidson suggest that with technology learning is streamlined and less boring—it is like speed learning. Children feel in control and smart. Ruddell (2000) says about a commercial in which children are promoting a dot.com site, "We need classrooms that 'crackle with the kind of energy I saw in the dot.com commercial' " (p. 2). She encourages teachers to embrace the possibilities of technology to promote "fully engaged learners who are excited, exhilarated, and passionately involved in school" (p. 2). Reinking (1997) comments that although technology itself is neutral, the way we use it to learn enables learners to be more creative and engaged.

5. Electronic text, as contrasted with paper text, is beneficial because it is easy to modify with the delete key. It can be adapted to the reader; it can be programmed to accept reader responses. Moving from place to place is easy in electronic text. Organization and retrieval skills are developed, and information can be stored more efficiently.

In summary, if technological instruction focuses on meaning, stresses comprehension, and lets students become actively involved with whole texts, then the technology can advance literacy.

TECHNOLOGY FOR CLASSROOM USE

 With some of these advantages of electronic literacy in mind, and the realization that the Net savvy generation is here to stay, we briefly look at some of these technologies and their impact on the classroom.

Word Processing and Other Production Applications

Maurer and Davidson (1999) tell the story of a first grader who seemed to be "giving up on school." When he realized that he could write on the computer, his whole attitude changed. He realized that he had the power to accomplish a literacy task in a way that enticed him.

Children's own work can become a learning resource for others. Term papers and reports that used to be submitted for only a teacher's eyes can be banished in favor of presentations for all learners to enjoy.

Many teachers know that writing is an effective means of learning. Learning logs and journals are two means of enabling students to express what they are learning and clarify difficult concepts. In today's world journals may be written on paper, but more likely they are posted at Internet sites, with access provided by the presenter to selected users. In Chapter 10 we explore the benefits of writing in the content areas more fully. In this chapter we point out that writing does not have to be done with pens or pencils; more often keyboards are used.

Visit the *Reading to Learn in the Content Areas* Web site, Chapter 7, where you will find Anderson-Inman's (1998) lists of several repositories of electronic text, one of which is "The Online Books Page." This site is a directory of full-text books available for reading on the Internet.

Many word processing programs are available. They range from simple free ones bundled with computer operating systems or downloadable, such as *Opennet,* to sophisticated applications such as Microsoft *Word.* Some software applications, such as *PowerPoint* (part of the Microsoft Office Suite) let users create slide shows with text. Audio and animation can also be included. Word processing programs let users create and edit text, insert pictures and graphics, and make appealing booklike products. Software tools such as *Inspiration* allow teachers to create maps, graphic organizers, Venn diagrams, outlines, and writing opportunities for—and with—students. Such software is not content specific; it provides numerous opportunities for content teachers to produce specific instructional materials. Haynes (2006) guided her fourth grade students to create graphic organizers describing places where they had fun. Then they expanded on a part of the graphic organizer and used that expansion to write paragraphs and then essays.

Applications such as *FrontPage* and *Dreamweaver* let users create presentations that can be published on the Web. Some textbooks are published entirely on the Internet with production applications. Students can read their electronic text, see the same illustrations that are included in the printed textbook, and *hear* the instructor explain points about a graph or lead them through a complicated set of directions. At given points, students can click and soar to other locations (using the hypertext feature), escaping the linear nature of a textbook for a nonlinear world. Teachers can create such presentations or search the Web for similar programs. Currently many simple programs for Web presentation are available, so a user does not have to purchase and learn advanced technology to post a Web site. Although studies have yet to be conducted that prove more learning occurs with such resources, informal evidence is all around us. Children are intrigued by the multisensual nature of production applications and seem to spend more time on learning when such resources are available.

Adding graphics to a report enhances student interest and understanding. Using scanners or digital cameras, learners can place graphics in text to create lively visual displays of their learning. Regular photographs can be transferred to a computer from a scanner. Digital cameras feed pictures directly to a computer or printer. Free sources of clip art, and clip art within such programs as *Inspiration* and *Word,* can also be used. Audio can be introduced to a presentation using applications such as *Garage Band, itunes,* or *Audacity.*

Databases are increasingly popular and efficient means of storing information. In fact, some form of database is used to check on the supply of items in any online store. When a shopper goes to the Internet to make a purchase, a database is searched to see whether that item is in stock. Teachers often use a database "to enter, store, update, access, and manipulate information" (Merkley, Schmidt, & Allen, 2001, p. 220). For instance, a teacher might store activity ideas in a database such as *Access* (from Microsoft) or *File Maker Pro.* Or students could enter, store, and retrieve data about planets. Other simple ways to organize information on a computer include the use of file folders and subfolders for categories.

Instructional Software

Software is delivered on CDs or over Internet downloads; it usually comes with supporting instructions and materials. Interactive computer books are available for students to read and respond to on screen (Chu, 1995). Programs like *Oregon Trail* and *Amazon Trail* have been around for some time and have undergone some improvements. *Leonardo the Inventor* takes learners to the Renaissance, where they experience da Vinci's ideas and inventions. Such programs simulate a situation and ask readers to make choices based on information. Careful thinking and interaction and literacy skills are required. Some software features a familiar text but provides multimedia, such as read-alongs and question/answer interaction. Students are expected to respond; their responses can be tracked to provide a score for the learner and instructor. This can be a helpful monitoring device for teachers who want to record which types of resources students use to learn about a topic and how effective those resources seem to be.

Instructional software programs can be wonderful learning resources. Software can track what users are doing, keeping records for students and teachers. As with textbooks, some are better than others. Willis, Stephens, and Matthew (1996) encourage teachers to look for attention to the subject matter, efficiency, approach to instruction, appeal, ease of use, and adaptability when they select software. Carter (1996) reviewed *Accelerated Reader* (AR), a software management program to record students' reading of selected books, and found that 89 percent of AR books had never been reviewed by a reputable publication.

Software should always be instructionally relevant as well as student and teacher friendly (Fox, 2003). When Quirk and Schwanenflugel (2004) analyzed the motivational appeal of five popular software programs for struggling readers, they found that each was somewhat stimulating, but all could have been much more motivating. A recent study (U.S. Department of Education, 2007) found that software programs have not been very effective at improving students' test scores. Software is not good simply because it is there; it must conform to educational standards and facilitate achieving the intended instructional goals.

How software is used makes a difference. Greenlee-Moore and Smith (1996) investigated the effects on reading comprehension when fourth grade students read either short and easy or difficult texts using either interactive software or printed text. When reading longer and more difficult narratives, the software group had higher scores. The authors speculate that students paid more attention to the text on computer than to the text in the book.

Quirk and Schwanen-flugel (2004) review the *DISTAR, PHAST, Early Steps, Reading Recovery,* and *Reading Apprentice* software programs.

Instructional software should teach about content as well as stimulate critical thinking rather than skill-and-drill or rote learning of isolated facts. One major advantage of software over Internet resources is that teachers can preview the software and be sure its content is suitable for the age group. Another advantage is that the teacher does not depend on an Internet connection, which might be expensive, unreliable, or sometimes inaccessible.

Visual Literacy

When films first became popular, Wise (1939) cautioned that films have benefits depending on the circumstances such as teacher, students, environment, and objectives. He noted that film does not equal a panacea.

A student in one of the authors' classrooms noted that visual learners find technology very helpful. "This correlation of visual stimulus and learning is obvious. Our generation is a visually stimulated generation. The children of our generation are visually stimulated and the generation from here on out will be visually stimulated. I feel that it cannot be avoided" (Evans, 2004). The use of TV, video, and movies as educational resources is well established. These visual media were available for many years before computers entered common use. Now they are being integrated with computers; users can record television programs, video, and movies directly to their computers for personal viewing. Technology lets people make movies with software that emulates that of professionals.

Video has replaced the old film projectors and film strips. And CDs and DVDs have replaced videos. These highly visual electronic devices can bring students closer to a topic, making it real. In 1998 Gersten and Tlusty described a video exchange between Czech and American students. Each group created a video that represented their lives and exchanged these videos. Content came alive through the careful planning, production, and viewing of different cultures through the medium of video. This project could be replicated via an interactive distance learning session or a site that lets users post videos and see those that others have posted.

Television is a less interactive and older form of visual literacy than is computer-based visual media. Many organizations, including the International Reading Association, sponsor "no TV" days or weeks to highlight the importance of an environment in which children can discover resources other than TV. When watching TV is simply a way to pass time, it probably is not stimulating much learning. As Elley (1992) reports in an international literacy study, people who often watch TV tend to score at lower levels of literacy than those who watch less TV. However, in some countries with high literacy scores, the average daily number of TV hours watched is three or four. In these countries, many foreign films with subtitles and informational films are shown on TV. Unfortunately the United States falls into the high-hours-of-TV-watching/low-literacy-scores category. After reviewing 30 years of research, Reinking and Wu (1990) stated that the evidence does not clearly show that TV is detrimental to literacy. It is reasonable to conclude that TV—documentaries, drama, and news shows, for example—can be a vehicle for learning opportunities (Reinking & Pardon, 1995).

What makes visual media so popular? They appeal to many of the senses, fostering visual literacy and more. We see and are entertained by them. Our eyes move from place to place rather than remaining focused on a page. Learning is a natural by-product. For instance, the movie *Clueless* barely credited the novel *Emma* by Jane

Austen—yet it became a starting point for discussing Austen's novel in many English classrooms. *Clueless* can guide students to the movie titled *Emma* and on to the novel itself. However, caution is urged in moving from movies to literature (Baines, 1996). Films often use less sophisticated vocabulary and language and "reduce the complexity of dialogue, plot, characters, and theme" (p. 616). But visual media lure students and can be the springboard to many projects linking movies and the literature.

Auditory Resources

Participating in cell phone conversations and listening to radio and music are popular pastimes that can be used as educational resources. Podcasts provide excellent examples of such possibilities. The term **podcast** combines the "pod" from Apple's iPod device with broadcasting audio (or video) files for anyone to download from the Internet and listen to. Podcasts use the Internet's Real Simple Syndication (RSS). Audio or video files can be transmitted directly to an iPod or another MP3 player. Anyone with a reasonably well-configured computer can create an audio file. And anyone with an Internet connection and enough bandwidth can download a podcast. In fact, Rainie and Madden report that an astounding number of people had listened to podcasts as of April 2005, and the number is growing daily. A device such as an iPod—which many young people possess or have easy access to—is portable and compact and is used for numerous listening purposes. Teachers can locate podcasts about topics they teach, or create their own podcasts about a topic. Then the podcasts can be posted where students can easily access and listen to them.

VoIP (Voice over Internet Protocol) has taken telephony—voice communication over distances—to the Internet. VoIP is often also called IP telephony. Transmission of digitized voice data has surpassed POTS (plain old telephone service) among the Net savvy. It is now possible for a person to "call" a number that transmits a voice message to an audio file that is received at an e-mail address. The recipient can then hear the message at leisure while checking e-mail. Educational applications could include these:

- Asking students to submit book reports via a VoIP service, using an expressive and compact delivery. The teacher can listen and respond via VoIP so that the student receives a personal critique.

- Having students record via VoIP and then listen to themselves, such as to practice a second language or to make sure they have not forgotten any steps in an explanation.

- Providing personal feedback to individual students.

- Posting an assignment that students and parents can listen to in order to clarify directions.

Electronic Books

An **electronic book** (or **e-book**) is a book presented on a computer; it is electronic text. The user's main focus is still on reading text, but the text can be augmented with pictures and hypertext links to create a nonlinear environment. For example, *A Survey*

Comments from a graduate student: "Before I began this class, I did not know what a podcast was. I had heard of the iPod and even purchased an MP3 player for my son, but I thought they only played music for the kids. Last weekend I had the pleasure of finding out what a valuable tool this is. Mind you, I would have not paid attention, if I had not already resisted taking a look at this activity. My brother and sister-in-law visited us from Texas for the weekend at my sister's lake home. We were all discussing some singer on a morning talk show, and she said she had some of his music on her iPod. She promptly let my sister listen. She also walks a few miles everyday, including getaway days. While walking, in addition to music, she listens to her favorite talk shows and devotional exercises she downloads to participate in. I listened to some, and I was amazed. No wonder kids love them. They are pricey, but now I see how worthwhile they can be."

She also had an office conference meeting to listen to on the plane going home. This activity helped me to understand what these useful devices are and how they can be used."
Linda Ford

of Western Art enables learners to view and read about art that they otherwise might never see. Navigating learning with electronic encyclopedias is an interesting and efficient way to support textbooks with literature (Wepner, Seminoff, & Blanchard, 1995). *Compton's Interactive Encyclopedia* and *Grolier Multimedia Encyclopedia*, offered on CDs, rival the print versions for number of articles. Ease of navigation from one article to another is good, and readability is fairly simple. Sound clips as well as pictures and animation are combined in these electronic books. But be careful! The package is modern, but these are still encyclopedias—which are secondary sources. Remind students that these are condensed sources, not deep treatments of any topic.

The Internet

The Internet makes electronic text easily accessible and has become "the medium of the future" (Anderson-Inman, 1998). We are now in the age of "Globalization 3.0" according to Friedman (2006), where using the Internet leads to "digitization, miniaturization, virtualization, personalization, and wireless" (p. 196). The Internet is a collection of many resource networks—an electronic library of information. The most commonly used part of the Internet is the part that supports multimedia: the World Wide Web. Every second something new is posted for viewers to find. A Web search engine lets a learner type in a topic using keywords and come up with many possible resources. Some are worthless, but many can enhance learning in content areas. Using the Internet to search for information is highly personal, but students need guidance to help them find the best and most completely verifiable information. Just as a reader should note the copyright date of a textbook, an Internet user should note when a Web site was posted and whether it has been revised (Rekrut, 1999). And just as a reader should want to know a text author's credentials, Internet users should be cautious about the sources of information they discover on the Web; the learner must judge the quality and reliability of the information. Content teachers can help by checking possible sites in advance of sending students to surf the Net.

The Internet is changing what it means to be literate (Leu, 1997):

1. Internet literacy requires new and sophisticated navigational skills. Getting around in the mass of information is a challenge.

2. Learning is endless; just as one masters a new literacy skill on the Net, a new challenge arises.

3. The Internet requires new ways of reasoning and thinking critically.

4. Content on the Net can be presented with multiple meanings and combinations.

To find out more about important holidays for people of different lands and cultures, visit the *Reading to Learn in the Content Areas* Web site, Chapter 7, for a Web link.

These literacy challenges are part of what makes the Internet appealing to students, but the challenge is for teachers to provide guidance so the Internet is used as a tool for effective learning. Teachers can use the Internet to help students learn, but they can't compete with Game Boys and iPods! Rather, they must look for ways to use them in an educational manner. For instance, teachers often find that the Internet can provide a means of extending literacy practice and proficiency (Karchmer, 2001).

Students find the Internet an appealing source of information (Leu, Castek, Henry, Coiro, & McMullan, 2004). They have opportunities to respond to literature, to view Web sites of authors, and to learn about diversity.

To view this site about Kid's Web, visit the *Reading to Learn in the Content Areas* Web site, Chapter 7.

As an example, a high school math teacher located a site that enlivens the study of the Pythagorean theorem. He found a high school posting about the short story "The Battle of Pythagorus." Here was a wonderful lesson about the theorem using the short story to lead into the lesson. In addition, Leu, Karchmer, and Leu (1999) provide numerous lessons in content areas that engage learners on the Internet. For example, they help learners find out about Japan by visiting "Kid's Web Japan." This site provides steps by which students can learn about Japan's climate, culture, and art.

The Internet can make it easy to consult an expert. Rather than traveling to the expert, which can be expensive and limit the audience, we can visit the expert online. We might even see him or her talking to us, listening, and responding. Van Horn (1999) discusses the merits of such a conference, provides tips on setting up a live conference, and explains what equipment works best in various circumstances. He calls the setting for such conferences the **e-classroom**.

The Internet also provides access to many libraries. Electronic journals let readers locate resources for immediate consideration. Professional development occurs online (Anderson-Inman, 1998) when current and back issues of journals are available for easy retrieval. The "card catalog" where one used to look for texts using an index card system in file cabinets has been revised to an online catalog one can visit in the library or from one's home via the Internet.

Visit the *Reading to Learn in the Content Areas* Web site, Chapter 7, to learn more about WebQuests.

WebQuests are a means of using the Internet to send students on a problem-solving journey to several preselected Web sites. The teacher poses a question and provides clues that are found within Web sites. WebQuests give students authentic problem-solving tasks. They guide purposeful reading and also can be used by cooperative groups of students. Teachers must search carefully each possible Web site to be used in a WebQuest, making sure the content is correct and suitable for the learners, and that the site does not link to any questionable sites. Clues must be thoughtfully prepared. This activity is time-consuming but very effective as a learning tool.

Throughout this textbook we have presented several WebQuest activities.

Treasure hunts are somewhat similar to WebQuests, although they are usually briefer and focus more on a fact-finding mission. Students are given a question that they answer by visiting teacher-selected sites. For both WebQuests and treasure hunts, the Internet offers numerous sites where teachers can follow directions to create and post their activities at no cost.

A HYPERTEXT ENVIRONMENT

Hypertext supports the use of a wide variety of resources in content classrooms. On the Web, a student can start at one location and click on a hyperlink (an icon or underlined text) to immediately link to another site where more information is located. Reinking (1997) demonstrates how hypertext works in an online and print format article as he discusses the possibilities of technology and literacy. The learner can go backward, forward, and sideways in many hierarchies. Instead of reading each line in

Find a link to Reinking's article at our *Reading to Learn in the Content Areas* Web site.

order on each Web page, the learner can branch from here to there in a nonlinear fashion. The student can click to view a footnote, then click back to the main article. Readers can check a reference without turning a page. This environment is similar to that of a learner who leaps from one idea to another, jumping between piles of information on a desk as needed to take care of several tasks. In short, Web hypertext and links create a typical learning environment.

E-Literacy Communication

The traditional view of communication and collaboration assumes face-to-face, same-time-same-place (**synchronous**) encounters. Online communication, however, is gaining in popularity. Learners are beginning to seek learning environments where they can work collaboratively over time and space in a variety of settings. Tse (1999) noted that participants who tend to be passive in face-to-face interactions tend to take a more active role in electronic discussions. **Electronic mail** is sent over the Internet; unlike paper letters (now sometimes called "snail mail"), **e-mail** can be received almost instantaneously. Sending letters by electronic mail lets learners contact favorite authors or content experts who have made their e-mail addresses available. Many legislators provide their e-mail addresses for constituents, giving students an opportunity to write and receive quick responses as they study political issues. Several studies have been conducted to determine the effect of e-mail correspondence on literacy skills and learning. Rekrut (1999) believes that e-mail is the best application with which to introduce the Internet to new users because it is so simple to learn.

Students today use e-mail and instant messaging to carry on conversations at least as often as they use cell phones. They are "tech-savvy" (Chandler-Olcott & Mahar, 2003). Such common informal writing can help boost more formal writing and communication skills. **Instant messages (IM)**, sent as short written notes over the Internet almost as quickly as a telephone conversation can be conducted, simplify the spelling and grammar of formal language. This is similar to what happens to language when many more users adopt it, and complexities are lost (Nettle & Romaine, 2000). Instant messages can also contain references that are familiar to the communicators but not to other speakers. Some might even call instant messaging a type of pidgin (an abbreviated form of communication adopted to allow speakers of different languages to use a very simple language, such as for trade). Lewis and Fabos (2005) examined how seven adolescents used instant messaging in their lives. These young people learned a great deal of literacy in "digitally mediated times" (p. 470) by using IM. Teachers cannot ignore the power of communication through text or instant messaging because students are using IM for all kinds of communication and sophisticated interaction.

Here are some common instant messaging terms:
LOL = Laugh out loud.
BRB = Be right back.
TTYL = Talk to you later.
CU = See you.
Cya = See ya.
FWIW = For what it's worth.
FAR = Free after rebate.

The possibilities for e-mail within content instruction are intriguing. The most obvious is that it provides a means for teachers, parents, and students to communicate outside classroom hours. E-pals allow students from different schools—or even countries—to talk to each other about content topics. Students can partner to instant message about a content topic and then "translate" it into more formal report language.

After discussing (insert your subject matter here), assign students to use either IM or e-mail to discuss it before the next class. Ask students to bring a copy of this conversation to the next class. In class, have them share with a partner a way to expand and elaborate on the language of IM/e-mail to create an explanation of the term that could be found in a content area glossary. This kind of expansion of language is similar to what English second language teachers do to help English language learners switch code from informal to formal language usage.

Quick electronic communication systems are just that: quick! It is up to teachers to help learners see how quick communication can be carried to a more academic level of communication. A recent letter to the editor was captioned, "Will Young PPL Gro Up 2 B Literate? OMG LOL! (*Richmond Times Dispatch*, 5/29/05). Activity 7.3 uses quick electronic communication as a way to move to writing about content learning.

Chat rooms (Morgan & Beaumont, 2003) are found online at various locations, usually through a host Internet service provider. Here users talk to each other about a topic of common interest. Teachers can create their own chat rooms on a school server, where their students can chat about a content topic. In chat rooms, several people can talk; the conversation can occur instantaneously or at a convenient time for users to submit their thoughts.

Discussion groups allow many people to discuss a topic either in real time or over a period of time on a Web site. (Regular e-mail does not allow real-time communication.) A respondent can receive replies from several different people, all of whom can then read one another's responses. This threaded discussion offers opportunities for reflection and allows numerous visits to consider and reconsider other points of view. Knowlton and Knowlton (2001) define **threaded discussion** as "the **asynchronous** (not face-to-face-same-time-same-place but in-own-time-own-place-own-time) exchange of messages using a bulletin board or e-mail software" (p. 39). Discussion groups are an excellent vehicle for students to learn from one another and to discuss a forthcoming test or a point they do not understand. They provide a kind of online tutorial. Discussion groups are somewhat like chat rooms in that people talk to each other about a set topic. But discussion groups usually are more formal and follow a specific thread, or thought, for a while. Chat rooms tend to be more spontaneous forms of conversation and are often very informal. Figure 7.1 shows an example of a threaded discussion board, where topics to be discussed are posted. Figure 7.2 is the threaded aspect for one of the threads in Figure 7.1. Discussion groups can be an excellent resource for content instruction.

Another form of electronic text communication is a **blog**, which is a Web log. It is a journal in which a person usually writes personal reflections and then shares them by posting them to a Web site. It is informal and written in one's natural voice. Once a blog is posted, others can visit it and add comments, although blog responses are not generally long or intense. The cyberjournal (Stefl-Mabry, 1998) is a type of

FIGURE 7.1

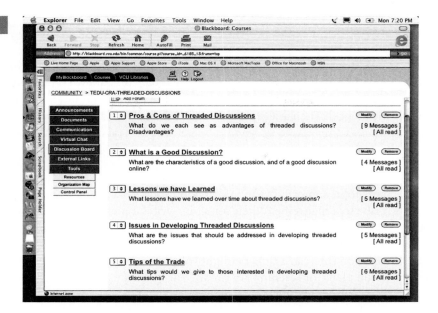

FIGURE 7.2

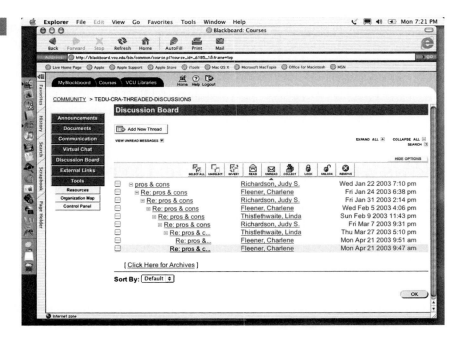

blog. Dieu (2004) notes that blogs work best as long-term assignments that can help students improve their writing and language fluency and competence. They can be excellent tools for English language learners but also help in content subjects when students are encouraged to write thoughts about their daily learning. Or teachers and students can blog. Activity 7.4 uses a social network, blogging, familiar to so many of the Net savvy generation.

Ask students to read a blog about a topic being studied in your content area. Ask students to present the most important statements in the blog in the exact words of the blogger. Then ask them to restate what they read in their own words. Finally, have them compare what the blogger believes to what the students know about this topic from their current study in your class.

To find some good links about blogs, especially for ELL students, visit the *Reading to Learn in the Content Areas* Web site, Chapter 7.

Participation in **listservs** is by subscription. People who are interested in the same topic subscribe to an information source—a listserv—much as they might subscribe to a magazine. When someone writes a message, it is sent to everyone on the listserv by e-mail. All the list members can read other members' comments. Listservs are a good means of disseminating information quickly to many people who have a common interest. Teachers might subscribe to a listserv where the common topic is lesson plans for teaching grammar. When one subscriber posts his or her plan, all the other listserv members receive it.

A teacher who is intrigued but does not yet have classroom access to the Internet and the forms of communication described in this section can use disks to create a discussion community (Cole, Raffier, Rogan, & Schleicher, 1998). One student writes a journal entry on disk and then passes the disk to another student, who reacts and passes the disk to another student. The teacher can read the final product.

These resources for electronic literacy create a community of learners. Students who might not speak out in class may feel freer to communicate via e-mail, discussion groups, and listservs. Thus many diverse perspectives become available in the learning environment (Morrison, 1999).

CAUTIONS ABOUT ELECTRONIC LITERACY

While the Net savvy generation—and we as authors—think that the advantages of technology and electronic literacy outweigh their disadvantages, cautions and concerns must be considered and overcome if possible. The series of panels about April, a teenager in the comic strip "For Better or for Worse" (written by Lynn Johnston in early December 2004) illustrates our first caution. April has finished her homework, which was to "write" an essay. Her mother discovers that she "wrote" it by visiting the Internet and copying and pasting from some sources there. Her mother makes her sit down with text material, including an encyclopedia, and read these materials in paper format, then write her own original essay. April mutters, "I was just told to do an essay. I wasn't told to LEARN anything." Our *first* caution, then, is that the ease of electronic literacy can lead to borrowing, plagiarism, or misappropriation of others' work because this can be so easy to do. Scanning, cutting and pasting, and assembling are simplified when one is working on a computer rather than having to use one's own handwriting to meet an assignment. Thus teachers need to be constantly vigilant to encourage careful selection of information and making the source part of new thoughts as well as incorporating information with attribution. This problem has become so prevalent that software companies have produced programs to "catch" overquotation without appropriation; many college instructors rely on such tools to help them locate plagiarized papers. Catching students in this act is the last desperate step in "solving" the problem—and probably not the best one! Much better is teaching our students to respect others' work, to value it, and to cite it appropriately while also adding their own critical thoughts about that work to the knowledge base. When students think of themselves as adding value to what they read, they are less likely to misappropriate. In Chapter 8 we present several activities for electronic study skills that give teachers ideas for how to accomplish this goal.

One of the best ways to avoid plagiarism is to encourage critical thinking. However, critical thinking—sometimes challenging for teachers to fit into test-based curricula—can be even more challenging to teach in computer-based environments. For background on critical thinking within a reading-to-learn context, please review Chapter 5 in this textbook. For some tips on how to encourage critical thinking in Internet environments, think about ways that the Web "turf" can be manipulated. The following notations, in the words of Dr. Dan Ream (2007), provide helpful considerations for practicing critical thinking; the more one understands what an Internet search is about, the better one can weigh the results:

- The average user does only a single-word search and does not look beyond the first 10 items on the list that is generated.
- The ranking of a page in a search engine's results (such as Google or Yahoo!) is determined by its relevance to the searched terms and—in Google searches—also the page's popularity as measured by the number of links to that page on the Web.
- A link is like a citation in a print journal in that it refers to a preexisting other source; in doing so, it is implied that the linker is recommending that page to others.
- Relevance ranking is done when the search engine looks at the occurrence of the item being searched for within the page (Google also looks at how many pages are linked to the one you are looking up, which is related to the page ranking formula).
- Search engine optimizers use various techniques to cause their clients' pages to be ranked higher in search results. These techniques include choosing different terms or adding more terms to the text of the page and using link farms to increase the number of links to an optimized page.
- Sponsored links in Google are highlighted across the top and along the right side. Other search engines allow companies to pay for having their pages ranked higher in search results (Google does not allow this latter practice).

Therefore, students need to realize that search engines do not locate infallible resources; they locate the number of "hits" for the query—the number of times this site has been visited by others, or its popularity with searchers. Web designers realize that a citation analysis will get their site in the first several "hits" to a query. So Web page creators may try to ensure that their sites contain the terms they think you might be searching for—not necessarily the content you may need. A critical reader should

You are going to find out how to read a Web site critically. Select your search engine, such as Google.com.

Type in "Martin Luther King."

Select the site titled "Martin Luther King Jr.—A True Historical Examination."

Scroll to the end of the page and click on the link "hosted by Stormfront."

Click that link and find answers to these questions: What is Stormfront? What do they advocate?

Now visit at least two other Web sites and one paper-based resource about MLK. Then answer this question: Is the Stormfront message consistent with what you know about MLK?

Let's check out whether we can trust this site to give us good information.

(We would expect that this site would be posted and maintained by credible authorities, correct?)

Copy the URL for the site; then go to a search engine such as Google.

Type in the search box the term "easywhois."

Select the site for Easy Who Is.

When the Easy Who Is site appears, paste in the link you copied for "Martin Luther King Jr.—A True Historical Examination" where the box says "Enter domain."

What do you find? Can you now tell if the creator of this site is biased toward one perspective and may be twisting facts?

---

think about the author's credentials; the objectivity of the site; the relevance and current nature of the site; and the quality of the presentation.

To determine whether a Web site contains credible information, students need to know how to conduct a Web page identity check. Any site should have a history that tells who posted the site, which can give important clues to its viability; it is just a click away from the Web site and is a useful tool for readers. Consider Activity 7.5, concerning a Martin Luther King Web site.

Another caution about using the Internet is that it is so easy to make permanent and visible to all what was a quick thought that should have been kept private! Some people use blogs as a way to write their personal diaries, thinking they are protected from unwanted readers by passwords. But who protects the passwords? Readership can expand without an author's knowledge when a password is shared or stolen. An e-mail is targeted at a specific user; but when that message arrives, what the reader does with it is now in his or her control. Of course this has always been true of paper too, but it's a bit harder to pass along than in the electronic environment. Consider Activity 7.6 as one way to impress this message on students.

Yet another caution is that technology and computers cannot teach; they can only facilitate. "It may be unreasonable to think that any innovation—technological or otherwise—would bring radical change to an institution as old, large, and as established as education" (Oppenheimer, 2003, pp. 23–24). When technology helps educators do their job better, this is a great bonus. But technology is no more a final solution to educational challenges than movies or television were. As Steve Jobs commented to Wolf (1996) in

Explain what the game Whisper Down the Lane is about: Within a circle of people, a "secret" is whispered to one person, then repeatedly whispered to the next person in the circle. By the time the "secret" comes back to the person who first shared it, the secret is usually garbled—and not at all what the sharer intended.

Play Whisper Down the Lane by giving a student a message about a topic you will be studying soon. Make sure the message is passed along to each other student in the room. Collect the message as the last recipient hears it.

Now try this game in a new way: Give a message to your students at the end of the day and ask them to share it with somebody in an e-mail by the next day. Tell your students to ask the recipient of the e-mail to forward it to at least one other person, and be sure to keep the student's name in the address. After one to two days, have the students bring in the path that this forwarded e-mail has followed. How many copies of this e-mail have been forwarded? About how many people will have seen this e-mail?

Make a comparison:

	What Happened to the Message?	How Many People Heard or Saw the Message?
Whisper Down the Lane	The message changed.	A limited number heard it.
Forward Down the Lane	The message did not change.	Many people read it in just two days!

Always make sure the message used for this activity is appropriate to the age group you teach.

---

an interview for *Wired*, "You're not going to solve the problems just by putting all knowledge onto CD-ROMS. We can put a Web site in every school—none of this is bad. It's bad only if it lulls us into thinking we're doing something to solve the problem with education" (p. 102). Even Thomas Friedman (2006), who gives us a very positive view of technology, writes, "There comes a time when you've got to put away the Game Boy, turn off the television, shut off the iPod, and get your kids down to work" (p. 383).

Finally, technology's globalization of communication has created a **digital divide** between those who have the resources to access and use electronic literacy and those who do not. In affluent communities, schools, and homes, students and teachers may own or have access to computers at almost any time However, not all communities, schools, and homes are affluent. Teachers and students in poorer communities may find that trying to access electronic literacy creates a chasm between their educational progress and that of the technologically advanced. Oppenheimer (2003) describes the digital divide as "the shortage of technological gear that has supposedly cheated the poor out of social and economic opportunities, but which is actually a very different problem" (p. xviii).

To close this section, consider several "techno-blunders" (Wepner, 2004) that can occur if educators assume that technology is a panacea. Wepner identifies some cautions:

- Always have a backup plan (of course this should be true for any lesson taught).
- Make sure that a technological tool is really easier and more effective than another way. Do not assume that students can use the technology.
- Understand that using technology takes time—it is not a quick fix.
- Use technology in creative ways—why replicate what can be done as effectively or better with paper?
- Select Web sites that fit the learners' skills, not because they are there!
- Beware of publisher claims (of course this should be true for paper materials too).
- Make sure there is a support system for the technology you plan to use.
- Make sure assistance is available.
- Make sure the technology works before starting the lesson.

Wepner, Seminoff, and Blanchard (1995) caution that teachers who understand their goals and are involved in planning for technological innovation will be more successful than those who do not understand what the cautions are. They encourage teachers making curricular decisions to ask the following questions:

- Where are we?
- Where do we want to be?
- How do we get there?
- How do we know we are there?

This chapter is available in a hypertext format so that readers can read it and also follow any links that the electronic text provides.

In the rest of this chapter we describe several varieties of technological resources. This information may help teachers answer questions and make wise decisions about integrating technology into their classroom instruction. Because this field is changing so rapidly, we invite readers to use the DVD that accompanies this textbook for access to current information.

TECHNOLOGY IN YOUR CLASSROOM

What will technology resources look like in future classrooms? They will surely take advantage of **distance learning** opportunities, such as videoconferencing. Two-way communication is improving, whereby students in one classroom can connect with other classrooms in geographically distant locations for real-time, or synchronous, discussion. Or individuals can go online for learning opportunities, choosing a convenient time to participate in a threaded discussion or locate Internet resources. Although many learners might access the same site, they may be there at different times, thus participating in an asynchronous manner.

Teachers will develop more and more Web sites, where they will post homework assignments, independent lessons, clarifications, notes to students and parents, streamed videos for home computer viewing about a topic, treasure hunts and WebQuests that guide students to appropriate sites to find content information, and much more. Web sites will be showcases for student work, so that others in schools far away—and students' relatives—can see. Students will send their homework and papers electronically, ask questions of teachers via e-mail, and share notes with other students, all online. Some students are now taking entire courses online.

More electronic devices will be brought to classrooms and used along with or instead of books. Some of these will be personal digital assistants (PDAs), laptop computers, and cell phones. Soon teachers will need an announcement similar to that of airlines: Please turn off all electronic devices.

All these possibilities can enhance content instruction and open new resources far beyond what a static, concise textbook can provide. Why should we consider technology as a resource for learning? "This is a nonquestion," according to Bruce (1998). Technology engages learners by providing motivation—a reason to learn and a need to know within a new environment. Technology engages learners by developing their contextual knowledge and showing the world in new ways. For instance, writing to friends via e-mail creates a new and vital use for reading in a social environment (Baker, 2001); and learners can compose questions to experts in distant locations and read replies to those self-generated questions. Technology can make personal inquiry and purposeful reading and writing powerful tools.

Technology engages learners because they want to know effective strategies to find discussion groups and listservs to read what others have said about a topic, to locate Web sites, and to access databases. Technology can engage learners because it can provide the means to a social process: From remote locations we can learn together.

Throughout this textbook we provide technological applications and notes to help readers make electronic literacy connections. Each chapter ends with PAR Online, where a threaded discussion topic may be suggested, and several Web sites are collected. The authors recognize that the field of electronic literacy is far outpacing the speed of publishing on paper. That is why we offer some technological alternatives along with this textbook.

ONE-MINUTE SUMMARY

Faced with an ever-expanding amount of content to be digested and learned in every content area subject, teachers increasingly realize that no single textbook can deliver all the concepts in, and differing viewpoints about, any unit of study. Thus many content area teachers are turning to electronic resources that complement textbooks. This chapter has presented information about technological literacy that can facilitate instruction. A rationale for electronic literacy was provided, featuring changes in culture and history that have led to electronic literacy and standards for instructional technology. Some advantages and cautions about electronic literacy were addressed, along with technology for classroom use, including visual media, production applications, software, e-books, the possibilities of the Internet in instruction, and e-literacy/communication. We ended with a brief look at the future.

PAR ONLINE

Visit the *Reading to Learn in the Content Areas* Web site at http://academic.cengage.com/education/richardson for links to the Web sites mentioned in this chapter, tutorial quizzing, and other resources.

END-OF-CHAPTER ACTIVITIES

Assisting Comprehension

1. Read this entire chapter online to experience a hyperlinked, electronic text environment.

2. A list of the applications and instructional software mentioned in this chapter can be found at the *Reading to Learn in the Content Areas* Web site; select the Chapter 7 resources.

Reflecting on Your Reading

The International Reading Association (2003) has developed a set of standards that identify the performance criteria relevant to classroom teachers. Standard 4 delineates two elements for creating a literate environment that a classroom teacher should possess. The classroom teacher should

4.1 Use technology to gather and to use this information in instructional planning. They can articulate the research base that grounds their practice.

4.2 Select books, technology-based information, and nonprint materials representing multiple levels, broad interests, and cultural and linguistic backgrounds. They can articulate the research that grounds their practice.

How were these two elements addressed in this chapter? How does being informed about these elements aid in content instruction?

CHAPTER 8

Study depends on the goodwill of the student, a quality that cannot be secured by compulsion.

QUINTILIAN (35–100 A.D.)

Study Skills in the Electronic Age

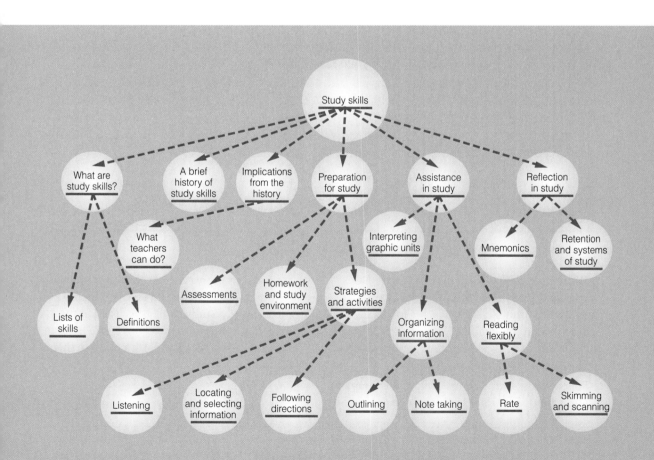

VOICES FROM THE CLASSROOM

Manny sits down to study in his bedroom. It is 9 p.m., and he plans to work on homework until at least 11 p.m. First he turns on the television—he has his own TV in his room and wants to watch his favorite show while studying—and then he boots up his laptop. Making sure his cell phone is beside him, he opens Instant Messenger to see who is ready to talk. He also connects to Skype in case he receives a phone call online from his friend across the country.

Opening his favorite browser, he finds the Web page his teacher assigned for the class to study, but then he remembers that he wanted to visit Facebook and post some comments on a friend's page, so he opens a second browser window and does that. Going back to the Web site, he considers the questions his teacher provided and begins to read to answer the questions. He moves to a second and third site the teacher listed. He decides to copy and paste some of the text into his own document so he can better make notes; he highlights the text he thinks is important, copies some sections into this new document, and finally answers all the questions he was assigned, some with direct quotations from the Web sites he has visited. Then he e-mails the homework file to his teacher.

At midnight he is wrapping up: He has talked on Skype to a friend, sent five text messages, participated in a lively IM discussion, visited Facebook and YouTube, and also studied three Web sites for homework.

In your opinion, is Manny studying? What differs between how he uses his time and how you might do so?

Look for a link to a similar story (found in *The Washington Post* on 2/26/07) at the Web links option of the Chapter 8 resources on this book's companion Web site.

PREPARING TO READ

1. What study skills do you use? List them. Do you teach study skills as you teach content? If so, list the study skills you teach. How many are described in this chapter? Can you add to your repertoire of study skills training methods after reading and studying this chapter?

2. Following is a list of terms used in this chapter. Some may be familiar to you in a general context, but in this chapter they may be used in unfamiliar ways. See if you can match the terms to a study strategy as listed in the following columns. Be ready to locate them in the chapter, and pay special attention to their meanings.

A Study Strategy or Category	A Study Behavior	A Term about Computer-Based Study	A Theory about Study	A Study Activity
Write term here	Write term here	Write term here	Write term here	Write term here

_____ study behaviors and tactics

_____ study strategy

_____ transmission versus transaction

_____ self-regulation

_____ information literate

_____ time management

_____ podcasts

_____ time-shifting

_____ Google Scholar

_____ Wikipedia

_____ previewing

_____ two-column note-taking system

_____ massed study

_____ mnemonics

_____ acronym

_____ acrostic

_____ method of loci

_____ chunking

_____ Go MAD

_____ fluency

_____ saccadic eye movements

_____ skimming

_____ scanning

_____ mental push-ups

_____ rapid reading drills

_____ preview and rapid reading drill

_____ study system

OBJECTIVES

As you read this chapter, focus your attention on the following purposes. You will

1. Understand the importance of developing students' ability to use study skills at all grade levels.

2. Learn the importance of self-regulation and deep thinking in study.

3. Be able to assess students' perceptions of study skills and how they study.

4. Describe several categories of study skills and see their place in the PAR Framework.

5. Describe several activities that lead students to effective study behaviors.

6. Note the differences between paper-based and Web-based study behaviors.

7. Understand the systems of study described in this chapter and be able to use them in your own classroom.

8. Find ways to integrate study strategies and activities into early elementary curricula.

9. Find ways to incorporate technology with study skills activities.

INTRODUCTION

Everyone recognizes that study skills are crucial to academic success, even though study skills do not seem to be the most popular topic in research and literature about reading. Jack Cassidy, who has offered a list of "what's hot and what's not" in *Reading Today* and the *Journal of Adolescent and Adult Literacy* for the past several years, notes that none of his lists since the first one in 1997 have ever included study skills (Cassidy, 2007). The closest the "hot" list comes to mentioning study skills is with the topics "technology" or "informational texts" (Cassidy & Cassidy, 2007; Cassidy, Garrett, & Barrera, 2007). An information sidebar in JAAL (Sebasta, 1997) notes the "hot literacy topics of the past" decades at IRA conventions from the 1960s to the 1990s. Study skills are nowhere on this list. Yet study skills may be the "premier practical attainment" (McBride, 1994, p. 461) of anything a student might learn in school. This chapter provides more references from the 1980s rather than more recent ones; this reflects the gap in information about study skills during the 1990s and 2000s.

WHAT ARE STUDY SKILLS?

Merriam-Webster's Online Dictionary (retrieved 2/17/07) defines *study* as the "application of the mental faculties to the acquisition of knowledge." The definition Harris and Hodges (1995) provide in the *Literacy Dictionary* states, "Study skills is a general term for those techniques and strategies that help a person read or listen for specific purposes with the intent to remember; commonly, following directions, locating, selecting, organizing, and retaining information, interpreting typographic and graphic aids, and reading flexibly" (p. 245). In 1984 Rogers defined *study skills* as the deliberate procedures (strategies) a learner uses to retain information. For instance, he noted that when studying, one reads more slowly and uses techniques such as underlining, note taking, rereading, and reading material aloud.

An important distinction should be made between **study behaviors and tactics** versus a **study strategy**, which is the learner's overall approach to selecting the best tactics for a study task (Lenz, Ellis, & Scanlon, 1996). Gettinger and Seibert (2002) explain the distinction in this way: "A study tactic is a sequence of steps or a specific procedure" (p. 352). A study strategy or skill, however, is "an individual's comprehensive approach to a task; it includes how a person thinks and acts when planning and evaluating his or her study behavior. A strategy consists of guidelines and rules related to selecting the best tactics and making decisions about their use" (p. 352). Those who read to learn are employing study strategies and skills. It is important to remember that students may use different behaviors and tactics to accomplish their study strategies and goals. Such an interpretation is important; it helps explain how study skills and strategies can remain constant over time while study behaviors and tactics may change as the environment for study changes.

Lists of study skills usually include listening and reading with attention, creating and understanding visual representations of information, previewing a text before reading, locating information, taking notes, and intending to learn. This list has remained consistent over several years. For instance, as far back as 1909, McMurry cited these important areas as the domain of study skills: setting specific purposes for study; identifying supplemental information; organizing ideas; judging the worth of the material; memorizing; keeping an open attitude; and relying on self-direction in learning. Dechant (1970) organized study skills into five categories: dictionary; location and reference; use of graphics; use of library resources; and organization. In their history of content reading, Moore, Readance, and Rickelman (1983) concluded that study skills included organizing skills, such as note taking, underlining, outlining, and summarizing. Blai (1993) identified comprehension of main ideas, self-monitoring, physical setting, organization, goal setting, and pacing as crucial to effective studying.

A Brief History of Study Skills

The topic of study skills has been written about since the early 1900s. For instance, Moore, Readance, and Rickelman (1983) cite such works as that of Hall-Quest (*Supervised Study,* 1916) and Woodring and Flemming (*Directing Study of High School Pupils,* 1935).

Consider these tenets from Huey (1908/1968, pp. 6–7); they show his emphasis on study skills (the italics are ours) as an important area of study in reading:

- Reading should always be accomplished with a *purpose* in mind that is known to the student.
- *Study skills* such as *library skills* and *note taking* should be taught as early as possible in the elementary grades.
- In high school, students should be given free reign to read widely on subjects of interest. This is preferable to a focused and analytical *study* of a few texts and authors.

In 1937 Gray stated that "pupils should be trained to study effectively as they read" (p. 580). Gray's summaries of early research depict his interest in effective means of study in subject matter. He looked at the value of reading for relationships, outlining, retention of material, and rate in social science materials. Strang published several texts and articles from the 1920s to the 1960s about improving reading and study in high school, such as "Another Attempt to Teach How to Study" (1928), "The Improvement of Reading in High School" (1937), and "Progress in the Teaching of Reading in High School and College" (1962).

A predominant theme in the 1970s was the impact of motivation or affect on study. In *Self-Directed Learning: A Guide for Learners and Teachers,* Knowles (1975) proposed that a learner should practice autonomy and inquiry, with the teacher facilitating that process. Study skills publications in the 1980s focused predominantly on college students. In this decade some significant studies of comprehension and retention were conducted. The intent of such studies was to construct models of curriculum and instruction that would raise literacy to a high standard (Bereiter & Scardamalia, 1987). Langer (1986) reported on her observations of high school juniors at study. She found that different study tasks caused different thinking patterns and learning.

In the 1990s articles describing new ways of perceiving literacy, especially studies about comprehension, often included some relevance for study skills. For instance, when Smith (1992) discussed reading as **transmission** versus reading as **transaction**, he found that students acknowledged being passive about reading and studying textbooks, often missing important clues. Waters and Waters (1992) stressed that there should be an underlying competence for study, especially the ability to think critically. Pressley and Afflerback (1995) reviewed several verbal protocol studies and identified these key study strategies: taking an overview before reading; looking for and paying great attention to important information; relating important points; activating prior knowledge; changing strategies when necessary; and monitoring and fixing up inaccuracies. These key strategies define the importance of metacognition and high literacy. Hattie, Biggs, and Purdie (1996) cautioned that study skills training needs to be conducted in the same context as the skill will be needed and used in order to promote learner active involvement and metacognition. In using the term *situated cognition,* Hattie, Biggs, and Purdie tied their analysis of study skills to a new, more active, and grounded way of looking at comprehension in the 1990s. The use of new technology—specifically computers—stimulated a new way of looking at study skills. Use of computers changed how students studied (Anderson-Inman, 1999a, 1999b). Stahl, Hynd, Britton, McNish, and Bosquet (1996) cautioned that students need specific instruction in the use of multiple resources and helpful notes to broaden their perspectives when studying from multiple sources in history.

The theme of studying as part of the greater picture of comprehension and metacognition continues into the 2000s. Simpson and Nist (2000) have cautioned that strategic learning requires mature and complex knowledge, such as task understanding, ability to generalize, and cognitive and metacognitive processing. A more descriptive term, **self-regulation**, was used by Barnett (2000) because self-regulation includes behavior and affect as well as cognitive awareness. According to Barnett, the more a person feels in control of his or her comprehension, the more self-regulated about study he or she should be. Students can be self-regulated only when they are motivated to be metacognitive and behave actively in their own learning (Young & Ley, 2001). Kitsantas (2002) found that those who performed best on tests regulated their study effectively. Cole and Goetz (2000) concluded from their study of underprepared college students that to be successful in school, a student must possess appropriate beliefs about learning and knowledge. This kind of knowledge is developed over time; it is not static. Holschuh (2001) found that high performers used more thoughtful and specific strategies and seemed to know when to use the most appropriate strategies.

The "age of multiliteracies" (Turbill, 2002), when one reads text plus "color, sound, movement, and visual representations," continued from the 1990s as a predominant consideration. The "information handling skills" students need to take advantage of electronic information became a popular topic of discussion (Macdonald, Heap, & Mason, 2001; Slaouti, 2002). For instance, students have to evaluate the quality of online documents and Web sites, realizing the difference between citing or plagiarizing a source and what copyright laws mean in the Web-based world (Goett & Foot, 2000). The term *new literacies* (Kist, 2000; Moje, 2000; Leu, Kinzer, Coiro, & Cammack, 2004; Moje, Ciechanowski, Kramer, Ellis, Carrillo, & Collazo, 2004) is being used to describe this electronic environment.

As in the early decades of the 20th century, the importance of teaching study skills in the early years has again become prominent in the 1990s and 2000s. There is growing awareness that basic study skills should be introduced to children as early as the first grade (Strauss, 2003). Making information relevant to students at all grade levels increases their motivation to study (Frymier & Schulman, 1995). Throughout this chapter, most strategies and activities presented can be adapted to suit students at every level. Table 8.2 shows where study strategies can be introduced in the curriculum.

What do the terms *metacognition*, *situated cognition*, *transaction*, and *self-regulation* have to do with study?

What Does This Brief History Tell Us about Study Skills?

With the advent of discussion about metacognition, self-regulation, and constructivism, reading processes—including study skills—are now thought to be much more complex and important than any activities, programs, or simple discussions of motivation can account for. Applefield, Huber, and Moallem (2000) have stated,

> The field of education has undergone a significant shift in thinking about the nature of human learning and the conditions that best promote the varied dimensions of human learning. As in psychology, there has been a paradigm shift in designed instruction: from behaviorism to cognitivism and now to constructivism. (p. 36)

Constructivism may be one of the most influential views of learning during the last two decades. It is a significant learning theory that emphasizes a student-centered approach to learning. In a constructivist model, learners build information with teachers' guidance. Readers must actively construct meaning by relating new material to the known, using reasoning and developing concepts. The search for a "perfect" study skills program or the "best" activities is probably fruitless. Certainly students need to be instructed in agreed-upon study skills and strategies, and told about the "tried and true" behaviors and tactics for study that others have found successful. But ultimately the learner must decide why to study and how to study.

Computer-based study skills are needed in today's world. Out of new literacies research has come a plethora of new activities. WebQuests and treasure hunts are now designed by content teachers to guide their students on the World Wide Web to content information that is informative and suitable. Hypertext lets students create their own quick references to word meanings. Outlining software such as *Inspiration* facilitates study.

While the actual technological literacy skills are not new, the *way* that electronic materials must be read is new. As Reinking noted in 1997, although technology itself is neutral, the way we use it to learn enables learners to be more creative and engaged. A reader still must use comprehension, vocabulary, and study skills to construct meaning; but the behaviors students must use differ from those required in a paper-based environment. For instance, when reading from a textbook, one may write notes on index cards or sticky notes. When reading on a computer, one may take notes by inserting remarks into a document in color, or even by using track editing or footnoting. The age of multiliteracies is helping to reintroduce study skills—an area dormant since the early 1900s—into content area reading. Readers must now be **information literate** (Henderson & Scheffler, 2004)—that is, able to find and use information in any paper or electronic form.

WHAT CAN TEACHERS DO?

Study strategies and skills require intensive reading and thinking; the more complex the strategy, the deeper the processing must be. More energy will be expended in study when several tactics or behaviors need to be used. For instance, to study one should read the information and then repeat the reading via note taking, highlighting, mapping, or other means of learning. Then one needs to organize that information by schematizing it. Next one needs to think about the information and how it is useful to the learning goal—perhaps by generating questions and linking answers from the organized notations. During all this study, the learner must plan, monitor, and assess how the study is progressing and when to alter a tactic for more effective and efficient study. This entire study process is based on an information-processing model, explained by Gettinger and Seibert (2002).

As Hubbard and Simpson (2003) suggest, we also recommend that assessments of study skills for today's students must find out if the behaviors and tactics students create and use are task-appropriate and sufficiently deep. Just asking students to complete a checklist won't discover students' personal theories about learning. Further, assessments have to consider both paper and electronic study contexts, as well as what tactics a student would self-select to study in either environment.

To rely on only demonstrations and lectures about study skills, or to assume that students can practice such skills independently or that students will see their importance, is a fallacy. Purdie and Hattie (1999), after analyzing 52 studies about outcomes of and relations between study skills, concluded that when students learn effective study behaviors and incorporate them into a meaningful approach to learning, they experience academic and affective results. Self-directed learning, as Sobrol (1997) noted, benefits most students.

Gee (2000) cautioned that working-class teens see uses of literacy differently than do upper-middle-class teens who are immersed in a more academic world. If we are to help all students study in the age of multiple literacy experiences, we must enable all students to find the value of study skills and their own way of accessing study in the electronic age. Students today are learning increasingly complex literacy practices and navigating complicated technologies (Moje, 2002). Are we ready to help them with study tactics that work?

To remain competitive in a global economy, students must know how to study in a different environment than they have in the past century. Web-based reading and study differ from paper-based study, and they sometimes produce less efficient study and resultant learning (Eveland & Dunwoody, 2002). It is not the study skills that are different, though; it is the tactics a learner must use to study in a computer-based environment. Studies by Eveland and Dunwoody (2002) and by Anderson-Inman, Knox-Quinn, and Szymanski (1999) show that learners can adapt to computer-based study tactics.

When we consider the students of this millennium and the themes raised within a historical perspective, the possibilities for study that is refreshing, challenging, exciting, and learner-controlled contribute to the makings of a crucial topic in the field of reading. Study is difficult and time-consuming, and many students do not know how to apply themselves sufficiently to become productive learners. Onwuegbuzie, Slate, and Schwartz (2001) found that graduate students responded appropriately only 57.8 percent of the time to statements about their study skills. If even graduate students are not good students, then what about younger, more diverse students? A survey conducted in 2000 (American School Counseling Association) showed that

- 70 percent of teachers say their students have poor study skills.
- 60 percent of guidance counselors say students are not prepared adequately to do homework assignments.
- Around 50 percent of schools do not offer study skills courses.
- Of those that do, only 11 percent require students to take these courses.
- Even though most counselors feel it is effective for learners to study in a group, 57 percent of students do their homework at home; only 9 percent study in a group.

Teachers can help students by providing opportunities whereby study leads to learning interesting information and where the payoff is worth the effort expended. Unfortunately most teachers do not seem to know about or to value study strategies and are unsure how to integrate study skills with content (Elliot, Foster, & Stinson, 2002; Jackson & Cunningham, 1994). This is so despite research showing that students who use a range of study skills achieve greater success in school (Purdie & Hattie, 1999) and research suggesting that good study habits lead to academic success (Jones, Slate, & Marini, 1995; Belzer, Miller, & Hoemake, 2003).

For the remainder of this chapter, we will use the PAR Framework to present ideas that can facilitate appropriate, self-regulated study skills.

Preparation for Study

ASSESSMENTS

Just as with any other reading-to-learn task, one must prepare for study. To be prepared, we must realize what we know and what we need to know. Therefore, an assessment of the reader's skills and strategies is an important first step. Most standardized achievement tests include subtests of study skills. However, these subtests are usually limited in scope, measuring students' knowledge of standard items such as reference skills, alphabetization, and the ability to read maps, charts, and graphs. Often neglected are important skills such as following directions, presenting a report, test taking, note taking, and memory training. In a review of past instruments to assess study, the authors have found that most assessments are outdated; they originated in the 1980s, such as Rogers's 1984 checklist. Rogers's informal checklist was intended to help teachers and students realize what they do while studying and what else they may need to do. In designing his checklist, he drew from Karlin's (1977) checklist and his own experiences and organized his checklist into four basic categories: (1) study and reading comprehension skills, including interpreting graphic aids and following directions; (2) location skills, including varying reading rate and location of information; (3) retention, including remembering what is studied; and (4) organizing information.

The LASSI (Learning and Study Strategies Inventory) was published in 1988 (Weinstein, Zimmerman, & Palmer). This commercially published instrument is still in use to evaluate learning and study strategies. It is a 76-item inventory that asks self-report questions about study. Eldredge (1990) developed the LASSI-HS, a high school version of the college-level LASSI.

In the early 2000s Mokhtari and Reichard (2002) designed the Metacognitive Awareness of Reading Strategies Inventory (MARSI). The intent of the MARSI is to help assess students' perception and use of strategies while reading to learn. The MARSI uses a self-report instrument that relies on students' metacognitive awareness and perceived use of reading to help them learn material.

None of these assessments reflects the current need for a way to assess what students actually do as they study. Smith (1992) developed a series of 18 questions to provoke thoughtful responses about how students encounter textbooks. The questionnaire is broader than study skills, including perceptions of interest in the textbook and judgments about the writing style and worth of the content. The questionnaire does not include any reference to the difference between paper and computer-based study environments. To address the need for a broader assessment of study skills, Rhodes, Robnolt, and Richardson (2005) used Harris and Hodges's definition of study skills (1995), creating seven categories of study skills. To clarify what each of these categories might mean and include, they referred to Rogers's list of study skills (1984), as well as what the literature indicated about study skills. The newest version of their study skills questionnaire has 11 categories of study skills (see Activity 8.1). These categories are grouped according to the PAR Framework. The questionnaire asks students to think about whether they use each skill, whether they use it with electronic and paper materials, and how they use the skill. This assessment is intended for student self-reflection; it is best administered either over time or in a nontimed session. While a teacher can immediately see what skills students think they use by the ratings, we also encourage teachers to talk with students about how they use the skills. Only when teachers realize what students actually do to achieve a study skill will they know how to guide effective study.

How can a study skills checklist be used in content area instruction? What else should teachers find out?

HOMEWORK AND STUDY CONDITIONS

Before study starts, the environment and conditions for study should be optimal. Students will attend to tasks better if they are taught to concentrate and think about what they are learning and to be responsible for their own learning. Study distracters can interfere significantly with learning information and completing assignments in a timely manner. To fend off external distracters, the following types of questions are useful: Where is one going to study? What interruptions may interfere, such as the telephone, instant messages, television, or enticing Web sites to wander into? Is the necessary study equipment at hand, such as pencils, highlighters, sticky notes, Internet access, and necessary software? To avoid internal distracters, questions such as these could be posed: Do I have a realistic study plan and enough time to study? Am I bringing unresolved issues to the study that might interfere with my concentration? To avoid physical distracters, key questions might be these: Have I had enough to eat to give me energy to study but not to weigh me down? Have I slept enough to be refreshed for study?

Time management can also contribute to successful study conditions. **Time management** has been defined by Francis-Smythe and Robertson (1999) as effectively using one's time through prioritizing, planning, and adhering to a schedule. Positive time management has been associated with higher achievement levels in

Demographic Information

NATIVE LANGUAGE _____ AGE _____

COUNTRY OF CITIZENSHIP _____ MALE OR FEMALE (CIRCLE ONE)

DO YOU READ FROM COMPUTER-BASED TEXTS?   YES   NO
(CIRCLE ONE)

Please complete the following checklist and add your description of how you would go about using each study skill. Please ask for help with any items you do not understand. Answer the questions in ALL columns.

	How often do you use this skill when reading text from the COMPUTER screen? Circle ONE: A—Always F—Frequently S—Sometimes N— Never	Study Behavior/ Tactic: How would you use this skill? Please describe what you would do for each skill when using an electronic (computer) text to study.	How often do you use this skill when reading a PAPER text? Circle ONE: A—Always F—Frequently S—Sometimes N—Never	Study Behavior/ Tactic: How would you use this skill? Please describe what you would do for each skill when using a traditional (paper) text to study.
Study Skills/Strategies for Reading				
Demonstrate good study habits (P–A–R):				
I know how to create a positive environment for study.	A F S N	Such as (circle and annotate): Few distractions. Equipment at hand. Plan time to study effectively. Use time to study effectively.	A F S N	Such as (circle and annotate): Few distractions. Equipment at hand. Plan time to study effectively. Use time to study effectively.
I do my homework successfully (P–A–R):	A F S N		A F S N	
Listening (P & A):				
I listen so I know what to study.	A F S N		A F S N	
I listen to take good notes.	A F S N		A F S N	
Locating and selecting information (P–A):				
I use an online library catalog.	A F S N		Not applicable	
I can find reference materials.	A F S N		A F S N	

(continued) ➤

Activity 8.1 *(continued)*

	Circle ONE:	Study Behavior/ Tactic:	Circle ONE:	Study Behavior/ Tactic:
I can use a card catalog.	Not applicable		A F S N	
I can use a search engine to find information.	A F S N		Not applicable	
I can find information in a dictionary.	A F S N		A F S N	
I can use guide words or letters to find a word.	A F S N	Such as (circle and annotate): Find feature.	A F S N	
I can find word origins.	A F S N		A F S N	
I can find information in a preface.	A F S N		A F S N	
I can find information in a table of contents.	A F S N		A F S N	
I can find information in a book chapter.	A F S N		A F S N	
I can find information in headings.	A F S N		A F S N	
I can find information in footnotes.	A F S N		A F S N	
I can find information in a glossary.	A F S N		A F S N	
I can find information in an index.	A F S N		A F S N	
I can find information in an appendix.	A F S N		A F S N	
I can find information in an encyclopedia.	A F S N		A F S N	
I can find a phone number.	A F S N		A F S N	
I can find a map and driving directions.	A F S N		A F S N	
I can find specific information in a newspaper.	A F S N		A F S N	
I can find information using book parts such as title, author's name, edition, and publisher.	A F S N		A F S N	
I can find information about the copyright of the text.	A F S N		A F S N	
I can use subheadings in text to find what I need to know.	A F S N		A F S N	

Activity 8.1 *(continued)*

	Circle ONE:				Study Behavior/ Tactic:	Circle ONE:				Study Behavior/ Tactic:
I ask myself questions while I am reading and studying so I can remember better.	A	F	S	N		A	F	S	N	
When I want to show something is important, I use a tactic to do so.	A	F	S	N	Such as (circle and annotate): Highlighting text. Underlining text.	A	F	S	N	Such as (circle and annotate): Highlighting text. Underlining text.
Following directions (P & A):										
I read to understand important information.	A	F	S	N		A	F	S	N	
I read to understand important relationships.	A	F	S	N		A	F	S	N	
I read to understand important details.	A	F	S	N		A	F	S	N	
Interpreting typographic and graphic aids (A):	A	F	S	N		A	F	S	N	
I can usually look at a picture or comic and understand it.	A	F	S	N		A	F	S	N	
I can usually look at a chart or graph and understand it.	A	F	S	N		A	F	S	N	
Study Skills/Strategies for Reading					**Study Behavior/ Tactic:** How would you use this skill? Please describe what you would do for each skill when using an electronic (computer) text to study.					**Study Behavior/ Tactic:** How would you use this skill? Please describe what you would do for each skill when using a traditional (paper) text to study.
Organizing information (A):										
I can create a way to remember information	A	F	S	N	Such as (circle and annotate): Mnemonic aids. Taking notes. Writing summary. Highlighting. Underlining.	A	F	S	N	Such as (circle and annotate): Mnemonic aids. Taking notes. Writing summary. Highlighting. Underlining.
Retaining information (R):										
I remember what I read.	A	F	S	N	Such as (circle and annotate): Repeating information. Drawing a picture. Taking notes. Writing a summary. Making an outline. Using text editing.	A	F	S	N	Such as (circle and annotate): Repeating information. Drawing a picture. Taking notes. Writing a summary. Making an outline. Using text editing.

Activity 8.1 *(continued)*

	Circle ONE:				Study Behavior/Tactic:	Circle ONE:				Study Behavior/Tactic:
Reading flexibly (A–R):										
I know how to read over text quickly to get the general idea.	A	F	S	N	Such as (circle and annotate): Using search and find. Skimming. Scanning.	A	F	S	N	Such as (circle and annotate): Using search and find. Skimming. Scanning.
I know how to locate information.	A	F	S	N		A	F	S	N	
I can change how fast I read when I want to find only one piece of information.	A	F	S	N		A	F	S	N	
I can change how fast I read when I need to think and remember important information.	A	F	S	N		A	F	S	N	
Systems of study (P–A–R):										
I study in a way that follows a system.	A	F	S	N	Such as (circle and annotate): SQ3R = survey, question, read, recite, review. 3Rs = read, review, reflect.	A	F	S	N	Such as (circle and annotate): SQ3R = survey, question, read, recite, review. 3Rs = read, review, reflect.

Developed by J. S. Richardson, J. Rhodes, and V. Robnolt (2004); updated (2007). Used by permission.

students (Britton & Tesser, 1991) and with improved self-evaluations of academic performance (Macan, et al., 1990).

An effective technique for teaching time management is to get students to monitor themselves with self-evaluation logs. An activity that can be modified for different grade levels is "How I Spend My Time." First students estimate how they think they spend their time. The teacher keeps these estimates. Next students record how they use their time for a given period. For first or second graders, one day is enough—from waking up until bedtime. Recording can be completed with teacher supervision during the school day. For upper elementary and middle school students, a week is an appropriate block of time. Students should keep records outside school hours, but the teacher might provide some class time for catching up. For high school and beyond, the block of time should be at least a week, with recording of all hours—even sleep—done outside class. Next students examine their records and compare the activities in which they spent their time with their estimates of how they thought they would spend it. Results are often revealing and help students see where they can make changes.

Eleventh graders who participated in such a time management study in their English class were asked to indicate

- How much time they spent on study and recreation.
- How much more study time was needed.
- Where time could be found in the schedule for more study.

The students wrote study goals such as "I will study 10 more minutes each evening for English class." They also wrote rewards that they might receive if they achieved a goal, such as "Because I studied wisely, I will probably get a better grade." A classmate had to sign the contract; a parent's signature was optional. Students were to consistently practice achieving their goals for a month. Here are some responses they recorded in their journals:

1. What was your time management goal?

   K: My time management goal was to spend more of my time studying—more quality time, that is—and thus achieve a better understanding of the material.

   J: My time management goal was to increase preparation—for instance, for tests, quizzes, and essays.

   E: My goal was to spend time studying and preparing for class.

2. Did you achieve this goal? Why or why not?

   K: I achieved my goal because I studied the material more extensively instead of just reading over it.

   J: I did not achieve my goal because of my lack of will and lack of time for preparation.

   E: Sort of. I did spend some more time, but not enough.

3. What did you discover about managing your time for study in English?

   K: I need to spend more time preparing for class instead of talking to friends on the phone. Also, I need to understand the material more fully.

   J: I found out that I spend most of my time working. I spent at least 7 hours a day on school days and 16–19 hours on weekends working. The rest of my time went to being at school and some time—very little—sleeping.

   E: I found that my priorities were not entirely in order. I previously would watch TV, eat dinner, and lie around before doing my homework. I now do my homework as soon as I get home, shower, and eat dinner, and then I take my leisure time. I sometimes study just before going to sleep as well.

4. Was this assignment helpful? Why or why not?

   K: The assignment was helpful to me because the chart helped me to budget my time more wisely.

   J: The assignment was helpful because it made me realize what I was doing and should be doing. I should spend more time on schoolwork, but at this time it is not possible.

   E: This assignment was helpful because it allowed me to get somewhat of a schedule together in order to get things done. I seem to work much more efficiently now, and my grades have improved.

The teacher observed progress in grades and attitudes. She attributed the success to students' involvement and control of their own progress. Students provided their own data about specific uses of time and then decided what they wanted to

When teachers can post a Web site where homework is placed, the contents can be printed out or placed on disk so that parents or supervisors in other study environments can help students do the assignments.

improve and how. The assignment did not take much class time, and responsibility improved.

For many students, changing the study environment at home might be difficult. Some children in inner cities have witnessed murders, dodged bullets, and gone to bed hungry on numerous occasions. Experimenting with study environments at home will not work under such conditions. However, arranging for the school or community to provide a study environment in another location might help (for example, in the school after hours or in a local community center or place of worship).

A particular area of concern in assessing study skills should be assessing homework study habits. Helping students find the best behaviors for homework is part of study preparation. Homework also provides practice for study, so it can be thought of as spanning the PAR stages. Schneider and Stephenson (1999) call students directionless, noting that they spend as much as 20 percent of their time alone and may have less oversight at home when 60 percent of mothers work outside the home. The researchers postulate that students today are particularly disadvantaged when it comes to homework. Besides not having strong parental guidance, students also encounter homework that is too difficult or boring and not of any inherent interest to them. Teachers need to consider whether the homework they assign is too difficult or too boring. If so, the first changes to be made toward successful homework can be made by teachers. If not, teachers can help students learn how to better handle homework. One way is to challenge students to think about how they do homework; are they like Manny in this chapter's opening scenario? Do they concentrate and accomplish the homework tasks in a reasonable amount of time? Are they engaged during homework time? As an experiment, teachers can ask students to conduct homework study in their usual way for a block of time (dependent on the age of the students) and then in the teacher's way (using behaviors the teacher has introduced as a result of his or her own study of the research) for the same amount of time. While studying, students can note how much they accomplish. Usually they discover by experimenting that at least some of the teacher's tips about a study environment really do help them study.

Homework is important; studies show that the amount of time spent doing homework is positively correlated with achievement (Keith, Reimers, Fehrmann, Pottebaum, & Aubey, 1986). Because of homework's importance, and because much study is done independently in the home, teachers also may want to assess what parents do to help their children study and how students evaluate their own study habits. Activity 8.2 provides examples for kindergartners and first graders, but adaptations can be made for any grade level. Teachers who have compared parents' to students' responses have discovered a difference in perception between the two groups. For instance, parents indicate that students do have a special place to study (see "Survey of Parents," Item 1), but students indicate that they do not ("Survey of Students," Item 6). Discussing such findings early in the school year with both students and parents can help establish positive study environments from the beginning of the school year.

The surveys in Activity 8.2 also provide several indicators about environments conducive to studying. Without a good study environment, study strategies will not be effective.

Preparation Strategies and Activities

The following strategies and activities are grounded in the preparation stage of study, but they can also be considered as part of the assistance stage of study, depending on the circumstances.

LISTENING

Listening is the foundation for all other study skills, and it can enhance learning in any classroom. Listening is a prerequisite for taking good notes from an oral presentation. In conjunction with teaching keywords and previewing, training in listening has been found to increase oral reading proficiency among low-achieving students (O'Donnell, Weber, & McLaughlin, 2003; Skinner, Cooper, & Cole, 1997). A classic listening activity is the directed listening technique (Gold, 1981) for motivating and guiding students to improve listening. Before the lesson, teachers ask students to listen for certain information in the presentation or in the oral reading. In this pre-presentation phase, students brainstorm areas of interest and questions to be answered. Teachers then deliver a presentation or read portions of a chapter from a textbook. In this way, students are trained to know what they must listen for and what they are expected to learn from listening.

Such an activity provides a means of study in a social context, which learners often find productive.

As a variation, listening guides can be constructed to point to parts of a lecture or oral reading that need to be emphasized. Here students are taught to listen more carefully for details and key points. Through such an active listening strategy, even primary students can be trained to be better listeners. Activity 8.3 presents such a listening guide for a high school class on the topic of genetics.

Another classic activity, listen–read–discuss or LRD, was developed by Alvermann (1987a). With this technique, the teacher first lectures about a selected portion of material. Students then read that portion with the purpose of comparing the lecture and the written content. Afterward students and teacher discuss the lecture and reading. LRD works best to promote discussion if the material is well organized.

Survey of Parents

Please circle YES or NO in front of each statement.

YES	NO	**1.** My child has a special place to study. Where? _____
YES	NO	**2.** My child has an independent reading time each night. When? _____
YES	NO	**3.** My child watches television while completing homework.
YES	NO	**4.** I always supervise my child's homework period.
YES	NO	**5.** I sometimes help my child with homework.
YES	NO	**6.** I listen to my child read.
YES	NO	**7.** My child has a set bedtime. When? _____
YES	NO	**8.** I check over my child's homework.
YES	NO	**9.** My child has a place to put materials that must be returned to school.
YES	NO	**10.** My child eats breakfast daily.
YES	NO	**11.** I discuss with my child how he or she does in school each day.
YES	NO	**12.** I read to my child often.

Survey of Students

Circle the true sentences as you read them.

1. I bring my books to school each day.
2. I listen in class.
3. I read the directions when I begin my work.
4. I ask questions when I don't know what to do.
5. I do my homework every night.
6. I have a special place to do my homework.
7. No one helps me with my homework.
8. I watch TV when I do my homework.
9. I bring my homework to school.
10. I am a good student.

These two surveys were adapted with permission from surveys done by Cornelia Hill.

The student listening activity (SLA) (Choate & Rakes, 1987) is another technique for improving listening skills. In using this strategy, the teacher first discusses concepts in the material and sets a clear purpose for listening, then reads aloud, interspersing several prediction cues with the reading. Finally, the teacher questions students about what they heard, using three levels of questions: factual, inferential, and applied.

The authors of this book have designed "first step to note taking," which also promotes listening and purpose setting. One result of this technique is that it offers

Listening purpose: Listen for the three aspects of genetics.
Directions: As you listen to the lecture, circle all of the topics you hear discussed. Feel free to make notes about the subjects as you hear about them in the lecture.

Heredity	**DNA**	**Mutation**
Traits	Replication	Inbreeding
Genes	Proteins	Hybridization
Dominant	Chromosomes	Producing insulin
Recessive		Cloning
Genotype		
Homozygous		
Heterozygous		
Phenotype		

Note: After listening to the lecture, get together with several of your classmates and see if they circled the same words you did. Discuss the meanings of the words.

---

practice in group note-taking strategies. Thus "first step to note taking" is a listening activity, a note-taking activity, and a cooperative grouping activity. The activity can be modified for teacher-based instruction or for an independent student learning experience, depending on the ages of students. The activity consists of five steps:

1. Either the teacher or a student defines a listening purpose. If, for instance, the student is completing an activity for independent practice, perhaps he or she will listen to the evening news for the purpose of identifying the major stories and two significant details of each story.

2. Listening with a purpose commences. Students might listen to the teacher read, listen to the news on television, or listen to a tape recording, for example. No writing is allowed during the listening.

Students can organize the listening and note taking in two-column form, as shown in a later example in this chapter when we discuss two-column note taking.

3. The students react by listing what they heard in relationship to the stated purpose. Responses are now recorded, but no modifications are made.

4. Students listen to the material again, with their lists in sight. No writing is allowed during the listening. (If students listened to the evening news, then either a recording of that news broadcast or a later news show would provide an appropriate second listening.)

5. Individually or in small groups, students edit their lists—adding, deleting, or modifying information—and organize them into information following a logical pattern. They have now generated notes for study.

These techniques can be adapted for a computer environment also. One way would be through PowerPoint presentations that use the voice feature. Technology today lets teachers use voice, either synchronously or asynchronously, in online teaching. Students

Visit the Pew Internet and American Life Project sites to learn more; check out some Web sites where you can download podcasts and create them free and simply. Go to the Web links option of the Chapter 8 resources on this book's companion Web site.

can practice using listening skills while in an online class that uses synchronous chats or voice with discussion threads.

Podcasts are popular with Internet users (see Chapter 7 for more information). The value of audio files for practicing listening skills is that students can listen as many times as they need to before they are ready to proceed to the lesson. A device such as an iPod—which many young people possess or have easy access to—is portable and compact, used for numerous listening purposes already. So listening to a podcast that lets students practice listening tactics for study is a great integration of modern technology with the academic world. Podcasts allow **time-shifting** in learning—study at all times rather than only at the "homework" hour. Podcasts offer a new way to deliver learning opportunities. Costa (2006) recommends that teachers post assignments in podcasts for students to listen to. After students become familiar with podcasts, they can create their own podcasts about a topic and post them for other class members to download and listen to, thus using listening to learn more about any topic. Activity 8.4 shows an assignment for listening to a podcast about microbes for middle school students.

LOCATING AND SELECTING INFORMATION

Until students understand the importance of locating information, they can't select what they should study. Knowing how information is organized can help students find information in a table of contents, index, preface, headings, footnotes, glossaries, or appendix. At the beginning of a school year, content teachers might use a textbook inventory as a class activity to help them learn about their students' proficiency in using textbooks. This activity assesses students' knowledge of the parts of a book and can be effective at any grade level—K through 12. Activity 8.5 is a parts-of-the-book search developed to help students in a computer class become familiar with a word processing manual.

The danger of locating incorrect information increases exponentially with the plethora of resources on the Web, many of which are questionable. Students must have guidance to know where to locate material for study in both paper and computer

---

ACTIVITY *8.4* LISTENING TO A PODCAST

1. Go to the Odeon Web site* and select a 90-second podcast from the American Society for Microbiology with the title "Propane and microbial accessories."
2. Play the podcast (either listen online or download it and listen on your podcasting device).
3. Listen as many times as you need to.
4. Write a statement that tells what this podcast is about, such as this: "Bugs—microbes—in the cold, deep sea sediment are turning organic matter into ethane and propane. They are extracting energy!"
5. How many people did you hear talking in this podcast? (Two voices)
6. How long was this podcast? (90 seconds)
7. Why did you like listening to this podcast?

   *Web sites are provided on our book's companion Web site.

BECOMING FAMILIAR AND COMFORTABLE WITH THE MANUAL

1. What are the titles of the three people named in the acknowledgments section of the book?

   a. _____

   b. _____

   c. _____

2. On what page do you find the explanation of the special symbols used in the table of contents? How many special symbols are used in the manual?

   Page _____

   Number of special symbols _____

3. How many appendixes does the manual contain? _____ Which appendix explains the features bars? _____

4. On what page does the manual begin talking about using columns, and how many different types of column does WordPerfect allow you to choose from?

   Page _____ Types of columns _____

5. What two things do you find at the end of each section?

   a. _____

   b. _____

6. What are the two types of "objectives" found in the manual? Explain the difference.

   a. _____

   b. _____

7. On what page will you find an explanation of the icons for drawing tools used in WP Draw? Page _____

8. On what page will you find an explanation of how to insert columns or rows into a table? Page _____

9. Where did you look to find the page number to answer the previous question—the table of contents or the index? _____ Would either one work?

   Yes _____ No _____

10. On what page would you find a table listing the different custom box types? Page _____ How many types are available to you?

    _____

11. Name the three major topics covered in the manual.

    a. _____

    b. _____

    c. _____

12. Where do you find an explanation of the keyboard shortcuts? _____

Developed by Mary L. Seward.

resources. Although past generations of learners remember the card catalog as their major resource for locating information, we seldom find any card catalogs today except in antique stores or in use as CD and DVD storage containers. Libraries now use online catalogs. Searching the Internet falls under the study skill of locating and selecting information; but in the information age this requires new behaviors. Teachers must know and share this important information about how to search and what the results of a search really mean in relation to the importance of citations and best choices. In Chapter 7 we presented an activity to demonstrate the importance of critical thinking by tracking authors of Web sites (the Martin Luther King activity). To successfully search the Internet, Henry (2006) proposes a searching system she calls SEARCH. The acronym stands for the following:

Set a purpose for searching.

Employ effective search strategies.

Analyze search engine results.

Read critically and synthesize information.

Cite your sources.

How successful was your search?

Teachers today can help themselves and their students gather information by subscribing to online services for deciphering and organizing incoming information, such as the free service InfoBeat or a pay service such as Lexis-Nexis Universe. InfoBeat offers a way to keep abreast of news without spending money; but caution must be observed because it can quickly overwhelm an e-mail account with volumes of information.

Search engines such as Google or Yahoo! are used often, but they can be a dubious source of help. Even though the information located may seem credible, it might be biased. A good alternative is **Google Scholar**, which searches scholarly journals and selected areas of the Web. Teachers can also create Google custom search engines. Kidsclick is a Web site for preschool through high school readers, reviewed by children's librarians and searchable by grade level. For a simple way to begin a search on Kidsclick, see Activity 8.6.

Because **Wikipedia**—the online encyclopedia/dictionary that users can not only read but also add to—contains so many topics, Wikipedia URLs usually come up in the first five hits of a search! However, this does not mean Wikipedia contains the best information; it means that the word being searched for has been cited the most times on Wikipedia during the search. Most searchers use only a single-word search rather than being more specific; this brings up more resources, some of which are not as credible as those a more specific search would have found. Domain names can reveal sources and credibility. For instance, "edu" means an education-sponsored site, whereas "org" means a general site that may not be as scholarly. KartOO is organized

> For URLs to search engines for better scholarship, visit the companion site for this chapter, accessed from the DVD.

ACTIVITY 8.6 KIDSCLICK AND MEASUREMENTS

Go to the Kidsclick Web site. Select Science and Math, then Space Kids.

Now you see some Web sites where you can convert from the way measurements are used in the United States—Fahrenheit—and the way measurements are used in much of the rest of the world—Celsius.

Try it out!

The way Wikipedia works should be presented to students as soon as teachers realize that students are beginning to use it. Although it may seem that Wikipedia is a resource only for older students, we have discovered that many children as young as first grade level are referring to it.

differently than most search engines; it is a visual search engine where students can realize how words and topics are connected.

A common trap for students is relying on the single simplest resource to locate. This used to be the set of encyclopedias in the library or on the home bookshelf. Now it is Wikipedia. The "wiki" in Wikipedia is derived from Hawaiian for "quick." When a student locates information in Wikipedia, that information may have been written by a scholar in the field—or by anyone else who wished to make the entry. Even if the entry was written by a scholar, it can also be altered by any reader. While this may seem disturbing, Wikipedia is actually a democratic resource: Everyone can have a voice in the creation of an entry. It is a wonderful example of how technology has influenced the way we learn. Wikipedia can be an excellent tool for helping students learn about locating and selecting information. By looking at the history of an entry, one can determine how many times the entry has been altered and how it was altered (authors can also ask to be notified when an entry has been altered so they can delete unwanted changes to their entries). This search for changes can help students understand that "facts" can be altered or biased and that one must exercise care in accepting resources. Many educators find this to be a good way to demonstrate lively interaction and critical thinking in process. Wikipedia is a good example of why one resource is not enough on which to base one's knowledge of a subject.

Activity 8.7 encourages thoughtful reading to locate resources by starting with Wikipedia. This activity is for middle school mathematics, but it can be adapted for other grade levels and content areas.

ACTIVITY *8.7* USING WIKIPEDIA

1. Go to Wikipedia and type in the word *circumference*.
2. How many selections do you find? (As of 3/13/07, there were 1,732.)
3. Select the definition and go to it. What is the definition? (The circumference is the distance around a closed curve. Circumference is a kind of perimeter.) You are reading the article about circumference (see the tabs above the entry).
4. Select the tab for "discussion." What is the discussion about? (It is about whether the definition of circumference should be merged with that of perimeter.) What would you add to this discussion?
5. Select the tab for "edit this page." What is the message you receive, and why could this be a good clue to how credible this definition is? (The message is that anyone can edit the page, but the IP address of the editor will be shown to anyone who looks at the history of the article. By registering, one can hide the IP address from viewers—not from the Wikipedia editor, though!)
6. Select the tab for "history." What do you find here? (Many links to the edits that have been done for this definition.)
7. Now go to the High Beam Encyclopedia and search for *circumference*. What is the definition? Is it the same as on Wikipedia?
8. What have you learned about how to search for a definition? When would you use Wikipedia? When should you use more than one resource to find an answer?

For URLs to
Web-based
bookmarking,
visit the com-
panion site for
this chapter,
accessed from
the DVD.

Teachers of elementary-aged students may find that using Web-based book-marks will help provide younger readers the structure and content they need to locate information (Forbes, 2004). Web-based bookmarking lets a teacher create a list of bookmarks and store them on the Web. In this way all sites will be previewed so Internet safety is improved. Because so many people mistype addresses, there is no telling where a child might land on the Internet without such guidance. Time on task is increased, frustration is reduced, and learning is facilitated. Services that help teachers create Web-based bookmarks make this process easy.

At the start of this chapter you saw a reference to a newspaper article about students studying in the electronic age. The authors read this article in a newspaper and wanted to save it. The old-fashioned way of saving it would have been to clip and laminate it. The new way is to locate it on the Web site for the newspaper and save the URL for easy access anytime. Students can be guided to scan a newspaper and locate an article they would like to save, then find it on the newspaper's site. In the same way, students can practice locating a phone number in a paper directory and then locating it online. Geography lessons can be enhanced by using both atlases and mapping Web sites.

PREVIEWING

Previewing may be the most important reading and study skill. Chapter 4 described the directed reading–thinking activity (DR–TA) (Stauffer, 1969a), the classic technique that teachers can use to model correct reading processes. Fundamental to the DR–TA is previewing, a process that is important for clarifying thinking before students read textbook material. Previewing has been found to help improve comprehension and achievement in students—especially low-achieving students (O'Donnell, et al., 2003; Skinner, et al., 1997).

In the previewing stage, students select strategies appropriate to the depth and duration of study needed. To select proper strategies—whether note taking, under-lining, or rapid reading—students must spend time clarifying their thinking about the topic. Then they need to ask themselves questions such as the following:

How interested am I in this section?

How deeply do I need to think and concentrate to learn this material?

How fast can I read this material?

What do I still need to learn about this topic?

Teachers might take students step-by-step through the previewing phase, then ask them to write down how they will study the material.

Just as one might size up a piece of clothing and decide whether it is too big and needs altering, a reader can size up a reading selection and realize that "mental alter-ations" are needed. Such assessment is the purpose of previewing. Sometimes a preview yields all the information a reader needs, so the material need not be read. In many instances, however, a preview builds anticipation for material that is not familiar to the reader.

Previewing to clarify thinking reduces uncertainty about reading assignments, allowing students to gain confidence, read in a more relaxed manner, gain interest, and improve their attitude toward the material. In addition, previewing strategies enable students to decide how much of the material is in their own background of experience. As a result of the previewing process, learners are clearer about what they know and what they need to know. In effect, they set a purpose for reading before they begin.

When previewing a technical chapter or a report, students should examine and think about the following:

1. *Title and subtitle:* We need to discover the overall topic of the chapter or article. This part of the chapter is often skipped entirely by students. This is where a student should figure out what she or he knows about the chapter as a whole and what this chapter has to do with the chapter that came before it. What will this chapter be about?

2. *Author's name:* We might ask whether the author is a recognized authority. What is the author's point of view?

3. *Copyright:* This is examined to see whether the material is current.

4. *Introduction:* Here we find out what the author intends to talk about. The main points that will be covered usually are discussed here, and sometimes objectives and goals are stated in the body of the paragraph(s) or highlighted in marginal notes.

5. *Headings and subheadings:* Identification of the topics of the sections that follow (forming these headings into questions gives purpose to the reading).

6. *Graphs, charts, maps, tables, pictures:* These are aids in understanding specific aspects of the chapter. It is important to study these because vital information might be gleaned here that is nowhere else in the reading.

7. *Summary:* Here we get an overview of what has been discussed in the reading. This is important to study in the preview to get a sense of where the entire reading is going.

8. *Questions:* These are examined to review important topics covered in the chapter.

In practicing with a group or a class, the teacher assists students in deciding what they already know about the material and what they need to learn. The reader turns things that are not known into questions, which provide a purpose for reading.

Students reading fiction need to preview the title, illustrations, and introduction in order to make hypotheses about the outcome of the story. This preview heightens suspense and helps maintain interest. Most important, predicting story structure gives the reader a purpose for reading: to find out whether the predictions are correct.

Whether students are reading fiction or expository material, an important reason for previewing is that it forces them to do the sophisticated kind of thinking required for drawing inferences and developing interpretations. Thus students think critically about a chapter or story before reading, operating at higher levels of cognition.

Students enjoy previewing, and their interest in the reading material is greatly heightened by using this strategy.

We find that students on any level generally will not preview material on their own unless teachers model and provide practice in this important skill. First teachers should make students aware that they are teaching both content and the strategy of previewing. Next teachers need to review with students the table of contents of a textbook to help them discover the theme or structure of the course material. In this way students will get the gist or overall idea of what the author is attempting to teach in the textbook. The teacher might ask, for example, why the author chose to organize the table of contents in a particular manner.

Students can learn to preview by using a preview guide that is easy to construct. Students fill in the guide as they preview a chapter, or part of a chapter, under the guidance of the teacher. Activity 8.8 is an example of such a guide.

ACTIVITY 8.8 CHAPTER PREVIEW GUIDE

1. Title of chapter: _____   From page _____ to page _____
   Subtitle of chapter: _____

2. Name(s) of author(s): _____   Is the author an authority?
   _____   Proof: _____

3. Copyright: _____   Is the material current? _____
                                                  _____

4. Introduction: _____   Tell what you know after reading
   _____   this introduction: _____
   _____   _____
   _____   _____

5. Headings and subheadings: _____   Subheading: _____
   _____
                                                  Page: _____

                                                  Subheading: _____
                                                  _____

                                                  Page: _____

                                                  Subheading: _____
                                                  _____

                                                  Page: _____

                                                  Subheading: _____
                                                  _____

                                                  Page: _____

                                                  Subheading: _____
                                                  _____

                                                  Page: _____

Subheading: _____
_____

Page: _____

6. Graphs, charts, maps, and pictures: _____
_____

Page: _____
Description: _____

Page: _____
Description: _____

Page: _____
Description: _____

7. Summary: _____
_____
Where summary section is found: _____
_____
_____

Write about the summary in your
own words: _____
_____
_____
_____
_____
_____

8. Vocabulary terms:

Word: _____
Page found: _____
Meaning: _____
_____
_____

Word: _____
Page found: _____
Meaning: _____
_____

Word: _____
Page found: _____
Meaning: _____
_____

Word: _____
Page found: _____
Meaning: _____
_____

For each new reading or unit of instruction, the teacher can ask students to return to the table of contents to see how this particular learning segment fits into the overall textbook scheme or pattern. Teachers with a class of poor readers can model the previewing strategy by using preview questions they have constructed and annotated.

Garber-Miller (2006) encourages the use of "playful textbook previews" that show students how to preview while having fun with textbook sales pitches and commercials, textbook picture walks, sticky note votes, and other lively ways to learn how to preview.

Previewing can be done for any type of reading material, including a Web site. Some of the eight steps in previewing may not apply to a particular Web site, but most will. Activity 8.9 shows how to preview a Web page to get the most out of research and study.

ACTIVITY 8.9 USING THE WEB

Eastern Virginia Medical School
Community Based • Nationally Recognized

I need to research medical schools. This looks like a good place to start.

Search | Home / Site Map / About EVMS / Patient Services
Education / Research / Departments / Library

Department Information

Francis J. Counselman, M.D. Chairman

Here is the chairman.

Emergency Medicine Department

The Department of Emergency Medicine at the Eastern Virginia Medical School is a fully accredited PGY-I through PGY-III program, approved by the Emergency Medicine Residency Review Committee. There are eight resident positions in each class. The program has maintained Continued Full Accreditation status since its inception in 1981. We received independent academic departmental status in 1992; we were only the twenty-sixth such academic department in the United States at that time.

Read the introductory paragraph.

Residency Program

Clinical Faculty

Core Faculty CVs

Awards

Publications

Tidewater Emergency Medical Services

Here are the faculty.

What are CVs? Maybe by clicking here I will find out.

All of the faculty of the Department of Emergency Medicine are board-certified or board-prepared in Emergency Medicine. A number of our faculty are double-boarded. In addition, all are members of our private practice group, Emergency Physicians of Tidewater, one of the country's oldest private practice Emergency Medicine groups. The faculty provide clinical supervision at all of our training sites, providing a uniformity of supervision and the guidance of academic practitioners as well as Emergency Medicine physicians in private practice. This provides a unique opportunity to experience first hand the different career paths available in Emergency Medicine.

◄

Home / Site Map / Search / About EVMS / Patient Services
Education / Research / Departments / Library

Feedback | Revised: November 29, 2001 | Copyright © 1999-2000 Academic Computer Center

What kind of library do they have?

I will click here to learn about the different departments.

FOLLOWING DIRECTIONS

Following directions is an important study skill. After finding information and selecting the best information for a study project, following the directions to complete the study is the next effective step. Of course the teacher must model by providing clear directions. The activities in this chapter model clear, step-by-step directions. Students need to rely, however, on their own deep thinking about directions to make any study successful. Hubbard (2003) encourages study that includes deep strategies rather than surface ones. Consider Activity 8.7, in which students follow the history of editing done on a definition at Wikipedia. The surface might be just following the directions provided in the activity, but the deep strategy of following the directions requires students to think about why following these directions helps them to direct their study now and in the future. The goal is to learn how to create one's own directions that can guide study successfully.

Assistance Strategies and Activities

The following strategies and activities are grounded in the assistance stage of study. But they can also be considered as part of the reflection and even preparation stages of study, depending on the circumstances.

INTERPRETING TYPOGRAPHIC AND GRAPHIC AIDS

Certainly visual aids help one preview and prepare to study; but interpretation of those visual aids also leads a student into the assistance phase of study. Visual representations in text are graphic clues and aids designed to help readers comprehend a content textbook. Teachers say that they use visual aids 84 percent of the time when they study (Barry, 2002). It is important for teachers to teach visual representations and never skip them. Yet one of the most common responses of students when questioned about such aids is that they "skip over them" (Gillespie, 1993). So often readers incorrectly assume that such visuals represent a "free page"! Many standardized state tests of learning assess graph, chart, and map reading. When teachers attend to the detail of reading visuals, they are directly helping students prepare for standardized tests of achievement.

Richardson and Forget (1995) illustrated the calculations that Mark Twain used in "proving" that the Mississippi River would be shortened to a length of a mile and three-quarters 742 years from the time he wrote *Life on the Mississippi*. By reading a graph that applies the formula for slope, readers can see how slope always reflects the relationship of one variable to another. Both Twain's humorous essay and the formula for slope are more interesting and clear when the graphic information is available.

If students are having particular difficulty reading visual information, teachers can use a modified textbook treasure hunt to teach the skill. Activity 8.10 shows how this procedure can help upper elementary and middle school students read about manatees while searching Internet sites on the subject. Lorenzo and Dziuban (2006) caution that digital images are easily altered to display falsehoods as fact. Cropping, enhancing, and altering images can seem to depict what is not really true. To prepare visually literate students who can look critically, Metors and Woosley (2006) suggest encouraging questions

Introduction

Surf's up! Grab your brain and head for the further reaches of cyberspace. There is a lot to learn in this information age. Using the Web allows you to discover tons more than you may have ever known possible. Below is a list of questions about manatees. Surf the Internet links on this page to find answers to the questions. Don't forget to go after the monster learning wave—the big question. Have fun and avoid any watery danger.

Questions

1. Give a detailed description of a manatee (color, size, weight, etc.).
2. Is the manatee population increasing or decreasing? Why?
3. Where does the West Indian manatee live? Does it migrate?
4. Do manatees have teeth?
5. Are manatees omnivores, carnivores, or herbivores? Give an example of their diet.

The Internet Resources

Your teacher will show you how to do an Internet search on manatees and provide you with some Web links.

The Big Question

How can we protect this endangered species?
Good luck and go find out about those manatees!

Activity developed by Jody Irvin.

---

such as these: Does this image tell the truth? How representative is this image? What is the source of this image? Are we responding to emotional issues or content? Also, as a form of study, students can draw their own pictures or make their own graphic outlines that depict the meaning of their reading (Haynes, 2006).

Pictures make a textbook interesting and vital. Teachers should frequently ask students to "read" pictures in an effort to clarify their thinking about concepts in a chapter. Cartoons are specialized pictures that carry significant messages or propaganda. What meaning does the comic depicted earlier in this chapter convey to you? Does it convey irony? Pessimism? Is it a satire on studying? Activity 8.11 demonstrates how teachers can teach students to label maps. It also models good directions. Labeling may be done either after students memorize a map or as they consult maps in their textbooks. We recommend map labeling as a primary way to get students to learn to use maps and to better remember certain important locations on a map.

Activity 8.12 illustrates how a digital camera, household objects, and the computer can help children in primary grades use visuals to organize and retain information about math shapes and simple geometry.

Complete this map. Use the map of the Colonial Southeast to help you complete this activity.

1. Color the water area BLUE.

2. Color the area covered by the 11 states of the Southeast LIGHT YELLOW.

3. Print the names of the states in the proper places on the map.

4. Print these names in the proper places:
   Mountains: Appalachians, Blue Ridge
   Plains: Atlantic Coastal, Gulf Coastal
   Rivers: Potomac, James, Savannah, Mississippi, St. Johns
   Bays: Chesapeake, Delaware

5. Print these names of early settlements in the proper places on the map:
   Jamestown   St. Mary's
   Charleston   Williamsburg
   Savannah

6. With a BLUE crayon trace over each of the rivers listed above.

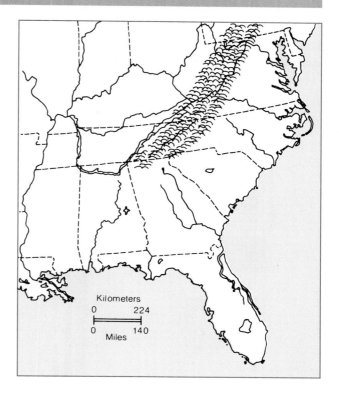

Organizing Information

When students organize for study, they are using study systems that help them direct study and use the most effective ways to remember. Behaviors can include adoption of a particular study system and use of mnemonics. Simpson and Nist (2000) indicate that organizing strategies may be the most researched study strategies. Organizational strategies should focus on cognitive and metacognitive processing. Which of the following methods of organizing should a student select? This is personal preference, based on individual study behaviors and needs; but it should be a deliberate and thoughtful choice.

UNDERLINING

Underlining is often cited as a way to help students organize their thinking enough to begin an outline. Underlining, then, can be a first step to outlining. McAndrew (1983), in a review of the literature about underlining, makes several suggestions

Have the students take pictures of household objects that show circles, rectangles, or triangles. Use digital cameras so the pictures can be downloaded to a computer. The teacher will download the pictures to the class computer and resize them to be small. Next the teacher will create a chart like the one in this activity. Then the students will open the file and select, copy, and paste pictures into the correct columns.

Circles	Rectangles	Triangles
Pilates ball	Bathroom tile	Shoji screen
Rug with a circle	Refrigerator door + pictures	Bread
Plate		

for teaching this skill if students own their textbooks. To begin, teachers should create "pre-underlining" reading assignments in handout materials that coincide with the textbook. Teachers need to show students how to underline relevant material. Students must learn how to underline superordinate statements rather than subordinate details. When they learn this, students will underline relatively little, but what they underline will be important. McAndrew notes that teachers should remind students that with underlining, less is more, and that any time they save by underlining can be put to good use in further study of the material. Teachers also need to teach students when to use techniques other than underlining. Even when underlining in textbooks is not possible, pre-underlining is an important study strategy for students to learn.

OUTLINING

Outlining is the traditional method of organization. There is no agreement, however, on the best way to teach this skill. Outlining is an organizational tool that lets readers create for themselves a condensed presentation of a chapter that they want to understand. Outlining is particularly useful because it actively involves the reader and because the notes are not made in the textbook, which the student might not own. A well-made outline shows the relationships of main ideas, supporting details, definitions of terms, and other data to the overall topic. Mapping can be an early, unstructured form of outlining. Outlines are valuable because they help students understand difficult texts, take notes, write papers, and give oral presentations.

When students first begin to practice outlining, they should not concentrate on form (no need for a B for every A). Teachers can help students learn to outline by preparing outlines with key words missing. By replacing missing words or terms, even very young children can begin to learn outlining. Teachers can give students partially finished outlines to complete as they read a chapter. These can even be done on sentence strips or index cards as a manipulative format to help young learners learn to order and organize. This example is from first grade:

MAPS

    I. Maps and Globes

        A. Legend

           1. Key

           2. Compass rose

        B. Flat

    II. Globes

        A. Sphere

The following are some features of successful outlines:

1. The material itself determines the number of headings and subheadings.
2. Each heading expresses one main idea.
3. Ideas are parallel. All ideas recorded with roman numerals are equally important.
4. All subheadings relate to the major heading above them.
5. In a formal outline, each category has more than one heading.

6. Each new level of heading is indented under the heading above it.

7. The first letter of the first word in each heading and subheading is capitalized.

An outline enables students to organize material in a hierarchical fashion. This can be accomplished by using a graphic pattern as well as in traditional ways. For instance, *Inspiration* and *Kidspiration* help students create maps that can be converted to outlines.

NOTE TAKING

Note taking, a common study skill, produces good study results. Teachers rate this skill highly for their own study, indicating that they use it during 74 percent of their study time (Barry, 2002). Research focusing on the time students spend on constructing their own study notes showed that their notes were more effective than instructor-provided notes (Crooks & Katayama, 2002). However, when middle school students were asked about their note-taking strategies, they reported understanding how to take notes but admitted that they did not practice note taking (Brown, 2005).

McAndrew (1983, p. 107) offers teachers these suggestions to help their students become effective note takers:

1. Be certain students realize that the use of notes to store information is more important than the act of taking the notes.

2. Try to use a spaced lecture format.

3. Insert questions, verbal cues, and nonverbal cues into lectures to highlight structure.

4. Write material on the board to be sure students will record it.

5. When using transparencies or slides, compensate for possible overload of information.

6. Tell students what type of test to expect.

7. Use handouts, especially with poor note takers.

8. Give students handouts that provide space for student notes.

To the students who are taking notes, Morgan and associates (1986) offer some practical advice:

1. *Do not use a spiral notebook (contrary to what is often advocated).* A two- or three-ring notebook filled with loose-leaf paper enables students to rearrange their notes or any other material and permits easy addition or subtraction of material.

2. *Write on every other line whenever possible or when it seems logical to separate topics.* By leaving a lot of white space, students give themselves room to correct errors or add points they missed. In addition, every-other-line note taking makes for easier reading when students review or study for an exam.

3. *Develop a shorthand system.* Students should reduce frequently used words to a symbol, such as "w" for *with*. Other commonly used words should be abbreviated. Morgan and associates (1986) offer examples of such abbreviations:

compare	comp	data bank	db
important	imp	evaluation	eval
advantage	advan	developed	dev
introduction	intro	literature	lit
continued	cont	definition	def
organization	org	individual	ind
information	info	psychology	psych
example	ex		

Content words should be recorded in full and spellings checked with a dictionary or a textbook.

4. *Underline, star, or record the teacher's pet theories or concepts.* Listen for key statements such as "I particularly agree with this theory" or "You'll probably be seeing this information again." Statements like those might mean that the material will appear on an exam. If the teacher writes terminology or math examples on the board, always record them word for word (or figure by figure). If the teacher lists or numbers remarks, such as "three significant facts stand out," those should be numbered and indented in the notes.

5. *Do not try to outline notes according to a roman numeral system with main ideas and supporting details.* No one thinks in roman numerals. Important points may be missed if students worry too much about how they are taking the notes. Until notes are organized later, students should not worry about the numerals.

6. *Do not disregard related discussions.* Teachers frequently use questions as a teaching tool. Students should write down questions that are introduced for discussion purposes. Often such discussions stray from the subject, but the teacher always has a reason for asking the question.

7. *Ask questions when there is misunderstanding.* If one student is confused by a concept or misses a point in a lecture, usually other students have missed it too. Students should not be embarrassed to ask for clarification.

8. *Review often and with different purposes in mind.* When rereading textbook assignments, students should coordinate the chapter with their notes. Make certain main ideas from the chapter are included directly in the lecture notes. For some students, rewriting notes is a helpful memory device. Even though this process is time-consuming, it may be worth the effort if it helps students retain the material.

Remember that note taking is usually somewhat messy. The process the mind uses while thinking and taking notes often resembles a webbing or mapping approach.

Richardson (1996) offers a tip for teachers. When teachers let students use notes during a test, they will see a great improvement over time in students' use of note taking. Of course students should not be able to find the answers to test questions directly in their notes; they should be required to use inference and application skills when forming their answers.

The role of summarizing is often embedded in note-taking activities and as part of outlining techniques. When one edits and reorganizes notes, summarizing and annotating them, deep thinking happens (Hubbard & Simpson, 2003). Summarizing is an excellent note-taking tactic (Friend, 2001).

The REST system (Morgan, Meeks, Schollaert, & Paul, 1986) has been proposed as a way to prepare for note taking before a lecture. This system takes into account the importance of note taking to help integrate lectures with textbooks. Using the REST system, students should follow these steps:

1. *Record*: Write down as much of what the teacher says as possible, excluding repetitions and digressions.
2. *Edit*: Condense the notes, editing out irrelevant material.
3. *Synthesize*: Compare the condensed notes with related material in the textbook, and jot down important points stressed in both the lecture and the textbook.
4. *Think*: Think and study to ensure retention.

To help students practice REST, teachers should distribute handouts for note taking that include space for writing notes about the lecture, for making notes to oneself, and for summarizing main ideas. An example of such a handout completed by a high school student in art history is shown in Activity 8.13.

The Cornell system (Pauk, 1997), a practical approach to taking notes, is an alternative to the REST system. Pauk's **two-column note-taking system,** or "5 R's," has an advantage over REST in that it can be used with younger children. To use this system, students divide the page in the following way: The main heading, the notes students make for themselves, and keywords all go in the narrow left column. The students also may use the left side as their side to record topics, questions, key

---

ACTIVITY *8.13* ART HISTORY NOTE-TAKING HANDOUT

Topics and Notes to Yourself

Purpose
   1) Slides
   (Mona Lisa)
   2) History
     1st & 2nd A.D.
☆ Learn for test
  term imp. → barbaric
   p. 327 "barbe"

Assignment

Lecture Notes

Make public understand what is the purpose of the art
Liz Taylor
         everybody recognizes
Marilyn Monroe

Ginger Rogers — almost forgotten

Greeks — naturalists
Romans — hedonists

→ Think about Andy Warhol's soup can

Summarization and Main Ideas

Art is a reflection of history.
Need to study both the purpose
and the style.

---

phrases, definitions, comments, and summaries of information from the lecturer or textbook. The wider right column is for information from the lecturer or the textbook.

The key to two-column note taking is space. Just as adolescents and even younger students need physical space, they also need intellectual space—that is, space to think. The left column provides space for students to question themselves about the big picture of the lesson and the major concepts to be learned. The system is based on the sound theory of categorization, with subordinate concepts consolidated and organized under superordinate headings.

Students practice these steps (the 5 R's):

Step 1: They *record* the information as they hear it or read it.

Step 2: They *reduce* the information by putting their abbreviated notes about it in the narrow left column.

Step 3: They *recite* the information by using their reduction notes with the recorded notes in the wider right column.

Steps 4 and 5: They *reflect on* and *review* the notes over time.

The two-column system allows students great flexibility. Pairs of students can "call" the notes to each other, covering either column and asking each other what belongs in that column. Teachers can ask students to form groups at the beginning or end of class and brainstorm two or three recently covered major topics (to go in the left column). In this manner note taking is made an integral part of all the class operations.

When this system is used effectively, students improve markedly. However, studies (Spor & Schneider, 1999) show that only 30 percent of teachers work with students on any outlining or note-taking procedures. Many simply tell students to "put a line down the page about one-third of the way across the page, creating two columns, and take notes like this from now on." Students do not continue (or even start) to use the method because they have no practice in using it.

Activity 8.14 is an example of a two-column note-taking handout from an early elementary classroom. The teacher is discussing a story and asks students to complete the notes. Teachers can prepare such handouts and give them to students before a lecture or before students read a chapter so that they can practice the two-column method. This handout employs a modified cloze procedure: Students fill in gaps as they listen to the lecture or read the chapter. In subsequent lessons, more and more notes are omitted (more blanks are used) until eventually students complete all the note taking themselves. Activity 8.15 is an example of a two-column note-taking handout from a high school health class about brain functioning's relations to diet and eating habits.

Knox and Anderson-Inmann (2001) studied how wireless note taking with laptops could enrich and support the study of Hispanic students in mainstreamed classrooms. An experienced note taker took and shared notes with English second language students during history classes. The notes helped these students

Two-column notes are often referred to by other names, such as double-entry notes or split-column notes.

NAME _____ DATE _____

Directions: Listen very closely as I discuss *Franklin Fibs* by Paulette Bourgeois. Fill in the missing words to complete these notes.

Main characters	Franklin, Bear, _____, Beaver, Mom, and _____.
Setting	Franklin's _____.
Beginning	Bear, Hawk, and _____ were _____ about things they could _____.
Middle	Franklin said he could eat _____ flies in the _____ of an eye.
End	Franklin did _____ seventy-six flies, but he ate them in a _____.
Problem	Franklin told a _____.
Solution	Franklin told the _____ and did something that he could brag about.

Developed by Stephanie Hunter.

---

understand the course, provided them with study notes, and taught them how to take notes. While replication of this experiment would be difficult without grant support, using the technique of the teacher simultaneously providing oral content and written notes easily accessed via computer could help many students get the gist of note taking.

Reflection Strategies and Activities

The following strategies and activities are grounded in the reflection stage of study; but they can also be considered as part of the assistance stage of study, depending on the circumstances. Students need to know that learning is difficult but always rewarding. Sternberg (1991) noted that learning and retention are enhanced when students study in fairly equal distributions over time rather than in what he calls **massed study**—last-minute cramming before a test or exam. Many students cram because it is human nature to put off study to the last minute. Also, students form this habit because teachers do not explain to them how distributed study enhances retention. Brinthaupt and Shin (2001) considered why college students crammed or procrastinated; they found differences between crammers, who waited until cramming felt like the good and appropriate way to study, and procrastinators, who waited because other behaviors felt better than studying. Crammers seemed to wait for a match between study challenge and study skills. It appears that how one views study is as important to how one does study, so teachers need to discover why their

Your brain	It is always _____.
	It is selective in the way it gets _____.
Two amino acids are important for brain function	Tyrosine is an amino acid that helps with _____ _____ , long term _____ , and feelings of being _____ .
	From tyrosine, the brain makes _____ and _____ .
	Tryptophan slows _____ time and makes you _____ .
	Scientists believe you can control the activity _____ of the mind with the foods you eat.
If you want to get tyrosine to the brain	eat _____ .
If you want to get tryptophan to the brain	eat _____ .
Protein lunches	enhance _____ performance.
Carbohydrates	can _____ thought processes of the brain.
	are good for helping you _____ .
	can _____ people with seasonal affective disorder (SAD).
Fats	are important for thinking.
	Brain _____ are made largely of fat.
	Take _____ hours for fats to reach the brain and affect thinking.
	Saturated fats _____ ability to think.
	Polyunsaturated fats _____ ability to think.

students cram and procrastinate before expecting them to become effective at distributing their learning.

The famous Ebbinghaus (1908) findings a century ago described the difficulty of learning. Ebbinghaus postulated that tremendous amounts of information are forgotten in a short period—up to 60 or 70 percent in only a few days. He also made these important discoveries:

1. Fatigue affects one's ability to remember.

2. Earlier study and learning tend to get buried by later learning.

3. Learned images may decay over time and end up changed in meaning from what was originally perceived.

4. Memories erode, and most information (an estimated 90 percent) is forgotten over prolonged periods.

In short, forgetting is natural and remembering is difficult.

For students who have Mac computers, notes can be programmed to pop up on the computer screen to remind them to study at a certain time for a predefined period. Within Microsoft Word, a feature is available to remind a reader to review a certain document at a prescribed time: Select Help/Tools/Flag for follow-up.

MNEMONICS

Fortunately the use of **mnemonics**—devices and techniques to improve memory—can help students in what Ebbinghaus describes as the difficult task of learning. Peters and Levin (1986) found that mnemonics benefited both above- and below-average readers when they read short fictional passages as well as longer content passages. Students instructed in mnemonic strategies remembered significantly more information on names and accomplishments than did those in the control group. Similarly, Levin, Morrison, and McGivern (1986) found that students given instruction in mnemonic techniques scored significantly higher on tests of immediate recall and on recall tests administered three days later than did either a group taught to memorize material or group members who were given motivational talks and then used their usual methods of study. Mnemonics instruction also has been found to be effective for learning new words in foreign language classes (Cohen, 1987) and as aids in learning Chinese and Japanese characters (Lu, Webb, Krus, & Fox, 1999). Studies (Levin, Levin, Glassman, & Nordwall, 1992; Scruggs, Mastropier, Brigham, & Sullivan, 1992) have found that keyword mnemonics significantly affect retention of text material, attesting to the benefits of mnemonic techniques. Mnemonics seem to work by taking the load off working memory, or short-term memory, by retrieving learning directly from long-term memory. This is completed through a single association with an existing memory code (Levin, 1993; Wang & Thomas, 1995). Not all research on the efficacy of using mnemonics has been positive, however. Hwang and Levin (2002) have found that students have trouble applying complex mnemonic strategies independently. They state that teachers must provide auxiliary support for a mnemonic strategy to be effective. It is not altogether certain whether children can discover effective learning strategies—such as mnemonics—on their own or apply them in learning environments (Pressley & Schneider, 1997).

Despite favorable studies, teachers don't seem to use mnemonics, even though it takes only a small effort to get students to try them. For example, a teacher can give vocabulary or chapter terms that need to be memorized and ask students to form groups in which they create their own mnemonics and share them with the class. The teacher can give rewards for the ones judged to be the best or perhaps the funniest. Through such practice, students can form the habit of creating mnemonics for themselves. Such creation is part of self-regulated study behavior, discussed at the beginning of this chapter.

In the remainder of this section we describe acronyms, acrostics, method of loci, and other mnemonic learning techniques. These can be welcome learning aids, especially for poor readers who find that they forget material too quickly (remember that the Ebbinghaus studies show that forgetting is natural). If we could help students to remember from 10 to 30 items with ease, think how their self-concepts and self-images might be improved. With practice, there seems to be almost no limit to improvement in long-term memory skill. We recommend familiarizing children in primary grades with these memory-enhancing techniques. Then they will possess a skill useful for the rest of their lives.

Remember that mnemonics have been used successfully for centuries!

The most time-honored of mnemonics, an **acronym**, is a word or phrase composed entirely of letters that are cues to words we want to remember. For example, PAR is an acronym for the instructional framework that we explain in this book. Or suppose you are reviewing musculoskeletal systems for a test, and among the things you want to remember are the six boundaries of the axilla: apex, base, anterior wall, posterior wall, medial wall, and lateral wall. The initial letters are A, B, A, P, M, and L. You could rearrange these letters to form the acronym A.B. PALM. Or consider the following list of the six branches of the axillary artery: supreme thoraces, thoracromial, lateral thoracic, anterior humeral circumflex, posterior humeral circumflex, and subscapular. You could use the initial letters S, T, L, A, P, and S to form the name of a fictitious patron saint of arteries: ST. LAPS. Here are a few examples of more common acronyms:

HOMES—The Great Lakes: Huron, Ontario, Michigan, Erie, Superior.

ROY G BIV—The colors of the spectrum: red, orange, yellow, green, blue, indigo, violet.

FACE—The notes represented by the spaces of the G clef.

An **acrostic** is a phrase or sentence in which the first letter of each word is a cue. For example, another way of remembering the boundaries of the axilla—initial letters A, B, A, P, M, and L—would be to create a phrase such as "above, below, and pretty much lost." To remember the names of our solar system's planets (as they used to be defined before Pluto was demoted from planet status)—Mercury, Venus, Earth, Mars, Jupiter, Saturn, Uranus, Neptune, Pluto—you might use the following acrostic: "My very elegant mother just served us nine pizzas (*or* sat upon nine porcupines)."

Acrostics can be made for any area. To improve reading study skills, ask students to RELAX by doing the following:

Rest plenty.

Exude enthusiasm.

Laugh often.

Anticipate what's coming.

Xcite yourself about the reading.

Suppose you had to remember these nautical terms: *bow, stern, cabin, traveler*. You could use this acrostic: "Big storms cause trouble."

Students can be taught to memorize words by associating the words to be learned with outrageous images. For instance, to memorize the words in the left column, students can imagine the images in the right column:

WORD	IMAGE
Sweater	Sweater
Horse	A gigantic horse wearing a gigantic sweater
Surf	A huge horse surfing
Iron gate	A surfer on a high surfboard flying over an iron gate
Typewriter	Tiny iron gates spewing out of a typewriter

In this manner, one word leads to the next to make a long list of associations.

Another means of associational learning is a *peg-word system,* which associates a target word with a numbered peg word. Listed here are 10 peg words that name familiar places found at many schools:

1. Computer center
2. Guidance office
3. Cafeteria
4. Auditorium
5. Library
6. Classroom
7. Hallway
8. Principal's office
9. Nurse's clinic
10. Gymnasium

The words to be memorized—*plot, setting,* and *character*—are linked to the peg words through outrageous images. You can remember the words *plot, setting,* and *character* by associating each with one of the numbered peg words:

1. A criminal with a *plot* to blow up the *library.*
2. Someone *setting* a tray down in the *cafeteria.*
3. A drunken *character* sitting in the back of a *classroom* filled with disbelieving students.

The peg words do not have to name places. They can be words that sound similar to or rhyme with the words to be learned. An example would be the peg word *commotion* for *commodities* in an economics class or *this criminal* for *discrimination.*

The **method of loci** (Latin for "places") improves students' ability to remember lists of unrelated objects. It also can be a sequencing task, enabling a student to remember items in a definite order. In this ancient method, used by Roman orators, a person mentally walks through a house that has familiar surroundings. Cicero and other classical orators constructed "memory places" and linked sections of their speeches to architectural features. Then, as they spoke, they imagined the place where they had established the links. This process enabled them to remember huge amounts of information. By choosing 15 to 20 distinct loci—for example, the stove, the closet, the desk, or the kitchen sink—students can mentally place objects to be learned in strategic spots throughout the house. In a variation, students memorize words by placing them in strategic places in each of the six or seven rooms where they have classes each day or in various places around the school.

An electronic drawing of a loci adds interest and permanence.

Chunking large amounts of information into categories can help students remember information more readily and retrieve it faster. Suppose you have to learn these 15 items in a language arts unit on puppetry:

Director	Equipment	Props	Create	Purchase
Lights Story	Story development	Size of puppets	Analysis	Microphone
Copyright	Budget	Sound	Stories	Spotlight

Chunking information into categories makes learning the 15 items much easier:

SCRIPTS	TECHNICAL
Director	Lights
Copyright	Equipment
Story development	Props
Budget	Size of puppets
Create	Sound
Analysis	Microphone
Stories	Spotlight
Purchase	

Chunking information through categorization exercises (which can be used to review for tests) is an excellent way to help poor readers understand text material. Chunking capitalizes on connecting prior knowledge to new knowledge, thus enhancing learning. Once students become more practiced at chunking, they can construct hierarchies of mnemonics to learn 15 to 50 items. Activity 8.16 provides an

ACTIVITY **8.16** CHUNKING THROUGH CATEGORIZATION

BEING A SUCCESSFUL BABYSITTER

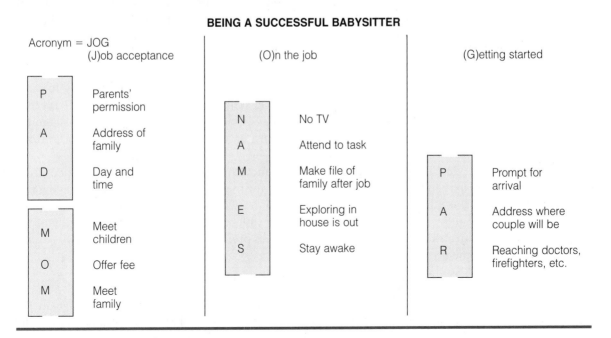

Acronym = JOG
(J)ob acceptance

P — Parents' permission
A — Address of family
D — Day and time

M — Meet children
O — Offer fee
M — Meet family

(O)n the job

N — No TV
A — Attend to task
M — Make file of family after job
E — Exploring in house is out
S — Stay awake

(G)etting started

P — Prompt for arrival
A — Address where couple will be
R — Reaching doctors, firefighters, etc.

example from a teen living class in home economics, where the total number of items to be learned is 14.

Remember that complicated hierarchies of mnemonics are best constructed by middle school and high school students who have considerable experience with using simple acronyms and acrostics. This level of chunking is the most difficult mnemonic to construct, but it allows students considerable leeway in memorizing prodigious amounts of information.

Children have a better chance of successfully using mnemonics if they create their own to help them learn certain concepts. One way to familiarize primary and upper elementary children with mnemonics is to **Go MAD**—use the mnemonic-a-day technique. Have students work in groups to make a mnemonic every day for 10 days. Each new mnemonic should be in a different content area than the one created the day before. Children keep MAD logs and periodically refer to them to make certain they remember all the accumulated mnemonics. Teachers can reward individuals or groups who can create a MAD example for the most days consecutively. This can be an enjoyable yet purposeful activity.

READING FLEXIBLY

Reading flexibly is at the heart of good study habits because students have to realize when to vary their speed according to the purpose for their reading and study. In recent years, the topic of **fluency** has become popular, due to the stress on fluency as one of the five keys in successful reading instruction (National Institute of Child Health and Human Development, 2000). Fluency refers mainly to "reading accurately, effortlessly and quickly, with appropriate expression and meaning" (Griffith & Rasinski, 2004, p. 126) and thus has taken on importance in theories about learning to read and beginning reading instruction. Discussions about fluency usually include word recognition to the point of automaticity—that is, recognizing words so quickly that comprehension takes over the act of decoding. The goal is more about comprehension and expressive reading than comprehension and study. Behaviors for developing fluency have included slowing reading rates, pausing while reading to make sure meaning is obtained, looking back, skipping and going back to difficult text, rereading, and reading aloud (Walczyk & Griffith-Ross, 2007). Activities suggested for gaining fluency include readers' theater, timed readings, and partner readings (Griffith & Rasinski, 2004).

Reading flexibly also includes fluency considerations; but here the focus is on reading to learn and varying one's rate for the intended study purpose. Varying rate starts with good previewing skills. By previewing, a student is actually scanning material to find what information is best to locate and select. In Barry's study of the strategies and tactics teachers themselves prefer, previewing was selected 45 percent of the time (Barry, 2002).

RATE OF READING

Rate of reading is a controversial topic. One of Edmund Burke Huey's tenets in *The Psychology and Pedagogy of Reading* (1908/1968) was that children should be taught, from the first reading instruction, to read as fast as the nature of the reading materials and their purpose will allow. Huey recommended speed drills to help students get information efficiently and effectively. After Huey, William S. Gray, in a 1925 review of the literature on speed of reading, endorsed rapid reading by concluding that such training could increase speed without concurrently reducing comprehension. Unfortunately many professionals have forgotten Huey's and Gray's work, and rapid reading has fallen into disfavor as a bona fide reading skill that students should acquire. In a recent history of study skills since the early 1900s, very little was found about rate of reading and speed reading (Richardson, Robnolt, & Rhodes, 2007). Yet in the same historical review, rate of reading was often a part of study skills assessments.

Probably no area of reading is as controversial as speed-reading (Carver, 1992). Perhaps one problem with speed-reading is the misconception that one can read faster simply by accelerating a physical activity. The physical process of reading requires the eyes to move in a jerky pattern over the page (**saccadic eye movements**), stopping to let the brain take in information (fixations), then moving again. These saccadic eye movements and eye fixations constitute the physical process of reading. A reader can get quite a headache by trying to accelerate this physical process too much. What is important is how readers manipulate the information taken in with each fixation, or as Frank Smith (1988) puts it, what goes on "between the eye and the brain" rather than from the page to the eye. This mental process requires chunking information into the largest meaningful units that one can assimilate and relating those chunks to an existing schema. We described this type of brain activity in the preceding discussion of mnemonic associations.

We do not recommend speed reading per se, but we do advocate rapid reading or speeding up one's reading along with an emphasis on encouraging the reader to decide what he or she needs and wants to know. Although early work on this topic stressed drills and techniques to learn to read faster, it neglected emphasizing the reader's purpose. In fact, when students read extensively and with purpose, they learn to vary their rate of reading (Bell, 2001). The strategy of SCAN and RUN (Salembier, 1999) reinforces this viewpoint. Students were taught a system of study that encourages not only **s**urveying, **c**apturing visuals, **a**ttacking boldface words, and **n**oting chapter questions, but also **r**eading and adjusting speed along with **u**sing word attack and **n**oticing when to check and reread.

> Timed readings can be created within some software programs.

SKIMMING AND SCANNING

Skimming is rapid glancing through text to find out generally what the reading is about (Jacobson, 1998). **Scanning** is rapid reading for some specific purpose—for instance, to find out where, when, or how something happened. When scanning, the reader may read an introduction or opening paragraph, a summary, and the first and last sentences of each paragraph, note material in bold print, and glance at visual aids. Unlike skimming, in which the reader glances at the whole text to get its general sense, scanning is searching for specific information, such as a word or detail. Students need much practice (beginning at an early age) to acquire these skills. We recommend scanning drills, in which teachers ask students to scan rapidly, looking for answers to *who, what, when,* and *where* questions in the reading material. Scanning can be practiced as students demonstrate how they confirmed predictions, or found a word's meaning, by returning to that place in the material.

RAPID READING EXERCISES

Teachers can use some easy rapid reading exercises to get students to practice and increase their reading speed. The first of these, **mental push-ups**, consists of rate and comprehension drills. At the beginning of class, the teacher asks students to use 3-by-5-inch cards to "mentally push" themselves down one page so quickly that they cannot absorb all the information on the page. (Older students who have had practice in the technique and who have better fine motor control can use a finger to pace themselves.) Then students close their books and write down what they learned. After the first reading, the amount retained is usually two or three words. The students repeat the procedure as many times as needed (usually two to four) until there is a rush of information—that is, until they comprehend and can express most of what is on the page. With extended practice, students will need fewer readings to comprehend material. This technique can clarify cognitive structure and increase student attention at the beginning of a class period. With practice, it will help make students more facile and mentally alert when reading short passages.

Another rapid reading activity is a variation on mental push-ups. Teachers can conduct three-minute **rapid reading drills** at the beginning of classes. In a straightforward rapid reading drill, students are asked to read as fast as possible. Again, young children can use a 3-by-5-inch card as a pacer; later they can use finger pacing. The teacher can conduct one or two three-minute drills without taking away too much time from the day's lesson. Students taking rapid reading drills are not asked to write out what they learned. As a variation, however, they could be asked to form groups in which each person discusses what she or he remembers from the reading.

A third exercise, the **preview and rapid reading drill**, can be used when the teacher is directing the reading of a content chapter. The teacher monitors the previewing phase, culminating with students writing specific questions that they wish to have answered in the reading. The previewing phase can be done by the whole class, in groups, or by individuals working on their own. The teacher asks the students to read more rapidly than usual to find the answers to their preview questions.

Retention and Systems of Study

The following systems of study are sometimes referred to as the best systems of learning that no one ever uses!

Retention should, in a self-regulated context, have as its goal that reading be transaction, not transmission (Smith, 1992). That is, retaining information is necessary to enhance readers' purposes, values, and beliefs rather being a mere accumulation of information to be regurgitated. Information is more easily retained when one wants to know it and add it to one's store of knowledge. Therefore, presenting subject matter through stimulating strategies and activities and following a framework of instruction such as PAR can facilitate student motivation to learn and study. Providing students with several study systems and letting them select the ones that work best for them enables students to practice good study techniques and retain information.

Many students do not use the systems because teachers do not take the time to model them. SQ3R and other learning systems need to be modeled in the classroom as many as 10 times for students to understand and begin to use them.

One of the first study systems teachers can model, starting in early elementary grades, is the directed reading–thinking activity (DR–TA) technique (Stauffer, 1969b). As such guided practice continues, teachers can gradually give more responsibility for learning to students, as illustrated in Pearson's (1985) model (see Figure 8.1). By the fourth or fifth grade, students can be introduced to a **study system**—a systematic set of steps for studying text. Study systems are a natural outgrowth of previewing, skimming, and teacher-modeled reading lessons such as the DR–TA. Study systems have not really permeated U.S. schools, although most teachers acknowledge their value. For example, Spor and Schneider (1999) found even though 44 percent of teachers had heard about the SQ3R system, only 17 percent had used it with students. There are probably three reasons for this low percentage. First, teachers themselves may not have learned through such a study system; thus they may give only lip service to the techniques described. Second, teachers may have been required to use a study system imposed by their own teachers, but they may not have understood the underlying reasons for the system. Teachers themselves need to practice previewing and study systems before they can believe in and teach such systems to others. Third, study strategies are not systematically introduced throughout educational systems from the early elementary years.

SQ3R

SQ3R (Robinson, 1961)—which stands for **s**urvey, **q**uestion, **r**ead, **r**ecite, **r**eview—is a study system that has been practiced for many years. Table 8.1 shows the SQ3R

FIGURE 8.1

The Gradual Release of Responsibility of Instruction

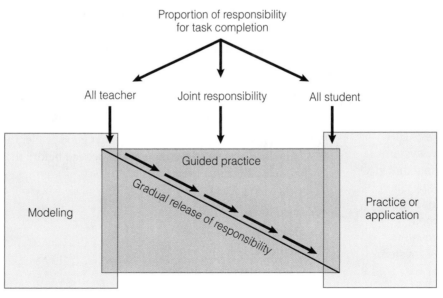

TABLE 8.1	SQ3R	
Technique	**Procedure**	**Values**
Survey	Read questions and summary at end of the chapter. Skim-read divisions of material, which usually are in boldface type. Read captions under pictures and graphs.	Highlights major ideas and emphases of chapter; helps organize ideas for better understanding later.
Question	Turn each heading into a question. (Practice will make this skill automatic.) Write questions in outline form.	Arouses curiosity; increases comprehension; recalls information known; highlights major points; forces conscious effort in applying the reading process.
Read	Read each section of the material to answer questions from headings.	Promotes active search for answers to specific questions; forces concentration for better comprehension; improves memory; aids in lengthening attention span.
Recite	After reading entire section, close book and write the answer to your question plus any significant cues; use your own words; write key examples; make notes brief.	Encourages students to use their own words and not simply copy from book; improves memory and ensures greater understanding.
Review	Study the topical outline and notes; try to see relationships; check memory by trying to recall main points; cover subpoints and try to recall them from seeing main points.	Clarifies relationships; checks short-term recall; prepares students for class.

steps. Lipson and Wixson (2003) call this the grandfather of study strategies. Spor and Schneider (1999) found in a survey of 435 teachers that 44 percent of teachers knew about the SQ3R study strategy and 31 percent said they would use it in their classrooms. Studies (Bhat, Rapport, & Griffin, 2000) generally speak to the benefits and positive results of using this approach. In a recent review of research concerning SQ3R, Huber (2004) found mixed results but overall asked for a renewed emphasis on researching the usefulness of the technique.

PQR2 ST+

PQR2 ST+ is a variation of the SQ3R study system. We feel that in this approach the added touches improve the SQ3R system.

The PQR2 ST+ study system developed by Morgan, Forget, and Antinarella (1996) is a complete study system. It consists of the following steps:

Preview: This is a very important step that good readers always do. Students take a quick overview of the material to be read before they start reading. Here is what to look for in a preview:

- Title.
- Introduction.
- Headings.
- Pictures.
- Charts, maps, and graphs.
- Bold print and italicized words.
- Summary.
- Review questions.

Question: In the left column of a page formatted for two-column notes, students write the questions or objectives to be achieved. A good way to do this is to turn the heading that introduces a passage into a question.

Read: Students read the subsection silently, thinking about how to express the information in *personal terms.*

Remember: In the right column of the notes, *with the book closed,* students write down the details of what they read. These notes must be in the student's own words! The students recall as much as possible but do not worry about missing some details.

Scan: Students rapidly scan the same text subsection to see whether they missed any details that were important or got anything wrong in their notes.

Touch up: Students add any important details to their notes.

+ (Plus): This last step should be done within the first 24 hours after the reading. Students return to study from their notes by folding the page so that only the questions show. Students see whether they can remember the details noted on the right side. Because of the way the notes are taken, students are able to recall important details. Students go over their notes one more time before a test.

SQRC

Sakta (1999) has proposed another study system similar to SQ3R. The SQRC procedure, which works best with expository readings, has four steps: **s**tate, **q**uestion, **r**ead, and **c**onclude. It is carried out in three phases of the reading process: before, during, and after reading. First students are given a general statement that they must support or refute based on what they find in the reading. Here are the phases of the strategy:

Phase 1—Before reading: The teacher introduces a topic and activates prior knowledge. Students then get a guide sheet (an example of such a guide sheet is shown as Activity 8.17), on which they write whether they are for or against the position statement given by the teacher, and why. Next students rewrite their position statements in question form.

Phase 2—During reading: Students read the text to find information that supports their positions. They also are instructed to take notes about salient points while reading. Immediately after reading, students review their notes and write brief conclusions.

Phase 3—After reading: The class is divided into two groups, each representing a position. With several students from each side acting as judges, students representing each position present arguments. The teacher serves as a consultant but does not offer opinions. After debate, the judges decide which side presented the stronger case.

NAME _____ CLASS _____

TITLE OF READING ASSIGNMENT: _____

Directions: Before reading the assignment, state your belief or position about the topic by selecting one of the two statements supplied by the teacher, or write your own position statement. Restate your position in the form of a question and write it in the space labeled "Question." As you read, use this question to guide your reading and thinking about the topic. Take notes on (1) facts that support your position and (2) facts that refute, or do not support, your position. When you are finished reading, review your notes and write your conclusion. The conclusion may or may not support your original position statement.

Statement: _____

_____

_____

_____

Question: _____

_____

_____

_____

_____

Facts that support my position statement:

_____

_____

_____

_____

_____

Facts that refute my position statement:

_____

_____

_____

_____

_____

Conclusion:

_____

_____

_____

_____

_____

Sakta (1999) presents results of a study she conducted that points to the effectiveness of the SQRC strategy for systematic study. The strategy is beneficial because, like SQ3R and PQR2 ST+, it combines key elements of cognitive learning theory and constructivist approaches. When study systems combine previewing, reading, reflection, and writing, they seem to net better success (Alber, Nelson, & Brennan, 2002).

ONE-MINUTE SUMMARY

Study skills are crucial but have not been highlighted in recent years. With the advent of the electronic age, though, study skills have resurfaced in academic discussions. The view that study must be self-regulated and is dependent on metacognition and deep thinking has changed the view of study skills from that of a set of specific steps one must follow to a set of behaviors from which a student selects based on the environment and purposes for study. This chapter presented an assessment technique designed to find out what study strategies students report using and what tactics they use to accomplish the strategies.

Study skills need to be demonstrated systematically and emphasized in early elementary grades through high school. As students mature and progress through school, the skills that are taught may include assessing one's study skills, creating good conditions for study, listening, locating and selecting information, following directions, interpreting visual information, organizing material for study, retaining information, being flexible, and using study systems. The teaching of study skills cannot be left to chance. Students at all levels need to be made aware of good study

TABLE 8.2 Study Strategies

	K	1	2	3	4	5	6	7	8	9	10	11	12
Assessing One's Study Skills	▬	▬	▬	▬	▬	▬	▬	▬	▬	▬	▬	▬	▬
Creating Good Conditions for Study	▬	▬	▬	▬	▬	▬	▬	▬	▬	▬	▬	▬	▬
Listening	▬	▬	▬	▬	▬	▬	▬	▬	▬	▬	▬	▬	▬
Locating and Selecting Information			▬	▬	▬	▬	▬	▬	▬	▬	▬	▬	▬
Following Directions	▬	▬	▬	▬	▬	▬	▬	▬	▬	▬	▬	▬	▬
Interpreting Visual Information	▬	▬	▬	▬	▬	▬	▬	▬	▬	▬	▬	▬	▬
Organizing Material for Study				▬	▬	▬	▬	▬	▬	▬	▬	▬	▬
Retaining Information				▬	▬	▬	▬	▬	▬	▬	▬	▬	▬
Being Flexible					▬	▬	▬	▬	▬	▬	▬	▬	▬
Using Study Systems					▬	▬	▬	▬	▬	▬	▬	▬	▬

practices through the use of a skills training model. Students must be convinced that study practices really will be more help than hindrance and that the hard work involved will pay off. Teacher modeling and involving students in practicing good study skills are the most effective ways to impart this message. Table 8.2 summarizes the strategies discussed in this chapter and indicates where each can be introduced in the school continuum.

PAR ONLINE

 Visit the *Reading to Learn in the Content Areas* Web site at http://academic.cengage .com/education/richardson for links to the Web sites mentioned in this chapter, tutorial quizzing, and other resources.

END-OF-CHAPTER ACTIVITIES

Assisting Comprehension

Select a study system that you prefer to use. Apply it to a content material of your choice in both a paper-based and a computer-based environment. Do you use the system in the same way for both environments? If not, how does your application differ? What is most helpful to your study and retention within this study system?

Reflecting on Your Reading

Standard 4.3 of the International Reading Association's Standards for Reading Professionals and Classroom Teachers states that teachers should model reading and writing strategies "enthusiastically" in the classroom:

> Model and share the use of reading and writing for real purposes in daily life. They use think-alouds to demonstrate good reading and writing strategies. They can articulate the research that supports modeling think-alouds and read-alouds to students.

Think about the study skills described in this chapter. Can you model them in your classroom? Think and reflect about ways that you can model these strategies in your classes.

CHAPTER 9

A word is not a crystal, transparent and unchanged; it is the skin of a living thought and may vary greatly in color and content according to the circumstances and time in which it is used.

OLIVER WENDELL HOLMES

Teaching Vocabulary

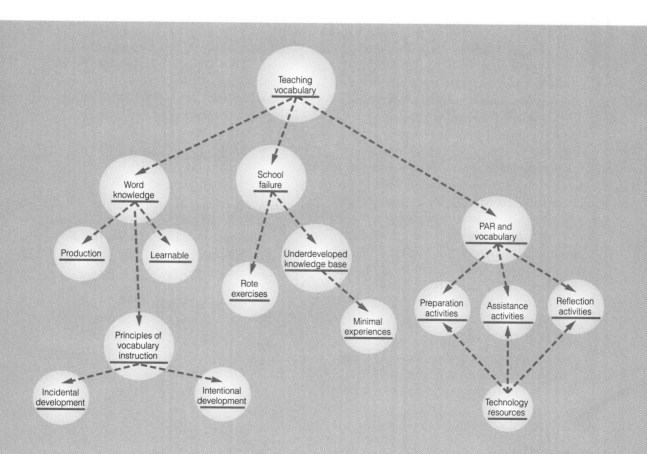

VOICES FROM THE CLASSROOM

Ms. Carson is eager to start a new unit in her first period junior English class. She has been teaching for seven years and knows her content well. She believes vocabulary is important for her students to understand in order for them to be able to master the concepts she teaches; so she consistently presents and makes assignments for each instructional unit in the same way. The following is her approach.

"Okay, it's Monday morning. Hope you had a great weekend and are ready to start fresh with our new unit on poetry. I have listed on the board the terms we will focus on for the duration of this study. You know the drill: Copy the terms, write the definitions, and write a sentence using each appropriately. Are there any questions?"

Why is this approach taken frequently in both elementary and secondary settings? Is it appropriate for both elementary and secondary students? Why or why not? How has this worked for you as a student?

PREPARING TO READ

1. What personal connections and associations come to mind when you think of vocabulary development? What do you remember about how you were taught vocabulary? Are your memories and associations pleasant or painful? Before beginning this chapter, list some ways in which you think content area teachers can generate enthusiasm for word study. How can we get students more interested in finding out the meanings of unfamiliar words? As you read the chapter, consider how your ideas can be added to or blended with those presented in the chapter to make vocabulary study appealing as a lifelong habit for your students.

2. Following is a list of terms used in this chapter. Some may be familiar to you in a general context, but in this chapter they may be used in unfamiliar ways. Rate your knowledge by placing a plus sign (+) in front of those you are sure you know, a check mark (✓) in front of those you have some knowledge about, and a zero (0) in front of those you don't know. Be ready to locate them in the chapter, and pay special attention to their meanings.

_____ production knowledge
_____ learnable knowledge
_____ contextual knowledge
_____ incidental vocabulary development
_____ intentional vocabulary development
_____ conceptual base of understanding
_____ free morphemes
_____ bound morphemes
_____ categorization
_____ closed word sort
_____ open word sort
_____ TOAST
_____ keyword strategy
_____ magic squares
_____ vocabulary illustrations

OBJECTIVES

As you read this chapter, focus your attention on the following purposes. You will

1. Understand the importance of vocabulary in reading comprehension.

2. Know and understand the underlying theory and research for vocabulary development in content areas.

3. Understand the four necessary mental operations for mastering new vocabulary.

4. Know the four guiding principles for vocabulary instruction.

5. Understand and be able to explain aspects of incidental and intentional vocabulary development.

6. Realize that a student's lack of understanding of concepts and vocabulary can contribute significantly to failure in school.

7. Use teaching strategies to increase a student's conceptual understanding of words.

8. Identify research-based practices to include strategies and activities for teaching vocabulary before, during, and after reading.

9. Learn a wide range of vocabulary enrichment activities considering student developmental, cultural, and linguistic differences.

10. Understand the role of oral language in vocabulary development.

11. Identify technology tools and applications for vocabulary development and enrichment.

In 1839 Edward George Bulwer Lytton wrote, "Beneath the rule of men entirely great, the pen is mightier than the sword." The words of language convey the essence of our thoughts, ideas, musings, and emotions. Having a command of our language—and specifically the vocabulary within that language—puts power in the hands of learners. A strong vocabulary equips us to actively participate in society as educated citizens and consumers.

Vocabulary plays a critical role in reading through the facilitation of comprehension (Blachowicz & Fisher, 2000, 2006; Graves, 2006a; Pressley, 2002c; Snow, Burns, & Griffin, 1998). The National Reading Panel (NRP; National Institute of Child Health and Human Development, 2000), upon examining numerous studies in the field, identified vocabulary instruction as one of the five key areas for emphasis necessary for successful reading among children. Vocabulary development is at least as important for secondary students because of specialized terms associated with content areas, as well as the importance of developing an understanding of numerous low-frequency terms typically assessed by standardized tests required for college entrance.

Low-frequency terms are vocabulary found in literature and texts associated with advanced schooling. Vocabulary scores on standardized tests of students entering college have declined over the past few years (Manzo, Manzo, & Thomas, 2006). With an influx of abbreviated language made popular by electronic devices and technology, among other influences, it seems that students are electing to use low-frequency terms less often. Manzo and colleagues suggest that a wider acceptance of coarse language within daily life and the media, along with the well-intentioned use of simpler terms to explain concepts, may contribute to vocabulary decline. One challenge, then, is to find ways to connect, include, and effectively integrate low-frequency terms in both elementary and secondary classrooms. Nagy and Scott (2000) explain that word usage within language indicates metalinguistic awareness, which ultimately affects academic achievement. In the next section we take a closer look at what is meant by *word knowledge* and ways in which it is both developed and encouraged.

A CLOSER LOOK AT WORD KNOWLEDGE

Over a half century ago, Davis (1944) and Thurstone (1946) wrote that knowledge of word meanings is one of the most important factors in reading comprehension. More recent studies (Blachowicz & Fisher, 2000; Cunningham & Stanovich, 1998; Pressley, 2002c; Snow, Burns, & Griffin, 1998) as well as the National Reading Panel (National Institute of Child Health and Human Development, 2000) in its review of research in reading instruction, have revealed the existence of a strong link between vocabulary and reading comprehension. Simply stated, if readers do not know the meanings of most words in a passage, they will be unable to understand the passage. Research attests to the correlation between vocabulary knowledge and unit test scores, oral reading rates, and teacher judgment (Lovitt, Horton, & Bergerud, 1987) as well as comprehension (Medo & Ryder, 1993). What constitutes vocabulary knowledge?

It is generally agreed that readers can "know" a word, but each person may relate it to a different experience. The sentence "John took a plane," for example, could be interpreted in different ways. A young child reading it might imagine playing with a toy; a high school student would imagine a scene in an airport; and an adult who is a carpenter might imagine a carpenter's tool. Simpson (1987) notes that "word knowledge is not a static product but a fluid quality that takes on additional characteristics and attributes as the learner experiences more" (p. 21). Knowing a word involves more than identification and pronunciation. Word knowledge has been described in various ways as being on a continuum (Dale, 1965; Stahl, 1999). We may think of word knowledge as being similar to coming to know a person. Initially a word is a *stranger,* one we have not seen or heard before. Then that word becomes an *acquaintance*; we have seen or heard it and know a little about it. As our depth of understanding grows and we become confident using the word in a variety of contexts, it takes on the status of *friend.*

Kibby (1995) proposes a continuum of word knowledge progressing from **production knowledge** to potentially **learnable knowledge**. Production knowledge is evident when a student knows a word so well that she or he can use it with facility in speech and writing. A student does not have learnable knowledge until background knowledge and pertinent information are provided concerning a concept about which students are unclear. Figure 9.1 shows this model.

When an association or a concept is known only vaguely or is not known at all, teachers need either to provide learning opportunities or to postpone instruction until students learn prerequisite knowledge. Teachers need ways to determine when to spend time on vocabulary. If they find that students already know a concept and words associated with it, time spent on vocabulary will be wasted. If they assume that

FIGURE 9.1

A Model of the Relation of Things and Words in an Individual's Lexicon.
Note: A "thing" is any real or imaginable object, feeling, action, or idea.

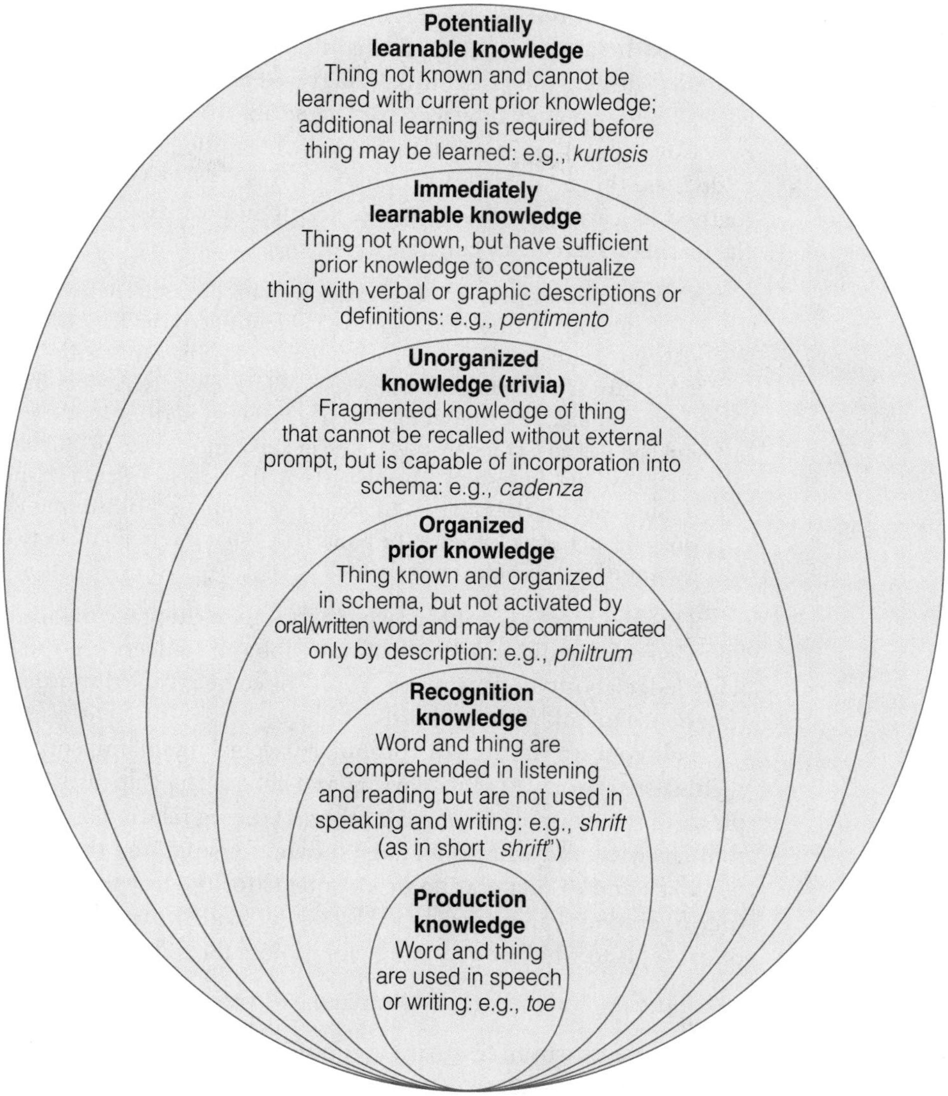

Potentially learnable knowledge
Thing not known and cannot be learned with current prior knowledge; additional learning is required before thing may be learned: e.g., *kurtosis*

Immediately learnable knowledge
Thing not known, but have sufficient prior knowledge to conceptualize thing with verbal or graphic descriptions or definitions: e.g., *pentimento*

Unorganized knowledge (trivia)
Fragmented knowledge of thing that cannot be recalled without external prompt, but is capable of incorporation into schema: e.g., *cadenza*

Organized prior knowledge
Thing known and organized in schema, but not activated by oral/written word and may be communicated only by description: e.g., *philtrum*

Recognition knowledge
Word and thing are comprehended in listening and reading but are not used in speaking and writing: e.g., *shrift* (as in short *shrift*")

Production knowledge
Word and thing are used in speech or writing: e.g., *toe*

From Kirby, M.W. (1995, November). The organization and teaching of things and the words that signify them. *Journal of Adolescent & Adult Literacy, 39*(3), 208–223. Reprinted by permission of the International Reading Association and Michael W. Kibby.

students know something that they do not know, not spending time on vocabulary will cripple the lesson. Biemiller (2001) and Stahl and Shiel (1999) argue that direct instruction of reading vocabulary is needed and appropriate for most students. However, the typical prereading vocabulary instruction that is given to students is one Nagy (1988) calls the "definition only" method, where students are asked to find definitions of 10 to 20 words in a dictionary and copy down the meanings before reading. This prescriptive approach has been described by researchers (Irvin, 1990; Ryder & Graves, 1994) as minimally effective, resulting in temporary retention of material, student disengagement, and little student understanding of text. Jitendra,

Edwards, Sacks, and Jacobson (2004) attest to the effectiveness of interventions and direct instruction that go beyond definitional learning for vocabulary growth among students with learning disabilities. Nagy and Scott (2000) describe true word knowledge as being applied knowledge or "being able to do things with it: to recognize it in connected speech or in print, to access its meaning, to pronounce it—and to be able to do these things within a fraction of a second" (p. 273). Unlike the "definition only" method of learning vocabulary, if concepts and words are to be learned, it is best for the teacher to start with concrete experiences. Consider this story:

> A 9-year-old was visiting a theme park with his parents. They walked past a ride named "Ribbault's Adventure." Although the father pronounced the ride's name, the boy kept asking when they would get a chance to ride "Rabbit's Adventure." In exasperation, the father turned to the mother and asked, "Why can't he remember the name of the ride?"
>
> The mother pointed out that the boy had read *Alice in Wonderland* and *Peter Rabbit* and had picked a name that was close in looks and sounds to "Ribbault's Adventure." "Perhaps," she suggested, "when he gets on the ride, he will call it what it is."
>
> Sure enough, the guide on Ribbault's Adventure explained who Ribbault was. And when the boy exited the ride, he remarked, "That was fun. I'd like to ride Ribbault's Adventure again before we go home."

This child was probably at what Kibby calls the stage of "immediately learnable knowledge." He did not know about Ribbault's adventure but had enough prior knowledge about adventures to "get it" once he received more information and an experience to link with the words.

Full-concept learning of vocabulary, according to Simpson (1987), requires four mental operations: (1) recognizing and generating critical attributes—both examples and nonexamples—of a concept; (2) seeing relationships between the concept to be learned and what is already known; (3) applying the concept to a variety of contexts; and (4) generating new contexts for the learned concept. The first of the four operations can be developed by asking students to exclude a concept from a list of concepts to which it does not belong. Note the following:

muezzin   mosque   minaret   *mangrove*

Also, students can brainstorm attributes and nonattributes of a given concept, as shown in Activity 9.1.

ACTIVITY 9.1 CONCEPT LEARNING: WORLD HISTORY

Use the textbook to brainstorm attributes and nonattributes of *nationalism*.

ATTRIBUTES		NONATTRIBUTES
honor	imperialism	maturity
pride	prestige	democracy
superiority	force	cooperation
wealth	fascism	isolationism
power		equality

Students can better understand relationships (operation 2) by brainstorming about targeted vocabulary concepts, then writing possible definitions. For mental operation 3, students can apply what they know about a vocabulary concept by being exposed to the word in different contexts. Stahl (1983) calls this teaching comprehension through developing **contextual knowledge**.

Students can learn how to generate new contexts for a learned vocabulary term (operation 4) by creating new sentences using previously learned concepts. To encourage frequent practice at this task, Simpson (1987) recommends a technique called *paired-word sentence generation:* Two words are given, and students are asked to write a sentence demonstrating the relationships between them. Possible examples are *method–analysis, genes–environment, graph–plot,* and *juvenile delinquency–recession.* A sentence for *juvenile delinquency–recession* might be "Incidents of juvenile delinquency occur more frequently during a recession."

Word knowledge results from both incidental and intentional learning experiences. Considerable word knowledge is developed naturally through exposure and daily living through incidental experiences. There is neither time nor is it necessary to teach every word that becomes part of an individual's store of knowledge (Beck, McKeown, & Kucan, 2002; Biemiller, 2001; Brabham & Villaume, 2002). Purposely setting up an environment for encouraging language play, inquiry, and discovery in addition to planning explicit instruction provides a means for positively influencing vocabulary acquisition to include both intentional and incidental learning pathways. Blachowicz and Fisher (2000), in their review of the research on vocabulary instruction, found and identified four guiding principles:

1. Students should be immersed in words (incidental).

2. Students should personalize word learning (intentional and incidental).

3. Students should continue to add to their word knowledge through varied and repeated exposures (intentional).

4. Students should be actively engaged in their own vocabulary development both to come to an understanding of words and to choose and apply strategies for independent word learning (intentional) (p. 504).

Incidental Vocabulary Development

Incidental vocabulary development occurs through conversation, word play (such as puns, rhymes, or jingles), exposure to spoken words from a variety of sources (such as television, radio, and video), and reading. Our earliest experiences with language are exposures to spoken words as parents and caregivers respond to our needs. Language development begins as a spontaneous and natural process as we listen, experiment, approximate, and put our understanding into practice. Through incidental experiences words are initially categorized and filed away in the mind based on personal connections and conceptions. Naive understandings may occur until explicit and intentional instruction clarifies and realigns faulty reasoning. For instance, young children believe that the sun actually "comes up" before learning the full meaning of planetary movements and distinctions between revolving and rotating.

As children are read stories and literature steeped in rich vocabulary, the initial and repeated exposure to language beyond daily conversation add to personal vocabulary growth. Cunningham and Stanovich (1998) found in their study examining vocabulary used in sources of spoken and written language that rare or "rich" words are more frequently found in children's literature than in adult conversation except for that which may occur in courtroom testimony. Biemiller and Boote (2006) made the case that during preschool and primary grade instruction, emphasis is typically on word recognition and decoding with little attention given to word meaning. Teachers in their study indicated reluctance to spend as much as 30 minutes a day on vocabulary instruction. Although decoding is critical to reading, being able to recognize and pronounce a word does not ensure its understanding. Devoting time and instruction to conceptual understanding of vocabulary terms should be considered as important for young readers as for their older counterparts (Padak, 2006). Given that many children begin school with limited vocabularies, inattention to concept development can set them up for academic disadvantages that are difficult to overcome (Hart & Risley, 2003). Biemiller and Boote's study provided evidence that primary grade, or preliterate, vocabulary instruction using repeated oral readings along with explanations and reviews of substantial numbers of words can improve vocabulary acquisition among young learners. They contend that

> if appropriate word meanings could be taught at a successful rate and during the three primary years, a child could acquire 1,000–1,500 additional word meanings. This would be enough to significantly improve the vocabulary of children with initially low vocabularies (p. 55).

As children come to understand that words are labels for things (Padak, 2006) and learn to transition from decoding to understanding terms to understanding sentences and passages, that vocabulary becomes a bridge to greater understanding (Kamil & Hiebert, 2005).

As children begin reading on their own, they can take greater responsibility for building their vocabulary. With modeling and scaffolded instruction they can learn to question unfamiliar words in the text and use root meanings and contextual clues. There is evidence that wide and extended independent reading experiences further contribute to vocabulary growth (National Institute of Child Health and Human Development, 2000).

Though language begins with listening and speaking experiences and moves and develops into reading and writing, all four channels contribute to our continued growth as literate individuals. In their study of building "meaning vocabulary" in primary grades, Biemiller and Boote (2006) cited several sources (Becker, 1977; Cunningham & Stanovich, 1998; Scarborough, 1998, 2001) providing evidence that limited oral vocabularies among children in early grades predict limited reading comprehension later in their schooling experiences. Activities that encourage classroom talk, including discussion, project work, role-playing, storytelling, and drama, are important for continued vocabulary development and are not reserved exclusively for young children.

Francis and Simpson (2003) found that one way of improving secondary and college students' vocabulary knowledge is to actively involve them in oral expression activities. Effective practices identified in this study included teachers making

Read about Pulido's (2004) study of the role of culture in incidental vocabulary development in *The Reading Matrix* 4(2). Look for it in the Web links option of the Chapter 9 resources on this book's companion Web site.

concerted efforts to apply and use new vocabulary in their daily classroom conversations. Students in such settings are given opportunities to try out and understand appropriate use and application of the terms they are learning. Graves (2006a) stresses the introduction of "meaty and somewhat academic topics" (p. 5) for discussion to ensure sophisticated and rich vocabulary development results. This level of vocabulary implementation takes the learning beyond memorization for tests.

Intentional Vocabulary Development

Making time to develop full word knowledge for **intentional vocabulary development** for depth and breadth of concept understanding has proven beneficial (Francis & Simpson, 2003; Nagy & Scott, 2000). Research supports practices that help students connect new vocabulary to known vocabulary and concepts. Francis and Simpson found that when teachers engaged students in explicit discussions identifying synonyms, antonyms, connotations, and nuances of the language, students were helped to clarify misunderstandings and were redirected to improve their reading comprehension.

Through direct instruction teachers may think aloud, model, and provide opportunities for practice and clarification to scaffold strategies and techniques for independent word learning. Interactive strategies in which students work together focusing on semantic connections using semantic maps, semantic feature analysis, and word sorts have been identified in the research as effective means for vocabulary development (Blachowicz & Fisher, 2000). The personal components of vocabulary learning that research supports include involving students in selecting words for study as well as choosing the strategies that work best for independent reading. Finally, instruction should go beyond introducing words prior to reading, the most common practice found in classrooms (Scott, Jamieson-Noel, & Asselin, 2003). Graves (2006b) advocates a four-part, long-term vocabulary program that includes "providing rich and varied language experiences, teaching individual words, teaching word-learning strategies, and fostering word consciousness" (p. 1). Vocabulary instruction, like comprehension and skills instruction, needs to be addressed prior to, during, and following the reading of text, providing repeated and reflective experiences with the words targeted for study.

VOCABULARY AND SCHOOL FAILURE

Often a mismatch occurs between school expectations and students' achievement, especially in the case of struggling readers. This is true despite a plethora of compensatory educational programs designed to reduce the conceptual and language deficits of culturally disadvantaged and minority children (Bryant, Goodwin, Bryant, & Higgins, 2003; Jitendra, Edwards, Sacks, & Jacobson, 2004; Moats, 2001). These children are often taught vocabulary through rote exercises that require dictionary definitions of extensive numbers of technical and specialized terms. In a typical exercise, the teacher informs students that before reading the chapter they must find, look up

Visit *Reading Online* to read an article by Curtis and Longo that describes a vocabulary intervention developed specifically for struggling adolescent readers. For further information about this reference, go to the *Reading to Learn in the Content Areas* Web site and select the Chapter 9 resources: http://academic.cengage.com/education/richardson.

in the dictionary, and define 30 words found in the chapter. It's no wonder reading is often thought of as decidedly dull by students who have to perform such rote tasks! This method of teaching vocabulary and concepts is product oriented; the rote production of the written word is the product. Rather than in-depth or thoughtful word exploration, what occurs is "considerable mentioning and assigning and little actual teaching" (Scott, Jamieson-Noel, & Asselin, 2003, p. 14). Such vocabulary exercises are used despite the fact that most disadvantaged students, at-risk populations, and generally poor readers use action words in much of their communication ("he gone," for example); they use processes to facilitate information rather than memorizing an extensive written vocabulary. Because rote vocabulary exercises present words and terms in the abstract, these students seem unable to grasp either their surface or their underlying meaning.

To help students learning words for which they seem to have no prior experiences or concepts, teachers need to present concepts in a very concrete manner, through direct and purposeful experiences followed by varied and repeated exposures (Bryant, Goodwin, Bryant, & Higgins, 2003; Jitendra, Edwards, Sacks, & Jacobson, 2004; Moats, 2001). Bryant and colleagues (2003) found in their review of the research on vocabulary instruction for students with learning disabilities a clear need for explicit, systematic instruction that includes opportunities for word manipulation, planned intervention, and personal connections and associations. It is especially important for instruction to include word examination that provides a means for deeper processing and retention at the word meaning level. Mnemonic devices and the keyword strategy were some techniques found to be effective for retention of content area vocabulary. A greater discussion of mnemonic devices can be found in Chapter 8.

When teaching students with learning disabilities, the number of words for study should be limited to those most needed; and multiple and varied exposures are critical. Snow (2002) has suggested that productive approaches that make the most of word learning may accelerate the process and help future learning. This may be done by creating semantic maps or by examining and manipulating word parts such as prefixes, suffixes, and roots. When hands-on experiences are not possible, students need "activities of observation," such as field trips, demonstrations, graphics, and visuals, to build a knowledge base for learning. Attention should be given to building and enriching oral language and basic concepts of study in an environment that encourages focused classroom talk and word play. "Just as a house needs a strong foundation, so reading comprehension depends on a strong base of oral language and concept development" (Blahcowicz & Fisher, 2003, p. 67).

Even if actual field trips are not possible, many virtual field trips are available on the Web. Visit this book's companion Web site, Chapter 9, to find links.

Remember that a reader's background knowledge is important in determining how much vocabulary she or he will understand and absorb. Students with broad background and understanding of the world will have an easier time learning vocabulary because of their wider background experience. This view has been substantiated in the research literature for decades (Blachowicz & Fisher, 2003; Ausubel, 1968; Carr & Wixson, 1986; Drevno, et al., 1994; Graves, 1985; Henry, 1974). For instance, students who have toured historic Philadelphia can relate to a passage about the influence of the Constitution more easily than can those lacking such firsthand experience.

Teachers who follow this view emphasize building on background knowledge in all phases of the PAR Lesson Framework. For example, a teacher might ask students what they know about small loan agencies in a business mathematics lesson about small loans. She might carefully present new vocabulary such as *collateral, passbook savings, debt,* and *consolidation loans.* At each phase of the lesson, she would try to identify how much students already know about the topic. In this manner, the teacher can help build students' general background knowledge.

Much of the discussion in this chapter so far has addressed ways to help students establish a **conceptual base of understanding**—an underlying knowledge of subject matter—with which to expand vocabulary knowledge. We feel that vocabulary instruction can be beneficial in increasing the base of knowledge at any phase of a lesson. Teachers need to make their own vocabulary lessons that will aid students before, during, and after reading. They cannot rely on basal reading series or textbook manuals' vocabulary exercises because these mostly stress teaching vocabulary before reading in the "definition only" method mentioned earlier. Teachers' manuals may also target words already known to your students or select words not particularly useful beyond the text selection. Letting students read freely in class or at home is important to vocabulary development but not sufficient for large vocabulary growth (Carver, 1994; Cunningham & Stanovich, 1998). Students struggling with reading either cannot or do not independently read the volume of material necessary to make a significant difference in vocabulary growth (Baker, Simmons, & Kame'enui, 1998).

Beck, McKeown, and Kucan (2002) propose a method for prioritizing and selecting words for specific instruction by considering words on a continuum of three tiers. Tier 1 words are those considered basic for understanding and communicating—those we consider high-frequency words. This would include words that label objects and actions with which children are familiar that are encountered in daily life. These are not generally necessary for special instruction because they are acquired incidentally. For example, Tier 1 words for a unit about the solar system might be *stars, moon, planets, sun,* and *earth.* Tier 2 words are often targeted for study in elementary settings and include words that label precisely and occur across subject areas. Some examples may be *comet, meteor, asteroid, orbit, galaxy, refraction, altitude, rotation,* and *revolution.* It is Tier 2 words that Beck, McKeown, and Kucan recommend as important for instruction for "mature language users." Facility with vocabulary at this level contributes to rich receptive and expressive language use across disciplines and situations. Tier 3 words are more technical and are most often used at advanced levels of study. Astronomy examples could be *chondrule, cosmology, occultation, nadir, zenith, perihelion, pulsar,* and *quasar.*

Students need preparation in vocabulary before reading a chapter or a lesson (the preparation phase of the PAR Lesson Framework); but the work should not stop there. Often students need assistance with vocabulary during or immediately after the reading (the assistance phase of PAR). For in-depth word learning students need longer periods of reflection to study vocabulary and attempt to understand how terms convey meaning and relationships (the reflection phase of PAR). Research by Memory (1990) suggests that vocabulary development can be effective when taught at any of these stages—before, during, or after reading assignments.

Effective readers consider their own background of understanding when trying to solve for unknown words encountered in a text. A former student told the story of her 6-year-old son trying to figure out the word *Kentucky* in a book he was reading. He asked for her help but explained that he knew the word had something to do with chicken. He apparently was drawing from his own experience with takeout food.

This three-step approach supports the specialized type of language development needed for students to come to full word understanding of the academic and content-specific vocabulary necessary for study and life application. Content area learning involves gaining a clear understanding of sets of terms that are critical to new concept development. This adds to the load because not only are the terms unfamiliar—the concepts too are new. The type of vocabulary associated with content area learning requires instruction that provides in-depth treatment going beyond superficial introduction. Because concepts often build on one another, gaining a clear understanding of terms basic to a concept is important for later learning and the complexity of advanced study. For example, students need to be able to understand, remember, and use the terms learned in basic mathematics as they move into algebra and geometry.

In the remainder of this chapter we describe several research-based practices and strategies for developing vocabulary. They can be used before reading, during reading, or shortly after reading. They also can be used as follow-up activities (usually the next day) after reading. We describe how teachers can use these strategies to teach vocabulary through understandable activities that are meaningful to students.

TEACHING VOCABULARY IN PREPARATION FOR READING

Research by Carney and associates (1984) shows that vocabulary instruction before reading improves student comprehension regardless of a student's reading ability. Teaching vocabulary before reading involves not so much the teacher "teaching" the terms as the students exploring and attempting to make sense of them before beginning the reading. As strategic learners, students need to recognize whether a link exists between words in the content material and their own knowledge. Douglas Barnes (1976) speaks to the matter in this way:

> Children are not "little vessels . . . ready to have imperial gallons of facts poured into them until they were full to the brim," as Dickens put it. They have a personal history outside the school and its curriculum. In order to arrive at school they have mastered many complex systems of knowledge; otherwise they could not cope with everyday life. School for every child is a confrontation between what he "knows" already and what the school offers; this is true both of social learning and of the kinds of learning which constitute the manifest curriculum. Whenever school learning has gone beyond meaningless rote, we can take it that a child has made some kind of relationship between what he knows already and what the school has presented. (p. 22)

Several activities—word inventories, graphic organizers, mapping, modified cloze, possible sentences, vocabulary connections, and capsule vocabulary—can be used before reading to strengthen the relationships between what students already know and what is provided in the text.

Word Inventories

Included in this book as self-inventories, word inventories are often at the start of each chapter. This activity encourages readers to assess their own prior knowledge and rate themselves. Although teachers can use such ratings to instruct, readers are in charge of their own assessment of conceptual knowledge. Activity 9.2 is an example of a word inventory developed for elementary school students.

Graphic Organizers

Reviews of graphic organizer research (Armbruster, 1992; Dunston, 1992; Egan, 1999; Rice, 1992) conclude that graphic organizers significantly aid students in remembering text. Graphic organizers can be an effective strategy for getting students on the same wavelength as the teacher in understanding the direction a lesson is taking. The teacher interacts with students by displaying a diagram and discussing why it is arranged in a particular way.

A semantic map is one of the most popular types of graphic organizers because it is excellent for depicting the interrelationships and hierarchies of concepts in a lesson. Research (Bos & Anders, 1990) demonstrates the effectiveness of semantic mapping for increasing reading comprehension and vocabulary learning. Mapping was introduced in Chapter 4 as a way to develop comprehension. A semantic map

Several Web sites offer a wide variety of printable graphic organizers. Visit some of those listed in Chapter 9 section of the Reading to Learn in the Content Areas *Web site.*

ACTIVITY *9.2* WORD INVENTORY IN ELEMENTARY ENGLISH

Directions: Use the happy faces to tell how well you know these words. This isn't a test and you won't be graded. Remember: You aren't supposed to know all the words.

I know it!

I think I've seen or heard it.

I don't know it.

_____ 1. Blanket	_____ 7. Burrowed
_____ 2. Question	_____ 8. Forever
_____ 3. Straight	_____ 9. Muckraker
_____ 4. Constantly	_____ 10. Shadow
_____ 5. Treacherous	_____ 11. Believe
_____ 6. Friend	_____ 12. Television

Developed by Terry Bryce.

can be used as a prereading or postreading exercise. To use semantic mapping before reading, follow these steps:

1. Select an important word from the reading assignment.

2. Ask students to think of as many related words and key concepts as possible that will help in understanding the keyword.

3. List these words on the board as they are identified.

4. As an extension of this activity, have students rank the words or categorize them as "most important" and "least important." This activity may help students begin to see that all words in the lesson are not equally important and that information needs to be categorized.

5. Organize the words into a diagram similar to the one in Activity 9.3 in elementary language arts.

ACTIVITY **9.3** SEMANTIC MAP IN ELEMENTARY LANGUAGE ARTS

ROTTWEILERS

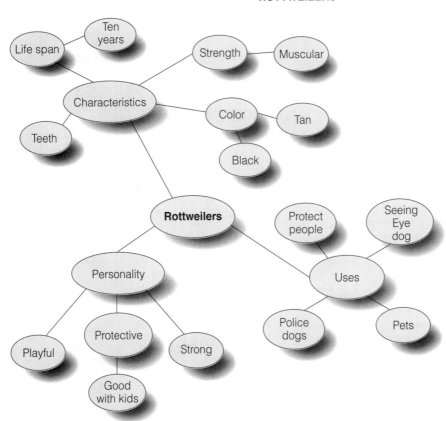

Visit the *Reading to Learn in the Content Areas* Web site for Chapter 9. Look for a link for *Inspiration* online to find and experience an interactive presentation/demonstration using graphic organizers and to discover further information about product utility.

Software like *Inspiration* and *Kidspiration* may fit seamlessly into a lesson using features like Rapid Fire to create graphic organizers with visual elements and vocabulary connections. The teacher may select a target word from the lesson and have students contribute words they associate with it. As the words are typed in using Rapid Fire, they are immediately added to a web with connecting lines providing a visual for all to see. Initial organizers can then be reorganized as students recognize groupings, headings, and subheadings. Activity 9.4 shows a variation of a semantic map. In this activity the Spanish teacher helped students learn about types of chili peppers.

Using the semantic map as their base, Schwartz and Raphael (1985) designed a word map. Directly under the keyword, which is circled or boxed, examples that remind students of that word are placed. To the right of the keyword, properties are written. The teacher might ask, "What is it like?" Directly above the keyword, the concept of the word is represented as a definition or description. In this way students are led in their understanding from concrete examples to abstract definitions and concepts. Activity 9.5 is a word map for the key word *metaphor*. Activity 9.6 presents

---

ACTIVITY 9.4 SEMANTIC MAP IN SPANISH

CHILI PEPPERS

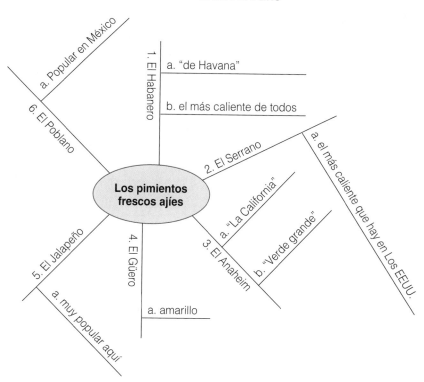

Developed by Brian Littman.

WORD MAP SIMILE
<KEY>

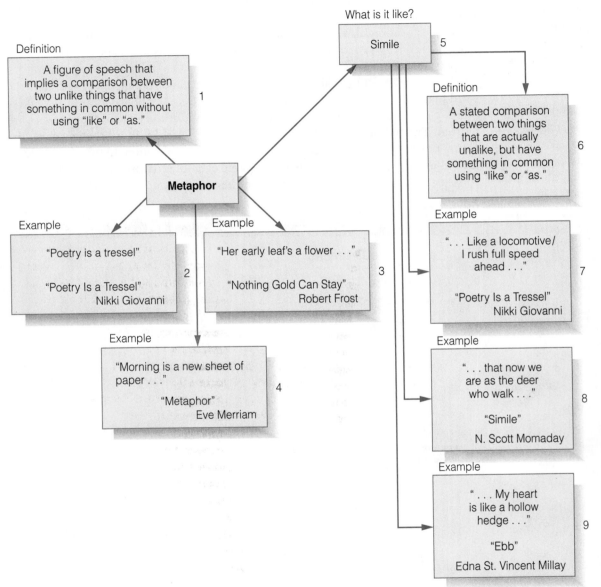

Definition

A figure of speech that implies a comparison between two unlike things that have something in common without using "like" or "as." 1

Metaphor

Example

"Poetry is a tressel"

"Poetry Is a Tressel"
Nikki Giovanni 2

Example

"Her early leaf's a flower . . ."

"Nothing Gold Can Stay"
Robert Frost 3

Example

"Morning is a new sheet of paper . . ."

"Metaphor"
Eve Merriam 4

What is it like?

Simile 5

Definition

A stated comparison between two things that are actually unalike, but have something in common using "like" or "as." 6

Example

". . . Like a locomotive/ I rush full speed ahead . . ."

"Poetry Is a Tressel"
Nikki Giovanni 7

Example

". . . that now we are as the deer who walk . . ."

"Simile"
N. Scott Momaday 8

Example

" . . . My heart is like a hollow hedge . . ."

"Ebb"
Edna St. Vincent Millay 9

Extra Credit
Why is this handout titled "Word Map Simile"?
Because it compares a metaphor to a simile and uses "like" or "as."

Developed by Tara Furges.

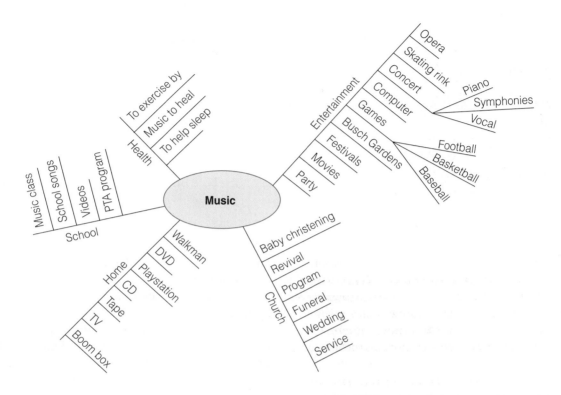

Developed by Audra Jones and her students.

a type of word map sometimes called a *spider map* because the graphic organizer resembles a spider's web. This activity is from an early elementary lesson on the benefits of music. Both semantic maps and word maps are excellent ways of getting students to clarify their thinking before reading an assignment.

Modified Cloze Procedures

Chapter 3 introduced cloze as a means of determining reader background. Cloze passages can also be constructed to teach technical or general vocabulary. Passages used in this manner are modified for instructional purposes. Instead of deleting words at predetermined intervals, as when measuring readability and checking students' reading ability, teachers select an important passage from the text and delete keywords. Teachers may also create their own cloze passages of 50 to 100 words to assess students' knowledge of vocabulary and concepts in a certain topic. Activity 9.7 presents a passage of more than 100 words constructed by a teacher to assess students' knowledge of the first settlers in North America. Students can fill in the blanks individually, then

The United States of America is a young country. It is only about _____ years old. North America had been explored for more than _____ years before any settlers came to live here. After the first settlement at _____ in 1607, many more European settlers came to North America. Some wanted to find _____ freedom. Others came for the chance to own _____ . Still others came to teach _____ to American Indians. At first, it was _____ for the colonists. Many did not know how to _____ the land and were not used to wild _____ . As a result, many colonists _____ .

---

discuss their answers in small groups. The best, or most unusual, answers can eventually be shared with the entire class.

Possible Sentences

Possible sentences (Moore & Arthur, 1981) is an activity that combines vocabulary and prediction. It is designed to acquaint students with new vocabulary that they will encounter in their reading and guide them as they attempt to verify the accuracy of the statements they generate. Additionally, it arouses curiosity concerning the passage to be read. This activity is best used when unfamiliar vocabulary is mixed with familiar terminology. When using this technique, the teacher might give students a worksheet such as the one shown in Activity 9.8. Teachers pick between five and eight vocabulary terms, such as those from elementary science in Activity 9.8.

For each term, students write a possible sentence on the left side of the worksheet. Then, during reading, they look for the real meaning of the term and write this meaning in a sentence. In doing so, students create a mnemonic, with the possible sentence cuing them to the real meaning of the word. This is a simple but powerful strategy for learning words. Research attests to the advantage of using such mnemonic devices to learn vocabulary (Levin, Levin, Glassman, & Nordwall, 1992; Moore & Surber, 1992; Scruggs, Mastropier, Brigham, & Sullivan, 1992). Mnemonic devices are discussed later in this chapter and in detail in Chapter 8.

Vocabulary Connections

Iwicki (1992) describes a strategy whereby students use a term from a previous book in shared literature study to describe a situation in a book currently being studied. In this way, connections are made between old vocabulary and the new book. For example, the word *pandemonium,* found in *Welcome Home, Jelly Bean* (Shyer, 1988), can be related to events in *The Black Stallion* (Farley, 1941). In other content areas, words from a previous chapter can be used to see relationships in a new one. In occupational mathematics, for example, the term *conversion* may be used with *product volumes* in one chapter and again in a chapter about the use of mathematics in leisure

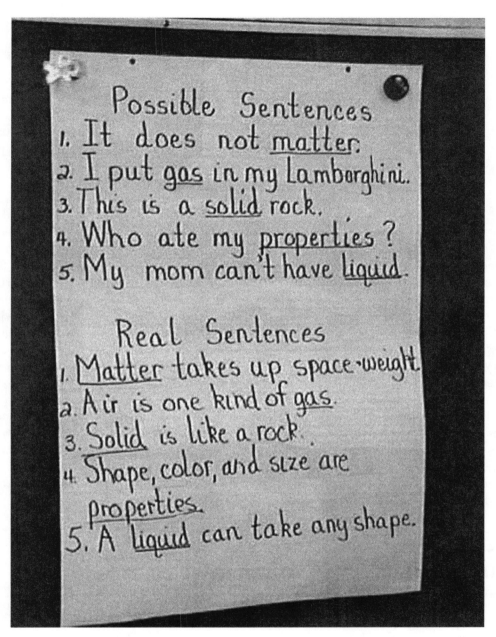

Possible Sentences
1. It does not <u>matter</u>.
2. I put <u>gas</u> in my Lamborghini.
3. This is a <u>solid</u> rock.
4. Who ate my <u>properties</u>?
5. My mom can't have <u>liquid</u>.

Real Sentences
1. <u>Matter</u> takes up space-weight.
2. Air is one kind of <u>gas</u>.
3. <u>Solid</u> is like a rock.
4. Shape, color, and size are <u>properties</u>.
5. A <u>liquid</u> can take any shape.

Developed by Suzanne McDaniel.

activities (such as converting international track and field times from English measurements to metrics). Iwicki reports that vocabulary connections retain their appeal to students throughout schooling. They provide an excellent way for students to use higher-level thinking skills in comparing vocabulary between content area subjects.

Capsule Vocabulary

Capsule vocabulary (Crist, 1975) is an activity that helps readers explore meaning relationships among words and helps students connect those relationships and what the students already know. The teacher selects a list (or capsule) of several words either found in the text or useful for understanding the text material. After the teacher briefly defines each word and uses it in a sentence, students work in pairs to use the terms in sentences. Next students write sentences or a summary using the words. Then they check their sentences against the text material.

Here is an example of the use of capsule vocabulary in an English as a second language class. Students worked in pairs to write sentences about new words they had encountered. Eighteen students from Cambodia, Vietnam, Korea, and Russia with widely different levels of English proficiency participated. Some had been in the United States for three years, some for less than two weeks. The teacher, Barbara Ingber, prepared a list of numbered words pertaining to shopping in a supermarket: *supermarket, cashier, coupons, groceries, food, detergent, diapers, bag, shopping cart, money,* and *change.* She dictated these words, and students wrote them in their notebooks using temporary spellings. Then the teacher asked for students to call the words back to her as she wrote each one on the chalkboard using the correct spelling. Students tried to define words as they were written on the board. For those they could not define, the teacher provided a definition with a sentence or an action (such as pretending to push a shopping cart). Next the students worked in pairs, creating sentences for each word. She was careful to pair students from different countries so that each had to communicate in English, the common language. Students then wrote their sentences on the board. The group studied each sentence and made corrections for standard English, with the teacher's help. Students copied the corrected sentences and read them aloud to their partners. This activity utilized paired learning, as well as listening, speaking, reading, and writing.

<aside>
Note
Ms. Ingber's use of listening, temporary (inventive) spelling, and oral interaction, as well as modeling and demonstration to prepare students for using vocabulary in writing and reading.
</aside>

TEACHING VOCABULARY TO ASSIST STUDENTS IN THEIR READING

Mealey and Konopak (1990), in an excellent review of the research on preteaching content area vocabulary, have questioned the value of solely preteaching content terms. Like these researchers, we maintain that students need to be assisted in all content areas and at every grade level in interpreting unfamiliar words. Teachers cannot "protect" students from words by teaching before reading every difficult term they will encounter. Teachers need to help students understand words that clarify text.

Encouraging students to develop word consciousness (Graves, 2000) may help them bring unfamiliar words that interfere with their understanding of the text to the forefront. Noticing new or unknown words is the first step in being proactive and taking responsibility for unlocking their meanings. Using sticky notes, highlighting tape, or flags to mark difficult or interesting words in the text engages the reader in actively attending to and identifying words for further consideration.

Revisit Chapter 8's discussion of study skills to read our suggestions for using Wikipedia and other dictionaries or encyclopedias that can enhance vocabulary in online environments.

Leading students to become independent strategists when encountering unknown vocabulary can begin as early as third or fourth grade with attention to context clues, morphology, and understanding appropriate use of dictionaries and reference sources (Blachowicz, Fisher, Ogle, & Watts-Taffe, 2006; Edwards, Font, Baumann, & Boland, 2004; Graves, 2004, 2006b). Even though context is not fool-proof, it can often provide a beginning point. The order of words within a sentence offer syntactic clues that can help students determine if an unfamiliar word is an action, a thing, or some type of description. Semantic clues can provide information in the form of examples, definitions, synonyms, antonyms, or descriptions. Students can be taught to recognize the various kinds of context clues as well as how to read ahead and use the clues to predict, infer, and reason out meanings. They also need to understand that context can sometimes be insufficient or even misleading. Other factors need to be considered to ensure accurate comprehension.

Five excellent techniques for assisting readers are context clue discovery, structural analysis, DISSECT, word attack paradigms, and vocabulary lists. Also, activities already introduced in this text, such as organizational (jot) charts, can be adapted to assist readers. Knowing how and when to use a dictionary, thesaurus, and online resources can provide one more strategy for achieving independent vocabulary acquisition.

Context Clue Discovery

To begin to understand the importance of "concepts in context," think of any word in isolation; then try to define it. Take, for example, the word *run*. It is not difficult to give a synonym for the word, but it does not have a clear meaning until it is placed in a context. You may have thought immediately of the most common definition, "to move with haste"; but "to be or campaign as a candidate for election," "to publish, print, or make copies," or even "to cause the stitches in a garment to unravel" would have been equally accurate. A precise meaning cannot be determined until *run* is seen in context. One way to help students recognize the importance of context to meaning is to do a brief word association activity (see Activity 9.9) with them. Have them number a sheet of paper from 1 to 10 and write a one- or two-word definition/association that comes to mind as you call words out orally. Select words that clearly have multiple meanings and words for which the students probably know two or three of the meanings.

Students often use context clues to help determine word meanings. Sometimes, however, students are unsuccessful at using context clues because they lack a systematic strategy for figuring out unknown words. To help students develop the ability to use context to discover the meaning of unfamiliar words, teachers can discuss specific clues that they should look for in text.

Word	Possible Definition	Possible Definition
1. Record	Musical disk	Data/information
2. Tie	Clothing for neck	Interlocking
3. Mouse	Furry animal	Computer device
4. Bad	Not good	Good
5. Story	A tale	Building level
6. Column	Newspaper story	Stone pillar
7. Break	Tear up	Brief relaxing period
8. Cell	Jail	Body part
9. Bank	Building for money	Land next to river
10. Bill	Bird part	Money owed

DEFINITIONS

Authors often define a word in the sentence in which it first appears. This technique is used frequently in textbooks when an author introduces terminology. Note the following examples:

The *marginal revenue product* of the input is the change in total revenue associated with using one more unit of the variable input.

The *peltier effect* is the production of heat at the junction of two metals on the passage of a current.

SIGNAL WORDS

Certain words or phrases may be used to signal the reader that a word or a term is about to be explained or that an example will be presented. Some of the most frequently used signal words are listed here, followed by two sentences using signal words:

for example	these (synonym)	in (the way) that
this way	especially	such
such as	like	

Martin Luther King was more than just a leader in America, *in that* he was recognized worldwide.

The man lost the sympathy of the judge, *especially* when he was found in a drunken stupor shortly after being let out of jail.

DIRECT EXPLANATIONS

Often authors provide an explanation of an unfamiliar term that is being introduced. This technique is used frequently in difficult technical writing.

> Joe was a *social being,* whose thoughts and behaviors were strongly influenced by the people and things around him and whose thoughts and behaviors strongly influenced the people he was around.

> Mead emphasized that the mind is a social product; indeed, one of the most important achievements of socialization is the development of *cognitive abilities*—intellectual capacities such as perceiving, remembering, reasoning, calculating, and believing.

SYNONYMS

A complex term may be followed by a simpler, more commonly understood word, even though the words may not be perfect synonyms. Again, the author is attempting to give the reader an explanation or definition—in this instance, by using a comparison. In the following example, *obscure* is explained by comparison to the word *unintelligible.* In the second sentence, *attacks* helps explain *audacious comments.*

> The lecture was so *obscure* that the students labeled it *unintelligible.*

> There were *audacious comments* and *attacks* on prominent leaders of the opposition.

ANTONYMS

An author may define or explain a term by contrasting it with words of opposite meaning:

> The young swimmer did not have the *perseverance* of her older teammates and *quit* at the halfway point in the race.

> All this is rather *optimistic,* though it is better to err on the side of hope than in favor of *despair.*

INFERENCES

Students can often infer the meaning of an unfamiliar word from the mood and tone of the selection. In this case, meaning must be deduced through a combination of the author's use of mood, tone, and imagery and the reader's background knowledge and experience. The author thus paints a picture of meaning rather than concretely defining or explaining a word within the text. In the passage that follows, the meaning of *opaque* is not made clear. The reader must infer the meaning from the mood and tone of the paragraph and from personal experience with a substance such as black asphalt:

> This is it, this is it, right now, the present, this empty gas station, here, this western wind, this tang of coffee on the tongue, and I am patting the puppy, I am watching the mountain. And the second I verbalize this awareness in my brain, I cease to see the mountain or feel the puppy. I am *opaque,* so much black asphalt. But at the same second,

the second I know I've lost it, I also realize that the puppy is still squirming on his back under my hand. Nothing has changed for him. He draws his legs down to stretch the skin out so he feels every fingertip's stroke along his furred and arching side, his flank, his flung-back throat. (From *Pilgrim at Tinker Creek,* by Annie Dillard. New York: Harper's Magazine Press, 1975.)

Research suggests that students can use context clue strategies to unlock the meaning of unfamiliar terms (Stahl, 1986). Therefore, it is a good idea to have these six clues (with explanations and sample sentences) posted at points around the classroom or on handouts to be kept in students' work folders:

CONTEXT CLUE TYPES AND EXAMPLES

Definitions: An *extemporaneous* speech is one that is given on the spot without prior preparation.

Signal words: There are several forms of *precipitation* like rain, sleet, snow, and hail.

Direct explanations: Carl was *despondent,* making him feel so downhearted that he didn't want to participate in anything.

Synonyms: When we looked into the jar we saw the *larva* stage, or worm, of the beetle we were studying.

Antonyms: Tamara was quite *gregarious* while her sister Mary was instead very shy.

Inferences: It was a good thing the locksmith only charged a *nominal* fee to unlock John's car because he had only a few dollars in his pocket.

Structural Analysis

Even if students practice and remember the strategy, context clues sometimes are not going to be of much help in decoding unfamiliar words (Blachowicz & Fisher, 2000; Nagy & Stahl, 2000). For example, readers probably would have trouble guessing the meaning of the following italicized terms from context clues:

Nations impose burdens that violate the laws of *equity.*

A very important finding about the effects of mass media relates to *latency.*

They put a *lien* on our house.

Using context clues alone in these sentences would probably give readers a vague idea of the meaning or no idea at all.

When a student is working alone, it can potentially be more helpful to use structural analysis, also known as morphemic analysis, along with contextual analysis to derive meaning. Instruction in morphology to learn word parts in the form of roots and affixes can be an advantage serving to unlock numerous words across disciplines (Baumann, 2005; Baumann, Edwards, Boland, Olejnik, & Kame'enui, 2003). Generally students are ready for using structural analysis to assist them in understanding unknown terms by the time they enter fourth grade (Edwards, Font, Baumann, & Boland, 2004; Graves, 2006a, 2006b; White, Sowell, & Yanagihara, 1989). Baumann and his colleagues (2002, 2003) have found empirical evidence that instruction and practice in using contextual and structural analysis together can improve independent vocabulary acquisition. Kieffer and Lesaux (2007) found in their study of fourth and fifth graders that apparently morphology (the study of word parts) and vocabulary development have a reciprocal relationship. As students develop a greater understanding of morphology, their vocabularies increase; and students with larger vocabularies tend to better understand morphology.

Structural analysis provides a way to examine words looking for roots and affixes as keys to unlocking word meanings. Roots (the most basic word parts) and affixes (prefixes and suffixes) are all morphemes. Morphemes are the smallest meaning-bearing units that make up words. In the word *unlock* there are two morphemes, *un* and *lock*. A **morpheme** can be **free** to stand alone like *lock* or **bound** like *un* (needing to be joined to another morpheme). Consider the following passage concerning sexual dimorphism:

> An interesting relationship between sexual dimorphism and domestic duties exists among some species. Consider an example from birds. The sexes of song sparrows look very much alike. The males have no conspicuous qualities which immediately serve to release reproductive behavior in females. Thus courtship in this species may be a rather extended process as pair-bonding (mating) is established. Once a pair has formed, both sexes enter into the nest building, feeding, and defense of the young. The male may only mate once in a season, but he helps to maximize the number of young which reach adulthood carrying his genes. He is rather inconspicuous, so whereas he doesn't turn on females very easily, he also doesn't attract predators to the nest.
>
> The peacock, on the other hand, is raucous and garish. When he displays to a drab peahen, he must present a veritable barrage of releasers to her reproductive IRMs. In any case, he displays madly and frequently and is successful indeed. Once having seduced an awed peahen, he doesn't stay to help with the mundane chores of child rearing, but instead disappears into the sunset looking for new conquests. (From R. A. Wallace, *Biology: The World of Life*. Copyright 1975 by Goodyear Publishing Co., Santa Monica, California.)

After reading this passage we know the following:

A relationship exists between sexual dimorphism and some species.

Sparrows share domestic duties.

Peafowl do not share domestic duties.

Mating and pair-bonding are different for sparrows and peafowl.

Visit the prefix/suffix sites using the links option of the Chapter 9 resources on the *Reading to Learn in the Content Areas* Web site.

What is the cause of the difference? Your response should be "sexual dimorphism." If you know that *di* means "two" and *morph* means "form or shape," then you can figure out the term *sexual dimorphism*. (The DVD for *Reading to Learn in the Content Areas*, at Chapter 9, contains a list of prefixes, suffixes, and roots of words, along with their meanings and examples.)

As few as 20 prefixes with consistent meanings and spellings are used in 97 percent of words containing prefixes found in texts and instructional materials commonly used in school (White, Sowell, & Yanagihara, 1989). Thus common prefixes make good candidates for use in instruction. As students find them in new words in a variety of texts and stories, they can use their understanding to unlock meanings independently. Knowing *un, re, in,* and *dis* gives students a key to the meanings of more than 1,500 words (Cunningham, 2006). Beyond prefixes, it is useful to teach commonly used suffixes, especially derivational suffixes like *less (regardless)* and *able (affordable)* because of their effect on meaning. Inflectional suffixes, often referred to as inflections, alter word forms but do not change the essential meanings of the roots. In the case of nouns, *cat* becomes *cats.* Verbs may change as *hop, hops, hopping,* and *hopped.* When comparing, *quick* may become *quicker* or *quickest.* As students mature in their vocabulary development, Greek and Latin roots can be effectively introduced as they become important to learning content-specific and specialized terminology. Edwards and colleagues (2004) suggest four guidelines for teaching morphemic analysis:

> *Guideline 1: Provide explicit instruction in how morphemic analysis works.* This includes modeling and practicing breaking words apart and putting them back together for the purpose of locating meaningful clues.
>
> *Guideline 2: Use word families to promote vocabulary growth.* Learning to recognize word families may help students make connections from common to less common derivations of a word.
>
> *Guideline 3: Promote independent use of morphemic analysis.* There are far too many affixes and roots used with the English language and not enough time or need to teach them all. Encouraging and challenging students to build their repertoire through vocabulary journals or notebooks can enhance independent vocabulary growth.
>
> *Guideline 4: Enhance students' awareness that morphemic analysis does not always work.* Word part meanings are not always consistent, and meanings of isolated parts when combined do not always produce true meanings of words. (pp. 164–166)

When putting together structural analysis with contextual analysis, the vocabulary rule strategy (Edwards, Font, Baumann, & Boland, 2004) of employing a whole–part–whole sequence is recommended. Students are directed first to read and make use of context, then consider the word parts of the key word(s), and finally put it all together again in the context of the passage. With explanations, modeling, and think-alouds, students can begin to adopt combinations of structural and contextual analysis strategies for continuing to develop mental habits that increase vocabulary understanding.

Take a look at two online sources of common prefixes, roots, and suffixes found on this book's companion Web site, Chapter 9.

Semantic maps make good vehicles for illustrating morphological relationships. *Kidspiration* and *Inspiration,* the well-developed software tools for creating semantic maps noted previously in this chapter, provide a way to include picture examples along with words and word parts being studied. Open and closed word sorts also work well for assisting students as they develop their understanding of words that share common morphemes. When working with young students, an activity called Affix Animals offers a playful way to experiment with prefixes and suffixes. Students are given a list of number and characteristic affixes from which

FIGURE 9.2   Biheaded, Trilegged Hydrosaur

they may choose to draw, create, and appropriately name an imaginary animal (see Figure 9.2)

DISSECT

This mnemonic, created by Deshler and Schumacher (1988), provides a ready reminder of several factors that help determine a word's meaning. When modeled and practiced, this may be a helpful tool for independent reading:

Discover the word's context.

Isolate the prefix.

Separate the suffix.

Say the stem or root word.

Examine the stem or root word.

Check with someone.

Try the dictionary.

WORD ATTACK PARADIGMS

Aguiar and Brady (1991) suggest that vocabulary deficits of less skilled readers stem from difficulty in establishing accurate phonological representations for new words. Their research points to the importance of structural analysis and the following strategy, called a *word attack paradigm,* to help students recognize words. In this

There are many free online dictionary sources. Visit this book's companion Web site, Chapter 9, to find links to several.

activity students are given a card with a series of steps to aid them in deciphering new words they encounter in reading. Such a paradigm might look like this:

1. Figure out the word from the meaning of the sentence. The word must make sense in the sentence.

2. Take off the ending of the word. Certain endings, such as *s, d, r, es, ed, er, est, al,* or *ing,* may be enough to make the word look "new."

3. Break the word into syllables. Don't be afraid to try two or three ways to break the word. Look for prefixes, suffixes, and root words that are familiar.

4. Sound the word out. Try to break the word into syllables several times, sounding it out each time. Do you know a word that begins with the same letters? Do you know a word that ends the same? Put them together.

5. Look in the glossary if there is one in the back of the book.

6. Ask a friend in class or the teacher. No one should be ashamed of asking someone for help in figuring out a word.

7. As a last resort, find the definition of the word in the dictionary.

Dictionaries should be the last source one uses in figuring out the meaning of a word—after all sources are exhausted. Unfortunately teachers (and parents) often tell students to use the dictionary as a first option in discovering the meaning of words. A word attack paradigm gives students a way to attempt newly found words without resorting to a dictionary. Students should keep the paradigm in their folders, or a large one can be posted on the wall by the teacher.

Vocabulary Lists

Visit the PBS Reading between the Lions site with vocabulary activities and a picture dictionary. The URL can be found on this book's companion Web site, Chapter 9.

Students can be encouraged to make vocabulary lists of new terms they have mastered, whether by context clue discovery, structural analysis, or the word attack paradigm. Students may keep such lists in notebooks or on file cards. If they use cards, first they can write a word and its dictionary pronunciation on the front side. Then on the back they can write the sentence in which the word was found and the dictionary definition. Periodically students can exchange their notebooks or file cards and call out vocabulary terms to one another, as they often do when spelling words: One student calls out the term, and another gives the definition and uses the word in a sentence. In this manner, students can make a habit of working daily and weekly with words to expand their content vocabulary. Activity 9.10 is an example of a vocabulary list with several words recorded.

Organizational (Jot) Charts

Students can compare and contrast words using organizational (jot) charts, as described in Chapter 4. For instance, a Spanish teacher had third-year students chart command words so they could see at a glance on one simple chart the relationship of the three types of commands in negative and affirmative statements. Activity 9.11 shows the chart. The table creation tool in any word processing program provides an interesting and useful computer application for this strategy.

Word	Page	Possible Definition	Verified Definition
Dwelling	132	Living area	A place where people live
Fossil	133	To harden or make like stone	The remains, trace, or impression of an animal or plant that lived long ago

ACTIVITY **9.11** LOS MANDATOS REGULARES

Key	Tú		Ud.		Uds.	
afirmativo hablar comer escribir	**-ar** **-er, ir**	habla- come escribe	**-ar** **-er, ir**	hable coma escriba	**-ar** **-er, ir**	hablen coman escriban
irregulares	decir-di hacer-haz ir-ve poner-pon	salir-sal ser-se´ tener-ten venir-ven	dar-de´ estar-este´ ir-vaya saber-sepa	ser-sea	dar-den estar-este´n ir-vayan saber-sepan	ser-sean
escribir **negativo** hablar comer	**-ar** **-er, ir**	no hables no comas no escribas	**-ar** **-er, ir**	no hable no coma no escriba	**-ar** **-er, ir**	no hablen no coman no escriban
irregulares	**dar-** **ir-** **estar-** **ser-**	no des no vayas no este´s no seas	dar- estar- ir- saber- ser-	no de´ no este´ no vaya no sepa no sea	dar- estar- ir- saber- ser-	no den no este´n no vayan no sepan no sean

Developed by Heather Hemstreet.

Using the Dictionary

Associations made for dictionary use are often those of being assigned a list of words that must be located in the dictionary for the purpose of writing definitions and relevant sentences. Although this exercise may provide some exposure and focus on selected words, it is not particularly useful for building and encouraging vocabulary development. However, dictionaries are valuable tools and sources of much more than definitions when students know how and when to use them as resources.

In everyday occurrences when someone asks for a word meaning, he or she is not typically expecting an answer that sounds like a dictionary definition, and may not appreciate being told to "look it up in the dictionary." A more common response is a description, example, or even an analogous connection offered in explanation. Although formal definitions are not often used in conversation or many forms of writing, they can help people learn the meanings of words. Explaining and providing instruction for making the most of a pronunciation key, guide words, word origins, and parts of speech give students yet another means for becoming independent learners.

PIQUING STUDENTS' INTEREST

Blachowicz and Fisher (2006) describe Piquing Students' Interest, a strategy developed by Smith (1983) for raising student awareness of the many pieces of information a dictionary entry may give about a word. In small groups students are given copies of a dictionary page and are challenged to list as many different pieces of information as they can find that the dictionary entry gives for a word specified by the teacher. The teacher may first share how many he or she found as a target or incentive. After 10 minutes students share their findings and compare them with the teacher's. This can provide an opening for discussion and exploration of elements with which students are less familiar.

THE DICTIONARY GAME

Koeze (1990) developed an activity, also recommended in Blachowicz and Fisher's (2006) vocabulary text, that challenges students to predict words that might be found in the definition of a selected term. One person in the group selects a term, such as *amphibian*; and starting with the person to the left each student in a small group of three to five gives a word that has a good possibility of being in the dictionary definition. Duplications, articles, and propositions are not allowed. When play returns to the person who selected the term, he or she gives a word and then looks up the term (*amphibian*) in the dictionary to verify predictions. Points are awarded for correct predictions, and play continues with the person to the left. This activity offers an interesting way to review and affirm understandings during or after completion of a unit of study.

Thesauruses, foreign language dictionaries, spelling dictionaries, and synonym/antonym dictionaries have been around for some time. A wide variety of subject and specialized dictionaries and reference sources can be found on the Internet. These can be a great source of interest and enjoyment and may include animation and sound dimensions not available in other formats.

TEACHING VOCABULARY AS A REFLECTION ACTIVITY

Even though considerable research shows the benefits of teaching vocabulary before reading (Carney, Anderson, Blackburn, & Blessing, 1984; Medo & Ryder, 1993), an intriguing finding consistently emerging from reading research is that it can be as beneficial—or more so—to teach vocabulary after reading (Mealey & Konopak, 1990; Memory, 1990). For years the conventional wisdom has been that vocabulary is best taught before reading. In fact, however, the more students are asked to discuss, brainstorm, and think about what they have learned, the more they comprehend and retain the material. Thus the reflection phase of vocabulary development holds much promise in helping students thoroughly grasp the meaning of difficult terms in their reading. In this section we offer a number of strategies for reflection. We feel that these are best carried out by students working in small groups.

Interactive Cloze Procedure

Meeks and Morgan (1978) describe a strategy called the *interactive cloze procedure,* which was designed to encourage students to pay close attention to words in print and to actively seek the meaning of passages by studying vocabulary terms. They offer the following paradigm for using the interactive cloze:

1. Select a passage of 100 to 150 words from a textbook. It should be a passage that students have had difficulty comprehending or one that the instructor feels is important for them to comprehend fully.

2. Make appropriate deletions of nouns, verbs, adjectives, or adverbs. The teacher can vary the form and number of deletions depending on the purpose of the exercise.

3. Have students complete the cloze passage individually, filling in as many blanks as possible. Set a time limit based on the difficulty of the passage.

4. Divide students into small groups of three to four. Instruct them to compare answers and come to a joint decision about the best response for each blank.

5. Reassemble the class as a whole. Read the selection intact from the text. Give students opportunities to express opinions on the suitability of the author's choice of terms compared to their choices.

6. Strengthen short-term recall by testing using the cloze passage.

Meeks and Morgan describe using the technique to teach imagery by omitting words that produce vivid images. Activity 9.12 is such a cloze, based on a passage from H. G. Wells's *The Red Room* (1896).

Semantic Feature Analysis

Semantic feature analysis (Pittleman, Heimlich, Berglund, & French, 1991) is a technique for helping a student understand deeper meanings and nuances of language. To accomplish the analysis, first the teacher lists terms vertically on the chalkboard and asks students to help choose the features that will be written across the top of the chalkboard. (Teachers can also choose the features beforehand.) Students then complete the matrix by marking a plus sign (+) for features that apply to each word. In certain situations, students can be asked to make finer discriminations: whether a vocabulary term always (A), sometimes (S), or never (N) happens with a feature. We recommend that students do this analysis after reading the lesson, having used a technique such as the guided reading procedure or the directed reading–thinking activity

I saw the candle in the right sconce of one of the mirrors _____ and go right out, and almost immediately its companion followed it. There was no mistake about it. The flame vanished, as if the wicks had been suddenly _____ between a _____ and a thumb, leaving the wick neither _____ nor smoking, but _____. While I stood _____, the candle at the _____ of the bed went out, and the _____ seemed to take another step towards me.

Vocabulary words:
finger
gaping
wink
black
shadows
foot
glowing
nipped

Visit a page from a reading WebQuest that spotlights semantic feature analysis. Go to the Web links option of the Chapter 9 resources on this book's companion Web site.

Discover the *Puzzlemaker* Web site using the Web links option of the Chapter 9 resources at the *Reading to Learn in the Content Areas* Web site.

(see Chapter 4). Activity 9.13 shows a semantic feature analysis used in a science class about energy.

We feel that semantic feature analysis is an excellent activity for teaching vocabulary—perhaps the best activity there is. It is powerful because students make fine gradations of meaning concerning vocabulary terms, stating whether a term is affiliated always, sometimes, or never with a given concept or feature. With some low achievers teachers will need to fill out both the vocabulary terms and features beforehand. We recommend that after considerable practice in doing the technique this way, students be allowed in groups to (1) brainstorm words in the reading that they find difficult and (2) find the major concepts that they are learning in the chapter—that is, the features. Eventually, then, students can both determine and fill out the matrix themselves. One caution is in order, however. This technique was originally suggested as both a prereading activity and a postreading activity, but in our informal research we have found that students do better with semantic features after they have completed a reading and have established a conceptual base of knowledge about the passage.

Word Puzzles

Almost all students enjoy word puzzles, and computer programs now make them easier to construct. The teacher enters vocabulary terms and definitions, and the computer program constructs the puzzle. If a computer is unavailable, teachers can construct their own puzzles by graphically displaying terms across and down and drawing boxes around the words. The boxes are numbered both across and down, and definitions are placed beside the grid. Activity 9.14 is a word puzzle in geography made for second grade students.

Post-Graphic Organizers

Earlier in this chapter we discussed how students could help construct their own graphic organizers before reading to learn new vocabulary terms and to attempt to construct a hierarchical pattern of organization. To enhance concept development, students can

Topic: __Energy__   (Chapter 11)

Directions: Mark those features that apply to each vocabulary term.

A = the vocabulary term always applies to the feature
S = the vocabulary term sometimes applies to the feature
N = the vocabulary term never applies to the feature

Features

Vocabulary Terms	Renewable resource	Nonrenewable resource	Fossil fuels—direct use	Nuclear material	Naturally occurs	Manmade materials	Conservable	Pro-environment	Pollutant		
Uranium^{235}											
Hydrogen											
Biomass											
Geothermal energy											
Hydroelectricity											
Wind energy											
Passive solar heating											
Active solar heating											
Deuterium + Tritium											
Oil											
Coal											
Natural gas											

Developed by Wendy Barcroft.

Visit some of the many graphic organizer sites online. Several links are available for you at the *Reading to Learn in the Content Areas* Web site Chapter 9 resources.

return to these organizers after reading. Chapter 5 described post-graphic organizers for use in the reflection phase of learning. Here we present a variation specifically for vocabulary. Students can construct a post-graphic organizer directly after the reading. Activity 9.15 shows an example of an elementary mathematics post-graphic organizer used following a basic unit about measurement.

Categorization

One of the best ways for students to learn relationships of concepts after a reading is through a categorization activity. **Categorization** is the act of assigning something to a class, a group, or a division. Categorization can be accomplished through a word

NAME _____

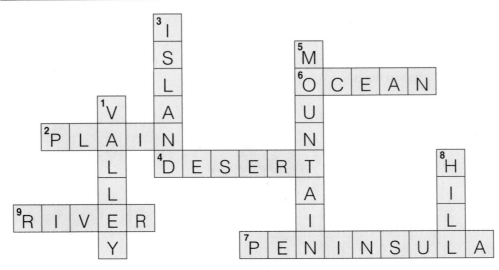

DOWN

   1. Low land between hills or mountains.

   3. Land that has water all around it.

   5. The highest kind of land.

   8. Land that rises above the land around it.

ACROSS

   2. Flat land.

   4. A dry place with little rain.

   6. A very large body of salt water.

   7. Land that has water on three sides.

   9. A long body of water that flows across the land.

Developed by Laurie Smith.

Maggie's Teachers' Lounge online provides suggestions for word sorts focusing on science topics. These sorts are based on phonetic elements and principles. Look for the Maggie's Teachers' Lounge link at the *Reading to Learn in the Content Areas* Web site Chapter 9 resources.

relationship activity that begins with the teacher suggesting a topic and asking students to supply words that describe the topic. The teacher may supplement the words given by the students or skim the text to find more words. If students' abilities or backgrounds are limited, the teacher can provide a list. Activity 9.16 is a list of body systems that was developed by a science teacher.

Students organize the list of words into smaller lists of items that have something in common, as shown in Activity 9.16. It is best during this phase for students to work in small groups to categorize and label the words. The groups explain their categories and labels to the entire class; then the whole class tries to reach a consensus on what the correct labels are and where the particular words belong. During this final phase, the teacher needs to act as a guide to make certain that discussion and labeling are being channeled in the proper direction. It is also essential that students be allowed to provide a rationale for their decisions.

The focus on explanation and discussion in this activity makes it an excellent strategy for teaching difficult vocabulary, concept development, and critical thinking,

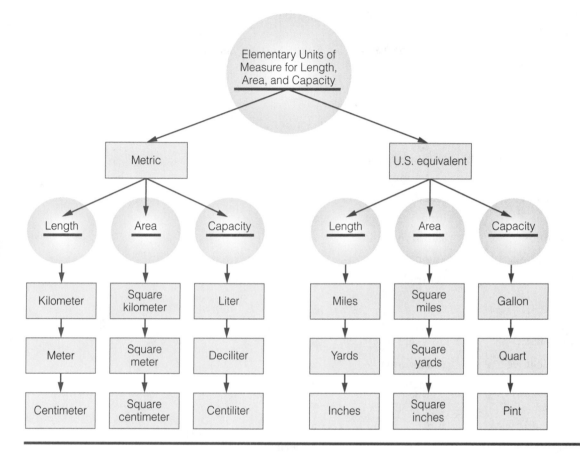

especially because much learning depends on students' ability to create meaningful categories of information. Practiced in a relaxed and purposeful atmosphere, this activity can be an excellent tool for helping students develop concepts, improve comprehension, and retain information. Gillett and Temple (1983) call this type of categorization activity a word sort. In a **closed word sort**, students are given the categories in advance. This teaches classification and deductive reasoning. In an **open word sort**, students have to group words as concepts and title their relationships. This teaches inference, or reading between the lines, which is an important concept for students to learn at any age.

DR–TA Vocabulary Search

When doing a directed reading–thinking activity in a content area classroom, the teacher can ask students to jot down difficult vocabulary terms. The student lists are

Below are three categories that describe functioning systems in the human body—the digestive, respiratory, and circulatory systems.

DIGESTIVE   RESPIRATORY   CIRCULATORY

Place each of the following vocabulary terms in the correct category:

aorta	gastric juice	trachea
esophagus	diaphragm	flatus
ulcer	lung	artery
atrium	salivary gland	asthma
pneumonia	angina pectoris	hypertension
bronchi	ventricle	peristaltic waves

Answers:

DIGESTIVE	RESPIRATORY	CIRCULATORY
ulcer	asthma	aorta
gastric juice	pneumonia	atrium
salivary glands	bronchi	angina pectoris
flatus	diaphragm	ventricle
peristaltic waves	lung	artery
esophagus	trachea	hypertension

Developed by Kim Blowe.

given to the teacher without student names, and these terms become the words to be studied after the DR–TA or at the beginning of the next class period.

The teacher first teaches word recognition by using a "word families" phonics approach to sound out words. If a word is *expressive,* for example, the teacher asks for other words in the same word family:

express

expression

press

pressure

Students work through the word family to sound out the word, thereby achieving word recognition.

Next comes a skimming and scanning exercise. The teacher begins by asking "Who can find *expressive* first in the story? Give me the page, column, and paragraph number, and then read the paragraph the word is in." After the word search, the paragraph is read, and with the aid of the teacher students try to figure out the meaning of the word in the context of the story or chapter. Here the teacher can ask students to use the context clue discovery strategy explained earlier in this chapter. This word search approach teaches word recognition, speed reading, and comprehension through the use of context clues. Keep in mind that the words to be studied are the ones with which students are actually having difficulty, not the ones a manual says are going to give them difficulty.

A Vocabulary Study System

Dana and Rodriguez (1992) have proposed a vocabulary study system using the acronym **TOAST**. They found this system more effective for learning vocabulary than other selected study methods. The steps in this vocabulary study technique are as follows:

Visit the Webster site for Building a Better Vocabulary. It offers tips, games, and clear explanations for building a strong vocabulary base. You can find a link for it at the *Reading to Learn in the Content Areas* Web site Chapter 9 resources.

T: Test. Students self-test to determine which vocabulary terms they cannot spell, define, or use in sentences.

O: Organize. Students organize these words into semantically related groups; arrange words into categories by structure or function, such as words that sound alike or are the same part of speech; and categorize words as somewhat familiar or completely unfamiliar.

A: Anchor. Students "anchor" the words in memory by using a keyword method (assigning a picture and a caption to a vocabulary term), tape-recording definitions, creating mnemonic devices, or mixing the words on cards and ordering them from difficult to easy.

S: Say. Students review the words by calling out the spellings, definitions, and uses in sentences to another student. The first review session begins 5 to 10 minutes after initial study and is followed at intervals by several more.

T: Test. Immediately after each review, students self-administer a posttest in which they spell, define, and use in context all the vocabulary terms with which they originally had difficulty. The response mode may be oral, written, or silent thought.

We recommend this vocabulary study system from early elementary grades through high school as a good method for getting students actively involved in the study of words. Keep in mind that TOAST encompasses all aspects of PAR.

Vocabulary Self-Collection Strategy

Another effective strategy for use after reading is the vocabulary self-collection strategy (VSS) (Haggard, 1986). VSS is a cooperative vocabulary activity that allows both teachers and students to share words that they wish to learn and remember. The strategy begins after students read an assignment. Each member of the class, including the teacher, is asked to bring a word that is perceived as important for the class to learn. Words usually come from the content area textbook but also may come from what students have heard within or outside the classroom. Students share their words in class, defining and elaborating on the presented words as the teacher writes them on the chalkboard. Then as a whole class, students decide which words are most important and should be learned by the class. The students record the chosen words in vocabulary notebooks. Class discussions ensue in which students use the words in purposeful sentences.

VSS can also be used as a cooperative assignment for groups. Each group member is expected to bring a word, and the groups decide what the words mean and which words are important enough for the entire class to learn. After working at length with their words, groups present their chosen words to the class. Words can be used for review and later study. A nice feature of VSS is that the vocabulary terms generated by this activity (with the exception of the one or two words suggested by the teacher) emanate from the students and are words in which they have shown interest.

Chase and Dufflemeyer (1990) have designed an adaptation of VSS for English classes that they call *vocab-lit strategy*. To begin this strategy, the teacher introduces a new vocabulary term; in a journal, the students write the term, the sentence where it is found, and a note about whether the student is acquainted with the word. Then students can work as a group to define the word and write sentences telling how the word is used in a story. As the story progresses and students get familiar with the technique, they can offer words and define and use them in this manner.

Language Enrichment through Reflection

Students find many of the activities described in this chapter so enjoyable that their interest in words is heightened. In this section, emphasizing word play, we offer additional techniques that will help students experience the pleasure of working with words. Specifically, we present seven techniques: imaging through keywords, word analogies, magic squares, vocabulary illustrations, vocabulary bingo, word bubbles, odd word out, and word inquiry.

USE OF KEYWORDS AND IMAGING

Probably no type of mnemonic device has been researched more thoroughly than the **keyword strategy** as an aid in learning new vocabulary terms. Much research over the past several decades has demonstrated the usefulness of this activity (Levin, Levin, Glassman, & Nordwall, 1992; McGivern & Levin, 1983; Zhang & Schumm, 2000). Atkinson (1975) describes the keyword method as a two-stage strategy. First the learner imagines a concrete and easily remembered word that sounds similar to the word to be learned. Next an image is remembered that cues the learner to the keyword and then, of course, to the word to be learned. For an example, say one wanted to

Visit Amanda's Mnemonics Page for a rich listing of devices for use among a variety of subjects and topics. You can find it using the *Reading to Learn in the Content Areas* Web site Chapter 9 resources.

remember the term *tryptophan* in a class about nutrition. The keyword would be *fan*. The image that would be conjured up would be of an attic. Someone trips over a *fan* and falls in the attic: He tripped the *fan* in the attic (hence *tryptophan*). It should be noted that although keywords have been shown to be effective, they do not work for all students and may not work with certain words. Also, some studies have found keyword gains in vocabulary growth to be temporary—sometimes the learned words stay with students as little as a week before fading. As with all mnemonic strategies, it is best to get students to make their own images rather than having keyword images dictated by the teacher. We included this strategy here because it has been shown to be effective in teaching vocabulary terms. As the reader will remember, we had a much more thorough discussion of mnemonics in Chapter 8.

WORD ANALOGIES

Word analogies are excellent for teaching higher-level thinking. To do word analogies, students must be able to perceive relationships between what amounts to two sides of an equation. This may be critical thinking at its best, in that the student is often forced to attempt various combinations of possible answers in solving the problem. At first students may have difficulty with this concept; therefore, the teacher should practice with students and explain the equation used in analogies:

_____ is to _____ as _____ is to

_____ .

or

_____ : _____ :: _____ : _____ .

For elementary students, teachers first spell out "is to . . . as" rather than using symbols. In addition, students say that analogies are easiest when the blank is in the fourth position, as in terms 1 and 2 in Activity 9.17, an early elementary activity in language arts. More difficult analogies can be constructed by varying the position of the blank, as in items 3 through 6. Analogies can also present a sophisticated challenge for older students, as illustrated in Activity 9.18, a high school Spanish activity.

MAGIC SQUARES

Any vocabulary activity can come alive through the use of magic squares, a technique that can be used at all levels—elementary, junior high, and high school. **Magic squares** are special arrangements of numbers that when added across, down, or diagonally always equal the same sum. Teachers can construct these vocabulary exercises by having students match a lettered column of words to a numbered column of definitions. Letters on each square of the grid match the lettered words. Students try to find the magic number by matching the correct word and definition and entering the number in the appropriate square or grid. Activity 9.19 gives explicit instructions for constructing magic squares. Activity 9.20 gives various magic square combinations, and Activity 9.21 is an example of a magic square in elementary mathematics.

1. Hot is to cold as day is to _____.
   up night long

2. Dog is to cat as small is to _____.
   little big short

3. Puppy is to _____ as young is to old.
   playful dog kitten

4. _____ is to white as on is to off.
   Red Black Door

5. Happy is to _____ as stop is to go.
   glad sad frown

6. Slow is to _____ as long is to short.
   silly happy fast

Developed by Colleen Kean.

Directions: Choose the answer that best completes the analogy.

Model: hot : cold :: up <u>down</u>   over   wet   down   under

1. él : ella :: ellos : _____   Juan   son   las   ellas

2. mira : televisión :: gana : _____   poco   dinero   mucho   ganar

3. viajar : nadar :: viajo : _____   viajan   nadan   nado   México

4. Juan : él :: Pablo y Sara : _____   ellos   los   ellas   las

5. mal : bien :: un poco : _____   ahora   mucho   dinero   siempre

6. invierno: _____ :: primavera : llueve   frío   viento   nieva   verano

7. toco : _____ :: escucho : discos   canto   ahora   tocar   guitarra

8. cantan : canto :: _____ : hablo   hablan   cantar   hablar   música

9. como : estás :: _____ : tardes   buenos   días   noches   buenas

10. _____ : Srta. :: señor : Sr.   señora   usted   hola   señorita

Developed by William Cathell.

Activity 9.22 represents a magic square history lesson on Greece, Rome, and the ancient world taught in an early elementary classroom.

VOCABULARY ILLUSTRATIONS

Joe Antinarella, an English teacher at Tidewater Community College in Chesapeake, Virginia, developed a creative way to enrich students' study of vocabulary that he

1. Start with a range of numbers, such as 1 to 9 or 4 to 12, to fill 9 squares in a 3 3 3 magic square.
2. Add the first and last numbers: $1 + 9 = 10$; $4 + 12 = 16$.
3. Determine the midpoint and put that number in the middle of the square: Between 1 and 9, put 5; between 4 and 12, put 8.

4. Add the first and last numbers: $1 + 5 + 9 = 15$.
5. Make combinations that add up to this magic square number and fill in the square.

8	1	6
3	5	7
4	9	2

As a shortcut to step 5, take the first number in your sequence, such as number 1; counting from that number, follow the directions below. In the diagram below, 1 is used as the first number.

1. Put the first number in the center of the top row.
2. Put the second number diagonally to the right; then place it in the corresponding position in the magic square.
3. Put the third number diagonally to the right; then place it in the corresponding position. Because you can't put the fourth number on the diagonal, you drop it below the third number.
4. Place the fifth number and then the sixth number on the diagonal.

5. You can't put the seventh number on the diagonal, so drop the seventh number down below the sixth.
6. Put the eighth number diagonally to the right, and move to the corresponding position.
7. Put the ninth number diagonally to the right; then move it to the corresponding position below.

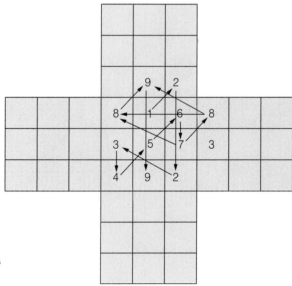

Variations on combinations:

672	294	438	618	492	834	276
159	753	951	753	357	159	951
834	618	276	294	816	672	438

9	2	7
4	6	8
5	10	3

18

16	2	3	13
5	11	10	8
9	7	6	12
4	14	15	1

34

19	2	15	23	6
25	8	16	4	12
1	14	22	10	18
7	20	3	11	24
13	21	9	17	5

65

ACTIVITY **9.21** MAGIC SQUARES: TWO-DIGIT SUBTRACTION

NAME _____ DATE _____

Directions: Put the number of the answer that best completes the statement listed in ABC order. Then place the number in the matching block. Check your answers to see if the sums of all rows, both across and down, add up to the magic number.

A. 56 minus 13 is
B. 72 minus 15 is
C. 40 subtract 10 is
D. 25
E. $68 - 24 =$
F. 75 apples less 45 apples is
G. 61
H. 80 apples less 22 apples is
I. $99 - 66 =$

1. 57
2. $78 - 17 =$
3. 30 apples
4. 33
5. 44
6. 43
7. $100 - 75 =$
8. 30
9. 58 apples
10. 32 apples

A. __6__	B. __1__	C. __8__	15
D. __7__	E. __5__	F. __3__	15
G. __2__	H. __9__	I. __4__	15
15	15	15	

The magic number is __15__ .

Developed by Laurie Smith.

NAME _____ DATE _____

Directions: Read each of the sentences below the magic square. Match the sentence to the correct word on the square. Put the number of the sentence in that box. If your answers are correct, the sum of the numbers when added across or down will be the same for each row.

Parthenon	Olympics	Slaves	
_____	_____	_____	_____
Athens	Columns	Arches	
_____	_____	_____	_____
Republic	Aqueduct	Rome	
_____	_____	_____	_____
_____	_____	_____	

1. The sporting event the Greeks invented to help train warriors.
2. This city ruled the largest empire in the world.
3. This city was the largest direct democracy in the world.
4. The type of government where citizens elect people to represent them.
5. The Greeks invented these to build temples and other important buildings.
6. These people could win their freedom by fighting in the Colosseum.
7. The Romans invented these to provide strong support for buildings.
8. The name of the temple built to honor the goddess Athena.
9. This carried water from the mountains to the city.

Developed by Ed Toscano.

calls **vocabulary illustrations**. He has students first define a word on a piece of drawing paper, then find a picture or make an original drawing that illustrates the concept. Below the picture, students use the term in a sentence that clarifies or goes along with what is happening in the picture or drawing. Activity 9.23 is a vocabulary illustration completed by a student in an elementary language arts classroom. Activity 9.24 shows an example created by a student in a seventh grade English class. Finally, Activity 9.25 shows a vocabulary illustration of a first grade student in a science lesson.

Goalie
A goalkeeper

by Michael

If I played socer I would be a goalie.

Developed by Barbara Wood.

Opulence

Definition - excessive wealth, grandeur

These four pictures are a good example of opulence because these things are things people with excessive wealth could afford to have.

Developed by Barbara Wood.

The sun has light and is warm.

The sun has light and is warm.

Developed by Barbara Wood.

VOCABULARY BINGO

Bingo is one of the most popular of all games. Playing vocabulary bingo lets teachers work with words in a relaxed atmosphere. The steps in playing vocabulary bingo are as follows:

1. Students make a "bingo" card from a list of vocabulary items. (The game works best with at least 20 words.) Students should be encouraged to select words at random to fill each square.

2. The teacher (or student reader) reads definitions of the words aloud, and the students cover the word that they believe matches the definition. (It's handy to have the definitions on 3-by-5-inch cards and to shuffle the cards between games.) The winner is the first person to cover a vertical, horizontal, or diagonal row.

3. Check the winner by rereading the definitions used. This step not only keeps everyone honest but serves as reinforcement and provides an opportunity for students to ask questions.

A sample bingo game in mathematics is shown in Activity 9.26.

Clues (also write on index cards):

Square—a shape with four equal sides and four right angles

Rectangle—a shape with four sides, two of them longer than the other two, and four right angles

Triangle—a shape with three sides

Circle—a round shape with no angles

Pentagon—a shape with five sides and five angles

Octagon—a shape with eight sides and eight angles

Trapezoid—a shape with four sides and four angles, which are not right angles

Cube—a solid with six equal square sides

Cylinder—a solid shaped like a can

Sphere—a solid shaped like a ball

Rectangular prism—a solid shaped like a box

Pyramid—a solid with sides shaped like triangles

Directions:

Each student should prepare a bingo card with 25 spaces. Write each term twice to fill up 24 boxes. The extra box can be a "free" box in the middle. The teacher shuffles the index cards and reads the *clues only*. The students decide which term matches the clue and cover one space with a chip. If all the clues are read without reaching a "Bingo," the cards can be reshuffled before continuing.

Square	Rectangle	Octagon	Trapezoid	Pentagon
Triangle	Circle	Cube	Cylinder	Sphere
Cylinder	Sphere	FREE	Rectangle	Rectangular Prism
Circle	Octagon	Square	Triangle	Trapezoid
Cube	Pentagon	Pyramid	Rectangular Prism	Pyramid

Developed by Mary Fagerland.

Bingo is an excellent game to play as a review. Most students enjoy the competition and participate enthusiastically. The constant repetition of the definitions can act as reinforcement for aural learners. Bingo can be played in any content area. For instance, in chemistry students can make bingo cards with symbols of elements, and the names of the elements are called out. For a higher level of difficulty, the caller can use other characteristics of elements such as atomic numbers or descriptions—for example, "a silvery liquid at room temperature" or "used to fill balloons." As a variation on Activity 9.26 in mathematics, the bingo cards can contain the pictures of the shapes, and the caller names the shapes.

WORD BUBBLES

The word bubble provides a good review of vocabulary. Students are given one clue to the word's meaning on a line below the bubble. Using this clue and the bank of words to be reviewed, they fill in the bubble and list other clues on the lines. Students are not limited to the word bank as they list new clues. Activity 9.27 is a sample word bubble for a third grade mathematics class.

ODD WORD OUT

Odd word out offers a way of considering similarities and differences among words and concepts as students try to determine which word does not belong and why. Students are given several groups of four words each. In each grouping one word must be selected as being different from the others. A rationale must be given for the word selected. Which word would you eliminate from each of the following sets?

A. Cottage, blue, American, cheddar.

B. Rectangle, triangle, quadrilateral, parallelogram.

C. Lincoln, Ford, Johnson, Bush.

D. Condensation, evaporation, dehydration, precipitation.

As you can see, there may be more than one right answer. In Set A *blue* may be chosen as the only word that is a color; or *American* may be chosen as the only one that begins with a capital letter. You will probably think of other selections for that set with yet other justifications. Students must carefully consider various aspects and attributes of each word to make their selections and state their rationale.

Another version of odd word out created by Ur and Wright (1992) begins with six words all purposefully selected from a broad category:

committee   bills   congress   senator   vote   gavel

Students select one word that doesn't belong and state why. From the remaining words students repeat the procedure. The steps are repeated until only two words are left. Students then decide on 10 ways the last two words are different.

MEASURE YOUR WORDS

Directions: Use the measurement word clue under each bubble to help you place the correct word from the word column in a bubble (in the example, "inch" is the word in the bubble). Then look at the word column again to add two more clue words on the blank lines extending below each bubble.

Words:

inch	pound
benchmark	temperature
foot	cup
yard	pint
mile	quart
perimeter	gallon
ounce	

Example:

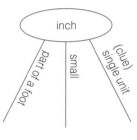

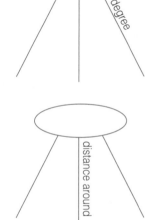

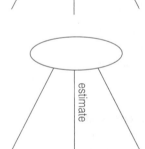

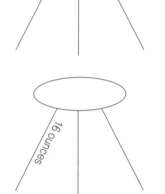

For extra credit, make your own word bubble game using words not found in this exercise.

Developed by Bessie Haskins.

WORD INQUIRY

Word inquiry uses the old 20 questions format. Ten to fifteen words are randomly placed on a page or transparency. Students work in groups of two (Partner A and Partner B). Each selects a word and writes it on a slip of paper so that the partner will not see it. Partner A may then ask questions of Partner B that can be answered with yes or no to determine the secret word. As questions are asked, a tally is kept. The one who figures out the secret word using the fewest questions is the winner. The value in this activity is the close examination of words as students consider what kinds of questions will narrow the field. Students can ask questions concerning prefixes, suffixes, word meanings, roots, compound words, parts of speech, and so on.

ONE-MINUTE SUMMARY

The main reason for vocabulary study is to develop concepts and help students see relationships inherent in their reading. Having a good understanding of most of the words in a text is necessary for optimal comprehension and fluency. Teachers need to take sufficient time to prepare for reading lessons by sometimes having students study difficult vocabulary terms before the reading. Preparation strategies help elevate word consciousness, provide personal connections, and build background to aid in understanding. Also, teachers need to assist students with long-term aids and strategies to help them grasp the meaning of unfamiliar words. These aids develop active reading habits as students negotiate meanings of unknown words encountered in the text. Often, however, it may be best to have students reflect on difficult vocabulary after reading, when they have established a conceptual base of knowledge with which to learn. By reconsidering and reflecting on selected vocabulary, students get opportunities for in-depth vocabulary knowledge development for later reference as independent learners. This chapter presented numerous vocabulary strategies that can be used at all phases of the PAR Framework. The central idea of this chapter is that students learn and grow intellectually when teachers spend time teaching vocabulary and vocabulary strategies that students may use independently to enrich their own understanding. Research was cited throughout the chapter to support the idea that increasing vocabulary knowledge is key to producing richer, deeper reading experiences for students.

PAR ONLINE

The Internet hosts numerous sites that students may reference for enriching and developing their vocabulary. However, as we all know, Web sites are moving targets; so frequent updating is necessary when suggesting or listing sites for use within the classroom. To provide current working links, we have located a variety of topics and sites for further reading, added resources, templates, and instructional development. Visit the *Reading to Learn in the Content Areas* Web site at http://academic.cengage.com/education/richardson for links to the Web sites mentioned in this chapter, tutorial quizzing, and other resources; select Chapter 9 resources.

END-OF-CHAPTER ACTIVITIES

Assisting Comprehension

See how well you remember the following strategies by placing them in categories (preparation, assistance, reflection) on this organizational chart. Be ready to explain your choices to a peer.

	Categories		
	Preparation	Assistance	Reflection
semantic map			
graphic organizers			
word bubbles			
odd word out			
structural analysis			
vocabulary self-collection			
strategy keyword			
context clue discovery			
word mapping			
modified cloze			
DISSECT			
word analogies			
word inquiry			
magic squares			
interactive cloze procedure			
semantic feature analysis			
word puzzles			
vocabulary connections			
vocabulary lists			
vocabulary illustrations			
capsule vocabulary			
post-graphic organizers			
word attack paradigms			
vocab-lit strategy			
word inventories			
DISSECT			
possible sentences			
TOAST			

	Categories		
	Preparation	Assistance	Reflection
categorization			
organizational (jot) charts			
DR–TA			
vocabulary search			
vocabulary bingo			
word sorts			
word inquiry			

Reflecting on Your Reading

1. The International Reading Association (2003) has developed a set of standards that identify the performance criteria relevant to classroom teachers. Standard 2 addresses three aspects of the use of instructional strategies and curriculum materials that a teacher should include. The teacher should

   • **2.1** Match instructional grouping options to specific instructional purposes that take into account developmental, cultural, and linguistic differences among students. They model and scaffold procedures so that students learn to work effectively. They provide an evidence-based rationale for their selections.

   • **2.2** Plan for the use of a wide range of instructional practices, approaches, and methods, including technology-based practices. Their selections are guided by an evidence-based rationale and accommodate the developmental, cultural, and linguistic differences of their students.

   • **2.3** Plan for the use of a wide range of curriculum materials. Their selections are guided by an evidence-based rationale and accommodate the developmental, cultural, and linguistic differences of their students.

   Considering the developmental, cultural, and linguistic differences of the students within your classroom, select a vocabulary strategy for each stage of PAR and write a reflection explaining how you plan to use this strategy to meet the needs of your students.

CHAPTER 10

*How do I know what I think
until I see what I say?*

E. M. FORSTER

Writing to Learn
in the Content Areas

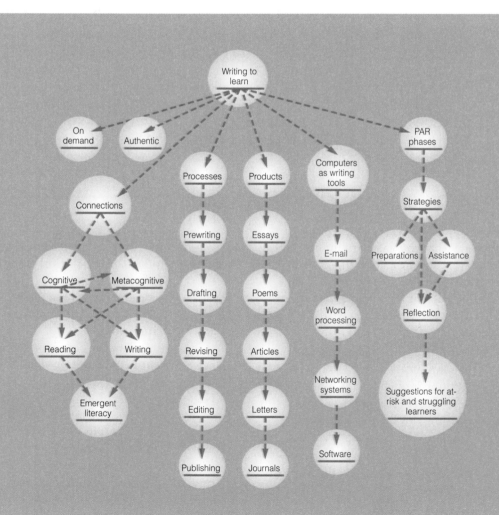

VOICES FROM THE CLASSROOM

Cooper Middle School was in the news again. In fact, student writing scores made front page headlines in the *Daily Gazette*. Large numbers of students were scoring below the state average. Mr. Lancaster, principal of Cooper Middle School, held a special faculty meeting to discuss concerns and a plan of action. He asked every teacher to find ways to include writing daily in their classrooms.

"It is just not possible, reasonable, or even necessary for writing to be a part of my math classes on a daily basis. What can I possibly do in math that makes sense? Besides that, I have too much to cover to waste time doing writing," commented Mr. Johnston.

"I know what you mean," said Mrs. Carson. "We do some writing in science, but certainly not daily. I just don't see that it is my responsibility when there are so many other things I have to teach. That should be the English teacher's job. I don't ask her to teach science in her English class, so why should I have to teach writing in mine?"

Use a discussion web (instructions following) to consider Mr. Lancaster's charge. Fold your paper into three parts or columns. In the center column put the question, "Should every teacher in every content area include writing in daily lessons?" In the right column place the word "No" at the top. In the left column place the word "Yes" at the top. In the right column list reasons you can think of for responding "No." In the left column list reasons you can think of for responding "Yes." Think of an equal number of reasons for each stance. After considering each side of the issue, write a conclusion or final response and your justification. Then reconsider this question after reading this chapter.

PREPARING TO READ

1. Anticipate what you will learn in this chapter by checking any of the following statements with which you agree. Be ready to explain your choices. After reading the chapter, return to decide whether you wish to reconsider any of your selections:

   _____ Writing is the most complex of the communicative arts.

   _____ Writing is often taught as a way of learning in the content areas.

   _____ Writing should not be taught to young children in kindergarten.

   _____ Elementary as well as college students may use metacognitive strategies to enhance their writing.

   _____ All writing should lead to a formal product, or publication of the writing.

   _____ Computers can provide an exciting way to help students improve their writing skills.

   _____ Writers may make major changes in their material during what is called the drafting stage.

2. Following is a list of terms used in this chapter. Some may be familiar to you in a general context, but in this chapter they may be used in unfamiliar ways. Consider what you know about the terms and decide how you might sort them into logical

groupings. Decide how the terms in each grouping are similar and make a label for each. Be ready to explain the rationale for your choices.

_____ on-demand writing
_____ authentic writing
_____ reading–writing connection
_____ metacognitive
_____ emergent literacy
_____ process writing
_____ write-alouds
_____ cubing
_____ brain-writing

_____ learning log
_____ double-entry journal
_____ annotating
_____ REAP
_____ biopoem
_____ geopoem
_____ first-person summary
_____ triangle truths
_____ RAFT
_____ guided writing procedure
_____ collaborative writing
_____ C3B4Me
_____ rubric

OBJECTIVES

As you read this chapter, focus your attention on the following purposes. You will

1. Learn about the connection between reading to learn and writing to learn.

2. Learn to distinguish between the process of writing and the products of writing.

3. See ways in which computers can aid students in learning to write.

4. Identify the stages of writing, from prewriting through revision and publishing strategies.

5. Learn strategies for preparing, assisting, and reflecting on writing.

6. See how writing can complement reading as a way to learn in the content areas.

7. Learn ways to grade students' writing.

THE IMPORTANCE OF WRITING

Writing involves complex higher levels of thinking, making it a potentially powerful learning tool.

Writing may be the most complex communication process within the communicative arts because of the ways it can be used to challenge and enhance thinking skills. "Like close reading, writing is thinking—perhaps in its most powerful and intense form" (Schmoker, 2007, p. 419). Writing is active involvement that allows students to explore subject matter. One can progress from a blank sheet to a page filled with statements about content learned, revelations about thoughts, and discoveries about self.

When writing is viewed as a way of discovering rather than as merely an avenue for testing knowledge, learning is the result. Brain research (Davis, 1997; Kotulak, 1996, as cited in Houston, 2004) has provided evidence in the form of PET (positron emission tomography) scans that writing activates numerous areas of the brain with more intensity than other activities investigated. Writing challenges us to communicate, at the same time, with others and with ourselves. The advantage afforded by vocal timbre, facial expression, and gestures must be accounted for in written communication through careful word choice and organization (Houston, 2004).

Writing includes both process and product in various stages of development. So although writing is often assumed to be the responsibility of the elementary school teacher or the English teacher, it is related to learning in all areas of the curriculum as well as to learning as a life pursuit. "Along with reading comprehension, writing skill is a predictor of academic success and a basic requirement for participation in civic life and in the global economy" (Graham & Perin, 2007, p. 3). Budig (2006) found in his study involving survey data collected from human resource directors that being able to communicate effectively though writing is a highly valued skill necessary for employment and critical to promotion in fast-growing industries.

Though some distinguish between learning to write and writing to learn, the two are intertwined. Even though the writer has to develop an understanding of the skills, form, and function of writing, without a purpose or focus there is no meaning. Writing requires abstract thinking, synthesis, and the ability and skill to apply several discrete skills as the writer describes or makes a case for his or her understanding of the content or topic. Writing is more than the sum of the skills necessary for creating an interesting piece: Collecting and organizing thoughts to communicate ideas and feelings lead to understanding and learning. When putting pen to paper to create an expository or informational piece, the writer has to ask herself or himself several questions:

1. What do reliable sources have to say?
2. What evidence is there?
3. What do I think?
4. What do others think?
5. What points and questions can I pose to encourage my readers to think about my topic?

If the purpose is to create a narrative, the author must consider aspects of good storytelling:

1. Where will the story take place, and how will I help the reader see it as I do?
2. Who are the characters, and what parts do they play in the story?
3. How does the story begin?
4. What problems are to be resolved? Will they be resolved?
5. Is the story interesting? Does it make sense to me and to others?
6. Does the story have a message?

In either case there is much to be learned through writing.

Writing is a true complement to reading when it enables students to clarify and think critically about concepts they encounter in reading. Reading and writing are often taught separately even though research has found that writing can be used in every content area as an effective means of learning (Bangert-Drowns, Hurley, & Wilkinson, 2004; Brown, Phillips, & Stephens, 1992). When reading and writing are taught as detached entities, students may adopt a superficial view of writing—an essay exercise for the purpose of producing a particular form of writing without connection to learning or understanding information related to a subject or content. Vacca (2002) submits that it is rare for students to assume or even consider writing as a vehicle for exploring or interpreting concepts and ideas found in textbooks. Students have to be made aware through direct instruction, modeling, and practice that writing can be a tool for learning. By using overhead transparencies, white boards, or projected word processing documents, teachers can demonstrate the process and enlist students in active discussion of the criteria and expectations for writing products.

Unfortunately writing is not used often enough as a way of learning in the content areas. Teachers may be reluctant to teach writing for some of the same reasons they often feel reluctant to teach mathematics and science concepts. If content teachers see writing as primarily prescribed forms and structures to be taught rather than as a means to clarify, reinforce, and support concept learning, they may feel unqualified or that it is not their domain. A lack of confidence in their own writing abilities can contribute to frustration and uncertainty as they try to instruct their students. Graves (1994) has pointed out that not enough teachers receive in-service and pre-service training in the effective teaching of writing. Although more needs to be done, writing programs and in-service training have increased with the emphasis and attention placed on writing scores and standardized testing in recent years. The National Center for Educational Statistics (2004) reported an improvement in writing performance for 4th and 8th graders between 1998 and 2002 while no significant change was found among 12th graders.

Why do you think writing is rarely used for learning in the content areas?

On-Demand Writing

On-demand writing involves writing to a prompt like that expected in high-stakes testing situations.

Caution must be taken to avoid a reductionist approach to writing, which may occur when the only writing students do is **on-demand writing** for a given prompt in preparation for high-stakes testing. Because the consequences are great, teachers and administrators are often reluctant to go beyond narrow instructional practices targeting good test performance. However, Higgins, Miller, and Wegmann (2006) have dared to pose this question: "Can best practices and demands of mandated testing truly coexist?" (p. 310). They cite research by Manzo (2001), Fletcher (2001), and Tchudi and Tchudi (1999) providing evidence that broader-based writing instruction that includes student choice, creativity, genre variety, feedback, and aspects of process writing and writing workshop yield higher scores on standardized tests than do more narrowly structured curriculum practices. Through professional development and collaborative discussions, teachers, administrators, and university partners can examine state literacy assessments in the context of developmentally appropriate and sound writing instruction to support "writing instruction, not destruction" (Brindley & Schneider, 2002, p. 339). This means raising awareness levels of all partners and working together to find solutions that support generative writing practices and give students the tools for success.

Setting aside or ignoring on-demand writing is not the solution. Helping students understand its purpose and proactive ways of approaching it can prepare them to do well in testing and real-life situations where this type of writing is important. Key questions and modeling can scaffold the process and help the learner gain confidence and develop a well-written response:

1. What is the prompt asking me to do? (Describe, explain, defend, compare, create, or what?)
2. What do I know about the topic?

3. What do I need to say? (Points and details.)

4. In what order do I want to say it?

5. Have I stated my points clearly, logically, and with enough detail?

6. When I reread, are my sentences grammatically correct? Is my spelling accurate?

Authentic Writing

What forms and for what purposes do you use authentic writing in your classroom?

Current studies (Purcell-Gates, Degener, Jacobson, & Soler, 2002; Purcell-Gates, Duke, & Martineau, 2007) provide strong evidence for the potential impact of authentic reading and writing tasks on both adults' and elementary students' abilities to read and write in a variety of genres. Purcell-Gates and her colleagues found that students given "real" purposes for reading and writing beyond classroom assignments, and for "real" audiences beyond a teacher, made significant progress in both reading and writing. Authentic literacy, and more particularly authentic tasks, can be defined in a variety of ways. Duke, Purcell-Gates, Hall, and Tower (2006) used an authenticity rating scale for differentiating levels when considering tasks for reading, writing, or listening (see Figure 10.1). Traditional, nonauthentic writing tasks include completing worksheets, writing for a given prompt, book reports, reports about a topic, and the like. Some tasks that are considered authentic include creating and distributing brochures for a local museum or upcoming community event; writing letters to community members, organizations, or businesses related to topics of study; and writing a speech to be given to an outside club, group, or community meeting. The studies' findings do not suggest replacing explicit instruction with authentic tasks, but rather give evidence of value added by thoughtful and purposeful inclusion of meaningful experiences that cross over into daily life.

Using writing as a means for learning as well as a tool to be learned and perfected provides a dual purpose contributing to achievement in writing as well as content. Content gives students something to write about. Bintz and Shelton (2004) explained that the power of a writing strategy and the potential of the curriculum for assisting students' learning are directly related to the teacher's adeptness for bringing the two harmoniously together.

THE IMPORTANCE OF THE READING–WRITING CONNECTION

Students need to write about what they are going to read about—and after that reading use writing again as a culminating activity to clarify what was read. This write–read–write model is sometimes referred to as the **reading–writing connection.** As students embrace this model, they use writing as a tool for learning content. Content teachers can through direct instruction emphasize writing as a way to learn. In their meta-analysis of the effects of school-based writing on learning, Bangert-Drowns, Hurley, and Wilkinson (2004) explained, "Students are more effective learners when they possess a rich arsenal of learning strategies, awareness of their

FIGURE 10.1

Authenticity
Rating Sheet

Brief description of activity, including (a) text students are reading, writing, or listening to, and (b) purpose of student's reading, writing, or listening:

_____

_____

_____

_____

Authenticity of purpose

Rating: 3   2   1

  3 = This reading, writing, or listening-to-text purpose exists in the lives of people outside a classroom, or it is as authentic as the use of that genre for that purpose can be.

  2 = This reading, writing, or listening-to-text purpose exists in the lives of people outside a classroom, but it differs in that for reading the impetus is less personal and for writing the audience is less compelling.

  1 = This reading, writing, or listening-to-text purpose is identified by its absence of any purpose beyond school work. This takes different forms depending on the genre and process (reading or writing).

Authenticity of text

Rating: 3   2   1

  3 = This text type occurs naturally in the lives of people outside a classroom. You can find it in bookstores or order it for home delivery. This category also includes texts that are written primarily for instructional purposes but that closely mimic the naturally occurring texts–the only difference being the publisher's audience.

  2 = This text is written primarily for use in schools and, although it mimics to an extent the genre style, form, and purpose of those texts that do occur naturally outside school, it includes enough school "stuff" to be recognizable. This type would include texts that have comprehension questions, special vocabulary sections, and perhaps even "Checking What You Have Learned" sections. These texts are hybrid forms reflecting school and authentic genres in different combinations and emphases.

  1 = This text would not occur anywhere except in a school or other teaching and learning contexts. It is written to teach skills and is used only for learning and practicing skills. You may be able to purchase these texts in stores but they reflect a skills-learning purpose.

Total authenticity rating: _____

Duke, Purcell-Gates, Hall, & Tower, Authentic literacy activities for developing comprehension and writing. *The Reading Teacher, 60*(4), 344–345. Reprinted with permission of the International Reading Association.

strategies, knowledge of the contexts in which the strategies will be effective, and a willingness to apply their strategies" (p. 32).

Both cognitive and **metacognitive** strategies may help students learn as they engage in writing tasks. Weinstein and Mayer (1986) categorized cognitive strategies as rehearsal strategies, elaboration strategies, organization strategies, and comprehension-monitoring strategies. As students consider points read and discussed during the planning and drafting stages of writing, they engage in repetition and rehearsal. Organization and elaboration strategies come into play while students order, reorder, and describe points related to their own understandings and backgrounds. Self-monitoring and reflection as well as peer review offer opportunities for using comprehension-monitoring strategies. Finally, Bangert-Drowns and colleagues (2004) cite several studies supporting the power of metacognitive comprehension-monitoring strategies for improving learning among K–college populations. Metacognitive strategies give students a tool for determining their own use of strategies and for evaluating how well those strategies may work in each situation for future reference and use.

Writing may improve academic achievement when metacognitive prompts are used and the length of the writing treatment is increased. Reduced effects may occur when longer writing assignments are given or writing-to-learn-assignments are used among students in grades 6–8 (Bangert-Drowns, et al., 2004).

Besides implementation of metacognitive prompts, longer treatment length was found to boost academic achievement (Bangert-Drowns, et al., 2004). It seems that repetition may produce a cumulative effect over time so that students internalize the strategies and use them to learn content. Conversely, reduced effects in achievement were found when longer writing assignments were used. It was posited that longer assignments may present problems for several reasons. For students already struggling with writing, greater length requirements may be discouraging. Longer assignments may take away class time needed for other instruction and provide less time for content coverage. Reduced effects were also found when considering one population: students in grades 6–8. Researchers suggested that the low effects for this age group may be due in part to the typical shift in school organizational structure at this level, in which subject matter is often distinctly differentiated. Developmental issues were also cited as a possible source of academic achievement difficulties. When considering studies of writing achievement among school populations, we must also recognize that students in control groups are capable of participating in writing tasks about content to at least some degree. This makes it particularly difficult to tease out and assess the power of writing to learn among populations.

We know now that writing can be taught to children at a younger age than was previously thought. Research on writing indicates that very young children can create forms of writing that they can explain to adults (Teale & Sulzby, 1986). Such writing includes pictures and scribbles, which Vygotsky (1978b) describes as gestures that represent children's thoughts. Figure 10.2 shows kindergartners' writing about and pictures of a bicycle and a bus.

Children in the early grades are capable of writing reports about content subjects (Calkins, 1986). Although these reports may contain inventive spelling and pictures that one might not expect to find in an older student's report, they reflect learning through language. Teachers are now encouraged to recognize this early reading and writing as a part of **emergent literacy** and to foster children's use of all of the communicative arts as early as possible in content subjects. Figure 10.3 contains two writing samples from a first grader. Both demonstrate learning about science through writing. The teacher made comments about the content of the writing, not about the "invented" or "temporary" spellings.

The sophistication of thinking and the composition process young writers are capable of bringing to the experience of writing informational text should not be underestimated. Read (2005), in her first grade study of informational text writing, created a writing workshop environment. She modeled and scaffolded thinking aloud, taking notes, reading, taking more notes, reading notes, and collaborating with students to create shared writings. Students then made their own topic selections. She

FIGURE 10.2

Writing to Learn
in Kindergarten

DaRius

Ride off Towfind
I can Not help
I see WhaTFlike Tow do
Isee a bicycle

I like the bus   Dennis

FIGURE 10.3

Writing to Learn
in First Grade

Andrew Pettit

(continued) ➤

FIGURE 10.3

(continued)

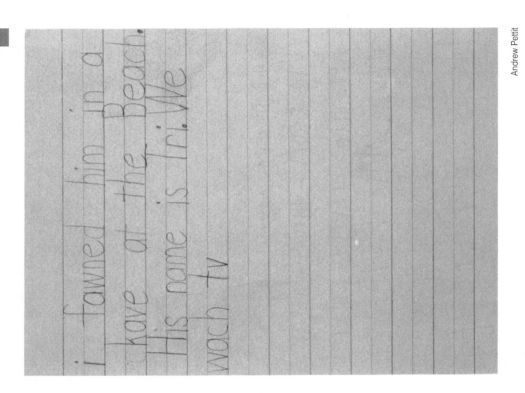

i fowned him in a
hove at the Beach
His name is Tri. We
woch tv

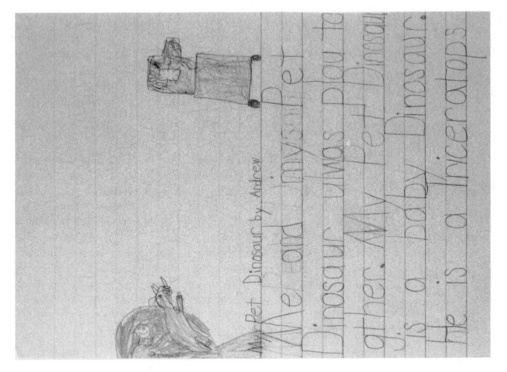

My Pet Dinosaur by Andrew
We ard my Pet
Dinosaur umas Dau to
gther. My Pet Dinosaur
is a baby Dinosaur.
He is a Inceratops

Andrew Pettit

paired them by topic for the purpose of creating a collaborative book. They were given considerable freedom to make choices and to work through the writing. Read discovered that contrary to her expectations, students did not spend most of their time grappling with sentence-level issues. Nor were their products like mini-encyclopedia articles. She found that these first graders, like older more experienced writers, could and did consider and negotiate the need for creating interest, using good form, and critically reflecting and making adjustments throughout the writing process. Even though the products were simple, they were nonetheless appropriate and indicated comprehension of both the content and the writing process.

WRITING AS A PRODUCT

Teachers often use the products of writing as a form of evaluation, such as evaluating a test essay or a research report. But teachers need to see products of writing not only as a versatile way of evaluating a student but also as a unique way to develop comprehension. For instance, many fiction writers confess that they did not know what a particular fictional character was going to do until they started writing. Their preparation gave them a direction but not exact knowledge of how the writing would turn out. Only by creating did they discover. The same held true for us as textbook writers. We learned more about our field of knowledge as we wrote this book. We discovered ways to express the information that we wanted to share with readers; before we drafted this text, we did not know all that we would write. In a similar way, readers learn as they read. Because both reading and writing can assist comprehension, it seems logical to use them in tandem when assisting readers. Unfortunately writing is not used often as an activity to help students understand content material (Knipper & Duggan, 2006; Pearce & Bader, 1984). Teachers like Miss K in *Ralph S. Mouse* by Beverly Cleary (1982) would turn anything into a writing project. When Miss K and her class discover that Ralph the mouse came to school with Ryan, she inspires the students to write about mice and later to write rejoinders to a newspaper article that contains misinformation about their projects. Many teachers, in contrast, seem to use writing activities that are mainly product oriented and graded. Products can take many forms, such as essays, poems, articles, journals, letters, and plays, to name a few.

Research shows, however, that writing doesn't always have to have an end product to be successful; that is, writing can be a powerful tool to assist comprehension (Von Glaserfeld, 1996). Writing requires the formation of an idea, or a cluster of ideas, generated from the writer's experiences, understanding, and imagination. It is a conscious shaping of the materials selected by the writer to be included in composition. In selecting what to put in and leave out, the student is using the elements of writing draftsmanship that he or she can manage.

A relationship exists between the process and the products of writing. Much process-oriented writing results in a formal product. The best products are generated when students are given opportunities for prewriting, writing, and revising. Not all writing leads to a formal product, but all writing can be a means of learning.

Computers as Writing Tools

The personal computer (PC) provides an exciting venue for students to improve their writing skills. A growing body of research indicates that computer use improves student learning in general and student writing in particular (Russell & Abrams, 2004).

A number of studies (Rekrut, 1999; Silva, Meagher, Valenzuela, & Crenshaw, 1996) recommend that students begin using the Internet by attempting electronic mail (e-mail) exchanges. Students can exchange e-mail with other students and even with authors and experts. Silva and colleagues found that students using such telecommunications progressed more quickly than students who were asked to use more traditional grammar practice and textbook readings. Wagner (1995) describes how vocational students used Internet relay chat (IRC) to talk with other students and learn about other cultures and lifestyles.

Word processing on the computer gives students an opportunity to improve their writing skills greatly. Students can write drafts quickly, revise them easily, and save anything they have written. Word processing programs can help students check for errors before making final copies. Studies (Bangert-Drowns, 1993; Cochran-Smith, 1991; Goldberg, Russell, & Cook, 2003) have shown that when computers are used for developing writing skills, students make more revisions during writing and before the final draft than those using traditional paper and pencil tools. Students using computers for writing produced longer products and demonstrated a tendency to more often share their writing with one another during the process—thus involving the social aspects of learning. Overall, Goldberg, Russell, and Cook's (2003) meta-analysis of research on the effects of computers on student writing revealed significant positive results for both quantity and quality of student writing when computers were used as tools for developing writing skills.

Using computers as tools for writing is not just for older students. Van Leeuwen and Gabriel's (2007) study of computer use for writing with first graders indicated that even young authors enjoy and benefit from this tool. With these children the quality of writing was comparable to paper-and-pencil products, but the products generally were shorter. More student-to-student interaction took place and was accepted as they asked one another for spelling and computer help. Fewer prewriting webs and plans were chosen for use, which may be attributed in part to the relative ease of making changes and editing using a computer. This seemed to be offset by frequent reading and rereading of composed text. This study lends support to the idea that different tools and means of producing writing provide different types of opportunities and challenges for developing and enhancing writing techniques and strategies.

Interestingly, despite positive effects found for using computers for developing writing skills among students, "across the nation, a higher percentage of teachers in urban locations and in lower-performing schools, as compared to suburban and high-performing schools, believe they have decreased instructional use of computers for writing because of the format of the state test" (Russell & Abrams, 2004, p. 1351).

Networking systems and databases available to students can assist and even motivate them to perform the research necessary for their writing. As Rekrut (1999) observed, "The depth and breadth of information available is virtually incomprehensible;

[margin note] Software that provides structure and tools for creating graphic organizers is useful and motivational for students for developing webs, graphs, charts, and tables before, during, and after writing.

[margin note] In what ways might the Russell and Abrams findings be cause for concern?

See Chapter 7 for more details and information about using technology for teaching reading and writing across the curriculum.

the World Wide Web is indeed aptly named" (p. 546). When students assess information and write about their findings, they are using real-world practices that increase overall competence in writing. Teachers need to encourage students both at home and at school to use this tool when it is available. Many course-authoring programs enable teachers to produce Web sites where their students can participate in online threaded discussions. When students write about a topic to one another online, and then read, consider, and reply within such a threaded discussion, they improve their writing skills in an electronic format.

WRITING AS A PROCESS

Graves (1983) and Calkins (1994) have been influential in getting teachers to view writing as a process that has as its components the generation of ideas, drafting, conferencing, and revision. Writers must think about a topic in a prewriting phase and develop a first draft from their initial thoughts. In the drafting phase, students think, change direction, organize, and reorganize their purposes. During this phase, students do not focus on such things as grammar and spelling or any other aspects of mechanics.

Also gone are the days when teachers maintained that one draft was all students needed to produce. Students now are often asked to revise their initial work. Such efforts can include major reorganization of the material, additions and deletions, and editorial changes. At this phase writers need to pay attention to the format of their work. The emphasis shifts to producing a product to be shared in the postwriting phase of the lesson.

Write-alouds make the stages of writing visible. How might you use them in your classroom?

The previous paragraphs describe **process writing**, whereby the student goes through many distinct phases in writing—from initial brainstorming of ideas to researching the topic and organizing information and ideas into a coherent piece of writing. A student working through this process may produce several drafts to clarify her or his message. An important part of this process is to have peers and others read drafts to help improve the writing. Activity 10.1 was developed by a primary science teacher to direct her students through the various phases of writing. **Write-alouds** (Cooper and Kiger, 2003) can make visible the thinking that forms each stage of writing, just as read-alouds help students understand the thinking that good readers use when reading. Using write-alouds, teachers can demonstrate thinking through the writing process on chart paper or overhead transparencies.

Though **rubrics** are typically used as instruments for assessment following an assignment, they can provide focus, direction, and clarification for helping students understand what is important and what must be included for a successful product (Knipper & Duggan, 2006). If students are invited to participate in developing rubrics, this gives them opportunities to thoughtfully consider and negotiate elements important to the writing. Rubrics describe specific criteria for several levels of achievement such as high, medium, and low or exemplary, satisfactory, and developing (look ahead to Activity 10.17). These will be discussed in greater detail later in the chapter. Checklists too can be useful before, during, and following the writing for self-assessment, peer reviewers, and teachers (look ahead to Activity 10.18). Checklists highlight "must-have" components for an assignment and can provide

I. Prewriting

The teacher will show the book *Desert Voices*, written by Byrd Baylor and Peter Parnall, to the class, and she will mention that these authors have worked together on three Caldecott Honor Books. (It may be necessary to refresh their minds about the annual Caldecott and Newbery Awards.)

"Byrd Baylor, who writes the words of the book, lives in the Southwest. I don't know which *particular* state in the southwestern portion of the United States. The title of this book has the word *desert* in it, and she has written another book called *The Desert Is Theirs*. If she lives in the Southwest and likes to write about deserts, could you guess a state where she *might* live?" (The students may remember that Arizona has desert land.)

"Peter Parnall illustrates the book. He lives on a farm in Maine with his wife and two children."

"If the title of the book is *Desert Voices*, who might be speaking? Who are the voices in the desert?" (Wait for responses.) "Byrd Baylor has written the words for 10 desert creatures as they tell us what it is like for the desert to be their home. I will read you what the jackrabbit and the rattlesnake have to say." (Teacher reads aloud.)

A. FACTSTORMING

The teacher will divide the class into small groups of four or five students. She lists on the chalkboard the names of the other creatures who "speak" in *Desert Voices*: pack rat, spadefoot toad, cactus wren, desert tortoise, buzzard, lizard, coyote. (The tenth voice is called "Desert Person.")

B. THE ASSIGNMENT

"Each group must select one of these creatures or any other desert animal or plant that has been mentioned in our unit. Each group member should jot down on a piece of paper any ideas he or she has about this creature's feelings relating to living in the desert. You may want to think about the appearance of this creature or thing. Does it have any body parts or habitat specifically suited to the desert's environment? After you jot down your ideas, place your paper in the center of the table and choose another member's paper. Add some of your ideas to his or her paper. After you have written something on every other group member's page, your group as a whole should compile the *best* list of ideas. Then we will begin to write our individual drafts."

II. Writing

III. Rewriting

Students may work in pairs to edit and proofread each other's work. The child's partner would be from another "creature's" group.

IV. Postwriting

Oral presentations

Room displays

Compilation of compositions dealing with the same "voice" into book form

Note: Naturally this project would continue for several days. Even the group factstorming might require more than one day, especially if some reference work were necessary.

Developed by Kathryn Davis.

possible point values for each component. By making them available as an assignment is introduced, students can see expectations from the beginning to help them monitor their own progress. Knipper and Duggan emphasize that using rubrics and checklists throughout the writing process must be encouraged and developed on a consistent basis.

Writing, just like reading, has phases that overlap, are recursive, and relate to the PAR Framework. The prewriting phase matches what happens before reading, which corresponds to what we have called *preparation.* The drafting, revising, and editing phases match what happens during reading, or what has been called *assistance.* The act of producing a product can be likened to the *reflection* phase of learning that occurs after reading. Breaking down the writing process into several phases is advisable because this process is new to many students. However, as stated previously, the phases truly overlap as they do in reading, so the process becomes relatively seamless. The remainder of this chapter discusses strategies for teaching writing during each of these phases of the learning process.

Just to summarize, excellent lessons in the content areas often include

- Teacher demonstration and modeling.
- Clear goals and expectations.
- Guided practice.
- Permission to make decisions and mistakes along the way.
- Feedback from both peers and teachers.
- An audience.
- A purpose that goes beyond a classroom assignment.

THE PREPARATION PHASE OF WRITING

Writing may be commonly used across the curriculum as a culminating project or report to demonstrate learning and understanding. But how often is it used to begin a lesson or unit of study? In their study of the use of writing for instruction in the area of junior high mathematics, Pearce and Davison (1988) found that writing was seldom used to guide thinking and learning, especially in the preparation phase of learning. In a follow-up study, Davison and Pearce (1988b) looked at five mathematics textbook series to determine whether these texts included suggestions for writing activities. Not surprisingly, they found few suggestions, and almost none were suggestions for writing before reading. Writing prompts are found in subject area textbooks published in the late 1990s and in the 2000s, but these generally appear as follow-up or extension activities. Teachers in various content areas confirm that they find few suggestions in their textbooks for using writing as a preparation activity. Because teachers rely on textbooks and teachers' manuals for the majority of their instruction, they may be missing a rich source of preparation through writing activities.

Beginning a lesson with writing invites students to explore what they know and to consider what they want to learn. Inquiry is a force that drives investigation and study. We often think of science as being inquiry-based; we think of mathematics as problem solving; and we ponder mysteries underlying history. By recording, in some form, current understandings and expectations before launching into reading or lesson activities, students are guided to clarify thinking and plan the next steps in learning.

Preparation is the stage of making connections and planning that gives direction to writing and learning.

In earlier chapters we presented a number of activities that pertain to writing in preparation for reading. Anticipation guides, factstorming, PreP, and What-I-Know Activities (Chapters 3 and 4) all use writing to prepare students to read. In this section we present additional writing activities to use before reading, to clarify students' thinking and spark interest in the material to be read.

A number web may be used as a prewriting strategy to help students recognize the roles that numbers play in their own lives. Students are charged with thinking of numbers that are important to them, such as phone numbers, home addresses, dates of birth, numbers of brothers, sisters, and pets, and the like. Students are instructed to write each number on a sticky note and place the notes on a file folder in a web format. Under each sticky note students write the significance of each number. Students share their number webs with a friend by asking the friend to try and guess the significance of each number; then answers are revealed and discussed. *The Math Curse* by Jon Scieszka complements this activity by providing numerous examples of how math is used in daily activities.

Cubing

Cubing is an activity that can prepare students as both writers and readers by having them think on six levels of cognition. Cowan and Cowan (1980) originated cubing as a way to stimulate writing, especially when writers have a block and can't think of anything to write. The writer imagines a cube, puts one of the six tasks on each of the six sides, and considers each task for no more than five minutes. Because all six sides are considered, the writer has to look at a subject from a number of perspectives. When applied to reading (Vaughan & Estes, 1986), cubing can lead to purposeful reading and help develop reading comprehension. Activity 10.2 shows the use of cubing in a mathematics class about linear equations.

The teacher may begin cubing by modeling the strategy for a simple construct such as a pencil. Then the teacher has students practice cubing for a concept that is in their sphere of prior knowledge. Finally, students practice cubing with difficult concepts to help clarify thinking.

A playful cube can easily be made from packing material or foam. There are even commercial blow-up cubes available from teacher supply companies that can be customized.

When a teacher actually constructs a cube and uses it as a visual prop, students can gain a rapid understanding of the reading material. Making the cube is simple. Cover a square tissue box with construction paper, and label each side; or use the outline that we provide in Figure 10.4 to construct a cube from a strong material such as cardboard. Most teachers, no matter what grade level they teach, find that the cube is an enticing prop for their students to manipulate. One teacher brought a cube to the classroom but did not have time to use it for several days. Left on her desk, the cube generated so much curiosity that the teacher was forced to use the activity.

A variation called *perspective cubing* (Whitehead, 1994) helps students consider concepts from perspectives other than their own. A number of teachers report excellent success with this approach. Students select a chart, map, graph, or picture in a textbook and then study and write about it from these six viewpoints:

Face One—Space: What would it look like up close? What would it look like from a distance?

Describe: It is the equation of a line, and it has two variables. It is written with the *y*-variable all by itself on one side.

Compare: Compared to the standard form, $Ax + By = C$, it is easier to use to find the line.

Associate: It makes me think of the coordinate plane with the X and Y axis.

Analyze: It is $y = mx + b$. The y is a variable, and so is the x. The m tells the slope of the line (how steep it is). The slope, m, is the rise over run, the change in y over the change in x. The b tells where the line crosses the y-axis. It is called the y-intercept.

Apply: For the line written $y = mx + b$, which has a slope of m and a y-intercept at b, there are an infinite number of solutions for x and y. For each x, there is a y, and vice versa. An example is $y = 2x + 3$. The slope is 2, which means the rise in the y-value is 2 for every increase in the run of the x-value. The line crosses the y-axis at 3. So it looks like this:

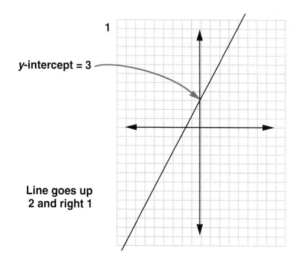

1

y-intercept = 3

Line goes up
2 and right 1

Argue: The slope-intercept form of writing linear equations is the easiest one to be able to see the line quickly. It is better than the standard form because you don't need to change the signs or anything to calculate the slope or intercept. I can just look at the equation and picture the line in my head.

Developed by Mark Forget.

FIGURE 10.4

Cubing: Making
the Cube

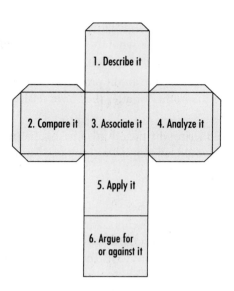

Face Two—Time: What do we think about it today? What will people think about it in 100 years?   What did people think about it 100 years ago?

Face Three—Location: What does it look like from above? What does it look like from the side? What does it look like from below?

Face Four—Culture: What would the indigenous people (first settlers of this land) think about it? What would visitors from another country think about it?

Face Five—Talk: If it could talk, what might it say?

Face Six—Size: If it changed size, how would that change affect the way we might think about it?

Brain-Writing

A variation of factstorming called **brain-writing** (Brown, Phillips, & Stephens, 1992) can help students generate ideas. Small groups of students respond to a topic, write down their ideas, and then exchange and add to one another's lists. While working in the brain-writing groups, students could do any of the following:

1. Predict and write down the definition of a new word in a chapter.

2. Write what they think a visual aid is illustrating or could have to do with a topic.

3. Write how a new topic might fit with previous topics studied.

4. For mathematics, students could write about what they think a particular symbol might mean, what the possible steps for solving a problem could be, or why a particular unit of study is presented at a particular place in the text. For example, a fourth grade mathematics textbook starts the chapter on fractions with a picture of a sectioned pizza, but no explanation is given. Elementary students could be asked to write why they think this illustration has been selected.

5. For science, students could write what they anticipate to be the steps in an experiment, what a formula will produce, what the composition of a substance is, or why certain conditions facilitate certain results.

6. For social studies, students could write about problems people might face when they move from one place to another or after they have settled in a new place (Pearce, 1987).

7. For English, students could write why they think a particular punctuation rule might be necessary: What would happen if we didn't use commas in our writing?

Three Warm-Up Writing Activities

When students first enter the classroom, teachers can direct them to write as a warm-up to the intended instruction for the day. One activity is called a *quick-write* because teachers ask students to jot down ideas and write for one or two minutes about the topic to be studied. Also, students can be asked to complete a *free-write*—writing that takes somewhat longer to complete, usually from three to five minutes. A free-write is an attempt to motivate students by getting them to write their perceptions of certain events or classroom operations. Students are encouraged to think and write without the encumbrance of worry about mechanics and correctness. The only rule is that once students put pencil to paper, they cannot stop until they are completely out of ideas or until the teacher calls an end to the free-write. In this way, students are guaranteed to exhibit free associations of ideas. If, however, students cannot sustain a free-write over five minutes, teachers can start with the easier quick-write for shorter practice and less frustration.

A third writing activity to begin a class is *student-generated questions*. Students can be asked in small groups to write questions that they would like answered about a topic to be studied. As a variation, the questions can be about anything the students have studied about which they are unsure, so that concepts learned in the past few classes can be clarified. Activity 10.3 presents a quick-write from an English class. Activity 10.4 presents a free-write from a high school geography class. Activity 10.5 presents student-generated questions from an elementary science class.

THE ASSISTANCE PHASE OF WRITING

The drafting or assistance stage of writing is much like the assistance phase in reading. Process is emphasized, and writers begin to realize what they have to say and what they understand about a topic. The flow of thought is represented in the writer's draft as it is in the reader's discussion. According to Self (1987), using writing to assist in teaching content material fulfills the following purposes:

1. Focusing students' attention.

2. Engaging students actively.

3. Arousing students' curiosity.

4. Helping students discover disparate elements in material.

5. Helping students make connections between material and themselves.

6. Helping students "make their own meaning" from material.

7. Helping students think out loud.

8. Helping students discover what they do and do not know.

9. Helping teachers diagnose students' successes and problems.

10. Preparing students to discuss material.

Think of three or four prospective audiences students may write for in science, math, social studies, music, art, and so on.

Gebhard (1983) suggests four principles for developing writing activities that assist comprehension. First, students need an audience other than the teacher. This was underscored recently by studies conducted by Purcell-Gates and her colleagues (Purcell-Gates, Degener, Jacobson, & Soler, 2002; Purcell-Gates, Duke, & Martineau, 2007). Peers are a fine resource because they can provide supportive comments and suggestions. Often students become much more active and committed to writing when the audience is someone other than the teacher. The use of peers as an audience conveys the message that the process of writing is more important than the final product, which is the case when writing is an activity to assist comprehension. Writing for peers may eliminate the teacher's need to "grade" the writing at all. If the teacher does decide to grade, then the revision and editing of the paper mean that the teacher will see a polished product. Correction will take second place to content.

A project at Tidewater Community College in Virginia Beach, Virginia, provided an interesting example of writing shared by peers. Students from nearby Salem High School shared their thoughts about poems and other readings with students in an

---

ACTIVITY *10.3* QUICK-WRITE ON MARK TWAIN'S *HUCKLEBERRY FINN*

I believe Mark Twain is one of the better writers of American literature. I actually read this book for my 11th grade lt. English class (which is a surprise because I rarely read the books we're assigned in English). I can see how the book was so controversial, being that the best character (I think) is black. He is very real and down to earth. The book is very easy to read and hard to put down. My only problem with it is when the character of Tom Sawyer comes in. I'm not very fond of this character. In fact I hate him. He just makes the story drag on, making me think "UGH! When is this going to end?!" Although I realize that he is only trying to make things more adventurous but I still find it very stupid. I was very angry in the end when Tom explains that Jim had been set free by Miss Watson and the whole escape plan was unnecessary. So much time wasted! I could have gone out with my friends instead of reading that stuff! Anyway, I think the book was done very well overall despite the Tom Sawyer character.

Dave N. Aznar

Students in a ninth grade geography class have been studying northern Eurasia (the former USSR). The teacher writes the following on the chalkboard

communism v. market economy
autocracy v. democracy

and asks students to discuss these terms in their own groups of three. After a few minutes of small-group discussion, the teacher informs students that they will perform a free-write as a prereading activity to prepare for the day's reading, the second chapter on northern Eurasia. The teacher reinforces the rules of free-write, stating to students that once they begin writing, they may not stop during the five minutes. Rather, they should rewrite the last phrase or sentence if they confront writer's block. The following are a few of the results. (They are reproduced with original student spelling and grammar.)

> Democracy is what we have in our country where the people have rights and freedoms. Autocracy is led by a couple of leaders and they own all the land. With a communist there is no freedom. The government does what it wants and there is no incentive to do well in life. The government gets the profits. Unlike with a democracy where the people keep the money that they make. So they want to do well in life and will work harder to make money and start new businesses. In communist countries the people must do whatever their government tells them to do and are not have the

> freedoms of other countries such as speech and religion. Russia was once communist and after they were no longer comunist they became poor because they people weren't use to it and wanted a leader. They had the freedoms but didn't know what to do with it.

> I know that capitalism is when you have ownership and it is not shared with the government. You are able to be richer or poorer than other people. Communism is the complete opposite. Everything is owned and controlled by the government and you don't own anything you have. If you won a million dollars, you'd own 0% of it. Or if you've been working in a factory for 40 years you can never buy it. That's just the way it goes!!!!!!!!!!!!!!!!!!!!!!!

> ¡Yep!

> Capitalism is a government that is more right wing and communism is far left wing because of its government trying to take care of the people too much which causes no insentive for the people, but under capitalism people have different wages and therefore have an incentive to work hard.

> Capitalism is when the businesses are owned by people. It is also called a market economy. Communist is when the government makes people work and get all the money. Democracy is when the people of a country get to select a leader. Autocracy is when a person is put into power without an election. In my view capitalism and democracy are the 2 top keys to true power of the people.

Developed by Mark Forget.

English class at the college. Student at both schools used the correspondence to clarify ideas and concepts while simultaneously improving their writing skills. Activity 10.6 is a letter from a student at Salem High School to a college student on interpreting the poem "Poetry" by Nikki Giovanni.

Second, the writing task needs to be of some importance to the student. Simply because the teacher may grade a piece of writing does not mean the student is

ACTIVITY 10.5 — STUDENT-GENERATED QUESTIONS IN ELEMENTARY SCIENCE

Student-Generated Questions

1. What does the sun do for plants?
2. Do all plants have seeds, leaves, and flowers?
3. Can the sun harm some plants?
4. Which plants grow best in deserts?
5. What do you call plants that come back every year?
6. Which part of the plant makes the food?
7. Do all plants need the same things to grow?
8. What are the four things that all plants need?
9. Do people need the same four things?
10. Can we eat some plants?

Answers

1. The sun helps the plant make food.
2. Yes, all plants have seeds, leaves, and flowers.
3. Yes, some plants only like shade and filtered sun (filtered sun is sun that has something blocking some of its rays).
4. Cacti grow best in deserts. They need very little water.
5. Perennials are plants that come back every year.
6. The leaves make the food by taking in the oxygen and sun.
7. No, some plants need more sunlight than others. Some need a lot of shade.
8. All plants need air, water, sunlight, and soil.
9. No, people do not need soil because we move around freely.
10. Yes, we can eat a lot of vegetables such as beans, tomatoes, and corn.

Developed by Susan W. Hamlin.

---

motivated. Students need to be able to write about topics that interest them. The Foxfire books illustrate this principle of consequential writing well. Eliot Wigginton (1986) inspired his English students in Rabun Gap, Georgia, to write about the crafts and habits of their own community. In this way he combined the subjects of English and social studies, using writing as the medium of instruction. This assignment itself was much more inspiring to students than receiving a grade. The audience consisted of their fellow students and their community. The work was collaborative, with many students planning and writing together. The collaboration helped students create a cultural history of their community. The result of their writing is the Foxfire books, whose success has been phenomenal.

Third, writing assignments should be varied. No one wants to do the same old thing again and again. Copying definitions, answering questions at the end of the chapter, and writing summaries get monotonous. Later in this section we provide several teacher-tried ideas to vary writing assignments. Several publications can also help content teachers find innovative and varied ways to introduce writing across the curriculum. Some are listed in the "Reflecting on Your Reading" section at the end of this chapter.

March 25, 1999

Dear Jason,

I, also must admit that I had to read "Poetry" by Nikki Giovanni, more than once to understand the poem secure enough to analyze it. Reading your letter and the verses in which you sighted, made me look at the poem in a different light. I didn't notice the "dark touch" it had.

My interpretation was much different. In lines 14-20 I understood it to say that poets, in general, are overwhelmed in their thoughts. They write what comes to mind, they understand it, but it really doesn't matter if we do. In lines 21-26 it sounds as if the writer is putting poets on a pedistool, that they are better than the average individual and their thoughts. The last three lines sum up the entire poem. I think the poem is not about poetry necessarily, but about the poets. There is a constant reinforcement of loniless, which you pointed out in your letter.

I enjoyed the poem and your letter. Please take in consideration my out look.

Sincerely,

Fourth, writing activities should connect prior knowledge to new information, providing students with a creative challenge. As we have shown, cubing does this well. Another excellent activity to encourage this connection is the jot chart, introduced in Chapter 4 as a way to promote comprehension; obviously jot charts can have more than one purpose. Jot charts provide a matrix for learning by giving students an organizational guide—a series of boxes in which they can enter their thoughts about content areas as they read and thereby see the connections between what they already knew, what they need to find out, and—when the chart is completed—what they have learned.

Davison and Pearce (1988a, pp. 10–11), by modifying Applebee's (1981) classification system, divide writing activities into five types:

1. *Direct use of language:* Copying and transcribing information, such as copying from the board or the glossary.
2. *Linguistic translation:* Translating words or other symbols, such as writing the meaning of a formula.
3. *Summary/interpretation:* Paraphrasing or making notes about material, such as explaining in one's own words or keeping a journal.
4. *Applied use of language:* Presenting new ideas in written form, such as writing possible test questions.

Writing assignments that target low-level thinking and copying may invite students to plagiarize because of the ease and convenience of locating information on the Internet.

5. *Creative use of language:* Using writing to explore and convey related information, such as writing a newspaper article, poem, or biographical sketch.

There is a dearth of current research concerning the types of writing tasks currently in use within content area classrooms. In their study, Davison and Pearce found that the copying tasks were predominantly used by junior high school mathematics teachers. Creative activities were seldom used, group writing opportunities were scarce, and the audience for the writing was usually the teacher. In practice, then, teachers do not seem to be following Gebhard's (1983) suggestions, probably because they do not realize how helpful writing activities can be in assisting students' comprehension. Yet the possibilities are great. Following are a number of ideas for content teachers, beginning with learning logs and annotations.

Learning Logs

Request that students write regularly in a journal called a **learning log**, under headings such as "Two new ideas I learned this week in science and how I can apply them to my life" or "How I felt about my progress in math class this week." These entries can be read by other students or by the teacher, but they should be valued for their introspective qualities and not graded. Richardson (1992a) found that such journal writing helps students work through problems they are having in learning material and verbalize concerns that the reader can respond to individually, also in written form. These types of activities tap the metacognitive aspects of learning to engage students in thinking about their own learning and the processes involved. Both a kindergarten study by Glaubman, Glaubman, and Ofir (1997) and a college study by McCrindle and Christensen (1995) found evidence of positive academic achievement when writing activities involving metacognitive thinking were used.

Sheryl Lam, a vocational education teacher, discovered that journal writing enabled her to better monitor the progress of her cooperative education students as they worked in their placements: "Since I have 13 students in five different concentration areas, it is not always easy to deal with all of their problems at once. For me as the teacher, I can focus on each student's problems or successes one at a time; no one gets left out. For the student it's a catharsis."

Learning logs are a relatively simple yet effective way to get all students to write in content area classes. They stimulate thinking. Normally students write in their logs every day, either in class or outside class. Students can be asked to write entries that persuade, that describe personal experiences and responses to stimuli, that give information, or that are creative and spontaneous. Activity 10.7, a learning log from a high school science class, demonstrates how a log can document students' problem-solving abilities.

Once students have practice in keeping logs, the teacher can ask them to respond in a more open-ended, less structured fashion. For instance, Page (1987) got the following response from a student, Carla, in exploring *Antigone* in a high school English class:

I get Sophocles and Socrates mixed up. Socrates is a philosopher. Athena is talked about a great deal in mythology. Wow, they had dramatic competitions. I wonder if he had the

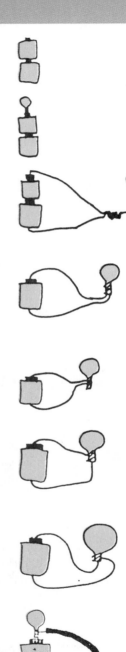

The only preknowledge I brought to this activity was how to put batteries in a flashlight. Using that knowledge, I immediately put the two batteries together like this:

Then, I ignored the wires to see what would happen if I just placed the bulb on top of the battery, because that is how a flashlight seems to work. It didn't work.

One person in my group said, "Remember, it's a circuit." So I held the wires to either end of both batteries and twisted them together and touched the bottom of the bulb. That did not work either, so I untwisted the wire ends and touched the bottom of the bulb with them separate from each other, but simultaneously. However, the bulb would not light.

I had a lot of trouble holding everything together, so I reasoned that I probably only had to use one battery since a positive charge from one end and a negative charge at the other end was all that two (or more) batteries really amounted to. I thought that maybe the problem was that the circuit was broken because of all my fumbling around. I retried touching the ends of the wires to the bulb, but it still would not light.

Then I remembered when I installed a new phone last year, I had to wrap the end of a wire around something that looked like a screw. So I tried wrapping the wire ends around the bulb. The bulb still would not light.

I unwrapped one of the wires from around the bulb, intending to try twisting it again with the end of the other wire and then wrapping that whole thing around the neck of the bulb. However, before I did that, I accidentally touched the end of that wire on the bottom of the bulb and I saw a very quick flicker. For a moment, I wasn't sure what I had done to make it work. Then I deliberately touched the bottom of the bulb again and got the bulb to light.

Next, I wondered if I could reverse the wrapping wire and the bottom-touching wire to make the bulb light up. The bulb lit up this way as well.

Next, I realized that my original "flashlight model" would work if I added a wire to complete the circuit, when working with my partner.

From Debby Deal (1998). "Portfolios, learning logs, and eulogies: Using expressive writing in a science methods class." In Sturtevant, E. G., Dugan, J. A., Linder, P., and Linek, W. M. *Literacy and Community: The Twentieth Yearbook of the College Reading Association.* Used with permission.

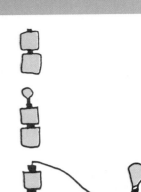

record for the most wins at a competition. I bet if Polynices were alive, he would be very proud of his sister. I would! The chorus seems similar to today's narrator.

Page notes also that students are more motivated to learn when they keep a journal or log. She cites the positive comments of three students about such writing:

> I love the writing journals. Having to keep a writing journal is the extra push I need to expand my ideas, when otherwise I would not. My journal has brought to life so many ideas that may have died if I had not been required to keep a journal. I am somewhat proud of it. —Carla

> Writing journals are my favorite. I like having a place to write down important events in my life, and literary ideas, poems, stories, etc. —Allison

> I feel that the writing journal by far is the most expressive and open writing that we have done in class. I always try to come up with original and creative entries. I feel that the journal has sparked some new creativity in me—and my essays (product paper) reflect it. They seem to be more imaginative than before. —Betsy

Another way of doing double-entry journals is using the left column for recording "what the author says" and the right column for "what you say."

Another journal activity, the **double-entry journal** (Vaughan, 1990), is a log in which students write on the left side of the page about their prior knowledge of a topic. After reading, they enter comments about what they learned on the right side of the page. These comments might include drawings or questions.

A class log, or class notebook (Richardson, 1992a), is a combined writing and note-taking activity that encourages students to take responsibility for writing about class content. Sometimes called content journals, they provide a way for students to review and interpret information to be discussed in class. Students can write in the journals during class—for instance, while reading a passage or text. Students also can write in journals at home as a way to clarify their thinking.

Written Conversation

Part of the learning that occurs as students engage in writing tasks involves social aspects of learning theory (Vygotsky, 1978a). Written conversation uses to advantage a mechanism students typically like to use to communicate on the sly. The very nature of the task provides active engagement for all students. Students work in pairs or triads to conduct a silent discussion. One sheet of paper and one pen or pencil is used to talk about a text, passage, or posed questions (Bintz & Shelton, 2004). Written conversation can be structured in a variety of ways to encourage idea and viewpoint exchange before, during, or after reading. Bintz and Shelton found in a study of written conversation among middle school students that the strategy encouraged students to really listen to one another, to take responsibility for their own participation and learning, and to take responsibility for supporting the learning of others. Different levels of participation and learning occurred based on partner satisfaction and compatibility. The data revealed several types of reading processes going on during written conversation: making a prediction, drawing an inference, making a personal connection, taking a position, asking a question, and detecting an anomaly. This writing strategy offers a means for engaging students in active processing and critical thinking as they read and write to learn.

Annotations

Students need frequent chances to practice critical thinking in their reading and writing. One way of providing these opportunities for older students—middle and secondary level—is through a system of annotation. **Annotating** (making notes about a reading) will help students think about their understanding of the material and enable them to get their reflections down in writing. One such system is **REAP** (**r**ead, **e**ncode, **a**nnotate, **p**onder), developed by Eanet and Manzo (1976). This procedure is designed to improve comprehension skills by helping students summarize material in their own words and develop writing as well as reading ability. The four steps in REAP are as follows:

R—Reading to discover the author's ideas.

E—Encoding into your own language.

A—Annotating your interpretation of the author's ideas.

P—Pondering whether the text information is significant.

Creating annotations helps students increase their maturity and independence in reading. Although annotations may be submitted for grading—perhaps as homework or class grades—they are probably more valuable as written notes to facilitate understanding. Next we describe seven different annotation styles, which students can use singly or in combination:

1. A *heuristic* annotation is a statement, usually in the author's words, that has two purposes: to suggest the ideas of the reading selection and to provoke a response. To write the statement, the annotator needs to find the essence in a stimulating manner. The quotation selected must represent the theme or main idea of the selection.

2. A *summary* annotation condenses the selection into a concise form. It should be brief, clear, and to the point. It includes no more or less than is necessary to convey adequately the development and relationship of the author's main ideas. For a story, the summary annotation is a synopsis—the main events of the plot.

3. A *thesis* annotation is an incisive statement of the author's proposition. As the word *incisive* implies, it cuts directly to the heart of the matter. With fiction, it can substitute for a statement of theme. One approach is to ask, "What is the author saying? What one idea or point is being made?" The thesis annotation is best written in precise wording; unnecessary connectives are removed to produce a telegram-like but unambiguous statement.

4. A *question* annotation directs attention to the ideas the annotator considers most germane; the question may or may not be the same as the author's thesis. The annotator must first determine the most significant issue at hand and then express this notation in question form. This annotation answers the question "What questions are the authors answering with the narrative?"

5. A *critical* annotation is the annotator's response to the author's thesis. In general, a reader may have one of three responses: agreement, disagreement, or a combination of the two. The first sentence in the annotation should state the

author's thesis. The next sentence should state the position taken with respect to the thesis. The remaining sentences are devoted to defending this position.

6. An *intention* annotation is a statement of the author's intention, plan, or purpose—as the student perceives it—in writing the selection. This type of annotation is particularly useful with material of a persuasive, ironic, or satirical nature. Determining intention requires that the annotator bring to bear all available clues—both intrinsic, such as tone and use of language, and extrinsic, such as background knowledge about the author.

7. A *motivation* annotation is a statement that attempts to speculate about the probable motive behind the author's writing. It is an attempt to find the source of the author's belief system and perceptions. Motivation annotation is a high form of criticism, often requiring penetrating psychological insight.

Poetry

Poetry, as a genre, may be used to introduce a concept, raise a question, provoke thought, or sum up an idea. Poetry, just like science, mathematics, social studies, and other content areas, involves reasoning, understanding, and making connections to the world. At the same time it provides a means for appreciating the power and subtleties found and expressed through words. Merging poetry with learning in content areas helps students develop basic understandings of principles and theories as well as experience ways those understandings can be described and enjoyed engaging the senses, feelings, and beliefs (Howes, Hamilton, & Zaskoda, 2003). Dickson (2002) found that characteristics inherent in poetry, such as brevity, repetition, and rhythm, often help students see a concept or idea in a fresh new way. Several types of poetry and poetry adaptations are described in the paragraphs to follow.

Here is a brief sampling of poetry books with science, social studies, or math connections:

Heller, R. (1983). *The reason for a flower.* Penguin Putnam Books.

Hopkins, L. B. (2001). *Marvelous math: A book of poems.* Aladdin Paperbacks.

Hopkins, L. B. (2002). *Spectacular science: A book of poems.* Aladdin Paperbacks.

Lewis, J. P. (2001). *A burst of firsts: Doers, shakers, and record breakers.* Dial Books.

Lewis, J. P. (2002). *A world of wonders: Geographic travels in verse and rhyme.* Dial Books.

Pollock, P. (2001). *When the moon is full: A lunar year.* Little, Brown.

Rice, D. L. (1997). *Lifetimes.* Dawn Publications.

Sceizska, J. (1995). *Math curse.* Viking Books.

Sceizska, J. (2004). *Science verse.* Penguin USA Viking Children's Books.

Shields, C. D. (2002). *American history fresh squeezed: 41 thirst for knowledge quenching poems.* Handprint Books.

Shields, C. D. (2003). *Brain juice: Science fresh squeezed!* Handprint Books.

Whitman, W. (2004). *When I heard the learn'd astronomer.* Simon and Schuster Children's Publishing.

BIOPOEMS

Pattern poems like biopoems provide structure for capturing main ideas and details important to content or topics.

The modified **biopoem** is a poem whose subject is the writer himself or herself. Gere (1985, p. 222) provides the following pattern for writing biopoems:

Line 1: First name.

Line 2: Four traits that describe the author.

Line 3: Relative of ("brother," "sister," "daughter," and so on).

Line 4: Lover of (list three things or people).

Line 5: Who feels (three items).

Line 6: Who needs (three items).

Line 7: Who fears (three items).

Line 8: Who gives (three items).

Line 9: Who would like to see (three items).

Line 10: Resident of.

Line 11: Last name.

An example of a biopoem written by an early elementary student is provided in Activity 10.8.

A biopoem can also be adapted to different subject matter, as illustrated in Activity 10.9. This is actually a variation called a **geopoem** that focuses on a country or region. A geopoem may include all or part of the following elements:

Line 1: City, state, or country name.

Line 2: Four physical features that describe this place.

Line 3: Three cultural features.

ACTIVITY *10.8* MODIFIED BIOPOEM

Andrea
who is blue-eyed, brown-haired and nice
relative of Aunt Kathy
lover of Mom, Aunt Kathy, and Louie (my dog)
who feels good, happy and tired
who needs more chapter books, friends, and long nails
who fears snakes, mom dying, mom's lupus
who gives clothes, toys, and money
who would like to see Spice Girls, 'N Sync and Backstreet Boys
resident of Virginia Beach

Developed by Terry Bryce.

Texas
Piney woods, rolling hills, grassy planes, and dry canyons
Fiestas, Octoberfests, Pow-Wows
Mexico's neighbor
Hot and dry or hot and wet
Home of the big open spaces, oil, and longhorn cattle
Battle of the Alamo, Juneteenth/Emancipation Proclamation, Southern hospitality
Rio Grande border, a hotbed of activity
Diamond of the Great Southwest!

Line 4: Neighbor of (bordering country or location).

Line 5: Climate (temperature and precipitation) description in a season.

Line 6: Home of (three items/resources/landmarks/famous people).

Line 7: Three events that have shaped this place.

Line 8: Issues or problems present.

Line 9: Country or region name.

CINQUAINS

Another writing strategy similar to the biopeom is the cinquain. A cinquain (pronounced sin-kān) is a five-line poem with the following pattern: The first line is a noun or the subject of the poem; the second line consists of two words that describe the first line (adjectives); the third line is three action words (verbs); the fourth line contains four words that

Junior high/middle school: After reading of the Boston Tea Party

Boston Tea Party
aggressive, risky
planning, breaking, entering
done for American independence
risk taking

High school business: After reading from *Introduction to Business*

Central Processing Unit
active, electronic
sorting, comparing, calculating
control center of computer
CPU

See What I Found
A wheel and axle
A type of simple machine
Right there on my bicycle
Makes my bicycle roll
Gets me from home to school
Awesome!

See What I Found
A STOP sign
A red octagon on the street
A signal meaning halt
Necessary for preventing crashes
A shape for saving lives

---

convey a feeling; and the fifth line is a single word that refers back to the first line. Students at all educational levels will be pleased to participate in this language enrichment activity. Cinquains require thought and concentration and can be tried in any content area. Activity 10.10 shows examples of cinquains written for middle and high school.

SEE WHAT I FOUND

This poetry pattern focuses on an object or concept critical to the area or topic being studied. Although the pattern is simple, it requires students to examine the object or idea critically "up close with new eyes." Activity 10.11 shows one example used during a simple machines unit and another for a stop sign that could be used in a social studies lesson.

PROCEDURE

1. Think of an object or item of significance that was a part of the passage read.
2. Write the word/object you chose on the first line.
3. Tell something about it on the second line.
4. Tell where you might find it on the third line.
5. Tell what purpose(s) that object has on the fourth and fifth lines.
6. Say anything you would like about it on the sixth line.

Real objects may be used, as well as pictures of objects, to provide concrete examples and models from which to work and consider.

First-Person Summary

A **first-person summary** is an excellent writing activity in which students write about something in the first person, as if they were part of the enterprise or the action. Often students read an assignment or memorize information without a true understanding

Another approach to first-person summary may take the form of an interview script. Students may take on the role of reporter and create a script to include relevant questions and responses.

of the material. First-person summaries allow them to process information by writing in their own words about a topic. Using the first person encourages them to become personally involved in the material. Teachers may be able to recognize and correct any deficiencies in students' understanding by reading their summaries. For instance, when studying photosynthesis in science, students might write first-person essays in which they take the part of a water molecule. They must explain how they get into a plant, where they journey in the plant, what happens once they reach the chloroplast, and so on. In this way students gain a deeper understanding of the photosynthesis process, and teachers can identify problems students are encountering. This type of assignment can work with a topic such as "A Day in the Life of a New Irish Immigrant in 1835" or "A Day in the Life of a Blood Cell," as demonstrated in Activity 10.12.

ACTIVITY 10.12 A DAY IN THE LIFE OF A BLOOD CELL

There I was, stuck on a boring day doing absolutely nothing. It was 1:32 in the afternoon. Agent 002 was in hot pursuit of the gangster known as Ned the Nucleus. Agent 0012 called me for backup because there was a shoot-out at the Cell Bank on 112 Membrane Street. I rode out there, but there was a backup in the bloodstream so I rode down the back way. Ned the Nucleus was threatening to blow the Cell Bank sky high. I snuck up and over the cell wall. I climbed up the Cell Bank with the help of Don the DNA. I went in and brought out Bob the Brain Cell. How could I be that stupid? Now Ned the Nucleus had a gun. He was shooting at the cops. What could we do?

I went back to the station and figured out a plan. I'd go in the bank disguised as a customer! He'd hold me hostage, then I'd hit him with my elbow and put him under arrest! I got into the building OK. Then I went up to the top floor. He had two other hostages. Their names were Rick the Red Blood Cell and Wally the White Blood Cell. He was arrested on the spot. I got promoted to Chief Lieutenant. Ned the Nucleus got 15–20 years and $500,000 cell bail. A very good lesson was learned today. Killing cells doesn't pay.

Headline!
Ned the Nucleus Breaks Out of Jail!
So now I had to get him back in jail. I went to headquarters so I could get all of the information. Then it hit me like a Mike Tyson jab. Where else would he be than Ned's Night Club in downtown Los Nucleus? So I took the bloodstream down there. He wasn't there, but I got some useful information. They told me he was at the dock. On San Fran Cellular's finest dock, Cells Wharf. I pulled up in the bad neighborhood. I wasn't alone, though. I had the help of Carl the Blood Clot and Priscilla the Spore. Ned the Nucleus was not alone; in fact, he had his whole gang there! I recognized some of their faces; they were Beau the Bruise, Cad the Cut, Rick the Red Blood Cell, and Wally the White Blood Cell, who had faked being a hostage at the bank. We called for backup and got out of there.

We missed the bullets shot at us and met the other cops at my house, where we had told them to go. We went back to the wharf with the SWAT team and the rest of the police squad. We had a stakeout. People shot at us from the water with their stun guns. Our snipers from the roof shot them. Then we had a shoot-out. But we had them surrounded, so they just gave up. I got a medal of honor and became head of the SWAT team and the police. But to me it was just another day in the life of a detective.

Written by Jon Morgan.

Triangle Truths and Smart Remarks

Two other activities described by Morgan, Forget, and Antinarella (1996) are triangle truths and smart remarks. **Triangle truths** can be described by students as they read or directly after they read a passage. In a log or a notebook, the student draws a triangle that contains four important pieces of information. One piece of information goes at each angle of the triangle (the clues), and one piece (the response that the reader must supply) goes in the center of the triangle. All the bits of information are connected to define, describe, or highlight a particular idea, person, or fact from the reading. The goal of the activity is to supply the correct response in the center of the triangle. A finished triangle could look like this:

> In the center of the triangle, one can use words to pose questions such as *who, what, where, when, how, why, tried, wanted, made,* and *found.*

Smart remarks are comments or questions that let students see in writing what they believe or need to know. The remarks are personal comments about what the reading says to the reader and how it makes the reader feel. The comments, when reviewed later by the students, show what was gained from the reading. After reading a passage about energy and catalysts, a student might make the following remarks:

> What is a catalyst? Look up or ask. Adding salt to water should be a chemical change. Heat must be energy released. *Exothermic* and *endothermic*—these words remind me of a "thermos" bottle. Energy must *exit* in exothermic reactions. Remember the prefix "ex." How do rechargeable batteries fit into this? Ask! I'm not sure how you can *add* energy.

The goal of smart remarks is to write to clarify thinking as one reads and to think deeply about what has been read.

Other Assisting Activities

Many writing activities can be practiced with students at the assistance phase of learning. Students can write out the steps they would follow to solve a math problem or complete an experiment. The teacher can ask them to speculate about what would happen if they altered one step. Students also can practice writing about mathematics problems through being asked to write questions about them: What is the sum of 15 and 30? The questions should reflect students' knowledge of the correct vocabulary and operations.

In a history class students can be asked to rewrite a historic event by altering one cause or one effect. For example, using the saying "If walls could talk. . ." students can write from the perspective of a historical structure describing the events and feelings experienced there during the time for which it is famous. Then students can contrast the way the event really happened with their invented version. In the same way, students in an English class can choose a topic they are studying and write about it from the perspective of the subject. For instance, one might become an author and, through the author's words, explain word, style, or plot choices. In science, one might become a blood cell and describe a journey through the body. Activity 10.12 presents a story by a child writing as a blood cell.

THE REFLECTION PHASE OF WRITING

A number of researchers (Atwell, 1987; Sanacore, 1998) maintain that the publication of writing is a natural motivation for writing. Atwell believes that teachers should support student publication efforts because students write better when they know someone will read their writing.

Publishing may take many forms. It can be a report, of course, but also a letter, an essay, a speech, an editorial, a manuscript, a diary, an invitation, a song, or the like.

When writing is to be published or finished as a product, writers should be concerned not only with content but also with form. This includes both revision and editing. Revision requires the writer to make decisions concerning content elaboration and organizational format to give the reader a clearly focused message. During revision writers are still learning to express what they understand about the information; but they also are learning to be considerate of their audience by putting the writing in a consistent, organized format. During the editing stage writers must attend to standard spelling, grammar, and mechanical issues to put the finishing touches on their work. After the writing has been revised and edited, an audience will read it and react in a formal way. Often teachers confuse the evaluation stage with the drafting stage and expect students to produce writing that meets format considerations before or while they are writing to express content. This is a difficult chore for even the most experienced writers. Here is a rule of thumb to use when analyzing a student's piece of writing:

Fluency → Clarity → Correctness → Eloquence and Style

Many students have poor handwriting, spelling, and grammar skills. In analyzing student writing, teachers first need to concentrate on the sincerity and fluency of the effort. Later they can ask for more clarity. Finally, the goal is to write correctly and with some style. Remember that for the student, motivation to write may come from the teacher, who follows this progression in grading and analyzing student writing.

RAFT (Vanderventer, 1979) offers one way for writers and their teachers to keep the appropriate audience in focus:

R stands for the role of the writer: What is the writer's role—reporter, observer, eyewitness?

A stands for audience: Who will be reading this writing—the teacher, other students, a parent, people in the community, an editor?

F stands for format: What is the best way to present this writing—in a letter, as an article, a report, a poem?

T stands for the topic: What is the subject of this writing—a famous mathematician, prehistoric cave dwellers, a reaction to a specific event?

Visit this book's companion Web site, Chapter 10, for links to RAFT examples and suggestions for use in content classrooms.

When teachers are clear about the purpose of the writing and students keep RAFT in mind, the product will be clearer and more focused. RAFT is a flexible strategy that can be used at various stages within a unit of study. It also provides a means to address the needs of students who struggle as well as those who desire a challenge. The strategy works well for controversial local, state, and national issues of concern such as those dealing with environment, social unrest, politics, or economic factors. One example focusing on global warming can be viewed in Activity 10.13. Groenke and Puckett (2006) describe several examples and ways of using RAFT within a science

Please note that the RAFT chart provides a few suggestions and possibilities and can be mixed and matched as needed.

Role	Audience	Format	Topic
Scientist	Scientific community	White paper or journal article	Global warming
Politician	Constituents	Letter	Environmental protection
Local citizen	CEO	Newspaper article or editorial	Global economy
High school student	Local community	Brochure or speech	Effects of global warming on the local community
Oil company CEO	Legislators	Interview	Global, state, and local economy
Journalist	Self	Journal or diary entry	Personal fears, hopes, and expectations concerning global warming

Students can be included in the particulars of this strategy by volunteering suggestions for specific problems to be addressed as well as additional role, audience, and formatting possibilities. Choices of role, audience, and format could be left to students. They also can help establish criteria or a rubric needed for assessment. A more elaborated example is as follows:

Role: You are a concerned high school student who has just been made aware of the dangers and impact of global warming.

Audience: You feel it is your responsibility as a well-informed citizen to alert the community of the potential harm that is being done to the environment and what they as private citizens can do to reverse or at least help correct the problem.

Format: Choose one of the following:

1. You are going to prepare and deliver a compelling speech to a local civic organization explaining the facts and what they as local citizens can do to help.

2. You are going to design a brochure explaining the dangers of global warming and the steps that local citizens can take to help. The local newspaper has agreed, upon approval of your final brochure copy, to distribute it through local delivery.

Topic: Causes and Effects of Global Warming

Whenever possible, as with RAFT, students should write for an audience, even if "publishing" means merely taking completed writing products home to family members. As students' writing skills develop, it becomes important to get students to write with attention to the finished product.

curriculum. An excellent example of criteria that can be used or adapted for assessment is provided as well.

Activities for Reflective Writing

A number of activities are well suited to helping students write reflectively with a goal of building a product.

GUIDED WRITING PROCEDURE

The **guided writing procedure** (Smith & Bean, 1980) is a strategy that uses writing specifically to enhance comprehension. Because guided writing leads to a graded product, we classify it as a reflection activity; however, guided writing also involves the preparation and assistance steps. Smith and Bean give seven steps for its implementation, to be completed in two days. On the first day the teacher (1) activates students' prior knowledge to facilitate prewriting, (2) has students factstorm and categorize their facts, (3) has students write two paragraphs using this organized list, and (4) has students read about the topic. On the second day the teacher (5) has students check their drafts for functional writing concerns, (6) assigns rewriting based on functional needs and revision to incorporate the information from the reading, and (7) gives a quiz. Alternatives to giving a quiz include submitting the rewritten paragraphs, which we think is just as appropriate.

Activity 10.14 is an example of a modified guided writing procedure used by a middle school English teacher to help her students write limericks.

ACTIVITY *10.14* GUIDED WRITING: LIMERICKS

Strategy: The purpose of this activity is to extend the students' abilities to compose a poem. They will achieve this purpose in a guided-writing exercise. I have students write poetry because they will understand poetry better after they have become poets. The exercise will begin with clustering, and from there the students will be guided through their first and final drafts. Because this is a guided exercise, I will first determine the students' background, build on that background, direct the study, and finally determine their comprehension. The final extension of this activity is publishing these poems.

First step: Prewriting (determining background) The teacher writes the word *limerick* on the board and then draws a circle around it. He/she then

asks the students to think about the characteristics of that word. As they give answers, the teacher writes them on lines extended from the main word. Then the teacher directs them to look at some limericks in the text.

Second step: Prewriting (building background) The limericks are read and studied for rhyme scheme and rhythm. The characteristics are listed as further subtopics of the main topic, "limericks."

Third step: Guiding the first draft (developing comprehension)

1. Tell the students that instead of writing limericks, they will be writing pigericks.

2. Pigericks are like limericks, except they are always about pigs. They are short, have lines

(continued) ➤

that rhyme, and contain a definite rhythm. Furthermore, they are humorous.

3. Pass out handouts on pigericks and show Arnold Lobel's book title *The Book of Pigericks.* Go over the poems, noticing the similarities between limericks and pigericks.

4. On the board or overhead, begin a line for a pigerick. Have the students continue brainstorming the remainder of the poem.

5. Assign the writing of a pigerick. Monitor.

Fourth step: Revising (reflection)

6. Have students exchange their poems and share suggestions.

7. Students then revise and rewrite onto large index cards. Next, they illustrate.

8. Post the finished products on the bulletin board.

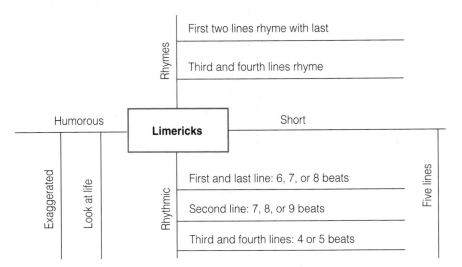

Students' Limericks:

There was a giant pig named Moe Cork
Who acted on a stage in New York
Said he, "Of we three
I am the greatest of thee
Because my head is made of more pork."

There once was a piggy named Lance,
Who wanted to do nothing but dance.
He danced every day,
In a very awkward way.
But that was okay for dancing Lance.

Developed by Frances Lively.

CONTENT-FOCUSED DRAMA

Cooter and Chilcoat (1991) describe how high school students can cooperatively study and perform content-focused melodramas to stimulate connections between what they know and what historical texts describe. Students pick a topic of interest within a unit of study and, in groups of five or six, develop a melodrama by writing the plot, developing characters, and making scenery. Students draft the writing in several stages: (1) the prewriting stage, in which they research the topic, organize facts, and develop characters, composing (2) the initial draft of the script, and

Performance of content-focused drama can be simplified through use of Readers' Theater. Visit the Web sites describing and providing examples using the Web links in the Chapter 10 resources on this book's companion Web site.

(3) conferencing with the teacher to revise, edit, and polish the final script. Cooter and Chilcoat advise that the teacher work with students on grasping the elements of melodrama: stereotyped characters, superheroes, archvillains as ruffians and cads, romantic loves, excessive acting, overblown conflict, and plenty of action. The authors list a number of benefits of such drama: development of cultural literacy, student collaboration and responsibility training, teacher support, teaching of creativity, and the teaching of reading–writing connections.

COLLABORATIVE WRITING

We mentioned **collaborative writing** in connection with the Foxfire books, cited earlier as an example of making writing relevant and relating it to students' backgrounds. Collaborative writing is most effective in demonstrating to students the necessity of finished products that reflect consideration for the intended reader. When students work together, they are less intimidated by what they see as the immense tasks involved in thinking, drafting, revising, and evaluating. Brunwin (1989) organized the students in an entire elementary school to produce a historical account of their neighborhood. They developed questions, targeted the best people to ask, conducted and transcribed interviews, organized their material, and wrote a book to report their findings.

However, collaborative writing need not involve such large groups. One teacher divided her class into several groups. Each individual read an article and reacted to it independently. Then individuals brought their reactions to their assigned groups. Within each group, a common draft was produced, using the individual reactions. Each group member then revised the draft and brought suggestions back to the group. Finally the groups evaluated and rewrote the papers, which the teacher then graded. She discovered that students were able to demonstrate their knowledge of the content well while practicing good writing skills—and as a bonus, she received fewer papers to grade. While working collaboratively in such teams, students can provide editing advice for each other using checklists, charts, or rubrics to help peers improve their final writing products. Explanations and examples for each of these tools are provided later in this chapter.

C3B4ME

Yeager (1991) introduced **C3B4Me** (See Three Before Me) to remind students that writing that is to be turned in for a grade must be carefully reviewed and revised. This can work well for collaborative writing as well as individual works to encourage students to assist one another in learning. As critical friends they can begin to understand how to give and take constructive criticism. For this strategy students should remember to see three other helpers before submitting their work to the teacher. First the writer should confer with himself or herself. Next the writer should confer with a peer, asking for specific advice about designated portions of the writing—not just "Do you like my work?" but "Do you think I have been clear enough in this section?" Last, the writer should be able to consult a "reading associate." Teachers can facilitate the revising/evaluating process by organizing the class into three types of associates. One type includes students who volunteer to be editors for other class members; they and the teacher should agree that they have this skill. The second type includes students who volunteer to illustrate others' written work. The third type helps writers find available editors and illustrators. In the C3B4Me process, students, or "associates," may find a checklist, criteria, or rubric chart helpful during the peer review process. These are discussed and examples are provided later in this chapter.

GIST

Several strategies exist for teaching students to summarize text effectively. One, called GIST (Cunningham, 1982)—"**g**enerating **i**nteractions between **s**chemata and **t**ext"—has been found to effectively improve students' reading comprehension and summary writing (Bean & Steenwyk, 1984). With GIST teachers must model and guide after the reading stage of a lesson. The reader is interrupted and directed to record a summary of the material just read. Cunningham recommends the following steps:

GIST is a great tool for scaffolding the difficult skill of summarizing.

1. Select a short passage in a chapter that has an important main idea. A passage containing from three to five paragraphs works best. Type the paragraphs on an overhead transparency.
2. Place the transparency on the projector, but display only the first paragraph (cover the others). Put 20 blanks on the chalkboard. Have students read the paragraph, and instruct them to write a summary with 20 or fewer of their own words.
3. Have students generate a class summary on the board in 30 or fewer words. Their individual summaries will function as guides for this process.
4. Reveal the next paragraph of the text and have students generate a summary of 30 or fewer words that encompasses both of the first two paragraphs.
5. Continue this procedure paragraph by paragraph until students have produced a GIST statement for the entire passage being taught. In time, they will be able to generate GIST statements for segments of text in a single step.

By restricting the length of students' GIST summaries, the teacher compels the students to use the three major strategies necessary for comprehension and retention of key ideas in any text. They must delete trivial information, select key ideas, and generalize in their own words (Kintch & Van Dijk, 1978). In this manner, GIST is beneficial for teaching reading and writing. Eventually the GIST can be constructed after the reading as an excellent reflective activity, although one should practice with the strategy in both the assistance and the reflection phases of the lesson. Activity 10.15 is an example of a GIST done following the reading of a passage about hurricanes.

SHORT STATEMENTS

Short pieces of writing can be quite motivational and provide a venue for exploring topics, synthesizing information, expressing the most critical parts clearly and concisely.

ACTIVITY *10.15* GIST: WHAT IS A HURRICANE?

Forming over warm waters in the Northern Hemisphere, this tropical storm has an "eye," 75+ mph counterclockwise winds, flooding rains.

Yell (2002) describes the short statement strategy as a way for students to learn to express points and ideas precisely while using research techniques. Students explore a topic and write one, two, or even three "information-rich" paragraphs to describe their findings. A shorter task may appear less daunting to students—but it often requires as much or more reading, research, and thought as does a longer assignment to accomplish writing an effective, concise product. Yell describes the steps for using this strategy to create a brief biography. First students are asked to explain the action, idea, or event for which the person is known. Next enough background information must be supplied to clarify the historical context. Writers must use action words. Finally the information must be condensed into five or fewer sentences per paragraph. This same strategy could be adapted and used to describe the procedure for solving a math problem.

WRITING FOR AT-RISK AND STRUGGLING READERS

Motivating poor readers and students at risk of failure requires techniques that engage them in both practical and creative writing. Teacher demonstrations, write-alouds, and scaffolding to build skills and understanding are important for developing the ability and confidence necessary for students to do well on their own. Students need to be given adequate time to write, opportunities to discuss questions and progress with their peers as well as with the teacher, and timely and appropriate feedback. A homework assignment in writing is often not successful with at-risk students because they may not be able to get answers to their questions or the support needed.

Go to the *Reading to Learn in the Content Areas* Web site and select Chapter 10 Web links for descriptions of means and ways of teaching students how to guard against plagiarism.

One teaching technique that has been used over time in all kinds of settings has been the telling of anecdotes and stories that connect to the principles being taught. Isolated facts are easily forgotten, but facts woven into a story become memorable. When comparing expository and narrative text in terms of reading difficulty among populations of children with learning disabilities, Saenz and Fuchs (2002) found narratives to be much easier for them to read. The emotions and human qualities present in stories, as well as familiar structure, help make them easier to understand. Hand (2006) has implemented a program called "History as Story" in her school system. This program is designed to guide students to research and use facts to create stories that will lead them to understand the significance of those facts. The information must come from reliable sources. "Literary nonfiction, also called creative nonfiction, serves to build deeper understanding of an historical time and place" (p. 42). Because students are weaving stories based on facts, plagiarism and encyclopedic-type reports are deterred.

In primary and intermediate grades, pictures can be motivational and serve as the basis for discussion that can be used to develop a story or informational text. The class can discuss characters in a picture, and students can be asked what is happening in the picture, what may be about to happen, and what may have happened in the past. To accompany the picture, the teacher may construct partial sentences for the students to complete, such as these for a picture showing the signing of the Declaration of Independence:

1. The man in the picture is . . .
2. He is signing . . .

3. If I were at the signing, I would . . .

4. The men in the picture look . . .

5. There are no women in the picture because . . .

6. The men will soon be . . .

In addition to practicing with closure, students can be motivated to write by being given a beginning to a story, such as the following:

> The man knew it was not wise to refuse the mugger, who was young and strong and mean looking. But he wanted to save his pocket watch. That watch was so special; it had a long history in his family. Should he refuse to give it to the thief?

By explaining why he should or should not surrender the pocket watch, students practice composing their own paragraphs.

The purpose of using writing as a means of learning is to help struggling students read and think better through awareness of their own ability to write. Research suggests that semiliterate students may have a writing vocabulary not exceeding 500 words (Tonjes & Zintz, 1981). Student understanding and confidence can be developed by starting small with sentences, moving to paragraphs, and then organizing and elaborating to create comprehensive texts that reflect their learning. Perhaps the most important factor in encouraging struggling learners is making certain not to emphasize mechanics too soon. Many students who fail have poor handwriting and are weak in spelling and grammar. Such students get discouraged when teachers find fault and dwell on their inadequacies. Teachers should tell these students that they will be graded on the sincerity and fluency of their efforts. Later teachers can ask for clearer student writing. Patience is the key when teaching students with these limitations. The goal is to produce students who write correctly and with some style.

Students at risk are generally characterized as passive learners who lack the ability to produce and monitor adequate reading behaviors (Harris & Graham, 1985; Torgensen & Licht, 1983). Yet as Adler (1982) points out, "genuine learning is active, not passive. It involves the use of mind, not just the memory. It is a process of discovery, in which the student is the main agent, not the teacher" (p. 50). Writing that stresses discovery and active learning represents an excellent way for passive students to become active learners who are responsible for creating their own concepts as they write. Such techniques can aid even children with severely limited capacity to learn.

More than six decades ago, Strauss and Lehtinen (1947) successfully used writing in helping to teach brain-injured children to read. They saw writing as valuable in developing the visual–motor perception and kinesthetic abilities of these children. Researchers since that time, including Myklebust (1965), Chomsky (1971), Moffett (1979), and Graves (1983), have advocated that writing programs be adopted in the schools. Research also has documented the benefits of teaching the writing process to learning-disabled students and other students with special needs (Barenbaum, 1983; Douglass, 1984; Kerchner & Kistinger, 1984; Radencich, 1985; Roit & McKenzie, 1985).

Zaragoza (1987) lists several fundamental elements of writing that, if followed, can help children identified as learning disabled and at risk gain control and become more active and involved in their learning. She says students need a 30-minute block

Students who struggle should not be limited to skill and drill exercises. They need opportunities to discover and create just like other learners.

of "time to write" each day—a period devoted expressly to writing so that they acquire the habit of writing. Zaragoza also calls for children to have considerable freedom in choosing topics to build self-confidence that what they say is important. The aim of process writing is to foster a feeling of control in students so that they "learn that the influence of their choices extends beyond their work to the larger classroom environment" (p. 292). She also recommends that a revision be done after the first draft and that teachers edit this revised version. Later children can "publish" their work in the form of student-made books.

According to Zaragoza (1987), the critical element in the writing process is the teacher–student conference. These conferences, which can take place during any phase of the program, allow for one-on-one advising, editing, and sharing. The researcher believes that emphasizing the writing process can help develop in children traits that may keep them from being tagged with an unflattering educational label.

Research shows that poor readers have trouble identifying important ideas in a passage and have trouble using the rules for summarizing (Winograd, 1984). Summary writing can help students by allowing them to reduce their thinking about the reading passage. The teacher can get these students to concentrate on the "big picture," or central theme, instead of getting caught up in minutiae. Zakaluk and Klassen (1992) report that Dan, a remedial ninth grader labeled as learning disabled, was taught to use check marks while reading so he could identify important points. Then he used the check marks to write headings for an outline. By going back to the text, he found supporting details. Then he was able to write summary paragraphs about what he had learned.

Another practical way to get students to concentrate on the gist of their reading is to start them with the ABOUT/POINT technique, discussed in Chapter 5: "This article on cumulus clouds is about, and the points are, and. . . ."

A number of reading professionals and researchers have formulated rules for condensing major ideas in a text (Brown, Campione, & Day, 1981; Kintch & Van Dijk, 1978). Here are six rules students generally should follow:

1. *Delete unnecessary detail:* With practice, students will become adept at separating important text information from minor facts and trivial statements.

2. *Delete redundant information:* Students should make lists and collapse information into broader categories of information as they notice redundancies.

3. *Use blanket terms:* Students should replace lists of smaller items of information with more encompassing terms.

4. *Select topic sentences; summarize paragraphs:* Often paragraphs have easily identifiable topic sentences. Sometimes there is no discernible topic sentence, however, and students have to create their own topic sentence for the summary. Doing this can be difficult for poor readers. Much practice is needed for these students to feel successful at this difficult step.

5. *Write a first draft of a summary:* Students need to integrate information by making more general certain topic sentences, keywords, and phrases already compiled in steps 1 through 4. The first four steps prepare students to write the first draft of the summary.

6. *Revise the summary:* With the help of other students or the teacher, students should rework the summary to make it more readable. By doing so, students will get a clearer idea of the major points covered in the material.

Hare and Borchardt (1984) used similar rules in an experimental study with minority high school students. Compared to a control group, which made little progress, the experimental group improved in summary writing ability as well as in the ability to use the rules to write summaries. It would appear from the results of this study and from our classroom observations that summary writing can help all students.

GRADING REFLECTIVE WRITING

Teachers sometimes question whether they should accept writing from students when it contains grammatical errors, misspellings, and other errors. "Surely seventh graders can write better than this!" they admonish. However, teachers must allow students to start where they are and to focus on one stage of writing at a time.

Errors are a normal part of learning, and they will occur in student writing. The amount and types of writing practice that students have had will determine their level of sophistication. If the pressure to focus on errors is eliminated during the prewriting and drafting stages, when the focus should be on content, then attention to errors can be greater during the revision and editing stages. If students have had prewriting and drafting opportunities, their revised writing will reflect both improved content and improved form.

Teachers can guide students in their writing activities by making clear their expectations for the final product. Students should understand exactly what will be evaluated. Of course the content of the writing is most important. But "content" is a vague criterion. To clarify expectations and grading criteria for students, a checklist or rubric may be developed. A **rubric** is an expectation guide that lists the qualities of a range of papers—from the strongest to the weakest (see Activities 10.16 and 10.17). A rubric helps students, who can refer to it as they revise, as well as the teacher, who can refer to it during grading. Similarly, checklists are useful because they list the features the teacher expects to find in students' writing (see Activity 10.18).

Teachers can use a checklist to quickly rate the features of a written assignment, and students can check their papers against this list during revision. Teachers might even provide their point scale for checklists or criteria for grading, as in Activity 10.19. Also, they can hand out the rubric or checklist when giving the assignment. In this way, students know in advance what factors will be considered in their grade, and they have a chance to organize their writing accordingly.

As with reflective reading, students should be involved at the evaluation and publishing stages of writing. Even if the teacher gives the final grade—as the teacher does if students take a test to demonstrate learning after reading—students should have opportunities to evaluate their own writing before giving it to the teacher. Only when students know that their own analysis is a crucial part of the process will they take responsibility for it.

WRITER'S NAME: _____ DATE: _____

PEER EDITOR'S NAME: _____ TITLE: _____

The writer would like this peer editor to examine and provide feedback for the following:

Content and ideas: _____

Organization: _____

Mechanics:_____

Questions the writer has for the peer editor:

Rubrics that Serve as a Guide for Each Domain

Domain	Needs Considerable Improvement 1	Needs Some Improvement 2	Well Done! 3
Content and ideas			
• Focus	• Information is scattered and random with no clear focus.	• Information is organized well enough to make the focus apparent.	• Information is clear, logical, and well focused.
• Major points	• Few to no major points are included.	• Most major points are included.	• All major points are addressed, and additional points of interest are appropriately included.
• Support	• Main points that are included are not supported by details and evidence.	• Main points are supported by some details and evidence.	• All main points are well supported by details and evidence.
• Interest	• Writing is bland with facts/thoughts just stated one after the other; uninteresting.	• Writing is interesting enough to hold the attention of the reader.	• Writing interests the reader and encourages further investigation of the topic.
Organization			
• Introduction	• There is no clear introduction.	• An adequate introduction is provided.	• The introduction is interesting and encourages the reader to think about the topic and read on.
• Order	• Points are randomly addressed and bounce back and forth.	• Most points and paragraphs follow a logical sequence appropriate for the topic.	• Points are clearly ordered to avoid confusing the reader or the issues.

(continued) ➤

Domain	Needs Considerable Improvement 1	Needs Some Improvement 2	Well Done! 3
• Transition	• Writing moves abruptly from one point to another with no apparent connection.	• Enough transitions are used to provide good flow from one sentence/paragraph/section to the next.	• Transitions move the reader seamlessly along from one sentence/paragraph/section to the next.
• Conclusion	• The writing just stops with no conclusion provided.	• The conclusion is appropriate and logical.	• The conclusion is strong, well stated, and well supported.
Mechanics			
• Spelling	• There are numerous spelling errors.	• Most words are spelled correctly.	• There are no spelling errors.
• Sentence structure	• Several sentences are poorly constructed or are not complete.	• Sentences are complete and are constructed well enough to make the meaning clear.	• Sentences are well constructed and easy to understand.
• Language	• Formal language conventions are not maintained.	• Most language conventions are followed.	• Formal language conventions are used throughout.
• Punctuation	• Several punctuation errors are present.	• Few punctuation errors are found.	• There are no punctuation errors.

Another way to facilitate such realization and responsibility is to allow preview and revision opportunities. Teachers can let students turn in drafts of assigned writing early for early review at no cost to their grades. After receiving a graded writing assignment, students can be encouraged to rewrite the paper and receive an average of the first grade and second grades. Using a computer and word processing program helps students become more receptive to polishing their writing (Bangert-Drowns, 1993; Brown, Phillips, & Stephens, 1992; Cochran-Smith, 1991; Goldberg, Russell, & Cook, 2003). Writing a draft and then returning to it with a critical eye is much easier when the major work does not have to be recopied. Cronin, Meadows, and Sinatra (1990) found that secondary students who used a computer for writing assignments across the curriculum improved their writing ability, attaining 100 percent success on a standard written essay test.

The Internet hosts numerous sites that suggest writing ideas for use by teachers as well as sites students may reference for enriching and developing their own writing skills and expertise.

Paper topic: 1960s approaches to civil rights in the United States.

High-quality papers contain

An overview of civil rights or their lack during the 1960s, with three specific examples.

A statement defining civil disobedience, with three examples of how it was used and Martin Luther King's role.

At least one other approach to civil rights, with specific examples, and a comparison of this approach with King's civil disobedience that illustrates differences or similarities in at least two ways.

Good organization, well-developed arguments, few mechanical errors (sentence fragments, grammatical errors, spelling errors).

Medium-quality papers contain

An overview of civil rights during the 1960s, with two specific examples.

A statement defining civil disobedience, with two examples of its use and Martin Luther King's involvement.

One other approach to civil rights, with examples, and a comparison of it with King's civil disobedience by their differences.

Good organization, few mechanical errors, moderately developed arguments.

Lower-quality papers contain

A general statement defining civil disobedience with reference to Martin Luther King's involvement and at least one example.

One other approach to civil rights and how it differs from civil disobedience.

Fair organization, some mechanical errors.

Lowest-quality papers contain

A general statement on who Martin Luther King was or a general statement on civil disobedience.

A general statement that not all Blacks agreed with civil disobedience.

A list of points, poor organization, many mechanical errors.

Content	Weak	Average	Strong
1. Clear and interesting topic or main idea.			
2. Topic appropriate to the assignment.			
3. Ideas and details support and develop the topic.			
4. Ideas stated clearly and developed fully.			
5. Good use of language.			

Form

6. Introduction, body, and conclusion.			
7. Details arranged logically; appropriate to the topic.			
8. Coherent; paragraphs constructed well.			

(continued) ➤

Activity 10.18 *(continued)*

Mechanics	Weak	Average	Strong
9. Grammar and usage.			
10. Spelling, capitalization, punctuation.			

Comments:

Key:

Strong—10 points
Average/strong—7 points
Average—5 points
Weak—3 points

Developed by Dianne Duncan.

ACTIVITY *10.19* CRITERIA FOR GRADING

NAMES _____

Used at least five facts   _____

Beginning   _____

Middle   _____

End   _____

Bat has a name   _____

Story has title   _____

Illustration(s)   _____

This is the evaluation form the teacher constructs for evaluating the students' performance. After the teacher completes this evaluation, it is kept and attached to the students' writing sample. These stories will be placed in a portfolio and made accessible to parents during visitation.

Developed by Polly Gilbert.

ONE-MINUTE SUMMARY

This chapter has described how to teach, emphasize, and apply writing across the content areas and at different grade levels. Writing to learn in various curricular areas gives students opportunities to rehearse, elaborate, and organize their thinking about the content while monitoring their understanding. Concurrently writing skills and techniques are practiced and reinforced. The connections between reading and writing were discussed in this chapter, as well as the importance of teaching writing in the earliest elementary grades. We differentiated between processes and products of writing and described a number of phases of writing across the curriculum. We provided some computer writing applications, cited research, and gave examples of how writing quality and quantity can be improved through using computers. To demonstrate how easily writing to learn can be incorporated into content instruction, we explained activities to promote writing at each phase of the PAR Lesson Framework. Real classroom applications were included to show teachers how content writing works in action. Considerations and techniques for working with at-risk students were described. A section about grading students' reflective writing demonstrated how important it is to be concise in grading writing through the use of rubrics, checklists, and set criteria. Writing is a skill, an art, and a tool that can be effectively used for learning in all curriculum areas.

PAR ONLINE

For a sampling of currently available sites related to using writing in the classroom, visit the *Reading to Learn in the Content Areas* Web site at http://academic.cengage.com/education/richardson, Chapter 10.

Threaded discussion suggestion: Given the challenges of limited numbers of computers within most classrooms, some students not having computers in their homes, and the current mismatch between state writing assessments and the use of computers for writing, how would you suggest teachers resolve these issues while preparing students for writing and technology within the workplace?

END-OF-CHAPTER ACTIVITIES

Assisting Comprehension

1. Try keeping your own learning log to record your reactions as you use the writing strategies described in this chapter. Assess how each activity helps you teach the writing process. Learn to practice writing in your log every day. Share the writing in your log with your students.

   a. Considering your own background of experience, training, and classroom practices, write three to five questions you have concerning the role, skills, approaches, and your feelings about the teaching of writing within content areas.

   b. Besides the material and suggestions in your text, what else will you do to find appropriate answers to your questions?

   c. Now answer your questions, using the resources and plan you selected for locating answers.

2. Try cubing. Write a short paragraph about this chapter on each of the following six sides of the cube:

   How would you describe this chapter?

   To what would you compare this chapter?

   What does this chapter make you think of?

   How would you analyze this chapter?

   Apply this chapter to your own life.

Do you agree with the tenets of this chapter?

Argue for or against writing to learn in the content areas. Do you favor writing as a product or process writing?

Reflecting on Your Reading

1. The International Reading Association (2003) has developed a set of standards that identify the performance criteria relevant to classroom teachers. Standard 5 describes four elements of literacy professional development necessary for a classroom teacher. The teacher should

    5.1 Ensure that all individuals project ethical and caring attitudes in the classroom. They work with families, colleagues, and communities to support students' learning.

    5.2 Identify specific questions related to knowledge, skills, and/or dispositions related to their teaching of reading and writing. They plan specific strategies for finding answers to those questions. They carry out those plans and articulate the answers derived. They indicate knowledge of and are members of some professional organizations related to reading and writing. They are informed about important professional issues and are effective advocates with administrators; school boards; and local, state, and federal policy-making bodies.

    5.3 Actively engage in collaboration and dialogue with other teachers and reading specialists to obtain recommendations and advice on teaching practices and ideas. They can articulate the evidence related to these recommendations. They may conduct action research as a part of these collaborations.

    5.4 Participate individually and with colleagues in professional development experiences.

2. The following textbooks provide excellent extension reading resources for finding out more about writing to learn in the content classrooms:

Blasingame, J., & Bushman, J. H. (2005). *Teaching writing in middle and secondary schools.* Upper Saddle River, New Jersey: Pearson Education.

Bright, R. (1995). *Writing instruction in the intermediate grades: What is said, what is done, what is understood.* Newark, DE: International Reading Association.

Bromley, K. (1993). *Journaling: Engagements in reading, writing, and thinking.* New York: Scholastic.

Graves, D. (1994). *A fresh look at writing.* Portsmouth, NH: Heinemann.

Houston, G. (2004). *How writing works: Imposing organizational structure within the writing process.* Boston: Pearson Education.

Irvin, J. L., Buehl, D. R., & Radcliffe, B. J. (2007). *Strategies to enhance literacy and learning in middle school content area classrooms,* 3rd ed. Boston: Pearson Education.

Maxwell, R. (1996). *Writing across the curriculum in the middle and high schools.* Boston: Allyn and Bacon.

Olson, C. B. (2007). *The reading/writing connection: Strategies for teaching learning in the secondary classroom,* 2nd ed. Boston: Pearson Education.

Routeman, R. (2004). *Writing essentials: Raising expectations and results while simplifying teaching.* Portsmouth, NH: Heinemann.

Scarborough, H. A. (Ed.). (2001). *Writing across the curriculum in secondary classrooms: Teaching from a diverse perspective.* Upper Saddle River, New Jersey: Pearson Education.

Wolfe, D., & Reising, R. (1983). *Writing for learning in the content areas.* Portland, ME: J. Weston Walch.

Wollman-Bonilla, J. (1991). *Response journals.* New York: Scholastic.

There will never be a single solution that will be a perfect fit for our diverse society. Don't wish for a unilateral answer to our educational dilemmas. Instead, we should work toward partnerships of families, communities, and educators who will enjoy the process of problem solving.

ELAINE GRIFFIN, 1995
UNITED STATES
TEACHER OF THE YEAR

Supporting Diverse Learners in Content Classrooms

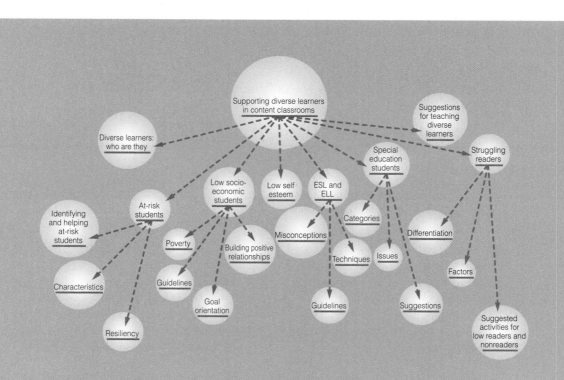

VOICES FROM THE CLASSROOM

Mr. Johnson was beginning his second year as a fifth grade teacher at Horseshoe Elementary. The community attracted migrant workers because there were a few large orchards on the edge of town and a poultry business. This year he had two new Hispanic students from south Texas, Laticia and Maria. They each had enough knowledge of English to speak socially and understand typical day-to-day conversation but had little knowledge of the form and subtleties of academic language. Last year Mr. Johnson had not had any ESL (English as second language) learners in his classroom, so he was both delighted and a little apprehensive about the possibilities. He asked Mrs. Carson, a seasoned teacher, what special accommodations and considerations he should make to provide the best learning experience for these students. Mrs. Carson assured him that they just needed good instruction as did his other students to help them get ready for the standards exam at the end of the year. She told him to be patient and not to expect too much from them. She found there were always one or two others in the class who were willing to help and work with them. She advised that children of migrant workers are generally shy and don't contribute much even when asked questions directly. She suggested he bring in special materials in May to highlight Cinqo de Mayo to help them feel included. After this conversation Mr. Johnson felt somewhat discouraged, but not daunted. He knew there must be techniques and strategies he could use that would make a positive difference for these students.

1. Why do you think Mrs. Carson had such low expectations for these students?
2. What beyond "just good instruction" should Mr. Johnson consider when planning lessons?
3. What suggestions would you give Mr. Johnson?

PREPARING TO READ

1. Answer the following statements thoughtfully and be ready to respond about your instruction for diverse students:

_____ I do not (or expect I will not) encounter students with cultural or language diversity in my classroom.

_____ I know how to accommodate instructional practices in my classroom—or future classroom—for learners with a wide range of needs.

_____ I can use student interests, reading abilities, and backgrounds to plan highly successful content lessons, no matter how diverse the students might be.

2. Following is a list of terms used in this chapter. Some may be familiar to you in a general context, but in this chapter they may be used in unfamiliar ways. Using prior knowledge and your understanding at this

point, decide how you could group the terms in four or five sets, and give each group an appropriate label. There may be several ways to group them, so there is no single right answer. Be ready to explain your selections. Next, using a piece of paper, make a three-column organizer with the following headings: terms, predicted definitions, chapter definitions. Select 10 terms with which you are least familiar, record them in your organizer, and predict how they might be defined for this chapter. As you read the chapter, verify your predictions and rewrite your definitions as necessary.

_____ diverse learners
_____ equity pedagogy
_____ at-risk students
_____ resilient students
_____ self-efficacy
_____ immigrants
_____ refugees
_____ acculturate
_____ assimilate
_____ i + 1
_____ affective filter hypothesis
_____ basic interpersonal communication skills (BICs)
_____ cognitive academic language proficiency (CALP)

_____ English for academic purposes (EAP)
_____ cultural discontinuity
_____ culture shock
_____ survivor guilt
_____ culturally responsive instruction
_____ English language learner (ELL)
_____ English as a second language (ESL)
_____ teaching English to speakers of other languages (TESOL)
_____ bilingual education
_____ sheltered content instruction
_____ group frame
_____ inclusion
_____ specific learning disorder (SLD)
_____ Individuals with Disabilities Education Act (IDEA)
_____ response to intervention (RTI)
_____ universal design
_____ comprehension monitoring
_____ PLEASE
_____ fix-up strategies
_____ reciprocal teaching
_____ ReQuest
_____ language experience approach (LEA)
_____ auditory discrimination
_____ visual discrimination
_____ concept formation study guides

OBJECTIVES

As you read this chapter, focus your attention on the following purposes. You will

1. Understand and identify characteristics of at-risk students.

2. Understand why teachers have to discourage passive approaches to reading.

3. Identify teacher-directed reading strategies for aiding at-risk, low-socioeconomic, and low-self-esteem learners.

4. Identify and clarify common misconceptions concerning instruction for English language learners.

5. Identify culturally responsive teacher-directed reading strategies for aiding English language learners.

6. Identify teacher-directed reading strategies for aiding special education students.

7. Identify teacher-directed reading strategies for aiding struggling readers.

Brian Basset © 2002. Distributed by the Washington Post Writers Group.

DIVERSE LEARNERS

Diverse learners defined.

Who are diverse learners? When we take the time to get to know each student in our classrooms, we begin to realize that all learners are actually diverse. Even in classrooms that may be designated as "homogeneous"—that is, where all learners are supposed to be grouped by a like factor such as giftedness or advanced or deficient academic ability—we discover a great range of diversity.

Within every classroom teachers find students who are diverse in intellectual ability, social and emotional background, language proficiency, racial background, cultural background, and physical attributes. Educators often define **diverse learners** as those who might be at risk for academic failure and need special understanding and attention. Teachers must be prepared to deal effectively with these individual differences (Au, 1992; Carolan & Guinn, 2007; Hammerberg, 2004; Heilman, Blair, & Rupley, 1994; Wassermann, 1999; Williams, 2006).

Equity pedagogy stresses instructional opportunity for all learners.

Current trends in the United States indicate that our population will continue to diversify. The population in the United States has experienced pattern shifts reflecting larger proportions of cultural, linguistic, and socioeconomic differences in recent years, and literacy as it relates to diversity has gained new attention (Au & Raphael, 2000; Xu, 2001). Achievement gaps between students in the mainstream population and their diverse peers remain a challenge. "A fundamental shift in teachers' knowledge, skills, and assumptions about children in high-poverty schools and students who are culturally and socioeconomically diverse is needed for the achievement gap to narrow" (Williams, 2006, p. 11). Content area teachers must practice **equity pedagogy** (Au, 2001; Banks, 1995), striving to educate every student, no matter what their heterogeneous or diverse qualities. This often means not treating or instructing each individual in the same way—but rather with respect to their differences and needs to provide effective instruction and ultimate learning success for them all. Every student must be prepared to take her or his rightful place in a workforce that is "ready with the technical and communication skills to compete in a global economy" (Brotherton, 2000, p. 21).

At-Risk Students

At-risk learners may have diverse characteristics. Some learners who come from low socioeconomic backgrounds find learning and the demands of literacy more difficult because they have had limited experience with reading; others have low self-esteem. Some are new to the English-speaking world. Some learners have special education needs. Some learners struggle with reading. And some learners may have combinations of these characteristics. Such learners cannot keep up with the majority in a content classroom. In this chapter we explore some of the characteristics of each of these groups of diverse learners, assist teachers in exploring their own understandings and beliefs associated with culture and diversity, and offer some strategies that can help content teachers teach diverse learners effectively. While all students can benefit from the information in this chapter, diverse students in particular need these strategies and suggestions.

Characteristics of At-Risk Students

At-risk students defined.

At-risk students are students who are in danger of dropping out of school, usually because of educational disadvantages, low socioeconomic status, or underachievement. Although poor minority children may be at greatest risk, many other students in our classrooms are also at risk of school failure. The reasons are varied: poverty, drug and alcohol abuse, crime, teen pregnancy, low self-esteem, ill health, poor school attendance, welfare dependence, and others.

NAEP statistics demonstrate the numbers of at-risk students teachers instruct.

The National Assessment of Educational Progress's (NAEP) *The Nation's Report Card* (Perie, Grigg, & Donahue, 2005) indicates that only 31 percent of fourth graders and only 31 percent of eighth graders attained a "proficient" level score—a standard that test officials say all students should reach. Thirty-six percent of fourth graders and 27 percent of eighth graders did not achieve a basic level of reading proficiency. Furthermore, children in families living below the poverty line often do not have opportunities to participate in preschools where they might receive early help to overcome at-risk factors; this situation applies to as many as 47 percent of our children. Such statistics should give us pause: Real wages are down, the incidence of poverty is up, the youthful population is declining, and the proportion of minorities and those for whom English is not the first language is growing. In addition, minorities and those with limited English proficiency are disproportionately represented among the poor and among those who are failed by our school system. Many of these students, also failed in many ways by society, will face a lifetime of debilitating poverty unless we, as educators, generate the imagination, will, and resources necessary to educate these at-risk students for independent, productive, and effective lives (Hornbeck, 1988).

Four affective needs of at-risk learners.

At-risk learners are desperate yet unfulfilled, trying to meet these four important affective needs: power, love, freedom, and fun (Glasser, 1986). Often their lives are governed by fear, threats, and negative thinking. They feel helpless and powerless and exhibit an external locus of control (discussed in Chapter 12), feeling that they lack control of their own destiny.

Pellicano (1987) defines at-risk students as "uncommitted to deferred gratification and to school training that correlates with competition, and its reward, achieved status" (p. 47). Pellicano sees at-risk students as "becoming unproductive, underdeveloped, and noncompetitive" (p. 47) in our technological and complex world. He sees at-risk youngsters as not so much "socially disadvantaged" (the label of the 1960s) but rather as economically disadvantaged. Pellicano cites a litany of dropouts, school failures, alcohol and drug abusers, and handicapped and poverty-stricken children—all putting the United States at risk of becoming a third-rate world power unable to respond to economic world market forces. He calls for a national policy agenda that "legitimates the school as a mediating structure for those who are powerless to develop their own potential" (p. 49).

Zaragoza (1987) describes at-risk first graders as children from a low socioeconomic background who often do not speak English, have poor standardized test scores, and perform unsatisfactorily on reading and writing exercises. Many of these students come from the inner city. The students that Pellicano (1987) and Zaragoza allude to manifest the poorest reading behaviors and are so fearful and negative that they often cannot be motivated, especially by threats (see Chapter 12). Psychologists tell us that when an organism is threatened, its perception narrows to the source of the threat. This may be why so many poor students "take it out" on the teacher. Feeling threatened, they don't pay attention to coursework, to commands, or to anything but how to repay the teacher for all the failure and frustration they feel. Like children who have not matured, at-risk students tend to focus entirely too much on the teacher, thus developing an external locus of control (see Chapter 12). Therefore, a teacher's attitude toward students and learning can be powerful; in fact, it appears to be a major factor in promoting interested readers (Wigfield & Asher, 1984).

Further characteristics of at-risk learners.

Identifying and Helping At-Risk Students

Some at-risk learners become successful learners.

The current attention on at-risk students can serve a useful purpose by helping educators focus on identifying and helping these students so that they become successful learners. Care must be taken, however, that the epithet "at risk" is not used as a prediction of failure, resulting in a negative label that perpetuates a self-fulfilling prophecy (Gambrell, 1990). In fact, studies have demonstrated that with careful attention and instruction, many students labeled as being at risk overcome this label to graduate from high school and attend college (Ferguson, 2000).

Some terms are more positive than others.

Of the many terms used to describe at-risk students, a less desirable term is "hard-to-reach/hard-to-teach," which resounds negatively and also seems to place responsibility on the students. The designation "students who present special challenges" may come closer to expressing the challenge to teachers rather than the deficiencies of students; for the present, the term "at risk" seems to be accepted as the popular terminology.

How do we develop the potential of this type of student? First and foremost, teachers need to be positive and caring enough to realize that behaviors that put these students at risk cannot be changed quickly. At-risk students have acquired bad study habits and negative thinking over their entire lifetimes. As Mark Twain once said, "A habit cannot be tossed out the window. It must be coaxed down the stairs a step at a time."

Hilliard (1988) contends that we already have the knowledge we need to help at-risk students. Hilliard draws the following conclusions from research on programs for these students:

Conclusions from research.

- At-risk students can be taught to perform successfully at demanding academic levels.
- Dramatic positive changes in the academic achievement of at-risk students are possible within a short time.
- There is no one way to achieve success with at-risk students.
- There are no absolute critical periods with human beings; it is never too late to learn.
- At-risk students thrive on intellectual challenge, not on low-level remedial work.
- There is no special pedagogy for at-risk students; the pedagogy that works for them is good for all students.

Resilient Students

Unless students can be resilient to challenges such as difficult environmental and academic challenges, as well as stress and setbacks in education, they will face great difficulty in school (Martin, 2002). Students who are resilient can adapt successfully to such challenges despite the difficult circumstances they may face (Borman & Overman, 2004). **Resilient students** are those who, despite hardships and at-risk factors, bounce back and succeed in school (Harvey, 2007; Howard & Johnson, 2000; Patterson, 2001). These students have chosen and learned to cope and respond positively to situations that often spawn anxiety, depression, withdrawal, and underachievement. Research has provided evidence that positive social relationships, positive attitudes and feelings, taking responsibility for controlling personal behaviors, and feelings of competence all encourage resilience (Harvey, 2007).

Teachers and administrators can help encourage resilience by finding means to foster positive teacher–student communication using journals or extracurricular events to uncover traits and talents to like and promote. Harvey (2007) emphasizes the importance of giving praise in public and criticism in private. Teachers can help students develop prosocial behaviors and attitudes of respect for peers and others by providing opportunities for cooperation, decision making, and collaborative problem solving. Listening to and allowing students time to recognize, name, and express emotions while discussing appropriate means for dealing with those emotions can validate feelings and produce positive outcomes. Including students in conversations on expectations, rules, and goals can give them a sense of responsibility and respect while encouraging self-regulation. Recognizing and supporting students' talents contributes to increased feelings of confidence. Harvey (2007) offers seven ways in which resilience can be fostered in school settings:

What factors influence resilience?

1. Provide a caring, supportive learning environment.
2. Foster positive attitudes.
3. Nurture positive emotions.
4. Foster academic self-determination and feelings of competence.
5. Encourage volunteerism.
6. Teach peace-building skills.
7. Ensure healthy habits. (p. 12)

Figure 11.1 depicts a model of factors influencing resilient students, developed by McMillan and Reed (1994). All the characteristics and problems associated with at-risk youth cannot be adequately dealt with in one chapter. Physical and mental disabilities, substance abuse, and many other issues are beyond the scope of this chapter. What we cover are some of the characteristics associated with at-risk youth and school failure that are critically linked to reading achievement: low socioeconomic environments, low self-esteem, English language learners (ELL), special education needs, and struggles with reading. These characteristics are not independent of one another. An at-risk student who speaks English as a second language may come from a low socioeconomic environment or suffer from low self-esteem. Rarely is a student at risk of school failure as a result of only one of these characteristics.

We do not claim that simply using the techniques and strategies described in this chapter will solve our nation's problem with at-risk students. The task is arduous and often frustrating for teachers, and no single set of strategies will solve such an overwhelming problem. We do suggest, however, that the PAR Lesson Framework and the techniques explained in this text, along with much attention to the affective domain of teaching, are steps in the right direction. Certainly studies such as Borman and Overman's (2004) look at mathematics students who "beat the odds" and McMillan

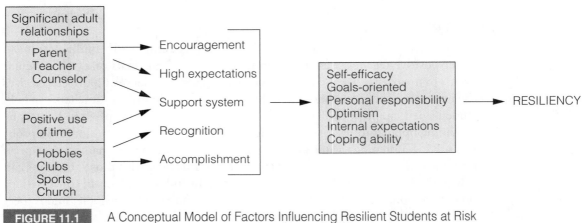

FIGURE 11.1 A Conceptual Model of Factors Influencing Resilient Students at Risk
From *The Journal of At-Risk Issues*, Vol. 1, No. 2 (Fall 1994), Fig 1, p. 32. Used with permission.

and Reed's (1994) interviews with resilient students indicate that this is true. We must begin now to enable this sizable group of failing students to become successful participants in the educational process.

Students from Low Socioeconomic Environments

Who are these students? They usually come from impoverished neighborhoods and often score in the low range on standardized tests. There is not much extra money for anything beyond food and basic clothing. Most of these students are interested in school and eager to learn, but many of them do not get the necessary educational or cultural exposure outside the classroom.

By all accounts far too many students in classrooms today suffer from the effects of living in poverty. The impact of poverty on students' lives is profound, and the consequences are complex. Pogrow (2006) decries the necessity for school reform and a call to action:

> We must confront the fact that, despite a century of alternating progressive and traditional reforms and despite the unselfish and creative efforts of many in high-poverty schools and of the profession as a whole, such schools generally remain highly ineffective in terms of their ability to reduce the learning gap or to accelerate their students after the third grade. (p. 233)

Poverty and School Achievement

The conditions in poor students' environments put them at serious risk of school failure. A study reported by the National Center for Educational Statistics (NCES) (2001) indicates that impoverished kindergarten children perform markedly less well on home educational and literacy experiences than do children from homes above the poverty index. Such low performance, seemingly influenced by poverty, contributes to continuing literacy struggles for adolescents (Hinchman, Alvermann, Boyd, Brozo, & Vacca, 2004). The differences between low-income and middle-income homes indicate that poverty leads to many fewer literacy resources for children (Neuman & Celano, 2001).

The NCES provides an excellent Web site where one can view study reports and charts that summarize data.

The NCES study was conducted in homes, but what about homeless children? They are often not available for such studies because they live in shelters, motels, or campgrounds. Without adequate shelter, they often go hungry and attend school sporadically. "The problem of meeting students' individual needs is compounded in high-poverty schools by student mobility and absenteeism, which make it difficult for teachers to establish continuity" (Pogrow, 2006, p. 225). Their literacy is at peril (Noll & Watkins, 2003).

Adams (1990) notes that children raised in high-literacy homes may have experienced more than 1,000 hours of reading and writing activities before they even arrive at school. Many students from low-socioeconomic families come from homes characterized by oral literacy rather than books, magazines, and adults who read. In an oral environment, children are socialized through the use of stories, parables, proverbs, and legends that are committed to memory (Egan, 1987). Although these are rich language experiences, they are not the ones many teachers assume children possess. Schools often fail to recognize the cultural and linguistic strengths of students from an oral literacy environment.

The effect of enriched language activities in the home.

Poverty is particularly associated with low achievement and dropping out of school, for reasons that include the following factors (Neckerman & Wilson, 1988):

- Poorly educated parents spend less time reading to their children.
- Class or ethnic differences in patterns of language acquisition contribute to difficulties in the early years of schooling.
- As poor children get older, they are much more likely to become teenage parents.
- As poor children get older, they are much more likely to get into trouble with the law or have disciplinary problems in school.

The impact of poverty on literacy.

Gee (2001) has tagged the ways we have of speaking, acting, communicating, and behaving with others as an "identity kit." We begin developing and building it early through interaction with families and communities. Children raised in middle or upper socioeconomic homes are often accustomed to print-rich environments using newspapers, library books, periodicals, and computers, as well as cultural experiences like museums and theaters, which may give them an advantage for negotiating the discourse expected in classroom environments. For students living in poverty, the ways of talking and responding learned in the home or community may conflict with or be a mismatch for the discourse expected in school. This may not only require an additional layer of learning for them but may serve as a source of tension between home and school communities (Williams, 2005/2006). Disadvantage where academic discourse is concerned is a high-stakes proposition. As Williams points out, "Access to power and cultural capital is why academic discourses that reflect the values of the dominant culture are the foundation for most literacy pedagogy" (p. 344).

It is still true that a large majority of teachers in the United States are females from white, middle-class families (NEA, 2003). Even though community populations in most parts of the country are more diverse, interactions and relationships do not often exist in settings where there are many people of color (Seidi, 2007). Smaller concentrations and less exposure to those of other cultures and socioeconomic levels may dilute or distort the differences and can create the illusion that we are all the same in how we think, act, and believe. Thus a teacher may mistakenly expect that a student from poverty should respond to prompts, praise, admonitions, directions, and instruction in the same way as those from middle- or upper-class homes. Some may also hold preconceived notions about poor students' capacity to learn that may result in less effective instruction for them (Lazar, 2006). "A fundamental shift in teachers' knowledge, skills, and assumptions about children in high-poverty schools and students who are culturally and socioeconomically diverse is needed for the achievement gap to narrow" (Williams, 2006, p. 11).

Goal Orientation and Low Socioeconomic Environments

Students who may seem lazy may instead be influenced by low socioeconomic environments.

Many students come to school with a future orientation—able to set goals and to set smaller subgoals in order to reach the larger goals. Some students from low socioeconomic environments, however, have not been exposed to and have not developed the traditional goal orientation associated with school achievement. These students have had little experience with the type of success in which most teachers believe. Teachers should be aware that lack of goal orientation does not necessarily mean that these students are lazy. It may simply mean that the teacher must try a variety of ways to motivate them. Behavior management techniques that require the teacher and student to establish short-range goals may help these students develop the skills necessary for successful school learning.

Instructional Guidelines for Working with Students from Low Socioeconomic Environments

Surveys show that even those at the poverty level in American society see education as the key to a better life (Orfield, 1988). Keep in mind the following guidelines for working with students from low socioeconomic environments:

1. Be sensitive to the home and community environmental conditions that may influence students' behavior and achievements. Students from deprived environments tend to have poor self-concepts and low aspirational levels, to be tardy and absent frequently, to be poorly oriented to school tasks, to display hostility toward school and authorities, and to resist or reject values that are foreign to them (Heilman, Blair, & Rupley, 1986). Examine your background knowledge and find resources (Noll & Watkins, 2003).

2. Be aware of the effect of poor nutrition and health on learning. The capacity to learn is obviously influenced by nutrition and health. Students without sound diets and with health problems are not likely to be able to concentrate and will lack the feeling of well-being that is essential to learning. Teachers must work with families and community social service agencies to diagnose and address the diet and health care needs of students to improve their capacity to learn (Levin, 1988).

3. Take action to change students' lives for the better. Rhodes's (1990) admonition "Don't be a bystander" should be taken to heart by every teacher who works with students who live in a culture of poverty. Richard Rhodes, recipient of the Pulitzer Prize and the National Book Award for his 1987 book *The Making of the Atomic Bomb,* suffered the effects of physical abuse and poverty during early adolescence. In contemplating why he survived with his capacity to love intact, Rhodes concludes that he did so because others not only cared

but acted. He cites several teachers who helped him—in particular, one teacher who saw that he was undernourished and managed to supplement his meager lunch and another who saw that he was poorly clothed and provided clothing.

Teachers should not be bystanders when they see students who suffer from the consequences of poverty. Many resources are available to teachers to help these students: social service agencies that can address the basic needs of families, including health care, shelter, nutrition, and counseling; youth agencies, such as Big Brothers and Big Sisters, that can offer enrichment programs after school, on weekends, and during summers; and adult tutors, particularly senior citizens, who can work with individual students. Timely teacher intervention can make a decisive difference.

STUDENTS WITH LOW SELF-ESTEEM

The relationship between self-esteem and learning is stressed continually throughout the current literature on at-risk students (Patterson, 2001). According to Coopersmith (1967), the four basic components of self-esteem are significance, competence, power, and virtue:

Four basic components of self-esteem.

Significance is found in the acceptance, attention, and affection of others—particularly significant others. At-risk students may feel rejected and ignored and believe that they do not belong.

Competence is developed as a person masters his or her environment. For the student, the school environment is of particular concern. Success in school tasks generates feelings of competence. The at-risk student may experience failure in school tasks, which in turn stifles motivation and promotes feelings of incompetence.

Power resides in the ability to control one's behavior and gain the respect of others. At-risk students may feel helpless and powerless, particularly with respect to school learning, and may feel that their failure cannot be overcome (Martin, 2002).

Virtue is worthiness, as judged by the values of one's culture and of significant others. Feelings of being worthy and valued are necessary for life to be fulfilling. The at-risk student may feel worthless and valueless as a result of school failure. Appearing and behaving somewhat differently from their peers may also make some students feel less worthy or acceptable (Harris & Smith, 1986).

Lack of self-esteem manifests itself most obviously during adolescence, when students are in a state of flux, constantly searching, focusing, and reevaluating themselves. During adolescence students are trying to find a stable image of themselves (Kerr, Nelson, & Lambert, 1987). Unfortunately, by the time some students enter middle school, they have a negative self-image, viewing themselves as helpless and without control over their level of achievement. They behave in ways that cause teachers to label them as unmotivated, immature, uncooperative, and even hostile. Although the behavior of these students may be inappropriate, it most likely reflects their distress at facing failure in the classroom day after day (Hinchman, Alvermann, Boyd, Brozo, & Vacca, 2004).

Motivation and Self-Esteem

Motivation has been defined as the process of initiating, directing, and sustaining behavior. Motivation is viewed as a drive toward competence that is sustained and augmented by the feelings of efficacy that accompany competent interaction with the environment (Connell & Ryan, 1984). Bandura (1977) popularized the term **self-efficacy**—an individual's belief in her or his own effectiveness to cope with given situations. Self-efficacy determines the degree and quality of effort and the limits of persistence of which an individual is capable.

What is self-efficacy?

Self-efficacy is related to a more specific form of motivation: achievement motivation. *Achievement motivation* is the need to try to reach a goal that is determined by expecting and valuing the successful completion of a task (Wigfield & Asher, 1986). According to Dweck (1985), two kinds of goals are important to achievement motivation: learning goals and performance goals. *Learning goals* help students strive toward increased competence; *performance goals* lead students to gain positive judgment and avoid negative judgment.

Building Positive Relationships

The importance of teachers' building positive relationships with at-risk students cannot be stressed too much. Brendtro, Brokenleg, and Bockern (1990) offer guidelines for building relationships that promote self-esteem; the following suggestions are adapted from their work (pp. 62–63).

Building a positive relationship is a process of giving that is typified by caring, knowledge, respect, and responsibility (Fromm, 1956). Caring is real concern for the life and growth of the student. Knowledge is genuine understanding of the students' feelings, even if they are not readily apparent. Respect is the ability to see and appreciate students as they are. Responsibility means being ready to act to meet the needs of the student.

Tracy Kidder (1989) writes in *Among Schoolchildren* about a boy who typifies low self-esteem and an impoverished environment. This fifth grader attempted to create a science project after much encouragement from his teacher. On the day the projects were due, he "forgot" his, and Chris, his teacher, was furious. She sent him home for it and when he returned, she started to scold him. When she saw that his project was an utter failure, she realized that he had tried but failed because of his lack of resources and low self-image. The teacher then demonstrated respect and responsibility for this troubled student.

CRISIS AS OPPORTUNITY

The struggling students who are most difficult to work with are those who create trouble rather than friendships. These students are often labeled "hard to reach": If one were to wait for them to warm up to the adult, one might wait forever. Many effective teachers have long recognized the great hidden potential of turning crisis into opportunity, as in the following story shared by a high school teacher:

Among Schoolchildren is a narrative account of a teacher who provides sound instruction in a caring manner to an at-risk child.

> Rob entered first period class 10 minutes after the bell, looking disheveled and agitated. I asked for his late pass and he swore and stormed from the room. I stepped into the hall to confront him about his behavior but recalled our discussion of "crisis as opportunity." I called him back and asked simply, "What's wrong, Rob?" "What's wrong!" he exclaimed. "I'm driving to school and my car gets hit. After I get through with the police, I'm late into the building and get stopped by the principal. When I tell him what happened he tells me to get to class. Now you send me out of class!" He whirled around starting down to the office. "Where are you going?" I asked. "To get a pass!" he replied. "That's OK, Rob, enough has gone wrong for one day; you're welcome in class." His hostility melted in tears. After a moment he regained his composure and thanked me, and we went back in the room. (Brendtro, Brokenleg, & Bockern, 1990, p. 62)

The teacher in this example could easily have responded in a manner that would have alienated this student. Instead the teacher used this crisis situation as an opportunity for relationship building. When a teacher manages a crisis with sensitivity, relationship bonds become more secure.

CARING FOR ALL STUDENTS

Struggling students—students who suffer from low self-esteem, those who are withdrawn, or those from a different economic or cultural background—may not find others lining up to build relationships with them. These are the students who are sometimes ignored or rejected. These students often believe that teachers are uncaring, unfair, and ineffective (Wehlange & Rutter, 1986). Teachers need to take affirmative action to enhance the standing of these students with their peers. Doing this requires that teachers actively focus on identifying the strengths of these at-risk students. Harvey (2007) recommends encouraging students to develop individual talents that will build feelings of competence and confidence. Talents like dancing, illustrating, or even rock climbing can provide multifaceted benefits that may serve as a source of joy and help when dealing with stress.

Lipsitz (1995) points out that "we are not being respectful or caring when we fail to teach children to read, compute, and write; nor are we respectful or caring when we hold different expectations for children because of their race, gender, or economic status" (p. 666). Bosworth's (1996) observations indicate that teachers tend to engage in neutral rather than caring interactions with students. Yet "for many nonwhite students, caring is more concrete and is translated through such activities as 'spending time with someone,' 'sharing,' and 'listening when someone has a problem'" (p. 689). It is not uncommon for children from adverse backgrounds to expect negative or apathetic responses from adults based on their past experiences. Harvey (2007) emphasizes that if we hope "to reverse this pattern, adults must deliberately, repeatedly, and genuinely communicate positive regard" (p. 11).

EARNING TRUST

Perhaps the central ingredient in building positive and effective relationships is trust. According to Brendtro, Brokenleg, and Bockern (1990), trust between the student and the teacher develops over time in three predictable stages:

Three stages of building relationships.

Casing: In this stage, the student needs to "check out" the teacher. The student observes how the teacher behaves, how much power the teacher wields, and how others respond to this adult. All these observations are crucial data to students who may view virtually all teachers and adults as threatening.

Limit testing: During this stage the student will "test out" interactions with the teacher. A student who distrusts a teacher's friendly manner may misbehave or provoke the teacher to determine whether this person is really different. In this situation the teacher should take a calm but firm approach to avoid either "giving in" or confirming the student's view that this adult is really just like all the others and not to be trusted.

Predictability: The previous two stages, casing and limit testing, provide a foundation for developing a more secure relationship between the student and the teacher. Consistency is important to building a trusting relationship. In such a relationship, each party—the student and the teacher—knows what to expect from the other. In some situations where trust building is difficult, it may be better for the teacher to simply acknowledge, "I know you don't feel you can trust me yet, and that's all right." It takes patience and persistence to build trust, and it is important to remember that trust begets trust.

Guidelines for Working with Students with Low Self-Esteem

Intuition tells us that when students feel better about themselves, they do better in school. Improving the self-esteem of students is a major concern of most teachers but especially for teachers of at-risk students.

1. Focus on the strengths of students with low self-esteem. At-risk students typically have low self-esteem because they have not been successful in school. These students, however, may have had many successful experiences outside the classroom. With some discussion and probing, students often identify successful aspects of their lives that they may not have recognized before. Spend time having students recall, write about, draw, and share their past achievements. Teachers must plan instruction that allows students with low self-esteem to demonstrate their strengths.

2. Make sure these students are given opportunities to read from materials that are within their reading proficiency level. Students need to be successful in their reading in order to build positive self-concepts as readers. This means that the material should be familiar enough so that the student can use sense-making strategies. When readers continually have to deal with text that is too difficult, they expend their energy constructing a hazy model of meaning and do not have the opportunity to elaborate on the content or strategies needed to enhance comprehension (Walker, 1990).

3. Provide opportunities for students to engage in cooperative learning. Research conducted by Johnson and Johnson (1987) and Slavin (1983) and his associates provides evidence that cooperative learning promotes higher self-esteem, greater social acceptance, more friendships, and higher achievement than competitive or individual learning activities. For instance, Forget and Morgan (1995) found that when reading to learn was emphasized in a school-within-a-school setting in working with at-risk youngsters in cooperative situations, attitudes and school attendance improved significantly. Cooperative learning experiences such as those described in Chapter 6 are beneficial for all students but especially for those with low self-esteem. Students can be organized into small groups that are monitored and rewarded for both individual and group accomplishments. Cooperative learning can be used in any content area, as well as for reading and writing lessons and activities. The major principle of cooperative learning is that members of a team can succeed only if all members of the group are successful. Students have a vested interest in ensuring that the other group members learn.

English Second Language Students

At the turn of this new century, increasing numbers of students whose first language is not English are arriving in classrooms daily (National Clearinghouse for Bilingual Education, 2002). While English second language (ESL) students are diverse members of our population, they are not necessarily at risk. Unfortunately, sometimes false assumptions are made when these children have difficulty demonstrating knowledge and skills considered "normal" for children in the grade level in which they are placed when they are assessed using traditional assessment measures (Williams, 2006). As a result, they may be inappropriately categorized, labeled, and identified for special education or alternative education. However, too many teachers have not been prepared to understand ESL students, so this section presents several issues that may affect their school performance. First some important terms that are used to describe ESL situations are introduced.

What is the difference between an immigrant and a refugee? How might this difference influence learning?

People for whom English is a second language are sometimes designated as non-native speakers of English, or by the abbreviation L2 for second language speakers (Leki, 1992). They are sometimes called ESL (English second language) students. Families from other countries come to the United States for various reasons. Students who left their home countries with families who purposefully chose to move, seeking a different way of life, are **immigrants**. Other families fled their home countries because of unstable and dangerous conditions in their homeland; they might not have wanted to move but left because they were no longer safe in their own countries. They are **refugees**. In either case, students might be confused and intimidated by their new surroundings; but refugees may have more challenges to overcome.

What is the difference between acculturation and assimilation? How might this difference influence learning?

How well ESL students settle into their new environment depends on several conditions. First students should be encouraged to feel proud of and retain their cultural heritage; when they integrate by maintaining their first language and culture and integrating as necessary, they are **acculturating** to English and the new country. If they feel forced to give up or deny their traditions, they may **assimilate**—or become much like others in this country—but lose an important part of themselves. In the case of assimilation, students may begin to resent the forced choice and develop low self-esteem. Schumann (1978) identifies conditions for successful acculturation and language acquisition in his now classic model. The best learning environment would include social variables such as an even balance between the target and native cultures, so that the learner does not rely more heavily on the native culture; an expectation that the two cultures will intermingle; a balance of the two cultures so that one does not dominate; an expectation that acculturation will occur; and positive attitudes toward both cultures.

The monitor model and five hypotheses.

In his monitor model, Krashen (1982, 1989) argues for a balance between determinism and environmental factors as contributors to second language acquisition. His model comprises five hypotheses. The first hypothesis is that any language is acquired unconsciously more than through direct learning. The power of acquisition ought to be used more effectively in teaching ESL. For instance, less reliance on organized learning through workbooks and more reliance on learner environment are necessary components of effective ESL instruction. The next two hypotheses are interrelated. Learners monitor their learning, but they need sufficient time to focus on form and specific knowledge of when to apply rules. Because these conditions are difficult to meet during most communication—which demands quick responses—explicit rule teaching and error correction will slow down or impede progress. The natural order hypothesis suggests that language learners acquire language "rules" in a natural, predictable sequence rather than by direct instruction. Grammatical features will evolve in spite of a prescribed sequence. Studies of English orthographic development (Bear & Templeton, 1996) seem to support this hypothesis. Fourth, as a logical extension, natural communication seems to provide a relaxed setting for language learning. Learners do best when language input is comprehensible and just beyond their current level of knowledge. Krashen calls this comprehensible input "$i + 1$," whereby i is input and 1 is the challenge level. Fifth, socioemotional factors strongly influence language learning and may account for older learners who master a second language despite the critical age factor. Krashen calls this the **affective filter hypothesis**; he writes that this is the single most important variable in language learning. When the filter is high, it represents a tense, highly anxious socioemotional climate. Learning is greatly impeded.

BICs and CALP.

Cummins (1979, 1994) argues that a distinction must be made between conversational language proficiency, which he calls **basic interpersonal communication skills (BICs)**, and **cognitive academic language proficiency (CALP)**, which is more formal academic instruction. Stoller (1999) calls this **English for academic purposes (EAP)** and notes its importance in a school content-based curriculum.

Learning English for conversational and functional purposes is less cognitively stressful and more immediately practical than is learning English for academic purposes. This notion supports Krashen's fourth hypothesis: that natural communication in a relaxed setting is the best vehicle for learning English as a starting point for ESL students.

Several second language experts discuss the variable of time in language acquisition. Cummins (1994) suggests that achieving conversational proficiency might take approximately two years, whereas achieving academic proficiency might take as much as five to seven years. Leki (1992) writes that time is the single most important factor in learning ESL, as do Peregoy and Boyle (1997). A study by Lee and Schallert (1997) suggests that solid second language proficiency is a better facilitator of literacy acquisition in a second language than is literacy proficiency in the first language. This second language proficiency takes time, as Snow, Burns, and Griffin (1998) indicate when they recommend that ESL children develop oral proficiency before beginning reading instruction; they indicate that oral proficiency may take as much as a year. Helping students make the transition from a first to a second language involves special attention to "linguistic bridges" that show the learner how the languages are similar and different (Gibbons, 2003). The process takes time.

ENGLISH LANGUAGE LEARNERS

 Public Law 93-380 (enacted in 1974) stipulates that there be provisions for bilingual education in virtually every aspect of the educational process. This law recognizes that students with limited English proficiency have special educational needs and that teachers must take into account the cultural heritage into which each student was born (Harris & Smith, 1986). With demographers continuing to predict increasing numbers of immigrant and refugee students from Central and South America, western Europe, and Asia, teachers must consider how instruction can be modified to meet the special needs of those with limited English proficiency. A major issue, cultural discontinuity, can have an impact on effective instruction.

Cultural discontinuity is the term that Reyhner and Garcia (1989) use to describe the serious internal conflict brought about by a disparity between the language and the culture of the home and of the school. Both immigrants and refugees may experience a language and cultural environment in the home that differs significantly from the language and cultural environment of the school. The differences may be so pronounced that, for some students, there is serious conflict. A student may be placed in the position of having to choose between the school's or the home's language and culture. According to Reyhner and Garcia (1989), such a choice is counterproductive to the educational development of the student. Rejection of the home background may result in a serious loss of self-esteem, while rejection of the language and culture of the school may result in a serious loss of educational opportunities (Williams, 2005/2006). This dilemma is called **culture shock**. When learners are refugees, the rejection is compounded by a deep sense of loss and guilt about fleeing, often called **survivor guilt**.

Visit the *Reading to Learn in the Content Areas* Web site at http://academic.cengage.com/education/richardson, Chapter 11, to find links to articles by Katherine Au about culturally responsive instruction.

Teachers should learn about the different cultures represented in their classrooms and provide instruction that encourages acceptance of native languages and cultures while facilitating the learning of English (Au, 2001; Mohr, 2004). By understanding cultural and even some language differences and similarities, teachers can create and blend examples and analogies into lessons to clarify meaning for students while building community and respect within the classroom. As lessons are prepared, it is important to pay attention to vocabulary, figurative language, and multiple-meaning words that may cause confusion so that appropriate background can be built. Making these considerations (among others) is **culturally responsive instruction (CRI)**:

> Successfully teaching students from culturally and linguistically diverse backgrounds—especially students from historically marginalized groups—involves more than just applying specialized teaching techniques. It demands a new way of looking at teaching that is grounded in an understanding of the role of culture and language in learning. (Villegas & Lucas, 2007, p. 29)

Another equally important aspect is enlisting support from the home. When the entire family is involved, cultural discontinuity is a less severe problem. Shanahan, Mulhern, and Rodriguez-Brown (1995) describe project FLAME, which helps Latino parents support their children's school learning. In fact, if a student must struggle with functioning in two disparate cultures, that of the home and that of the school, the child's literacy learning may actually be impeded (Schmidt, 1995).

Differences among cultures with respect to social style and attitudes also have implications for instruction. A number of studies (Downing, 1973; Downing, Ollila, & Oliver, 1975; Heath, 1986; Schieffelin & Cochran-Smith, 1984) confirm that students from non–school-oriented cultures do not have the same literacy skills as students from school-oriented cultures. The value and utility of literacy in the culture, and particularly in the home environment, influence the development of literacy skills. A study by Lee, Stigler, and Stevenson (1986) found that the superior reading performance of Chinese students in Taiwan, as compared to their American counterparts, was related to social and cultural variables such as time spent in class, amount of homework, and parental attitudes. This study suggests that the Chinese students were better readers because they worked harder and were encouraged and supervised more frequently by parents and teachers. High motivation is the most powerful factor in successful learning of a second language (Leki, 1992).

Visit *Reading Online* and read Nagel's (2002) article about the ABCs of the cultural and communication model. The URL is located in the references for this book.

One model that can raise cultural awareness levels of both teachers and students within a classroom or school community is the ABCs of cultural understanding and communication, developed by Schmidt (1998) (see Activity 11.1). Everyone has a life story, and this gives us permission to thoughtfully consider and tell that story, learn about the stories of others, and discover in what ways we are alike and different. The steps of Schmidt's model are adaptable for a variety of grade levels. This type of experience helps students better understand their own culture and that of another. Nagel (2002) found that when she paired students with others within their classroom, they were quite surprised to find they had so much in common as well as many interesting and admirable qualities not previously known.

1. *Autobiography:* Students can talk with family members, reflect, and record events that have shaped their own life stories. They can include descriptions of personal, educational, athletic, or other accomplishments; special family, holiday, and religious traditions; successes and disappointments; and even accounts of family or ancestral milestones.

2. *Biography:* Students select and interview someone from a culture other than their own. Depending on the confidence and ability of the students, these interviews could be unstructured or semistructured. In small or large groups, students could brainstorm possible questions to select from, modify, or add to for an interview framework. The interview could be audiotaped or conducted over more than one sitting. Once the interview is completed, students write a biography, including key events and important details to best describe the individual and his or her culture. The student should then give the person interviewed the opportunity to read what was written in order to clarify or correct misinformation or misinterpretations.

3. *Cross-cultural analysis and appreciation of differences:* Students consider and chart the similarities and differences between their own life stories and those of the people interviewed. This can be done independently or with the people interviewed.

4. *Cultural self-analysis of differences* (Finkbeiner & Koplin, 2002): In this step students reflect upon and react to the findings in the chart created in Step 3. As differences and similarities are uncovered, students need to think about their feelings of comfort or discomfort and examine the causes. The results can be written or simply discussed.

5. *Communication and home–school connections:* Findings and understandings resulting from previous steps can be used to modify classroom activities and communication with the home and community to build relationships and tolerance.

Adapted from Nagle's ABC model, 2002.

The elements of the assignments include several aspects that are motivating and contribute to persistence necessary for group relationships. Knowledge, power, and affection are all interwoven within the steps. We all have knowledge of self and generally consider it engaging to explore. Each has the power to select what will be shared. The type of listening associated with caring is involved as interviews are conducted and findings are negotiated to come to an understanding. Finally, students and teachers can come to value new perspectives and viewpoints by seeing the world through another's eyes.

School Programs for English Language Learners

When ESL students arrive at school with some proficiency, but not fluency, in English, they are often labeled as limited English proficient (LEP) or as students with limited English proficiency (SLEP). However, a more recent and less deficit-implying term is **English language learner (ELL)**. Also, some designate these ESL students as "speakers of other languages."

Two types of programs are prevalent in American schools for ELL pupils: an ESL/TESOL approach or a bilingual approach. These programs are usually conducted by a specialist in teaching **English as a second language (ESL)**. When students receive language instruction in special programs, classroom teachers should be aware of what the specialist is doing and monitor student progress to ensure that students receive adequate classroom opportunities to develop English, reading, and writing skills (Mason & Au, 1990; Mohr, 2004).

The first type of program is ESL (English second language) or **TESOL** (teaching English to speakers of other languages); this program emphasizes the learning of English exclusively. Instruction in English progresses from oral skills (listening and speaking) to written skills (reading and writing). The methodology emphasizes English language skills and learner-centered activities that stress meaningful communication. ESL/TESOL is somewhat similar to programs that teach English-speaking students a second language. The latter usually focus more on CALP, whereas the former focuses on basic communication. The main goal of ESL/TESOL is to help students attain the language skills needed for success in school as quickly as possible. Most ESL/TESOL programs now include not only oral but also reading and writing skills. Chamot & O'Malley (1994) describe the cognitive academic language-learning approach (CALLA) as a "method of reading instruction for second language learners which provides students with authentic texts that include both content area material and literature to integrate oral and written language skills so that students can develop all aspects of academic language and develop strategic reading and writing through explicit instruction in learning strategies" (p. 94). The goal of ESL/TESOL classes is to move students to the regular classroom as soon as possible. Many ESL/TESOL classrooms have learners from 10 or more different countries, and the only common language is English.

The second type of program is **bilingual education**, which provides instruction in both English and the native language in the same classroom. Separate instructional periods are provided, one in English and one in the students' native language. In a variation of this approach—transitional bilingual education—bilingual teachers begin instruction in the students' native language and gradually introduce English. A review of the history of bilingual education indicates that this approach can be very effective (Rothstein, 1998). Of course it works only where all learners speak a common language and need to learn English as their second language.

Instructional programs for ELL students may emphasize English, emphasize the students' first language, or give equal attention to both languages. Mason and Au (1990) caution that teachers should realize that bilingual education is a controversial topic. Teachers must be aware of the view of the community and school system concerning bilingual education. In some communities, parents may feel strongly that their children's education should emphasize bilingual competence; in other communities, parents want their children to speak and read only in English.

Instructional Guidelines for Working with ELL Students

Russell (1995) describes a program called **sheltered content instruction**, which focuses on "teaching subject matter through the principles of second language acquisition" (p. 30). First, the teacher activates students' prior knowledge and introduces new experiences. Second, new concepts and ideas are added. Third, students are encouraged to apply the new knowledge. This method is similar to the PAR system. Russell explains that sheltered language instruction calls for a balance of top-down (emphasis on prior knowledge, context, and cognition) and bottom-up (emphasis on text and language features) because the needs of the ESL learner are different from those of a proficient user of English. But the focus is on subject matter. Sheltered language instruction might best occur in an ESL classroom rather than in a regular content classroom; but knowing about it may help regular classroom teachers accommodate ESL learners. Immersion in English without any sheltered instruction becomes most effective only with the third generation of English-as-a-second-language speakers (Rothstein, 1998).

When ELL students are included in regular classrooms, teachers of content subjects will be their instructors too. These students certainly can learn the same curriculum in language arts, science, and math as native English speakers (Minicucci, et al., 1995). By studying eight schools with exemplary programs for ELL students, Minicucci, and her colleagues identified several characteristics of successful instruction:

1. Innovative approaches encouraging students to become independent learners.
2. Use of cooperative learning.
3. Making parents feel comfortable at the school.
4. Intercommunication with teachers, parents, and community.
5. "Families" within the school to create strong attachments.
6. Innovative uses of time, particularly so students have more learning time.
7. A concentrated focus on the goal of learning English.

Teachers should not underestimate ELL competencies. Verplaeste (1998) found that teachers issued more directives to and asked fewer and lower-level cognitive questions of ESL students in their content classes. Teachers were protective but also impatient about waiting for ESL students' responses. Mohr and Mohr (2007) recommend that teachers anticipate difficulties and proactively scaffold classroom talk for these students rather than allowing them to remain silent. A response protocol they have developed offers specific examples and ways for building language skills within the general classroom. To avoid instructional traps when working with ELL students, teachers should keep the following guidelines in mind:

1. ESL students should be assessed and placed in appropriate programs. Specialists should be available in school districts to perform this kind of assessment. Content teachers should communicate with these specialists. Further, teachers

should make sure they consistently evaluate student work and make sure that ELL learning opportunities are maximized (Mohr, 2004).

2. Teachers need to learn as much as possible about students' languages and cultures. Ample evidence indicates that background knowledge is a significant factor in reading comprehension (see Chapters 3 and 4). Teachers should become as knowledgeable as possible about the native cultures of students. Field and Aebersold (1990) suggest that the teacher determine answers to the following questions: Is a student's native culture literate? What is the common method of instruction in this native culture? Are the relatives living in the present home literate in English? Is English spoken in the home? Is reading (in any language) a part of their home activities? It is relatively easy for a teacher to determine answers to these questions by interviewing the student, parents, relatives, or other members of the culture. Using local reference sources such as community groups, libraries, and knowledgeable professionals can also provide insights about other cultures. Culturegrams—brief descriptions of a culture—can be obtained by writing embassies or searching on the Internet.

3. Model how oral language ability precedes reading. Students can read what they can say and understand. Accordingly, students should begin reading instruction in their native language, or they should receive instruction that focuses on language development before formal reading instruction. Snow, Burns, and Griffin (1998) recommend that "an adequate level of proficiency in spoken English" (p. 10) is necessary before reading instruction begins.

4. Whenever possible, use reading materials for instruction that reflect the backgrounds and cultures of students. Teachers can supplement existing reading materials with literature representative of the native cultures represented in the classroom. Teachers can implement daily teacher read-aloud sessions using trade books that feature minority cultures. Students can be encouraged to contribute proverbs, recipes, and stories from parents and grandparents that can be used as the basis for experience stories (Reyhner & Garcia, 1989).

5. Create learning situations in which students can develop a sense of security and acceptance. Language proficiency is developed through oral and written activities that direct students' attention to significant features of English. Students can gain fluency in English through working with proficient English-speaking peers, learning key phrases for school tasks, and reading predictable texts. For instance, threaded discussion boards can facilitate practice in meaningful use of English in the content context (Bikowski & Kessler, 2002).

6. Employ thematic units (Chapter 6) and literature so ELLs can explore their own identities as they learn about your content (Vann & Fairbairn, 2003; Vyas, 2004).

7. Be conscious of the issues related to working successfully with students from other cultures, without feeling restricted by them. Teachers are in a unique position to positively affect the attitudes of children from different cultures by adopting methods, materials, and ideas that are linguistically and culturally sympathetic to the students' backgrounds (Cooter, 1990).

Field and Aebersold (1990) suggest, "What is most important is that we remain aware of how culture functions as a cognitive filter for all of us, shaping our values and assumptions, the ways we think about reading, and the ways we teach reading" (p. 410).

8. Practice patience. Time is the single greatest factor influencing success for ESL learners (Leki, 1992; Peregoy & Boyle, 1997); they need time to acculturate, to learn language, and to apply that learning to the act of reading. Teachers need to be willing to provide L2 students enough time, get to know them, consult with them often, and adapt their curricula.

Instructional Misconceptions about ELL Students

It is easy to fall into the trap of believing that teaching ELL students is just a matter of good teaching. Harper and de Jong (2004) explain four commonly held misconceptions:

1. Exposure and interaction will result in English language learning. Though daily exposure and opportunities for verbal exchange are important for language development, they are not sufficient. Inclusion of grammatical, morphological, and phonological elements is important for building understanding and facilitating use. Social interchange with native English-speaking peers in small-group exercises is frequently reduced to one- or two-word exchanges that limit language development. Frequent practice and appropriate feedback are needed to extend and develop both language and content development.

2. All ELLs learn English in the same way and at the same rate. Younger learners often readily develop social language skills as they work on building their understanding of more formal academic language. Older learners, having already well-developed academic language skills in their first languages, may instead learn to read and write formal English first as they grapple with affective and sociocultural issues experienced by adolescents. Rate is an individual matter, just as it is with learning other skills and concepts.

3. Good teaching for native speakers is good teaching for ELLs. Though good research-based instructional strategies used with native speakers are important for ELLs, the demands imposed by the terms and language inherent to the subject or topic, as well as the procedures for activities and assignments, must be recognized and reconciled.

4. Effective instruction means nonverbal support. While visuals and graphic organizers can be valuable tools for decreasing the language demands of instruction, care should be taken as well to use nonverbal aids as a means to encourage vocabulary and concept development.

So although strategies that work well for native English-speaking students may also work well for ELLs, additional consideration must be given to particular needs and instructional demands posed by language.

Techniques That Work Well with ELL Students

The majority of techniques and approaches that ESL experts propose are centered around language arts, of course. These approaches use some of the strategies that we stress in this text, such as cooperative learning, response journals, higher-level thinking skills, use of visuals to teach vocabulary and concepts, directed readings, and use of predictions in reading. Writing (discussed further in Chapter 10) is an excellent tool for content teachers. Cook and Gonzales (1995) suggest that ESL students be encouraged to visualize and manipulate literature they read because "second language learners need a social context for both understanding and producing English." Although such activities are not new—visualization through drawing is much like post-graphic organizers—they encourage students to use what they already know in making connections to the new language and culture. ESL learners who regard text as "only a tool to learn that language" (p. 639), rather than as a way to learn about a new culture, do not learn as effectively and efficiently (Chi, 1995).

The **group frame** from the guided language experience model is recommended for reading and writing and is directly applicable to content area material (Brechtel, 1992). Using this strategy, the teacher takes dictation (pertaining to the content area) from the class and records the information on a chart. This information is used to model revising and editing for the group. The revised dictation is reproduced and used for the reading lesson. Activity 11.2 shows a group frame from an elementary mathematics lesson about flowcharts and algorithms. In this example the teacher can begin with the child's native language (in this case Spanish) or start with English and dictate later in the second language.

ACTIVITY *11.2* GROUP FRAME: ELEMENTARY MATHEMATICS

Dictation from Students	Dictation from Students
We use a series of steps to solve a problem.	Usamos una serie de pasos para resolver un problema.
We can make a chart showing how we solved the problem.	Podemos hacer un esquema que nos muestra cómo resoldimos el problema.
The answer to the problem should be at the end of the chart.	La solución del problema debería estar al final del esquema.
Revised Dictation	**Revised Dictation**
A series of steps to solve a problem is called an *algorithm*.	Una serie de pasos para resolver un problema se llama un "algorithm."
The picture of this is called a *flowchart*.	El diagrama se llama un "flowchart."
Shapes of things in the flowchart tell you something.	Las formas de los pasos en el esquema te indican algo.

A modified anticipation guide (introduced in Chapter 3) can net very positive results. A group of 10 adult ESL students, 7 men and 3 women, from Vietnam, Egypt, Bangladesh, China, El Salvador, Colombia, and Hong Kong, reacted to the statements shown in Activity 11.3. First the teacher wrote the statements on the chalkboard to encourage reading in English. Class discussion about the students' opinions, based on their experiences in the United States, was conducted. After discussion, a passage about an American family was read. The students were eager to volunteer information and were interested in finding out about family life in one another's cultures as well as in the United States. The teacher noted that she had fewer requests during the reading time for explanation of vocabulary, and she speculated that coming to the passage with a good idea of the concepts helped the students use context clues to make sense of unfamiliar vocabulary. This activity engaged ESL students in listening, speaking, and reading in English, and it respected their various cultures.

A vocabulary activity that requires ESL students to work in pairs to write sentences about new words is similar to capsule vocabulary. For an ESL example, see Chapter 9.

Multitext activities are especially important for ESL learners. When books are provided at many levels and on many topics, ESL learners have opportunities to select, read, reread, and practice (Gee, 1999; Koskinen et al., 1999). Hadaway and Mundy (1999) share how they used picture books about science topics to create

---

ACTIVITY *11.3* MODIFIED ANTICIPATION GUIDE FOR ESL ADULTS

MOST MARRIAGES LAST A LONG TIME

Most students felt that marriages in the United States do not last a long time. Discussion turned to the question "What is a long time?" The students decided it meant a lifetime. We talked about divorce in the United States and how divorce is viewed in other cultures.

WOMEN IN AMERICA ARE EQUAL TO MEN IN THE UNITED STATES

Most students agreed that women in the United States are equal to men. After much laughter, the Vietnamese men commented that American women seem to be superior to American men because they always get to go first!

TELEVISION IS BAD FOR CHILDREN

Although the class generally disagreed with the statement, several students commented that television can be both good and bad for children. We talked about the need for parents to be selective and to monitor programs. Watching TV is one way to learn English.

WORKING MOTHERS NEGLECT THEIR CHILDREN

This statement generated the most controversy and debate among the students. The student from Egypt felt that mothers needed to be with children for long times; other students brought up the idea of quality time.

Developed by Karen Curling.

compare/contrast maps, poetry, semantic maps, and jot charts with secondary ESL students. Watching videos and movies and then discussing the content and American culture depicted in them is a good way to combine oral and written media (Pally, 1998). Sadly, books representing children from other countries are not as available as teachers and students would prefer.

Special Education Students

Special education is defined as schooling for students "very different in one or more ways in intellectual, physical, social, or emotional development from the usual student" (Harris & Hodges, 1995, p. 238). Special education students are diverse learners, and their differences may place them at risk unless they receive appropriate accommodations. If their differences are severe, students are usually placed in special classrooms for all or part of their accommodations. The current educational preference, however, is **inclusion** (called *mainstreaming* in the 1990s), which is designed to include students in regular classrooms as often as possible.

In 2005–2006, 6.7 million children (ages 3–21) received special education services; this was an increase of 81 percent from 3.7 million in 1976–1977 (U.S. Department of Education, NCES, 2007). This means that 14 percent of the total public school enrollment for 2005–2006 qualified for and received services. When students are included in regular classrooms, content teachers must understand what special education needs their students possess and how to provide appropriate accommodations. In this section we introduce some terms that may be helpful, issues that content teachers should be aware of, and suggestions and strategies that content teachers should use.

Categories of Disability

Some students possess significant developmental disabilities. These are usually children born with birth defects, serious sensory or physical disabilities, or cognitive delays. They are most often diagnosed early in life and begin receiving intervention even before beginning kindergarten. Although PL (Public Law) 94-142, Education of All Handicapped Children, was originally passed for this group, they constitute only 10 percent of children now included in special education (Horn & Tynan, 2001). Accommodations made for them include interpreters, Braille resources, curb cuts for wheelchairs, and enough space to use appropriate equipment for learning.

A second subgroup of special education students includes those with conduct or behavioral problems. These students might be labeled as having "oppositional defiant disorder" or "conduct disorder." They will often be enrolled in special programs to help them become accountable for their behaviors and cope calmly with stress.

The largest group of students with special education needs includes those with mild forms of neurological dysfunction—learning disabilities, often labeled as **SLD** for **specific learning disorder** and encompassing seven areas of disability: listening, speaking, basic reading of words, reading comprehension, written expression, mathematics problem solving, and mathematics calculations. The number of students classified as SLD has increased dramatically over the past 20 years (Swanson, 2000). Also included are students with mild forms of neurological dysfunction or mild mental retardation, such as educable mentally retarded (EMR) students and those with attention deficit disorders (ADD). These students are most often included in regular classrooms and must receive appropriate accommodation.

Gifted children present special challenges also.

Although they are not usually thought of as having a disability or as special education students, gifted students also require accommodation in their learning to engage them beyond the regular curriculum. These students are a challenge because teachers must ensure that they will become autonomous learners who have appropriate skills and attitudes. Gifted students need a differentiated curriculum so that they can learn at their own pace within the classroom (Betts, 2004). Sometimes the feeling is that these students will learn and thrive no matter what is done within the classroom. Though they may be quick to grasp a concept, unless they are challenged and guided to explore and think analytically and creatively, boredom and ambivalence may impede their progress. And although gifted students can help struggling learners, repeatedly using them in this way may not enhance their learning appropriately. Research has indicated that gifted learners need opportunities to work in homogeneous groupings at times to better facilitate and accelerate their learning (Kulik & Kulik, 1987).

Technology is an excellent resource to tap the creativity of gifted children (DelSiegle, 2004).

Gallagher (1998) points out that gifted students do not receive the challenges they need; their test scores often inflate a school's test performance, but they themselves do not benefit from the curriculum they should have. Gifted students who are also learning disabled present a special challenge. They do best when identified early, especially when their specific gifts are recognized. They require a supportive environment that stresses resilience (Dole, 2000).

Issues in Special Education

Laws govern special education, as well as ELL instruction.

PL (Public Law) 94-142, Education of All Handicapped Children, was renamed the **Individuals with Disabilities Education Act (IDEA)** in 1990. This law states that all children with disabilities will receive a free and appropriate education in the least restrictive environment. In 1997 the act was amended to become IDEA 97. The most significant change for regular education teachers was the expansion of the term "other health impaired" to include specific language for students with ADD or ADHD (H=Hyperactivity). Final regulations for IDEA 97 were released in March 1999. These regulations are meant to ensure that all children with disabilities receive a free and appropriate public education, with special education emphases and services that meet the children's needs. The effectiveness of educational efforts are to be assessed.

Visit this book's companion Web site, Chapter 11, to find links for IDEA and others related to teaching students with learning disabilities.

The reauthorization of IDEA (2004) gave states a new option to use in identifying students for special education services. They may now choose to use **response to intervention** (**RTI**) criteria in place of the IQ–achievement discrepancy formulas. This is considered particularly good news for linguistically and culturally diverse students in that the number of inappropriate referrals and placements should be reduced (Vaughn & Fuchs, 2003). The idea is that before placing students in special education services based primarily on a battery of tests, a student would be provided instruction using evidenced-based interventions in tiers or stages; decisions would result based on the student's responses and progress. In this way students would get reasonable opportunities to learn skills and concepts in a general classroom setting with the benefit of relevant quality intervention before being labeled as having learning disabilities. The first tier would involve quality intervention and careful monitoring within a regular classroom. If a student did not progress to levels expected for his or her age and grade level, then the second tier of more intensive instruction would be provided. Again, if the student failed to progress adequately, a third tier or special education placement might be necessary. RTI models vary in method and implementation, but the structure and framework must be the same (Fuchs & Fuchs, 2006; Klingner & Edwards, 2006).

Klingner and Edwards (2006) caution that study results should be carefully considered when selecting instruction for each RTI tier. Interventions found to be effective in studies conducted in laboratory or clinical settings may not meet with the same success in public school environments. Another consideration is that students participating in studies should have attributes closely resembling those of the students for which an intervention is to be used. Often samples include few, if any, culturally and linguistically diverse students, making it difficult to generalize findings or effects of interventions for special populations. This again goes back to the idea that evidence-based instruction without culturally responsive elements may not affect the learning of diverse individuals in the same way as those of the dominant culture. A final caution is to consider the possibility that the classroom instruction a student is receiving may be inadequate. Poor progress can result from deficient instruction instead of student disability. When a model or intervention is selected, care must be taken to remain true to the model when putting it into practice. Deviations can negatively affect outcomes.

Retention and transfer of knowledge learned in school is a critical problem for special education students (Gersten & Baker, 1998). Mastropieri, Scruggs, and Butcher (1997) found that 35 percent of students with learning disabilities could not transfer a general rule of physical science when 95 percent of average-ability students could do so. "Nearly every student with whom we worked used an approach to solving word problems that was mechanical and procedural, rather than based on an attempt to understand the problem. . . . Students consistently attempted to use the irrelevant information in every problem we gave them. They demonstrated poor comprehension of the problems they were being asked to solve" (Goldman, et al., 1996, p. 201).

Some special education students show poor postschool outcomes (Cimera, 2000). In 1984 Will proposed a bridge model for transition and adjustment for special education students after the completion of high school studies. But his model has not been actualized. Cimera writes that the goal "should be to give students the skills they will need to accomplish whatever they wish to achieve" (p. 124), but many are not able to determine this for themselves or to become self-sufficient.

Teaching Special Education Students in the Content Classroom

Teachers of content subjects will teach special education students. Instruction must be in the best interest of the special education students while also serving all other students in the classroom. Following are some suggestions from experts in special education.

First, **universal design** should guide all instruction. The basic principle of universal design in education is that instruction that takes into account the needs of special education will also benefit all students in the classroom.

Borden and Lytle (2000) provide a checklist and scoring procedure to make us aware of special education students' instructional needs. The instructional setting should include social support, such as parent support groups, resources, and classroom volunteers. The instructional setting should also encompass a team approach that includes parents, teachers, students, and administrators; steady positive comments to parents and students via telephone, notes, or e-mail; and a consistent view of strengths more than weaknesses.

Gersten and Baker (1998) recommend that teachers know and practice a variety of strategies and effective adaptations. Situated cognition—placing or situating activities into the context and concepts being studied—makes sense. Situated cognition helps anchor learning and application in real-world problems.

Gallagher (1998) proposes differentiated education: the opportunity to allow different opportunities for different learners to learn the content beyond the regular curriculum. Personal inquiry (see Chapter 6) is one established way to differentiate instruction.

Lankutis (2001) encourages teachers to provide instruction in more than one mode. Brain research (see Chapter 12) tells us that when learners receive information in more than one way, they process it more effectively. Using technology can be an aid to multimode presentation (see Chapter 7). For instance, *Co-Writer 4000,* a software program (Don Johnston, Inc.), helps a student who has difficulty moving ideas from thought to print. The program "guesses" what word the student might mean to write from clues given so the student can make good writing choices: "I want to r-" might be translated as "I want to read." *L & H Kurweil 3000* is a program that scans and reads text to students. It also has study skills features.

Maroney (1990) tells teachers that to make it easier for students to do what is expected, teachers should *tell* students exactly what is expected; *teach* by modeling; *watch* students in action to see if they understand; *coach* students who seem unsure; *remind* students frequently; and *practice, practice, practice* to make perfect!

Universal design, a feature of special education, should be a feature of all education.

READING INSTRUCTION FOR STRUGGLING STUDENTS

 Proficiency in reading stands at the center of academic learning. The student who is struggling in reading avoids reading at all costs. Such students read when instructed to do so but only to "get through" the assignments. Their view of themselves as helpless and unable to overcome failure results in lack of participation and passive reading at best. In short, these students do not learn how to read to learn.

Struggling readers often manifest other problems in a classroom.

Those who struggle with reading from elementary school onward are more likely to become violent and to engage in delinquency and substance abuse (Fleming, et al., 2004). Bad behavior and poor reading habits are difficult to break. However, through modeling and guided practice in using techniques such as those listed in Table 11.1, even the poorest students can change their reading patterns. Using a think-aloud, a teacher can demonstrate thought processes and steps a strategic reader may take before, during, and after reading a story or text.

TABLE 11.1 Becoming a Self-Regulating, Strategic Reader: An Incomplete List of What to Do When

Prereading	Reading	Postreading
As you select and/or consider a text …	*Now that you're in the midst of it …*	*Now that you have read the entire text …*
Consider your purpose:	**Predict, monitor, and regulate:**	**Deepen your sense of the text:**
Consider the assigned purpose.	Anticipate the "next move."	Pose new questions, revisit same text.
Develop a self-selected purpose.	Anticipate relations between concepts.	Discuss/debate it with someone.
Pose umbrella questions.	Ask if it is making sense.	Write about it.
	Read to confirm or reject.	Search for its significance, its impact.
Consider what you bring to the text:	Adjust your reading pace.	Reduce or summarize it.
Recall the key players.	Look back in the text.	Rehearse and study it.
Recall the key point of view.	Look forward in the text.	
Recall the key jargon/vocabulary.	Look inside your thinking.	
Recall key facts, concepts, and relations.		**Find a place in your mind for the text:**
Search for gaps in your understanding.	**Plan for gist or summary retrieval:**	
Find the outer limits of your own knowledge.	Attend to key vocabulary.	Assess it in light of original purpose.
Create a framework (web, outline, etc.).	Attend to textual and graphic cues.	Place this author among others.
	Attend to the author's style and angle.	Place this text among others.
Consider what the text offers you: Will it support your purpose?	Select important ideas/delete trivia.	Extend your thinking along the same purpose or question.
Preview title and overall focus.	Make connections within the text.	Develop a new purpose or question.
Preview table of contents, headings, subheadings.	Make connections outside the text.	
Preview pictures and graphics.	Summarize segments, if needed.	
Preview organizational patterns.	Reduce the information (web, etc.).	
Preview author's biography.	Visualize the relations.	

Source: From O'Flanahan & McDonell (1990). Is practice keeping pace with research? *Reading in Virginia, XV*, 1–9. Reprinted with permission of the Virginia State Reading Association.

We know that virtually all students can learn to read. We also know a great deal about how to succeed with students who are at risk of reading failure. To succeed with these students is not always easy; in some cases it is extremely difficult. The routes to success, however, are not mysterious (Au, 1992; Gambrell, 1990). The work of Allington (1991) and Pallas, Natriello, and McDill (1989) suggests that improvement in the teaching and learning of struggling students does not lie in special remedial programs. Rather, we need to change the approaches we use with these students in the regular classroom (Au, 1992, 1998). Ivey and Broaddus (2000), for instance, encourage teachers to "tailor the fit" of their instruction by being responsive to the needs and interests of their students.

Differentiation

Differentiation has long been the topic of many professional development training sessions, journal articles, and governmental mandates. Though it is done well in numerous classrooms, many make only halfhearted attempts while maintaining that true differentiation is not feasible (Schumm & Vaughn, 1991; Tomlinson, 2005). An already full instructional schedule and high-stakes assessment pressures have teachers feeling overwhelmed with expectations and responsibilities. From some of their training in learning styles, brain-based instruction, and special adaptations, they mistakenly assume that every concept needs to be instructed in separate and multiple ways (Carolan & Guinn, 2007). But differentiation can be accomplished in small and subtle ways using student interests, cultural backgrounds, flexible grouping, and visual and tactile experiences that fit naturally into a lesson. Tomlinson (2005) explains that "in effectively differentiated classrooms, teachers use a variety of graphic organizers, reading materials at different levels of complexity, direct instruction in small groups, curriculum compacting, upfront teaching of vocabulary to support reading success, and so on" (p. 10). Differentiation is both learner- and knowledge-centered instruction. It is often easy to incorporate topics of student interest within instruction without sacrificing specific skills, strategy, and concept objectives. Research has shown that effective teachers take care to structure a safe environment, use consistent routines, and believe all students can be successful (Lazar, 2006). Some students who still struggle have learned over time that it is easier to quickly give up and not try. That way they do not have to risk "doing it wrong."

Visit this book's companion Web site, Chapter 11, to find tips and example instructional units helpful for differentiation.

Factors to Consider

Vacca and Padak (1990) have identified four factors associated with the learned helplessness that typifies many struggling students:

1. Struggling students may not understand the reading process and, as a result, may have trouble identifying appropriate purposes for reading and resolving comprehension failure. Struggling readers who experience reading difficulty must learn to be aware of the demands of the reading task and learn how to handle these demands.

This awareness is important for readers to make decisions about the strategies needed either to meet their purposes or to resolve their comprehension difficulties.

2. Struggling readers typically view themselves as poor, ineffective readers. They do not see themselves as competent, proficient readers. This self-view may manifest itself in avoidance behaviors related to reading. These students don't read because they don't believe they will be successful.

3. When students fail to value reading as a source of information and enjoyment, they are at risk of reading failure. As explained in Chapter 12, motivation is a central component of the reading comprehension process (Gambrell, 1996; Guthrie, 2000; Mathewson, 1976). When students are motivated, they will want to pick up materials to read. Encouraging students to choose reading as an activity should be a primary goal of reading instruction. The teacher plays a critical role in motivating students to read. One of the keys to motivating a student to read is a teacher who values reading and is enthusiastic about sharing a love of reading with students. If a teacher associates reading with enjoyment, pleasure, and learning, students will be more likely to become voluntary lifelong readers (Wilson & Gambrell, 1988).

4. Struggling readers may lack the ability to monitor their own comprehension. Because they lack experience in constructing meaning, they read words passively instead of actively questioning their understanding (Walker, 1990). **Comprehension monitoring** is the conscious control of one's own level of reading comprehension (Brown, 1980). Comprehension monitoring occurs when readers begin to scrutinize their comprehension processes and actively evaluate and regulate them. In short, comprehension monitoring occurs when readers think about their own comprehension. This awareness of processing allows readers to take remedial action to rectify comprehension failure. Before readers can independently employ specific strategies to enhance comprehension, they must be aware that their comprehension is less than adequate.

Forgan and Mangrum (1997) remind content teachers that there are many possible causes of reading failure. They use the acronym **PLEASE** to remind teachers what to consider:

Use PLEASE to help guide understanding of struggling readers.

1. **P**hysical factors may have caused difficulties, such as poor vision, hearing, or health at an early age.
2. **L**anguage problems or delays may cause a child to fall behind in development.
3. **E**nvironment—the home or the community may not stress literacy or may distract from learning.
4. **A**ptitude may be over- or underestimated, causing lower or higher expectations than are fair.
5. **S**ocioeconomic status may influence the will to learn; interests and attitudes may conflict with learning.
6. **E**ducational factors may play a role—for example, poor educational facilities, teachers without the proper background, or lack of materials.

Steps for Content Teachers

Refer to the reading specialist for help with content instruction that incorporates reading.

To help struggling readers, the first step is for content teachers to rely on the reading specialists in their schools. Yes, every school should have a reading specialist on board! According to Tatum (2004), the reading specialist should be ready to assess students who are struggling and share assessment results, along with suggestions that incorporate appropriate strategies within content classrooms. Also, this specialist should select and demonstrate curriculum materials and resources that aid content teachers. Dole (2004) suggests that reading teachers should coach teachers in how to teach reading within their subject areas.

Second, content teachers need to understand how their students view literacy. The story of Jacques (Knobel, 2001) provides a sobering illustration. Jacques declared that he was "not a pencil man" (p. 407). He used many avoidance strategies, such as fooling around to distract attention from the reading task assigned; remarking on "how boring" the assignment is; and not listening—or pretending not to listen. When teachers realize what these avoidance behaviors might be, they can counter them with relevant use of text and activities that pull those nonpencil students into literacy.

Third, content teachers need to ask hard questions and seek answers rather than abdicating responsibility. Ganske, Monroe, and Strickland (2003) pose some of these hard questions and provide brief responses. One question posed is "Why don't students come to each grade level more prepared?" (p. 126). The answer is not easy, but the authors point out that early literacy experiences, background knowledge, choice of materials used in classrooms, and difficulty of tests are all contributors. In this text the authors present information about each of these issues. The next section provides concrete suggestions.

Strategy Repertoire

Striving readers often do not realize that reading calls upon them to know what to do at a given point with the text they are reading (Gee, 1996). Even if they know they should take action, their repertoire of strategies to comprehend material is very limited (Olshavsky, 1975; Paris, 1986). Proficient readers use such strategies deliberately and flexibly, adapting them to fit a variety of reading situations (Duffy & Roehler, 1987). When used for resolving comprehension difficulties, these are often referred to as **fix-up strategies**. When struggling readers encounter difficulty with text, their response may be to "shut down," to stop, to give up because the text is too difficult. The proficient reader, in contrast, is aware of specific strategies—such as visual imagery, self-questioning, and rereading—that can be used to fix up or resolve the comprehension difficulty (see Activity 11.4).

Research suggests that proficient readers spontaneously use fix-up strategies, whereas struggling readers do not—even though they can and do use fix-up strategies under teacher direction (Gambrell & Bales, 1986). Kletzein (1991) investigated students' self-reports of strategies when reading different kinds of materials. He found little difference in the strategies used by good and poor readers, but good

VISUALIZATION

Visualize a tree house that you and your friends would like to build in your backyard or in a nearby forest.

How would you measure it? In yards? In feet? In inches?

Visualize how big it would be and your measuring of it.

Visualize some objects that are one inch long.

Visualize some objects that are one foot long.

Visualize some objects that are one yard long.

Visualize something that is one mile long.

SELF-QUESTIONING

What are the standard units of length?

Why do I need to know them?

Why do we measure in fractions?

What if we couldn't measure in fractions?

---

readers were more flexible and persistent. Poor readers did not seem to know when to use appropriate strategies. In fact, the most important goal of reading instruction for the struggling reader may be to develop the ability to use strategies to enhance comprehension (Winograd & Paris, 1988). Embedding strategy instruction within content is an efficient way to help struggling readers in content classrooms (Hinchman, et al., 2004). To do so, teachers must have a repertoire from which to draw. The following activities have been found to be especially effective with struggling readers, but the reader will also find numerous other activities that can be effective in each chapter of this text.

RECIPROCAL TEACHING

Palincsar and Brown (1986) describe a strategy to promote independent learning from a text. In this strategy, called **reciprocal teaching,** students and teachers establish a dialogue and work together in comprehending text. At the heart of reciprocal teaching are four shared goals: prediction, summarization, questioning, and clarification. First the teacher assigns a paragraph. Next the teacher summarizes the paragraph and asks students several questions about it. The teacher then clarifies any misconceptions or difficult concepts. Finally the students predict in writing what will be discussed in the next paragraph or segment. When the next cycle begins, roles are reversed and students become the modelers.

We recommend this strategy because reciprocal teaching uses small segments of reading; thus struggling readers are not overwhelmed by too much reading. It is a highly structured method that incorporates all the language arts—listening, writing, reading, and speaking. According to Palincsar and Brown (1986), this technique succeeds with small and large groups, in peer tutoring, in science instruction, and in teaching listening comprehension.

Reciprocal teaching has been successfully adapted and used with English language learners (Klingner & Vaughn, 1996). Explicit explanations of language needed for each role (predictor, summarizer, questioner, and clarifier) are provided as roles are demonstrated. Cue cards having language prompts are provided for practicing each role and as students work in small groups (Harper & de Jong, 2004). In this way linguistic skills are scaffolded as reading skills, and critical thinking is developed.

REQUEST

Manzo (1969) describes a questioning strategy called **ReQuest** that encourages students to ask informed questions. This procedure seems to work especially well in a remedial situation or with poor readers. The key to this technique is that it requires students to "open up" their thinking—to question and think critically. Also, a short selection is involved, usually a paragraph, which doesn't overwhelm the slow reader.

With this technique, the teacher and students first read silently a selected portion of the text (usually one or two paragraphs). The students then ask the teacher questions about what they read. The teacher must keep the book closed during this phase. When the students exhaust their questions, the teacher begins asking questions. During this phase, the students must also keep their books closed. The activity can be repeated with other paragraphs as time allows. The teacher then sets purposes for reading the remainder of the lesson, referring to the questions asked and information received during the ReQuest.

Because Manzo had remedial readers and small groups in mind when designing ReQuest, some modifications for the content class are in order. The teacher probably should select a small but representative portion of text and not try to use ReQuest for a long period. The teacher also might want to limit the questioning time. It is likely that students' questions will be mainly literal; the teacher can then concentrate on inferences and applications. If ReQuest is used often, students will readily adapt to asking more sophisticated questions. After focusing on listening, speaking, and reading in this activity, teachers can follow the same steps using written rather than oral questions. Written questions tend to be more intricate than oral questions and will thus enhance students' levels of sophistication with writing as well. The results of a sixth grade mathematics teacher using ReQuest are reported in Activity 11.5.

Ciardiello (1998) added a training model to ReQuest that encourages formal questioning. In Stage 1, divergent questions are identified; in Stage 2, divergent questions are classified; in Stage 3, divergent questions are generated. The model enhances ReQuest by enabling struggling readers to comprehend at higher levels.

MYSTERY CLUE GAME

The mystery clue game, described in Chapter 4, is useful for helping students understand the sequential listing organizational pattern. The example provided in Activity 11.6 is adapted for first graders in an inner-city school. The teacher used this activity to help students recognize the sequence of steps in a science experiment about fire and air. The question they were to answer was "Can fire burn without air?" The teacher wrote each step on a different card. When she presented the cards to the students, she said that she had "dropped them and needed to get the cards back in order." She had "found" the first card and placed it at the top of the pile. Their job was to put the rest of the cards in order. She read each card aloud, pointing to the picture and word clues. After the students sequenced the cards, they completed the experiment.

ReQuest was used to introduce the chapter about integers. Students read the first two pages of the chapter, then asked the teacher questions directly pertaining to those pages. The students referred to their pages, but the teacher could not. After two minutes, the teacher had students close their books, and she asked questions. The teacher, Ms. Marshall, comments:

> This activity was enjoyed by all—teacher and students. I noticed that even students who don't participate orally did so with "stump the teacher." Students were better able to answer the questions I asked them because they had already listened to the answers I had given to their questions. Overall, comprehension was greatly increased over past reading.

STUDENTS' SAMPLE QUESTIONS

What was the coldest temperature recorded in the United States? (80 below)

What was the name of the weather station? (Prospect Creek Camp)
In what state was the weather station located? (Alaska)
How do you write a negative integer? (-4)

TEACHER'S SAMPLE QUESTIONS

What are some examples other than those on these pages where integers are used? (profit/loss; elevation . . .)
Which number is larger, 0 or -5? (0: it is farther to the right on the number line)
Describe the locations of 2 and -2 on the number line. (Positive 2 is two units to the right of 0, and negative 2 is two units to the left of 0.)

Developed by Beverly Marshall.

For follow-up, students received an ordered copy of the clues, which they cut apart and then pasted in correct sequence again. The teacher found that her students, often distracted, paid attention and participated enthusiastically. She thought that their understanding was greatly enhanced.

ANALOGIES

Analogies (see Chapter 3) are especially helpful to struggling readers, who often require relational (concrete, gestalt, example-oriented, relevant) rather than analytical (abstract, detail- and lecture-oriented, definitional) learning experiences (Anderson & Adams, 1992). At-risk readers might be better equipped to understand what they read after hearing analogies such as these:

> When I begin a new year of teaching mathematics, I always draw a little house on the board, starting with a foundation of bricks, and I explain that the foundation in math is being able to do the four basic operations—first with whole numbers, then with decimals, then with fractions. As we get into time, measurement, money, percents, and geometry, having a good foundation is absolutely necessary in order to do the work. So I tell my students that we cannot have any "loose bricks," or else doing multistep problems, story problems, solving for one or more unknowns, and graphing will be

CAN A FIRE BURN WITHOUT AIR?

First — Use a knife to cut off the top of the pumpkin.

Fifth — Put the top back on the pumpkin.

Third — Put a candle inside the pumpkin.

Then
Relight the candle.

Second — Clean the inside of the pumpkin with a spoon.

Next
Cut eyes, nose, and a mouth in the pumpkin.

Fourth — Light the candle.

Last
Put the lid back on.

Developed by Megan K. Houston.

impossible. Students seem to appreciate the foundation analogy and can accept that doing calculations well is as important as grasping the new concept. The teaching of the new concepts must be "laid down" on a solid understanding of old concepts and the ability to apply them.

—Kerry Blum, middle school mathematics teacher

When a student does not understand new words or does not have any prior knowledge to link with new content, the student is likely to reject the new information. Deoxyribonucleic acid is a very complex molecule made up of different nucleotides linked together and is very difficult to understand. However, Watson and Crick's double helix model of DNA can be taught easily by taking the very basic approach of comparing it to something the students already know. By drawing a picture in students' minds of a circular staircase, and by describing the links of nucleotides as building blocks that can match up only in specific pairs (cytosine to guanine and adenine to thymine), the mystery of the DNA molecule dissolves.

—Diana Freeman, high school biology teacher

Additional Strategies for Struggling Readers and Nonreaders

What can the content area teacher do with the student who can barely read or who is a nonreader? The teacher can (1) pretend such a student is really not that bad a reader and do nothing, (2) get help from a reading specialist, or (3) assign extra work to help a student in this situation. Ideally content area teachers do both (2) and (3). The reading specialist can help with basic skills while aiding the content teacher in adapting assignments for this type of student. Most of the techniques that we describe in this book will help the very poor reader or nonreader. But here we present some techniques that are especially important for the success of such students.

LANGUAGE EXPERIENCE APPROACH

The **language experience approach (LEA)** has been used by reading specialists for a long time (Ashton-Warner, 1959). Fisher and Frey (2003) suggest its use once again as part of what they term a "gradual release model." In this model teachers move from teacher-controlled to student-directed writing. Students dictate to a teacher or another individual their thoughts about a topic; then they copy to their own notebooks the words they have said and now see. The words next become the topic of discussion, which can also generate new words, phrases, and sentences. Next students are encouraged to try to write just a few more sentences. In the Fisher and Frey model, students go on to interactive writing, relying on models of good writing to expand their own writing, and generating sentences. Eventually students are able to expand their writing and move beyond the teacher's help with dictation. The model can also apply to reading. In the same way, by having struggling readers dictate their impressions about a subject, then use that dictation to talk about the subject and add to it, a very beginning reader—even in a content classroom—will have some text material to read and use for study.

AUDITORY AND VISUAL DISCRIMINATION GUIDES

Auditory discrimination can be defined as a student's ability to differentiate between sounds, including differences in rhythm, volume, and tone. **Visual discrimination** is a student's ability to perceive similarities and differences in forms, letters, and words. As children mature and develop, they usually acquire basic auditory and visual discrimination abilities. However, auditory and visual discrimination problems may continue for many children into middle school and even high school. Weaknesses in these two important areas may hinder students severely in learning to read.

We suggest that content area teachers ask reading specialists to evaluate nonreaders on these two important factors. Nonreaders weak in these areas can be helped through auditory and visual discrimination games and activities. For instance, the teacher or another student can call out to a nonreader words similar or alike in beginning, middle, and ending sounds to selected words in the unit: Are the beginning (middle, ending) sounds of these two words alike or different? *zygoma* [word in unit], *xylophone*

CONCEPT FORMATION STUDY GUIDES

The ability to create superordinate generalizations is a skill often completely lacking in reluctant readers and at-risk learners. **Concept formation study guides** (Thompson & Morgan, 1976) are excellent motivational tools for such readers. Such guides use a fundamental learning operation: the categorization of facts (subordinate concepts) under more inclusive, superordinate concepts. Thompson and Morgan note that "once a key concept has been acquired, we use it at different levels of abstraction, complexity, and generality, depending upon our stage of motivation" (p. 132). The function of this type of study guide is to teach the key concepts of a passage and to provide practice in applying those concepts to more complex and more general situations.

Activities 11.7 and 11.8 present two examples of concept formation study guides. The first is for elementary students, the second for high school social studies.

ACTIVITY 11.7 CONCEPT FORMATION STUDY GUIDE FOR ELEMENTARY STUDENTS

I. Read the story. Put an X before each statement you think is true.

  _____ 1. A person should find out how the neighborhood feels about pets.

  _____ 2. Some small pets grow into large pets.

  _____ 3. Someone must care for your pet if you are sick.

  _____ 4. A kangaroo will not make a good pet.

  _____ 5. Do not read about a pet before you buy it.

  _____ 6. It is hard to keep a pet in a small apartment in the city.

II. Put true statements from Part I where they fit below.

  Choosing a pet depends on:

  Size   Care   Space

III. When you are finished, get together with a classmate and discuss your answers.

THE MOVE TO WINTER GRASSLANDS

Key Concept: Social Transience

Main Idea: Interaction between people and the physical and social environment that surrounds them influences how they meet the basic needs of life.

Part I

Directions: Think of a family that you know who recently moved. What reasons did this family have for moving? In the chart below, complete a listing of reasons American families and Al'Azab families have for moving from one place to another.

Reasons for Moving

American Families	Bedouin Al'Azab Clan
1. Dad's new job	1. Good grasslands
2.	2.
3.	3.
4.	4.
5.	5.
6.	6.
7.	7.
8.	8.
9.	9.
10.	10.

PART II

Directions: From your list in Part I, answer the following questions:

1. Select those items under the "American" list that are related to making a living. Do the same thing for the Al'Azabs. How are the reasons different? Alike?

2. Based on the information you have organized above, make a list of the Al'Azab basic needs of life. Are they different from the American family's basic needs?

3. Based on the information you have organized above, define in your own words what you think *social transience* is.

EMBEDDED QUESTIONS

Weir (1998) encourages the use of questions embedded in reading material to engage struggling readers. When they are confronted with questions during reading, they will be more likely to practice metacognitive strategies. Weir actually cut up reading material and inserted questions and response slots to keep students' attention while reading. Students began to make more and more elaborate responses as they answered embedded questions. Their test scores reflected increased comprehension.

Embedded questions must be carefully considered to maintain balance and variety. Selections will actually be cut up and pasted back together with questions and response slots—unless a teacher uses a computer and a word processing program to create the activity. This is a fix-up activity that is best reserved for struggling readers, but the investment of time does help students become active, more proficient readers.

BEGINNER-ORIENTED TEXTS

The texts used in content classes are too difficult for many struggling readers. Texts that contain fewer words per sentence and page, simpler words, less metaphoric language, fewer complex sentences, and illustrations that provide context will be more successful (Cole, 1998). Media specialists can help content teachers locate such texts. Low-interest, low-readability, content-oriented books are also available from a few publishers. They are a good choice because they enable practice with material at the readers' instructional level (Ivey, 1999). Activity 11.9 lists some of these books and publishers.

INTERACTIVE NOTEBOOKS

Interactive notebooks have been used for a variety of purposes but may be best known for their use in science and social studies. As Chesbro (2006) notes when discussing the value of interactive science notebooks, they "encapsulate and promote the most cutting-edge constructivist teaching strategies while simultaneously addressing standards, differentiation of instruction, literacy development, and maintenance of an organized notebook as laboratory and field scientists do" (p. 31). The concept of an interactive notebook provides a great deal of flexibility for teachers to structure designs and parameters to reflect the needs and organization of the content and skills to be learned. Pages on the right side of the notebook are used for "input" or incoming information in the form of notes taken from lectures, presentations, textbook or other readings, audiotapes, videotapes, lab sessions, or class activities. Pages on the left are reserved for "output" in the form of student responses or connections to the information on the right. These could be charts, graphs, webs, tables, illustrations, diagrams, poems, cartoons, reflections, or the like. Entries may be written or drawn right on the page or taped in and folded to the size of the page. Interactive notebooks are some ways quite similar to double-entry journals except that instead of dividing a page in half, the entire left page is used for student responses and the entire right page is used for notes or information. An interactive notebook allows creativity and modification appropriate to the various needs and differences among students. Assessment can be based on rubrics and criteria provided by the teacher or decided collaboratively among students and teachers.

From The Globe Readers' Collection (Globe Fearon, 4350 Equity Drive, Columbus, OH 43216):

Myths and Stories from the Americas
Stories of Adventure and Survival
Eight Plays of U.S. History

From The Reading Success Series (Curriculum Associates, Inc., P.O. Box 2001, North Billerica, MA 01862):

The Inside Story
Sneakers
Burgers
Jeans
Bikes
Skateboards

From Dominie Press, Inc. (1949 Kellogg Avenue, Carlsbad, CA 92008):

Global Views
American Voices
Knowing about Places

The Horn Book Guide: interactive database, reviews more than 29,000 books, searchable by level and topic (Heinemann, 88 Post Road West, P.O. Box 5007, Westport, CT 06881).

An alternative to beginner-oriented texts is rewriting (see Chapter 3). This requires teacher time, but it tailors the text to the specific content to be taught.

Teaching Diverse Learners in the Content Classroom

Horn and Tynan (2001) state that the most effective educational strategies for special education students are the same ones that help most students in regular education. Likewise, the strategies we present next are ones that work for all students, and especially for all diverse learners. This list of suggestions is a positive way to end this chapter of our textbook, reminding the content teacher that PAR works for all content students:

- Gee (1999) encourages teachers to remember that reading is the best way to become a good reader. Good readers read. Practice makes perfect, and those who are at risk and struggling need to read also. Direct instruction in reading skills is important, but written language is too complex to master without extended practice in the actual process of reading. We feature this suggestion throughout the textbook.

- Technology can help diverse learners put reading into practice in different and challenging ways. Use of discussion forums, e-mail, Internet treasure hunts, WebQuests, videotapes, and audiotapes will provide variety and use several modes to stimulate learning (Dahlman & Rilling, 2001; Lankutis, 2001). We feature this suggestion in Chapter 7.

- Writing helps diverse learners reflect on their behavior, builds literacy skills, and increases willingness to learn (Haley & Watson, 2000). We feature this suggestion in Chapter 10.

- Collaborative strategic reading (CSR) promotes reading comprehension and content learning with support from other learners (Klingner & Vaughn, 1999). Students with different reading skill levels assist one another in small groups as they apply previewing, comprehension monitoring, retelling, and summarizing. Using such strategies is featured throughout this text. CSR goes beyond cooperative grouping because the learners in the group collaborate, making their own decisions and going far beyond what the teacher has designated should occur in a cooperative group. Thus in successful group work there are no longer masters and apprentices but "equally competent learners in a learning community" (Leki, 2001, p. 60).

ONE-MINUTE SUMMARY

This chapter has considered several groups of diverse learners: students at risk, students from low socioeconomic environments, students with low self-esteem, students with limited English proficiency, special education students, and struggling readers. We suggested that at-risk learners can become successful, as studies of resilient students indicate. The types of intervention suggested for all diverse learners include cooperative grouping; teacher interaction and high expectations; boosting students' confidence and encouraging an internal locus of control; and interesting, systematic, and strategy-based learning. Most of the techniques presented in this textbook are appropriate with some modifications. Some additional strategies were also suggested in this chapter.

There is an old saying in education that teachers must work with the haves, the "halves," and the have-nots. The true art of teaching is in coming to know and value the similarities and differences among them while using those as advantages to teach them. The haves may easily learn and understand, but still must be challenged to stretch to their potential. The halves have marginal skills to learn a subject but are not motivated to do so. The have-nots usually are not motivated to learn and do not have the necessary thinking, reading, and study skills to be successful. This chapter presented unique strategies for unique individuals—diverse learners who need teacher assistance and empathy to help them become productive citizens in a technological society. The challenge that such students pose for teachers is great, and the rewards may be few. But these diverse students can and must be reached if our society is to prosper.

PAR ONLINE

Visit the *Reading to Learn in the Content Areas* Web site at http://academic
.cengage.com/education/richardson for links to the Web sites mentioned in this
chapter, tutorial quizzing, and other resources.

Post a threaded discussion to share your ideas for high-needs activities. High-
needs activities are targeted for diverse learners who may be hard to teach or
have greater needs than many others.

Locate a Web site that provides information about one kind of diverse learner
discussed in this chapter. Describe to others in your class how this Web site can
be useful in content instruction.

END-OF-CHAPTER ACTIVITIES

Assisting Comprehension

1. In a jigsaw named for the jigsaw puzzle,
cooperative reading and study occur as
students read, share, and teach one another.
Students in a base group (numbers 1–4)
are given unique information about a
topic. After reading the material,
students meet in "expert" groups
(all As together, all Bs together, and
so forth) with their counterparts from
other groups to discuss and master the
information. Students share their "expert"
knowledge in their base groups, each
taking a turn. In this way the puzzle is
completed. The following diagram
illustrates the structure of this activity.

For this jigsaw, Group A is to read and teach
the information about diverse learners:
at-risk, low-socioeconomic, and low self-
esteem students. Group B is to read and
teach the information about ESL and ELL
students. Group C is to read and teach the
information about special education
students. Group D is to read and teach the
information about struggling readers and
the chapter summary.

Base Group 1

A	B
C	D

Base Group 2

A	B
C	D

Base Group 3

A	B
C	D

Base Group 4

A	B
C	D

Reflecting on Your Reading

1. Read *Among Schoolchildren* by Tracy Kidder
(1989), particularly the chapter titled "The
Science Fair," in which Chris, the teacher,
confronts Robert about his failed science
project. *Supporting Struggling Readers* by
Barbara Walker (1992) gives many practical
instructional suggestions. Also, Mary
Ashworth's (1992) *First Step on the Longer
Path: Becoming an ESL Teacher* will help you
understand ESL learners.

2. The International Reading Association (2003) has developed a set of standards that identify the performance criteria relevant to classroom teachers. Standard 1.3 indicates that teachers should

> Demonstrate knowledge of language development and reading acquisition and the variations related to cultural and linguistic diversity. They can describe when students are meeting developmental benchmarks; they know when to consult other professionals for guidance.

Standard 2.2 indicates that teachers should

> Use a wide range of instructional practices, approaches, and methods, including technology-based practices, for learners at differing stages of development and from differing cultural and linguistic backgrounds.

Standard 2.3 indicates that teachers should

> Use a wide range of curriculum materials in effective reading instruction for learners at different stages of reading and writing development and from different cultural and linguistic backgrounds.

Standard 4.1 indicates that teachers should

> Use students' interests, reading abilities, and backgrounds as foundations for the reading and writing program.

Standard 4.2 indicates that teachers should

> Use a large supply of books, technology-based information, and nonprint materials representing multiple levels, broad interests, and cultural and linguistic backgrounds.

How were these elements addressed in this chapter? How does being informed about these elements aid in content instruction?

12

In training a child to the activity of thought, above all things we must beware of what I will call inert ideas— that is to say, ideas that are merely received into the mind without being utilized, or tested, or thrown into fresh combinations.

ALFRED NORTH
WHITEHEAD

Teaching in the Affective Domain

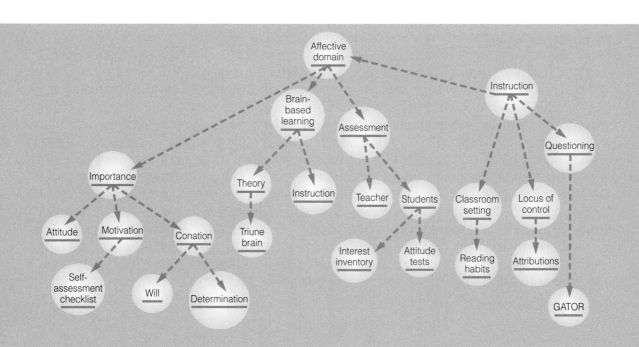

VOICES FROM THE CLASSROOM

Johnny has had difficulty in school since the third grade. Now in middle school he finds himself daily moving from classroom to classroom in which little or no talking is allowed among students except during the five minutes between classes. In his history class the typical lesson is going over the questions at the end of the chapter. He is supposed to read the chapter for homework, but he is so disenchanted with school that he rarely does. The teacher gives a brief lecture about the reading material and addresses a stern lecture to the class about the value of homework and the apparent laziness shown by many students. This lecture is punctuated by the threat of a quiz at the end of the class and the warning that "all this will be on the test on Friday." Students are not allowed to talk to one another (although several write notes by text messaging when they are supposed to be studying via the computer). The teacher spends a great deal of time and energy on discipline, preventing students from talking. Students spend much of the class filling in words in spaces provided on textbook worksheets created by the publisher. To accomplish this task, Johnny rarely reads the text. He simply finds the answers by scanning for boldface words and other clues that show where he might find the answer that will fill the blank. He seldom does well on either the end-of-class multiple-choice quizzes or the teacher's tests, but he always acts as though he doesn't care. When the bell rings to change classes, Johnny always feels as though he hasn't learned much. In fact what he is learning is that history is not interesting and that reading in history is pretty much about filling in spaces on worksheets to keep the teacher happy. Johnny dislikes reading and never reads a book on his own.

Sally is a ninth grade student who also has had some difficulty since third grade, but her day is different from Johnny's. She starts the day in a 100-minute-long interdisciplinary "earth class" in which the same teacher teaches both geography and earth science. The class begins with the teacher writing a single word on the chalkboard and then getting all the students involved by writing about what they think they will find about the topic. The anticipation is obvious as the students busily make their predictions. After this prediction phase, the teacher asks each student to share aloud as she paraphrases each response on the chalkboard. Students at this point are simultaneously helping the teacher discover what students know about the topic and helping build background knowledge about the topic. There is an air of importance to what each student has to offer, and the teacher frequently asks the students to explain why they gave certain responses. Both teacher and students respect what each person brings to the pursuit of knowledge. The teacher then introduces a skill the students will use to make sense of the reading they are about to do. She points out that "good readers" always use this skill when they read nonfiction text. Then she shows students how they can practice the skill in class that day. Throughout the practice of the skill to be learned, students are active, engaged, and thoughtful. When Sally leaves her class, she is happy that she has learned both science content and a new reading skill, all in a friendly class with a positive environment. Sally never feels threatened in this class. She knows the teacher is interested not just in teaching geography and earth science but also in sharing important skills that Sally has found out can help her in other subjects as well.

Have you ever been in a class like Johnny's history class? Or participated in a class like Sally's? What makes these classes so different? If you were a student, in which class do you think you would learn more, and why? In what ways can the classes you teach benefit from this lesson?

PREPARING TO READ

1. Before you read Chapter 12, try to answer the following questions to test your background knowledge concerning the affective domain of learning. Then read the chapter and expand your knowledge and see how your answers change:

   a. Why is the affective domain of learning important?

   b. What are conative factors of learning?

   c. How can attitude affect learning?

   d. How can we use attitude tests and interest inventories to improve instruction?

   e. How can brain function influence students' actions?

   f. What is locus of control? Why is it an important construct for teaching?

2. Match the words in the left column with their definitions in the right column:

   1. Affective domain

   2. Attitude

   3. Conation

   4. Brain-based learning theory

   5. Neocortex

   6. Locus of control

   7. Internal locus of control

   8. Attribution theory

   a. The will and determination to learn.

   b. The disposition, temperament, or feeling one has about something or someone.

   c. Accepting responsibility for one's own behavior.

   d. The way someone explains their successes and failures affects learning.

   e. The domain of learning dealing with feelings and emotions.

   f. The perceived control one has over a condition or situation.

   g. The newest and largest portion of the brain that deals with verbal acuity and logical reasoning.

   h. A theory that the brain is modular, and as such it helps form and shape certain kinds of learning behaviors.

OBJECTIVES

As you read this chapter, focus your attention on the following purposes. You will

1. Learn what is meant by *affective domain of teaching*.

2. Understand why affect is important to reading.

3. Learn the importance of attitudes in teaching.

4. Learn the importance of conative factors in reading.

5. Understand what constitutes a brain-based approach to learning.

6. Understand the importance of attitude tests.

7. Learn about three examples of attitude tests.

8. Better understand the construct of locus of control and its importance for content area instruction.

9. Understand attribution theory and its importance for teachers.

10. Be able to incorporate a number of affective strategies into the content area curriculum.

"SOON AS YOU LEARN TO READ, JOEY, THE WHOLE WORLD'S AGAINST YOU."

Dennis the Menace® used by permission of Hank Ketcham and © North American Syndicate.

THE IMPORTANCE OF AFFECT IN LEARNING

There are many kinds of emotional reactions that one exhibits in learning. The term *affect* (coming from the Latin "affectus," meaning to afflict or to touch) refers to the response to a stimuli that causes feelings or emotions. Such evoked feelings and emotions are said to be part of the **affective domain** of learning. Affective constructs, such as feelings, emotions, attitudes, self-concepts, values, self-esteem, and locus of control, connote slightly different meanings but all influence a student's ability to learn.

Feelings and emotions are essential elements in learning. It takes such affective domain variables as feelings and emotions to make students care about a topic; and only through caring can students adequately begin the process of cognition (Cardoso, 2003). It is easier for fiction to stir our emotions—we can all remember a poem or story that made us reach deep inside to encounter strong emotions. But try to think about one of the more engaging and moving sections of a textbook you have read. It is not as easy to remember such an experience with a nonfiction textbook. Informational textbooks do not usually have the power to move students to be passionate about remembering them. That is why content area teachers need to engage students with strategies that stress intensity of interaction with text.

Students from kindergarten to 12th grade "dwell" in the affective domain—that is, their lives are often ruled by strong feelings and emotions, and they often exhibit very positive or very negative attitudes about their school environment. Conversely, teachers often neglect the affective domain, instead concentrating solely on student achievement and cognitive development of students as the criteria for success (Sherry, Cronje, Rauscher, & Obermeyer, 2005).

Teachers have to pay attention to both cognitive and affective aspects of learning.

Students and teachers are physically in the same classroom, but their needs are quite different. Teachers are driven to impart knowledge and assist students in their learning, whereas students tend to focus on discovering how they relate to people and events inherent in living each new day that involves a range of emotions. Thus real communication sometimes does not occur in classrooms where the focus of instruction is only on content. Throughout this book we have asserted that it is the teacher's job to get students to think more clearly. Sometimes students can be lazy in their thinking habits, and some students have not been trained to think. However, we also contend that teachers need to pay more attention to the affective domain—to make learning more interesting by making class more fun, functional, and rewarding. We think that this is important enough to devote an entire chapter to engaging students through good affective teaching. In this chapter we explain why we agree with the researchers we cite that the affective domain plays an important role in learning. We present both theory and applications (strategies) to enhance the teaching of affect in content area classrooms.

Researchers (Adler, 1931; Bandura, 1986, 1997; Dechant, 1970; Glasser, 1986) have for decades been writing about the importance of the social aspects of learning. Because so many of the reports referred to in Chapter 1 emphasized the lack of achievement of our students, research on such affective variables as attitude and self-concept has waned. Initiatives and reform efforts have resulted in rigorous national standards, and specific performance measures have been mandated for students in many states; therefore, studies examining affective variables have been largely absent from funding proposals. This is so despite research showing that affective variables have an important connection to outcome performance measures such as memory and recall (Hager & Gable, 1993; Wolfe, 2001). Recently Van Valkenburg and Holden (2004) have written that "every cognitive behavior has an affective counterpart" (p. 347) and that every cognitive approach is concerned with as much affection as cognition.

The most outward manifestation of the affective domain is **attitude**—the mental disposition one exhibits toward others. For a long time educators have known that student attitude is a critical variable in reading achievement (Purves & Bech, 1972; Walberg & Tsai, 1985). Frank Smith (1988) notes that the emotional response to reading "is the primary reason most readers read, and probably the primary reason most nonreaders do not read" (p. 177). M. Cecil Smith (1990) found, in a longitudinal study, that reading attitudes tend to be stable over time from childhood through adulthood, adding to the notion that poor attitudes toward reading (or good attitudes) are inculcated early in schooling and tend to remain stable throughout life. However, Wolfe and Antinarella (1997) maintain that teachers can win over and inspire students by developing in them attitudes and dispositions for learning that cause them to honor, respect, and value themselves and others. Researchers such as Maurer and Davidson (1999) call for teachers not to ignore the affective domain, and what they call the "power of the heart," in using new technologies in the classroom for teaching the skills of reading and writing.

To change student attitudes about reading, teachers first need to listen actively when students are commenting and discussing. Teachers need to concentrate on what students are saying and reply to their comments, not formulate in advance a stock reply. Also, teachers need whenever possible to make reading fun and rewarding. They can do this by encouraging students to read on their own and making certain that reading assignments are not long and overwhelming. Yoon (2002) found that providing time for students to read material of their own choosing improved student attitudes toward reading. Teachers also can have students take part in frequent group sharing experiences. As another element of good teaching, teachers should always speak well of reading and be readers who share the books they are reading. To promote affect, teachers should bring good literature into the classroom whenever possible, even in content area classrooms. Bottomley and colleagues (1999) found that a literature-based approach to reading and writing had a greater effect on intermediate-age children's affective orientations toward literacy than did whole language or basal reader literacy instruction. Purkey and Novak (1984) suggest that teachers can change attitudes of students by making classrooms more affectively inviting. They outline four levels of invitation that directly affect student learning. Figure 12.1 shows Purkey's four levels from intentionally disinviting to intentionally inviting. They stress that at the highest level teachers must consciously work to make students feel that they are part of a learning community. Teachers must further

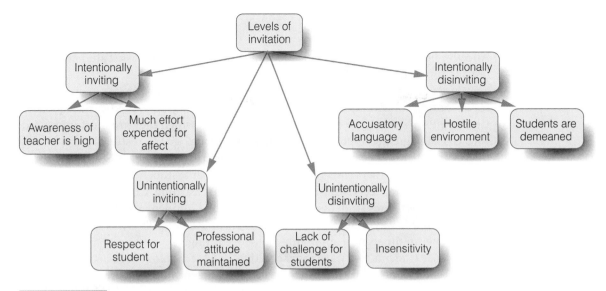

FIGURE 12.1 Purkey's Four Levels of Invitation

From W. W. Purkey and J. M. Novak, *Inviting School Success*. (1984). Adapted with permission of Wadsworth, a Division of Thomson Learning.

be aware that students want to learn and that each day teachers must nurture that innate desire and quest for knowledge from students.

Van Valkenburg and Holden (2004) suggest that the following activities can also improve student attitudes and can be sustaining methods of teaching in the affective domain:

- Keeping student journals about experiences.
- Developing student portfolios of learning experiences.
- Incorporating volunteerism into class assignments.
- Using learning contracts with measurable desired results.
- Adding a value component to each syllabus.

Researchers (Fisher & Berliner, 1985; Palmer, 1998) have stressed the importance of creating a positive classroom climate. Teachers should provide a climate that says, "I am never going to give up on you; I believe in you." Many famous people did poorly in school—for example, Albert Einstein, Woodrow Wilson, Thomas Edison, George Bernard Shaw, Pablo Picasso, William Butler Yeats, Henry Ford, and Benjamin Franklin. Paul Harvey, in *Destiny* (Aurandt, 1983), relates how Charles Schulz struggled with rejection in school for years. Schulz was a "loser" in school—no one had faith in him, yet he created *Peanuts,* one of the most popular comic strips. If we emphasize the positive, each of us someday may play a central role in helping a future genius realize his or her potential. Most important of all, teachers must value inquiry, problem solving, and reasoning. By keeping an open mind and letting students take part in open-ended discussions, a teacher makes a statement about the true art of teaching that even the most limited students cannot ignore or misinterpret.

MOTIVATING STUDENTS TO LEARN

 Affective bonds can be strengthened for students when teachers assist students during lessons by designing tasks that influence children's motivation. Turner and Paris (1995) explain how the context for literacy includes student choice, challenge, personal control, collaboration, the construction of meaning, and specific consequences. Choice allows students to select from those areas in which they are most interested, thus ensuring greater attention during the task. Challenge keeps students from being bored, as long as the learning tasks are not at the frustration level. Students need to feel that a class is "their class" as much as the teacher's; students are more willing as learners when they feel that they control their own learning. Collaboration or social interaction motivates students to be more curious, confident about, and engaged in learning. In this way, emotions come into play in learning. This is important, as we explain later in the section about brain-based learning.

Because students today are accustomed to using technology regularly in their lives outside school, and because they may see literacy differently than their teachers do (Gee, 2000), instruction that incorporates technology in academics can be highly motivating.

Another way to motivate students is for the teacher to develop a checklist for student self-assessment on certain affective variables. Such a checklist may make students more cognizant of their feelings, attitudes, and motivation to learn. In addition, it can help teachers focus their instruction on the affective domain. It could be used once a week or at the beginning of a unit of instruction. A sample checklist, adapted from one developed by Gallo and associates (2003), is presented in Activity 12.1. Remember that any teacher using this checklist can add, subtract, or change items based on the particular lesson or unit of study.

THE ROLE OF CONATION IN TEACHING READING

 In *Hooked on Books,* Fader (1976) relates his encounter with remedial students in Los Angeles whom he "catches" reading an article in *Playboy.* They explain to him that it isn't that they can't read—they won't read. An aspect that teachers sometimes overlook is students' lack of determination, persistence, and will to gain information through reading. Energy, persistence, desire, determination, and will to learn are defined as *conative variables* in learning (Cooter, 1994). Even though **conation** has been used for almost 200 years in psychological literature, it is a fairly obscure term. Paris, Lipson, and Wixson (1983) were among the first modern researchers to affirm the importance of intrinsic motivation and determination in a student's ability to become an independent learner. They noted that becoming a good reader requires both the skills of reading and the will to learn in increasingly complex educational environments. More recent research (Wang & Guthrie, 2004) has corroborated what Paris, Lipson, and Wixson found about the importance of intrinsic motivation in reading comprehension.

Researchers such as Cooter (1994), Raven (1992), and Berlak (1992) have argued for the emergence and realization of the importance of conative components of

Check which of these four levels applies to you:

I always feel this way.
I feel this way most of the time.
I sometimes feel this way.
I never feel this way.

	Always	Most of the Time	Sometimes	Never
Determination: I am determined to learn. I care about learning. I must get better in this class. I am clear in my goals for this class. I take responsibility for my learning.				
Fair treatment of others: I play fair. I accept defeat and do not complain. I do not gloat in victory. Everyone needs to be treated fairly.				
My self-control in class: People are always bothering me. People make fun of me. I control my fate in this class. People do not bother me much. The teacher is unfair in this class. What I say matters in this class.				
How I communicate with fellow students: I listen to others. I interact well with other students. I want other students to do well. I encourage others. I am respectful of all my peers.				
How I treat my teacher: I respect what my teacher tells me. I respond positively to instruction. I daydream when the teacher talks. I ask for clarification from the teacher.				

Adapted from Gallo, A. M. (2003). Assessing the Affective Domain. *The Journal of Physical Education, Recreation and Dance.*

learning. These researchers maintain that conative aspects of human behavior are necessary for a student to function cognitively.

Gholar and Riggs (2004), in an excellent book called *Connecting with Students' Will to Succeed: The Power of Conation*, were the first to write an entire textbook dealing with conation. In it they offer a conative paradigm of learning, reproduced here as Figure 12.2. This paradigm progresses from what Gholar and Riggs call

FIGURE 12.2

A Conative
Paradigm of
Learning

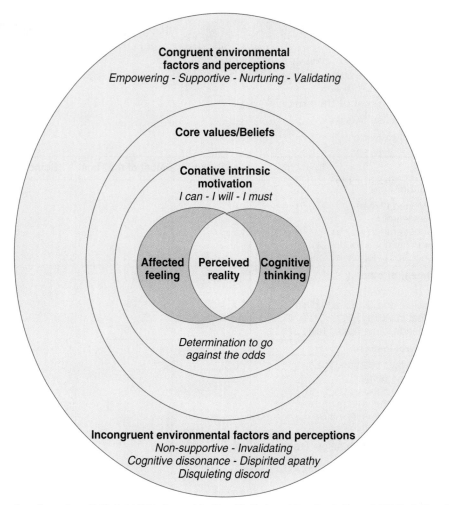

From *Connecting with Students' Will to Succeed*, by Cheryl R. Gholar and Ernestine G. Riggs. © 2004 by Pearson Professional Development. Reprinted by permission of LessonLab, a Pearson Education Company, www.lessonlab.com

an "incongruent environment" to a "congruent environment." In an incongruent environment, much cognitive dissonance (see Chapter 3), apathy, and discord are evident because affected feelings and conation are not being nurtured. Conversely, in a congruent environment, students are empowered and actively engaged in learning. This is so, according to Gholar and Riggs, because teachers in this environment are supportive and nurturing. In such an environment, teachers stress intrinsic motivation through the use of positive conative experiences. According to the authors, conation can be stressed through (1) activities and strategies that give students choices in the learning experience, (2) pretend situations where students learn self-efficacy by being challenged to succeed in difficult encounters, and (3) use of activities that ask students to decide whether a real or imagined historical or fictional character exhibits good or bad intentions. WebQuests, discussed earlier in this text, can be set up for students to do all three of these activities. Activity 12.2 shows possible WebQuest questions for small groups of students.

INTRODUCTORY TASK

We are going to a new school and have no one to plant and maintain our flower gardens for the year. We are being asked to help to produce and maintain the flower gardens to make the school more beautiful. A local store has agreed to donate the materials needed to grow the garden. Are you ready to help?

FIRST STEP

You will be divided into four horticultural teams, and each team will have special roles. The roles will be

Soil investigators.
Weather interpreters and predictors.
Flower fanciers.
Survivors.

QUESTIONS FOR THE SOIL INVESTIGATORS

What types of soil do flowers grow in?
What types of soil are in our area?
What needs to be done to prepare our soil for planting?

QUESTIONS FOR THE WEATHER INTERPRETERS AND PREDICTORS

What is the weather like in our area?
Is the weather in our area favorable for flower growth?

What would you predict the weather will be like here for the next week?
What will it be like for the next month?

QUESTIONS FOR THE FLOWER FANCIERS

What are some flowers that will do well in our area?
When and where do they grow?
What is a perennial flower?
What is an annual flower?
Will it be easier to plant perennials or annuals in our area?
Can you name five different flowers that could grow in our garden?

QUESTIONS FOR THE SURVIVORS

What is a plant?
What is a flower?
What is the plant life cycle?
What does a flower need to grow?
What does a flower need to sustain life?

Fleener and associates (2000) propose that conation be treated as a viable component of the reading development of children. They suggest a model of literacy development that integrates conation, cognition, affect, and social environment as connecting domains that interact to enable successful teaching and learning. These researchers propose that successful literacy development happens when teachers tend to affect and conation and demonstrate the value of inquiry, sharing, and curiosity about learning within a social context. The four key contexts in which these social attributes occur are child, teacher, text, and task. Table 12.1 lists the key attributes of learning that these researchers feel are important for each of the four contexts.

TABLE 12.1 Factors Contributing to Teaching and Learning Success

Child	Teacher	Text	Task
Quality of prior knowledge The learner's prior knowledge may be clear and factual, or unclear and represent false knowledge.	**Quality of time on task** Teachers must develop caring relationships with children in completing the task.	**Perception of difficulty** Students cannot perceive the book in a negative way, as being too difficult to comprehend.	**Interest** Tasks must be interesting to students.
Task-intrinsic motivation The child's readiness to perform an activity is a goal in itself.	**Modeling the value of thought processes** Teachers must value thinking and discussion as tools to develop the thought processes of children.	**Aesthetics** Texts must be appropriate for the audience, with pleasing formats.	**Appropriateness** Tasks must be appropriate to the intellectual, psychological, social, and moral development of students.
Insight Reflective awareness comes through cooperative interchange among students.	**Fostering curiosity** Teachers must believe that inquisitiveness and curiosity are most important in the learning process.	**Good writing** Subjects must come alive through the author's use of good writing.	**Cohesive context** Students must perceive that the task assigned makes sense in relation to what is read.
Perception of self as a reader Children must see themselves as generators of information, not passive receptors of knowledge.			**Perception of difficulty** Students cannot perceive the task in a negative way, as being too difficult to perform.
Will to succeed Persistence and internal locus of control must be present.			**Will to succeed** Internal locus of control and a desire to be competitive with others or oneself—that is, persistence must be operational.

From Fleener, C., Hager, J., Morgan, R. F., & Childress, M. (2000). The integration of conation, cognition, affect, and social environment in literacy development. In P. Linder, W. M. Linek, E. G. Sturtevant, & J. Dugan (Eds.), *Literacy at a New Horizon: 22nd Yearbook of the College Reading Association*. Used with permission of the College Reading Association.

AFFECT AND BRAIN-BASED TEACHING

 It might surprise the reader to know that the interconnections that transpire in a human brain outnumber all possible connections on the Internet by a large margin. The brain is tremendously complex, and science is just beginning to discover how this marvelous organ operates. In the last 10 years, because of advances in functional magnetic resonance imaging, researchers have been able to pinpoint more precisely how the brain functions (Pink, 2005). Increasingly educators are relying on **brain-based learning theory** to take advantage of a growing body of knowledge that neurologists are uncovering about how humans learn (Palombo, 2000). The newest imaging technology, such as magnetic resonance imaging (MRI) and positron emission tomography (PET scans), has shown us how the brain is structured in an incredible network of approximately 100 billion neurons, each connected to thousands of other neurons to form more connections than there are atoms in the entire universe. Sylwester (1994) describes the brain as modular, with separate components learning over time to combine information to form complex cognitive environments. Sylwester maintains that the brain is powerfully shaped by genetics, development, and experiences. The brain works to shape the nature of our experiences and is active in formulating the culture in which we live.

Sylwester's work is a natural outgrowth of the research of MacLean (1978), who described the *triune brain* theory of how the brain functions. This model clarifies how the brain works in general and precisely why affect is so important in reading. MacLean explains that the brain has evolved into three principal parts, each of which handles a different function. The most primitive part is the brain stem, often referred to as the "reptilian brain" because reptiles as well as mammals possess this limited brain function. This lowest section of the brain deals with only the most basic needs, such as reaction to immediate threat. This part of the brain holds no memories—which is why, when the reptilian brain is in charge, we have no recollection of what occurred.

The middle section of the brain, which MacLean calls the "old mammalian brain" because it is present in all mammals, is a larger and newer portion of the brain. It controls emotions and plays a great role in the learning process by determining whether the newest portion of the brain will be able to function fully. Here is the seat of the limbic system, which secretes different chemicals when a mammal is confronted with stimuli. For instance, a negative event may stimulate chemicals that affect the reptilian brain, which may then produce an automatic response to danger, much like freezing or "shutting down." Hart (1983a) describes this process by which negative messages are sent from the old mammalian to the reptilian brain as "downshifting."

The upper section of the brain, which MacLean calls the "new mammalian brain," is the **neocortex**. This newest and largest portion of the brain deals with abilities such as mathematical and verbal acuity and logical reasoning. This is the most complex part of the human brain and, as a result, the one that functions most slowly. The neurological makeup of the neocortex allows learning to take place through associations that can number in the high trillions. Medical researchers know that through the release of limbic system neurotransmitters, cells of the neocortex are either helped or hindered in their functioning.

Possible applications of the triune brain theory might include actions such as the following: A student perceives an academic climate as threatening; chemicals may be secreted to the reptilian brain, telling the brain to, in effect, revert to the instinct of freezing, thereby impeding learning and retention. The primary concern for educators ought to be that the neocortex function to its fullest potential through the elimination of the possibility of threats. Students such as Sally, described earlier, who feel positive and happy about a learning experience, will be better able to process and retain information. Students such as Johnny, who are uncertain and unhappy in a learning situation, either at school or at home, will become emotionally unable to attend to a task for any length of time. Just as the reptilian brain takes over in situations of panic, the limbic system can take over from the highest levels of thinking possible in the neocortex if an emotional climate is threatening or stressful.

Researchers (Caine & Caine,1994; Palombo, 2000) stress the importance of brain-based learning for educators. They describe the brain as a parallel processor that performs many functions simultaneously, making all meaningful learning complex and nonlinear. Many researchers (Diamond & Hopson, 1998; Sylwester, 1995; Weiss, 2000) assert that the brain is constantly in a search for meaning. Green (1999) has asserted that "learning is enhanced by combining a rich environment with complex and meaningful challenges. Isolated pieces of information unrelated to what makes sense to a student [are] resisted by the brain" (p. 685).

The affective environment seems to have everything to do with how well a student learns content (Jensen, 1998). Positive emotions lead to greater ability to attend to the learning task, whereas negative emotions can impede learning. Therefore, the roles of affect, emotions, conation, and brain development should be of uppermost importance to educators. To disregard what we are finding out about how the brain works in successful learning environments would be irresponsible. Yet most educators either are not aware of these findings or choose to ignore them. Schools continue to teach separate, often nonmeaningful and segmented concepts to students, who "chew" them in bite-sized bits of uninteresting learning. Such an approach is inherently uninteresting because it is not compatible with how the human brain works and has evolved. In addition, the primary means of controlling students who have difficulty learning in this stifling system is through the use of threats—either of failure or of disciplinary measures. Because the brain does not function at its best or at its highest level in a threatening environment, the use of threats can guarantee only failure in the learning process.

It can be further postulated that a teacher's attitude toward the reasons for learning, and toward learners themselves, may be a more important factor in how well something is learned than the specific content. In making learning interesting and challenging, teachers activate brain subsystems responsible for alertness and emotional tone. Teachers who are aware of the role of affect in brain functioning can create an environment in which the brain is allowed to function at its highest level. Such classrooms exhibit important attributes. Slater (2002) lists these four attributes as important to learning in content areas: challenge, relevance, novelty, and a positive emotional climate. In addition, Marzano (2003) maintains that the affective classroom needs enhancement with appropriate teacher feedback, engagement, opportunities for students to construct and work on long-term projects, and explicit instruction in motivation to learn.

Research also has shown that brain functioning increases significantly when novelty is present (Restak, 1979) and when subjects experience feelings of pleasure and joy (Sagan, 1977). Conversely, researchers have found that removing touch and movement can increase violent behavior (Penfield, 1975). All this gives credence to the importance of attitudes, feelings, emotions, motivation, and conative factors in reading and learning. The neocortex, according to Leslie Hart (1983b), is what separates humans from most animals. It is the newest part of the brain, which enables us to make plans and carry them out. Hart suggests that pattern seeking—efforts to make sense out of complex and often chaotic realities—is the key to human intelligence. Such pattern seeking can be fostered by what Greenough, Withers, and Anderson (1992) call "enriched environments," where students encounter substantial and varied input, problem-solving efforts, and immediate feedback in the context of real-world problems.

The human brain did not develop because of evolutionary needs for rote memory, manipulation of symbols, or dealing with tight, sequential structures or work systems, which today constitute the main concerns of conventional schooling and much training. If a learner already knows at least something about a topic, then a logical, sequential, and fragmented presentation may serve well enough to transfer some new information about that topic to his or her neocortex. But if a learner is not already familiar with the topic, this kind of presentation produces consistently poor learning results. In a recent book, Friedman (2006) warns that jobs of the future will go to those who can master novel challenges, as opposed to the routine, and to those who can "synthesize the big picture rather than analyzing a single component" (p. 307). He calls for schools to heighten student abilities to use the right hemisphere of the brain for increased intuitive, creative, empathetic thinking, rather than emphasizing only left hemisphere thinking that deals with linear, logical, analytical thinking.

Focusing on what brain research is telling us about how students learn (Diamond & Hopson, 1998; Friedman, 2006; Lowery, 1998; Wolfe & Brandt, 1998), we believe the following guidelines are important to teaching:

1. Students remember material best that is structured and meaningful (Jensen, 1998).
2. Because the environment in which a brain operates determines to a large degree the functioning ability of that brain, the classroom should always be a rich environment in which students interact.
3. An enriched environment allows students to make sense of what they are learning.
4. Opportunities to talk and move about are important in allowing for heightened brain activity.
5. Threats and pressures need to be held to a minimum because they cause the neocortex (the newest and highest level of the brain) to function poorly.
6. Because the brain is essentially curious, learning must be a process of active construction by the learner, whereby students relate what they learn to what they already know.
7. Because learning is strongly influenced by emotion, when positive emotion is added to learner input, retention is enhanced.
8. Teachers should stress intuitive learning as much as step-by-step logic to allow creative thinking to emerge.

To get students more motivated to master the task of mature silent and oral reading, Forget (2004) asks teachers to do the following in their classrooms:

- Value student responses.
- Use cooperative learning.

- Combine challenge with support.
- Establish relevance.
- Connect to what students already know.
- Make learning concrete and immediately important.
- Measure success in more than one way.
- Model expected behavior.
- Stress specific information but get students to see the overall meaning.
- Be enthusiastic.
- Call on students by their preferred names.
- Use a variety of activities.
- Apply appropriate strategies to different kinds of text.

By taking advantage of what we now know about the way the human brain functions, we can create in our classrooms an environment in which all students can perform at their highest potential, developing patterns that will carry them through life as successful learners. In an affective environment that facilitates optimal use of the higher brain functions, students are empowered to become effective, self-motivated learners.

Teacher Self-Assessment in the Affective Domain

An important part of preparing to teach is to find out what attitudes students exhibit toward school in general and toward your course in particular. However, we suggest that before doing this, teachers conduct some self-assessment on whether they are exhibiting an enthusiastic and positive attitude about reading in their classrooms. One factor found to be positively correlated with both teacher affectivity and attitudinal changes is teacher enthusiasm (Streeter, 1986). According to Collins (1977), teacher enthusiasm affects vocal delivery, eyes, gestures, body movements, facial expressions, word selection, acceptance of ideas and feelings, and overall energy. As a first self-assessment, the teacher can fill out the checklist presented as a student assessment in Activity 12.1. This checklist should show whether appropriate teacher behaviors are being exhibited. Also, the teacher survey shown as Activity 12.3, called *The Teacher's View of Reading—A Self-Assessment,* can be taken by any K–12 teacher. It assesses whether teachers are exhibiting an enthusiastic and positive attitude about reading in their classroom.

Student Assessment in the Affective Domain

The *Mikulecky Behavioral Reading Attitude Measure* (Mikulecky, Shanklin, & Caverly, 1979) for older students (see Activity 12.4) and the *Elementary Reading Attitude Survey* (McKenna & Kear, 1990) for early elementary grade students (see Activity 12.5) were designed to cover a broad range of affective interest and developmental stages. Appendix A provides keys for interpreting these two surveys, along with technical

Directions: Please read each of the following questions, and then circle *often, sometimes, seldom,* or *never* after each question.

1. Do you have patience with those who are having difficulty reading?
   Often   Sometimes   Seldom   Never

2. When you finish a guided reading lesson, do you ask your students whether they want to find out more about the topic?
   Often   Sometimes   Seldom   Never

3. Do your students ever get so interested in reading that they talk about the assignment after it is completed?
   Often   Sometimes   Seldom   Never

4. Do you ask thought-provoking, higher-order thinking questions about the reading assignments?
   Often   Sometimes   Seldom   Never

5. Do you check the prior knowledge of your students before assigning reading?
   Often   Sometimes   Seldom   Never

6. Do you ensure students are choosing reading material appropriate for their reading level?
   Often   Sometimes   Seldom   Never

7. Do you help students find resource books for assignments?
   Often   Sometimes   Seldom   Never

8. Are you always careful to select reading material that is on the students' appropriate reading grade level?
   Often   Sometimes   Seldom   Never

9. Do you explain or define new concepts and vocabulary in reading assignments?
   Often   Sometimes   Seldom   Never

10. Do you praise students for good reading effort?
    Often   Sometimes   Seldom   Never

11. Do you give reading assignments of appropriate length?
    Often   Sometimes   Seldom   Never

12. Do you provide a quiet atmosphere for independent reading and study?
    Often   Sometimes   Seldom   Never

13. Do you explain the importance of reading to your students?
    Often   Sometimes   Seldom   Never

14. Do you modify the reading material to meet the needs of individual students, especially students with disabilities?
    Often   Sometimes   Seldom   Never

15. Do you provide your students with extended literacy experiences?
    Often   Sometimes   Seldom   Never

16. Do you know how interested your students are in reading?
    Often   Sometimes   Seldom   Never

17. Are you interested in reading in your daily life?
    Often   Sometimes   Seldom   Never

18. Do you read books for pleasure?
    Often   Sometimes   Seldom   Never

19. Are you flexible in your reading—that is, do you read at different rates for different purposes?
    Often   Sometimes   Seldom   Never

20. Do you find yourself exhibiting enthusiasm when discussing a favorite book?
    Often   Sometimes   Seldom   Never

All 20 items should be answered *often* or *sometimes.*

(continued) ➤

Activity 12.3 (*continued*)

Scoring key:

15–20 *often* or *sometimes* responses	Very effective
12–14 *often* or *sometimes* responses	Reasonably effective; fair in the affective areas
8–11 *often* or *sometimes* responses	OK; need some improvement
0–7 *often* or *sometimes* responses	Poor; do some rethinking!

Adapted from a questionnaire developed by James Laffey in *Successful Interactions in Reading and Language: A Practical Handbook for Subject Matter Teachers*, by J. Laffey and R. Morgan, 1983, Harrisonburg, VA: Feygan.

ACTIVITY *12.4* MIKULECKY BEHAVIORAL READING ATTITUDE MEASURE

Following are 20 descriptions. You are to respond by indicating how much these descriptions are either unlike you or like you. For *very unlike* you, circle the number 1. For *very like* you, circle the number 5. If you fall somewhere between, circle the appropriate number.

Example:
You receive a book for a holiday present. You start the book, but decide to stop halfway through.

Very Unlike Me   1   2   3   4   5   Very Like Me

1. You walk into the office of a doctor or dentist and notice that there are magazines set out.

    Very Unlike Me   1   2   3   4   5   Very Like Me

2. People have made jokes about your reading in unusual circumstances or situations.

    Very Unlike Me   1   2   3   4   5   Very Like Me

3. You are in a shopping center you've been to several times when someone asks where books and magazines are sold. You are able to tell the person.

    Very Unlike Me   1   2   3   4   5   Very Like Me

4. You feel very uncomfortable because emergencies have kept you away from reading for a couple of days.

    Very Unlike Me   1   2   3   4   5   Very Like Me

5. You are waiting for a friend in an airport or supermarket and find yourself leafing through the magazines and paperback books.

    Very Unlike Me   1   2   3   4   5   Very Like Me

6. If a group of acquaintances would laugh at you for always being buried in a book, you'd know it's true and wouldn't mind much at all.

    Very Unlike Me   1   2   3   4   5   Very Like Me

7. You are tired of waiting for the dentist, so you start to page through a magazine.

    Very Unlike Me   1   2   3   4   5   Very Like Me

(continued) ➤

8. People who are regular readers often ask your opinion about new books.
   Very Unlike Me   1   2   3   4   5   Very Like Me

9. One of your first impulses is to "look it up" whenever there is something you don't know or whenever you are going to start something new.
   Very Unlike Me   1   2   3   4   5   Very Like Me

10. Even though you are a very busy person, there is somehow always time for reading.
    Very Unlike Me   1   2   3   4   5   Very Like Me

11. You've finally got some time alone in your favorite chair on a Sunday afternoon. You see something to read and decide to spend a few minutes reading just because you feel like it.
    Very Unlike Me   1   2   3   4   5   Very Like Me

12. You tend to disbelieve and be a little disgusted by people who repeatedly say they don't have time to read.
    Very Unlike Me   1   2   3   4   5   Very Like Me

13. You find yourself giving special books to friends or relatives as gifts.
    Very Unlike Me   1   2   3   4   5   Very Like Me

14. At holiday time, you look in the display window of a bookstore and find yourself interested in some books and uninterested in others.
    Very Unlike Me   1   2   3   4   5   Very Like Me

15. Sometimes you find yourself so excited by a book you try to get friends to read it.
    Very Unlike Me   1   2   3   4   5   Very Like Me

16. You've just finished reading a story and settled back for a moment to sort of enjoy and remember what you've just read.
    Very Unlike Me   1   2   3   4   5   Very Like Me

17. You choose to read nonrequired books and articles fairly regularly (a few times a week).
    Very Unlike Me   1   2   3   4   5   Very Like Me

18. Your friends would not be at all surprised to see you buying or borrowing a book.
    Very Unlike Me   1   2   3   4   5   Very Like Me

19. You have just gotten comfortably settled in a new city. Among the things you plan to do are check out the library and bookstore.
    Very Unlike Me   1   2   3   4   5   Very Like Me

20. You've just heard about a good book but haven't been able to find it. Even though you've tried, you look for it in one more bookstore.
    Very Unlike Me   1   2   3   4   5   Very Like Me

Reprinted with permission of Dr. Larry Mikulecky, Professor of Education, Indiana University. Data regarding the construction, validation, and interpretation of this test are contained in Appendix A.

SCHOOL _____ GRADE _____ NAME _____

1. How do you feel when you read a book on a rainy Saturday?

2. How do you feel when you read a book in school during free time?

3. How do you feel about reading for fun at home?

4. How do you feel about getting a book as a present?

5. How do you feel about spending free time reading?

6. How do you feel about starting a new book?

7. How do you feel about reading during summer vacation?

8. How do you feel about reading instead of playing?

9. How do you feel about going to a bookstore?

10. How do you feel about reading different kinds of books?

11. How do you feel when the teacher asks you questions about what you read?

12. How do you feel about doing reading workbook pages and worksheets?

13. How do you feel about reading in school?

14. How do you feel about reading your school books?

15. How do you feel about learning from a book?

16. How do you feel when it's time for reading class?

17. How do you feel about the stories you read in reading class?

18. How do you feel when you read out loud in class?

19. How do you feel about using a dictionary?

20. How do you feel about taking a reading test?

information about their construction and validation. These tests can be given as pretests and again after several months as posttests to determine whether students' attitudes have changed significantly.

Sometimes simply by finding out what students like to do in their spare time, but being aware of their goals and perceived needs, teachers can ensure a more positive atmosphere in the classroom. To this end, teachers can create general-interest inventories such as the one shown for middle school and high school in Activity 12.6, and the one for early elementary school in Activity 12.7.

Through the use of an inventory a high school English teacher asked her eleventh graders to indicate what types of writing experiences they liked best. She discovered that they enjoyed writing letters but disliked writing essays. The curriculum expectation was that all students would learn and practice writing persuasive essays. While teaching "Sinners in the Hands of an Angry God" by Jonathan Edwards, the teacher talked about this sermon as an example of a persuasive essay. Then she asked the students to relate some of their own experiences in trying to convince someone of something important to them and to estimate how successful their efforts had been. After developing a list of successful persuasion strategies, she told the students to write a persuasive essay to a real person, trying to persuade that person about an important issue. The teacher told the students that they could use any chosen way—such as text messaging—or blogs—to get the letter across to someone else (see Chapter 7 for ideas to expand informal to formal language). The assignment was a huge success.

ACTIVITY	12.6	STUDENT SURVEY

Name _____

What do you prefer to be called? _____

Home address _____ Phone _____

Name of parent/guardian _____

Parent's place of employment _____

Parent's work phone _____

Your usual grade in Math _____, Social Studies _____, English _____, Science _____.

The grade you plan to earn this year in Math _____, Social Studies _____, English _____, Science _____.

What percentage of your grades should come from tests? _____.

In what other ways do you want to earn grades? _____

Complete the following:

My favorite subjects in school are _____.

My least favorite subjects are _____.

Circle all the words that describe you:

healthy	quiet	good sport	friendly
dependable	likable	hard worker	lazy
honest	nervous	cooperative	lonely
worthless	quick-tempered	shy	artistic
sense of humor	cheerful	easily upset	clean, neat appearance
forgetful	easygoing	good leader	easily discouraged

(*continued*) ➤

Activity 12.6 (*continued*)

If I could change anything about myself, it would be _____

_____.

If I could change anything about school, it would be _____

_____.

My favorite hobby is _____.

My favorite sport is _____.

At home it is fun to _____.

I like to read about _____.

Ten years from now I would like to be _____.

Things I do well are _____.

What I dislike about classes are _____.

What I dislike about teachers are _____.

Sports I play at school are _____.

Clubs I belong to at school are _____.

ACTIVITY 12.7 ELEMENTARY INTEREST INVENTORY

My name is _____.

I am happy because _____.

My family likes that I am _____.

I am good at _____.

I think reading is _____.

If I could be another person it would be _____.

My favorite book is _____.

My favorite thing to do is to _____.

My favorite subject in school is _____.

You can describe me as (circle one)

     happy   sad   bored   shy   friendly

My hero is _____ because _____.

My favorite time at school is _____ because _____.

I enjoy reading because _____.

The assessment instruments described here enable teachers to determine their own attitudes and interests as well as those of their students. This will help teachers design effective instruction that is sensitive to the students as individuals. When teachers show students that they are interested in them as people, significant changes can occur in student behavior. In the next section we present ways to use the assessment results.

The Importance of the Classroom Setting

Classroom settings can make a difference in how well the affective domain is stressed. Forget and Morgan (1995) found that when reading to learn was emphasized in a school-within-a-school setting for improved conditions for working with at-risk youngsters (dividing the school into smaller learning units for more individualized care), attitudes and school attendance improved significantly. In addition, they found that students' abilities to use and think critically about textbook material improved measurably. The way a classroom is arranged also affects the learning and teaching climate. Classrooms where all students face forward and are always in straight rows seem to convey the message that learning takes place through lecture and teacher control. To engage all students in learning, redefinitions of the classroom climate must be made (Kowalski, 1995). A seminar approach, as is used in the Paideia schools (Strong, 1995), calls for long tables with all learners seated facing one another for intensive discussion. If such tables are not available, teachers and students might move several desks together to create the same effect. Group work calls for small clusters of chairs in several parts of a room.

Daily (1995) asks teachers to motivate students by modeling the classroom after the workplace. Students are "paid" as a reward for performing well in assignments and completing long-term projects. Activity 12.8 is a teacher's adaptation of Daily's

---

ACTIVITY 12.8 A VERSION OF BRAINMAKERS INCORPORATED

Materials
- Each student is issued a packet of five checks and one check register. (I go to the bank and beg for donations, but you could make your own for the students.)

Payments
- Each student is paid $50 per day based on a full day's attendance. Sickness and doctors' appointments are not excused. A student who is not there doesn't get paid even if the absence is not his or her fault.
- Paydays are the 15th and 30th of each month.

Deductions (I don't distinguish between types of assignments.)

- Students lose $20 for each missed homework assignment in the first nine weeks, $25 in the second nine weeks, $30 in the third nine weeks, and $40 in the fourth nine weeks.
- Students lose $10 for a negative phone call home or a scheduled parent conference due to a student's not being responsible.
- Students lose $10 for being tardy.
- When a student is out of checks, he or she will be charged $25 for a new set.
- Students unable to make rent should be charged all that they have in their accounts and then docked a $20 late fee from the next paycheck in addition. (Consider taking away a privilege until enough money is earned to cover rent.)

(*continued*) ➤

Activity 12.8 (*continued*)

- No checks or check registers are allowed to go home. Any student losing the checking materials is out of the game for the rest of the year.

Employees' Responsibilities

- Students must pay $600 in rent on the first of every month for the use of desks, books, cafeteria, playground equipment, computers, etc.
- September rent may be prorated at $15 per day because students won't have any money in their accounts. I actually charged my students rent for September at the end of September and then collected October's rent on the first of October. All other rent should be collected on the first (or the first available school day closest to the first) of each month.
- Students must endorse their checks when they are paid and then enter the amount correctly in their check registers. (Doing this as a class lesson with an overhead is very important for the first four or five payments until they get the hang of it.) You should have to write rent checks with them for only two months; they should be able to do it by themselves by November.
- Students write a check to you paying for items purchased in the auction (see below).

Auctions

- Auctions are held at the end of each nine-week period, for a total of four auctions. Good marketing in weekly newsletters to parents or sending home flyers can bring in donations to your auction that will save you time and money.
- Have as many parents volunteer for the auctions as you can. They can help move the merchandise to you as you auction it and help the students keep track of how much they are spending so no child spends more than allowed. Also, at the conclusion of the auction the students write you a check for the auction items they just purchased, and parents can help with this and help check the registers for accuracy.

- Allow time before the auction for students to browse and decide what they want to buy. Some will spend all their money on one large item; others will buy several small things.
- Allow time after the auction for students to admire their purchases and, in some instances, trade off with other students for something else.
- Students must always keep a balance in their accounts for emergencies (groceries, medical bills, etc.); thus they should not be allowed to go below $700 in their accounts. Most times, if rent has been paid, I let them go down to $150 but no lower. They write the amount of money they can spend on a piece of paper before the auction and deduct the amount every time they purchase something so they can keep a running total of what they have left to spend. At the end of the auction, they add up all that they spent and write a check to "Brain-Makers, Inc." for the correct amount, putting "auction" on the memo line of the check.

Hints

- Have students (or parent volunteers) cut out the checks, and always keep plenty on hand.
- Have a student fill in the date and the names on the checks so all the teacher has to do is write the amount owed.
- Sign the checks that the teacher uses to pay them before you photocopy them so you won't have to keep signing your signature.
- Consistently check the registers to help students who are having subtraction difficulties, aren't dating the transactions, or are placing their numbers in an incorrect area of the register. Ensuring that students keep accurate records all along is very important and will prevent them from not knowing their account balance because of errors in the register.

(*continued*) ➤

- No ink in the registers—pencils only.
- Get auction volunteers to help the students keep track of how much they are spending and to help at the end with check writing.

You will be tired after talking the whole auction and trying to keep the students from playing with their new toys. Parents can help with classroom management.

BrainMakers, Inc.

_____

Pay to the Order of _____ $_____

_____ Dollars

Memo _____

05100001: 9541 8741 0100

Developed by Chris White, fourth grade teacher, Shady Grove Elementary, Henrico County, Virginia. This activity was adapted from "A Glimpse of the Real World" by Garrison Daily. *Learning Magazine* (September 1995).

---

system. Teachers can also develop thematic units that cross content areas and that are developed around "themes of caring" (Nodding, 1995), such as caring for strangers through study of war, poverty, and tolerance. When teachers collaborate on such units, students see the value of collaboration more clearly.

Fostering the Habit of Reading

The authors have seen many classrooms where it is evident that students individually and collectively are avoiding reading whenever possible. Students will often listen to the teacher or to peers to glean information to be covered on tests. To combat this resistance to reading, teachers must be careful to design instruction that includes reading as a crucial component and that ensures that the consequences of reading are important as well as interesting. Richardson (1995a) shares a personal story of using three techniques to keep her middle-school son reading: reading aloud from democratically chosen selections, reserving a period of time for sustained reading, and respecting her son's choices of reading material. Restrictions were not made, and the new climate of sharing, time, and choice fostered the reading habit. Teachers can implement all three of these techniques in some form in their classrooms. Enlisting parent support and being on the lookout for interesting newspaper articles in your content area are two ways to start.

When students are presented with reading opportunities that combine their academic and social experiences with technology, they may "discover" reading to learn with new zeal. It may be more enticing to read on an iPod or a Palm than in a paper text. The content of the material remains the same, but the literacy environment seems more like the world students experience.

Martin and Martin (2001) suggest a number of strategies for fostering reading habits in students who are having reading difficulty. First, they maintain that students should progress at a pace that is comfortable enough to bring success. Many poor readers are rushed to finish exercises, and this only brings more frustration. To help in monitoring pace, teachers can give students small and manageable portions of reading so students will find it easier to stay focused. Martin and Martin also recommend Paris and Oka's (1989) idea of acting as a coach to students to motivate them to acquire a habit of reading. Another important component is the motivational aspects of reading. Teachers should bring in the emotions of literature, making the reading more personal and relevant to the student. Finally, they recommend that student self-checks (as shown in Activity 12.1) be employed often to give students more responsibility and more of a stake in the activities.

No chapter on the importance of the affective domain in reading would be complete without a discussion of the particular problem we have in this country with boys and literacy. Researchers (Sommers, 2000) are documenting that by many measures boys are having far more problems with schooling than girls. Young and Brozo (2001) have gathered statistics on literacy and learning for boys, and they are alarming. According to some findings, boys are more violent than girls, get in trouble with the law with much greater frequency, have much more trouble with alcohol and drug abuse than girls, and are far more likely to commit suicide. The most outstanding schooling statistic is that boys have far more reading problems than girls. Also, they are three to five times more likely to be diagnosed with attention deficit disorder and learning disabilities, as well as 50 percent more likely to be retained in school. Of course far more boys drop out of school than girls. These facts are so disconcerting that Brozo says boys "are fast becoming the culturally and academically dispossessed" (p. 318).

There is no easy answer to help the plight of boys in our schools (which Brozo says now amounts to a crisis in our nation). Certainly, though, ways must be found to foster the habit of reading in boys. Most boys still view reading as not the most masculine of ventures. One of this book's authors still remembers playing at recess and in the school yard and how the subject of books simply never came up when boys got together. Sports heroes, television, movie stars, and events of the day were discussed. But no boy in the group ever said, "Let me tell you about a great book I'm reading." Boys never made such statements, and we think they still do not make such claims today. Ways must be found to make reading a more acceptable pastime for boys. A first step might be for the teacher to discuss with male students the books that interest them. Then teachers, whenever possible, need to supply boys with readable books that have high interest for them.

Reinforcing Internally Controlled Behaviors

Locus of control, based on Rotter's (1966) social learning theory, refers to a person's belief that life events can be controlled. The term is often used interchangeably with self-efficacy. However, they are not the same. Self-efficacy deals with a feeling one has of acting competently, whereas locus of control is thought of as an issue of control—from outside agents or from within (Spector & O'Connell, 1994). People with an **internal locus of control** accept responsibility for the consequences of their own behavior. In addition, internally controlled people are much more likely to change their behavior following reinforcement than are individuals who do not have an internal locus of control. Those with an external locus of control blame fate, chance, other individuals, or task difficulty for their successes and failures. External locus of control has been found to be related to poor attitude in the workplace (Duvdevany & Rimmerman, 1996). The concept of locus of control is a legitimate construct for affective teaching because it helps teachers understand certain behaviors in the classroom.

Studies have specifically tested locus of control and achievement (Borman & Overman, 2004; Culver & Morgan, 1977; Moore, 2006). These studies support the notion that internally controlled students make greater gains in achievement in general, in reading achievement, and in classroom adjustment. Studies have found internally controlled individuals to be more cognitively active in the search and learning activities involved in reading (Creek, McDonald, & Ganley, 1991; Curry, 1990; DeSanti & Alexander, 1986). Chan (1996) found that gifted students in Australia had greater motivation and confidence in their own ability to control successes or failures in school tasks than did a group of average-achieving peers. Borman and Overman (2004) found that low-socioeconomic students with an internal locus of control had higher mathematics scores on standardized tests than did low-socioeconomic students with an external locus of control. And in a recent study of test anxiety and locus of control, Moore (2006) found that underachieving gifted students were more externally oriented than achieving gifted students, and males exhibited more externally controlled behaviors than did females.

Locus of control is similar to **attribution theory** (Weiner, 1995). This theory declares that the way students explain their successes and failures influences learning-related affect and achievement (Marzano, 2003). According to this theory, students often fail at tasks because they are influenced by their perceptions of the causes of past behavior. That is, students who see their performance in tasks as based mainly on chance factors, on luck, and on other factors they can't control get discouraged easily and are prone to give up when trying to complete a difficult task.

Morgan and Culver (1978) have proposed certain guidelines to help teachers in both of these problem areas. First teachers need to minimize anxiety over possible failure by building patterns of success for each student in the class. They can accomplish this in several ways. To begin, teachers need to develop a realistic reward system of praise for work completed. The system of rewards can be kept simple if the teacher uses a contractual arrangement that specifies a sequence of graduated tasks, each of which is attainable. The teacher should stress the concept of task mastery in grading students, thereby eliminating arbitrary grading, which is a source of agitation to students who are external in their thinking. The teacher can deemphasize the concept of time and thus lessen compulsiveness by allowing students unlimited time to complete and master certain tasks. In addition, teachers should help school guidance staff counsel students toward realistic life goals because externally controlled people often have unrealistic aspirations or no aspirations at all.

Teachers also can adopt strategies that foster self-direction and internal motivation. For instance, they can let students make a set of conduct rules for the class and start their own class or group traditions, thus reinforcing the importance of both the group and the individuals in the group. Such an activity, which relies on listening and speaking, can be implemented even in early grades. Teachers might want to let students collaboratively create rubrics for projects and assignments along with their teachers. Another excellent activity for older students is an "internal–external" journal, in which students record recent events that have happened to them. In the journal they can explain whether the events were orchestrated and controlled by someone other than themselves and, if so, whether these externally controlled events frustrated them. As a variant of the journal idea, students can make a "blame list" to indicate whether positive and negative events that happen to them are their own fault or the fault of others. These activities rely on the use of writing, thus integrating another communicative art into affective education.

One of the most important classroom strategies for helping students develop an internal locus of control is to have them practice decision making whenever possible. Study guides and worksheets can be constructed so that individuals and groups are asked to reason and react to hypothetical situations in which decisions need to be made. Group consensus in decision making about a possible conclusion to a story can be a powerful way to teach self-awareness and self-worth and to teach about relationships with others. The directed reading–thinking activity (Stauffer, 1969b) is another excellent strategy for teaching group decision making through hypothesizing the outcome of a story. This activity, explained in Chapter 4, helps students believe in themselves and feel that what they have to say has dignity and worth.

Questioning

Questions in the affective domain provide linkage among emotions, attitudes, and thoughts or knowledge (Jones, Morgan, & Tonelson, 1992). For example, when students, examining the problems faced by Abraham Lincoln when he was president of the United States, are asked to consider their own feelings about these problems, they are connecting knowledge and feelings.

The GATOR (**g**aining **a**cceptance **to**ward **r**eading) system can improve instruction by allowing the teacher to ask more reflective questions. To help gain student acceptance of reading, the teacher announces that all questions asked about a lesson, by either the teacher or the students, must be based on "feeling," as must all responses. The entire lesson is taught with questions such as these:

How did that make you feel?

Why is this lesson important?

How did you feel about the main character?

Why would you have done or not done what the main character did?

Why is this chapter important?

Why do you like what you just read?

GATOR also can be used when students are working in small groups. Students are asked to discuss only emotion-laden questions. As an example, consider these affective questions, which were generated in a kindergarten class during a brainstorming session after reading *No, David* by David Shannon (1999):

Have you ever done any of the things David did in the story?

If so, did your mom say no?

How did David feel when his mom said no?

At any time in the story, did you feel like David?

How do you feel when you are told you cannot do something?

Even though David's mom said no, how do you know she still loved him?

Did you like this story? Why or why not?

Using expository materials in a middle school lesson about seasons and climate from an earth science textbook, a teacher could ask the following affective questions:

How do you feel about today's weather?

Can weather affect your mood and how you feel? Give examples.

How do you feel about the seasons?

What if there was never any change of seasons? Describe what your feelings would be.

Course-related environmental and social issues offer clear possibilities for including affective questions and perspectives. Closely connected to the topic of weather and seasons is the highly controversial issue of global warming. Newspaper and journal articles as well as information on the Internet can give rise to relevant affective questions that are authentic and timely.

ONE-MINUTE SUMMARY

This chapter has discussed the affective domain—attitudes, emotions, interests, attributions, and conative factors that are important in content area teaching. The chapter began with a discussion of the importance of the affective domain for learning. A section explained how to change students' attitudes through using strategies we described. A section about conation in learning described the importance of will and determination in following through in the pursuit of academics. A brain-based approach to teaching and learning was explained. Brain-based learning strategies can heighten students' brain activity, thereby helping students overcome threats and pressures.

This chapter also addressed the importance of the classroom setting and environment. A positive, wholesome classroom environment helps students feel that they are capable of learning and becoming successful. One way to create a positive classroom setting is to foster the habit of reading in every aspect of class work. In this chapter we explained how to foster the habit of lifelong reading.

Teacher and student attitude tests were presented, as well as general-interest inventories and a student checklist. Two important constructs—locus of control and attribution theory—were discussed, and strategies were given for stressing internal locus of control to improve learning and achievement. We also described questioning in the affective domain and a strategy called GATOR, which helps students focus on affect as they read.

Throughout the chapter we exhorted teachers to bring about lasting achievement by paying attention to both the cognitive and affective domains of learning. Classroom teachers who stress affect in their teaching of cognitive skills and course content will be considerably more successful than those who omit such emphasis from their classrooms.

PAR ONLINE

Visit the *Reading to Learn in the Content Areas* Web site at http://academic .cengage.com/education/richardson for links to the Web sites mentioned in this chapter, tutorial quizzing, and other resources.

Create a model or diagram of the triune brain using a software program such as *Inspiration* or *KidPix*.

For direct links to topics such as Internet treasure hunts, creative writing, fun with making postcards, online books, and poetry for children, visit the *Reading to Learn in the Content Areas* Web site and select **the Chapter 12 resources:** http://academic.cengage.com/education/richardson.

END-OF-CHAPTER ACTIVITIES

Assisting Comprehension

1. Why is it important for teachers to know about locus of control? What are some teaching methods that can help students gain a more internal locus of control?

2. What is brain-based learning? What are some brain-based learning principles?

3. What is conation? How does knowing about this construct prove beneficial in teaching?

Reflecting on Your Reading

International Reading Association standards for classroom teachers say that teachers should display positive dispositions toward reading and that teachers should motivate students to become lifelong readers. Both of these standards relate to ideas discussed in this chapter. Think to yourself and then jot down ways this chapter has helped you to focus more positively on reading. Also, how have discussions in this chapter taught you to motivate students to read?

Assessing Attitudes toward Reading
Elementary Reading Attitude Survey

Directions for Use

The Elementary Reading Attitude Survey (ERAS) provides a quick indication of student attitudes toward reading. It consists of 20 items and can be administered to an entire classroom in about 10 minutes. Each item presents a brief, simply worded statement about reading, followed by four pictures of Garfield. Each pose is designed to depict a different emotional state, ranging from very positive to very negative.

ADMINISTRATION

Begin by telling students that you wish to find out how they feel about reading. Emphasize that this is *not* a test and that there are no "right" answers. Encourage sincerity.

Distribute the survey forms. If you wish to monitor the attitudes of specific students, ask all students to write their names in the space at the top. Hold up a copy of the survey so that the students can see the first page. Point to the picture of Garfield at the far left of the first item. Ask the students to look at this picture on their own survey form. Discuss with them the mood Garfield seems to be in (very happy). Then move to the next picture and again discuss Garfield's mood (this time, a *little* happy). In the same way, move to the third and fourth pictures and talk about Garfield's moods—a little upset and very upset. It is helpful to point out the position of Garfield's *mouth,* especially in the middle two figures.

Explain that together you will read some statements about reading and the students should think about how they feel about each statement. They should then circle the picture of Garfield that is closest to their own feelings. (Emphasize that the students should respond according to their own feelings, not as Garfield might respond!) Read each item aloud slowly and distinctly; then read it a second time while students are thinking. Be sure to read the item *number* and to remind students of page numbers when new pages are reached.

SCORING

To score the survey, count four points for each leftmost (happiest) Garfield circled, three for each slightly smiling Garfield, two for each mildly upset Garfield, and one point for each very upset (rightmost) Garfield. Three scores for each student can be obtained: the total for the first 10 items, the total for the second 10, and a composite total. The first half of the survey relates to attitude toward recreational reading; the second half relates to attitude toward academic aspects of reading.

INTERPRETATION

You can interpret scores in two ways. One is to note informally where the score falls in relation to the four nodes of the scale. A total score of 50, for example, would fall about midway on the scale, between the slightly happy and slightly upset figures, therefore indicating a relatively indifferent overall attitude toward reading. The other approach is more formal. It involves converting the raw scores into percentile ranks by means of Table A.1. Be sure to use the norms for the right grade level and to note the column headings (*Rec* = recreational reading; *Aca* = academic reading; *Tot* = total score). If you wish to determine the average percentile rank for your class, average the raw scores first; then use the table to locate the percentile rank corresponding to the raw score mean. Percentile ranks cannot be averaged directly.

Technical Aspects

THE NORMING PROJECT

To create norms for the interpretation of scores, a large-scale study was conducted in late January 1989, at which time the survey was administered to 18,138 students in grades 1 through 6. A number of steps were taken to achieve a sample that was sufficiently stratified (that is, reflective of the American population) to allow confident generalizations. Children were drawn from 95 school districts in 38 U.S. states. The number of girls exceeded by only 5 the number of boys. Ethnic distribution of the sample was also close to that of the U.S. population (*Statistical Abstract of the United States,* 1989). The proportion of blacks (9.5%) was within 3 percent of the national proportion, while the proportion of Hispanics (6.2%) was within 2 percent.

Percentile ranks at each grade for both subscales and the full scale are presented in Table A.1. These data can be used to compare individual students' scores with the national sample, and they can be interpreted like achievement test percentile ranks.

RELIABILITY

Cronbach's alpha, a statistic developed primarily to measure the internal consistency of attitude scales (Cronbach, 1957), was calculated at each grade level for both subscales and for the composite score. These coefficients ranged from .74 to .89 and are presented in Table A.2.

It is interesting that with only two exceptions, coefficients were .80 or higher. These were for the recreational subscale at grades 1 and 2. It is possible that the stability of young children's attitudes toward leisure reading grows with their decoding ability and familiarity with reading as a pastime.

Scoring Sheet

Student name _____

Teacher _____

Grade _____ Administration date _____

<table>
<tr><td colspan="2">Scoring guide</td></tr>
<tr><td>4 points</td><td>Happiest Garfield</td></tr>
<tr><td>3 points</td><td>Slightly smiling Garfield</td></tr>
<tr><td>2 points</td><td>Mildly upset Garfield</td></tr>
<tr><td>1 point</td><td>Very upset Garfield</td></tr>
</table>

Recreational reading	Academic reading
1. _____	11. _____
2. _____	12. _____
3. _____	13. _____
4. _____	14. _____
5. _____	15. _____
6. _____	16. _____
7. _____	17. _____
8. _____	18. _____
9. _____	19. _____
10. _____	20. _____
Raw score: _____	Raw score: _____

Full scale raw score (recreational + academic): _____

Percentile ranks   Recreational

                    Academic

                    Full scale

Raw Scr	Grade 1 Rec Aca Tot	Grade 2 Rec Aca Tot	Grade 3 Rec Aca Tot	Grade 4 Rec Aca Tot	Grade 5 Rec Aca Tot	Grade 6 Rec Aca Tot
80	99	99	99	99	99	99
79	95	96	98	99	99	99
78	93	95	97	98	99	99
77	92	94	97	98	99	99
76	90	93	96	97	98	99
75	88	92	95	96	98	99
74	86	90	94	95	97	99
73	84	88	92	94	97	98
72	82	86	91	93	96	98
71	80	84	89	91	95	97
70	78	82	86	89	94	96
69	75	79	84	88	92	95
68	72	77	81	86	91	93
67	69	74	79	83	89	92
66	66	71	76	80	87	90
65	62	69	73	78	84	88
64	59	66	70	75	82	86
63	55	63	67	72	79	84
62	52	60	64	69	76	82
61	49	57	61	66	73	79
60	46	54	58	62	70	76
59	43	51	55	59	67	73
58	40	47	51	56	64	69
57	37	45	48	53	61	66
56	34	41	44	48	57	62
55	31	38	41	45	53	58
54	28	35	38	41	50	55
53	25	32	34	38	46	52
52	22	29	31	35	42	48
51	20	26	28	32	39	44
50	18	23	25	28	36	40
49	15	20	23	26	33	37
48	13	18	20	23	29	33
47	12	15	17	20	26	30
46	10	13	15	18	23	27
45	8	11	13	16	20	25

Raw Scr	Grade 1 Rec	Aca	Tot	Grade 2 Rec	Aca	Tot	Grade 3 Rec	Aca	Tot	Grade 4 Rec	Aca	Tot	Grade 5 Rec	Aca	Tot	Grade 6 Rec	Aca	Tot
44			7			9			11			13			17			22
43			6			8			9			12			15			20
42			5			7			8			10			13			17
41			5			6			7			9			12			15
40	99	99	4	99	99	5	99	99	6	99	99	7	99	99	10	99	99	13
39	92	91	3	94	94	4	96	97	5	97	98	6	98	99	9	99	99	13
38	89	88	3	92	92	3	94	95	4	95	97	5	96	98	8	97	99	10
37	86	85	2	88	89	2	90	93	3	92	95	4	94	98	7	95	99	8
36	81	79	2	84	85	2	87	91	2	88	93	3	91	96	6	92	98	7
35	77	75	1	79	81	1	81	88	2	84	90	3	87	95	4	88	97	6
34	72	69	1	74	78	1	75	83	2	78	87	2	82	93	4	83	95	5
33	65	63	1	68	73	1	69	79	1	72	83	2	77	90	3	79	93	4
32	58	58	1	62	67	1	63	74	1	66	79	1	71	86	3	74	91	3
31	52	53	1	56	62	1	57	69	0	60	75	1	65	82	2	69	87	2
30	44	49	1	50	57	0	51	63	0	54	70	1	59	77	1	63	82	2
29	38	44	0	44	51	0	45	58	0	47	64	1	53	71	1	58	78	1
28	32	39	0	37	46	0	38	52	0	41	58	1	48	66	1	51	73	1
27	26	34	0	31	41	0	33	47	0	35	52	1	42	60	1	46	67	1
26	21	30	0	25	37	0	26	41	0	29	46	0	36	54	0	39	60	1
25	17	25	0	20	32	0	21	36	0	23	40	0	30	49	0	34	54	0
24	12	21	0	15	27	0	17	31	0	19	35	0	25	42	0	29	49	0
23	9	18	0	11	23	0	13	26	0	14	29	0	20	37	0	24	42	0
22	7	14	0	8	18	0	9	22	0	11	25	0	16	31	0	19	36	0
21	5	11	0	6	15	0	6	18	0	9	20	0	13	26	0	15	30	0
20	4	9	0	4	11	0	5	14	0	6	16	0	10	21	0	12	24	0
19		2	7		2	8		3	11		5	13		7	17		10	20
18		2	5		2	6		2	8		3	9		6	13		8	15
17		1	4		1	5		1	5		2	7		4	9		6	11
16		1	3		1	3		1	4		2	5		3	6		4	8
15		0	2		0	2		0	3		1	3		2	4		3	8
14		0	2		0	1		0	1		1	2		1	2		1	3
13		0	1		0	1		0	1		0	1		1	2		1	2
12		0	1		0	0		0	0		0	1		0	1		0	1
11		0	0		0	0		0	0		0	0		0	0		0	0
10		0	0		0	0		0	0		0	0		0	0		0	0

		Recreational Subscale				**Academic Subscale**				**Full Scale (Total)**			
Grade	N	M	SD	S_eM	Alpha[a]	M	SD	S_eM	Alpha	M	SD	S_eM	Alpha
1	2,518	31.0	5.7	2.9	.74	30.1	6.8	3.0	.81	61.0	11.4	4.1	.87
2	2,974	30.3	5.7	2.7	.78	28.8	6.7	2.9	.81	59.1	11.4	3.9	.88
3	3,151	30.0	5.6	2.5	.80	27.8	6.4	2.8	.81	57.8	10.9	3.8	.88
4	3,679	29.5	5.8	2.4	.83	26.9	6.3	2.6	.83	56.5	11.0	3.6	.89
5	3,374	28.5	6.1	2.3	.86	25.6	6.0	2.5	.82	54.1	10.8	3.6	.89
6	2,442	27.9	6.2	2.2	.87	24.7	5.8	2.5	.81	52.5	10.6	3.5	.89
All	18,138	29.5	5.9	2.5	.82	27.3	6.6	2.7	.83	56.8	11.3	3.7	.89

TABLE A.2 Descriptive Statistics and Internal Consistency Measures

[a]Cronbach's alpha (Cronbach, 1951).

VALIDITY

Evidence of construct validity was gathered by several means. For the recreational subscale, students in the national norming group were asked (a) whether a public library was available to them and (b) whether they currently had a library card. Those to whom libraries were available were separated into two groups (those with and without cards), and their recreational scores were compared. Cardholders had significantly higher ($p < .001$) recreational scores ($M = 30.0$) than noncardholders ($M = 28.9$), evidence of the subscale's validity in that scores varied predictably with an outside criterion.

A second test compared students who presently had books checked out from their school library with students who did not. The comparison was limited to children whose teachers reported not requiring them to check out books. The means of the two groups varied significantly ($p < .001$), and children with books checked out scored higher ($M = 29.2$) than those who had no books checked out ($M = 27.3$).

A further test of the recreational subscale compared students who reported watching an average of less than one hour of television per night with students who reported watching more than two hours per night. The recreational mean for the low televiewing group (31.5) significantly exceeded ($p < .001$) the mean of the heavy televiewing group (28.6). Thus the amount of television watched varied inversely with children's attitudes toward recreational reading.

The validity of the academic subscale was tested by examining the relationship of scores to reading ability. Teachers categorized norm-group children as having low, average, or high overall reading ability. Mean subscale scores of the high-ability readers ($M = 27.7$) significantly exceeded the mean of low-ability readers ($M = 27.0$, $p < .001$), evidence that scores were reflective of how the students truly felt about reading for academic purposes.

The relationship between the subscales was also investigated. It was hypothesized that children's attitudes toward recreational and academic reading would be moderately but not highly correlated. Facility with reading is likely to affect these two areas similarly, resulting in similar attitude scores. Nevertheless, it is easy to imagine children inclined to read for pleasure but disenchanted with assigned reading and children academically engaged but without interest in reading outside school. The intersubscale correlation coefficient was .64, which meant that just 41 percent of the variance in one set of scores could be accounted for by the other. It is reasonable to suggest that the two subscales, while related, also reflect dissimilar factors—a desired outcome.

To tell more precisely whether the traits measured by the survey corresponded to the two subscales, factor analyses were conducted. Both used the unweighted least squares method of extraction and a varimax rotation. The first analysis permitted factors to be identified liberally (using a limit equal to the smallest eigenvalue greater than 1). Three factors were identified. Of the ten items composing the academic subscale, nine loaded predominantly on a single factor while the tenth (item 13) loaded nearly equally on all three factors. A second factor was dominated by seven items of the recreational subscale, while three of the recreational items (6, 9, and 10) loaded principally on a third factor. These items, however, did load more heavily on the second (recreational) factor than on the first (academic). A second analysis constrained the identification of factors to two. This time, with one exception, all items loaded cleanly on factors associated with the two subscales. The exception was item 13, which could have been interpreted as a recreational item and thus apparently involved a slight ambiguity. Taken together, the factor analyses produced evidence extremely supportive of the claim that the survey's two subscales reflect discrete aspects of reading attitude.

GARFIELD REVISITED: PERMISSION TO USE THE ERAS

Michael C. McKenna / Georgia Southern University
Dennis J. Kear / Wichita State University

Educators wishing to use the scale should copy and paste the legend on each page of the scale.

Since its appearance, the ERAS has grounded a number of research studies of reading attitudes, and each of these studies has contributed to an understanding of the instrument. The following sources may be useful to educators who have used the ERAS:

Allen, L., Cipielewski, J., & Stanovich, K. E. (1992). Multiple indicators of children's reading habits and attitudes: Construct validity and cognitive correlates. *Journal of Educational Psychology, 84,* 489–503.

Bromley, K., Winters, D., & Schlimmer, K. (1994). Book buddies: Creating enthusiasm for literacy learning. *The Reading Teacher, 47,* 392–399.

Grisham, D. L. (1993, December). *The integrated language arts: Curriculum enactments in whole language and traditional fourth grade classrooms.* Paper presented at the meeting of the National Reading Conference, Charleston, SC.

Kush, J. C., Watkins, M. W., McAleer, M. T., & Edwards, V. A. (1995). One-year stability of the elementary reading attitude survey. *Mid-Western Educational Researcher, 8,* 11–14.

McKenna, M. C., & Kear, D. J. (1990). Measuring attitude towards reading: A new tool for teachers. *The Reading Teacher, 43,* 626–639.

McKenna, M. C., Kear, D. J., & Ellsworth, R. A. (1995). Children's attitudes toward reading: A national survey. *Reading Research Quarterly, 30*:4, 934–956.

McKenna, M. C., Stratton, B. D., & Grindler, M. C. (1992, November). *Social desirability of children's responses to a reading attitude survey.* Paper presented at the meeting of the College Reading Association, St. Louis, MO.

McKenna, M. C., Stratton, B. D., Grindler, M. C., & Jenkins, S. (1995). Differential effects of whole language and traditional instruction on reading attitudes. *Journal of Reading Behavior, 27,* 19–44.

Payne, D. A. (1994, April). *Two-year evaluation of a continuous progress K–3 program.* Paper presented at the meeting of the American Educational Research Association, New Orleans.

Rasinski, T. V., & Linek, W. (1993, November). *Do students in whole language classrooms like reading more than students in traditional classrooms?* Paper presented at the meeting of the College Reading Association, Richmond, VA.

Reinking, D., & Watkins, J. H. (1996). *A formative experiment investigating the use of multimedia book reviews to increase elementary students' independent reading* (Technical Report). Athens, GA: National Reading Research Center.

Stanovich, K. E. (1993). Does reading make you smarter? Literacy and the development of verbal-intelligence. In H. Reese (Ed.), *Advances in child development and behavior* (Vol. 24, pp. 133–180). Gilsum, NH: Academic Press.

Whitney, P. (1994). *Influences on grade-five students' decisions to read: An exploratory study of leisure reading behavior.* Unpublished doctoral dissertation, University of British Columbia, Vancouver.

MIKULECKY BEHAVIORAL READING ATTITUDE MEASURE

 Norming and Validation Information[*]

The *Mikulecky Behavioral Reading Attitude Measure* (MBRAM) was developed to be a sound reading-attitudes measure appropriate for use with mature readers. To establish the instrument on sound theoretical foundations, all items were written with direct

[*]*Mikulecky, L. J. The developing, field testing, and initial norming of a secondary/adult level reading attitude measure that is behaviorally oriented and based on Krathwohl's Taxonomy of the Affective Domain.* Unpublished doctoral dissertation, University of Wisconsin–Madison, 1976.

Mikulecky Behavioral Reading Attitude Measure

Name _____ Instructor's Name _____

Age _____ Sex _____ School _____

Example

You receive a book for a holiday present. You start the book, but decide to stop halfway through.

VERY UNLIKE ME   1   2   3   ④   5   VERY LIKE ME

1. You walk into the office of a doctor or dentist and notice that there are magazines set out.

   VERY UNLIKE ME   1   2   3   4   5   VERY LIKE ME

2. People have made jokes about your reading in unusual circumstances or situations.

   VERY UNLIKE ME   1   2   3   4   5   VERY LIKE ME

3. You are in a shopping center you've been to several times when someone asks where books and magazines are sold. You are able to tell the person.

   VERY UNLIKE ME   1   2   3   4   5   VERY LIKE ME

4. You feel very uncomfortable because emergencies have kept you away from reading for a couple of days.

   VERY UNLIKE ME   1   2   3   4   5   VERY LIKE ME

5. You are waiting for a friend in an airport or supermarket and find yourself leafing through the magazines and paperback books.

   VERY UNLIKE ME   1   2   3   4   5   VERY LIKE ME

6. If a group of acquaintances would laugh at you for always being buried in a book, you'd know it's true and wouldn't mind much at all.

   VERY UNLIKE ME   1   2   3   4   5   VERY LIKE ME

7. You are tired of waiting for the dentist, so you start to page through a magazine.

   VERY UNLIKE ME   1   2   3   4   5   VERY LIKE ME

8. People who are regular readers often ask your opinion about new books.

   VERY UNLIKE ME   1   2   3   4   5   VERY LIKE ME

9. One of your first impulses is to "look it up" whenever there is something you don't know or whenever you are going to start something new.

   VERY UNLIKE ME   1   2   3   4   5   VERY LIKE ME

10. Even though you are a very busy person, there is somehow always time for reading.

    VERY UNLIKE ME   1   2   3   4   5   VERY LIKE ME

11. You've finally got some time alone in your favorite chair on a Sunday afternoon. You see something to read and decide to spend a few minutes reading just because you feel like it.

    VERY UNLIKE ME   1   2   3   4   5   VERY LIKE ME

12. You tend to disbelieve and be a little disgusted by people who repeatedly say they don't have time to read.

    VERY UNLIKE ME   1   2   3   4   5   VERY LIKE ME

13. You find yourself giving special books to friends or relatives as gifts.

    VERY UNLIKE ME   1   2   3   4   5   VERY LIKE ME

14. At holiday time, you look in the display window of a bookstore and find yourself interested in some books and uninterested in others.

    VERY UNLIKE ME   1   2   3   4   5   VERY LIKE ME

(continued)

Mikulecky Behavioral Reading Attitude Measure (*concluded*)

15. Sometimes you find yourself so excited by a book you try to get friends to read it.

    VERY UNLIKE ME   1   2   3   4   5   VERY LIKE ME

16. You've just finished reading a story and settle back for a moment to enjoy and remember what you've just read.

    VERY UNLIKE ME   1   2   3   4   5   VERY LIKE ME

17. You *choose* to read nonrequired books and articles fairly regularly (a few times a week).

    VERY UNLIKE ME   1   2   3   4   5   VERY LIKE ME

18. Your friends would not be at all surprised to see you buying or borrowing a book.

    VERY UNLIKE ME   1   2   3   4   5   VERY LIKE ME

19. You have just gotten comfortably settled in a new city. Among the things you plan to do are check out the library and bookstores.

    VERY UNLIKE ME   1   2   3   4   5   VERY LIKE ME

20. You've just heard about a good book but haven't been able to find it. Even though you're tired, you look for it in one more book store.

    VERY UNLIKE ME   1   2   3   4   5   VERY LIKE ME

reference to the Hovland-Rosenberg tricomponent model of attitude and to the stages of Krathwohl's *Taxonomy of the Affective Domain*. A pool of 40 items, each of which was designed to reflect a specific Krathwohl substage, was reduced to 20 items after considering the evaluations of a panel of judges familiar with Krathwohl's taxonomy and after an item analysis that eliminated all items that correlated at $r = .600$ or less with the sum of items reflecting the Krathwohl stage appropriate to each item. The hierarchical framework hypothesized by Krathwohl was supported by an analysis of subjects' item responses using a method for Scaling a Simplex developed by Henry Kaiser (*Psychometrika,* 1962). The MBRAM hierarchy gave evidence of a .933 out of a possible 1.000 goodness-of-fit to an ideal hierarchy. This was interpreted as empirical support for the Krathwohl theoretical foundation of the MBRAM.

A graduate-level seminar on affective domain measurement helped survey and refine all items to reflect everyday reading-related behaviors, thereby establishing *face validity*. Correlations of *concurrent validity* ranging from .446 to .770 were established with such formal reading attitude measures as the Estes Scale, the Dulin-Chester Scale, and the Kennedy-Halinski Reading Attitude Measure. The MBRAM correlated more highly with the Estes Scale and the Dulin-Chester Scale than either of those measures did with the other.

To establish *construct validity,* five informal criteria for reading attitude (self-reported liking and amount of reading, teacher and classmate judgment of reading attitude, and number of books read in six months) were administered along with the MBRAM. All MBRAM correlations with these informal criteria were significant to the $p < .001$ level, and the majority of correlations ranged from .500 to .791. The MBRAM correlated significantly more highly with these informal measures than did the other, formal reading attitude measures used in the study. Analysis of variance statistically demonstrated the ability of the MBRAM to discriminate subjects of high, average, and low reading attitude as measured by the informal criteria.

The MBRAM demonstrated a test–retest reliability of .9116.

The MBRAM was administered to 1,750 subjects ranging from seventh grade through college–adult. 1,343 of the subjects were public school students selected from urban, suburban, and rural populations. These subjects were randomly sampled to create a composite, stratified Wisconsin Population Model. Norms for the MBRAM are reported for each grade level in terms of this model and also in terms of urban, suburban, and rural populations. For ease of interpretation of scores, attitude-level scoring bands are provided. No significant differences in scores of urban, suburban, or rural subjects were found from seventh to tenth grade, but rural subjects exhibited slightly higher MBRAM mean scores in the upper grades. Reading attitude scores decreased slightly in all locations with each year in school. (See Tables A.3 and A.4.)

Stages of Krathwohl's Taxonomy as Reflected by Mikulecky Behavioral Reading Attitude Measure Items

Stage 1 (attending) of Krathwohl's taxonomy is reflected by items 1, 3, 5, and 7 (see Table A.5). Each item provides from 1 to 5 points. A perfect score at this stage would be 4 items × 5 points, or 20 points. A student can be said to have attained a stage if he or she has 75 percent of the possible points at that stage. By interpreting items and stages, a deeper understanding of a student's reading attitude is possible.

TABLE A.3 Summary Statistics: Junior High School (Grades 7–9) and Senior High School (Grades 10–12); Urban, Suburban, and Rural Subjects, MBRAM Scores

	Urban				Suburban				Rural			
Level	N	Mean	Range	S.D.	N	Mean	Range	S.D.	N	Mean	Range	S.D.
Jr	127	55.93	27–90(63)	12.11	276	59.60	25–98(73)	14.33	182	60.81	22–92(70)	13.91
Sr	332	55.24	20–90(70)	12.51	144	58.29	24–95(71)	15.55	190	59.28	29–97(68)	15.17

Attitude Bands for Junior and Senior High School by Location

	Urban		Suburban		Rural	
Attitude Level	Jr. High	Sr. High	Jr. High	Sr. High	Jr. High	Sr. High
Above average	66–100	62–100	68–100	67–100	69–100	68–100
Average	53–65	49–61	52–67	59–66	54–68	52–67
Below average	20–52	20–48	20–51	20–59	20–53	20–51

Adult Norms: Results of Analyses of Variance and Post Hoc Scheffe Tests of Attitude toward Reading (MBRAM Score) by Each Demographic Variable

TABLE A.4

All Cases	N	Mean	S.D.	F-Ratio	Post Hoc Test of Significance
Sex					
M	118	65.02	14.15	33.58	***
F	166	74.47	13.10		
Race					
W	262	70.78	14.36	.43	Not significant
B	20	67.90	14.22		
O	2	65.50	0		
Education					
Less than high school	40	66.87	12.13	2.48	*
High school	88	68.69	15.79		
Post high school	93	71.07	14.19		
College	42	73.71	13.34		
Graduate work	22	77.09	11.13		
Family Income					
Less than 3,000	13	69.38	12.72	2.79	*
3–5,000	17	70.12	13.37		
5–10,000	39	71.69	10.76		
10–20,000	112	69.26	15.23		
Greater than 20,000	86	73.85	12.89		
No response	17	60.94	19.46		
Employment					
Full time	141	68.38	15.75	3.008	**
Part time	20	75.45	11.80		
Housewife	49	74.96	11.45		
Unemployed	9	78.67	17.33		
Student	36	67.81	11.57		
Retired	29	71.10	12.26		

*$p<.05$
**$p<.01$
***$p<.001$

From Mikulecky, Shanklin, & Caverly (1979).

	Stages of Krathwohl's Taxonomy as Reflected by Mikulecky Behavioral Attitude
TABLE A.5	Measure Items

Krathwohl Stages	Items (1–5 Points Possible Each Item)	Criterion Score (75 Percent of Possible Points)
I. *Attending:* The individual is generally aware of reading and tolerant of it.	1, 3, 5, 7	15 pts.
II. *Responding:* The individual is willing to read under certain circumstances. He or she begins to choose and occasionally enjoy reading.	11, 14, 16	11 pts.
III. *Valuing:* The individual begins to accept the worth of reading as a value to be preferred and even to extend to others.	13, 15, 17 18, 19, 20	23 pts.
IV. *Organization:* For the individual, reading is part of an organized value system and is so habitual that it is almost "instinctive."	9, 10, 12	11 pts.
V. *Characterization:* For the individual, reading is so much a part of life that both the reader and others see reading as crucial to this person.	2, 4, 6, 8	15 pts.

Readability Information
Using the Fry Graph for Short Selections

The Procedure

The Fry graph can be used with selections of fewer than 100 words if some conversions are made (Forgan & Mangrum, 1985). This technique will be useful to teachers of primary grades, where material is partly visual and partly verbal, or for teachers using newspaper or magazine articles to supplement instruction. It also can help teachers measure the difficulty of word problems in math or of essay questions on tests. The material should contain fewer than 100 words; if the material contains at least 100 words, then the Fry graph can be applied. To use this short-selection version, a teacher should do the following:

1. Count the total number of words.

2. Round *down* to the nearest 10.

3. Refer to the conversion chart (Figure B.1), and identify the conversion number corresponding to the rounded number.

4. Count the number of syllables and sentences in the rounded-down number of words (see steps 1 and 2).

5. Multiply the number of syllables by the number on the conversion chart; multiply the number of sentences by the number on the conversion chart.

6. Plot the final numbers on the regular Fry graph.

FIGURE B.1	If the number of words in the selection is:	Multiply the number of syllables and sentences by:
Conversion Chart for Fry's Graph for Selections with Fewer Than 100 Words	30	3.3
	40	2.5
	50	2.0
	60	1.67
	70	1.43
	80	1.25
	90	1.1

From *Teaching Content Area Reading Skills*, 3rd ed., by Harry W. Forgan and Charles T. Mangrum II, copyright © 1985. Merrill Publishing Co., Columbus, OH. Used with permission.

An Example

The following two essay questions have been assessed using
this procedure.

	Syllables
1. To what extent do you believe it is possible for people of different races, religions, or political beliefs to live together in harmony? What suggestions can you make to help people become more tolerant?	17
	21
	16
	6
2. It is often said that communism develops fastest in those countries where people do not have the basic necessities of life. Why do you think this might be possible?	16
	16
	6
60 words *Total*	98

Counting the words, you will find a total of 63. Rounding down to the nearest 10, you will use 60 words in our sample. There are 98 syllables and 3.8 sentences in the 60 words. Both numbers are then multiplied by 1.67 to convert them to a scale of 100 words. Thus we have 162 syllables and 6.3 sentences, indicating readability at the eleventh grade level.

 __60__ Nearest 10 (# of words used in determining readability)

 __98__ Number of syllables × __1.67__ = __163.7__

 __3.8__ Number of sentences × __1.67__ = __6.3__

 __11th__ Estimate of readability

USING THE SMOG FORMULA

McLaughlin (1969) named his readability formula SMOG as a tribute to another formula—the FOG—and after his birthplace, London, where "smog first appeared" (p. 641). Some have said that SMOG stands for the Simple Measure of Gobbledygook! Although its name is very lighthearted, this formula is a serious solution to the problem of measuring the readability of material that students may have to read on their own.

The SMOG formula is very easy to compute. However, the teacher needs to use a calculator that computes square roots or have a table of square roots handy. To use the SMOG formula, follow these steps:

1. Count three sets of 10 sentences (a total of 30 sentences).

2. Count all words of three or more syllables.

3. Take this number, and determine the nearest perfect square root.

4. Add 3 to this square root.

5. The final number is the readability level.

DIFFERENCES BETWEEN THE FRY GRAPH AND THE SMOG FORMULA

The differences between the Fry graph and the SMOG formula are important to note. Each formula is based on a different premise, so the readability scores must be read differently. The Fry formula measures the readability of material used in an instructional setting. Because the teacher will explain the difficult words and sentences, the score is based on students' understanding 65 to 75 percent of the material at a given grade level. The SMOG formula is intended to measure the readability of material that a teacher will not be teaching. Perhaps it is material that the teacher has suggested a student use independently. Because the teacher will not be explaining the difficult words and sentences, the score is based on students' understanding 90 to 100 percent of the material. If a Fry and a SMOG were calculated on the same material, the Fry score would probably be lower. Table B.1 illustrates the basic differences between these two popular measures of readability.

TABLE B.1   A Comparison of the Fry Graph and the SMOG Readability Formula

Readability Measure	Provides Readability Score for	Teacher Will Be Assisting Instruction?	Student Is Expected to Comprehend	Readability Score May Be	Apply This Formula When
Fry	Instructional reading settings	Yes	65–75% of material	Lower*	Teacher will instruct the group using the material being measured
SMOG	Independent reading settings	No	90–100% of material	Higher*	Student will be reading the measured material on her or his own, as in report writing, homework, etc.

*As measured on the same passage.

References

Abrami, P. C., Chambers, B., d'Apollonia, S., Farrell, M., & DeSimone, C. (1992). Group outcome: The relationship between group learning outcome, attributional style, academic achievement, and self-concept. *Contemporary Educational Psychology, 17,* 201–210.

Abruscato, J. (1993). Early results and tentative implications from the Vermont portfolio project. *Phi Delta Kappan, 74,* 474–477.

Adams, M. J. (1990). *Beginning to read: Thinking and learning about print.* Cambridge, MA: MIT Press.

Adler, A. (1931). *What life should mean to you.* New York: Capricorn.

Adler, M. J. (1982). *The Paideia proposal.* New York: Macmillan.

Adler, M. J. (1994). *Socrates: Art, the arts, and the great ideas.* New York: Simon and Schuster.

Afflerbach, P. (1987). How are main idea statements constructed? Watch the experts. *Journal of Reading, 30,* 512–518.

Afflerbach, P. (2002). The road to folly and redemption: Perspectives on the legitimacy of high-stakes testing. *Reading Research Quarterly, 37*(3), 348–360.

Agbenyega, S., & Jiggetts, J. (1999). Minority children and their overrepresentation in special education. *Education, 119*(4), 619–628.

Aguiar, L., & Brady, S. (1991). Vocabulary acquisition and reading ability. *Reading and Writing: An Interdisciplinary Journal, 3*(3), 413–425.

Alber, S. R., Nelson, J. S., & Brennan, K. B. (2002). A comparative analysis of two homework study methods on elementary and secondary school students' acquisition and maintenance of social studies content. *Education & Treatment of Children, 25*(2), 172–197.

Albright, J. (2001). The logic of our failures in literacy practices and teaching. *Journal of Adolescent & Adult Literacy, 44,* 644–658.

Alexander, P. A., & Jetton, T. L. (2000). Learning from text: A multidimensional and developmental perspective. In M. L. Kamil, P. B. Mosenthal, P. D. Pearson, & R. Barr (Eds.), *Handbook of Reading Research* (Vol. 3, pp. 285–310). Mahwah, NJ: Erlbaum.

Alexander, P. A., & Judy, J. E. (1998). The interaction of domain-specific and strategic knowledge in academic performance. *Review of Educational Research, 58,* 375–404.

Alexander, P. A., & Murphy, P. K. (1998). *The research base for APA's learner-centered psychological principles.* Washington, DC: American Psychological Association.

Ali, A. (2004). Applying constructivism in a traditional environment. *Academic Exchange Quarterly, 8*(1), 71–76.

Allen, R., Brown, K., & Yatvin, J. (1986). *Learning language through communication: A functional approach.* Belmont, CA: Wadsworth.

Allington, R. L. (1991). How policy and regulation influence instruction for at-risk learners: Or why poor readers rarely comprehend well and probably never will. In L. Idol & B. F. Jones (Eds.), *Educational values and cognitive instruction: Implications for reform* (pp. 277–299). Hillsdale, NJ: Erlbaum.

Altea, R. (1995). *The eagle and the rose.* New York: Warner Books.

Alvarez, M. C., & Rodriguez, W. J. (1995). Explorers of the universe: A pilot case study. In *Generations of literacy, seventeenth yearbook of the College Reading Association* (pp. 221–236). Commerce, TX: East Texas State University.

Alvermann, D. (1999). Modes of inquiry into studying engaged reading. In J. Guthrie & D. Alvermann (Eds.), *Engaged reading: Processes, practices, and policy implications* (pp. 134–149). New York: Teachers College Press.

Alvermann, D. E., O'Brien, D. G., & Dillon, D. R. (1990). What teachers do when they say they're having discussions of content reading assignments: A qualitative analysis. *Reading Research Quarterly, 25,* 296–321.

Alvermann, D. E., Young, J. P., Weaver, D., Hinchman, K., Moore, D., Phelps, S., Thrash, E. C., & Zalewski, P. (1996). Middle and high school students' perceptions of how they experience text-based discussions: A multicase study. *Reading Research Quarterly, 31*(3), 244–267.

American Psychological Association (2001). Appropriate use of high-stakes testing in our nation's schools. *APA Online.* Retrieved Sept. 7, 2004, from http://www.apa.org/pubinfo/testing.html.

American School Counseling Association (2000). *Study skills survey.* Alexandria, Virginia.

Amlund, J. T., Kardash, C. A. M., & Kulhavy, R. W. (1986). Repetitive reading and recall of expository text. *Reading Research Quarterly, 21,* 49–53.

Ammons, R. I. (1987). *Trade books in the content areas.* Tempe, AZ: Jan V.

Anderson, J., & Adams, M. (1992, Spring). Acknowledging the learning styles of diverse student populations: Implications for instructional design. In L. L. B. Border & N. Van Note Chism (Eds.), *Teaching for Diversity, 49,* 21–33.

Anderson, R. C., & Pearson, P. D. (1984). A schematheoretic view of basic processes in reading comprehension. In P. D. Pearson (Ed.), *Handbook of reading research* (pp. 255–291). New York: Longman.

Anderson, V. A., & Roit, M. (1993). Planning and implementing collaborative strategy instruction for delayed readers in grades 6–10. *The Elementary School Journal, 94,* 121–137.

Anderson-Inman, L. (1998a). Electronic journals in technology and literacy: Professional development online. *Journal of Adolescent & Adult Literacy, 41*(15), 400–405.

Anderson-Inman, L. (1998b). Electronic text: Literacy medium of the future. *Journal of Adolescent & Adult Literacy, 41*(8), 678–682.

Anderson-Inman, L. (1999, July–Sept). Computer-based solutions for secondary students with learning disabilities: Emerging issues. *Reading and Writing Quarterly: Overcoming Learning Difficulties, 15*(3), 239–249.

Anderson-Inman, L., Knox-Quinn, C., Szymanski, M. (1999). Computer-supported studying: Stories of successful transition to postsecondary education. *Career Development for Exceptional Individuals, 22*(2), 185–212.

Anderson-Inman, L., & Zeitz, L. (1993). Computer-based concept mapping: Active studying for active learners. *The Computing Teacher, 21*(1), 6–10.

Apple, M. (1998). *Teachers and texts: A political economy of class and gender relations in education.* New York: Routledge and Kegan.

Applebee, A. N. (1981). *Writing in the secondary school.* Urbana, IL: National Council of Teachers of English.

Applefield, J. M., Huber, R, I., & Moallem, M. (2000). Constructivism in theory and practice: Toward a better understanding. *High School Journal, 84*(2), 35.

Ariail, M., & Albright, L. K. (2006). A survey of teachers' read-aloud practices in middle schools. *Reading Research and Instruction, 45*(2), 69–89.

Arlin, P. K. (1984). *Arlin test of formal reasoning.* East Aurora, NY: Slosson Educational Publications.

Armbruster, B. (1992). Content reading in RT: The last two decades. *The Reading Teacher, 46,* 166–167.

Armbruster, B., & Anderson, T. (1984). *Producing "considerate" expository text: Or easy reading is damned hard writing* (Reading Education Report No. 36). Champaign: University of Illinois, Center for the Study of Reading.

Armbruster, B., Anderson, T., Armstrong, J., Wise, M., Janisch, C., & Meyer, L. (1991). Reading and questioning in content areas. *Journal of Reading Behavior, 23,* 35–59.

Armbruster, B. B., Anderson, T. H., & Meyer, J. L. (1991). Improving content area reading using instructional graphics. *Reading Research Quarterly, 26*(4), 393–416.

Aronson, E. (1978). *The jigsaw classroom.* Beverly Hills, CA: Sage.

Ashby-Davis, C. (1985). Cloze and comprehension: A qualitative analysis of critique. *Journal of Reading, 28,* 585–593.

Ashton-Warner, S. (1959). *Spinster.* New York: Simon & Schuster.

Ashworth, M. (1992). *First step on the longer path: Becoming an ESL teacher.* Markham, Ontario: Pippin.

Atkinson, R. C. (1975). Mnemotechnics in second language learning. *American Psychologist, 30,* 821–828.

Atwell, N. (1987). *In the middle: Writing, reading, and learning with adolescents.* Portsmouth, NH: Heinemann.

Atwell, N. (1989). *Coming to know: Writing to learn in the intermediate grades.* Portsmouth, NH: Heinemann.

Au, K. H. (1992). *Literary instruction in multicultural settings.* Fort Worth, TX: Harcourt Brace Jovanovich.

Au, K. H. (1998). Social constructivism and the school literacy learning of students of diverse backgrounds. *Journal of Literacy Research, 30,* 297–331.

Au, K. H. (2001). Culturally responsive instruction as a dimension of new literacies. *Reading Online, 5*(1). Retrieved Dec. 7, 2004, from http://www.readingonline.org/newliteracies/lit_index.asp?HREF=/newliteracies/xu/index.html.

Au, K. H., & Raphael, T. E. (2000). Equity and literacy in the next millennium. *Reading Research Quarterly, 35,* 171–188.

Aurandt, P. (1983). *Destiny.* New York: Bantam Books.

Ausubel, D. (1960). The use of advance organizers in learning and retention of meaningful verbal material. *Journal of Educational Psychology, 51,* 267–272.

Ausubel, D. (1963). *The psychology of meaningful verbal learning.* New York: Grune and Stratton.

Ausubel, D. (1968). *Educational psychology: A cognitive view.* New York: Holt, Rinehart and Winston.

Ayers, S. F. (2001). Developing quality multiple-choice tests for physical education. *The Journal of Physical Education, Recreation & Dance, 72*(16), 23–30.

Babbs, P., & Moe, A. (1983). Metacognition: A key for independent learning from text. *The Reading Teacher, 36,* 422–426.

Bader, L. (1987). *Textbook analysis chart: Reading, writing, speaking, listening, and critical thinking in content area subjects.* Unpublished manuscript, Michigan State University.

Baerwoald, T. J., & Fraser, C. (1992). *World geography.* New Jersey: Prentice-Hall.

Baines, L. (1996). From page to screen: When a novel is interpreted from film, what gets lost in the translation? *Journal of Adolescent & Adult Literacy, 39*(8), 612–622.

Baker, E. A. (2001). The nature of literacy in a technology-rich, fourth grade classroom. *Reading Research and Instruction, 40,* 159–184.

Baker, S. K., Simmons, D. C., & Kame'enui, E. J. (1998). Vocabulary acquisition: Research bases. In D. C. Simmons & E. J. Kame'enui (Eds.), *What reading research tells us about children with diverse learning needs* (pp. 183–218). Mahwah, NJ: Erlbaum.

Ball, D. L., & Cohen, D. K. (1999). Developing practice, developing practitioners: Toward a practice-based theory of professional education. In L. Darling-Hammond & G. Sykes (Eds.), *Teaching as the learning profession: Handbook of policy and practice* (pp. 3–32). San Francisco: Jossey-Bass.

Bandura, A. (1977). Self-efficacy: Toward a unifying theory of behavioral change. *Psychological Review, 84,* 191–215.

Bandura, A. (1986). *Social foundations of thought and action: A social–cognitive theory.* Upper Saddle River, NJ: Prentice-Hall.

Bandura, A. (Ed.). (1995). *Self-efficacy in changing societies.* New York: Cambridge University Press.

Bandura, A. (1997). *Self-efficacy: The exercise of control.* New York: W. H. Freeman.

Bangert-Drowns, R. L. (1993). The word processor as an instructional tool: A meta-analysis of word processing in writing instruction. *Review of Educational Research, 63*(1), 69–93.

Bangert-Drowns, R. L., Hurley, M. M., & Wilkinson, B. (2004). The effects of school-based writing-to-learn interventions on academic achievement: A meta-analysis. *Review of Educational Research, 74,* 29–58.

Banks, J. A. (1995). Multicultural education: Historical development, dimensions, and practice. In J. A. Banks & C. A. M. Banks (Eds.), *Handbook of research on multicultural education* (pp. 3–24). New York: Macmillan.

Banks, L. R. (1990). *The Indian in the cupboard.* Garden City, NY: Doubleday.

Bardovi-Harlig, K., & Dornyei, Z. (1998). Do language learners recognize pragmatic variations? *TESOL Quarterly, 32*(2), 233–259.

Barenbaum, E. (1983). Writing in the special class. *Topics in Learning and Learning Disabilities, 3,* 12–20.

Barnako, F. (2004). Life without the Net is unbearable. Retrieved Sept. 23, 2004, from http://cbs .marketwatch. com/news/archivedStory.asp? archive=true&dist=ArchiveSplash&siteid=mktw& guid=%7BB0361CD7%2D6B85%2D4808%2D860B %2D9EE55739D9BE%7D&returnURL=%2Fnews% 2Fstory%2Easp%3Fguid%3D%7BB0361CD7% 2D6B85%2D4808%2D860B%2D9EE55739D9BE %7D%26siteid%3Dmktw%26dist%3Dnbc% 26archive%3Dtrue%26param%3Darchive% 26garden%3D%26minisite%3D.

Barnes, D. (1976). *From communication to curriculum.* New York: Penguin Books.

Barnett, J. E. (2000). Self-regulated reading and test preparation among college students. *Journal of College Reading and Learning, 31*(1), 42–61.

Barry, A. (2002). Reading strategies teachers say they use. *Journal of Adolescent and Adult Literacy, 46*(2), 132–141.

Bartlett, F. C. (1932). *Remembering.* Cambridge: Cambridge University Press.

Barton, J. (1995). Conducting effective classroom discussions. *Journal of Reading, 38,* 346–350.

Baumann, J., Edwards, E., Font, G., Tereshinski, C., Kame'enui, E., & Olejnik, S. (2002). Teaching morphemic and contextual analysis to fifth-grade students. *Reading Research Quarterly, 37,* 150–176.

Baumann, J. F. (2005). Vocabulary comprehension relationships. In B. Maloch, J.V. Hoffman, D. L. Schallert, C. M. Fairbanks, & J. Worthy (Eds.), *54th yearbook of the National Reading Conference* (pp. 117–131). Oak Creek, WI: National Reading Conference.

Baumann, J. F., Edwards, E. C., Boland, E. M., Olejnik, S., & Kame'enui, E. J. (2003). Vocabulary tricks: Effects of instruction in morphology and context on fifth-grade students' ability to derive and infer word meanings. *American Educational Research Journal, 40,* 447–494.

Baumann, J. F., Seifert-Kessell, N., & Jones, L. A. (1992). Effect of think-aloud instruction on elementary students' comprehension monitoring abilities. *Journal of Reading Behavior, 24,* 143–172.

Baxter, J. (1985). *Designing a test.* Unpublished paper, submitted in partial fulfillment of course requirements for Reading in the Content Areas. Virginia Commonwealth University, Richmond.

Bean, T. W. (1988). Organizing and retaining information by thinking like an author. In S. Glazer, L. Searfoss, & L. Gentile (Eds.), *Reexamining reading diagnosis* (pp. 103–127). Newark, DE: International Reading Association.

Bean, T. W. (2001). An update on reading in the content areas: Social constructivist dimensions. *Reading Online, 5*(5). Retrieved Dec. 7, 2004, from http://www.readingonline.org/articles/art_index.asp?HREF=handbook/bean/index.html.

Bean, T. W., & Readance, J. E. (2002). Adolescent literacy: Charting a course for successful futures as lifelong learners. *Reading Research and Instruction, 41*(3), 203–210.

Bean, T. W., & Steenwyk, F. L. (1984). The effect of three forms of summarization instruction on sixth graders' summary writing and comprehension. *Journal of Reading Behavior, 16,* 297–306.

Beane, J. (1990). *A middle school curriculum: From rhetoric to reality.* Columbus, OH: National Middle School Association.

Bear, D. R., & Templeton, S. (1996). Explorations in developmental spelling: Foundations for learning and teaching phonics, spelling, and vocabulary. *The Reading Teacher, 52,* 222–242.

Beck, I., McKeown, M., & Kucan, L. (2002). *Bringing words to life: Robust vocabulary instruction.* New York: Guilford.

Beck, I. L., & McKeown, M. G. (1988, August–September). Toward meaningful accounts in history texts for young learners. *American Educational Research Journal,* 31–39.

Beck, I. L., McKeown, M. G., & Kucan, L. (2002). *Bringing words to life: Robust vocabulary development.* New York: Guilford Press.

Beck, I. L., McKeown, M. G., Sinatra, G. M., & Loxterman, J. A. (1991). Revising social studies text from a text processing perspective: Evidence of improved comprehensibility. *Reading Research Quarterly, 26,* 251–276.

Becker, W. C. (1977). Teaching reading and language to the disadvantaged: What we have learned from field research? *Harvard Educational Review, 47,* 518–543.

Beers, T. (1987) Schema-theoretic models of reading: Humanizing the machine. *Reading Research Quarterly, 22*(3), 369–377.

Bell, T. (2001). Extensive reading: Speed and comprehension. *The Reading Matrix, 1*(1). Retrieved March 14, 2007 from http://www.readingmatrix.com/articles/bell/article.pdf.

Belzer, S., Miller, M. & Hoemake, S. (2003). Concepts in biology: A supplemental study skills course designed to improve introductory students' skills for learning biology. *The American Biology Teacher, 65*(1), 30–40.

Bereiter, C., & Scardamalia, M. (1987). An attainable version of high literacy: Approaches to teaching higher-order skills in reading and writing. *Curriculum Inquiry, 17*(1), 9–30.

Bergenske, M. D. (1987). The missing link in narrative story mapping. *The Reading Teacher, 41,* 333–335.

Berlak, H. (1992). The need for a new science of assessment. In H. Berlak et al. (Eds.), *Toward a new science of educational testing and assessment.* New York: State University of New York Press.

Berliner, D. C. (2001). Mythology and the American system of education. In K. Ryan & J. M. Cooper (Eds.), *Kaleidoscope: Readings in education* (pp. 106–115). Boston: Houghton Mifflin.

Berube, C. T. (2004). Are standards preventing good teaching? *The Clearing House, 77*(6), 264–267.

Betts, F. (1991). What's all the noise about? Constructivism in the classroom. In K. Ryan & J. M. Cooper (Eds.), *Kaleidoscope: Readings in education.* Boston: Houghton Mifflin.

Betts, G. (2004). Fostering autonomous learners through levels of differentiation. *Roeper Review, 26*(4), 190–192.

Beyer, B. K. (1983). Common sense about teaching thinking skills. *Educational Leadership, 41,* 44–49.

Beyer, B. K. (1984). Improving thinking skills: Defining the problem. *Phi Delta Kappan, 65,* 486–490.

Bhat, P., Rapport, M. J., & Griffin, C. C. (2000). A legal perspective on the use of specific learning methods for students with learning disabilities. *Learning Disabilities Quarterly, 23*(4), 283–297.

Bieger, E. M. (1995). Promoting multicultural education through a literature-based approach. *The Reading Teacher, 49,* 308–311.

Biemiller, A. (2001). Teaching vocabulary. *American Educator,* 143–148.

Biemiller, A., & Boote, C. (2006). An effective method for building meaning vocabulary in primary grades. *Journal of Educational Psychology, 98*(1), 44–62.

Biggs, S. A. (1992). Building on strengths: Closing the literacy gap for African-American students. *Journal of Reading, 35,* 624–628.

Bikowski, D., & Kessler, G. (2002). Making the most of discussion boards in the ESL classroom. *TESOL Journal, 11*(3), 27–30.

Bintz, W. P., & Shelton, K. S. (2004). Using written conversation in middle school: Lessons from a teacher researcher project. *Journal of Adolescent & Adult Literacy, 47*, 492–507.

Blachowicz, C. L. Z., & Fisher, P. (2000). Vocabulary instruction. In M. Kamil, P. Mosenthal, P. D. Pearson, & R. Barr (Eds.), *Handbook of reading research: Vol. III* (pp. 503–523). Mahwah, NJ: Erlbaum.

Blachowicz, C. L. Z., & Fisher, P. (2004). Vocabulary lessons. *Educational Leadership, 61*(6), 66–69.

Blachowicz, C. L. Z., & Fisher, P. J. L. (2006). *Teaching vocabulary in all classrooms* (3rd ed.). Upper Saddle River, NJ: Pearson Education.

Blachowicz, C. L. Z., Fisher, P. J. L., Ogle, D., & Watts-Taffe, S. (2006). Vocabulary: Questions from the classroom. *Reading Research Quarterly, 41*(4), 524–539.

Blai, B. (1993). A study guide for students. *The Clearing House, 67*(2), 98–103.

Blasingame, J., & Bushman, J. H. (2005). *Teaching writing in middle and secondary schools.* Upper Saddle River, NJ: Pearson Education.

Block, C. C. (2004). *Teaching comprehension: The comprehension process approach.* Boston: Allyn & Bacon.

Block, C. C., & Israel, S. E. (2004) The ABCs of performing highly effective think-alouds: Effective think-alouds can build students' comprehension decoding, vocabulary, and fluency. *The Reading Teacher, 58*(2), 154–168.

Bloom, A. (1987). *The closing of the American mind.* New York: Simon and Schuster.

Bloom, B. C. (1956). *Taxonomy of educational objectives: Cognitive domain.* New York: David McKay.

Blumenfeld, P. C., Marx, R., Soloway, E., & Krajcik, J. (1997). Learning with peers: From small group cooperation to collaborative communities. *Educational Researcher, 25*, 37–40.

Boaler, J. (2006). Promoting respectful learning. *Educational Leadership, 63*(5), 74–78.

Bohan, H., & Bass, J. (1991, Fall). Teaching thinking in elementary mathematics and science. *Educator's Forum, 1*, 4–5, 10.

Borden, J., & Lytle, R. K. (2000). All together now . . . ? *The Exceptional Parent, 30*(9), 79–82.

Borko, H., & Putnam, R. T. (1996). Learning to teach. In D. C. Berliner & R. C. Calfee (Eds.), *Handbook of educational psychology* (pp. 673–708). New York: Macmillan.

Borman, G. D., & Overman, L. T. (2004). Academic resilience in mathematics among poor and minority students. *The Elementary School Journal, 104*(3), 177–197.

Bormouth, J. R. (1969). *Development of a readability analysis.* (Final Report, Project No. 7-0052, Contract No. OEC-3-7-070052-0326). Washington, DC: USOE, Bureau of Research, U.S. Department of Health, Education, and Welfare.

Bormouth, J. R. (1975). Literacy in the classroom. In W. D. Page (Ed.), *Help for the reading teacher: New directions in research* (pp. 60–90). Urbana, IL: National Conference on Research in English and ERIC/RCS Clearinghouse.

Bos, C. S., & Anders, P. L. (1990). Effects of interactive vocabulary instruction on the vocabulary learning and reading comprehension of junior-high learning disabilities students. *Learning Disabilities Quarterly, 13*(1), 31–42.

Bos, C. S., & Vaughn, S. (2002). *Strategies for teaching students with learning and behavior problems,* 5th ed. Boston: Allyn & Bacon.

Bosworth, K. (1996). Caring for others and being cared for: Students talk about caring in school. *Phi Delta Kappan, 76*, 686–693.

Bottomley, D. M., Truscott, D. M., Marimak, B. A., Henk, W. A., & Melnick, S. A. (1999). An affective comparison of whole language, literature-based, and basal reader literacy instruction. *Journal of Research and Instruction, 38*(2), 115–130.

Boyd, W. L. (2004, February). Relaunching the *American Journal of Education* in "interesting times." *The American Journal of Education, 110*, 105–107.

Boyd-Batstone, P. (2004). Focused anecdotal records assessment: A tool for standards-based, authentic assessment. *The Reading Teacher, 58*(3), 230–239.

Brabham, E. G., & Villaume, S. K. (2002). Vocabulary instruction: Concerns and visions. (Questions and answers). *The Reading Teacher, 56*, 264–269.

Bracey, G. (1992). The condition of public education. *Phi Delta Kappan, 74*, 104–117.

Bracey, G. (1997). *Setting the record straight: Responses to misconceptions about public education in the United States.* Alexandria, VA: Association for Supervision and Curriculum Development.

Bradbury, R. (1983, July). Goodbye grandma. *Reader's Digest, 23*, 139–142.

Brady, M. (1993). Critical issues that will determine the future of alternative assessment. *Phi Delta Kappan, 74*, 444–456.

Brechtel, M. (1992). *Bringing the whole together: An integrated whole-language approach for the multilingual classroom.* San Diego: Dominie Press.

Brendtro, L. K., Brokenleg, M., & Bockern, S. V. (1990). *Reclaiming youth at risk: Our hope for the future.* Bloomington, IN: National Educational Service.

Bright, R. (1995). *Writing instruction in the intermediate grades: What is said, what is done, what is understood.* Newark, DE: International Reading Association.

Brindley, R., & Schneider, J. J. (2002). Writing instruction or destruction: Lessons to be learned from fourth-grade teachers' perspectives on teaching writing. *Journal of Teacher Education, 53,* 328–341.

Brinthaupt, T. M., & Shin, C. M. (2001). The relationship of academic cramming to flow experience. *College Student Journal, 35*(3), 457–472.

Britton, B. K., & Tesser, A. (1991). Effects of time-management practices on college grades. *Journal of Educational Psychology, 83,* 405–410.

Bromley, K. (1993). *Journaling: Engagements in reading, writing, and thinking.* New York: Scholastic.

Brooks, J. G., & Brooks, M. G. (1993). *The case of constructivist classrooms.* Alexandria, VA: Association for Supervision and Curriculum Development.

Brotherton, P. (2000). Diverse solutions. *Techniques, 75*(2), 18–21.

Brown, A. L. (1980). Metacognitive development and reading. In R. J. Spiro, B. Bruce, & W. F. Brewer (Eds.), *Theoretical issues in reading comprehension* (pp. 453–481). Hillsdale, NJ: Erlbaum.

Brown, A. L., Campione, J. C., & Day, J. D. (1981). Learning to learn: On training students to learn from texts. *Educational Researcher, 10,* 14–21.

Brown, A. L., & Day, J. D. (1983). Macrorules for summarizing texts: The development of expertise. *Child Development, 48,* 1–8.

Brown, A. L., & Smiley, S. S. (1977). Rating the importance of structural units of prose passages: A problem of metacognitive development. *Child Development, 48,* 1–8.

Brown, J., Phillips, L., & Stephens, E. (1992). *Toward literacy: Theory and applications for teaching writing in the content areas.* Belmont, CA: Wadsworth.

Brown, J., & Stephens, E. (1995). *Teaching young adult literature.* Belmont, CA: Wadsworth.

Brown, R. (2005). Seventh-graders' self-regulatory note-taking from text: Perceptions, preferences, and practices. *Reading Research and Instruction, 44*(4), 1–26.

Bruce, B. (1998). Dewey and technology. *Journal of Adolescent & Adult Literacy, 42*(3), 222–226.

Brunwin, B. (Ed.). (1989). *The Bucktrout swamp.* Written by first- to sixth-grade students at Greenbriar Elementary School, Chesapeake, VA.

Bryant, D. P., Goodwin, M., Bryant, B. R., & Higgins, K. (2003). Vocabulary instruction for students with learning disabilities: A review of the research. *Learning Disability Quarterly, 26,* 117–128.

Bryant, D. P., Vaughn, S., Linan-Thompson, S., Ugel, N., Hamff, A., & Hougen, M. (2000). Reading outcomes for students with and without reading disabilities in general education middle-school content area classes. *Learning Disability Quarterly, 23*(3), 24–38.

Bryant, J. A. R. (1984). Textbook treasure hunt. *Journal of Reading, 27,* 547–548.

Budig, G. A. (2006). Writing: A necessary tool. *Phi Delta Kappan, 87,* 663.

Burns, M. (1975). *The I hate mathematics! book.* New York: Little Brown and Co.

Bushaw, W. J., & Fujloka, J. (2006, Feb. 22). Education week. Retrieved June 2007 from http://www.pdkintl.org/newsroom/publicst/0602advt_ew.htm.

Butler, G., & McManus, F. (1998). *Psychology: A very short introduction.* Oxford: Oxford University Press.

Byrnes, J. P. (1995). Domain specificity and the logic of using general ability as an independent variable or covariable. *Merrill-Palmer Quarterly, 41,* 1–24.

Cadenhead, K. (1987). Reading level: A metaphor that shapes practice. *Phi Delta Kappan, 68,* 436–441.

Caine, G., & Caine, R. (1994). *Mindshifts.* Tucson: Zephyr Press.

Caine, R. N., & Caine, G. (1991). *Teaching and the human brain.* Alexandria, VA: Association for Supervision and Curriculum Development.

Calfee, R. C. (1987). *The role of text structure in acquiring knowledge: Final report to the U. S. Department of Education* (Federal Program No. 122B). Palo Alto, CA: Stanford University, Text Analysis Project.

Callison, D. (2003). Concept mapping. *School Library Media Activities Monthly, 17*(10), 30–32.

Calkins, L. (1986). *The art of teaching writing.* Portsmouth, NH: Heinemann.

Calkins, L., Montgomery, K., & Santman, D. (1998). *A teacher's guide to standardized reading tests.* Portsmouth, NH: Heinemann.

Calkins, L. M. (1994). *The art of teaching writing,* 2nd ed. Portsmouth, NH: Heinemann.

Cantrell, S. C. (2002). Promoting talk: A framework for reading discussions in teacher education courses: Using reading discussion groups with preservice teachers leads to greater comprehension and engagement. *Journal of Adolescent & Adult Literacy, 45*(7), 642–652.

Cardoso, S. (Ed.) (2003). *Brain and mind: Electronic magazine and neuroscience.* http://www.epub.org.br/cm/n05/mente/estados_i.htm.

Carmen, R., & Adams, W. (1972). *Study skills: A student's guide to survival.* New York: Wiley.

Carolan, J., & Guinn, A. (2007). Differentiation: Lessons from master teachers. *Educational Leadership, 64*(5), 44–47.

Carney, J. J., Anderson, D., Blackburn, C., & Blessing, D. (1984). Preteaching vocabulary and the comprehension of social studies materials by elementary school children. *Social Education, 48*(3), 195–196.

Carr, E., & Ogle, D. (1987). KWL plus: A strategy for comprehension and summarization. *Journal of Reading, 30,* 626–631.

Carr, E., & Wixson, K. K. (1986). Guidelines for evaluating vocabulary instruction. *Journal of Reading, 29,* 588–595.

Carter, B. (1996, Fall). Hold the applause! Do *Accelerated Reader* and *Electronic Bookshelf* send the right message? *School Library Journal,* 22–25.

Carter, K. (1986). Test-wiseness for teachers and students. *Educational Measurement: Issues and Practices, 5,* 20–23.

Carver, R. P. (1990). *Reading rate: A review of research and theory.* New York: Academic Press.

Carver, R. P. (1992). Reading rate: Theory, research, and practical applications. *Journal of Reading, 36*(2), 84–95.

Carver, R. P. (1994). Percentage of unknown vocabulary words in text as a function of the relative difficulty of the text: Implications for instruction. *Journal of Reading Behavior, 25*(4), 413–437.

Cassidy, J. (2007). Email communication with author on February 8, 2007.

Cassidy, J., & Cassidy, D. (2007). What's hot, what's not for 2007. *Reading Today, 24*(4), 1, 10.

Cassidy, J., Garrett, S. D., & Barrera, E. S. (2007). What's hot in adolescent literacy 1997–2006. *Journal of Adolescent and Adult Literacy, 50*(1), 30–36.

Chall, J. (1958). *Readability: An appraisal of research and application.* Columbus: Ohio State University, Bureau of Educational Research.

Chall, J. (1983). *Stages of reading development.* New York: McGraw-Hill.

Chamot, A. U., & O'Malley, J. M. (1989). The cognitive academic language learning approach. In P. Rigg (Ed.), *When they don't all speak English: Integrating the ESL student into the regular classroom* (pp. 108–125). Urbana, IL: National Council of Teachers of English.

Chamot, A. U., & O'Malley, J. M. (1994). Instructional approaches and teaching procedures. In K. Spangenberg-Urbschat & R. Pritchard (Eds.), *Kids come in all languages: Reading instruction for ESL students* (pp. 82–107). Newark, DE: International Reading Association.

Chan, L. K. S. (1996). Motivational orientations and metacognitive abilities of intellectually gifted students. *Gifted Child Quarterly, 40*(4), 184–193.

Chandler-Olcott, K., & Mahar, D. (2003). "Tech-savviness" means multiliteracies: Exploring adolescent girls' technology mediated literacy practices. *Reading Research Quarterly, 38*(3), 356–385.

Chang, I. (1991). *A separate battle: Women and the Civil War.* New York: Lodestar Books/Dutton.

Chase, A. C., & Dufflemeyer, F. A. (1990). VOCAB-LIT: Integrating vocabulary study and literature study. *Journal of Reading, 34*(3), 188–193.

Chesbro, R. (2006). Using interactive science notebooks for inquiry-based science. *Science Scope, 29*(7), 30–34.

Chi, F. (1995). ESL readers and a focus on intertextuality. *Journal of Reading, 38,* 638–644.

Chi, K. (2004, Spring). No Child Left Behind and emerging trends. *Spectrum.* Retrieved Nov. 26, 2004, from http://www.csg.org.

Childress, H. (1998). Seventeen reasons why football is better than high school. Retrieved Nov. 26, 2004, from http://www.pdkintl.org/kappan/kchi9804.htm.

Chinn, C. A., & Anderson, R. C. (1998). The structure of discussions that promote reasoning. *Teachers College Record, 100,* 315–368.

Chinn, C. A., Anderson, R. C., & Waggoner, M. A. (2001). Patterns of discourse in two kinds of literature discussion. *Reading Research Quarterly, 36*(4), 378–411.

Choate, J. S., & Rakes, T. A. (1987). The structured listening activity: A model for improving listening comprehension. *The Reading Teacher, 41,* 194–200.

Chomsky, C. (1971). Write first, read later. *Childhood Education, 47,* 296–299.

Chu, M. L. (1995). Reader response to interactive computer books: Examining literacy responses in a nontraditional reading setting. *Reading Research and Instruction, 43,* 352–366.

Ciardello, A. V. (1998). Did you ask a good question today? Alternative cognitive and metacognitive strategies. *Journal of Adolescent & Adult Literacy, 42*(3), 210–219.

Ciardiello, A. V. (2004). Democracy's young heroes: An instructional model of critical literacy practices. *The Reading Teacher, 58,* 138–147.

Cimera, R. E. (2000). From bridges to beyond: A perspective of special education's future. *Journal of Disability Policy Studies, 11*(2), 124–125.

Clark, D. (1999). Critical reflection. Retrieved November 22, 2003, from http://www.nwlink.com/~donclark/hrd/development/reflection.html.

Cleary, B. (1982). *Ralph S. Mouse.* New York: William Morrow.

Cleland, J. V. (1999). We can charts: Building blocks for student-led conferences. *The Reading Teacher, 52*(6), 588–595.

Cochran-Smith, M. (1991). Word processing and writing in elementary classrooms: A critical review of related literature. *Review of Educational Research, 61*(1), 107–155.

Cohen, A. D. (1987). The use of verbal and imagery mnemonics in second-language vocabulary learning. *Studies in Second Language Acquisition, 9,* 43–61.

Cohen, M. R., Cooney, T. M., Hawthorne, C., McCormack, A. J., Pasachoff, J. M., Pasachoff, N., Rhines, K. L., & Siesnick, I. L. (1991). *Discover science.* Glenview, IL: Scott, Foresman.

Coiro, J. (2003). Reading comprehension on the Internet: Expanding our understanding of comprehension to encompass new literacies. *The Reading Teacher, 56,* 458–464.

Cole, A. D. (1998). Beginner-oriented texts in literature-based classrooms: The segue for a few struggling readers. *The Reading Teacher, 51*(6), 488–501.

Cole, R., Raffier, L. M., Rogan, P., & Schleicher, L. (1998). Interactive group journals: Learning as a dialogue among learners. *TESOL Quarterly, 32*(3), 556–568.

Cole, R. P., & Goetz, V. W. (2000). Epistemological beliefs of underprepared college students. *Journal of College Reading and Learning, 31*(1), 60–70.

College Board, Touchtone Applied Science Associates. (1986). *Degrees of reading power.* New York: College Board.

Collins, M. L. (1977). *The effects of training for enthusiasm on the enthusiasm displayed by pre-service elementary teachers.* Unpublished doctoral dissertation, Syracuse University, Syracuse, NY.

Colwell, C. G., Mangano, N. G., Childs, D., & Case, D. (1986). Cognitive, affective, and behavioral differences between students receiving instruction using alternative lesson formats. *Proceedings of the National Reading and Language Arts Conference.*

Commission on No Child Left Behind. (2007). Commissioner Messina Gives Remarks at Annual State School Board Conference. Press release downloaded June 14, 2007, from http://www.aspeninstitute.org/site/c.huLWJeMRKpH/b.938015/k.40DA/Commission_on_No_Child_Left_Behind.htm.

Committee on Education and the Workforce. (2002). *President Bush signs landmark reforms into law* [press release]. Washington, DC: White House Committee on Education and the Workforce.

Conley, M. W., & Hinchman, K. A. (2004). No Child Left Behind: What it means for U.S. adolescents and what we can do about it. *Journal of Adolescent & Adult Literacy, 48*(1), 42–48.

Connell, J. P., & Ryan, R. M. (1984). A developmental theory of motivation in the classroom. *Teacher Education Quarterly, 11,* 64–77.

Conner, J. (2003). Instructional reading strategy: Anticipation guides. Retrieved from http://www.indiana.edu/~1517/anticipation_guides.htm.

Cook, L., & Gonzales, P. (1995). Zones of contact: Using literature with second language learners. *Reading Today, 12,* 27.

Coombe, C. A., & Hubley, N. J. (2004). *Fundamentals of language assessment.* Presentation and booklet, TESOL conference, Long Beach, CA.

Cooper, J., & Kiger, N. (2003). *Literacy: Helping children construct literacy.* Boston: Houghton Mifflin.

Coopersmith, S. (1967). *The antecedents of self-esteem.* San Francisco: Freeman.

Cooter, R. B. (1990, October/November). Learners with special needs. *Reading Today,* 28.

Cooter, R. B., Jr. (1994). Assessing affective and conative factors in reading. *Reading Psychology, 15*(2), 77–90.

Cooter, R. B., & Chilcoat, G. W. (1991). Content-focused melodrama: Dramatic renderings of historical text. *Journal of Reading, 34,* 274–277.

Cooter, R. B., Joseph, D., & Flynt, E. (1986). Eliminating the literal pursuit in reading comprehension. *Journal of Clinical Reading, 2,* 9–11.

Cornu, B. (2001). *Winds of change in the teaching profession.* The report of the French National Commission for UNESCO. Paris: UNESCO.

Costa, C. (2006). My adventure in Podland. *Essential Teacher, 3*(4), 38–41.

Covey, S. (1990). *Seven habits of highly effective people.* New York: Simon and Schuster.

Cowan, G., & Cowan, E. (1980). *Writing.* New York: Wiley.

Cox, J., & Wiebe, J. (1984). Measuring reading vocabulary and concepts in mathematics in the primary grades. *Reading Teacher, 37,* 402–410.

Cox, Matthews, & Associates. (2001). Blacks are more likely to be placed in special education. *Black Issues in Higher Education, 18*(3), 22.

Crapse, L. (1995). Helping students construct meaning through their own questions. *Journal of Reading, 38*(5), 389–390.

Creek, R. J., McDonald, W. C., & Ganley, M. A. (1991). *Internality and achievement in the intermediate grades.* (ERIC Document No. ED 330 656).

Crist, J. (1975). One capsule a week—painless remedy for vocabulary ills. *Journal of Reading, 31,* 147–149.

Cronbach, L. J. (1951). Coefficient alpha and the internal structure of tests. *Psychometrika, 16,* 297–334.

Cronbach, L. J. (1957). *Psychological tests and personnel decisions.* Urbana: University of Illinois Press.

Cronin, H., Meadows, D., & Sinatra, R. (1990). Integrating computers, reading, and writing across the curriculum. *Educational Leadership, 48,* 57–62.

Crooks, S. M., & Katayama, A. D. (2002). Effects of online note-taking format on the comprehension of electronic text. *Research in the Schools, 9,* 22–23.

Cullinan, B. E., Karrer, M. K., & Pillar, A. M. (1981). *Literature and the child.* New York: Harcourt Brace and Jovanovich.

Culver, V. I., & Morgan, R. F. (1977). *The relationship of locus of control to reading achievement.* Unpublished manuscript, Old Dominion University, Norfolk, VA.

Cummins, J. (1979). Linguistic interdependence and the educational development of bilingual children. *Review of Educational Research, 49,* 222–251.

Cummins, J. (1994). The acquisition of English as a second language. In Spangenberg-Urbschadt and R. Pritchard (Eds.), *Kids come in all languages.* Newark, DE: International Reading Association.

Cunningham, A. E., & Stanovich, K. E. (1998). What reading does for the mind. *American Educator 22*(1, 2), 8–15.

Cunningham, J. W. (1982). Generating interactions between schemata and text. In J. A. Niles & L. A. Harris (Eds.), *New inquiries in reading research and instruction: Thirty-first yearbook of the National Reading Conference* (pp. 42–47). Rochester, NY: National Reading Conference.

Cunningham, P. (1995). *Phonics they use.* New York: Harper Collins.

Cunningham, P. (2006). What if they can say the words but don't know what they mean? *The Reading Teacher, 59*(7), 708–711.

Cunningham, P., & Stanovich, K. E. (1997). Early reading acquisition and its relation to reading experience and ability 10 years later. *Developmental Psychology, 33,* 934–945.

Cunningham, R., & Shablak, S. (1975). Selective reading guide-o-rama: The content teacher's best friend. *Journal of Reading, 18,* 380–382.

Currie, H. (1990). Making texts more readable. *British Journal of Special Education, 17,* 137–139.

Curry, B. A. (1990). The impact of the Nicholls State Youth Opportunities Unlimited Program as related to academic achievement, self-esteem, and locus of control. Master's thesis, Nicholls State University, Thibodaux, LA.

Curtis, M. E., & Longo, A. M. (2001). Teaching vocabulary to adolescents to improve comprehension. *Reading Online, 5*(4). Available at http://www.readingonline.org/articles/art_index.asp?HREF=curtis/index.html.

Dahlman, A., & Rilling, S. (2001). Integrating technologies and tasks in an EFL distance learning course in Finland. *TESOL Journal, 10*(1), 4–8.

Daily, G. (1995, September). A glimpse of the real world. *Learning,* 62–63.

Dale, E. (1965). Vocabulary measurement: Techniques and major findings. *Elementary English, 42,* 395–401.

Dale, E., & Chall, J. (1948). A formula for predicting readability. *Educational Research Bulletin, 27,* 11–20, 37–54.

Dale, E., & O'Rourke, J. (1976). *The living word vocabulary.* Elgin, IL: Dome.

Dale, E., O'Rourke, J., & Bamman, H. (1971). *Techniques of teaching vocabulary.* Palo Alto, CA: Field Educational Publications.

Dana, C., & Rodriguez, M. (1992). TOAST: A system to study vocabulary. *Reading Research and Instruction, 31*(4), 78–84.

Daniels, H. (1994). *Literature circles: Voice and choice in the student-centered classroom.* Portsmouth, NH: Heinemann.

Danielson, K. E. (1987). Readability formulas: A necessary evil? *Reading Horizons, 27,* 178–188.

Darling-Hammond, L. (2000). Teacher quality and student achievement: A review of state policy evidence. *Education Policy Analysis and Archives, 8,* 1. Retrieved May 30, 2007, from: http://epaa.asu.edu/epaa/v8n1/.

Davey, B. (1983). Think aloud: Modeling the cognitive processes of reading comprehension. *Journal of Reading, 27,* 44–47.

Davidson, J. L. (1982). The group mapping activity for instruction in reading and thinking. *Journal of Reading, 26,* 52–56.

Davis, B. (1985). *The long surrender.* New York: Random House.

Davis, F. B. (1944). Fundamental factors of comprehension in reading. *Psychometrika, 9,* 185–197.

Davis, J. (1997). *Mapping the mind: The secrets of the human brain and how it works.* Secaucus, NJ: Carol Publishing Group.

Davis, M. (1998). The Amish teachers' supper. *The Reading Professor, 21*(1), 158–164.

Davis, N. (2000). Information technology for teacher education at its first zenith: The heat is on! *Journal of Information Technology for Teacher Education, 9*(3), 277–286.

Davis, S., & Winek, J. (1989). Improving expository writing by increasing background knowledge. *Journal of Reading, 33,* 178–181.

Davis, W. C. (1985). *Touched by fire: A photographic portrait of the Civil War.* Boston: Little, Brown and Co.

Davis, W. C. (1990). *Diary of a Confederate soldier.* Columbia, SC: University of South Carolina Press.

Davison, A. (1984). Readability formulas and comprehension. In G. Duffy, L. Roehler, & J. Mason (Eds.), *Comprehension instruction* (pp. 128–143). New York: Longman.

Davison, D., & Pearce, D. (1988a). Using writing activities to reinforce mathematics instruction. *Arithmetic Teacher, 35,* 42–45.

Davison, D., & Pearce, D. (1988b). Writing activities in junior high mathematics texts. *School Science and Mathematics, 88,* 493–499.

Day, B., & Anderson, J. (1992). Assessing the challenges ahead. *Delta Kappa Gamma Bulletin, 58*(4), 5–10.

Deal, D. (1998). Portfolios, learning logs, and eulogies: Using expressive writing in a science methods course. In E. G. Sturtevant, J. A. Dugan, P. Linder, & W. M. Linek (Eds.), *Literacy and community: Twentieth yearbook of the College Reading Association* (pp. 243–256). Commerce, TX: Texas A & M Press.

De Bono, E. (1976). *Teaching thinking*. London: Temple Smith.

Dechant, E. (1970). *Improving the teaching of reading*. Englewood Cliffs, NJ: Prentice-Hall.

Deen, M. Y., Bailey, S. J., & Parker, L. (2001). *Life skills evaluation system*. Wenatchee, WA: Washington State University Cooperative Extension.

Delgardo, B. (2001). Interpretations of constructivism and consequences for computer assisted learning. *British Journal of Educational Technology, 32*(2), 183–194.

Dember, W. M., Warm, J. S., & Parasuraman, R. (1996). Olfactory stimulation and sustained attention. In A. Gilbert (Ed.), *Compendium of olfactory research* (pp. 39–46). New York: Olfactory Research Fund, Ltd.

Derby, T. (1987). Reading instruction and course-related materials for vocational high school students. *Journal of Reading, 30,* 308–316.

DeSanti, R. J., & Alexander, D. H. (1986). Locus of control and reading achievement: Increasing the responsibility and performance of remedial readers. *Journal of Clinical Reading, 2,* 12–14.

Deshler, D. D., & Schumaker, J. B. (1988). An instructional model for teaching students how to learn. In J. L. Graden, J. E. Zins, & M. J. Curtis (Eds.), *Alternative educational delivery systems: Enhancing instructional options for all students* (pp. 391–411). Washington, DC: National Association of School Psychologists.

Devault, R., & Joseph, L. M. (2004). Repeated readings combined with word boxes phonics technique increases fluency levels of high school students with severe reading delays. *Preventing School Failure, 49*(1), 22–28.

DeVoogd, G. (2006). Question authority. *School Library Journal, 52*(4), 48–52.

Dewey, J. (1933). *How we think*. Boston: Heath.

Diamond, M., & Hopson, J. (1998). *Magic trees of the mind: How to motivate your child's intelligence, creativity, and healthy emotions from birth through adolescence*. New York: Penguin Putnam.

DiCecco, V. M., & Gleason, M. M. (2002). Using graphic organizers to attain relational knowledge from expository text. *Journal of Learning Disabilities, 35*(4), 306–321.

Dickson, R. (2002). Creating joy: Adolescents writing poetry with young children. *Voices from the Middle, 10*(2), 38–42.

Dieu, B. (2004). BLOGs for language learning. *The Essential Teacher, 1*(4), 28–30.

Dillard, A. (1975). *Pilgrim at Tinker Creek*. New York: Harper's Magazine Press.

Dillon, J. T. (1983). *Teaching and the art of questioning*. Bloomington, IN: Phi Beta Kappa Educational Foundation. Fastback No. 194.

Dixon, F., Cassady, J., Cross, T., & Williams, D. (2005) Effects of technology on critical thinking and essay writing among gifted adolescents. *Journal of Secondary Gifted Education, 16*(4), 180–190.

Dole, J. A. (2004). The changing role of the reading specialist in school reform. *The Reading Teacher, 57*(5), 462–471.

Dole, S. (2000). The implications of the risk and resilience literature for gifted students with learning disabilities. *Roeper Review, 23*(2), 91.

Douglass, B. (1984). Variations on a theme: Writing with the LD adolescent. *Academic Therapy, 19,* 361–362.

Dove, M. K. (1998). The textbook in education. *Delta Kappa Gamma Bulletin, 64*(3), 24–30.

Downing, J. (1973). *Comparative reading*. New York: Macmillan.

Downing, J., Ollila, L., & Oliver, P. (1975). Cultural differences in children's concepts of reading and writing. *British Journal of Educational Psychology, 45,* 312–316.

Drevno, G. E., Kimball, J. W., Possi, M. K., Howard, W. L., Gardner, R., & Barbetta, P. M. (1994). Effects of active student response during error correction on the acquisition, maintenance, and generalization of science vocabulary by elementary students: A systematic replication. *Journal of Applied Behavior Analysis, 27*(1), 179–180.

Drum, P. (1985). Retention of text information by grade, ability, and study. *Discourse Processes, 8,* 21–51.

Duffelmeyer, F. A., & Baum, D. D. (1992). The extended anticipation guide revisited. *Journal of Reading, 35,* 654–656.

Duffy, G. G., & Hoffman, J. V. (1999). In pursuit of an illusion: The flawed search for a perfect method. *The Reading Teacher, 53,* 10–16.

Duffy, G. G., & Roehler, L. R. (1987). Teaching reading skills as strategies. *The Reading Teacher, 40,* 414–418.

Duke, N. (2003). Information text? The research says, "Yes!" In L. Hoyt, M. Mooney, & B. Parkes (Eds.), *Exploring informational texts: From theory to practice* (pp. 2–7). Portsmouth, NH: Heinemann.

Duke, N., & Pearson, P. D. (2002). Effective practices for developing reading comprehension. In A. E. Farstrup & S. J. Samuels (Eds.), *What research has to say about reading instruction,* 3rd ed. (pp. 205–242). Newark, DE: International Reading Association.

Duke, N. K. (2000). 3.6 minutes per day: The scarcity of informational texts in first grade. *Reading Research Quarterly, 35,* 202–224.

Duke, N. K., Purcell-Gates, V., Hall, L. A., & Tower, C. (2006). Authentic literacy activities for developing comprehension and writing. *The Reading Teacher, 60,* 344–355.

Dunlap, J. C., & Grabinger, R. S. (1996). Rich environments for active learning in the higher education curriculum. In B. Wilson (Ed.), *Constructivist learning environments: Case studies in instructional design.* Englewood Cliffs, NJ: Educational Technology Publications

Dunston, P. J. (1992). A critique of graphic organizer research. *Reading Research and Instruction, 31,* 57–65.

Durkin, D. (1979). What classroom observations reveal about reading comprehension. *Reading Research Quarterly, 14,* 481–533.

Durkin, D. (1981). Reading comprehension instruction in five basal reading series. *Reading Research Quarterly, 16,* 515–544.

Durkin, D. (1984). Is there a match between what elementary teachers do and what basal reader manuals recommend? *The Reading Teacher, 37,* 734–744.

Duvdevany, I., & Rimmerman, A. (1996). Individuals with work-related disabilities: Locus of control, attitudes toward work, and cooperation with the rehabilitation worker. *Journal of Applied Rehabilitation Counseling, 27*(2), 30–35.

Dweck, C. S. (1985). Intrinsic motivation, perceived control, and self-evaluation maintenance: An achievement goal analysis. In C. Ames & R. Ames (Eds.), *Research on motivation in education: Vol. 2* (pp. 289–305). Orlando, FL: Academic Press.

Dwight, J. (2001). An epistemology of hypertexts. *VSTE Journal, 15*(2), 22–26.

Dzaldov, B. S., & Peterson, S. (2005). Book leveling and readers. *The Reading Teacher, 59,* 222–229.

Eanet, M., & Manzo, A. V. (1976). REAP—A strategy for improving reading/writing/study skills. *Journal of Reading, 19,* 647–652.

Earle, R., & Barron, R. F. (1973). An approach for teaching vocabulary in content subjects. In H. L. Herber & R. F. Barron (Eds.), *Research in reading in the content areas: Second year report* (pp. 84–100). Syracuse, NY: Syracuse University, Reading and Language Arts Center.

Ebbinghaus, H. (1908/1973). *Abriss der psychologie* (M. Meyer, Trans. and Ed.). New York: Arno Press.

EDUCAUSEConnect (May, 2005). 7 Things you should know about clickers. Retrieved June 2007 from http://connect.educause.edu/library/abstract/ 7ThingsYouShouldKnow/39379?time=1182561758.

Edwards, E. C., Font, G., Baumann, J. F., & Boland, E. (2004). Unlocking word meanings: Strategies and guidelines for teaching morphemic and contextual analysis. In J. F. Baumann & E. B. Kame'enui (Eds.), *Vocabulary instruction: Research to practice* (pp. 159–176). New York: Guilford Press.

Egan, K. (1987). Literacy and the oral foundations of education. *Harvard Educational Review, 57,* 445–472.

Egan, M. (1999). Reflections on effective use of graphic organizers. *Journal of Adolescent & Adult Literacy, 42*(8), 641–645.

Ehlinger, J., & Pritchard, R. (1994). Using think-alongs in secondary content areas. *Reading Research and Instruction, 33*(3), 187–206.

Eldredge, J. L. (1990). Learning and study strategies inventory—high school version. *Journal of Reading, 34*(2), 146–149.

Elley, W. B. (1992). *How in the world do students read?* The Hague, The Netherlands: International Association for the Evaluation of Educational Achievement.

Elliot, L., Foster, S., & Stinson, M. (2002). Student study habits using notes from a speech-to-text support service. *Exceptional Children, 69*(1), 25–41.

Erickson, B. (1996). Read-alouds reluctant readers relish. *Journal of Adolescent & Adult Literacy, 40*(3), 217–221.

Evans, E. (2004, Spring). Comments on electronic learning. In the course Reading Instruction in the Content Areas, Virginia Commonwealth University, Spring 2004.

Eveland, W. P., & Dunwoody, S. (2002). An investigation of elaboration and selective scanning as mediators of learning from the Web versus print. *Journal of Broadcasting and Electronic Media, 46*(1), 34–54.

Facione, P. A. (1984). Toward a theory of critical thinking. *Liberal Education, 30,* 253–261.

Fader, D. (1976). *The new hooked on books.* New York: Berkeley.

Fahey, K., Lawrence, J., & Paratore, J. (2007). Using electronic portfolios to make learning public. *Journal of Adolescent and Adult Literacy, 50*(9), 460–471.

Farley, W. (1941). *The black stallion.* New York: Random House.

Feldhusen, J. (1989). Synthesis of research on gifted youth. *Educational Leadership, 46*(6), 6–11.

Ferguson, D. B. (2000). Reexamining at-risk. *Curriculum Administrator, 36*(6), 79–90.

Fiedler E., Lange, R., & Winebrenner, S. (2002). In search of reality: Unraveling the myths about tracking, ability grouping, and the gifted. *Roeper Review, 24,* 108–111.

Field, M. L., & Aebersold, J. A. (1990). Cultural attitudes toward reading: Implications for teachers of ESL/ bilingual readers. *Journal of Reading, 33,* 406–410.

Fielding, L. G., & Pearson, P. D. (1994). Reading comprehension: What works? *Educational Leadership, 51,* 62–68.

Fillmore, L. W. (1981). Cultural perspectives on second language learning. *TESL Reporter, 14,* 23–31.

Finkbeiner, C., & Koplin, C. (2002, October). A cooperative approach for facilitating intercultural education. *Reading Online, 6*(3). Retrieved June 3, 2007, from http://www.readingonline.org/newliteracies/ lit_index.asp?HREF=finkbeiner/index.html.

Fisher, C. W., & Berliner, D. (Eds.). (1985). *Perspectives on instructional time.* New York: Longman.

Fisher, D., Flood, J., Lapp, D., & Frey, N. (2004). Interactive read-alouds: Is there a common set of implementation practices? *The Reading Teacher, 58*(1), 8–17.

Fisher, D., & Frey, N. (2003). Writing instruction for struggling adolescent writers: A gradual release model. *Journal of Adolescent & Adult Literacy, 46*(5), 395–405.

Fisher, D., & Frey, N. (2008). *Improving adolescent literacy: Content area strategies at work.* Upper Saddle River, NJ: Merrill Prentice Hall.

Fisher, M. (2004, October 12). Falls Church School won't teach to the test. *The Washington Post,* B1.

Fleener, C., Hager, J., Morgan, R. F., & Childress, M. (2000). *The integration of conation, cognition, affect, and social environment in literacy development.* In P. Linder, W. M. Linek, E. G. Sturtevant, & J. Dugan (Eds.), *Literacy at a new horizon: Twenty-second yearbook of the College Reading Association* (pp. 88–98). Commerce, TX: Texas A & M University–Commerce.

Fleming, C. B., Harachi, T. W., Cortes, R. C., Abbott, R D., & Catalano, R. F. (2004). Level and change in reading scores and attention problems during elementary school as predictors of problem behavior in middle school. *Journal of Emotional and Behavioral Disorders, 12*(3), 130–144.

Flesch, R. (1949). *The art of readable writing.* New York: Harper and Row.

Forgan, H. W., & Mangrum, C. T. (1985, 1997). *Teaching content area reading skills.* Columbus, OH: Merrill.

Fletcher, R. (2001). *Writing workshop: The essential guide.* Portsmouth, NH: Heinemann.

Forbes, L. S. (2004). Using Web-based bookmarks in K–8 settings: Linking the Internet to instruction. *The Reading Teacher, 58*(2), 148–153.

Forget, M. A. (2004). *MAX teaching with reading and writing: Classroom activities for helping students learn new subject matter while acquiring literacy skills.* Victoria, BC: Trafford Publishing.

Forget, M. A., & Morgan, R. F. (1995, November). *An embedded curriculum approach to teaching metacognitive strategies.* Paper presented at the College Reading Association, Clearwater Beach, FL.

Fox, B. J. (2003). Teachers' evaluations of word identification software: Implications for literacy methods courses. In M. B. Sampson, P. E. Linder, J. R. Dugan, & B. Brancato (Eds.), *Celebrating the freedom of literacy: The twenty-fifth yearbook of the College Reading Association.* Commerce: Texas A & M University.

Francis, M. A., & Simpson, M. L. (2003). Using theory, our intuitions, and a research study to enhance students' vocabulary knowledge. *Journal of Adolescent & Adult Literacy, 47*(1), 66–78.

Francis-Smythe, J. A., & Robertson, I. T. (1999). On the relationship between time management and time estimation. *British Journal of Psychology, 90*(3), 333–334.

Frand, J. L. (2000). The information-age mindset. *Education Review, 35*(5), 15–24.

Friedman, T. L. (2006). *The world is flat.* New York: Farrar, Straus & Giroux.

Friend, R. (2002). Teaching summarization as a content area reading strategy. *Journal of Adolescent and Adult Literacy, 44*(4), 320–329.

Fromm, E. (1956). *The art of loving.* New York: Harper and Row.

Fry, E. (1968). The readability graph validated at primary levels. *The Reading Teacher, 3,* 534–538.

Fry, E. (1977). Fry's readability graph: Clarifications, validity, and extension to level 17. *Journal of Reading, 21,* 242–252.

Fry, E. (1987). The varied uses of readability measurement today. *Journal of Reading, 30,* 338–343.

Fry, E. (1989). Reading formulas—maligned but valid. *Journal of Reading, 32,* 292–297.

Fry, E. (1990). A readability formula for short passages. *Journal of Reading, 33,* 594–597.

Frymier, A. B., & Schulman, G. (1995). "What's in it for me?" Increasing content relevance to enhance students' motivation. *Communication Education, 44,* 40–50.

Fuchs, D., & Fuchs, L. S. (2006). Introduction to response to intervention: What, why, and how valid is it? *Reading Research Quarterly, 41,* 93–99.

Fulwiler, T. (1987). *Teaching with writing.* Portsmouth, NH: Boynton/Cook.

Gagne, R. (1974). Educational technology and the learning process. *Educational Researcher, 3,* 3–8.

Galeman, D. (1995). *Emotional intelligence: Why it can matter more than IQ.* New York: Bantam.

Gallagher, J. J. (1998). Accountability for gifted students. *Phi Delta Kappan, 79*(10), 739–743.

Gallagher, J. M. (1995). Pairing adolescent fiction with books from the canon. *Journal of Adolescent & Adult Literacy, 39,* 8–14.

Gallo, A. M. (2003). Assessing the affective domain. *The Journal of Physical Education, Recreation & Dance, 74*(4), 44–49.

Gambrell, L. (2005). Reading literature, reading text, reading the Internet: The times, they are a'changing. *The Reading Teacher, 58*(6), 588–591.

Gambrell, L. B. (1990). Introduction: A themed issue on reading instruction for at-risk students. *Journal of Reading, 33,* 485–488.

Gambrell, L. B. (1995). Motivation matters. In *Generations of Literacy: Seventeenth Yearbook of the College*

Reading Association (pp. 2–24). Commerce, TX: East Texas State University.

Gambrell, L. B. (1996). Creating classroom cultures that foster reading motivation. *The Reading Teacher, 50*(1), 14–25.

Gambrell, L. B., & Almasi, J. F. (1996). *Lively discussions: Fostering engaged reading.* Newark, DE: International Reading Association.

Gambrell, L. B., & Bales, R. J. (1986). Mental imagery and the comprehension-monitoring performance of fourth- and fifth-grade poor readers. *Reading Research Quarterly, 21,* 454–464.

Ganske, K., Monroe, J. K., & Strickland, D. S. (2003). Questions teachers ask about struggling readers and writers. *Journal of Adolescent & Adult Literacy, 57*(2), 118–128.

Garber-Miller, K. (2006). Playful textbook previews: Letting go of familiar mustache monologues. *Journal of Adolescent and Adult Literacy, 50*(4), 284–288.

Gardner, J. E., & Wissick, C. A. (2002). Enhancing cooperative learning using the World Wide Web: Tools and strategies that integrate technology for students with mild disabilities. *Journal of Special Education Technology, 17,* 27–38.

Gardner, J. E., Wissick, C. A., Schweder, W., & Canter, L. S. (2003). Enhancing interdisciplinary instruction in general and special education: Thematic units and technology. *Remedial and Special Education, 24*(3), 161–173.

Garner, R., Alexander, P., Slater, W., Hare, V. C., Smith, J., & Reis, R. (1986, April). *Children's knowledge of structural properties of text.* Paper presented at the meeting of the American Educational Research Association, San Francisco.

Garner, R., & Gillingham, M. (1987). Students' knowledge of text structure. *Journal of Reading Behavior, 29,* 247–259.

Garner, R., Hare, V. C., Alexander, P., Haynes, J., & Winograd, P. (1984). Inducing use of a text lookback strategy among unsuccessful readers. *American Educational Research Journal, 21,* 789–798.

Garner, R., Macready, G. B., & Wagoner, S. (1985). Reader's acquisition of the components of the text-lookback strategy. *Journal of Educational Psychology, 76,* 300–309.

Garrison, W. B. (1992). *Civil War trivia and fact book.* Nashville, TN: Rutledge Hill Press.

Gebhard, A. (1983). Teaching writing in reading and the content areas. *Journal of Reading, 27,* 207–211.

Gee, J. P. (1996). *Social linguistics and literacies: Ideology in discourses,* 2nd ed. Bristol, PA: Taylor & Francis.

Gee, J. P. (2000). Teenagers in new times: A new literacy studies perspective. *Journal of Adolescent and Adult Literacy, 43*(5), 412–420.

Gee, J. P. (2001). Literacy discourse and linguistics: Introduction. In E. Cushman M. Rose, B. Kroll, & E. R. Kitgen (Eds.), *Literacy: A critical sourcebook* (pp. 525–544). Boston: Bedford/St. Martin's.

Gee, R. W. (1999). Encouraging ESL students to read. *TESOL Journal, 8*(1), 3–7.

George, J. C. (1971). *All upon a stone.* New York: Crowell.

Gere, A. (1985). *Roots in the sawdust: Writing to learn across the disciplines.* Urbana, IL: National Council of Teachers of English.

Gersten, B. F., & Tlusty, N. (1998). Creating international contexts for cultural communication: Video exchange projects in the EFL/ESL classroom. *TESOL Journal, 7*(6), 11–16.

Gersten, R., & Baker, S. (1998). Real world use of scientific concepts: Integrating situated cognition with explicit instruction. *Exceptional Children, 65*(1), 23–36.

Gettinger, M., & Seibert, J. K. (2002). Contributions of study skills to academic competence. *School Psychology Review, 31*(3), 350–366.

Gholar, C. R., & Riggs, E. G. (2004). *Connecting with students' will to succeed: The power of conation.* Glenview, IL: Pearson Education.

Gibbons, P. (2003). Mediating language learning: Teacher interaction with ESL students in a content-based classroom. *TESOL Quarterly, 37*(2), 247–273.

Gill, S., & Dupre, K. (1998). Constructivism in reading education. *The Reading Professor, 21*(1), 91–108.

Gillespie, C. (1993). Reading graphic displays: What teachers should know. *Journal of Reading, 36,* 350–354.

Gillett, J. W., & Temple, C. (1983). *Understanding reading problems: Assessment and instruction.* Boston: Little, Brown.

Gillies, R. M., & Ashman, A. F. (1998). Behavior and interactions of children in cooperative groups in lower and middle elementary grades. *Journal of Educational Psychology, 90*(4), 746–757.

Gillies, R. M., & Boyle, M. (2006). Ten Australian elementary teachers' discourse and reported pedagogical practices during cooperative learning. *The Elementary School Journal, 106*(5), 429–452.

Glasser, W. (1986). *Control theory in the classroom.* New York: Harper and Row.

Glatthaar, J. T. (1990). *Forged in battle: The Civil War alliance of black soldiers and white officers.* New York: Free Press.

Glaubman, R., Glaubman, H., & Ofir, L. (1997). Effects of self-directed learning, story comprehension, and self-questioning in kindergarten. *Journal of Educational Research, 90,* 361–374.

Glickman, C. (2004). *Letter to the next president: What we can do about the real crisis in public education.* New York: Teachers' College Press.

Glynn, S. M. (1997). *Learning from science text: Role of an elaborate analogy.* College Park, MD: National Reading Research Center.

Godwin, K., & Sheard, W. (2001). Education reform and the politics of 2000. *Publius: The Journal of Federalism, 31*(3), 11–129.

Goett, A., & Foot, K. E. (2000). Cultivating student research and study skills in Web-based learning environments. *Journal of Geography in Higher Education, 24*(1), 92–99.

Gold, P. C. (1981). The directed listening–language experience approach. *Journal of Reading, 25,* 138–141.

Goldberg, A., Russell, M., & Cook, A. (2003). The effect of computers on student writing: A meta-analysis of studies from 1992 to 2002. *Journal of Technology, Learning, and Assessment, 2*(1). Retrieved Nov. 26, 2004, from http://www.bc.edu/research/intasc/jtla/journal/v2n1.shtml.

Goldman, S., & Rakestraw, J. (2000). Structural aspects of constructing meaning from text. In M. Kamil, P. Mosenthal, P. D. Pearson, & R. Barr (Eds.), *Handbook of reading research,* Vol. 3 (pp. 311–335). Mahwah, NJ: Erlbaum.

Goldman, S. R., Hasselbring, T. S., & the Cognition and Technology Group at Vanderbilt (1996). Achieving meaningful mathematics literacy for students with learning disabilities. *Journal of Learning Disabilities, 30*(2), 198–208.

Goodson, F. T. (2007). The electronic portfolio: Shaping an emerging genre. *Journal of Adolescent and Adult Literacy, 50*(9), 432–434.

Gottleib, M. (2003). *Large scale assessment of English language learners.* Alexandria, VA: TESOL.

Grady, M. P. (1990). *Whole brain education.* Bloomington, IN: Phi Delta Kappa Educational Foundation.

Graham, S., & Perin, D. (2007). *Writing next: Effective strategies to improve writing of adolescents in middle and high schools—a report to Carnegie Corporation of New York.* Washington, DC: Alliance for Excellent Education.

Graves, D. (1983). *Writing: Teachers and children at work.* Portsmouth, NH: Heinemann.

Graves, D. (1994). *A fresh look at writing.* Portsmouth, NH: Heinemann.

Graves, D., Prenn, M., & Cooke, C. (1985). The coming attraction: Previewing short stories. *Journal of Reading, 28,* 594–598.

Graves, M. F. (1985). *A word is a word . . . or is it?* New York: Scholastic.

Graves, M. F. (2000). A vocabulary program to complement and bolster a middle-grade comprehension program. In B. M. Taylor, M. F. Graves, & P. van den Broek (Eds.), *Reading for meaning: Fostering comprehension in the middle grades* (pp. 116–135). New York: Teachers College Press.

Graves, M. F. (2004) Teaching prefixes: As good as it gets? In J. F. Baumann & E. B. Kame'enui (Eds.), *Vocabulary instruction: Research to practice* (pp. 81–99). New York: Guilford Press.

Graves, M. F. (2006a). Building a comprehensive vocabulary program. *The New England Reading Association Journal, 42*(2), 1–7.

Graves, M. F. (2006b). *The vocabulary book: Learning and instruction.* New York: Teachers College Press, International Reading Association, National Council of Teachers of English.

Gray, W. (1925). *Summary of investigations related to reading* (Supplementary Educational Monographs No. 28). Chicago: University of Chicago Press.

Gray, W. (1960). The major aspects of reading. In H. Robinson (Ed.), *Development of reading abilities* (Supplementary Educational Monographs No. 90). Chicago: University of Chicago Press.

Gray, W. S. (1937). The nature and organization of basic instruction in reading. In G. M. Whipple (Ed.), *The teaching of reading: A second report* (thirty-eighth yearbook of the National Society for the Study of Education, Part I). Bloomington, IL: Public School Publishing Company.

Green, F. E. (1999). Brain and learning research: Implications for meeting the needs of diverse learners. *Education, 119*(4), 682–687.

Green, J. F., & Smyser, S. O. (1996). *The teacher portfolio: A strategy for professional development and evaluation.* Lancaster, PA: Technomic Publishing.

Green, S. K., & Gredler, M. E. (2002). A review and analysis of constructivism for school-based practice. *School Psychology Review, 31*(1), 53–71.

Greenlee-Moore, M., & Smith, L. (1996). Interactive computer software: The effects on young children's reading achievement. *Reading Psychology: An International Quarterly, 17,* 43–64.

Greenough, W. T., Withers, G. S., & Anderson, B. J. (1992). Experience-dependent synaptogenesis as a plausible memory mechanism. In I. Gormezano & E. A. Wasserman (Eds.), *Learning and memory: The behavioral and biological substrates* (pp. 209–299). Hillsdale, NJ: Erlbaum.

Griffith, L. W., & Rasinski, T. V. (2004). A focus on fluency: How one teacher incorporated fluency with her reading curriculum. *The Reading Teacher, 58*(2), 126–137.

Groenke, S. L., & Puckett, R. (2006). Becoming environmentally literate citizens. *The Science Teacher, 73*(8), 22–27.

Groff, P. (1981). Direct instruction versus incidental learning of reading vocabulary. *Reading Horizons, 21*(4), 262–265.

Gronlund, N. (1993). *How to make achievement tests and assessments.* Boston: Allyn & Bacon.

Gross, S. J. (2003). A case of American education flu. *Reading Online.* Retrieved Sept. 7, 2004, from http://www.readingonline.org/international/ inter_ index.asp?HREF=gross/index.html.

Guillaume, A. M. (1998). Learning with text in the primary grades. *The Reading Teacher, 51*(6), 476–486.

Gunderson, L., & Siegel, L. S. (2001). The evils of the use of IQ tests to define learning disabilities in first and second language learners. *The Reading Teacher, 55*(1), 48–55.

Gusak, F. J. (1967). Teacher questioning and reading. *The Reading Teacher, 21,* 227–234.

Guthrie, J. (2000). Contexts for engagement and motivation in reading. In M. L. Kamil, P. B. Mosenthal, P. D. Pearson, & R. Barr (Eds.), *Handbook of reading research: Vol. III* (pp. 403–422). Retrieved Oct. 1, 2004, from http://www.readingonline.org/ articles/handbook/guthrie/index.html.

Guthrie, J. T. (2004). *CORI: Classroom practices promoting engagement and achievement in comprehension.* Keynote address PowerPoint slides. International Reading Association Annual Conference, May 1.

Guthrie, J. T., Burnam, N., Caplan, R. I., & Seifert, M. (1974). The maze technique to assess and monitor reading comprehension. *The Reading Teacher, 28,*161–168.

Guthrie, J. T., Hoa, L. W., Wigfield, A., Tonks, S. M., Perencevich, K. C. (2006). From spark to fire: Can situational reading interest lead to long-term reading motivation? *Reading Research and Instruction, 45*(2), 91–117.

Guthrie, J. T., Schafer, W. D., Von Secker, C., & Alban, T. (2000). Contributions of instructional practices to reading achievement in a statewide improvement program. *Journal of Educational Research 93*(4), 211.

Guthrie, J. T., Wigfield, A., & Perencevich, K. C. (Eds.). (2004). *Motivating reading comprehension: Concept-oriented reading instruction.* Mahwah, NJ: Erlbaum.

Guzzetti, B. (1990). Enhancing comprehension through trade books in high school English classes. *Journal of Reading, 33,* 411–413.

Guzzetti, B., Hynd, C. R., Skeels, S. A., & Williams, W. O. (1995). Improving physics texts: Students speak out. *Journal of Reading, 38,* 656–663.

Guzzetti, B., Kowalinski, B. J., & McGowan, T. (1992). Using a literature-based approach to teaching social studies. *Journal of Reading, 36,* 114–122.

Guzzetti, B., Snyder, T., & Glass, G. (1992). Promoting conceptual change in science: Can texts be used effectively? *Journal of Reading, 35,* 642–649.

Hadaway, N., & Mundy, J. (1999). Children's informational picture books visit a secondary ESL classroom. *Journal of Adolescent & Adult Literacy, 42*(6), 464–475.

Hager, J. M., & Gable, R. A. (1993). Content reading assessment: A rethinking of methodology. *The Clearing House, 66,* 269–272.

Haggard, M. R. (1986). The vocabulary self-collection strategy: Using student interest and world knowledge to enhance vocabulary growth. *Journal of Reading, 29,* 634–642.

Haley, A. N., & Watson, D. C. (2000). In-school literacy extension: Beyond in-school suspension. *Journal of Adolescent & Adult Literacy, 43*(7), 654–661.

Hall, L. A. (2007). Understanding the silence: Struggling readers discuss decisions about reading expository text. *The Journal of Educational Research, 100,* 3, 132–141.

Hall-Quest, A. L. (1916). *Supervised study.* New York: Macmillan.

Halladay, M. A. K. (1994). *An introduction to functional grammar,* 2nd ed. London: Edward Arnold.

Hamachek, D. E. (1975). *Behavior dynamics in teaching, learning, and growth.* Boston: Allyn & Bacon.

Hammerberg, D. D. (2004). Comprehension instruction for socioculturally diverse classrooms: A review of what we know. *The Reading Teacher, 57*(7), 648–658.

Hancock, D. (2004). Cooperative learning and peer orientation effects on motivation and achievement. *Journal of Educational Research, 97*(3), 159–167.

Hand, D. (2006). Adolescent literacies: Reading, thinking, writing. *Knowledge Quest, 35,* 40–43.

Hansen, J. (1981). The effects of inference training and practice on young children's comprehension. *Reading Research Quarterly, 16,* 391–417.

Hansen, J., & Pearson, D. (1983). An instructional study: Improving the inferential comprehension of fourth grade good and poor readers. *Journal of Educational Psychology, 75,* 821–829.

Hapgood, S., & Palincsar, A. S. (2006/2007). Where literacy and science intersect. *Educational Leadership, 64,* 56–60.

Hare, V. C., & Borchardt, K. M. (1984). Direct instruction of summarization skills. *Reading Research Quarterly, 20,* 62–78.

Harper, C. & de Jong, E. (2004). Misconceptions about teaching English language learners. *Journal of Adolescent & Adult Literacy, 46,* 152–162.

Hart, B., & Risley, T. R. (2003). The early catastrophe: The 30 million word gap by age 3. *American Educator, 27*(1), 4–9.

Hart, L. (1983a). Programs, patterns, and downshifting in learning to read. *The Reading Teacher, 37,* 5–11.

Hart, L. (1983b). *Human brain and human learning.* New York: Longman.

Harris, K., & Graham, S. (1985). Improving learning disabled students' composition skills: Self-control strategy training. *Learning Disability Quarterly, 8,* 27–36.

Harris, L. A., & Smith, C. B. (1986). *Reading instruction: Diagnostic teaching in the classroom.* New York: Macmillan.

Harris, T. L., & Hodges, R. E. (1995). *The literacy dictionary: The vocabulary of reading and writing.* Newark, DE: International Reading Association.

Hart, L. (1975). *How the brain works.* New York: Basic Books.

Hart, L. (1983). *Human brain and human learning.* New York: Longman.

Harvey, V. S. (2007). Schoolwide methods for fostering resiliency. *Principal Leadership, 7*(5), 10–14.

Hattie, J., Biggs, J., & Purdie, N. (1996). Effects of learning skills interventions on student learning: A meta-analysis. *Review of Educational Research, 66,* 99–136.

Haussamen, B. (1995). The passive-reading fallacy. *Journal of Reading, 38,* 378–381.

Hawkes, K. S., & Schell, L. M. (1987). Teacher-set prereading purposes and comprehension. *Reading Horizons, 27,* 164–169.

Hayes, H., Stahl, N., & Simpson, M. (1991). Language, meaning, and knowledge: Empowering developmental students to participate in the academic community. *Reading Research and Instruction, 30*(3), 89–100.

Haynes, J. (2006). DSL—Digital as a second language. *Essential Teacher, 3*(4), 6–7.

Heath, S. B. (1986). Critical factors in literacy development. In S. de Castell, A. Luke, & K. Egan (Eds.), *Literacy, society, and schooling: A reader* (pp. 209–229). New York: Cambridge University Press.

Heilman, A. W., Blair, T. R., & Rupley, W. H. (1986, 1994). *Principles and practices of teaching reading.* Columbus, OH: Merrill.

Heller, M. (1986). How do you know what you know? Metacognitive modeling in the content areas. *Journal of Reading, 29,* 415–422.

Henderson, M. V., & Scheffler, A. J. (2004). New literacies, standards, and teacher education. *Education, 124*(2), 390–395.

Henk, W. A., & Helfeldt, J. P. (1987). How to develop independence in following written directions. *Journal of Reading, 30,* 602–607.

Henry, G. H. (1974). *Teach reading as concept development: Emphasis on affective thinking.* Newark, DE: International Reading Association.

Henry, L. A. (2006). SEARCHing for an answer: The critical role of new literacies while reading on the Internet. *The Reading Teacher, 59*(7), 614–627.

Herber, H. (1978). *Teaching reading in the content areas,* 2nd ed. Englewood Cliffs, NJ: Prentice-Hall.

Herber, H. (1987). Foreword. In D. Alvermann, D. Moore, & M. Conley (Eds.), *Research within reach: Secondary school reading.* Newark, DE: International Reading Association.

Herman, J. L., Aschbacher, P. R., & Winters, L. W. (1992). *A practical guide to alternative assessment.* Alexandria, VA: Association for Supervision and Curriculum Development.

Hiebert, E. H. (1999). Text matters in learning to read. *The Reading Teacher, 52*(6), 552–566.

Higgins, B., Miller, M., & Wegmann, S. (2006/2007). Teaching to the test. . .not! Balancing best practice and testing requirements in writing. *The Reading Teacher, 60,* 310–319.

Hill, W., & Erwin, R. (1984). The readability of content textbooks used in middle and junior high schools. *Reading Psychology, 5,* 105–117.

Hillerich, R. L. (1979). Reading comprehension. *Reporting on Reading, 5,* 1–3.

Hilliard, A. G. (1988). Public support for successful instructional practices for at-risk students. In D. W. Hornbeck (Ed.), *School success for at-risk youth: Analysis and recommendations of the Council of Chief State School Officers* (pp. 195–208). Orlando, FL: Harcourt Brace Jovanovich.

Hillocks, G., Jr. (2002). *The testing trap: How state writing assessments control learning.* New York: Teachers College Press.

Hinchman, K. A., Alvermann, D. E., Boyd, F. B., Brozo, W. G., & Vacca, R. T. (2004). Supporting older students' in-and-out-of-school literacies. *Journal of Adolescent & Adult Literacy, 47*(4), 304–310.

Hirsch, E. D. (1987). *Cultural literacy.* Boston: Houghton Mifflin.

Hittleman, D. R. (1978). Readability, readability formulas, and cloze: Selecting instructional materials. *Journal of Reading, 22,* 117–122.

Hmelo, C. E., Nagarajan, A., & Day, R. S. (2000). Effects of high and low prior knowledge on construction of a joint problem space. *The Journal of Experimental Education, 69*(1), 36.

Hoffman, J. (1992). Critical reading/thinking across the curriculum: Using I-charts to support learning. *Language Arts, 69,* 121–127.

Hoffman, S. (1983). Using student journals to teach study skills. *Journal of Reading, 26,* 344–347.

Hogan, K., Nastasi, B. K., & Pressley, M. (2000). Discourse patterns and collaborative scientific reasoning in peer and teacher-guided discussions. *Cognitive Instruction, 17,* 379–432.

Holiday, W. G. (1983). Overprompting science students using adjunct study questions. *Journal of Research in Science Teaching, 20,* 195–201.

Holmes, B., & Roser, N. (1987). Five ways to assess readers' prior knowledge. *The Reading Teacher, 40,* 646–649.

Holschuh, J. P. (2000). Do as I say, not as I do: High, average, and low-performing students' strategy use in biology. *Journal of College Reading and Learning, 31*(1), 94–132.

Honebein, P. C. (1996). Seven goals for the design of constructivist learning environments. In B. G. Wilson (Ed.). *Constructivist learning environments: Case studies in instructional design* (pp. 11–24). Englewood Cliffs, NJ: Educational Technology Publications.

Horn, W. F., & Tynan, D. (2001). Revamping special education. *The Public Interest, 36*–42.

Hornbeck, D. W. (1988). All our children: An introduction. In D. W. Hornbeck (Ed.), *School success for at-risk youth: Analysis and recommendations of the Council of Chief State School Officers* (pp. 3–9). Orlando, FL: Harcourt Brace Jovanovich.

Hornberger, T. R., & Whitford, E. V. (1983). Students' suggestions: Teach us study skills! *Journal of Reading, 27,* 71.

Houston, G. (2004). *How writing works: Imposing organizational structure within the writing process.* Boston: Pearson Education.

Houston, P. D. (2005). NCLB: Dreams and nightmares. *Phi Delta Kappan, 86*(6), 469–471.

Howard S., & Johnson, B. (2000). What makes the difference? Children and teachers talk about resilient outcomes for children "at risk." *Educational Studies, 26,* 321–337.

Howes, E. V., Hamilton, G. W., & Zaskoda, D. (2003). Linking science and literature through technology: Thinking about interdisciplinary inquiry in middle school. *Journal of Adolescent & Adult Literacy, 46,* 484–504.

Howland, J. (1995). Attentive reading in the age of canon clamor. *English Journal, 84,* 35–38.

Hubbard, B. P., & Simpson, M. (2003). Developing self-regulated learners: Putting theory into practice. *Reading Research and Instruction, 42*(4), 62–89.

Huber, J. (2004). A closer look at SQ3R. *Reading Improvement, 41*(2), 108–113.

Huck, C., Hepler, S., & Hickman, J. (1987). *Children's literature in the elementary school.* Fort Worth, TX: Holt, Rinehart and Winston.

Huey, E. (1908/1968). *The psychology and pedagogy of reading.* Cambridge, MA: MIT Press.

Hughes, J. (2007). Rotting principals, persistent teachers. *Essential Teacher, 4*(2), 7–8.

Hunter, K. (2006). A textbook case. *T.H.E. Journal, 33*(15), 48–50.

Hurd, P. (1970). *New directions in teaching secondary school science.* Chicago: Rand-McNally.

Huss, J. A. (2006). Gifted education and cooperative learning: A miss or a match? *Gifted Child Today, 29*(4), 19–23.

Hwang, Y., & Levin, J. (2002). Examination of middle school students' independent use of a complex mnemonic system. *The Journal of Experimental Education, 7*(1), 25–39.

Hynd, C. (1999.) Teaching students to think critically using multiple texts in history. *Journal of Adolescent & Adult Literacy, 42*(6), 428–436.

Individuals with Disabilities Education Improvement Act of 2004, Pub. L. 108-466.

Inspiration Software. (2000). *Kidspiration* (computer software). Portland, OR: Author.

Inspiration Software. (2002). *Inspiration 7.0* (computer software). Portland, OR: Author.

International Reading Association. (1988). *New directions in reading instruction.* Newark, DE: Author.

International Reading Association. (1999). *High stakes testing.* Newark, DE: Author. Retrieved Sept. 7, 2004, from http://www.reading.org/resources/issues/positions_high_stakes.html.

International Reading Association. (2003). *Standards for reading professionals.* Newark, DE: Author, Professional Standards and Ethics Committee.

Irvin, J. L. (1990). *Vocabulary knowledge: Guidelines for instruction. What research says to the teacher.* Washington, DC: National Education Association.

Irvin, J. L., Buehl, D. R., & Klemp, R. M. (2007). *Reading and the high school student: Strategies to enhance literacy,* 2nd ed. Boston: Pearson Education.

Irvin, J. L., Buehl, D. R., & Radcliffe, B. J. (2007). *Strategies to enhance literacy and learning in middle school content area classrooms,* 3rd ed. Boston: Pearson Education.

Ivey, G. (1999). Reflections on teaching struggling middle school readers. *Journal of Adolescent & Adult Literacy, 42*(5), 372–381.

Ivey, G., & Broaddus, K. (2000). Tailoring the fit: Reading instruction and middle school readers. *The Reading Teacher, 54*(1), 68–78.

Iwicki, A. L. (1992). Vocabulary connections. *The Reading Teacher, 45,* 736.

Jackson, F. R., & Cunningham, J. (1994). Investigating secondary content teachers and preservice teachers' conceptions of study strategy instruction. *Reading Research and Instruction, 34,* 11–135.

Jacobs, J., & Paris, S. (1987). Children's metacognition about reading: Issues in definition, measurement, and instruction. *Educational Psychologist, 22,* 255–278.

Jacobson, J. M. (1998). *Content area reading: Integration with the language arts.* Albany, NY: Doman.

Jaimes, J. (2005). Critical thinking, reflective writing: Learning? *Academic Exchange Quarterly, 9*(1), 192–197.

Jenkins, C., & Lawler, D. (1990). Questioning strategies in content area reading: One teacher's example. *Reading Improvement, 27,* 133–138.

Jensen, E. (1998). *Teaching with the brain in mind.* Alexandria, VA: Association for Supervision and Curriculum Development.

Jetton, T. L., & Alexander, P. A. (2000). Learning from text: A multidimensional and developmental perspective. In M. L. Kamil, P. B. Mosenthal, P. D. Pearson, & R. Barr (Eds.), *Handbook of reading research: Vol. III.* Retrieved Sept. 7, 2004, from http://www.reading online.org/articles/handbook/jetton/index.html.

Jitendra, A. K., Edwards, L. L., Sacks, G., & Jacobson, L. A. (2004). What research says about vocabulary instruction for students with learning disabilities. *Exceptional Children, 70,* 299–322.

Johnson, D. (2002, March). Web watch: Writing resources. *Reading Online, 5*(7). Retrieved Dec. 12, 2004, from http://www.readingonline.org/electronic/elec_index .asp?HREF=webwatch/writing/index.html.

Johnson, D. (2002, October). Web watch: Poetry workshop. *Reading Online, 6*(3). Retrieved Dec. 12, 2004, from http://www.readingonline.org/electronic/ elec_index.asp?HREF=webwatch/poetry/index.html.

Johnson, D., & Johnson, B. (2002, August/September). The unfairness of uniformity. *Reading Today, 20,* 18.

Johnson, D. D. (2001). *Vocabulary in the elementary and middle school.* Boston: Allyn & Bacon.

Johnson, D. W., & Johnson, R. T. (1974). Instructional goal structure: Cooperative, competitive, or individualistic. *Review of Educational Research, 44,* 213–240.

Johnson, D. W., & Johnson, R. T. (1987). *Learning together and alone: Cooperative, conjunctive, and individualistic learning.* Englewood Cliffs, NJ: Prentice-Hall.

Johnson, D. W., & Johnson, R. T. (2003). *Joining together: Group theory and group skills.* New York: A and B Publishing.

Johnson, D. W., Johnson, R. T., & Stanne, M. B. (2000). Cooperative learning methods: A meta-analysis. Retrieved June 24, 2007 from http://www .co-operation.org/pages/cl-methods.html.

Jones, C. H., Slate, J. R., & Marini, I. (1995). Locus of control, social interdependence, academic preparation,

age, study time, and the study skills of college students. *Research in the Schools, 2,* 55–62.

Jones, F. R., Morgan, R. F., & Tonelson, S. W. (1992). *The psychology of human development,* 3rd ed. Dubuque, IA: Kendall/Hunt.

Jones, H. J., Coombs, W. T., & McKinney, C. W. (1994). A themed literature unit versus a textbook: A comparison of the effects on content acquisition and attitudes in elementary social studies. *Reading Research and Instruction, 34,* 85–96.

Juel, C., & Deffes, R. (2004). Making words stick. *Educational Leadership, 61*(6), 30–34.

Juster, N. (1961). *The phantom tollbooth.* New York: Random House.

Kagan, S. (1994). *Cooperative learning.* San Clemente, CA: Resources for Teachers, Inc.

Kahn, E. A. (2000). A case study of assessment in a grade 10 English course. *The Journal of Educational Research, 93*(5), 276–286.

Kaiser, Henry F. (1962). Scaling a simplex. *Psychometrika, 27*(2), 155–162.

Kamil, M. L., & Hiebert, E. H. (2005). The teaching and learning of vocabulary: Perspectives and persistent issues. In E. H. Hiebert & M. L. Kamil (Eds.), *Teaching and learning vocabulary: Bringing research to practice* (pp. 1–23). Mahwah, NJ: Erlbaum.

Kane, B. (1984). *Remarks made at the regional meeting on reading across the curriculum.* Reading to Learn in Virginia, Capital Consortium.

Kapinus, B. (1986). *Ready reading readiness.* Baltimore: Maryland State Department of Education.

Karabenick, S. A. (1998). Help seeking as a strategic resource. In S. A. Karabenick (Ed.), *Strategic help seeking: Implications for learning and teaching* (pp. 1–11). Mahwah, NJ: Erlbaum.

Karchmer, R. (2001). The journey ahead: Thirteen teachers report how the Internet influences literacy and literacy instruction in their K–12 classrooms. *Reading Research Quarterly, 36*(4), 442–466.

Karlin, R. (1977). *Teaching reading in the high school.* Indianapolis: Bobbs-Merrill.

Katayama, A. D., & Robinson, D. H. (2000). Getting students "partially" involved in note-taking using graphic organizers. *Journal of Experimental Education, 68*(2), 119.

Keith, T. Z., Reimers, T. M., Fehrmann, P. G., Pottebaum, S. M., & Aubey, L. W. (1986). Parental involvement, homework, and TV time: Direct and indirect effects on high school achievement. *Journal of Educational Psychology, 78,* 373–380.

Kellogg, R. (1972). Listening. In P. Lamb (Ed.), *Guiding children's language learning* (pp. 141–170). Dubuque, IA: William C. Brown.

Kerchner, L., & Kistinger, B. (1984). Language processing/word processing: Written expression, computers, and learning disabled students. *Learning Disability Quarterly, 7,* 329–335.

Kerr, M. M., Nelson, C. M., & Lambert, D. L. (1987). *Helping adolescents with learning and behavior problems.* Columbus, OH: Merrill.

Kibby, M. W. (1995). The organization and teaching of things and the words that signify them. *Journal of Adolescent & Adult Literacy, 39,* 208–223.

Kidder, T. (1989). *Among schoolchildren.* Boston: Houghton Mifflin.

Kieffer, M. J., & Lesaux, N. K. (2007). Breaking down words to build meaning: Morphology, vocabulary, and reading comprehension in the urban classroom. *The Reading Teacher, 61,* 134–144.

Kinder, D., Bursuck, B., & Epstein, M. (1992). An evaluation of history textbooks. *Journal of Special Education, 25,* 472–491.

King, S. (2002). *On writing: A memoir of the craft.* New York: Pocket Books.

Kintch, W., & Van Dijk, T. (1978). Toward a model of text comprehension and production. *Psychological Review, 85,* 363–394.

Kist, W. (2000). Beginning to create the new literacy classroom: What does the new literacy look like? *Journal of Adolescent and Adult Literacy, 43,* 710–718.

Kitsantas, A. (2002). Test preparation and performance: A self-regulatory analysis. *The Journal of Experimental Education, 70*(2), 101–114.

Kleiner, A., & Lewis, L. (2003). *Internet access in U. S. public schools and classrooms: 1994–2002.* National Center for Educational Statistics 2004–011. Retrieved Dec. 14, 2004, from http://nces.ed.gov.

Kletzein, S. B. (1991). Strategy use by good and poor comprehenders reading expository text of differing reading levels. *Reading Research Quarterly, 26,* 67–86.

Klingner, J. K., & Edwards, P. A. (2006). Cultural considerations with response to intervention models. *Reading Research Quarterly, 41,* 108–117.

Klingner, J. K., & Vaughn, S. (1996). Reciprocal teaching of reading comprehension strategies for students with learning disabilities who use English as a second language. *The Elementary School Journal, 96,* 275–292.

Klingner, J. K., & Vaughn, S. (1999). Promoting reading comprehension, content learning, and English acquisition through collaborative strategic reading. *The Reading Teacher, 52*(7), 738–747.

Knickerbocker, J. L., & Rycik, J. A. (2006). Reexamining literature study in the middle grades: A critical response framework. *American Secondary Education, 34*(3), 43–56.

Knipper, K. J., & Duggan, T. J. (2006). Writing to learn across the curriculum: Tools for comprehension in content area classes. *The Reading Teacher, 59,* 462–470.

Knobel, M. (2001). "I'm not a pencil man": How one student challenges our notions of literacy "failure" in school. *Journal of Adolescent & Adult Literacy, 44*(5), 404–414.

Knowles, M. S. (1975). *Self-directed learning: A guide for learners and teachers.* New York: Association Press.

Knowles, M. S. (1980). *The modern practice of adult education: From pedagogy to andragogy.* New York: Cambridge Books.

Knowlton, D. S., & Knowlton, H. M. (2001). The context and content of online discussions: Making cyberdiscussions viable for the secondary school curriculum. *American Secondary Education, 29*(4), 38–52.

Knox, C., & Anderson-Inman, L. (2001) Migrant ESL high school students succeed using networked laptops. *Learning and Leading with Technology, 28*(5), 18–28.

Koeze, S. (1990). The dictionary game. *Reading Teacher, 43,* 613.

Koskinen, P., et al. (1999). Shared reading, books, and audiotapes: Supporting diverse students in school and at home. *The Reading Teacher, 52*(5), 430–444.

Kowalski, P., & Taylor, A. K. (2004). Ability and critical thinking as predictors of change in students' psychological misconceptions. *Journal of Instructional Psychology, 31*(4), 297–304.

Kowalski, T. (1995). Chasing the wolves from the schoolhouse door. *Phi Delta Kappan, 76,* 486–489.

Kozen, A. A., Murray, R. K., & Windell, I. (2006). Increasing all students' chance to achieve: Using and adapting anticipation guides with middle school learners. *Intervention in School & Clinic, 4*(4), 195–201.

Krashen, S. (1982). *Principles and practices in second language acquisition.* New York: Pergamon Press.

Krashen, S. (1989). *Language acquisition and language education.* Englewood Cliffs, NJ: Prentice-Hall.

Krathwohl, D. R., Bloom, B. S., & Masia, B. B. (1964). *Taxonomy of educational objectives: Handbook II: Affective domain.* New York: David McKay.

Kropiewnicki, M. (2006). Comprehending comprehension: Training pre-service teachers in reading comprehension strategies. *The Reading Professor, 28,* 1, 20–24.

Kulik, J., & Kulik, C. (1987). Effects of ability grouping on student achievement. *Equity and Excellence, 23*(1), 22–30.

Kulik, J. A., & Kulik, C. C. (1990). Ability grouping and gifted students. In N. Colangelo & G. A. Davis (Eds.), *Handbook of gifted education* (pp. 178–196). Boston: Allyn & Bacon.

Laffey, J., & Morgan, R. (1983). *Successful interactions in reading and language: A practical handbook for subject matter teachers.* Harrisonburg, VA: Feygan.

Laing, S. P., & Kamhi, A. G. (2002). The use of think-aloud protocols to compare inferencing abilities in average and below-average readers. *Journal of Learning Disabilities, 35*(5), 436–448.

Lambiotte, J. G., & Dansereau, D. F. (1992). Effects of knowledge maps and prior knowledge on recall of science lecture content. *The Journal of Experimental Education, 60,* 189–201.

Langer, J. (1981). From theory to practice: A prereading plan. *Journal of Reading, 25,* 152–156.

Langer, J. (2001). Beating the odds: Teaching middle and high school students to read and write well. *American Educational Research Journal, 38,* 837–880.

Langer, J. A. (1986). Learning through writing: Study skills in the content areas. *Journal of Reading, 29,* 5, 400–406.

Lankutis, T. (2001). Reaching the struggling reader. *Technology and Learning, 21*(10), 24–30.

Larson, C., & Dansereau, D. (1986). Cooperative learning in dyads. *Journal of Reading, 29,* 516–520.

Last, D. A., O'Donnell, A., & Kelly, A. E. (2001). The effects of prior knowledge and goal strength on the use of hypertext. *Journal of Educational Multimedia and Hypermedia, 10,* 1, 3.

Lauber, P. (1995). *Who eats what? Food chains and food webs.* New York: Harper Collins.

Lazar, A. (2006). Literacy teachers making a difference in urban schools: A context-specific look at effective literacy teaching. *Journal of Reading Education, 32,* 13–21.

Lederer, J. M. (2000). Reciprocal teaching of social studies in inclusive elementary classrooms. *Journal of Learning Disabilities, 33*(1), 91.

Lederer, R. (1987). *Anguished English.* New York: Dell/Bantam Doubleday.

Lee, J., & Schallert, D. (1997). The relative contribution of L2 language proficiency and L1 reading ability to L2 reading performance: A test of the threshold hypothesis. *TESOL Quarterly, 31,* 713–739.

Lee, P., & Allen, G. (1981). *Training junior high LD students to use a test-taking strategy* (Eric Document No. ED 217 649).

Lee, S., Stigler, J. W., & Stevenson, H. W. (1986). Beginning reading in Chinese and English. In B. Foorman and A. W. Siegel (Eds.), *Acquisition of reading skills* (pp. 123–149). Hillsdale, NJ: Erlbaum.

Leki, I. (1992). *Understanding ESL writers: A guide for teachers.* Portsmouth, NH: Heinemann.

Leki, I. (2001). "A narrow thinking system": Nonnative English-speaking students in group projects across the curriculum. *TESOL Quarterly, 35*(1), 39–67.

Lemkuhl, M. (2002, May). Pen-pal letters: The cross-curricular experience. *The Reading Teacher, 55*(8), 720–722. Retrieved Dec. 12, 2004, from http://www.readingonline.org/electronic/elec_index.asp?HREF=/electronic/RWT/lemkuhl/index.html.

Lent, R. (2006). In the company of critical thinkers. *Educational Leadership, 64*(2), 68–72.

Lenz, B. K., Ellis, E. S., & Scanlon, D. (1996). *Teaching learning strategies to adolescents and adults with learning disabilities.* Austin, TX: Pro-Ed.

Leonard, J., & McElroy, K. (2000). What one middle school teacher learned about cooperative learning. *Journal of Research in Childhood Education, 14*(2), 239.

Lesesne, T. S. (2001). Timing: The right book at the right moment. *Voices from the Middle, 9,* 68–72.

Lester, J. H., & Cheek, E. H., Jr. (1998). The "real" experts address the textbook issues. *Journal of Adolescent & Adult Literacy, 41*(4), 282–291.

Leu, D. J., Jr. (1997). Caity's question: Literacy as deixis on the Internet. *The Reading Teacher, 51*(1), 62–67.

Leu, D. J., Jr. (2000). Literacy and technology: Deictic consequences for literacy education in an information age. In M. L. Kamil, P. B. Mosenthal, P. D. Pearson, & R. Barr (Eds.), *Handbook of reading research: Vol. III* (pp. 743–770). Mahwah, NJ: Erlbaum.

Leu, D. J., Castek, J., Henry, L. A., Coiro, J., & McMullan, M. (2004). The lessons that children teach us: Integrating children's reading and the new literacies of the Internet. *The Reading Teacher, 57*(5), 496–504.

Leu, D. J., Jr., Karchmer, R., & Leu, D. D. (1999). Exploring literacy on the Internet. *The Reading Teacher, 52*(6), 636–642.

Leu, D. J., Jr., Kinzer, C. K., Coiro, J., & Cammack, D. W. (2004). Toward a theory of new literacies emerging from the Internet and other communication technologies. In R. Ruddell & N. Unrau (Eds.), *Theoretical models and processes of reading,* 5th ed. (pp. 1570–1613). Newark: DE: International Reading Association.

Leu, D. J., Jr., & Leu, D. D. (1999). *Teaching with the Internet: Lesson from the classroom.* Norwood, MA: Christopher Gordon.

Levin, H. M. (1988). Accelerating elementary education for disadvantaged students. In D. W. Hornbeck (Ed.), *School success for at-risk youth: Analysis and recommendations of the Council of Chief State School Officers* (pp. 209–226). Orlando, FL: Harcourt Brace Jovanovich.

Levin, J. R. (1993). Mnemonic strategies and classroom learning: A 20-year report card. *Elementary School Journal, 94,* 235–244.

Levin, J. R., Levin, M. E., Glassman, L. D., & Nordwall, M. B. (1992). Mnemonic vocabulary instruction: Additional effectiveness evidence. *Contemporary Educational Psychology, 17,* 156–174.

Levin, J. R., Morrison, C. R., & McGivern, J. E. (1986). Mnemonic facilitation of text-embedded science facts. *American Educational Research Journal, 23,* 489–506.

Lewis, C. & Fabos, B. (2005). Instant messaging, literacies, and social identities. *RRQ, 40*(4), 470–501.

Liaw, S. (2004). Consideration for developing constructivist Web-based learning. *International Journal of Instructional Media, 3*(3), 309–322.

Lin, L. M., Zabrucky, K., & Moore, D. (1997). The relations among interest, self-assessment comprehension, and comprehension performance in young adults. *Reading Research and Instruction, 36*(2), 127–139.

Lindfors, J. W. (1980). *Children's language and learning.* Englewood Cliffs, NJ: Prentice-Hall.

Linn, R., Baker, E., & Dunbar, S. (1991). Complex, performance-based assessment: Expectations and validation criteria. *Educational Researcher, 20*(8), 15–21.

Lipsitz, J. (1995). Why we should care about caring. *Phi Delta Kappan, 76,* 665–666.

Lipson, M. Y., & Wixson, K. K. (2003). *Assessment and instruction of reading and writing disability* (3rd ed.). New York: Longman.

Liston, D., Whitcomb, J., & Borko, H. (2007). NCLB and scientifically based research. *The Journal of Teacher Education, 58*(2), 99–107.

Loschert, K. (2003). High-tech teaching. *Tomorrow's Teachers, 9,* 2–5.

Lotan, R. (2003). Group-worthy tasks. *Educational Leadership, 60,* 6. Alexandria, VA: Association for Supervision and Curriculum Development.

Lorenzo, G., & Dziuban, C. (2006). Ensuring the Net generation is net savvy. *EDUcause Learning Initiative.* Retrieved from http://www.educause.edu/LibraryDetailPage/666?ID=ELI3006.

Lovitt, T. C., Horton, S. V., & Bergerud, D. (1987). Matching students with textbooks: An alternative to readability formulas and standard tests. *British Columbia Journal of Special Education, 11,* 49–55.

Lowery, L. F. (1998). *The biological basis for thinking and learning* (monograph). Berkeley, CA: Lawrence Hall of Science.

Lowry, L. (1989). *Number the stars.* Boston: Houghton Mifflin.

Lu, M., Webb, J. M., Krus, D. J., & Fox, L. S. (1999). Using order analytic instructional hierarchies of mnemonics to facilitate learning Chinese and Japanese Kanji characters. *The Journal of Experimental Education, 67*(4), 293.

Luke, A. (2000). New literacies in teacher education. *Journal of Adolescent and Adult Literacy, 43*(5), 424–435.

Lund, J. (1997). Authentic assessment: Its development and applications. *JOPERD—The Journal of Physical Education, Recreation, and Dance, 68*(7), 25.

Lynch-Brown, C., & Tomlinson, C. M. (1993). *Essentials of children's literature.* Boston: Allyn & Bacon.

Macan, H. T., Shahani, C., Dipboye, R. L., & Phillips, A. P. (1990). College students' time management: Correlations with academic performance and stress. *Journal of Educational Psychology, 82,* 760–768.

MacDonald, J. (1986). Self-generated questions and reading recall: Does training help? *Contemporary Educational Psychology, 11,* 290–304.

Macdonald, J., Heap, N., & Mason, R. (2001). "Have I learnt it?" Evaluating skills for resource-based study using electronic resources. *British Journal of Educational Technology, 32*(4), 419–433.

MacLean, P. (1978). A mind of three minds: Educating the triune brain. In J. Chall and A. Mirsley (Eds.), *Education and the brain* (pp. 308–342). Chicago: University of Chicago Press.

Madrid, L. D., Canas, M., & Ortega-Medina, M. (2007). Effects of team competition versus team cooperation in classwide peer tutoring. *Journal of Educational Research, 100*(3), 155–160.

Mahler, W. R. (1995). Practice what you preach. *The Reading Teacher, 48,* 414–415.

Manz, S. L. (2002). A strategy for previewing textbooks: Teaching readers to become THIEVES. *The Reading Teacher, 55,* 434–435.

Manzo, A. V. (1969). The ReQuest procedure. *Journal of Reading, 11,* 123–126.

Manzo, A. V. (1975). The guided reading procedure. *Journal of Reading, 18,* 287–291.

Manzo, A. V., Manzo, U. C., & Thomas, M. M. (2006). Rationale for systematic vocabulary development: Antidote for state mandates. *Journal of Adolescent & Adult Literacy, 49*(7), 610–619.

Manzo, K. (2001, December 12). Schools stress writing for the test. *Education Week on the Web.* Retrieved March 31, 2007, from http://www.edweek.org/ew/newstory.cfm?slug=15write.h21.

Marashio, P. (1995). Designing questions to help students peel back the layers of a text. *Interdisciplinary Humanities, 12*(1), 27–31.

Maria, K., & Junge, K. (1993). *A comparison of fifth graders' comprehension and retention of scientific information using a science textbook and an informal storybook.* Paper presented at the annual meeting of the National Reading Conference, Charleston, SC.

Maria, K., & MacGinitie, W. (1987). Learning from texts that refute the readers' prior knowledge. *Reading Research and Instruction, 26,* 222–238.

Marks, L. I., (1998). Deconstructing locus of control: Implications for practitioners. *Journal of Counseling and Development, 76,* 251–260.

Maroney, S. A. (1990). Step by step. *Instructor, 110*(2), 101–102.

Martin, A. (2002). *Australian Journal of Education, 46*(16), 34.

Martin, N., D'Arcy, P., Newton, B., & Parker, R. (1976). *Writing and learning across the curriculum.* Montclair, NJ: Boynton/Cook.

Martin, S. H., & Martin, M. A. (2001). Using literature response activities to build strategic reading for students with reading difficulties. *Reading Improvement, 38*(2), 85–94.

Marzano, R. (2003). *What works in schools: Translating research into action.* Alexandria, VA: Association for Supervision and Curriculum Development.

Mason, J. M., & Au, K. H. (1990). *Reading instruction for today.* Glenview, IL: Scott, Foresman.

Massey, D. D., & Heafner, T. L. (2004). Promoting reading comprehension in social studies. *Journal of Adolescent & Adult Literacy, 48*(1), 26–40.

Mastropieri, M. A., Scruggs, T. E., & Butcher, K. (1997). How effective is inquiry learning for students with mild disabilities? *Journal of Special Education, 31*(2), 199–211.

Mastropieri, M. A., Scruggs, T. E., Mantzicopoulos, P. Y., Sturgeon, A., Goodwin, L., & Chung, S. (1998). "A place where living things affect and depend upon each other": Qualitative and quantitative outcomes associated with inclusive science teaching. *Science Education, 82,* 163–179.

Mathewson, G. (1976). The function of attitudes in the reading process. In H. Singer and R. Ruddell (Eds.), *Theoretical models and processes of reading* (pp. 908–919). Newark, DE: International Reading Association.

Maurer, M. M., & Davidson, G. (1999). Technology, children, and the power of the heart. *Phi Delta Kappan, 80*(6), 458–461.

Maxwell, R. (1996). *Writing across the curriculum in the middle and high schools.* Boston: Allyn & Bacon.

McAndrew, D. A. (1983). Underlining and note taking: Some suggestions from research. *Journal of Reading, 27,* 103–108.

McBride, J. P. (1994). Study habits of Isaac Newton. *Education, 114*(3), 461–464.

McCombs, B. L. (1986). The role of the self-system in self-regulated learning. *Contemporary Educational Psychology, 11,* 314–332.

McCrindle, A. R., & Christensen, C. A. (1995). The impact of learning journals on metacognitive and cognitive processes and learning performance. *Learning and Instruction, 5,* 167–185.

McDonald, S., & Stevenson, R. J. (1998). Effects of text structure and prior knowledge of the learner on navigation in hypertext. *Human Factors, 40*(1), 18–28.

McGivern, J. E., & Levin, J. R. (1983). The keyword method and children's vocabulary learning: An interaction with vocabulary knowledge. *Contemporary Educational Psychology, 8*(1), 46–54.

McInnes, A., Humphries, T., Hogg-Johnson, S., & Tannock, R. (2003). Listening comprehension and working memory are impaired in attention-deficit hyperactivity disorder irrespective of language impairment. *Journal of Abnormal Child Psychology, 31*(4), 427–444.

McKeachie, W. J. (2002). *McKeachie's teaching tips: Strategies, research, and theory for college and university teachers,* 11th ed. Boston: Houghton Mifflin.

McKenna, M. C., & Kear, D. J. (1990). Measuring attitude toward reading: A new tool for teachers. *The Reading Teacher, 43,* 626–639.

McKeown, M. G., & Beck, I. L. (2003). Taking advantage of read-alouds to help children make sense of decontextualized language. In A. van Kleeck, S. A. Stahl, & E. B. Bauer (Eds.), *On reading books to children* (pp. 159–176). Mahwah, NJ: Erlbaum.

McKeown, M. G., Bede, I. L., & Worthy, J. (1992). *Engaging students with text.* Paper presented at the annual meeting of the National Reading Association Conference, San Antonio, TX.

McLaughlin, H. (1969). SMOG grading—a new readability formula. *Journal of Reading, 12,* 639–646.

McLaughlin, M., & DeVoogd, G. (2004). Critical literacy as comprehension: Expanding reader response. *Journal of Adolescent & Adult Literacy, 48,* 52–62.

McLuhan, M. (1995). *Understanding media: The extensions of man.* New York: Routledge.

McMaster, K. N., & Fuchs, D. (2002). Effects of cooperative learning on the academic achievement of students with learning disabilities: An update of Tateyama-Sbuezej's review. *Learning Disabilities Research and Practice, 17,* 107–117.

McMaster, K. N., & Fuchs, D. (2005, Spring). Cooperative learning for students with disabilities. *Current Practice Alerts, 11.* Retrieved from http://www.teachingld.org/pdf/alert11.pdf.

McMillan, J. H., & Reed, D. F. (1994). Resilient at-risk students: Students' views about why they succeed. *Journal of At-Risk Issues, 1,* 27–33.

McMurry, F. M. (1909). *How to study, and teaching how to study.* Boston: Houghton Mifflin.

McPeck, J. (1981). *Critical thinking and education.* New York: St. Martin's Press.

McQuillan, J. (1998). *The literacy crisis: False claims, real solutions.* Portsmouth, NH: Heinemann.

McTighe, J., & Lyman, F. T. (1988). Cueing thinking in the classroom: The promise of theory embedded tools. *Educational Leadership, 45*(7), 18–24.

McWilliams, L., & Rakes, T. (1979). *The content inventories.* Dubuque, IA: Kendall/Hunt.

Mealey, D., & Konopak, B. (1990). Content area vocabulary instruction: Is preteaching worth the effort? *Reading: Exploration and Discovery, 13*(1), 39–42.

Medo, M. A., & Ryder, R. J. (1993). The effects of vocabulary instruction on readers' ability to make causal connections. *Reading Research and Instruction, 33*(2), 119–134.

Meeks, J., & Morgan, R. (1978). New use for the cloze procedure: Interaction in imagery. *Reading Horizons, 18,* 261–264.

Meloth, M. S., & Deering, P. D. (1992). Effects of two cooperative conditions on peer-group discussions, reading comprehension, and metacognition. *Contemporary Educational Psychology, 17,* 175–193.

Memory, D. M. (1990). Teaching technical vocabulary: Before, during, or after reading assignment? *Journal of Reading Behavior, 22,* 39–53.

Menke, D. J., & Pressley, M. (1994). Elaborative interrogation: Using "why" questions to enhance the learning from text. *Journal of Reading, 37*(8), 642–645.

Merkley, D. J., Schmidt, D. A., & Allen, G. (2001). Addressing the English language arts technology standard in a secondary reading methodology course. *Journal of Adolescent & Adult Literacy, 45*(3), 220–231.

Merriam-Webster's Online Dictionary. Retrieved February 17, 2007, from http://www.m-w.com/dictionary/study.

Mesmer, H. A. E. (2005). Text accessibility and the struggling reader. *Reading and Writing Quarterly, 21,* 1–5.

Mesmer, H. A. E., & Hutchins, E. J. (2002). Using QARs with charts and graphs. *The Reading Teacher, 56,* 21–27.

Metors, S. E., & Woosley, K. (2006). Visual literacy: An institutional imperative. *EDUCAUSE Review, 41*(3), 80. Retrieved March 13, 2006, from http://www.educause.edu/LibraryDetailPage/666?ID=ERM0638.

Metzger, M. (1989). *Voices from the Civil War.* New York: Crowell.

Mevarech, Z. R. (1999). Effects of metacognitive training embedded in cooperative settings on mathematical problem solving. *Journal of Educational Research, 92*(4), 195.

Meyer, B. J. F. (2003). Text coherence and readability. *Topics in language disorders, 23,* 204–224.

Meyer, B. J. F., Brandt, D. M., & Bluth, G. J. (1980). Use of top-level structure in text: Key for reading comprehension of ninth grade students. *Reading Research Quarterly, 16,* 72–103.

Mikulecky, L., Shanklin, N., & Caverly, D. (1979). Mikulecky behavioral reading attitude measure. In *Adult reading habits, attitudes, and motivations: A cross-sectional study.* Bloomington: Indiana University, School of Education.

Minicucci, C., Berman, P., McLaughlin, B., McLeod, B., Nelson, B., & Woodworth, K. (1995). School reform and school diversity. *Phi Delta Kappan, 77,* 77–80.

Miyake, N., & Norman, D. (1979). To ask a question, one must know enough to know what is not known. *Journal of Verbal Learning and Verbal Behavior, 18,* 357–364.

Moats, L. C. (2001). When older students can't read. *Educational Leadership, 58*(6), 36–40.

Moffett, J. (1979). Integrity in the teaching of writing. *Phi Delta Kappan, 61,* 276–279.

Mohr, K. A. J. (2004). English as an accelerated language: A call to action for reading teachers. *The Reading Teacher, 58*(1), 18–26.

Mohr, K. A. J., & Mohr, E. S. (2007). Extending English language learners' classroom interactions using the response protocol. *The Reading Teacher, 60,* 440–450.

Moje, E. B. (2000). What will classrooms and schools look like in the new millennium? *Reading Research Quarterly, 35,* 128–134.

Moje, E. B. (2002). Reframing adolescent literacy research for new times: Studying youth as a resource. *Reading Research and Instruction, 41,* 3, 211–228.

Moje, E. B., Ciechanowski, K. M., Kramer, K., Ellis, L., Carrillo, R., & Collazo, T. (2004). Working toward the third space in content area literacy: An examination of everyday funds of knowledge and discourse. *Reading Research Quarterly, 39,* 38–70.

Molden, K. (2007). Critical literacy, the right answer for the reading classroom: Strategies to move beyond comprehension for reading improvement. *Reading Improvement, 44*(1), 50–56.

Moore, D. W., Readance, J. E., & Rickelman, R. J. (1983). An historical exploration of content area reading instruction. *Reading Research Quarterly, XVIII,* 419–438.

Moore, J. C., & Surber, J. R. (1992). Effects of context and keyword methods on second language vocabulary acquisition. *Contemporary Educational Psychology, 17,* 286–292.

Mokhtari, K., & Reichard, C. A. (2002). Assessing students' metacognitive awareness of reading strategies. *Journal of Educational Psychology, 94*(2), 249–259.

Montague, M., & Applegate, B. (2000). Middle school students' perceptions, persistence, and performance in mathematical problem solving. *Learning Disabilities Quarterly, 23*(3), 215–228.

Moore, D., & Arthur, S. V. (1981). Possible sentences. In E. K. Dishner, T. W. Bean, & J. E. Readance (Eds.), *Reading in the content areas: Improving classroom instruction.* Dubuque, IA: Kendall/Hunt.

Moore, D., & Murphy, A. (1987). Selection of materials. In D. Alvermann, D. Moore, & M. Conley (Eds.),

Research within reach: Secondary school reading (pp. 94–108). Newark, DE: International Reading Association.

Moore, J. C., & Surber, J. R. (1992). Effects of context and keyword methods on second language vocabulary acquisition. *Contemporary Educational Psychology, 17,* 286–292.

Moore, M. M. (2006). Variations in test anxiety and locus of control orientation in achieving and underachieving gifted and nongifted middle school students. (Recent dissertation research in gifted studies.) *Roeper Review, 28*(4), 252–253.

Morgan, R., & Culver, V. (1978). Locus of control and reading achievement: Applications for the classroom. *Journal of Reading, 21,* 403–408.

Morgan, R., Otto, A., & Thompson, G. (1976). A study of the readability and comprehension of selected eighth grade social studies textbooks. *Perceptual and Motor Skills, 43,* 594.

Morgan, R. F., Forget, M. A., & Antinarella, J. C. (1996). *Reading for success: A school to work approach.* Cincinnati, OH: South-Western.

Morgan, R. F., Meeks, J. W., Schollaert, A., & Paul, J. (1986). *Critical reading/thinking skills for the college student.* Dubuque, IA: Kendall/Hunt.

Morgan, W., & Beaumont, G. (2003). A dialogic approach to argumentation: Using a chat room to develop early adolescent students' argumentative writing. *Journal of Adolescent & Adult Literacy, 47*(2), 146–157.

Morrison, J. L. (1999). The role of technology in education today and tomorrow: An interview with Kenneth Green. *On The Horizon, 7*(1), 1–4.

Morrison, T. G., Jacobs, J. S., & Swinyard, W. R. (1999). Do teachers who read personally use recommended literacy practices in their classrooms? *Reading Research and Instruction, 38*(2), 81–100.

Mosenthal, P. B., & Kirsch, I. S. (1998). A new measure for assessing document complexity: The PMOSE/IKIRSCH document readability formula. *Journal of Adolescent & Adult Literacy, 41*(8), 638–657.

Moss, B., & Hendershot, J. (2002). Exploring sixth graders' selection of nonfiction trade books. *The Reading Teacher, 56,* 6–17.

Moss, J. (1990). *Focus units in literature: A handbook for elementary school teachers,* 2nd ed. Urbana, IL: National Council of Teachers of English.

Muller-Kalthoff, T., & Moller, J. (2003). The effects of graphical overviews, prior knowledge, and self-concept on hypertext disorientation and learning achievement. *Journal of Educational Multimedia and Hypermedia, 12*(2), 117–135.

Murray, D. (1982). *Learning by teaching.* Montclair, NJ: Boynton/Cook.

Murray, J. (2002). Creating placement tests. *ESL Magazine Online.* Retrieved Nov. 26, 2004, from http://eslmag.com/modules.php?name=News&file=article&sid=30.

Myers, J. W. (1984). *Writing to learn across the curriculum.* Bloomington, IN: Phi Delta Kappa.

Myers, P. (1998). Passion for poetry. *Journal of Adolescent & Adult Literacy, 41*(4), 262–271.

Myklebust, H. (1965). *Development and disorders of written language.* New York: Grune and Stratton.

Nagel, G. K. (2002, November). Building cultural understanding and communication: A model in seven situations. *Reading Online, 6*(4). Retrieved June 3, 2007, from http://www.readingonline.org/newliteracies/lit_index.asp?HREF=nagel/index.html.

Nagy, W., Herman, P., & Anderson, R. C. (1985). Learning words from context. *Reading Research Quarterly, 20,* 233–253.

Nagy, W., & Scott, J. A. (2000). Vocabulary processes. In M. Kamil, P. Mosenthal, P. D. Pearson, & R. Barr (Eds.), *Handbook of reading research: Vol. III* (pp. 269–284). Mahwah, NJ: Erlbaum.

Nagy, W., & Stahl, S. (2000). *Promoting vocabulary development.* Austin: Texas Education Agency.

Nagy, W. E. (1988). *Teaching vocabulary to improve reading comprehension.* Newark, DE: International Reading Association.

National Assessment of Educational Progress. (1998). Denver, CO: Education Commission of the States. National Assessment of Educational Progress's (NAEP) *The Reading Report Card* (2003). Retrieved Nov. 15, 2004, from http://nces.ed.gov/nations reportcard/reading/.

National Assessment of Educational Progress. (2007). *The Nation's Report Card: Reading 2007.* Retrieved October 12, 2007, from http://nces.ed.gov/nationsreportcard/pubs/main2007/2007496.asp.

National Board for Professional Teaching Standards Assessment. (2007). Retrieved June 2007 from http://www.nbpts.org/help_and_faqs/assessment.

National Center for Education Statistics. (1996). *Reading literacy in the United States: Findings from the IEA reading literacy study.* Washington, DC: U.S. Department of Education.

National Center for Education Statistics. (1999). *Digest of educational statistics, 1998.* Washington, DC: U.S. Department of Education.

National Center for Education Statistics. (2001). *Early childhood longitudinal study, kindergarten class of 1998–99.* U.S. Department of Education. Retrieved Sept. 9, 2004, from http://www.ed.gov/programs/coe/2003/charts/chart36/asp.

National Center for Education Statistics. (2003). *The nation's report card: Reading highlights, 2003.* U.S. Department of Education, NCES 2004–452.

National Center for Educational Statistics. (2003). The NAEP reading achievement levels. *The nation's report card, 2003.* Retrieved from http://nces.ed.gov/nationsreportcard/reading/achieveall.asp#grade12.

National Center for Education Statistics. (2004). Learner outcomes: Academic outcomes: Indicator 10: Writing performance of students in grades 4, 8, and 12. *The condition of education.* Retrieved Nov. 27, 2004, from http://nces.ed.gov/programs/coe/2004/section2/indicator10.asp.

National Clearinghouse for Bilingual Education. (2002). Rate of LEP growth in the United States. Retrieved Sept. 9, 2004, from http://www.ncbe.gwu.edu.

National Commission on Excellence in Education. (1983). *A nation at risk: The imperative report to the nation and the secretary of education.* Washington, DC: U.S. Government Printing Office.

National Council of Teachers of English. (1996). *Standards for the English language arts.* Urbana, IL: National Council of Teachers of English and International Reading Association.

National Council of Teachers of Mathematics. (2000). *High-stakes testing.* Reston, VA: NCTM. Retrieved Sept. 9, 2004, from http://www.nctm.org/position_statements/highstakes.htm.

National Education Association (NEA). (2002). National Education Association 2002 Instructional Materials Survey. Retrieved June 24, 2007 from http://www.publishers.org/SchoolDiv/research/research_02/NEA2002InstrMatReport.pdf.

National Education Association (NEA). (2003). *Status of the American Public School Teacher 2000–2001.* Washington, DC: Author.

National Institute of Child Health and Human Development (2000). *Report of the National Reading Panel. Teaching children to read: An evidence-based assessment of the scientific research literature on reading and its implications for reading instruction* (NIH Publication No. 00–4769). Washington, DC: U.S. Government Printing Office.

Neckerman, K. M., & Wilson, W. J. (1988). Schools and poor communities. In D. W. Hornbeck (Ed.), *School success for at-risk youth: Analysis and recommendations of the Council of Chief State School Officers* (pp. 25–44). Orlando, FL: Harcourt Brace Jovanovich.

Nessel, D. (1987). Reading comprehension: Asking the right questions. *Phi Delta Kappan, 68,* 442–445.

Nettle D., & Romaine, S. (2000). *Vanishing voices: The extinction of the world's languages.* New York: Oxford University Press.

Neufeld, P. (2005). Comprehension instruction in content area classes. *The Reading Teacher, 59*(4), 302–313.

Neuman, S. B., & Celano, D. (2001). Access to print in low-income and middle-income communities: An ecological study of four neighborhoods. *Reading Research Quarterly, 36*(1), 8–26.

Newman, J. M. (2000). Following the yellow brick road. *Phi Delta Kappan, 81,* 774–779.

Nichols, W. D., & Rupley, W. H. (2004). Matching instructional design with vocabulary instruction. Reading Horizons, 45(1), 55–71.

Nodding, N. (1995). Teaching themes of caring. *Phi Delta Kappan, 76*(9), 675–679.

Noll, E., & Watkins, R. (2003). The impact of homelessness on children's literacy experiences. *The Reading Teacher, 57*(4), 362–371.

Nuthall, G. (1999). The way students learn: Acquiring knowledge from an integrated science and social studies unit. *Elementary School Journal, 99*(4), 303.

O'Brien, R. (1971). *Mrs. Frisby and the rats of NIMH.* New York: Atheneum.

O'Dell, Scott. (1987). *The serpent never sleeps.* New York: Ballantine.

O'Donnell, P., Weber, K. P., & McLaughlin, T. F. (2003). Improving correct and error rate and reading comprehension using key words and previewing: A case report with a language minority student. *Education & Treatment of Children, 26*(3), 237–255.

Ogle, D. (1986). KWL: A teaching model that develops active reading of expository text. *The Reading Teacher, 39,* 564–570.

Ogle, D. (1992). KWL in action: Secondary teachers find applications that work. In E. K. Dishner, T. W. Bean, J. E. Readance, & D. W. Moore (Eds.), *Reading in the content areas: Improving classroom instruction,* 3rd ed. (pp. 270–281). Dubuque, IA: Kendall/Hunt.

Olshavsky, J. (1975). Reading as problem solving: An investigation of strategies. *Reading Research Quarterly, 12,* 654–674.

Olson, C. B. (2007). *The reading/writing connection: Strategies for teaching learning in the secondary classroom,* 2nd ed. Boston: Pearson Education.

Olson, M. W., & Gee, T. (1991). Content reading instruction in the primary grades: Perceptions and strategies. *The Reading Teacher, 45,* 298–307.

Onwuegbuzie, A. J., Slate, J. R., & Schwartz, R. A. (2001). Role of study skills in graduate-level educational research courses. *The Journal of Educational Research, 94*(4), 238–248.

Opitz, M. (1992). The cooperative reading activity: An alternative to ability grouping. *The Reading Teacher, 45,* 736–738.

Opitz, M., & Rasinski, T. (1998). *Goodbye round-robin: Twenty-five effective oral reading strategies.* Portsmouth, NH: Heinemann.

Oppenheimer, T. (2003). *The flickering mind: False promise of technology in the classroom and how learning can be saved.* New York: Random House.

Orfield, A. (1988). Race, income, and educational inequity. In *School success for at-risk youth: Analysis and recommendations of the Council of Chief State School Officers* (pp. 45–71). Orlando, FL: Harcourt Brace Jovanovich.

Oster, L. (2001). Using the think-aloud for reading instruction. *The Reading Teacher, 55,* 65–69.

Padak, N. (2006). What's in a word? Teaching vocabulary from the inside out. *The New England Reading Association Journal, 42*(2), 8–11.

Page, B. (1987). From passive receivers to active learners in English. In J. Self (Ed.), *Plain talk about learning and writing across the curriculum* (pp. 37–50). Richmond: Virginia Department of Education.

Palincsar, A. S., & Brown, A. L. (1986). Interactive teaching to promote independent learning from text. *The Reading Teacher, 39,* 771–777.

Pallas, A. M., Natriello, G., & McDill, E. L. (1989). Changing nature of the disadvantaged population: Current dimensions and future trends. *Educational Researcher, 18,* 16–22.

Pally, M. (1998). Film studies drive literacy development for ESL university students. *Journal of Adolescent & Adult Literacy, 41*(8), 620–628.

Palmer, P. J. (1998). *The courage to teach.* San Francisco: Jossey-Bass.

Palmer, R. G., & Stewart, R. A. (2003). Nonfiction trade book use in primary grades. *The Reading Teacher, 57,* 38–48.

Palmer, R. G., & Stewart, R. A. (2005). Models for using nonfiction in the primary grades. *The Reading Teacher, 58,* 426–434.

Palombo, R. (2000). Brain based learning. *Training & Development, 54*(7), 21–35.

Pappas, C. (1991). Fostering full access to literacy by including information books. *Language Arts, 68,* 449–462.

Pappas, C. C. (1993). Is narrative "primary"? Some insights from kindergartners' pretend readings of stories and information books. *Journal of Reading Behavior, 25,* 97–129.

Paris, S. G. (1986). Teaching children to guide their reading and learning. In T. E. Raphael and R. Reynolds (Eds.), *Context of literacy* (pp. 115–130). New York: Longman.

Paris, S. G., Lipson, M. Y., & Wixson, K. K. (1983). Becoming a strategic reader. *Contemporary Educational Psychology, 8,* 393–396.

Paris, S. G., & Oka, E. R. (1989). Strategies for comprehending text and coping with reading difficulties. *Learning Disability Quarterly, 12,* 32–42.

Parker, W. C. (1991). Achieving thinking and decision-making objectives in social studies. In J. P. Shaver (Ed.), *Handbook of research on social studies teaching and learning.* New York: Macmillan.

Patrick, H., Bangel, N. J., Jeon, K., & Townsend, M. A. R. (2005). Reconsidering the issue of cooperative learning with gifted students. *Journal for the Education of the Gifted, 29,* 90–108.

Patterson, J. H. (2001, Spring). Raising resilience in classrooms and homes. *Childhood Education, 77*(3), 180.

Pauk, W. (1997). *How to study in college,* 6th ed. Boston: Houghton Mifflin.

Paul, D. G. (2004). The train has left: The No Child Left Behind Act leaves black and Latino literacy learners waiting at the station. *Journal of Adolescent & Adult Literacy, 47*(8), 647–656.

Paulsen, G. (1990). *Canyons.* New York: Delacorte Press.

Pearce, D. (1983). Guidelines for the use and evaluation of writing in content classrooms. *Journal of Reading, 17,* 212–218.

Pearce, D. (1987). Group writing activities: A useful strategy for content teachers. *Middle School Journal, 18,* 24–25.

Pearce, D., & Bader, L. (1984). Writing in content area classrooms. *Reading World, 23,* 234–241.

Pearce, D., & Davison, D. (1988). Teacher use of writing in the junior high mathematics classroom. *School Science and Mathematics, 88,* 6–15.

Pearson, P. D. (1985). Changing the face of reading comprehension. *The Reading Teacher, 38,* 724–738.

Pearson, P. D., & Johnson, D. (1978). *Teaching reading comprehension.* New York: Holt, Rinehart and Winston.

Pearson, P. D., & Santa, C. M. (1995). Students as researchers of their own learning. *Journal of Reading, 38,* 462–469.

Pearson, P. D., & Tierney, R. (1983). In search of a model of instructional research in reading. In S. Paris, G. Okon, & H. Stevenson (Eds.), *Learning and motivation in the classroom.* Hillsdale, NJ: Erlbaum.

Pellicano, R. (1987). At-risk: A view of "social advantage." *Educational Leadership, 44,* 47–50.

Penfield, W. (1975). *The mystery of the mind: A critical study of consciousness and the human brain.* Princeton, NJ: Princeton University Press.

Peregoy, S., & Boyle, O. (1997). *Reading, writing, and learning in ESL: A resource book for K–12 teachers.* White Plains, NY: Longman.

Perie, M., Grigg, W., & Donahue, P. (2005). *The Nation's Report Card: Reading 2005* (NCES 2006-451).

U.S. Department of Education, National Center for Education Statistics. Washington, DC: U.S. Government Printing Office.

Peters, E. E., & Levin, J. R. (1986). Effects of a mnemonic imagery strategy on good and poor readers' prose recall. *Reading Research Quarterly, 21,* 179–192.

Peterson, S. E., & Miller, J. A. (2004). Comparing the quality of students' experiences during cooperative learning and large-group instruction. *Journal of Educational Research, 97*(3), 123–134.

Piaget, J. (1963). *The origin of intelligence in children.* New York: Norton.

Pink, D. (2005) *A whole new mind: Moving from the information age to the conceptual age.* New York: Riverhead Publishing.

Pittleman, S. D., Heimlich, J. E., Berglund, R. L., & French, M. P. (1991). *Semantic feature analysis.* Newark, DE: International Reading Association.

Pogrow, S. (2006). Restructuring high-poverty elementary schools for success: A description of the hi-perform school design. *Phi Delta Kappan, 88,* 223–229.

Pressler, M. W. (2006, October 11). The handwriting is on the wall. *The Washington Post,* A 01.

Pressley, M. (2000). What should comprehension instruction be the instruction of? In M. L. Kamil, P. B. Mosenthal, P. D. Pearson, & R. Barr (Eds.), *Handbook of reading research,* Vol. 3 (pp. 545–561). Mahwah, NJ: Erlbaum.

Pressley, M. (2002a). Comprehension strategies instruction: A turn-of-the-century status report. In C.C. Block & M. Pressley (Eds.), *Comprehension instruction: Research-based best practices* (pp. 11–27). New York: Guilford.

Pressley, M. (2002b). *Reading instruction that works: The case for balanced teaching,* 2nd ed. New York: Guilford.

Pressley, M. (2002c, September). Comprehension instruction: What makes sense now, what might make sense soon. *Reading Online, 5*(2). Retrieved July 30, 2004, from http://www.readingonline.org/articles/art_index.asp?HREF=/articles/handbook/pressley/index.htm.

Pressley, M., & Afflerbach, P. (1995). *Verbal reports of reading: The nature of constructively responsive reading.* Hillsdale, NJ: Erlbaum.

Pressley, M., & Schneider, W. (1997). *Introduction to memory development during childhood and adolescence.* Mahwah, NJ: Erlbaum.

Pressley, M., Wharton-McDonald, R., Hampson, J., & Echevarria, M. (1998). The nature of literacy instruction in ten fourth and fifth grade classrooms in upstate New York. *Scientific Studies in Reading, 2,* 159–191.

Pulido, D. (2004, September). The effect of cultural familiarity on incidental vocabulary acquisition through reading. *The Reading Matrix, 4*(2). Retrieved April 1, 2004, from http://www.readingmatrix.com/articles/pulido/article.pdf.

Purcell-Gates, V., Degener, S. C., Jacobson, E., & Soler, M. (2002). Impact of authentic adult literacy instruction on adult literacy practices. *Reading Research Quarterly, 37,* 70–92.

Purcell-Gates, V., Duke, N. K., & Martineau, J. A. (2007). Learning to read and write genre-specific text: Roles of authentic experience and explicit teaching. *Reading Research Quarterly, 42,* 8–45.

Purdie, N., & Hattie, J. (1999). The relationship between study skills and learning outcomes: A meta-analysis. *Australian Journal of Education, 43*(1), 72.

Purkey, W. W., & Novak, J. M. (1984). *Inviting school success: A self-concept approach to teaching and learning,* 2nd ed. Belmont, CA: Wadsworth.

Purmensky, K. (2006). Weblogs transform service-learning reflection. *Academic Exchange Quarterly, 10*(1), 3–5.

Purves, A. C., & Bech, R. (1972). *Literature and the reader: Research in response to literature, reading interests, and the teaching of literature.* Urbana, IL: National Council of Teachers of English.

Quirk, M. P., & Schwanenflugel, P. J. (2004). Do supplemental remedial reading programs address the motivational issues of struggling readers? An analysis of five popular programs. *Reading Research and Instruction, 43*(3), 1–19.

Radencich, M. (1985). Writing a class novel: A strategy for LD students? *Academic Therapy, 20,* 599–603.

Rainie, L., & Madden, M. (2005). Podcasting catches on. Pew Internet and American Life Project. Retrieved on March 11, 2007, from http://www.pewinternet.org/PPF/r/194/report_display.asp.

Rakes, G. C., Rakes, T. A., & Smith, L. J. (1995). Using visuals to enhance secondary students' reading comprehension of expository texts. *Journal of Adolescent & Adult Literacy, 39,* 46–54.

Rakes, T., & Chance, L. (1990). A survey of how subjects remember what they read. *Reading Improvement, 27,* 122–128.

Ralph, J., Keller, D., & Crouse, J. (1994). How effective are American schools? *Phi Delta Kappan, 76,* 144–150.

Raphael, T. (1984). Teaching learners about sources of information for answering comprehension questions. *Journal of Reading, 27,* 303–311.

Raphael, T. (1986). Teaching question/answer relationships, revisited. *The Reading Teacher, 39,* 516–522.

Raphael, T. E., & Au, K. H. (2005). QAR: Enhancing comprehension and test taking across grades and content areas: The authors describe how question and answer relationships (QAR) can provide a framework for comprehension instruction with the potential of closing the literacy achievement gap. *The Reading Teacher, 5*(3), 206–222.

Rasinski, T. V., & Padak, N. D. (1993). *Inquiries in literacy learning and instruction: Fifteenth yearbook of the College Reading Association.* Kent, OH: Kent State University.

Raven, J. (1992). A model of competence, motivation, and behavior, and a paradigm for assessment. In H. Berlak et al. (Eds.), *Toward a new science of educational testing and assessment.* New York: State University of New York Press.

Read, S. (2005). First and second graders writing informational text. *The Reading Teacher, 59,* 36–44.

Readance, J. E., Bean, T. W., & Baldwin, R. S. (1981). *Content area reading: An integrated approach.* Dubuque, IA: Kendall/Hunt.

Ream, D. (2007, June). Personal e-mail communication.

Reinking, D. (1997). Me and my hypertext:) A multiple regression analysis of technology and literacy (sic). *The Reading Teacher, 50*(8), 626–643.

Reinking, D., & Pardon, D. (1995). Television and literacy. In T. V. Rasinski (Ed.), *Parents and teachers helping children learn to read and write* (pp. 137–145). Ft. Worth, TX: Harcourt Brace.

Reinking, D., & Wu, J. H. (1990). Reexamining the research on television and reading. *Reading Research and Instruction, 29,* 30–43.

Rekrut, M. D. (1999). Using the Internet in classroom instruction: A primer for teachers. *Journal of Adolescent & Adult Literacy, 42*(7), 546–557.

Restak, R. (1979). *The brain: The last frontier.* Garden City, NY: Doubleday.

Reutzel, D. R., & Daines, D. (1987). The text-relatedness of reading lessons in seven basal reading series. *Reading Research and Instruction, 27,* 26–35.

Reyes, D. J. (1986). Critical thinking in elementary social studies text series. *Social Studies, 77,* 151–157.

Reyhner, J., & Garcia, R. L. (1989). Helping minorities read better: Problems and promises. *Reading Research and Instruction, 28,* 84–91.

Reynolds, R. E., Sinatra, G. M., & Jetton, T. L. (1996). Views of knowledge acquisition and representation: A continuum from experience centered to mind centered. *Educational Psychologist, 21,* 93–104.

Rhodes, J. A., Robnolt, V. J., & Richardson, J. S. (2005). Study skills in the electronic age. In P. Linder, M. B. Sampson, J. A. R. Dugan, & B. Brancato (Eds.), *The College Reading Association yearbook* (pp. 221–235). Logan, UT: College Reading Association.

Rhodes, L. K., & Shanklin, N. (1991). *Windows into literacy: Assessing learners K–8.* Portsmouth, NH: Heinemann.

Rhodes, R. (1990, October 14). Don't be a bystander. *Parade,* 4–7.

Rice, G. E. (1992, April). *The need for explanations in graphic organizer research.* Paper presented at the annual meeting of the American Educational Research Association, San Francisco.

Richardson, J. (1991). Developing responsibility in English classes: Three activities. *Journal of the Virginia College Reading Educators, 11,* 8–19.

Richardson, J. (1992a). Generating inquiry-oriented projects from teachers. In A. Frager and J. Miller (Eds.), *Using inquiry in reading teacher education* (pp. 24–29). Kent, OH: Kent State University, College Reading Association.

Richardson, J. (1992b). Taking responsibility for taking tests. In N. Padak and T. Rasinski (Eds.), *Literacy research and practice: Foundations for the year 2000* (pp. 209–215). Kent, OH: Kent State University, College Reading Association.

Richardson, J. S. (1994). Great read-alouds for prospective teachers and secondary students. *Journal of Reading, 38,* 98–103.

Richardson, J. S. (1995a). Three ways to keep a middle school student in the "reading habit." *Affective Reading Education, 14,* 5–7.

Richardson, J. S. (1995b). A read-aloud for cultural diversity. *Journal of Adolescent & Adult Literacy, 39,* 160–162.

Richardson, J. S. (1996). *The survival guide: Reading to learn in the English class.* Toronto, Canada: Pippin.

Richardson, J. S. (1999). *Reading is drudgery; reading is deeper meaning.* Paper presented at the 43rd conference of the College Reading Association, Hilton Head, North Carolina.

Richardson, J. S. (2000a). *Read it aloud! Using literature in secondary content classrooms.* Newark, DE: International Reading Association.

Richardson, J. S. (2000b). *Voices of adolescents and strategies for change.* Paper presented at the World Congress on Reading, Aukland, New Zealand.

Richardson, J. S. (2002). *Forum on adolescent literacy: Reading is drudgery.* Paper presented at the World Congress on Reading, Edinburgh, Scotland.

Richardson, J. S. (2004, July/August). Content area literacy lessons go high tech. *Reading Online, 8*(1). Retrieved July 10, 2004, from http://www.reading online.org/articles/art_index.asp?HREF=richardson/index.html online.

Richardson, J. S., Fleener, C. E., & Thistlethwaite, L. (2005). Using threaded discussions to learn about threaded discussions. In J. R. Dugan, P. Linder, M. B. Sampson, B. Brancato, & L. Elish-Piper (Eds.), *Celebrating the power of literacy* (pp. 439–461). Commerce: Texas A&M University, College Reading Association.

Richardson, J. S., & Forget, M. A. (1995). A read-aloud for algebra and geometry classrooms. *Journal of Adolescent & Adult Literacy, 39,* 322–326.

Richardson, J. S., & Morgan, R. F. (1991). Crossing bridges by connecting meaning. *Texas Affect in Reading Journal, 34*(1).

Richardson, J. S., & Morgan, R. F. (1997). *Reading to learn in the content areas.* Belmont, CA: Wadsworth ITP.

Richardson, J. S., Rhodes, J. A., & Robnolt, V. J. (2004). *Electronic study skills: What do the new study skills look like?* Paper presented at the College Reading Association, October 30, 2004, Delray Beach, FL.

Richardson, J. S., Robnolt, V. J., & Rhodes, J. A. (2007). A history of study skills: Not hot, but not forgotten. Paper presented at the College Reading Association, November 3, 2007, Salt Lake City, UT.

Rifkin, J. (1987). *Time wars.* New York: Henry Holt.

Rifkin, J. (2002). *The hydrogen economy.* New York: Tarcher/Putnam.

Ritter, S., & Idol-Mastas, L. (1986). Teaching middle school students to use a test-taking strategy. *Journal of Educational Research, 79,* 350–357.

Robelen, E. (2005, February 23). PTA members are split on NCLB's effectiveness. *Education Week, 24,* 2(4), 30.

Robertson, J. I. (1992). *Civil War: America becomes one nation.* New York: Knopf.

Robinson, A. (2003). Cooperative learning and high ability students. In N. Colangelo & G. Davis (Eds.), *Handbook of gifted education,* 3rd ed. (pp. 282–292). Boston: Allyn & Bacon.

Robinson, D. H. (1998). Graphic organizers as aids to text learning. *Reading Research and Instruction, 37*(2), 85–105.

Robinson, D. H., & Schraw, G. (1994). Computational efficiency through visual argument: Do graphic organizers communicate relations in text too effectively? *Contemporary Educational Psychology, 19,* 399–415.

Robinson, F. P. (1961). *Effective study,* rev. ed. New York: Harper and Row.

Roblyer, M. D., Edwards, J., & Havriluk, M. A. (1997). *Integrating educational technology into teaching.* Upper Saddle River, NJ.

Rogers, D. B. (1984). Assessing study skills. *Journal of Reading, 27,* 346–354.

Rohrbeck, C. A., Ginsburg-Block, M. D., Fantuzzo, J. W., & Miller, T. R. (2003). Peer-assisted learning interventions with elementary school students: A meta-analytic review. *Journal of Educational Psychology, 95,* 240–257.

Roit, M., & McKenzie, R. (1985). Disorders of written communication: An instructional priority for LD students. *Journal of Learning Disabilities, 18,* 258–260.

Romance, N. R., & Vitale, M. R. (1997). *Knowledge representation systems: Basis for the design of instruction for undergraduate course curriculum.* Paper presented at the Eighth National Conference on College Teaching and Learning, Jacksonville, FL.

Romance, N. R., & Vitale, M. R. (1999). Concept mapping as a tool for learning. *College Teaching, 47*(2), 74.

Rose, L. C., & Gallup, A. M. (2006). The 38th Annual Phi Delta Kappa/Gallup Poll of the public's attitudes toward the public schools. *Phi Delta Kappan, 88,* 41–53.

Rose, L. C., & Gallup, A. M. (2007). The 39th Annual Phi Delta Kappa/Gallup Poll of the public's attitudes toward the public schools. *Phi Delta Kappan, 89*(1), 33–51.

Rose, M. C. (1999). Don't stop now. *Instructor, 108*(8), 28.

Roser, N. L., & Keehn, S. (2002). Fostering thought, talk, and inquiry: Linking literature and social studies. *The Reading Teacher, 55,* 416–426.

Rothstein, R. (1998). Bilingual education: The controversy. *Phi Delta Kappan, 79*(9), 672–678.

Rotter, J. B. (1966). Generalized expectancies for internal versus external control of reinforcement. *Psychological Monographs: General and Applied, 80*(1), 1–28.

Routeman, R. (2004). *Writing essentials: Raising expectations and results while simplifying teaching.* Portsmouth, NH: Heinemann.

Ruddell, M. R. (2000, July). Dot.com lessons worth learning: Student engagement, literacy, and project-based learning. *Reading Online, 4*(1). Retrieved Sept. 7, 2004, from http://www.readingonline.org/articles/ruddell/.

Rudestam, K. E., & Schoenholtz-Read, J. (2002). Overview: The coming of age of adult online education. In K. E. Rudestam and J. Schoenholtz-Read (Eds.), *Handbook of online learning* (pp. 3–29). Thousand Oaks, CA: Sage.

Ruiz-Primo, M. A., & Shavelson, R. J. (1996). Problems and issues in the use of concepts maps in science assessment. *Journal of Research in Science Teaching, 33*(6), 569–600.

Rumelhart, D. E. (1980). Schemata: The building blocks of cognition. In R. J. Spiro, B. C. Bruce, & W. F. Brewer (Eds.), *Theoretical issues in reading comprehension* (pp. 33–58). Hillsdale, NJ: Erlbaum.

Russell, M. (1999.) *Testing on computers: A follow-up study comparing performance on computer and on paper.* Education Policy Analysis Archives, 7, 20. ERIC EJ588928.

Russell, M., & Abrams, L. (2004). Instructional uses of computers for writing: The effect of state testing programs. *Teachers College Record, 196,* 1332–1357.

Russell, S. (1995). Sheltered content instruction for second language learners. *Reading Today, 13,* 30.

Ryder, R. J., & Graves, M. F. (1994). Vocabulary instruction presented prior to reading in two basal readers. *Elementary School Journal, 95*(2), 139–153.

Sadoski, M., Paivio, A., & Goetz, E. T. (1991). A critique of schema theory in reading and a dual coding alternative. *Reading Research Quarterly, 26*(4), 463–484.

Saenz, L. M., & Fuchs, L. S. (2002). Examining the reading difficulty of secondary students with learning disabilities: Expository versus narrative text. *Remedial and Special Education, 21,* 31–41.

Sagan, C. (1977). *The dragons of Eden.* New York: Random House.

Sakta, C. G. (1999). SQCR: A strategy for guiding reading and higher level thinking. *Journal of Adolescent & Adult Literacy, 42*(4), 265–269.

Salembier, G. B. (1999). SCAN and RUN: A reading comprehension strategy that works. *Journal of Adolescent & Adult Literacy, 42*(5), 386–401.

Salvia, J., & Ysseldyke, J. (1998). *Assessment,* 7th ed. Boston: Houghton Mifflin.

Sanacore, J. (1998). Promoting the lifelong love of reading. *Journal of Adolescent & Adult Literacy, 41*(5), 392–396.

Scarborough, H. A. (Ed.). (2001). *Writing across the curriculum in secondary classrooms: Teaching from a diverse perspective.* Upper Saddle River, NJ: Pearson Education.

Scarborough, H. S. (1998). Early identification of children at risk for reading disabilities: Phonological awareness and some other promising predictors. In B. K. Shapiro, P. J. Accardo, & A. J. Capute (Eds.), *Specific reading disability: A view of the spectrum* (pp. 75–119). Timonium, MD: York Press.

Scardamalia, M., & Bereiter, C. (1984). Development of strategies in text processing. In H. Mandl, N. L. Stein, & T. Trabasson (Eds.), *Learning and comprehension of text* (pp. 379–406). Hillsdale, NJ: Erlbaum.

Schaeffer, R. K. (2003). Globalization and technology. *Phi Kappa Phi Forum, 83*(4), 30–33.

Shermis, S. (1999). Reflective thought, critical thinking. *Eric Digest.* Retrieved November 30, 2003, from http://www.ericfacility.net/databases/ERIC_Digests/ed436007.html.

Schieffelin, B. B., & Cochran-Smith, M. (1984). Learning to read culturally: Literacy before schooling. In H. Goelman, A. Oberg, & F. Smith (Eds.), *Awakening to literacy* (pp. 3–23). Portsmouth, NH: Heinemann.

Schmidt, P. R. (1995). Working and playing with others: Cultural conflict in a kindergarten literacy program. *The Reading Teacher, 48,* 404–412.

Schmidt, P. R. (1998). The ABC's of cultural understanding and communication. *Equity and Excellence in Education, 31*(2), 28–38.

Schmoker, M. (2007). Radically redefining literacy instruction: An immense opportunity. *Phi Delta Kappan, 88,* 488–493.

Schneider, B., & Stephenson, D. (1999). *The ambitious generation: America's teenagers motivated but directionless.* New Haven, CT: Yale University Press.

Schoenbach, R., Greenleaf, C. L., Cziko, C., & Hurwitz, L. (1999). *Reading for understanding.* San Francisco: Jossey-Bass.

Schumann, J. (1978). Second language acquisition: The pidginization hypothesis. In E. Hatch (Ed.), *Second language acquisition.* Rowley, MA: Newbury House.

Schumm, J. (1992). Content area textbooks: How tough are they? *Journal of Reading, 36,* 47.

Schumm, J., Mangrum, C., Gordon, J., & Doucette, M. (1992). The effect of topic knowledge on the predicted test questions of developmental college readers. *Reading Research and Instruction, 31,* 11–23.

Schumm, J., & Vaughn, S. (1991). Making adaptations for mainstreamed students: General education teachers' perspectives. *Remedial and Special Education, 12*(4), 18–27.

Schwartz, D. M. (1999). *If you hopped like a frog.* New York: Scholastic Press.

Schwartz, R. M., & Raphael, T. E. (1985). Concept of definition: A key to improving students' vocabulary. *Journal of Reading, 39,* 198–205.

Scieszka, J. (1995). *The math curse.* New York: Penguin Books.

Scott, J. A., Jamieson-Noel, D., & Asselin, M. (2003). Vocabulary instruction throughout the day in twenty-three Canadian upper-elementary classrooms. *The Elementary School Journal, 103*(3), 269–288.

Scruggs, T., Mastropieri, M. A., Brigham, F. J., & Sullivan, G. S. (1992). Effects of mnemonic reconstructions on the spatial learning of adolescents with learning disabilities. *Learning Disability Quarterly, 15*(3), 154–167.

Scruggs, T., White, K., & Bennion, K. (1986). Teaching test-taking skills to elementary students: A meta-analysis. *Elementary School Journal, 87,* 69–82.

Sebasta, S. (1997). Hot literacy topics of the past. *JAAL, 40*(6), 500.

Seidi, B. (2007). Working with communities to explore and personalize culturally relevant pedagogies. *Journal of Teacher Education, 58,* 168–183.

Self, J. (1987). The picture of writing to learn. In J. Self (Ed.), *Plain talk about learning and writing across the curriculum* (pp. 9–20). Richmond: Virginia State Department of Education.

Shanahan, T. (1997). Reading–writing relationships, thematic units, inquiry learning . . . in pursuit of effective integrated literacy instruction. *The Reading Teacher, 51*(1), 12–19.

Shanahan, T., Mulhern, M., & Rodriguez-Brown, F. (1995). Project FLAME: Lessons learned from a family literacy program for linguistic minority families. *The Reading Teacher, 48,* 586–593.

Shanahan, T., Robinson, B., & Schneider, M. (1995). Avoiding some of the pitfalls of thematic units. *The Reading Teacher, 48,* 718–719.

Shannon, D. (1999). *No, David.* New York: The Blue Sky Press, Scholastic Books.

Shapiro, A. M. (1999). The relationship between prior knowledge and interactive overviews during hypermedia-aided learning. *Journal of Educational Computing Research, 20,* 143–167.

Sharan, S., & Sharan, Y. (1976). *Small-group teaching.* Englewood Cliffs, NJ: Educational Technology Publications.

Sherry, L., Cronje, J., Rauscher, W., & Obermeyer, G. (2005). Mediated conversations and the affective domain: Two case studies. *International Journal of E-Learning, 4*(2), 177–191.

Short, K. (1997). *Reading as a way of knowing.* York, ME: Stenhouse.

Shyer, M. F. (1988). *Welcome home, jelly bean.* New York: Macmillan.

Sideridis, G. D., Mouzaki, A., Simos, P., & Protopapas, A. (2006). Classification of students with reading comprehension difficulties: The roles of motivation, affect, and psychopathology. *Learning Disabilities Quarterly, 29*(3), 159–181.

Siedow, M. D., & Hasselbring, T. S. (1984). Adaptability of text readability to increase comprehension of reading disability students. *Reading Improvement, 21,* 276–279.

Siegle, D. (2004). The merging of literacy and technology in the twenty-first century: A bonus for gifted children. *Gifted Child Today, 27*(2), 32–36.

Silva, P. U., Meagher, M. E., Valenzuela, M., & Crenshaw, S. W. (1996). E-mail: Real-life classroom experiences with foreign languages. *Learning and Leading with Technology, 23*(5), 10–12.

Simon, K. (1993). Alternative assessment: Can real-world skills be tested? *The Link, 12,* 1–7.

Simpson, M. L. (1987). Alternative formats for evaluating content area vocabulary understanding. *Journal of Reading, 30,* 20–27.

Simpson, M. L., & Nist, S. (2000). An update on strategic learning: It's more than textbook reading strategies. *Journal of Adolescent and Adult Literacy, 43*(6), 528–541.

Sinatra, R. (1986). *Visual literacy connections to thinking, reading, and writing.* Springfield, IL: Charles C. Thomas.

Singer, H., & Bean, T. (1988). Three models for helping teachers to help students learn from text. In S. J. Samuels and P. D. Pearson (Eds.), *Changing school reading programs* (pp. 161–183). Newark, DE: International Reading Association.

Singer, H., & Donlan, D. (1985). *Reading and learning from text.* Hillsdale, NJ: Erlbaum.

Skinner, C. H., Cooper, L., & Cole, C. L. (1997). The effects of oral presentation rates on reading performance. *Journal of Applied Behavior Analysis, 30,* 331–334.

Slater, R. (2002). Brain compatible classroom practices. Presentation, 16th Annual *High Schools That Work* Staff Development Conference, Nashville, TN.

Slaouti, D. (2002). The World Wide Web for academic purposes: Old study skills for new? *English for Specific Purposes, 21*(2), 105–124.

Slavin, R. E. (1980). Cooperative learning. *Review of Educational Research, 50,* 315–342.

Slavin, R. E. (1983). *Cooperative learning.* New York: Longman.

Slavin, R. E. (1990). Cooperative learning and the gifted: Who benefits? *Journal for the Education of the Gifted, 14,* 28–30.

Slavin, R. E. (1991). Synthesis of research on cooperative learning. *Educational Leadership, 48,* 71–82.

Slavin, R. E. (1995). *Cooperative learning,* 2nd ed. Boston: Allyn & Bacon.

Slavin, R. E. (1996). Research on cooperative learning and achievement: What we know, what we need to know. *Contemporary Educational Psychology, 21,* 43–69.

Slavin, R. E. (2000). *Educational psychology: Theory and practice,* 6th ed. Boston: Allyn & Bacon.

Slavin, R. E. (2001). Cooperative learning and the cooperative school. In K. Ryan and J. M. Cooper (Eds.), *Kaleidoscope: Readings in education,* 9th ed. Boston: Houghton Mifflin.

Sloan, G. D. (1984). *The child as critic: Teaching literature in elementary and middle schools,* 2nd ed. New York: Teachers College Press.

Smith, D. J. (1992). Common ground: the connection between reader response and textbook reading. *Journal of Reading, 35*(8), 630–635.

Smith, F. (1971). *Understanding reading.* New York: Holt, Rinehart and Winston.

Smith, F. (1973). *Psycholinguistics and reading.* New York: Holt, Rinehart and Winston.

Smith, F. (1988). *Understanding reading: A psycholinguistic analysis of reading and learning to read,* 4th ed. Hillsdale, NJ: Erlbaum.

Smith, F. (1989). Overselling literacy. *Phi Delta Kappan, 70,* 352–359.

Smith, F. (1994). *Understanding reading: A psycholinguistic analysis of reading and learning to read,* 5th ed. Hillsdale, NJ: Erlbaum.

Smith, J. B. (1983). "Pique": A group dictionary assignment. *Exercise-Exchange, 29*(1), 35.

Smith, M. C. (1990). A longitudinal investigation of reading attitude development from childhood to adulthood. *Journal of Educational Research, 83,* 215–219.

Smith, N. B. (1965). *American reading instruction.* Newark, DE: International Reading Association.

Smith, S., & Bean, R. (1980). The guided writing procedure: Integrating content reading and writing improvement. *Reading World, 19,* 290–294.

Smuin, S. (1978). *Turn-ons.* Belmont, CA: Fearon Pitman.

Snow, C. E. (2002). *Reading for understanding. Toward an R&D program in reading comprehension.* Santa Monica, CA: RAND.

Snow, C. E., Burns, M. S., & Griffin, P. (Eds.). (1998). *Preventing reading difficulties in young children.* Washington, DC: National Academy Press.

Sobrol, D. T. (1997). Improving learning skills: A self-help group approach, *Higher Education, 33,* 39–50.

Sommers, C. H. (2000). *The war against boys: How misguided feminism is harming our young men.* New York: Simon and Schuster.

Sosniak, L. A., & Perlman, C. L. (1990). Secondary education by the book. *Journal of Curriculum Studies, 22,* 427–442.

Sousa, D. (2005). *How the brain learns to read.* Thousand Oaks, CA: Corwin Press.

Spache, G. (1953). A new readability formula for primary grade reading materials. *Elementary School Journal, 53,* 410–413.

Sparks, D. (1995). A paradigm shift in staff development. *The ERIC Review, 3*(3), 5–7.

Spector, P. E., & O'Connell, B. J. (1994). The contribution of personality traits, negative affectivity, locus of control, and type A to the subsequent reports of job stressors and job strains. *Journal of Occupational and Organizational Psychology, 67,* 1–12.

Speigel, D. (1998). Silver bullets, babies, and bath water: Literature response groups in a balanced literacy program. *The Reading Teacher, 52,* 114–124.

Spor, M., & Schneider, B. (1999). Content reading strategies: What teachers know, use, and want to learn. *Reading Research and Instruction, 38*(3), 221–231.

Stahl, S. (1983). Differential word knowledge and reading comprehension. *Journal of Reading Behavior, 15,* 33–50.

Stahl, S. (1986). Three principles of vocabulary instruction. *Journal of Reading, 29*(1), 662–668.

Stahl, S. A. (1999). *Vocabulary development.* Cambridge, MA: Brookline.

Stahl, S. A., Hynd, C. R., Britton, B. K., McNish, M. M., & Bosquet, D. (1996). What happens when students read multiple source documents in history? *Reading Research Quarterly, 31,* 430–456.

Stahl, S. A., & Shiel, T. G. (1999). *Teaching meaning vocabulary: Productive approaches for poor readers. Read all about it! Readings to inform the profession.* Sacramento: California State Board of Education.

Statistical abstract of the United States—1989. Prepared by the chief of the Bureau of Statistics, Treasury Department. Washington, DC: U.S. Government Printing Office.

Stauffer, R. G. (1969a). *Directing reading maturity as a cognitive process.* New York: Harper and Row.

Stauffer, R. G. (1969b). *Teaching reading as a thinking process.* New York: Harper and Row.

Steen, P. (1991). Book diaries: Connecting free reading with instruction, home and school, and kids with books. *The Reading Teacher, 45,* 330–333.

Stefl-Mabry, J. (1998). Designing a Web-based reading course. *Journal of Adolescent & Adult Education, 41*(7), 556–571.

Sternberg, R. J. (1985, November). Teaching critical thinking: 1. Are we making critical mistakes? *Phi Delta Kappan,* 194–198.

Sternberg, R. J. (1991). Are we reading too much into reading comprehension tests? *Journal of Reading, 34,* 540–545.

Sternberg, R. J. (1994). Answering questions and questioning answers. *Phi Delta Kappan, 76,* 136–138.

Sternberg, R. J. (1997). What does it mean to be smart? *Educational Leadership, 5,* 20–24.

Sternberg, R. J., & Baron, J. B. (1985). A statewide approach to measuring critical thinking skills. *Educational Leadership, 43,* 40–43.

Stewart, M. T. (2004). Early literacy instruction in the climate of No Child Left Behind. *The Reading Teacher, 57*(8), 732–743.

Stien, D., & Beed, P. L. (2004). Bridging the gap between fiction and nonfiction in the circle setting: Reading circles can be a valuable tool for engaging students with nonfiction texts. *The Reading Teacher, 57*(6), 510–519.

Stoller, F. (1999). Time for a change: A hybrid curriculum for EAP programs. *TESOL Journal, 8*(1), 8–13.

Strahan, D. B. (1983). The emergence of formal reasoning during adolescence. *Transescence, 11,* 7–14.

Strang, R. (1928). Another attempt to teach how to study. *School and Society, 28,* 461–466.

Strang, R. (1937). The improvement of reading in high school. *Teachers College Record, 39,* 197–206.

Strang, R. (1962). Progress in the teaching of reading in high school and college. *The Reading Teacher, 16,* 170–177.

Strauss, A. A., & Lehtinen, L. (1947). *Psychopathology and education in the brain-injured child: Vol. 1.* New York: Grune and Stratton.

Strauss, V. (2003). Start early with study skills instruction. *Curriculum Review, 42*(8), 3.

Streeter, B. (1986). The effects of training experienced teachers in enthusiasm on students' attitudes toward reading. *Reading Psychology, 7*(4), 249–259.

Strong, M. (1995). Socratic practice as an organizing principle. *Paideia Next Century, 4,* 5–6.

Strong, M. (2000). Students lack needed study skills. *USA Today, 128*(2659), 15.

Sturtevant, E. (1992). *Content literacy in high school social studies: Two case studies in a multicultural setting.* Unpublished doctoral dissertation, Kent State University, Kent, Ohio.

Sturtevant, E. G., & Linek, W. M. (2003). The instructional beliefs and decisions of middle and secondary teachers who successfully blend literacy and content. *Reading Research and Instruction, 4*(3), 74–90.

Summers, J. J. (2006). Effects of collaborative learning in math on sixth graders' individual goal orientation from a socioconstructivist perspective. *The Elementary School Journal, 106*(3), 273–291.

Swafford, J. (1995). "I wish all my groups were like this one": Facilitating peer interaction during group work. *Journal of Reading, 38,* 626–631.

Swanson, H. L. (2000). Issues facing the field of learning disabilities. *Learning Disability Quarterly, 23*(1), 37–48.

Sylwester, R. (1994, October). How emotions affect learning. *Educational Leadership, 52*(2), 60–68.

Sylwester, R. (1995). *A celebration of neurons: An educator's guide to the human brain.* Alexandria, VA: Association for Supervision and Curriculum Development.

Tatum, A. W. (2004). A road map for reading specialists entering schools without exemplary reading programs: Seven quick lessons. *The Reading Teacher, 58*(1), 28–39.

Taylor, B. M., Frye, B. J., & Maruyama, G. M. (1990). Time spent reading and reading growth. *American Educational Research Journal, 72,* 351–362.

Taylor, B. M., Pressley, M., & Pearson, P. D. (2002). Research supported characteristics of teachers and schools that promote reading achievement. In B. M. Taylor & P. D. Pearson (Eds.), *Teaching reading* (pp. 361–374). Mahwah, NJ: Erlbaum.

Taylor, W. (1953). Cloze procedure: A new tool for measuring readability. *Journalism Quarterly, 30,* 415–433.

Tchudi, S. J., & Tchudi, S. N. (1999). *The English language arts handbook,* 2nd ed. Portsmouth, NH: Heinemann.

Teale, W., & Sulzby, E. (1986). *Emergent literacy: Writing and reading.* Norwood, NJ: Ablex.

Templeton, S. (1991). *Teaching integrated language arts.* Boston: Houghton Mifflin.

Thoman, E. (1999). Skills and strategies for media education. *Educational Leadership, 56,* 50–54.

Thompson, G., & Morgan, R. (1976). The use of concept formation study guides for social studies reading materials. *Reading Horizons, 7,* 132–136.

Thornburg, D. D. (2001, May/June). Pencils down! How decontextualized standardized testing can destroy education. *MultiMedia Schools.* Retrieved April 2007 from http://www.infotoday.com/MMSchools/may01/dcon0105.htm.

Thorndike, E. L. (1917/1932). *Educational psychology.* New York: Columbia University, Teachers College Press.

Thurstone, L. L. (1946). A note on a reanalysis of Davis's reading tests. *Psychometrika, 11,* 185–188.

Tierney, R. J. (1998). Literacy assessment reform: Shifting beliefs, principled possibilities, and emerging practice. *The Reading Teacher, 51*(5), 374–390.

Toch, T. (1984, March 7). Bell calls on education to push publishers for better materials. *Education Week,* 11.

Todd, C. J. (1995). The semester project: The power and pleasures of individualized study. *English Journal, 84,* 73–76.

Tomlinson, C.A. (2005). Traveling the road to differentiation in staff development. *JSD, 26*(4), 8–12.

Tonjes, M. J., & Zintz, M. V. (1981). *Teaching reading/thinking study skills in content classrooms.* Dubuque, IA: William Brown Co.

Torgensen, J., & Licht, B. (1983). The learning disabled child as an inactive learner: Retrospect and prospects. In J. McKinney and L. Feagans (Eds.), *Current topics in learning disabilities, Vol. 1* (pp. 3–31). Norwood, NJ: Ablex.

Trier, J. (2007). "Cool" engagements with YouTube: Part two. *Journal of Adolescent and Adult Literacy, 50*(7), 598–603.

Tse, A. (1999). Conducting electronic focus group discussions among Chinese respondents. *Journal of the Market Research Society, 41*(4), 407.

Turbill, J. (2002, February). The four ages of reading philosophy and pedagogy: A framework for examining theory and practice. *Reading Online, 5*(6). Retrieved

Dec. 10, 2004, from http://www.reading online.org/international/inter_index.asp?HREF= turbill4/index.html.

Turner, J., & Paris, S. G. (1995). How literacy tasks influence children's motivation for literacy. *The Reading Teacher, 48,* 662–673.

Twenty-fourth yearbook of the national society of the study for education. (1925). Bloomington, IN: Public School Publishing Company.

Tyner, K. (1998). *Literacy in a digital world: Teaching and learning in the age of information.* Mahwah, NJ: Erlbaum.

Unks, G. (1985). Critical thinking in the social studies classroom. *Social Education, 44,* 240–246.

Unsworth, L. (1999). Developing critical understanding of the specialized language of school science and history texts: A functional grammatical perspective. *Journal of Adolescent & Adult Education, 42*(7), 508–521.

Ur, P., & Wright, A. (1992). *Five-minute activities: A resource book of short activities.* New York: Cambridge University Press.

U.S. Department of Education. (1993). *The condition of education 1993.* Washington, DC: Author.

U.S. Department of Education. (1997). *President Clinton's call to action for American education in the 21st century: Technological literacy.* Retrieved April 8, 2003, from http://www.ed.gov/updates/PresEDPlan/part11.html.

U.S. Department of Education, National Center for Education Statistics. (2006). *The Condition of Education 2006* (NCES 2006–071). Washington, DC: U.S. Government Printing Office.

U.S. Department of Education, National Center for Education Statistics. (2007). *The Condition of Education 2007* (NCES 2007-064). Washington, DC: U.S. Government Printing Office.

Uzzell, L. (2005, September). Cheat sheets. *American Spectator, 36*(7), 26–30.

Vacca, R. T. (2002). From efficient decoders to strategic readers. *Educational Leadership, 60*(3), 6–11.

Vacca, R. T., & Padak, N. (1990). Who's at risk in reading? *Journal of Reading, 33,* 486–488.

Valencia, S. W., & Wixson, K. K. (1999, April 1). *Policy-oriented research on literacy standards and assessment.* Ann Arbor, MI: Center for the Improvement of Early Reading Achievement (CIERA Report No. 3-004).

Valeri-Gold, M. (1987). Previewing: A directed reading–thinking activity. *Reading Horizons, 27,* 123–126.

Van Blerkom, D. L., Van Blerkom, M. L., & Bertsch, S. (2006). Study strategies and generative learning: What works? *Journal of College Reading and Learning, 37*(1), 7–19.

Van der Heuval, G. (1988). *Crowns of thorns and glory: Mary Todd Lincoln and Varina Howell Davis, the two first ladies of the Civil War.* New York: Dutton.

Vanderventer, N. (1979, Winter). RAFT: A process to structure prewriting. *Highway One: A Canadian Journal of Language Experience, 26.*

Vandiver, F. E. (1992). *Blood brothers: A short history of the Civil War.* College Station: Texas A&M Press.

Van Horn, R. (1999). The electronic classroom and video conferencing. *Phi Delta Kappan, 80*(5), 411–412.

Van Leeuwen, C. A., & Gabriel, M. A. (2007). Beginning to write with word processing: Integrating writing process and technology in a primary classroom. *The Reading Teacher, 60,* 420–429.

Vann, R . J., & Fairbairn, S. B. (2003). Linking our worlds: A collaborative academic literacy project. *TESOL Journal, 12*(3), 11–16.

Van Sertima, T. (1976). *The African presence in ancient America: They came before Columbus.* New York: Random House.

Vaughan, C. L. (1990). Knitting writing: The double-entry journal. In N. Atwell (Ed.), *Coming to know: Writing to learn in the intermediate grades* (pp. 69–75). Portsmouth, NH: Heinemann.

Vaughan, J., & Estes, T. (1986). *Reading and reasoning beyond the primary grades.* Boston: Allyn & Bacon.

Vaughn, S., & Fuchs, L. (2003). Redefining learning disabilities as inadequate response to instruction: The promise and potential problems. *Learning Disabilities Research & Practice, 18,* 137–146.

Van Valkenburg, J., & Holden, L. K. (2004). Teaching methods in the affective domain. *Radiologic Technology, 75*(5), 347–355.

Veatch, J. (1968). *How to teach reading with children's books.* New York: Citation Press.

Verdugo, R. R. (2007). English language learners: Key issues. *Education and Urban Society, 39,* 167–193.

Verkoeijen, P., Rikers, R., & Schmidt, H. G. (2005). The effects of prior knowledge on study-time allocation and free recall: Investigating the discrepancy reduction model. *The Journal of Psychology, 139*(1), 67–80.

Vermette, P. (1994). The right start for cooperative learning. *High School Journal, 77,* 255–260.

Vermette, P., Foote, C., Bird, C., Mesibov, D., Harris-Ewing, S., & Battaglia, C. (2001). Understanding constructivism: A primer for parents and school board members. *Education, 122*(1), 87–94.

Vermette, P., Harper, L., & DiMillo, S. (2004). Cooperative and collaborative learning with 4–8 year olds: How does research support teachers' practice? *Journal of Instructional Psychology, 31*(2), 130–135.

Verplaeste, L. S. (1998). How content teachers interact with English language learners. *TESOL Journal, 7*(5), 24–28.

Villaune, S. K. (2000). The necessity of uncertainty: A case study of language arts reform. *Journal of Teacher Education, 51*(1), 18.

Villaune, S. K., & Hopkins, L. (1995). A transactional and sociocultural view of response in a fourth-grade literature discussion group. *Reading Research and Instruction, 34,* 190–203.

Villano, T. L. (2005). Should social studies textbooks become history? A look at alternative methods to activate schema in the intermediate classroom. *The Reading Teacher, 59,* 122–130.

Villegas, A. M., & Lucas, T. (2007). The culturally responsive teacher. *Educational Leadership, 64,* 28–33.

Viorst, J. (1978). *Alexander who used to be rich last Sunday.* New York: Atheneum.

Virginia Grade Level Alternative Procedural Manual. (2006). Retrieved June 2007 from Virginia Department of Education Web site: http://www.pen.k12.va.us/go/VDOE.

Von Glaserfeld, E. (1996). Introduction: Aspects of constructivism. In C. T. Fosnot (Ed.), *Constructivism: Theory, perspectives, and practice* (pp. 3–7). New York: Teachers College Press.

Vyas, S. (2004). Exploring bicultural identities of Asian high school students through the analytic window of a literature club. *Journal of Adolescent & Adult Literacy, 48*(1), 12–23.

Vygotsky, L. (1978a). Interaction between learning and development. In M. Cole, V. John-Steiner, S. Scribner, & E. Souberman (Eds.), *Mind in society: The development of higher psychological process* (pp. 79–91). Cambridge, MA: Harvard University Press.

Vygotsky, L. (1978b). The prehistory of written language. In M. Cole, V. John-Steiner, S. Scribner, & E. Souberman (Eds.), *Mind in society: The development of higher psychological process* (pp. 105–119). Cambridge, MA: Harvard University Press.

Vygotsky, L. S. (1962). *Thought and language.* Cambridge, MA: MIT Press.

Wade, S. E., & Adams, R. B. (1990). Effects of importance and interest on recall of biographical text. *Journal of Reading Behavior, 22,* 331–353.

Waggoner, M., Chinn, C., Yi, H., & Anderson, R. C. (1995). Collaborative reasoning about stories. *Language Arts, 72,* 582–589.

Wagner, C. L., Brock, D. R., & Agnew, A. T. (1994). Developing literacy portfolios in teacher education courses. *Journal of Reading, 37*(8), 668–674.

Wagner, J. O. (1995). Using the Internet in vocational education. *ERIC Digest No. 160* (ERIC Document Reproduction Service No. ED. 385-777).

Walberg, H. J., & Tsai, S. (1985). Correlates of reading achievement and attitude: A national assessment study. *Journal of Educational Research, 78,* 159–167.

Walczyk, J. J., & Griffith-Ross, D. A. (2007). How important is reading skill fluency for comprehension? *The Reading Teacher, 60*(6), 560–569.

Walker, B. (1992). *Supporting struggling readers.* Markham, Ontario: Pippin.

Walker, B. J. (1990). *Remedial reading.* Washington, DC: National Education Association.

Wallace, C. S., Hand, B., & Yand, E. (2004). The science writing heuristic: Using writing as a tool for learning in the laboratory. In W. S. Saul (Ed.), *Crossing borders in literacy and science instruction: Perspectives on theory and practice* (pp. 355–368). Newark, DE: International Reading Association.

Wallace, R. A. (1975). *Biology: The world of life.* Santa Monica, CA: Goodyear.

Walpole, P. (1987). Yes, writing in math. In J. Self (Ed.), *Plain talk about learning and writing across the curriculum* (pp. 51–59). Richmond: Virginia State Department of Education.

Walpole, S. (1999). Changing texts, changing thinking: Comprehension demands of new science textbooks. *The Reading Teacher, 52*(4), 358–369.

Walpole, S., Hayes, L., & Robnolt, V. J. (2006). Matching second graders to text: The utility of a group-administered comprehension measure. *Reading Research and Instruction, 46*(1), 1–22.

Walton, S., & Taylor, K. (1996). How did you know the answer was boxcar? *Educational Leadership, 54*(4), 38–40.

Wang, A. Y., & Thomas, M. H. (1995). The effects of key words on long-term retention: Help or hindrance? *Journal of Educational Psychology, 87,* 468–475.

Wang, J. H., & Guthrie, J. T. (2004). Modeling the effects of intrinsic motivation, extrinsic motivation, amount of reading, and past reading achievement on text comprehension between U.S. and Chinese students. *Reading Research Quarterly, 39*(2), 162–184.

Warm, J. S., Dember, W. M., & Parasuraman, R. (1991). Effects of olfactory stimulation on performance and stress in a visual sustained attention task. *Journal of the Society of Cosmetic Chemists, 42,* 199–210.

Wassermann, S. (1999). Shazam! You're a teacher. *Phi Delta Kappan, 80*(6), 464–468.

Waters, M., & Waters, A. (1992). Study skills and study competence: Getting the priorities right. *ELT Journal, 46*(3), 264–273.

Watts-Taffe, S., Gwinn, C. B., Johnson, J. R., & Horn, M. L. (2003). Preparing preservice teachers to integrate technology with the elementary literacy program. *The Reading Teacher, 57*(2), 130–138.

Weaver, C. (1994). *Reading processes and practice.* Portsmouth, NH: Heinemann.

Wehlange, G. G., & Rutter, R. A. (1986). Dropping out: How much do schools contribute to the problem? *Teachers College Record, 87,* 374–392.

Weiner, B. (1995). *Judgments of responsibility: A foundation for a theory of social conduct.* New York: Guilford Press.

Weinstein, C. E. (1987). Fostering learning autonomy through the use of learning strategies. *Journal of Reading, 30,* 590–595.

Weinstein, C. E., & Mayer, R. E. (1986). The teaching of learning strategies. In M. C. Wittrock (Ed.), *Handbook of research on teaching* (pp. 315–327). New York: Macmillan.

Weinstein, C. E., Zimmerman, S. A., & Palmer, D. R. (1988). Assessing learning strategies: The design and development of the LASSI. In C. E. Weinstein, P. A. Alexander, & E. T. Goetz (Eds.), Learning and study strategies: Issues in assessment, instruction, and evaluation (pp. 25–39). New York: Academic Press.

Weir, C. (1998). Using embedded questions to jumpstart metacognition in middle school readers. *Journal of Adolescent & Adult Literacy, 41*(6), 458–467.

Weiss, R. P. (2000). Brain based learning. *Training and Development, 54*(7), 21–27.

Wells, H. G. (1987). *The complete short stories of H. G. Wells.* New York: St. Martin's Press.

Wepner, S. B. (1995). Using technology for literacy instruction. In S. B. Wepner, J. T. Feeley, & D. S. Strickland (Eds.), *The administration and supervision of reading programs.* New York: Teachers College Press.

Wepner, S. B. (2004). Technology run amok: The top ten technoblunders. *Reading Online, 7*(6). Retrieved Dec. 10, 2004, from http://www.readingonline.org/electronic/elec_index.asp?HREF=wepner2/index.html.

Wepner, S. B., Seminoff, N. E., & Blanchard, J. (1995). Navigating learning with electronic encyclopedias. *Reading Today, 12,* 28.

White, E. B. (1951). Calculating machine. In *The second tree from the corner* (pp. 165–167). New York: Harper and Row.

White, T. G., Sowell, J., & Yanagihara, A. (1989). Teaching elementary students to use word-part clues. *The Reading Teacher, 42,* 302–308.

Whitehead, D. (1994). Teaching literacy and learning strategies through a modified guided silent reading procedure. *Journal of Reading, 38,* 24–30.

Whittington, D. (1991). What have 17-year-olds known in the past? *American Educational Research Journal, 28,* 759–783.

Wigfield, A., & Asher, S. R. (1984). Social and motivational influences on reading. In P. D. Pearson (Ed.), *Handbook of reading research.* New York: Longman.

Wigfield, A., & Asher, S. R. (1986). Students' thought processes. In M. C. Wittrock (Ed.), *Handbook of research on teaching.* New York: Macmillan.

Wiggins, G. (1989). A true test: Toward more authentic and equitable assessment. *Phi Delta Kappan, 70,* 703–713.

Wigginton, E. (1986). *Sometimes a shining moment: The Foxfire experiences.* New York: Anchor/Doubleday.

Wilcox, B. L. (1997). Writing portfolios: Active vs. passive. *English Journal, 86*(6), 34–37.

Wiley, J., Griffin, T. D., & Thiede, K. W. (2005) Putting the comprehension in metacomprehension. *Journal of General Psychology, 132*(4), 408–429.

Wilkinson, L. C., & Silliman, E. R. (2001, February). Classroom language and literacy learning. *Reading Online, 4*(7). Retrieved Nov. 11, 2004, from http://www.readingonline.org/articles/art_index.asp?HREF=/ articles/handbook/wilkinson/index.html.

Will, M. (1984). *Bridges from school to working life: OSERS programming for the transition of youth with disabilities.* Washington, DC: U.S. Department of Education, Office of Special Education and Rehabilitative Services.

Williams, B. (2006). Lessons along the cultural spectrum. *JSD, 27*(4), 10–14.

Williams, B. T. (2005/2006). Home and away: The tensions of community, literacy, and identity. *Journal of Adolescent & Adult Literacy, 48,* 342–347.

Willis, J., Stephens, E., & Matthew, K. (1996). *Technology, reading, and language arts.* Boston: Allyn & Bacon.

Wilson, M. (2004). Assessment, accountability, and the classroom: A community of judgment. In M. Wilson (Ed.), *Toward coherence between classroom assessment and accountability: 103rd yearbook of the National Society for the Study of Education.* Chicago: University of Chicago Press.

Wilson, R. M., & Gambrell, L. B. (1988). *Reading comprehension in the elementary school.* Boston: Allyn & Bacon.

Window on the classroom: A look at teachers' tests. (1984). *Captrends, 10,* 1–3.

Winne, P. H., & Perry, N. E. (2000). Measuring self-regulated learning. In M. Boekaerts, P. Pintrich, & M. Zeidner (Eds.), Handbook of self-regulation (pp. 531–566). New York: Academic Press.

Winograd, P. (1984). Strategic difficulties in summarizing texts. *Reading Research Quarterly, 19,* 404–425.

Winograd, P., & Paris, S. (1988). A cognitive and motivational agenda for reading instruction. *Educational Leadership, 46,* 30–36.

Wise, H. A. (1939). *Motion pictures as an aid in teaching American history.* New Haven, CT: Yale University Press.

Wolf, G. (1996, February). Steve Jobs: the next great thing. *Wired,* 102–163.

Wolfe, D., & Antinarella, J. (1997). *Deciding to lead: The English teacher as reformer.* Portsmouth, NH: Heinemann.

Wolfe, D., & Reising, R. (1983). *Writing for learning in the content areas.* Portland, ME: J. Weston Walch.

Wolfe, P. (2001). *Brain matters: Translating research into classroom practice.* Alexandria, VA: Association for Supervision and Curriculum Development.

Wolfe, P., & Brandt, R. (1998). What do we know from brain research? *Educational Leadership, 56*(3), 8–13.

Wollman-Bonilla, J. (1991). *Response journals.* New York: Scholastic.

Wood, K. D. (1987). Fostering cooperative learning in middle and secondary level classrooms. *Journal of Reading, 31,* 10–18.

Wood, K. D. (1992). Fostering collaborative reading and writing experiences in mathematics. *Journal of Reading, 36,* 96–103.

Wood, K. D., Lapp, D., & Flood, J. (1992). *Guiding readers through text: A review of study guides.* Newark, DE: International Reading Association.

Wood, T. M. (1996). Evaluation and testing: The road less traveled. In S. J. Silverman and C. D. Ennis (Eds.), *Student learning in physical education: Applying research to enhance instruction* (pp. 199–219). Champaign, IL: Human Kinetics.

Woodring, M. N., & Flemming, C. W. (1935). *Directing study of high school pupils.* New York: Columbia University Teacher's College.

Woodward, A., Elliott, D. L., & Nagel, K. C. (1986). Beyond textbooks in elementary social studies. *Social Education, 50,* 50–53.

Woolf, V. (1967; c. 1966). *Collected essays.* New York: Harcourt, Brace and World.

Worthen, B. (1993). Critical decisions that will determine the future of alternative assessment. *Phi Delta Kappan, 74,* 444–456.

Worthy, J., & Broaddus, K. (2002). Fluency beyond the primary grades: From group performance to silent, independent reading. *The Reading Teacher, 55*(4), 334–343.

Worthy, J., & Hoffman, J. V. (2000). Critical questions— the press to test. *The Reading Teacher, 53*(7), 596–598.

Wray, D. (1994). Text and authorship. *The Reading Teacher 48*(1), 52–57.

Wray, D., & Lewis, M. (1998). An approach to factual writing. *Reading Online.* Retrieved Dec. 12, 2004, from http://www.readingonline.org/articles/art_index.asp?HREF=writing/index.html.

The writing report card: Writing achievement in American schools. (1987). Princeton, NJ: National Assessment of Educational Progress and the Educational Testing Center.

Xu, S. H. (2001, July/August). Exploring diversity issues in teacher education. *Reading Online, 5*(1). Retrieved June 3, 2007, from http://www.readingonline.org/newliteracies/lit_index.asp?HREF=action/xu/index.html.

Yanowitz, K. L. (2001). Using analogies to improve elementary school students' inferential reasoning about scientific concepts. *School Science and Mathematics, 101*(3), 133.

Yeager, D. (1991). *The whole language companion.* Glenview, IL: Goodyear.

Yell, M. M. (2002). Putting gel pen to paper. *Educational Leadership, 60*(3), 63–66.

Yochum, N. (1991). Children's learning from informational text: The relationship between prior knowledge and text structure. *Journal of Reading Behavior, 23,* 87–108.

Yolen, J. (Ed.). (1986). *Favorite folktales from around the world.* New York: Pantheon Books.

Yoon, J. (2002). Three decades of sustained silent reading: A meta-analytic review of the effects of SSR on attitude toward reading. *Reading Improvement, 39*(4), 186–196.

Young, D. B., & Ley, K. (2000). Developmental students don't know what they don't know. Part I: Self-regulation. *Journal of College Reading and Learning, 31*(1), 54–62.

Young, J. P., & Brozo, W. G. (2001). Boys will be boys, or will they? Literacy and masculinities. *Reading Research Quarterly, 36*(3), 316–325.

Young, J. P., Mathews, S. R., Kietzmann, A. M., & Westerfield, D. T. (1997). Getting disenchanted adolescents to participate in school literacy activities: Portfolio conferences. *Journal of Adolescent & Adult Literacy, 40*(5), 348–360.

Young, T. A., & Daines, D. (1992). Students' predictive questions and teachers' prequestions about expository text in grades K–5. *Reading Psychology, 13*(4), 291–308.

Yovanoff, P., Duesbery, L., Alonzo, J., & Tindal, G. (2005). Grade-level invariance of a theoretical causal structure predicting reading comprehension with vocabulary and oral reading fluency. *Educational Measurement: Issues and Practice,* 4–12.

Yurick, A. L., Robinson, P. D., Cartledge, G., Lo, Y., & Evans, T. L. (2006). Using peer-mediated repeated readings as a fluency-building activity for urban learners. *Education & Treatment of Children, 29*(3), 469–507.

Zakaluk, B., & Klassen, M. (1992). Enhancing the performance of a high school student labeled learning disabled. *Journal of Reading, 36,* 4–9.

Zaragoza, N. (1987). Process writing for high-risk learning disabled students. *Reading Research and Instruction, 26,* 290–301.

Zeilik, M., Schau, C., Mattern, N., Hall, S., Teague, K. W., & Bisard, W. (1997). Conceptual astronomy: A novel model for teaching postsecondary science courses. *American Journal of Physics, 66*(10), 987–996.

Zhang, Z., & Schumm, J. S. (2000). Exploring effects of the keyword method on limited English proficient students' vocabulary recall and comprehension. *Reading Research and Instruction 39*(3), 202–221.

Zimmerman, B. J., & Schunk, D. H. (2001). *Self-regulated learning and academic achievement*. Mahwah, NJ: Erlbaum.

Activity Contributors

Dawn Watson and Walter Richards: PAR Diagram, p. 16

Alex Seeley, Richmond, VA: Examples for primary social studies lesson (pp. 18–19) and Activity 1.1

Elisabeth Groninger, Richmond, VA.: Example for fourth grade science (pp. 19–22) and Activity 1.2

Michael Tewksbury, Richmond, Va.: Examples for middle school mathematics (pp. 22–23) and Activity 1.3

Mark A. Forget, Yogi Hightower Boothe, and James DiNardo II, Examples for ninth grade health and physical education (pp. 23–26) and Activity 1.4

Lori Levy: Activity 2.1, p. 42.

Ginger Banta: Activity 2.1, p. 42

Mary Broussard: A homework strategy, p. 44

Charles Carroll: Activity 2.2, p. 44

Amy Nowlin: Activity 2.3, p. 45

Jane Baxter: test design, p. 46

Bessie Haskins: Activity 2.4, p. 47

Dr. Jeff Nugent: Activity 2.5, p. 51

Frances Reid: Activity 2.6, p. 53

Sandra Zeller and Brenda Winston: Activity 2.7, p. 54

Jeannette Rosenberg: Activity 3.1, p. 74

Grace Hamlin: example of incorrect knowledge, p. 78

Travis Sturgill: Activity 3.4, p. 82

Dr. Mark Forget: Activity 3.7, p. 87

Dr. Mark Forget: Activity 3.9, p. 90

Dr. Mark Forget: Activity 3.10, p. 91

Kathy Feltus, Activity 3.13, p. 93

Travis Sturgill: Activity 4.1, p. 100

Dr. Mark Forget: Activity 4.5, p. 111

Lori Lambert: Activity 4.7, p. 113

Laura Clevinger: Activity 4.9, p. 120

Serena Marshall, Activity 4.14, p. 125

Nancy S. Smith, Activity 4.16, p. 131

Gail Perrer: Activity 5.2, p. 144

Dana S. Jubilee: Activity 5.9, p. 158

Marvette Darby: Activity 6.4, p. 191

Stephen D. Rudlin: Activity 6. 5, p. 193

Cheryl Keeton: Activity 6.10, p. 206

Shawn Nunnally: Activity 6.12, p. 208

Dr. Jim McLeskey, Jr.: Activity 6.13, p. 209

Elizabeth Evans: visual literacy + technology, p. 221

Linda Ford: comments about podcasts, p. 222–223

Dr. Dan Ream: comments about critical thinking on the Internet, p. 229

Drs. Judy Richardson; Joan Rhodes; & Valerie Robnolt: Activity 8.1, pp. 245–248

Connie Hill: Activity 8.2, p. 252

Mary L. Seward: Activity 8.5, p. 255

Jody Irvin: Activity 8.10, p. 264

Terry Bryce: Activity 9.2, p. 299

Brian Littman: Activity 9.4, p. 301

Tara Furges: Activity 9.5, p. 302

Audra Jones: Activity 9.6, p. 303

Suzanne McDaniel: Activity 9.8, p. 305

Barbara Ingber: example Capsule Vocabulary, p. 306

Heather Hemstreet: Activity 9.11, p. 315

Wendy Barcroft: Activity 9.13, p. 319

Laurie Smith: Activity 9.14, p. 320

Kim Blowe: Activity 9.16, p. 322

Colleen Kean: Activity 9.17, p. 326

William Cathell: Activity 9.18, p. 326

Laurie Smith: Activity 9.21, p. 328

Ed Toscano: Activity 9.22, p. 329

Barbara Wood: Activities 9.23, 9.24, 9.25, pp. 330–332

Mary Fagerland: Activity 9.26, p. 333

Bessie Haskins: Activity 9.27, p. 335

Andrew Pettit: Figure 10.3, p. 348–349

Kathryn Davis: Activity 10.1, p. 353

Dr. Mark Forget: Activity 10.2, p. 356

Dr. Mark Forget: Activity 10.4, p. 360

Susan W. Hamlin: Activity 10.5, p. 361

Sheryl Lam: example of journal writing, p. 363

Terry Bryce: Activity 10.8, p. 368

Jon Morgan: Activity 10.12, p.371

Frances Lively: Activity 10.14, pp. 375–376

Dianne Duncan: Activity 10.18, pp. 385–386

Polly Gilbert: Activity 10.19, p. 386

Karen Curling: Activity 11.3, p. 414

Beverly Marshall: Activity 11.5, p. 425

Megan K. Houston: Activity 11.6, p. 426

Kerry Blum: math analogy, p. 427

Diana Freeman: biology analogy, p. 427

Chris Birdsong White: Activity 12.8, pp. 457–459

Author Index

Blackburn, C., 316
Blai, B., 238
Blair, T. R., 392, 399
Blanchard, J., 232
Blessing, D., 316
Block, C. C., 160
Bloom, A., 6, 36
Bloom, B. C., 111
Blumenfeld, P. C., 197
Boaler, J., 197, 198
Bockern, S. V., 401, 403
Bohan, H., 138
Boland, E., 307, 310, 312
Boote, C., 294
Borchardt, K. M., 381
Borden, J., 418
Borko, H., 38, 43, 72
Borman, G., 395, 396, 461
Bormouth, J. R., 185
Bos, C. S., 83, 299
Bosquet, D., 240
Bosworth, K., 402
Bottomley, D. M., 440
Boyd, D. E., 397, 401
Boyd, W., 7
Boyd-Batstone, P., 65
Boyle, M., 139, 149
Boyle, O., 406, 412
Brabham, E.G., 293
Bracey, G., 5, 37
Brady, M., 59
Brady, S., 313
Brandt, R., 449
Brechtel, M., 413
Brendtro, L. K., 401, 403
Brennan, K. B., 284
Brigham, F. J., 274, 304
Brindley, R., 343
Brinthaupt, T. M., 272
Britton, B. K., 240, 248
Broaddus, K., 77, 420
Brock, D. R., 61
Brokenleg, M., 401, 403
Brooks, J. G., 104
Brooks, M. G., 104
Brotherton, P., 392
Brown, A. L., 153, 381, 421
Brown, J., 75, 342, 357, 384
Brown, R., 268
Brozo, W. G., 397, 401, 460
Bruce, B., 233
Brunwin, B., 377
Bryant, B. R., 295, 296

Bryant, D. P., 83, 295, 296
Bryant, J. A. R., 194
Budig, G. A., 342
Buehl, D. R., 155
Bulwer-Litton, E., 289
Burnam, N., 188
Burns, M. S., 289, 290, 406, 411
Bushaw, W. J, 38, 42
Butcher, K., 417
Butler, G., 73
Byrnes, J. P., 71

Cadenhead, K., 182
Caine, G., 448
Caine, R. N., 448
Calfee, R. C., 167, 172
Calkins, L., 38, 346, 352
Callison, D., 83
Cammack, D. W., 240
Campione, J. C., 381
Canas, M., 197
Caplan, R. I., 188
Cardoso, S., 439
Carmen, R., 56
Carney, J. J., 298, 316
Carolan, J., 392, 420
Carr, E., 192, 296
Carrillo, R., 240
Carter, B., 220
Carter, K., 56
Cartledge, G., 150
Carver, R. P., 279, 297
Cassady, J., 142
Cassidy, D., 237
Cassidy, J., 237
Caverly, D., 450
Celano, D., 397
Chall, J., 179
Chambers, B., 201
Chamot, A. V., 409
Chan, L. K. S., 461
Chance, L., 103
Chandler-Olcott, K., 225
Chase, A. C., 324
Cheek, E. H., 174
Cheek, L., 76
Chesbro, R., 430
Chi, F., 413
Chi, K., 5
Chilcoat, G. W., 376, 377
Chinn, C. A., 118
Choate, J. S., 253
Chomsky, C., 380

Christensen, C. A., 363
Chu, M. L., 220
Ciardiello, A. V., 127, 424
Ciechanowski, K. M., 240
Cimera, R. E., 417, 418
Clark, D., 140
Cleary, B., 350
Cleland, J. V., 61
Cochran-Smith, M., 351, 384, 407
Cohen, A. D., 274
Cohen, D. K., 72
Coiro, J., 166, 240
Cole, A. D., 430
Cole, C. L., 252
Cole, R., 228
Cole, R. P., 240
Collazo, T., 240
Collins, M. L., 450
Colwell, C. G., 114
Conley, M., 37
Conner, J., 85, 401
Cook, A., 351, 384
Cook, L., 413
Cooke, C., 82
Coombe, C. A., 48
Cooper, J., 352
Cooper, L., 252
Coopersmith, S., 400
Cooter, R. B., 126, 376, 377, 411, 442
Cornu, B., 215
Costa, C., 254
Cowan, G., 355
Cowan, E., 355
Creek, R. J., 461
Crenshaw, S. W., 351
Crist, J., 306
Cronin, H., 384
Cronje, J., 439
Crooks, S. M., 268
Cross, T., 142
Culver, V., 461
Cummins, J., 405, 406
Cunningham, A. E., 290, 294, 297
Cunningham, J., 243
Cunningham, J. W., 154, 378
Cunningham, P., 312
Cunningham, R., 132
Currie, H., 80
Cziko, C., 100

Dahlman, A., 432
Daily, G., 457
Daines, D., 126

Dale, E., 179, 290
Dalgarno, B., 105, 106
Dana, C., 323
Daniels, H., 94
Danielson, K. E., 176
Dansereau, D., 83, 202
d'Apollonia, S., 201
Darling-Hammond, L., 5
Davey, B., 159
Davidson, G., 154, 218, 440
Davis, F. B., 290
Davis, J., 341
Davis, M., 156
Davis, N., 215
Davison, A., 183
Davison, D., 354, 362, 363
Day, J. D., 153, 381
Day, R. S., 71
deBono, E., 14
Dechant, E., 238, 439
Deen, M. Y., 197
Deering, P. D., 201
Degener, S. C., 70, 344, 359
de Jong, E., 412
Dember, W. M., 31
DeSanti, R. J., 461
Deshler, D. D., 313
DeSimone, C., 201
Devault, R., 150
Devoogd, G., 142
Dewey, J., 106, 136, 141
Diamond, M., 448, 449
DiCecco, V. M., 83
Dickson, R., 367
Dieu, B., 227
Dillard, A., 310
Dillon, D. R., 124
Dillon, J. T., 127
DiMillo, S., 201
Dixon, F., 142
Dole, J. A., 422
Dole, S., 416
Donahue, P., 393
Donlan, D., 15, 131
Dornyei, Z., 38
Doucette, M., 76
Douglass, B., 380
Dove, M. K., 166
Downing, J., 407
Drevno, G. E., 296
Drum, P., 75
Duffelmeyer, F. A., 156, 324
Duffy, G. G., 138, 422

Duggan, T. J., 350, 352, 353
Duke, N., 101, 141, 172
Duke, N. K., 344, 359
Dunbar, S., 58
Dunlap, J. C., 105
Dunston, P. J., 299
Dunwoody, S., 242
Dupree, K., 105
Durkin, D., 126, 127
Durkin, D., 126, 127
Duvdevany, I., 461
Dweck, C. S., 401
Dwight, J., 215
Dzaldov, B. S., 174
Dziuban, C., 215, 263

Eanet, M., 366
Ebbinghaus, H., 184, 273, 274
Echevarria, M., 102
Edwards, E. C., 307, 310, 312
Edwards, J., 104
Edwards, L. L., 291, 295, 296
Edwards, P. A., 417
Egan, K., 398
Egan, M., 2, 299
Ehlinger, J., 128
Eldredge, J. L., 244
Elley, W. B., 221
Elliott, D. L., 142
Elliott, L., 243
Ellis, E. S., 238
Ellis, L., 240
Erickson, B., 169
Estes, T., 15, 355
Evans, E., 221
Evans, T. L., 150
Eveland, W. P., 242

Fabos, B., 225
Facione, P. A., 140
Fader, D., 442
Fahey, K., 62
Fairbairn, S. B., 411
Fantuzzo, J. W., 197
Farrell, M., 201
Faulkner, W., 179
Fehrman, P. G., 250
Feldhusen, J., 198
Ferguson, D., 394
Fiedler, E., 198
Field, M. L., 411, 412
Fielding, L. G., 102
Fisher, C. W., 441
Fisher, D., 108, 169, 427

Fisher, M., 41
Fisher, P., 289, 290, 293, 295, 296, 307, 310, 316
Fleener, C. E., 10, 104, 445
Fleming, C. B., 419
Flemming, C. W., 239
Fletcher, R., 343
Flood, J., 169, 205
Flynt, S., 126
Font, G., 307, 310, 312
Foot, K. E., 240
Forbes, L. S., 258
Forgan, H. W., 181, 421
Forget, M. A., 83, 137, 263, 282, 404, 449, 457
Foster, S., 243
Fox, B. J., 220
Fox, L. S., 274
Francis, M. A., 294, 295
Francis-Smythe, J. A., 244
Frand, J., 6
French, M. P., 317
Frey, N., 108, 427
Friedman, T. L., 6, 12, 214, 215, 223, 231, 449
Friend, R., 153
Fromm, E., 401
Frost, R., 123
Frye, B. J., 10, 169
Fry, E., 179, 183
Frymier, A. B., 240
Fuchs, D., 197, 417
Fuchs, L. S., 379, 417
Fujloka, J., 38, 42

Gable, R. A., 59, 440
Gabriel, M. A., 351
Gallagher, J. J., 416, 418
Gallagher, J. M., 75
Gallico, P., 112
Gallo, A. M., 442
Gallup, A. M., 5, 6, 37, 38
Gambrell, L. B., 12, 170, 214, 215, 394, 420–422
Ganley, M. A., 461
Ganski, K., 422
Garber-Miller, K., 262
Garcia, R. L., 406, 411
Garner, R., 118, 151–153
Garrett, S. D., 237
Gebhard, A., 359, 363
Gee, J. P., 118, 217, 242, 398, 422, 442
Gee, R. W., 414, 431

Shiel, T. G., 291
Shinn, C. M., 271
Sideridis, G. D., 101
Siedow, M. D., 80
Silva, P. U., 351
Simmons, D. C., 297
Simos, P., 101
Simpson, M., 242
Simpson, M. L., 6, 7, 11, 240, 265,
    290, 292, 294, 295
Sinatra, G. M., 71
Sinatra, R., 8, 9, 384
Sinclair, U., 156
Singer, H., 15, 131
Sizer, T., 33
Skinner, C. H., 252
Slaouti, D., 240
Slate, J. R., 242, 243
Slater, R., 448
Slavin, R. E., 197, 198, 204, 205, 404
Sloan, G. O., 172
Smiley, S. S., 153
Smith, C. B., 400, 406
Smith, D. J., 174, 239, 247, 280
Smith, F., 73, 100, 279, 440
Smith, L., 220
Smith, L. J., 83
Smith, M. C., 440
Smith, N. B., 8
Smith, S., 375
Smuin, S., 118
Snow, C. E., 289, 290, 296, 406, 411
Snyder, T., 94
Sobrol, D. T., 242
Soler, M., 70, 344, 359
Soloway, E., 197
Sommers, C. H., 460
Sousa, D., 74
Sowell, J., 310, 311
Sozniak, L. A., 173
Spache, G., 179
Sparks, D., 104
Spector, P. E., 461
Speigel, D. L., 94
Spor, M.W., 271, 281, 282
Stahl, N., 7
Stahl, S. A., 240, 290, 291, 293, 310
Stanne, M. B., 197
Stanovich, K. E., 290, 294, 297
Stauffer, R. G., 108, 258, 281, 462
Steenwyk, F. L., 378
Stefl-Mabry, J., 226
Stephens, E., 75, 220, 342, 357, 384

Stephenson, D., 250
Sternberg, R. J., 76, 126, 140
Stevenson, H. W., 407
Stevenson, R. J., 71, 272
Stewart, M., 6, 33
Stewart, R. A., 169, 172
Stigler, J. W., 407
Stinson, M., 243
Stoller, F., 405
Strahan, D. B., 142
Strang, R., 151
Strauss, A. A., 380
Strauss, V., 240
Streeter, B., 450
Strickland, D. S., 422
Strong, M., 457
Sturtevant, E., 126
Sullivan, G. S., 274, 304
Sulzby, E., 346
Summers, J. J., 139
Surber, J. R., 304
Swafford, J., 201
Swinyard, W. R., 10
Sylwester, R., 447, 448
Szymanski, M., 242

Taylor, A. K., 136
Tatum, A.W., 422
Taylor, B. M., 10, 124
Taylor, K., 43, 44, 46
Taylor, W., 184, 185
Tchudi, S. J., 343
Tchudi, S. N., 343
Teague, K. W., 106
Teale, W., 346
Temple, C., 321
Templeton, S., 405
Tesser, A., 248
Thiede, K. W., 138
Thistlethwaite, L., 104
Thoman, E., 166
Thomas, M. H., 274
Thomas, M. M., 289
Thompson, G., 428
Thornburg, D. D., 39
Thorndike, E. L., 99
Thurstone, L. L., 290
Tierney, R., 27, 60
Tlusty, N., 221
Toch, T., 175
Todd, C. J., 155
Tomlinson, C. M., 420
Tonelson, S. W., 462

Tonjes, M. J., 380
Tonks, S. M., 172
Torgenson, J., 380
Tower, C., 344
Townsend, M. A. R., 198
Trier, J., 217
Tse, A., 225
Turbill, J., 240
Turner, J., 442
Twain, M., 214, 263, 395
Tynan, D., 415, 416, 431
Tyner, K., 166

Unks, G., 139
Unsworth, L., 173
Uzzell, L., 38

Vacca, R. T., 342, 397, 401, 420
Valencia, S., 6, 33
Valenzuela, M., 351
Van Blerkom, D. L., 127, 156
Van Blerkom, M. L., 156
Vanderventer, M., 373
Van Dijk, T., 378, 381
Van Leeuwen, C. A., 351
Vann, R. J., 411
Van Valkenburg, J., 440, 441
Vaughan, C. L., 365
Vaughan, J., 15, 355
Vaughn, S., 83, 417, 420, 432
Von Glaserfeld, E., 350
Veatch, J., 176
Verkoeijen, P., 71
Vermette, P., 106, 201
Verplaeste, L. S., 410
Villano, T. L., 168, 169
Villaune, S. K., 138, 172, 293
Villegas, A. M., 407
Vitale, M. R., 106
Von Secker, C., 100
Vyas, S., 411
Vygotsky, L., 106, 346, 365

Wade, S. E., 76
Wagner, C. L., 61
Wagner, J. O., 351
Waggoner, M. A., 118
Wagoner, S., 151, 153
Walczyk, J. J., 278
Walker, B. J., 421
Walpole, S., 72, 174
Walton, S., 43, 44, 46
Wang, A. Y., 274

Subject Index

PAR Cross-Reference Guide

	SCIENCE	MATH
Primary	Activity 2.8, p. 61 Activity 3.8, p. 89 Activity 5.9, p. 158 Activity 5.11, p. 158 Activity 6.4, p. 191 Activity 9.25, p. 332 Activity 10.1, p. 353 Activity 11.6, p. 426 Activity 11.7, p. 428	Activity 2.4, p. 47 Activity 8.6, p. 256 Activity 8.12, p. 266
Intermediate	Activity 1.2, p. 21 Activity 3.5, p. 84 Activity 4.7, p. 113 Activity 4.8, p. 116 Activity 4.11, p. 122 Activity 4.13, p. 124 Figure 5.2, p. 154 Activity 6.9, p. 204 Activity 8.7, p. 264 Activity 9.8, p. 305 Activity 10.5, p. 361 Activity 10.11, p. 370 Activity 12.2, p. 445	Activity 3.11, p. 92 Activity 8.7, p. 257 Activity 9.15, p. 321 Activity 9.21, p. 328 Activity 9.27, p. 335 Activity 11.2, p. 413 Activity 11.4, p. 423 Activity 12.8, pp. 457–459
Middle	Activity 2.5, p. 51 Activity 4.3, p. 108 Activity 4.16, p. 132 Activity 6.3, p. 190 Activity 8.4, p. 254 Activity 10.12, p. 371 Activity 10.15, p. 378	Activity 1.3, p. 23 Activity 6.10, p. 206 Activity 9.26, p. 333 Activity 11.5, p. 425 Math analogy, p. 427
Secondary	Activity 4.13, p. 131 Activity 6.13, p. 210 Activity 8.3, p. 252 Activity 9.10, p. 315 Activity 9.13, p. 319 Activity 10.7, p. 364 Biology analogy, p. 427	Activity 2.3, p. 53 Activity 3.1, p. 74 Activity 3.9, p. 90 Activity 6.11, p. 207–208 Activity 10.2, p. 356